Victorian Poets

Victorian Poets

A Critical Reader

Edited by
Valentine Cunningham

WILEY Blackwell

This edition first published 2014
© 2014 John Wiley & Sons, Ltd

Registered Office
John Wiley & Sons, Ltd, The Atrium, Southern Gate, Chichester, West Sussex, PO19 8SQ, UK

Editorial Offices
350 Main Street, Malden, MA 02148–5020, USA
9600 Garsington Road, Oxford, OX4 2DQ, UK
The Atrium, Southern Gate, Chichester, West Sussex, PO19 8SQ, UK

For details of our global editorial offices, for customer services, and for information
about how to apply for permission to reuse the copyright material in this book please
see our website at www.wiley.com/wiley-blackwell.

The right of Valentine Cunningham to be identified as the author of the editorial
material in this work has been asserted in accordance with the UK Copyright, Designs
and Patents Act 1988.

Library of Congress Cataloging-in-Publication Data
Victorian Poets : a Critical Reader / edited by Valentine Cunningham.
    pages   cm. – (Blackwell Critical Reader; 10)
  Includes index.
    ISBN 978-0-631-19913-7 (hardback) – ISBN 978-0-631-19914-4 (paper)   1. English
poetry–19th century–History and criticism.   I. Cunningham, Valentine, editor of
compilation.
  PR593.V57 2014
  821′.809–dc23
                                                                        2013038471
A catalogue record for this book is available from the British Library.

Cover image: Flora, details from tapestry weaving in wool and silk by Edward
Burne-Jones and William Morris, with verses by Morris on borders, made by Morris &
Company at Merton Abbey, 1885. Whitworth Art Gallery, The University of Manchester /
Bridgeman Art Library.
Cover design by Richard Boxall Design Associates

Set in 10/12.5pt Palatino by SPi Publisher Services, Pondicherry, India
Printed in Malaysia by Ho Printing (M) Sdn Bhd

1   2014

Contents

Contents

Contributors

Isobel Armstrong is Emeritus Professor of English at Birkbeck College, University of London, and a Senior Research Fellow at the London University Institute of English Studies. An eminent scholar-critic especially of Victorian poetry, her publications include *Arthur Hugh Clough* (1962), *The Major Victorian Poets: Reconsiderations* (1969), *Victorian Scrutinies* (1972), *Robert Browning* (1974), *Language as Living form in Nineteenth-Century Poetry* (1982), *Victorian Poetry: Poetry, Politics and Poetics* (1993), *Women's Poetry, Late Romantic to late Victorian: Gender and Genre* (1999), *The Radical Aesthetic* (2000), *Victorian Glassworlds* (2008).

Joseph Bristow is a Professor of English at UCLA, the University of California, Los Angeles. A specialist in nineteenth- and twentieth-century literature, with strong lines on gender and gay writing. His books include *The Victorian Poet: Poetics and Persona* (1987), *Robert Browning* (1991), *Empire Boys: Adventures in a Man's World* (1991), *Sexuality* (1997), *Effeminate England: Homoerotic Writing after 1885* (1997), *The Fin-de-Siècle Poem: English Literary Culture and the 1890s* (2005). His many editions include *Victorian Women Poets: Emily Brontë, Elizabeth Barrett Browning, Christina Rossetti* (1995), *Nineteenth-Century Women Poets: An Oxford Anthology* (1996, with Isobel Armstrong), Oscar Wilde's *The Picture of Dorian Gray* (2004), *Wilde Writings: Contextual Conditions* (2003), *The Cambridge Companion to Victorian Poetry* (2000), and *Oscar Wilde and Modern Culture: the Making of a Legend* (2008).

Timothy A J Burnett has retired from his job as a manuscript librarian in the Department of Western Manuscripts at the British Library, London. Writing as T A J Burnett, he is the author of *The Rise and Fall of a Regency Dandy: The Life and Times of Scrope Berdmore Davies* (1981), and the editor of Charlotte Brontë's *The Search after hapiness* (sic): *a Tale*

(1969), *Childe Harold's Pilgrimage Canto III: a Facsimile of the Autograph Fair Copy found in the 'Scrope Davies' Notebook* (1988), and of *The British Library Catalogue of the Ashley Manuscripts* (1998) – the collection of the notorious faker-bibliographer T J Wise.

Mary Wilson Carpenter is Professor Emerita of English, Queen's University, Kingston, Ontario, Canada. She writes as a literary historian about Victorian literature with an emphasis on feminism and gender. Her main publications are *George Eliot and the Landscape of Time: Narrative Form and Protestant Apocalyptic History* (1986), *Imperial Bibles, Domestic Bodies: Women, Sexuality and Religion in the Victorian Market* (2003) and *Health, Medicine and Society in Victorian England* (2010).

Mary Ann Caws is distinguished Professor of English, French and Comparative Literature at the Graduate School of City University, New York. An art historian, literary critic, and biographer of Proust, Virginia Woolf, Henry James, Picasso and Salvador Dalí, she has edited anthologies on Manifestoes, Surrealism, and twentieth-century French literature. Her many translations of modern French poets include Stéphane Mallarmé.

Carol T Christ became the tenth President of Smith College, Northampton, Massachusetts in 2002 after a distinguished career as Professor of English and administrator at the University of California, Berkeley. A strong champion of women's issues and diversity, her critical interests have focussed on Victorian women poets and novelists. As a Professor of English at Smith she teaches seminars on science and literature and on the arts. Her books include *The Finer Optic: the Aesthetic of Particularity in Victorian Poetry* (1975), *Victorian and Modern Poetics* (1984), the Norton edition of George Eliot's *The Mill on the Floss* (1994), and *Victorian Literature and the Victorian Visual Imagination*, edited with John O Jordan (1995).

Valentine Cunningham is a Professor of English Language and Literature at Oxford University and a Senior Research Fellow of Corpus Christi College, Oxford. His books include *Everywhere Spoken Against: Dissent in the Victorian Novel* (1975), *British Writers of the Thirties* (1988), *In the Reading Gaol: Texts, Postmodernism and History* (1993), *Victorian Poetry Now: Poets, Poems, Poetics* (2011), *The Connell Guide to King Lear* (2012). He has edited *The Penguin Book of Spanish Civil War Verse* (1980), *Spanish Front: Writers on the Civil War* (1986), *Adam Bede* (1998), and *The Victorians: An Anthology of Poetry and Poetics* (2000).

Eric Griffiths is a Fellow in English at Trinity College, Cambridge. He teaches, and writes widely about, poetry from the Restoration to the present. Poetry of all sorts: like his critical father-in-the-faith Christopher Ricks, he's a devotee of Bob Dylan. His books are *The Printed Voice of Victorian Poetry* (1989) and his Penguin edition *Dante in English* (2005, with Matthew Reynolds).

Antony Harrison is Distinguished Professor of English at North Carolina State University, at Raleigh, North Carolina. An eminent Victorianist, editor, critical theorist and student of gender, his books are *Christina Rossetti in Context* (1988), *Swinburne's Medievalism: a Study in Victorian Love Poetry* (1988), *Victorian Poets and Romantic Poems: Intertextuality and Ideology* (1990), *Victorian Poets and the Politics of Culture: Discourse and Ideology* (1998), and *The Cultural Production of Matthew Arnold* (2009). He's the editor of *The Letters of Christina Rossetti* (4 vols., 1997–2004), and coeditor of *Gender and Discourse in Victorian Literature and Art* (1992), *The Culture of Christina Rossetti: Female Poetics and Victorian Contexts* (1999), and of *The Blackwell Companion to Victorian Poetry* (2002).

Geoffrey Hill is widely regarded as the greatest living English poet. Professor Emeritus of English Literature and Religion at Boston University, Massachusetts; former co-director (with Christopher Ricks) of the Boston University Editorial Institute; currently Professor of Poetry at Oxford. He has published many volumes of poetry since his first, *For the Fallen* (1959). The best of his agonist critical writing, amounting to a radically conservative, compellingly ethical and religious philosophy of literature, is generously gathered in his bumper *Collected Critical Writings* (2008).

Gerhard Joseph is Professor of English at Lehman College and the Graduate Centre of the City University of New York. He's a theoretically clued-up critic of modern literature with a special stake in Victorian writing, whose books are *Tennysonian Love: The Strange Diagonal* (1969), *Tennyson and the Text: The Weaver's Shuttle* (1992) and the edited volume *Victorian Classicism* (1982).

Angela Leighton is a Professor of English, and Fellow of Trinity College, Cambridge University. A poet in her own right (*Sea Level*, 2007), she's a leading feminist critic with main, though not exclusive, interests in the nineteenth century. Her books are *Shelley and the Sublime* (1984), *Elizabeth Barrett Browning* (1986), *Victorian Women Poets: Writing Against the Heart*

(1992), and *On Form: Poetry, Aestheticism and the Legacy of a Word* (2007). She has edited *Victorian Women Poets: An Anthology*, with Margaret Reynolds (1995), and *Victorian Women Poets: A Critical Reader* (1996).

Dorothy Mermin is Professor Emerita of English, Cornell University, with a concentration on Victorian literature and women's poetry. Her main publications are *The Audience in the Room: Five Victorian Poets* (1983), *Elizabeth Barrett Browning: The Origins of a New Poetry* (1989), and *Godiva's Ride: Women of Letters in England, 1830–1880* (1993). She edited *Victorian Literature 1830–1900* (2001) with Herbert Tucker.

J Hillis Miller is Distinguished Research Professor of English and Comparative Literature of the University of California, at Irvine (to which he moved from Yale where he was member of the so-called Yale School of deconstruction, which also included Jacques Derrida, Paul de Man, Geoffrey Hartman and Harold Bloom). A very influential American deconstructionist, he started off as a rather straightforward literary-historical critic specializing in the nineteenth-century (best early book: *The Disappearance of God: Five Nineteenth-Century Writers*, 1963), but from the later 1970s works of a deconstructive, and soon post-deconstructive cast (he was rather scarred like his colleagues and graduate students by the Paul de Man scandal), have poured out. Representative titles (and concerns): *Fiction and Repetition* (1982), *Tropes, Parables, Performatives* (1990), *Ariadne's Thread* (1992), *Topographies* (1995), *Black Holes* (1999), *Others* (2001), *For Derrida* (2009), *The Conflagration of Community: Fiction Before and After Auschwitz* (2011).

Christopher Ricks is William M and Sarah B Warren Professor of the Humanities at Boston University, Massachusetts, and co-director with Archie Burnett of the Boston University Editorial Institute, which he founded. He was Oxford's Professor of Poetry, 2004–9. Often hailed as the greatest living Anglophone critic, this very eminent scholar-critic and editor is extraordinarily prolific. He has produced major critical books on Milton (1963), Tennyson (1972), Keats (1974), T S Eliot (1988), Beckett (1993), and Bob Dylan (2003). The advocate of Johnsonian *principles* rather than critical *theories*, he's the witty scourge of the over-solemn, the pretentious, and weak theorists. As well as his mag-isterial editions of Tennyson (one volume 1972; 3 volumes 1987– after the Tennyson family lifted its embargo against the quoting of the manuscripts), he's produced *Inventions of the March Hare: T S Eliot Poems 1909–1917* (1996), a *Selected* edition of James Henry, *The Complete Poems of T S Eliot* (2011, with Jim McCue), and, among many other anthologies, *The New Oxford Book of Victorian Verse* (1987) and *The Oxford Book of English Verse* (1999).

David G Riede is Professor of English at the Ohio State University. A strong investigator of nineteenth-century literary production, with a concentration on the Victorians, his many books include *Swinburne: A Study of Romantic Mythmaking* (1978), *Dante Gabriel Rossetti and the Limits of Victorian Vision* (1983), *Matthew Arnold and the Betrayal of Language* (1988), *Oracles and Hierophants: Constructions of Romantic Authority* (1991), *Allegories of One's Own Mind: Melancholy in Victorian Poetry* (2005). He has also edited *Critical Essays on Dante Gabriel Rossetti* (1992).

Herbert F Tucker is John C Coleman Professor of English at the University of Virginia. A specialist in nineteenth-century British literature with a close interest in the poetry of the period, he's the author of many flashy critical articles in the area. His books include *Browning's Beginnings: the Art of Disclosure* (1981), *Tennyson and the Doom of Romanticism* (1988), and *Epic: Britain's Heroic Muse 1790–1910* (2008). He has edited *Critical Essays on Alfred Lord Tennyson* (1993), *The Blackwell Companion to Victorian Literature and Culture* (1999), *Victorian Literature 1830–1900* (2001, with Dorothy Mermin), and *Under Criticism: Essays in Honor of William H Pritchard* (1998) – Tucker's old Professor at Amherst, the composer of superior satirical songs about Theorists.

Jennifer A Wagner-Lawlor is Associate Professor of English and Women's Studies in the Department of Women's Studies at Penn State, Pennsylvania State University. She writes on sonnets, parody, cultural context, women and utopia. Her books are (as Jennifer Wagner), *A Moment's Monument: Revisionary Poetics and the Nineteenth-Century English Sonnet* (1996); and, as Wagner-Lawlor, *The Victorian Comic Spirit: New Perspectives* (2000). With Barbara Ching, she has edited *The Scandal of Susan Sontag* (2009).

Chris White is a former teacher of Literature at the Bolton Institute of Higher Education, subsequently Bolton University. She writes with combative force on homosexuality and lesbianism. With her then partner Elaine Hobby (now Professor of Seventeenth-Century Studies at Loughborough University) she edited *What Lesbians do in Books* (1991), and by herself the no-holds-barred *Nineteenth-Century Writings on Homosexuality: A Sourcebook* (1999).

Ann Wordsworth taught in Oxford's Faculty of English Language and Literature, especially for St Hugh's College and the Department for

Continuing Education. A spirited (and in Oxford terms a pioneering) theorist, she was one of the three 1970s founders of the *Oxford Literary Review* – the journal founded to ginger up literary study in Britain, but especially in Oxford, by promoting Theory and Theorists, not least Derrida and Harold Bloom. A keen Bloomian, she published many Theory-disposed articles and reviews, particularly in the *Oxford Literary Review*.

Susan Zlotnick is Associate Professor of English at Vassar College, New York. She teaches and writes on the intersection of history and literature, especially in Victorian literature and in the case of women's and working-class writing. She's the author of *Women, Writing and the Industrial Revolution* (1999).

Introduction

This collection of critical essays presents some of the Newest New Criticism of the Victorian Poets. It illustrates the range of new, or newish, critical approaches to this extraordinary body of poetry and poetics, to the poets and their ways with their texts, their words, their forms, their modes and sub-genres. Here are Now re-readings and re-interpretations – contentious often (and often contended) – driven variously by contemporary ideological interests, including especially gender questions, selfhood and body issues, compelled too by recent textualities promoted by structuralism, post-structuralism and deconstruction, all applied in critical practice to the grand, and less grand, masters of the traditional canon and to the newer arrivals in the now greatly afforced canon, women, homosexuals, regional and working-class poets.

The number of Victorian poets now demanding and getting reader attention, the canon of Victorian poets, the authors of the poems now on the syllabus, makes a vast crowd. The bulkier modern anthologies shout the story of currently accepted Victorian largesse – Christopher Ricks's *New Oxford Book of Victorian Verse* (1990: 112 poets), Daniel Karlin's *Penguin Book of Victorian Verse* (1997: 145 poets), my own *The Victorians: An Anthology of Poetry and Poetics* (Blackwell, 2000: 158 poets). At the core of the canon, as they have been for a long time, are the two uncontestedly major figures, Alfred Lord Tennyson, Victoria's Poet Laureate, and Robert Browning. They're the quality of the quality, assisted by a still highly regarded troupe of male producers: Gerard (Manley) Hopkins , Matthew Arnold and his friend Arthur Clough, Algernon Swinburne, A E Housman and Oscar Wilde, Dante Gabriel Rossetti and William Morris, Edward Fitzgerald, Robert Bridges and

Victorian Poets: A Critical Reader, First Edition. Edited by Valentine Cunningham.
© 2014 John Wiley & Sons, Ltd. Published 2014 by John Wiley & Sons, Ltd.

Thomas Hardy. A strong male band rather cleanly divided on educational, which is to say, class lines. On the one hand, the gentlemen poets from the ancient English universities of Oxford and Cambridge – Tennyson and Fitzgerald (Trinity, Cambridge), Hopkins, Arnold, Clough and Swinburne (Balliol, Oxford), Morris (Exeter, Oxford), Housman (St John's, Oxford), Wilde (Magdalen, Oxford), Bridges (Corpus Christi College, Oxford). On the other hand, the Others, who didn't go to an ancient English university: Browning, D G Rossetti, Hardy, denigrated in their own time, and even after that, as not educated enough, too philistine and uncouth to be taken as seriously as the scholarly gents. But nonetheless a group comprising a coherent all-male school, until it was, as it were, forced to go mixed, with women admitted as literary equals, and sometimes more than equals. Notably, of course, Elizabeth Barrett Browning and Christina G Rossetti, now thought of as very powerful women poets, a canonized pair more and more supported by a host of other women canonistas – the likes of Felicia Hemans, George Eliot, Emily Brontë, Mary Coleridge, Augusta Webster, Constance Naden, Lizzie Siddal, Dora Greenwell, Alice Meynell, Margaret Woods, Amy Levy. Many of them, of course, bourgeois, even rather posh and well-off (like Elizabeth Barrett Barrett and Alice Meynell), daughters of vicars (like the Brontës), comfortably-off wives (like Margaret Woods, wife of the President of Trinity College, Oxford, or Augusta Webster, wife of a Fellow of Trinity, Cambridge), even undergraduates (like Amy Levy, who spent two terms at the new women's Cambridge College, Newnham). Women put firmly on the literary map not least by anthologies such as *Victorian Women Poets 1830–1900* (Dent, 1994), edited by Jennifer Breen, and *Victorian Women Poets*, edited by Angela Leighton and Margaret Reynolds (Blackwell, 1995).

If not all that long ago the Big Four Victorian Poets were Tennyson, Browning, Arnold and Hopkins, now – supposing it's not too silly to go on talking in these terms – they are Tennyson, Browning, Christina Rossetti and Elizabeth Barrett Browning. Though many critics and syllabus-makers would prefer that quartet to play as a quintet, with the fifth chair going to Hopkins, or Swinburne, or Wilde. (My own preference is for Hopkins.) Women critics, and feminist criticism, are, of course, largely responsible for the strong upgrade of Barrett Browning, Christina G, and the other women canonistas. And it's modern shifts of critical interest and ideology, of Theory in other words – the latest moves in the ever shifting, shoving, tilting, switching politics of reading, of literary history, of canon-making – which are responsible likewise for the other party and partisan inclusions in the Victorian canon, as well as for the recent/recentish re-readings, re-envisionings of established canon members.

The present presence of so many proletarian poets in the canon, for example, is the result of potent Marxist and Marxized critical preachments, especially, though not exclusively, as they draw breath in the long shadow of revived historicism, the so-called New Historicism. The House of Poetry now gives bed and board to lots more residents than heretofore, the onetime poetic homeless, rescued from the aesthetic ghetto, working men and women from the provinces, from proletarian quarters of cities, the field, factory and mine, the loom and the kitchen-sink: Ebenezer Elliott the 'Corn-Law Rhymer'; John Clare the poor-boy ruralist; Thomas Cooper the Chartist; charity-boy James ('The City of Dreadful Night') Thomson; Ebenezer Jones another Chartist; Gerald Massey, the 'Red Republican', son of illiterate bargee parents put to work thirteen and a half hours day in a silk mill at the age of eight; Joseph Skipsey, Northumberland coal-miner; John ('Thirty Bob a Week') Davidson; blind Scottish spinner and weaver Janet Hamilton; self-educated Eliza Cook; the 'Factory Girl' from Glasgow, Ellen Johnston; Dundee ploughman's daughter Elizabeth Duncan; Ruth Willis, lame Leicester factory worker; Mary Smith, the one-time domestic servant from Cropredy, Oxfordshire; and so on. (Sterling propagandizing and availability of poems in Brian Maidment's compendium *The Poorhouse Fugitives: Self-Taught Poets and Poetry in Victorian Britain* (1987) and Florence S Boos's *Working-Class Women Poets in Britain: An Anthology* (2008).)

The hand of Michel Foucault is to be felt everywhere in these canonical recruitments. His Marxized historiographical criticism, all about the rescue of the subjugated, the disregarded and the disapproved, from under the oppressive gaze of marginalizing power, has had great critically recreative effect. It has revitalized older feminisms of course, and is uniquely responsible for the massively important Post-Colonial and Queer Studies of recent times. The post-colonial awareness, which has attended to the blackness of the West Indian Creole Bertha Mason in Charlotte Brontë's *Jane Eyre*, the woman liberated by feminist criticism from her house-arrest as 'The Mad Woman in the Attic', nowadays homes in on the blackness of Elizabeth Barrett Browning, of her husband Robert Browning, and for that matter, of Alice Meynell, all offspring of miscegenated planter families in the West Indies. It has made attending to the orientalism of Tennyson's *Maud* a *sine qua non* of reading that poem now. Queer (or Q) criticism, a main branch of the big field of modern gender studies, has resulted in the canonizing of once ignored homosexual poets – chief among these the pair of lesbians Katherine Harris Bradley and her niece Edith Emma Cooper writing under the name of Michael Field (important not least for their major part in the significant Victorian poetic cult of Sappho, whose female pronouns for the desired beloved they restored in their translations and adaptations; 'my two dear Greek women' Browning called them, with large liberal affection). Q studies are also responsible for the way long well-regarded poets Hopkins and Housman and Wilde have been as it were officially re-branded, re-stamped, as gay poets (their homosexuality and homoerotic interests coming to matter as much as if not more than anything else that matters about them). Q interests have made sure that the homosexual tenor of Tennyson's cult of his dead friend Arthur Hallam will be given what's now thought of as due prominence.

So: new readings, new scenes and focusses of reading, and new tools for reading. The politicized considerations that have burst the old canon's banks to let in onetime occluded and marginalized, even excluded writers – women, homosexuals, proletarians, the poor and the proletarian, miscegenated women in the attic, political and religious dissenters and nonconformists, the regionally accented, dialect speakers, the many far from and short on what Matthew Arnold, Oxford's massively influential Professor of Poetry, praised as 'the tone of the centre' – have released for critical attention, indeed made mandatory attention to, literature's dealings as subject matter with questions of gender and race, as well as sharpening up the attention paid to class (that rather long-established British critical interest: less so, traditionally, in the USA). All this is a grand politicizing and historicizing, which inevitably motor an awkward-squad nagging away at the doings of power, and at how selves, persons, their bodies as well as their minds and souls, people in their skin as well as in the societies they inhabit and compose, are, as they say, 'constructed' in literature. This is to see literature, in other words, as a main actor in what Michel Foucault called the 'discourses' that collaborate to imagine and so create persons and societies. 'Discourses', because Foucault recognized the collaboration in these imperious ideological doings of all forms of textual activity. Texts of all kinds, medical, political, religious as well as fictional; art of all sorts, especially in Victorian times painting and the latest medium of representation the photograph, but all modelled on writing, the stuff of literature, which gives literature a main place in these considerations. And Foucault's political analyses greedily, and for his time naturally, inhabit what we now think of as the mid-twentieth-century 'linguistic turn', that granting of precedence to language and its ways in all thinking about cultural production. The textuality, the linguistic work, the rhetoric, metaphoricity, the 'figurality', of the historical, empirical, ideological: it's a contentious convergence, obviously; in fact, a difficult marriage teetering always on divorce.

The linguistics in question, of course, is that of the most influential linguist ever, the great Ferdinand de Saussure in his early twentieth-century lectures, which became his (posthumous) *Cours de Linguistique Générale*, the famous *Course of General Linguistics*. The linguistics that gave rise to structuralism, and eventually post-structuralism, to the idea of literature, and literary practice, as being above all self-reflexively about itself as writing, the way the text works, the internal play of its words as such, as (in de Saussure's terms) *signifiers*, not *signifieds* (or signata), that is words pointing to the world outside. In other words, texts as systems of verbal *difference* rather than *reference*. The assumption being that a poem is a self-mirroring space, utterly inward looking – *abysmal*, as the code has it, that is plunging for meaning deeper and deeper into its own textual self. Hotly self-referential, intra-textual, the poem on this view does as it were squint beyond itself, but always in a textually constrained way: it has outside relations, but with other writings, the writings near and distant, which generate it and which it generates, its 'intertextual' relations. And, according to the influential German theorist, Wolfgang Iser, the text's self-subjectivity builds in possible ways of reading it – 'implicit' or 'implied' readings, which in effect construct an 'implicit' or 'implied' reader. All in all, though, this is the *autotelic* text, influentially refigured by Jacques Derrida as 'deconstructive', that is made of language at war with itself, with language's ancient and persisting desire for presence and fullness of meaning, for reference to the world; and so here language is stuck on a border, a threshold, where access to meaning and value is frustrated, even barred. The Derridean word for this is aporia: the *aporetic* text.

Such textual/intertextual assumptions have animated literary criticism, and not least the reading of Victorian poetry, as much as, if not more so than, the pressing ideological concerns. Together they comprise the interests of what is known as Theory. Interests that are not as innovatory as they are sometimes claimed, but which have certainly been strongly renovatory. Literary criticism proceeds historically, of course, by from time to time refuelling and retooling the persistent Basic Trio of critical concerns, the Big Three (as old as Aristotle) of *text-producer*, *produced text* and its meanings, and the *contexts of production*.

5

Literary criticism survives by, thrives on, such shifts. But they are Turns, rather than Breaks. So that contemporary reading practice is always more of a palimpsestic blending than a case of cleanly wiped slates. But still the recent renovations, ideological and textual, have been so loud and deep and wide as to suggest more breaking than mere turning. And resistance to critical *renoving* (Joyce's portmanteau word for modernism's paradoxical mix of removing and renewing), though historically normal , has never been so strong as recently, because the renovators' polemics about literary ideologies and the ways of textualizing have never, perhaps, been so fierce. Never before so much blood on the coal, which means never such interesting critical times as now.

The business of this collection of essays is to show some of the new Theorized, and post-Theory, ways of reading Victorian poetry in action, the engagement with the now stretched canon, the application of renovating ideological and textual insistences to canonistas old and new. It welcomes the polemics, the partisanships, on behalf of the new, but also the resistances: that is, the serious contending and argumentativeness of current critical proceedings. Above all it wants to illustrate the exciting range of current critical attention, the bustling play of the exhilaratingly various possibilities of things to notice, things to say, ways of thinking and saying them, now available to readers of Victorian poetry.

In 'The Echo and the Mirror *en abîme* in Victorian Poetry' Gerhard Joseph, enthusiastic Derridean, explains the notion of abysmality, connecting it with Derrida's concept of *différance* (a dual term Derrida coined to denote language as a practice of *difference*, words as fields of meaning, and of *deferring*, words as slippery evaders of your grasp as they retreat down the signifying plughole), and linking it with the large practice of self-echoing, self-mirroring, repetivity in poems by Tennyson, Browning and Arnold. Joseph doesn't want precisely to argue that Victorian poets are post-structuralists *avant la lettre*, but he is arguing the strong applicability to them of abysmality. Characteristically of a lot of users of postmodernist assumptions Joseph is at pains to suggest abysmality has, in practice, a long and established history; not unknown to older criticism (think, e.g., *Tristram Shandy*) but needing recent Theory to give it due prominence.

There's more textual mirroring and echoing in 'The Mirror's Secret: Dante Gabriel Rossetti's Double Work of Art' by J Hillis Miller's, doyen of Anglophone deconstructionism (personal friend and colleague of Derrida; founder member of the so-called Yale School of Criticism in which Derrida was a member; in many ways Derrida's echo-chamber): treatment of Dante Gabriel Rossetti's poems about mirrors and which are verbal mirrors of his own paintings, as the paintings are mirrors of the poems – paintings in the mirror of poems, and vice versa. A strong case of modern ekphrastic analysis, that is critique of poems about paintings (*ekphrasis*: the literary description of a 'plastic' work of art), poems that are now not uncommonly taken as prime examples of the textually self-mirroring, 'post-modernist' poem. John Hollander, the most thorough analyst of ekphrastic poems, gets an honourable mention.

Three takes follow on what literary history has long accepted as the main sub-genre of Victorian poetry, namely the great Victorian poetic practice of the dramatic monologue. In 'Browning's Anxious Gaze' Ann Wordsworth seeks to shake any sense of successful outcomes for the dramas of perception mounted by the mode's greatest exponent Robert Browning. She reads the anxieties powering Browning's gazing narratives through the lens of Lacan's insistent problematizing of the gaze, but especially with the help of Harold Bloom's influential thoughts about the anxieties of poetic influence, the ephebic, successor poet's struggle with his strong predecessors. (The piece first appeared in the collection of critical essays in the *Robert Browning* volume of the Prentice-Hall Twentieth Century Views series, edited by Harold Bloom himself with Adrienne Munich.)

In 'The Pragmatics of Silence and the Figuration of the Reader in Browning's Dramatic Monologues' Jennifer A Wagner-Lawlor inspects the handling by the mode's greatest exponent Robert Browning of what tradition accepts is an absolute of the form, namely the silence of the monologuist's addressee. For Wagner-Lawlor this silence is central to the animation, the construction, of the reader as this poetry's main subject – the implied reader (and the implicit readings) of Iserian instantiation. This reader is stuck in enticing, suggestive, but frustrating 'dialogue' with the poem, as the original addressees are held in their irkingly loaded silence by their unstoppable addressers. So the dramatic monologue becomes a key modernist business: the poem presenting its subject as 'figuration', metaphoricity, rhetoric, of course, and in the matter of what a literary text is held, modernistically, to be all about – silence, the withholding of certainties, the insistence upon enigma rather than revelation. As Wagner-Lawlor notes, John Ruskin cantankerously accused Browning of being gratuitous and self-indulgent about: utterly missing what is for her Browning's uncannily far-reaching linguistic and poetic principle.

For his part Herbert F Tucker's 'Dramatic Monologue and the Overhearing of Lyric' offers an historical and critical repositioning of the genre of dramatic monologue (practised by Tennyson, but still mainly a Browning affair) as a form of lyric. Lyric for Tucker is an affair of over-hearing – intertextual overhearing, but mainly overhearing by persons – the implied hearers of these poems, and by us the poems' readers (shades of Wagner-Lawlor's concerns). What's at stake in these poems is 'the intersubjective confirmation of the self': the dramatics of the lyrical. This, Tucker argues, was a great gift to the modernists, especially Yeats, Pound, Frost and Eliot – all exploiters of dramatic monologue. 'Poetry became modern once again in its return to the historically responsive and dialogical mode that Browning, Tennyson, and others had brought forward from the Romantics'. (*Dialogical* is a handy, and still popular, term of approval in Theory-driven criticism – taken from the Russian critic Mikhail Mikhailovich Bakhtin who notoriously applied it to the novels of Dostoevsky in order to bring them in from the cold, which Soviet Socialist Realism would assign them to.) Tucker is throughout keen to weigh Browning's 'lyricism' within the history of its reception. He suggests that the personal concerns of Browning were why the dominant mid-twentieth-century New Critics, who valued impersonality in poetry and criticism, found Browning so awkward a case. Typically of some post-Theory reading, Tucker wants his story of a particular mode's reception to be an allegory of the problems of reading that mode as such.

Antony Harrison's 'Matthew Arnold's Gipsies: Intertextuality and the New Historicism' looks at the gipsy poems of the extremely important poet-critic/critical poet Matthew Arnold, in particular 'The Scholar Gipsy', the poem rightly regarded as quintessential to Arnold's poetic delvings into the role of the artist in Victorian times. This is an intertextual analysis conducted under the flag of New Historicism: the practice founded by Stephen Greenblatt of reading a literary text in parallel with non-literary texts, here non-aesthetic writings about gipsies; a practice which, according to Greenblatt's original formulation, shows that a literary text's main existence is within a 'circulation of texts' rather than bound into a relationship with real things outside the text. Whether Harrison succeeds in this is as moot as with any of Greenblatt's own 'new-historical' readings. It's a good try, though, even if here, as elsewhere, 'New Historicist' reading seems quite close to Old Historicism – old historicizing just writ a bit larger, or more shoutily. A common enough charge against 'New Historicist' proceedings.

In 'A New Radical Aesthetic: The Grotesque as cultural critique: Morris', Isobel Armstrong, experienced materialist and grounded feminist critic, *grande dame* in fact of Victorian poetry studies, looks at the poetry of Socialist aesthete William Morris in terms of a form his

8

politicized poetry went in for greatly, the Grotesque. The Grotesque was a poetic mode defined powerfully, albeit despisingly, by John Ruskin, so Morris's radical social and aesthetic theory is addressed in dialogue with Ruskin's different and more conservative thinking. Morris's volume *The Defence of Guenevere and Other Poems* provides rich material for discussion of how ideologically contentious sex and sexuality play in Victorian poetry and culture; especially in the matter of hair, the most prevalent synecdoche of the body in Victorian poetry, a dominant of Victorian poets' clamant obsession with the body – or 'fleshly' consciousness as contemporary body-aesthetics were labelled in Robert Buchanan's stroppy attack on the Pre-Raphaelites and their ilk, 'The Fleshly School of Poetry: Mr D G Rossetti' ('By "Thomas Maitland"'). A better example of the way this essay has ideology and form intersecting and interacting – embracing what Hayden White, the pioneer of (post)modern considerations of the rhetoricity of historiography, called *The Content of the Form* (his title of 1987) – would be hard to find. It finely justifies the claim of its title in Armstrong's important *Victorian Poetry: Poetry, Poetics and Politics* (1993) that Morris was engaged in 'A New Radical Aesthetic'.

The important lecture by Geoffrey Hill, 'Alienated Majesty: Gerard M Hopkins', on Hopkins in relation to Walt Whitman , the American poet he was so greatly taken with, is a critique exemplary as a comparative study but also as an awkwardly forthright political one. Whitman the radical democrat, Hopkins the Christian Tory democrat: at first sight similar only in their shared homosexuality, but truly united, as Hill argues in his wonderfully gritty, lexically deep-digging fashion, in their shared interest in what Hill calls *civil polity* (a subject uniting many of the lectures Hill is giving as Matthew Arnold's successor as Oxford Professor of Poetry). It's a case pushing with canny strategy along, but against, the grain of much recent Hopkins criticism, which Hill plainly feels, if not gone totally astray, is at least often wide of the mark. Loudly rebuking here is Hill's refusal to address Hopkins's, or Whitman's, homosexuality. That major preoccupation of recent criticism is, he implies, a diversion from the main track in reading either poet. Hill embraces Hopkins's politics as a peculiar but still authentic democratic vision, in the face of the now common fleering at this priest as a hierarchical conservative despiser of tramps, the unemployed, farriers and such. And (at first surprisingly) central to Hopkins's Whitmanite affinities is his dutifulness as a never not quite alienated Jesuit: the serious Roman Catholicism of the poet and the poetry cannot be discounted as some modern critique would prefer. Hill is here doing criticism in the modern way as massively political, but his is modern criticism reversed, in the mirror of the usual. Hill is as polemically aggressive as any of the implied critics he's spurning, fights over their ground, but always from the opposite corner. This produces a conservative criticism by no means simplistic, whose wonderfully individualistic strength is to be differently radical.

My 'Fact and Tact: post-Arnoldian Fact-finding and Modern Q Tactlessness in the Reading of Gerard Hopkins' is a polemical piece (originating in a tribute to the scholar-critic-editor F W Bateson founder and General Editor of the great Longman's Annotated Poets series, which brought out Ricks's *Tennyson*, the Allotts' *Arnold*, and the Woolford/Karlin/Phelan *Robert Browning*) suggesting as an essential principle and methodology for good reading a combination of the accumulation of *facts*, as advocated by Bateson's favourite Matthew Arnold ('more and more' fact), and readerly tact (heedful, lovingly attentive critical touch), as suggested by Christopher Ricks (the magisterial editor of Tennyson). The combination gets a test run in relation to the way Hopkins's 'Felix Randal', a main Hopkins poem, and one touchingly about touching between men, has been read – on the one hand rescued from serious mistaking by the accession of facts about Hopkins's farrier subject and the true meaning of key words in the poem, and on the other misjudged in tactless misprizing at the hands of strong Q critics Joseph Bristow and Gregory Woods.

Susan Zlotnick's essay '"A Thousand Times I'd be a Factory Girl": Dialect, Domesticity, and Working-Class Women's Poetry in Victorian Britain' is admirably pugilistic in its multi-focussed restoration work. It brings in from the critical cold the variously regional, dialect-speaking, proletarian, female domesticity, woman factory-worker subject and poeticity. Compellingly centred on the distinguished work of Ellen Johnston, the Scottish 'Factory Girl', this is radical feminist canon-busting. Its politico-historical-critical strengths include its feminizing of the traditionally male scene of regional dialect-speaking verse, and its moving pondering of the mountainous difficulties in the way of the aspirant proletarian housewife-worker poet.

'"The fruitful feud of hers and his": Sameness, Difference, and Gender in Victorian Poetry' has Dorothy Mermin doing a classic job of what Jonathan Culler has called 'reading as a woman'. Her big subject is gender in Victorian poetry: how sexual sameness, difference and androgyny play, in both male and female poetry. The great Victorian problematic is the speaking subject (focussed especially in dramatic monologues), and this for Mermin is a necessarily gendered matter.

Her forte is the challenging sweeping claim. 'In some important ways all the Victorian poets, male and female, can be read as women'.

Mary W Carpenter's '"Eat me, drink me, love me": The Consumable Female Body in Christina Rossetti's *Goblin Market*' works with feminism's favourite Christina Rossetti poem to bring out the poet's, and the period's, obsession with the variously sexualized female body, especially the body of the fallen woman (of great interest to Christina G in daily life as well as in her poetry). These well-aired (Victorian) contemporary moral and religious questions are shown to be heavily infected by assumptions about class and social hierarchy; by nationalist prejudices too, Carpenter thinks, since fallen Laura's blondeness signs her as emphatically English. Hers is an English female body destroyed by sexuality – a nationalizing of the body provocation emphasized by the parallel Rossetti poem 'In the Round Tower at Jhansi', about an English officer during the 'Indian Mutiny' who shot his wife and then himself to save her from rape by the dark uprising horde. Here feminist critique segues adroitly into post-colonialist awareness: the obsessive Victorian body a terrifying pivot of multivalent fear and threats.

Entrancing body horrors are Carol T Christ's concern too, in her 'Browning's Corpses': focussing in particular Browning's, and his period's, necrophilia: the constant imminence of death in the poetry, and, in a time of fading faith in Christian orthodoxy's afterlife, a clinging to poetic fictions of bodily resurrection.

Striking bodily matters, and in particular head-hair that especial focus of Victorian body consciousness, are the grave centre of Christopher Ricks's subtly adroit 'A E Housman and "the colour of his hair"'. Ricks's concern is with what Housman might have meant by saying four times in his 'Oh who is that young sinner with the handcuffs on his wrists?' that the gravamen of Oscar Wilde's offence, the cause of his jailing, was 'the colour of his hair'. Ingenious speculation leads to a paralleling of Wilde's outcasting with traditional hostility to Jews for the colour, the stereotyping redness, of their hair. Ricks has been a loud Theory sceptic, declaring that what criticism needs is *principles* of reading not theories, and he is frequently linked rather with promoting the actual texts of Victorian poets than theorizing about them (and indeed, singlehandedly his unimprovable editions have made Tennyson's poems available in all their detail forever; and his *Selected* poems of the Irish poet James Henry (2002) does a lovely resurrection job; and Housman editor Archie Burnett's great (2007) edition of Housman letters is a product of the Boston University Editorial Institute Ricks and Geoffrey Hill founded, and which Burnett now co-directs with Ricks). But like Geoffrey Hill, whose poetry Ricks has enthusiastically promoted, Ricks enjoys nothing more than running onto the Theory pitch in order to show the Theory team how to score goals better. Housman, Wilde, homophobia, anti-semitism, the arbitrary making of outcasts to be scourged by oppressive authority: up-to-date concentrations don't come more concentrated than this. But, of course, that anti-Theory Ricks is taking them up does indicate how unavoidable they've become.

In David G Riede's 'Tennyson's "Little *Hamlet*"' the huge Victorian emotional turmoil of mourning turning into melancholia, so central to the poets' fraught engagement with the self, is cannily analysed in melancholic Tennyson's work, especially 'Maud' (his 'little *Hamlet*') – the poem that with Tennyson's *In Memoriam* and James Thomson's 'The City of Dreadful Night' makes up the Big Trinity of Victorian sadness poems. This is a finely instructive essay in its rich array of important critical engagements: particularly in relating Tennyson and the Victorians to Walter Benjamin's classic account of Protestant (post-Hamletian) melancholy and its allegorical outcomes; in drawing out the imperialist and orientalist aspects of 'Maud'; and in the consideration of Ruskin's 'pathetic fallacy' indignations.

Different, though not unrelated melancholies, are the concerns of Eric Griffiths' 'The Disappointment of Christina G Rossetti', with its stress on the theology-driven, practical Christianity of her tortured selfhood, as she waited Beckettianly for the Second Advent of Christ, which never happened (hopes deferred, in Biblical words, making her heart sick). Here's a continually astute close reading of Christina G's poems, especially good on her verbal repetitions (her *twice-ness* fondness). Griffiths reads with forceful, even tetchy, combativeness; this is criticism in the midst of contemporary debate. 'Poems do not have insides and outsides', as recent criticism believes they do. Feminist readings are put in their place. It's wrong of Angela Leighton to offer Rossetti's 'doubleness' as gender-specifically female: this is 'normal also for male writers'. Isobel Armstrong is misguided to take Rossetti's prosodic irregularity as revolutionarily feminist. Adrienne Rich mistakenly reads Rossetti's religion as sexual 'sublimation' (Griffiths dislikes Freudianism). Importantly, he wants to get Rossetti's religiosity straight (an often embarrassing subject for secularizing feminism), and he mainly succeeds – though his refusal to accept that the *sisterhood* aspects of Rossetti concerns, her large interest in nuns, for example, might be even proto-feminist does not carry a lot of weight.

Angela Leighton's 'Stirring "a Dust of Figures": Elizabeth Barrett Browning and Love' takes up Barrett Browning's estranging and estranged *discourse* of love, in a demonstration where the normality of this woman's great contribution to the Victorian 'language of the heart', to Victorian erotics (Leighton is right to oppose the modern cliché about repressed Victorians) cries out for, and gets, definition in its womanly distinctiveness. The impressively calm concentration – much of Leighton's polemical force comes from her refusal to get heated – is *Sonnets from the Portuguese*, Elizabeth Barrett's private courtship poems for Robert Browning. These poems, this poet, are shown ghosted by the 'Mariana' poems of Tennyson. Barrett Browning, a prisoner, in her own words, 'scrawling mottos on the walls', is offered as representing the imprisoned self of the Victorian woman poet: the poet figured as, and figuring in, distance, doubleness and foreignness (metaphoricized first as 'Bosnian' then as 'Portuguese'). Her particular language of the heart: a kind of foreign language, certainly hard to learn, and like all foreign languages easily misunderstood.

In '"Love, let us be true to one another": Matthew Arnold, Arthur Hugh Clough and "our Aqueous Ages"' the serious Q theorist Joseph Bristow brings together Matthew Arnold and Arthur Clough as friends patrolling the fluid borders of gender, where their maleness is much troubled by fear of women and of emasculation. They're as it were together on Arnold's Dover Beach, site of the most famous watery margin of Victorian poetry's many, worried by the female 'bearded well', the 'Fuosich' of the original title of Clough's same-sex College-boy poem *The Bothie of Tober-na-Vuolich*. The undergirding assumption is that gender is entirely an affair of self-making, as popularized by Judith Butler and Eve Kosofsky-Sedgwick. Bristow disclaims wanting to present Arnold and Clough as a gay pair, but he certainly convinces about their shared fluctuating masculinity and their poetic intertwining (not least in the appearance of Clough, the 'liminal bachelor' as Kosofsky-Sedgwick calls him, as Thyrsis in Arnold's 'The Scholar Gipsy').

In '"Poets and lovers evermore": the poetry and journals of Michael Field' Chris White carefully complicates the nature of the writing of 'Michael Field', the most celebrated Victorian pair of 'Sapphic', lesbian, lovers and poets, too readily limited and simplified by the enthusiasm of their feminist enthusiasts. White's critical force lies in her sense of the variety of discourses this pair of poets tried out in their never finally resolved quest for the 'lesbian' words to say it: classical scholarly (the translations and versions of Sappho), heterosexual, the language of friendship, Roman Catholic (at the end). White dwells sympathetically on the naming and self-naming issue around Bradley and Cooper's choice of 'Michael Field', and is very informative in her literary-historical story of the deployment of Greek cultural precedent by Victorian gays of all genders.

Timothy A J Burnett's focus is Victorian poetry's most industrious sexual bad boy Swinburne at work on the notorious 'Anactoria', one of the most offending offerings in his publicly horrifying *Poems and Ballads* volume. This is a Sapphic poem, indeed, as relished by feminist and lesbian critics; but even more one steeped in Swinburne's sado-masochistic fetishism after the Marquis de Sade. These sexual matters are revealingly approached by an analysis of Swinburne hard at work on the first page of his poem. This is close-up textual reading of Swinburne as a most diligently attentive wordsmith. It's important to include in this collection of contemporary approaches because it indicates the kind of reception enabled now by the assiduously garnered textual data in modern editions (the Longmans Annotated Poets, Margaret Reynolds' *Aurora Leigh*), as well as putting to flight, to the sword in fact, the old canard that Victorian poets were merely slapdash knockers-off of their verses. That was a lie especially hurtful to Swinburne whose onetime reputation as the 'poet with the fatal facility' gave him awful prominence among the slandered.

And, finally, a chronologically forward-looking discussion of what's argued is the perennial and on-going poetic struggle with naming. It's worked by Mary-Ann Caws and Gerhard Joseph through a look at the devotion of the Symbolist and ur-modernist Stéphane Mallarmé to High Victorian Tennyson – an attraction evinced not least in Mallarmé's prose translations of Tennyson's 'Mariana' and 'Godiva'. Richly Derridean in its interest in a normative aporetic convergence of naming and not naming, the piece is a very good example not only of the now large recognition of Victorian poetry's effect and influence on modern/modernist/postmodernity, but of the proto-modernism of Tennyson (and many of his contemporaries). Modernists on this reckoning are characterized by their naming, which is also a refusal to name; and so also is Tennyson, the loudly 'sonorous' namer. A deceptive sonorousness, because it too, for all its audibility, is what T S Eliot, adapting Lancelot Andrewes, called the 'word unheard', the 'word within a word, unable to speak a word'.

Style Note: the different practices of the original articles in spelling (English/American), use of inverted commas, and referencing methods have been preserved.

14

1

The Echo and the Mirror *en abîme* in Victorian Poetry

Gerhard Joseph

In recent French theory, the term *en abîme* describes any fragment of a text that reproduces in small the structure of the text as a whole. Introduced by André Gide in a passage of his *Journal* in 1893, the phrase, which he intended as a characterization of his own reduplicative techniques, had as its origin an ancient visual device – that of the miniature heraldic shield enclosed within another shield whose shape and inner divisions it repeats exactly. There had, to be sure, been earlier examples of internal mirror effects in painting and literature – Gide cites the literary instances of *Hamlet, Wilhelm Meister,* and "The Fall of the House of Usher."[1] But in order to distinguish his own strategies from those of simple doubling, he felt the need to fashion a new critical term – *"en abîme"* – to indicate the idea of multiple replication. From Gide's coinage in the *Notebooks* and exemplary practice in *Narcisse, La Tentative,* and *Les Faux- Monnayeurs,* it is but a short step to the *mise en abîme* of post-Saussurean, post-structuralist theory, where we are invited to follow, in Jacques Derrida's words, "a book in the book, an origin in the origin, a center in the center"[2] beyond the inmost bound of human thought. In short, the *mise en abîme* generated by Derrida's elaboration of bottomless *différance* uncovers a frame within a frame in endless replication – what one thinks of in more homely terms as the Dutch-Cleanser, Quaker-Oats or Morton-Salt effects of commercial packaging.

Joseph, Gerhard. 1985. "The Echo and the Mirror *en abîme* in Victorian Poetry." In *Victorian Poetry*, 23, iv (Winter), pp. 403–12. Reproduced with permission of Gerhard Joseph.

Victorian Poets: A Critical Reader, First Edition. Edited by Valentine Cunningham.
© 2014 John Wiley & Sons, Ltd. Published 2014 by John Wiley & Sons, Ltd.

It is no accident that the concept was given its initial literary definition in the nineteenth century. In his famous characterization of "the Piranesi effect," for instance, Thomas De Quincey recalls the play within a play in *Hamlet* and compares this to a room on whose wall is a picture of that room, on whose wall is a picture of that room, on whose wall is a picture of that room…, and concludes that "we might imagine this descent into a life below a life going on *ad infinitum*" into "abysses that swallow…up abysses."[3] And Alfred Tennyson conveys to perfection what Gide meant by *en abîme* in the very context of Gide's heraldic etymology: Lancelot's shield in "The Lady of Shalott" with its image of a knight forever kneeling to his lady gives us in microcosm the larger structure of desire in the poem. That is, whatever its history in French theory and literature, the device, or something very much like it, also accentuated itself in English Victorian poetry in the auditory guise of the echo and the visual one of the mirror, sometimes in tandem. It demonstrated thereby the nineteenth-century English sources – Arnold's tortured and unending "dialogue of the mind with itself" – of modernist reflexiveness.

The formal expression of man's cognitive self-enclosure for the period is the dramatic monologue, with its limited aperture of the single personality's straitened vista upon the world.[4] The very narrowness of the "single window" in the monologue, however, makes for a compensatorily rich depth; the outer frame can compose a wildly proliferative inner cosmos, the receding strata of voices, for instance, within Robert Browning's poems. As John Hollander suggests in his exhaustive study of the figure of echo in English literature, dramatic form is an implicit echo chamber whenever a speaker is made to echo a prior voice,[5] the typical situation in Browning's monologues. In the simplest and most accessible of the monologues, the speaker's outer voice merely brackets a single interlocutory one – the Duke's voice, say, in "My Last Duchess" containing the implied answers of the Count's envoy. But more often that framing impulse leads Browning to the more dazzling rhetorical acrobatics which attract his sophistical protagonists, those "wheel within a wheel" replications their perverse, complex natures require, as his Bishop Blougram insists.[6] At his most convoluted (and increasingly in the later monologues), Browning approaches the frame within-a-frame recessiveness that Erving Goffman has anatomized in *Frame Analysis*, his breakdown of social intercourse at its labyrinthine extreme where only the most patient of listeners can follow.[7]

While others may have their own favorite Browning echo chamber, my candidate for his most recursive Chinese-box instance – or at any rate the one easiest to exfoliate in brief as a paradigm for auditory regressiveness – is "Dîs Aliter Visum; or Le Byron de Nos Jours." In this maddening tour de force, Browning's *Last Year at Marienbad*, a woman addresses a famous French poet who out of timidity and a passion for respectability had refused to seize the moment of love with her ten years earlier. Then, they had met by a cliff brow at the seaside; now, she reminisces to him at a windowseat in an enclosed room. As quotation marks envelop quotation marks, point of view becomes ever more recessively entangled until, at the echolalial center of the poem, the woman is imagining what her lover would have imagined himself saying in reply to the speech (sts. xv–xvii) which he had just imagined her making had they indeed decided, as they had not, to marry! And the challenge to the audience becomes even more forbidding in such late monologues as *Balaustion's Adventure, Red Cotton Night-Cap Country; or Turf and Towers*, or *Prince Hohenstiel-Schwangau, Saviour of Society*. Perhaps we have not yet reached, even in the most impenetrable of such later mazes, the systematic vocal dislocations of Alain Robbe-Grillet and Nathalie Sarraute or the deepset games of R. D. Laing's *Knots*. Arguably we are not quite at the seventh remove from the outer voice (" ' " ' " ' "in print) where John Barth locates the innermost voice of his "menelaiad," one of the auditory experiments in *Lost in the Funhouse*. But Browning is surely moving in such directions, and the pleasurable strain we experience in disentangling the voices of his intricate echo chambers prepares us for the late games of modernist theory and practice, for an epistemological vertigo that stages itself rhetorically as auditory confusion.

The original sound that the Victorian poet's voice projects into the world is not of course inevitably indecipherable, or so the situations in some of Tennyson's poetry assure us. In a brief, early Shelleyan phase, unmediated sound fills the soul of the Tennysonian bard upon the height (as in, say, "Timbuctoo" or "Armageddon"), from which remove he is able to "shake the world" with prophecy. The sound of the Dying Swan, one of Tennyson's recurring images of the poet's prophetic voice,[8] flows forth into the world with such a bracing force, flooding an otherwise desolate wasteland with "eddying song." But very quickly Tennyson's artist figures suffer an "Icarian fall"[9] from a semidivine to a human condition. As a result, prophecy now floats down from the heights upon a melodic stream to be received by such fallen or "cursed" maidens as Claribel, Mariana, and the Lady of Shalott – artist figures immured within a garden of the mind who try in their turn to reach an audience or a single auditor with their voices. As song flows out of the aesthetic garden, the important question Tennyson considers is how or even whether the bard's inspired flow will be received by listeners in the cities of man. Tennyson conceives of a variety of answers to that question in the course of his career from the perspective both of the artist and of the audience, but for the sake of brevity, I will abstract first the positive and then the negative force of his notion of sound, especially of reverberative sound – i.e., the echo.

One of the critical truisms about Tennyson is that he is the poet of the remote in time and space, a poet of the "far, far away" – to echo one of his favorite echoing phrases. "It is the distance," he maintained to his friend James Knowles late in life, "that charms me in the landscape, the picture and the past, and not the immediate to-day in which I move."[10] If that recessional quality characterizes his visual sense, it informs his sense of sound as well. Sound like sight is most evocative when it is experienced at a "far, far" remove from the original source, and the appeal of echo over simple sound is that the former gives the impression of having traveled great distances, of having bounced off various surfaces on the way to the auditor and of having been rendered numinous in the process. Music, as it moves from the bugle in the lyric "The splendour falls on castle walls" (from *The Princess*), grows "thinner" and "clearer" the further it travels, the greater the number of wild echoes it achieves. That is, the artist's sound may dissipate at its source – it is ever "dying, dying, dying." But the very repetition of the word, like the repetition of "far" in "Far Far-Away" or "break" in "Break, break, break"[11] denies that death since it implies an endless life in an answering nature and in the ears of distant auditors:

> O love, they [the echoes] die in yon rich sky,
> They faint on hill or field or river:
> Our echoes roll from soul to soul,
> And grow for ever and for ever.
> (ll. 13–16 of "The splendour falls
> on castle walls")

To the extent that the echo is nature's correspondent instrument to the impulse of human speech and sound, theoretically unto infinity, it implies the emergence of sound's life out of sound's death – not merely life dying out but also life rolling from soul to soul forward to the starry track. Of the several other instances of a death-and-rebirth pattern one might educe to illustrate Tennyson's treatment of the answering echo, perhaps the most haunting occurs at the conclusion of the *Idylls of the*

King. There, the dying wail of the three queens as they escort Arthur toward the distant great deep is answered by a sound from that deep:

> Then from the dawn it seemed there came, but faint
> As from beyond the limit of the world,
> Like the last echo born of a great cry,
> Sounds, as if some fair city were one voice
> Around a king returning from his wars.
>
> ("The Passing of Arthur," ll. 457–461)

But the Tennysonian echo is not always so expressive of life rolling to and from the limit of the world, especially in works where the poet-figure does not have much of an impact upon or is misunderstood by his – or rather "her" – audience (since, as Lionel Stevenson demonstrated in a Jungian analysis of the matter, Tennyson in his early poetry habitually rendered himself as an *"anima"* figure in the guise of isolated maidens[12]). Perhaps the situation in "The Lady of Shalott" may illustrate the auditory gap as well as any of the early poems ("Anacaona," "Claribel," "The Kraken," "Oenone" or "The Hesperides") that one might have chosen. In the 1832 version of the poem, a reaper, arguably representing the audience of the Lady's art, hears the song she sings in her tower:

> Underneath the bearded barley,
> The reaper, reaping late and early,
> Hears her ever chanting cheerly,
> Like an angel, singing clearly,
>   O'er the stream of Camelot.
>
> (ll. 28–32)

By the time of Tennyson's 1842 revision, the Lady's "clear" song has been transformed into something more mysterious:

> Only reapers, reaping early
> In among the bearded barley,
> Hear a song that echoes cheerly
> From the river winding clearly,
>   Down to towered Camelot.
>
> (ll. 28–32)

While the single reaper of the first version hears the song directly, the several reapers of the second encounter it as a reverberation off the river, to which the epithet "clear" has now been shifted. It is tempting

19

to read something thematic into this change partly for reasons of interpretive originality: to my knowledge no one has argued for its significance. To be honest, however, the change from straight sound to deflected echo in a single stanza may not by itself be very important, but it becomes so if we hear it as a concomitant and reinforcement of a like change in visual emphasis between the 1832 and 1842 versions of "The Lady of Shalott."

In the 1832 version of the poem, the Lady

> lives with little joy or fear.
> Over the water, running near,
> The sheepbell tinkles in her ear.
> Before her hangs a mirror clear,
> Reflecting towered Camelot.
> (ll. 46–50)

The mirror into which the Lady gazes is primarily that, a literal mirror which is figuratively unremarkable. Since tapestry is woven from the reverse side, a mirror would have been necessary for the Lady to see the design being woven, and that technical craft function is the primary emphasis or is at any rate more obvious in the 1832 than in the equivalent lines in the 1842 version of the poem:

> And moving through a mirror clear
> That hangs before her all the year,
> Shadows of the world appear.
> There she sees the highway near
> Winding down to Camelot.
> (ll. 46–50)

Now the "mirror clear" has moved to the first line of the stanza to become associated with "Shadows of the world" (l. 48) of which, after catching sight of Lancelot, the Lady becomes "'half sick'" (l. 71). Because of that change, both the ontological and aesthetic oppositions of the poem receive sharpened definition, so that the poem is now usually read as a parable concerning the problematics of mimesis in Tennyson's early art. Within that "parabolic drift" (Tennyson's term for his figurative methods), the fact that Lancelot's image flashes into the Lady's glass "From the bank and from the river" (l. 105) seems crucial. In the semiotic exchange of the poem, the reapers have to decipher a song that echoes off the river, a second order deflection; but the Lady in her reaction to the sight of Lancelot has to contend not only with his mirror image but also with a reflection of that same river's reflection of him, not only with a second but also with a third order reflection,[13] i.e. with the *mise en abîme*.

In the historical context of representation theory, it seems important to distinguish between the metaphorical implications of the "Shadows of the world" of which the Lady is "half sick" on the one hand and the mirror on the other as alternative figures of aesthetic imitation. Both the shadow and the mirror of the poem are traceable back to a Platonic ontological dualism. But while the shadow in the famous parable of the cave in *The Republic* assumes the possibility of only a single duplication – one cannot imagine a shadow of an opaque shadow – that is not true of Plato's mirror. Because a mirror relies upon reflection, there can be a mirror image of a mirror image – indeed, there can theoretically be an infinite series of reflections of reflections of a single putative original. And that is precisely the inner cosmic play of frames implied by the optical situation of "The Lady of Shalott" (not to mention the infinity-of-mirrors conclusion to Orson Welles' *Lady from Shanghai*), a perceptual abyss in which the "original" image of Lancelot bounces endlessly and without grounding between river and glass, teasing the Lady (or at any rate some recent commentators upon her plight) out of thought as doth eternity.

Consequently, "The Lady of Shalott" has of late achieved a paradigmatic force that extends well beyond the status of the poem as a part of Tennyson's early work. I have myself argued that the Lady's movement from mirror to window epitomizes the motion of other nineteenth-century epistemological rebels who seek, at whatever cost, a windowed release from Romantic self-absorption and solipsism,[14] while Geoffrey Hartman has read her passion for direct, unmediated contact with the world, her unwillingness to rest content with ungrounded representation, as *the* best poetic symbol of a Western "desire for reality-mastery as aggressive and fatal as Freud's death instinct":

> "I am half-sick of shadows," says the Lady of Shalott, and turns from her mirror to the reality of advent. She did not know that by her avertedness, by staying within representation, she had postponed death. The most art can do, as a mirror of language, is to burn through, in its cold way, the desire for self-definition, fulness of grace, presence; simply to expose the desire to own one's own name [Hartman's context is Lacanian], to inhabit it numinously in the form of "proper" noun, words, or the signatory act each poem aspires to be.[15]

Thus, when the knights and burghers of Camelot gather around the barge which has floated her body down to Camelot, all they can know of her being is her name, "The Lady of Shalott," inscribed upon the prow of her barge. The Lady thus becomes in death what she was, unbeknownst to herself, in life: a "floating signifier," in Hartman's inspired pun (p. 107). That is, "The Lady of Shalott" serves for Hartman precisely what "The Purloined Letter" did for Lacan in his now famous seminar on Poe's story – as an allegory of the signifier floating through the abyss.

To be sure, such an abyss – like the *mise en abîme* itself – is hardly the invention of the present or even the Victorian age, whatever the current fashion of the concept. Possibly alluded to as early as Euripides, it served as a model for Neo-Platonic notions of Being from Plotinus to Macrobius. In the transition from the dualistic Platonic philosophy with its divisions of Being into Ideas and their Forms to a hierarchy with several gradations, the Neo-Platonists evidently preferred Plato's mirror figure to his shadow figure because it is possible to have mirror images of a mirror but not even a single shadow of a shadow; and Richard Rorty, arguing for a "philosophy without mirrors," has recently shown in his influential *Philosophy and the Mirror of Nature* the systematic centrality of the mirror metaphor in ontology from Plato to Kant.[16] There is a running debate these days, chronicled in Herbert Grabes' *The Mutable Glass*, concerning the extent to which the fashion for mirrors and mirror imagery from the late Middle Ages onward is attributable to the improvement and cheap mass production by the Venetians of glass mirrors and the extent to which that fashion demonstrates a new Hamletic consciousness, a post-Cartesian increase in reflexiveness of thought, and a deep shift in reciprocity of subject and object.[17] Within the frame of that debate, if the 1832 version of "The Lady of Shalott" with its concentration upon the craft function of the mirror may be said to support the former technological explanation, the 1842 version with its profusion of mimetic reflectors supports the latter epistemological one. Indeed, as Christopher Ricks has shown, the parabolic use of the mirror in the poem is directly imitative of an earlier Neo-Platonic mirror scene, the one in Book III, Canto ii of *The Faerie Queene* where Britomart in her tower first spies and falls in love with Artegall in a "wondrous myrrhour."[18]

Nineteenth-century adaptations of the ontological and aesthetic mirror are, as I have said, generally traceable to a Platonic paradigm of the twofold remove of art from archetypal forms. Specifically, in the tenth book of *The Republic*, Socrates explains the mimetic nature of art by an analogy: while the maker of an actual table or bed imitates the

Ideas of those things, the artist has another way. "What way?" asks Glaucon. "An easy enough way," Socrates replies,

> or rather, there are many ways in which the feat might be *quickly* and *easily* accomplished, none quicker than that of turning a mirror round and round – you would soon enough make the sun and the heavens, and the earth and yourself, and the other animals and plants, and all the other things of which we were just now speaking, in the mirror (italics added).[19]

While Plato – or Socrates for him – evolves several negative consequences of this turning mirror as an instrument of cognitive deception, one can see its more positive potential for a later Aristotelian tradition of mimesis. Accepting the truth value of sense experience, that tradition would find Plato's whirling mirror quite congenial to the view that the world of objects could be seen accurately and "easily" – could be seen with the visual acuteness Matthew Arnold attributed to a Sophocles who saw life "steadily" and "whole." Consider the Arnoldian echo in order to allude momentarily to the third of the major Victorian poets, because in what he does with Plato's whirling mirror Arnold illustrates even more pointedly than Tennyson the distance the West has traveled toward a cognitive nihilism. For in the despairing words of Arnold's Empedocles,

> The out-spread world to span
> A cord the Gods first slung,
> And then the soul of man
> There, like a mirror, hung,
> And bade the winds through space impel the gusty toy.
>
> Hither and thither spins
> The wind-borne, mirroring soul,
> A thousand glimpses wins,
> And never sees a whole;
> Looks once, and drives elsewhere, and leaves its last employ.
>
> The Gods laugh in their sleeve
> To watch man doubt and fear,
> Who knows not what to believe
> Since he sees nothing clear,
> And dares stamp nothing false where he finds nothing sure.[20]

Victorian poetry, then, presents us at key points with the opposition of sound and answering echo and of image and mirrored repetition, and Victorian paintings (say, those of William Holman Hunt) and photographs (especially those of the fascinating, relatively unknown Lady Clementine Hawarden)[21] contain comparable iconographic mirrors that raise epistemological questions. When they do, we are, to return to the outer frame of my argument, well on our way to Gide's image *en abîme* – and beyond, to the infinite play of substitution and replication that, for a highly influential Derrida at any rate, constitutes the fundamental operation of any text. I am not of course asserting the identity of a Victorian and a post-structuralist view of representation: for recent theorists the *mise en abîme* describes the operation of the text as mirror or echo of a previous mirror or echo beyond recoverable origin, which is why the two conceptual metaphors are appropriate pendants for the idea of a textuality beyond which the readers (or reapers?) of the world cannot get. (The Greeks, to be sure, also combined the story of Echo and Narcissus into a single myth.[22]) Consequently, the *mise en abîme* can have no existence outside of the mirror and the echo. Since it does not partake of the property of objects, it cannot be grounded in them. Representation always appears in the text as the representation of representation, as the mirror of a mirror or the echo of an echo.

In contrast, the Victorian poet as implied pre-Saussurean theorist would have us believe that the echo has a firm origin in the sound of the bugle, that the images of the world are grounded (if somewhat shakily) in its objects. In "Le Byron de Nos Jours" (unlike *Last Year at Marienbad*) a definable something *did* happen ten years ago, and the ever so patient reader can unravel what it was; and even for the perplexed Lady of Shalott, a palpable Lancelot does undoubtedly exist beside the river and the bank. In terms of the poet's belief in linguistic referentiality, we are still well within what the post-structuralist mind would deconstruct as a naively confident Metaphysics of Presence. Still, while the structures of representation within Victorian poetry have not brought us to the infinite regress of contemporary theory and lost-in-the-funhouse fictional practice, they do predict, we retrospectively see, the modernist endgame of bottomless indeterminacy.[23]

Notes

1   André Gide, *Journal 1889–1939*, "Pléiade" (Paris, 1951), pp. 41–42. For a historical treatment of the *mise en abîme* in literary theory, see Lucien Dällenbach, *Le récit spéculaire: essai sur la mise en abîme* (Paris, 1977).

2   "Ellipsis," in *Writing and Difference*, trans. Alan Bass (Univ. of Chicago Press, 1978), p. 296.

The specific source for the Derridean *mise en abîme* would seem to be Edmund Husserl's Dresden gallery passage in *Ideas*. Husserl's sentences, which become the epigraph that introduces Derrida's *Speech and Phenomena*, trans. David Allison (Northwestern Univ. Press, 1973), p. 1, read as follows: "A name on being mentioned reminds us of the Dresden gallery and of our last visit there: we wander through the rooms, and stop in front of a painting by Tenier which represents a gallery of paintings. Let us further suppose that the paintings of the gallery would represent in their turn paintings, which, on their part, exhibited readable inscriptions and so forth...."

3   Thomas De Quincey, *Collected Writings*, ed. David Masson, 14 vols. (London, 1896–97), X, 344, 416.

4   See F. H. Bradley, *Appearance and Reality: A Metaphysical Essay* (Oxford Univ. Press, 1893), p. 229: "Contact with reality is through a limited aperture. For [we] cannot get at it directly except through...one small opening." W. David Shaw considers Tennyson's habit of opening different "windows" upon the same event throughout *Tennyson's Style* (Cornell Univ. Press, 1976), and I examine the prevalence of windows and mirrors as metaphor in "Victorian Frames: The Windows and Mirrors of Browning, Arnold, and Tennyson" in *VP*, 16 (1978), 70–87. Two other works to which the present essay is indebted in a general way are W. David Shaw, "The Optical Metaphor: Victorian Poetics and the Theory of Knowledge," *VS*, 23 (1980), 293–324; and Michael Greenstein, "The Window in Post-Romantic Aesthetics," Diss. York University, Canada, 1974.

5   John Hollander, *The Figure of Echo: A Mode of Allusion in Milton and After* (Univ. California Press, 1981), p. 44.

6   *Bishop Blougram's Apology*, l. 389. Citations of Browning are from *The Works of Robert Browning*, Centenary Edition, ed. F. G. Kenyon (London, 1912).

7   *Frame Analysis: An Essay on the Organization of Experience* (Harvard Univ. Press, 1974). I would like to thank Mary Ann Caws for letting me profit from the manuscript of *Reading Frames in Modern Fiction*, her phenomenological study of framing structures in the novel from Austen to Woolf (Princeton Univ. Press, 1985).

8   See Catherine Stevenson, "Tennyson's Dying Swans: Mythology and the Definition of the Poet's Role," *SEL*, 20 (1980), 621–35; citations of Tennyson's poetry are from *The Poems of Tennyson*, ed. Christopher Ricks (London, 1969).

9   The phrase, as well as the generalized theory, is A. Dwight Culler's in *The Poetry of Tennyson* (Yale Univ. Press, 1977), pp. 27–8.

10 James Knowles, "Aspects of Tennyson, II: (A Personal Reminiscence)," *The Nineteenth Century*, 33(1893), 170.

11 On Tennysonian repetition, see "Tennyson, Tennyson, Tennyson," Chapter 1 of Culler's *Poetry of Tennyson*.

12 Lionel Stevenson, "The 'High-Born Maiden' Symbol in Tennyson," *PMLA*, 63 (1948), 234–43.

13 David Martin was the first to emphasize this twofold detachment in "Romantic Perspectivism in Tennyson's 'The Lady of Shalott'," *VP*, 11 (1973), 255–66.

14 Joseph, pp. 85–6. "Victorian Frames: The Windows and Mirrors of Browning, Arnold and Tennyson, VP (1978). See also Jennifer Gribble, *The Lady of Shalott in the Victorian Novel* (London, 1983).

15 Geoffrey Hartman, "Psychoanalysis: The French Connection," in *Psychoanalysis and the Question of the Text*, ed. Geoffrey Hartman (Johns Hopkins Univ. Press, 1978), p. 8.

16 Princeton Univ. Press, 1979.

17 *The Mutable Glass: Mirror Imagery in Titles and Texts of the Middle Ages and the English Renaissance*, trans. Gordon Collier (Cambridge Univ. Press, 1983), p. 118. Grabes argues for the technological explanation, while Alastair Fowler in his review of Grabes' study (*TLS*, August 19, 1983, p. 872) criticizes him for that emphasis, seeing instead "a most profound alteration in sensibility" and a new, more reflective mode of consciousness.

18 Ricks, p. 357. The Platonic context of Britomart's mirror is spelled out succinctly in the notes to *The Faerie Queene* III. ii. 22, 5–6 in A. C. Hamilton's recent edition (New York, 1977), p. 320: "In Plato, *Phaedrus* 255 d, the lover is said to be a mirror in which he beholds himself; cf. the fountain of Narcissus in the *Romance of the Rose* [ll.] 1571–602. Britomart's inward-looking gaze projects an image of beauty which arouses love for Artegall; hence the vision of him follows. It leads to self-division; hence she compares herself to Narcissus at 44.6–9."

19 Trans. Benjamin Jowett (New York, 1932), 596.

20 *Empedocles on Etna* I. ii. 77–91, in *Matthew Arnold: Poetical Works*, ed. C. B. Tinker and H. F. Lowry (Oxford Univ. Press, 1950).

21 I have discussed the symbolic opposition of window and mirror in Hunt's *The Awakening Conscience* as an example of the figural strategies that the Victorian painters employed (Joseph, op.cit., pp. 71–2), and Craig Owen considers the same opposition in the work of Lady Hawarden (in "Photography *en abyme*," *October*, 5 [1978], 73–88).

22 For a most interesting treatment of the convergence of the two figures, see John Barth's experimental story about life "on the autognostic verge" – "Echo" in *Lost in the Funhouse* (Garden City, 1968), pp. 98–103. At the end of the story, he writes, "Narcissus would appear to be opposite from Echo: he perishes by denying all except himself; she persists by effacing herself absolutely. Yet they come to the same: it was never himself Narcissus craved, but his reflection, the Echo of his fancy; his death must be partial as his self-knowledge, the voice persists, persists" (pp. 102–3).

23 I wish to thank Michael Greenstein and especially Stuart Davis for their generous help at different stages in the composition of this essay.

2

The Mirror's Secret
Dante Gabriel Rossetti's Double Work of Art

J Hillis Miller

> And still she sits, young while the earth is old,
> And, subtly of her self contemplative,
> Draws men to watch the bright web she can weave,
> Till heart and body and life are in its hold.[1]

If Rossetti's Lilith looks only, speculatively, at her own image in the mirror, she also looks self-consciously aware of the looks of all those men whom she draws by her indifference into her fatal net. Rossetti's source here is that text from Goethe which he translated:

> Hold thou thy heart against her shining hair,
> If, by thy fate, she spread it once for thee;
> For, when she nets a young man in that snare,
> So twines she him he never may be free.
> ("Lilith – from Göthe," *W*, p. 541)

Lilith's mirroring of herself and our fatal mirroring of ourselves in the painting are doubled by the mirror imaged on the canvas. Moreover, the painting mirrors a Victorian Pre-Raphaelite boudoir, and also Rossetti's feelings about Fanny Cornforth. The painting, in addition, mirrors the poem, "Body's Beauty," Sonnet 78 of *The House of Life*, of which it is an "illustration." Or is it the other way around, the poem a "caption" for the painting? Ultimately, both poem and painting are

Miller, J Hillis. 1991. "The Mirror's Secret: Dante Gabriel Rossetti's Double Work of Art." In *Victorian Poetry*, 29, iv (Winter), pp. 333–49. Reproduced with permission of J Hillis Miller.

Victorian Poets: A Critical Reader, First Edition. Edited by Valentine Cunningham.
© 2014 John Wiley & Sons, Ltd. Published 2014 by John Wiley & Sons, Ltd.

mirrors of, mirrored by, other works, echoing before and after, works in painting and in poetry by Rossetti himself, and multitudinous works in a complex tradition – graphic, literary, and philosophical – going back to the Bible and to the Greeks, in one direction, and forward, to our day, for example to John Hollander's admirable *The Head of the Bed*. In this tangled network of relations, "Mirror on mirror mirrored is all the show."[2]

These mirrorings are all, however, in one way or another odd, ambiguous, subversive, irrational. The mirrored image undoes what seeks its image there. Each mirrored image is somehow different from the exact reflection which tells the truth unequivocally, as when I look at my face in the mirror in the morning. There I am, as I am. "I am that I am." The mirror tells me so. I suffice to myself, like God. Or do I?

Far from producing an emblem of such fullness and completion, image matching image, Lilith's subtle contemplation of herself weaves a net, and behind the net there is a gulf. Into this abyss the men she fascinates will fall. This gulf is that "orchard pit" which was Rossetti's constant dream, that ugly ditch beside the apple tree with the Lilith or Siren figure in the crotch of its branches, offering a fatal apple and a fatal kiss. Why is it that when we men contemplate not ourselves in the mirror but our incongruous other self, a desirable woman contemplating herself, our own integrity is mutilated, destroyed?

> Men tell me that sleep has many dreams; but all my life I have dreamt one dream alone.
>
> I see a glen whose sides slope upward from the deep bed of a dried-up stream, and either slope is covered with wild apple-trees. In the largest tree, within the fork whence the limbs divide, a fair, golden-haired woman stands and sings, with one white arm stretched along a branch of the tree, and with the other holding forth a bright red apple, as if to some one coming down the slope. Below her feet the trees grow more and more tangled, and stretch from both sides across the deep pit below: and the pit is full of the bodies of men.
>
> They lie in heaps beneath the screen of boughs, with her apples bitten in their hands; and some are no more than ancient bones now, and some seem dead but yesterday. She stands over them in the glen, and sings for ever, and offers her apple still. ("The Orchard Pit," *W*, pp. 607–8)

If *Lady Lilith* mirrors Fanny Cornforth and a certain kind of Victorian decor (its furniture, costume, and psychosocial structures, its domestic economy), this mimetism is peculiar, since this Victorian boudoir, with its mirror, double candlestick, cosmetic bottle, chest, and settee, seems to be out of doors. What is mirrored in the mirror on the wall is not an interior but an exterior woodland scene, a scene of branches going from left to right matching in reverse Lilith's tresses, which spread from right to left. The branches duplicate themselves in smaller and smaller repetitions out to invisibility in a *mise en abîme*. The scene in the mirror is in fact the orchard pit. Or is the mirror a window? No, it cannot be so, since the roses and the candles are reflected there. How odd, however, that the Lady Lilith should be combing her hair outdoors, surrounded by all those bedroom appurtenances and by roses and poppies which might be either inside or out. In Eden there was no inside or out, but this scene is the diabolical mirror image of Eden, as Lilith is of Eve.

The confusion of interior and exterior, mirror and window, is characteristic of all that art Walter Pater called "aesthetic." In such art, nature has been made over into the images of art, and those images made over once more, at a double remove. As Pater puts it in a splendid formulation:

> Greek poetry, medieval or modern poetry, projects, above the realities of its time, a world in which the forms of things are transfigured. Of that transfigured world this new poetry takes possession, and sublimates beyond it another still fainter and more spectral, which is literally an artificial or "earthly paradise." It is a finer ideal, extracted from what in relation to any actual world is already an ideal. Like some strange second flowering after date, it renews on a more delicate type the poetry of a past age, but must not be confounded with it. The secret of the enjoyment of it is that inversion of home-sickness known to some, that incurable thirst for the sense of escape, which no actual form of life satisfies, no poetry even, if it be merely simple and spontaneous.[3]

In "aesthetic" poetry and painting even the most meticulously naturalistic scene, in what Pater calls, apropos of Rossetti, an "insanity of realism" (p. 209), is emblematic. Such a scene is absorbed into a spiritualized human interior, inside and outside at once, since the distinction, uneasily, no longer exists, just as the distinction between the spiritual and material no longer exists. To go outside is not to be outside but to remain claustrophobically enclosed, and the interior is no safe enclosure. It is exposed to the dangers of a fatal encounter. The orchard pit is within and without at once, just as the window in Sir John Everett Millais' *Mariana* (an illustration of Tennyson's "Mariana") is also a mirror of her state, and just as the same ambiguity functions in the mirror of Tennyson's "The Lady of Shalott," in this case illustrated by Holman

Hunt. Pater, with his characteristic genius as a critic, has once more provided a definitive formulation of this aspect of Rossetti's work:

> With him indeed, as in some revival of the old mythopoeic age, common things – dawn, noon, night – are full of human or personal expression, full of sentiment. The lovely little sceneries scattered up and down his poems, glimpses of a landscape, not indeed of broad open-air effects, but rather that of a painter concentrated upon the picturesque effect of one or two selected objects at a time – the "hollow brimmed with mist," or the "ruined weir," as he sees it from one of the windows, or reflected in one of the mirrors of his "house of life" (the vignettes for instance seen by Rose Mary in the magic beryl) attest, by their very freshness and simplicity, to a pictorial or descriptive power in dealing with the inanimate world, which is certainly also one half of the charm, in that other, more remote and mystic, use of it. For with Rossetti this sense of lifeless nature, after all, is translated to a higher service, in which it does but incorporate itself with some phase of strong emotion. Everyone understands how this may happen at critical moments of life; what a weirdly expressive soul may have crept, even in full noonday, into "the white-flower'd elder-thicket," when Godiva saw it "gleam through the Gothic archways in the wall," at the end of her terrible ride [Tennyson, "Godiva"]. To Rossetti it is so always, because to him life is a crisis at every moment (pp. 532–3).

What that "crisis" is, cutting off before from after, and dividing the moment too within itself, and what feeling every moment as a crisis has to do with this particular version of the pathetic fallacy, remains to be identified. Window or mirror, as Pater has seen, are means to the same vision. What is seen there is natural, human, and spiritual, all at once. The framed image is always, as Pater's brilliantly chosen quotations from Rossetti indicate, some version of the orchard pit, the "hollow brimmed with mist," the "ruined weir," or that maelstrom into which the lovers are swept in the poetic fragment of "The Orchard-Pit":

> My love I call her, and she loves me well:
> But I love her as in the maelstrom's cup
> The whirled stone loves the leaf inseparable
> That clings to it round all the circling swell,
> And that the same last eddy swallows up.
>   (*W*, p. 240)

In "Lady Lilith" the mirroring of a boudoir which turns out to be an abyssal wood of storm-tossed branches also mirrors the reflection of

Lilith in her hand-held mirror. Though the back of that mirror is turned toward the spectator, the image in the mirror on the wall tells him what chasm is no doubt pictured there behind the screen of reflected hair. This chasm is imaged over and over throughout Rossetti's work by way of displaced figures in the "outside" framed in a window or in a mirror.

The other mirrorings are equally alogical. The relation between Rossetti's painting and his poetry is asymmetrical, skewed. This is true not in the sense that one overtly contradicts the other, but in the sense that each exceeds the other, however deliberately they may be matched, as in the case of *Lady Lilith* and "Body's Beauty." Each says more or less than the other, and says it differently, in ways which have only in part to do with the differences of medium. Either may be taken as the "original" of which the other is the "illustration" or the explanatory poetic "superscription," writing on top of another graphic form. This relation does not depend, of course, on the chronology of Rossetti's actual creation of the two works in question. In each case, however, the secondary version in the other medium is always in one way or another a travesty, a misinterpretation, a distorted image in the mirror of the other art.

The relation to "the tradition" of the double, self-subversive work of art is, once more, a false mirroring. Whether one takes the more immediate context of Rossetti's other work or, as does John Dixon Hunt in *The Pre-Raphaelite Imagination*, the wider context of Pre-Raphaelite work generally, or Rossetti's relation to his immediate predecessors, Shelley and Tennyson, or the relation of his work to the whole Western tradition, this relation of work to context, as the passage from Pater quoted above suggests, is not a straightforward copying, continuation, or reflection. It is a strange second flowering after date, a sublimation or rarefaction which is also a swerving, a distortion.

Nonetheless, this subversive mirroring is already part of the tradition, traditional even in Plato or Milton, however much that deconstructive mirroring may have been apparently suppressed. "Aesthetic" poetry was already a part, though sometimes a secret part, of "ancient" and "modern" poetry. Pater's chronology of the development of Western poetry in fact describes a synchronic tension within it among patterns which may not be reconciled in any synthesis, dialectic, or historical movement. Rossetti's false mirroring of the tradition does but tell a secret which is already there, everywhere within that "tradition," but often hidden.

What is the secret that the distorting mirror always tells and keeps? Loss. All Rossetti's work is haunted by an experience of devastating loss. That loss has always already occurred or is about to occur or is occurring, in memory or in anticipation within the divided moment.

It occurs proleptically, antileptically, metaleptically, the feared future standing for the already irrevocable past, and vice versa, in a constant far-fetching reversal of late and early. The longed-for future may not be. The poet of "The Stream's Secret" knows or is told by the mirroring stream that it may not be. The past was disastrous, even if it held moments of joy. Those moments have passed, their joy turned into the desolation of their loss. "What whisper'st thou?" the poet asks that moving and murmuring, mirroring stream:

> Nay, why
> Name the dead hours? I mind them well:
> Their ghosts in many darkened doorways dwell
> With desolate eyes to know them by.
> ("The Stream's Secret," *W*, p. 114)

The loss in question is experienced perpetually in that everlasting moment of crisis (in the etymological sense of division) in which the mind dwells. Of that division the mind makes an emblem in those natural scenes glimpsed through a window or reflected in a mirror. These scenes in turn become human figures which then become those personified abstractions, Life, Death, Time, and so on, which populate, as Pater observed, Rossetti's work. These personifications constitute in their humanized particularity the "insanity of realism" in Rossetti. "And this delight in concrete definition," says Pater, "is allied with another of his conformities to Dante, the really imaginative vividness, namely, of his personifications – his hold upon them, or rather their hold upon him, with the force of a Frankenstein, when once they have taken life from him. Not Death only and Sleep, for instance, and the winged spirit of Love, but certain particular aspects of them, a whole 'populace' of special hours and places, 'the hour' even 'which might have been, yet might not be,' are living creatures, with hands and eyes and articulate voices" (Pater, "Dante Gabriel Rossetti," p. 531).

These personifications result from a process miming the progressive sublimation of aesthetic poetry. They are a further refinement of what is already a transfigured or humanized nature. Their meaning is always some aspect of that absolute loss which is exacerbated, always, by having almost been its opposite, like a swimmer who almost makes the shore and then is swept away:

> Look in my face; my name is Might-have-been;
> I am also called No-more, Too-late, Farewell;
> Unto thine ear I hold the dead-sea shell

Cast up thy Life's foam-fretted feet between;
Unto thine eyes the glass where that is seen
    Which had Life's form and Love's, but by my spell
    Is now a shaken shadow intolerable,
Of ultimate things unuttered the frail screen.
("A Superscription," W, p. 107)

The figure in the glass, "Might-have-been," is one's own face, just as Pater's metonymic "mistake" in naming the monster with the name of its creator catches accurately the relation between Doctor Frankenstein and his creature, the made making and unmaking the maker. Rossetti's personifications keep their hold upon him because they are figures for himself. All those persons, personifications, and scenes – the orchard pit, the ruined weir, the stormy branches – are one's own face in the mirror, caught in the eternal moment of crisis as the confrontation of a perpetual loss.

Loss of what? Loss as such, total and irrevocable. Absence. To name this loss one's own death or (fear of) castration, or the confrontation with the woman who has (or who does not have) the phallus (Lilith as snake), or the death of the beloved, or that betrayal by the beloved which is always the story of love for Rossetti, is only to conjure one more shadow in the glass, one more frail screen, like all the other images in Rossetti, for "ultimate things unuttered," and, in any literal way, unutterable. It is as if I looked in the mirror and saw nothing there, or were to see an image which is not myself but a figure of my absence or of my incompletion.

Precisely this happens in a little poem, "The Mirror." Here the poet's failure to find a reciprocating feeling in the lady he loves is imaged as the unsettling experience of seeing what he thinks is his own image in a distant mirror and then finding it is not himself, so that he is for the moment imageless:

She knew it not: – most perfect pain
    To learn: this too she knew not. Strife
        For me, calm hers, as from the first.
        'Twas but another bubble burst
    Upon the curdling draught of life, –
My silent patience mine again.
As who, of forms that crowd unknown
    Within a distant mirror's shade,
        Deems such an one himself, and makes

> Some sign; but when the image shakes
> No whit, he finds his thought betray'd,
> And must seek elsewhere for his own.
> ("The Mirror," *W*, p. 194)

"For his own": the phrase has a straightforward enough grammatical ellipsis and yet, dangling uncompleted in the open as it does at the end of the poem, possessive adjective without a noun, it shimmers with alternative possibilities. He must seek elsewhere for his own image, and the missing noun mimes the absence of what the speaker seeks. As the logic of the figurative relation between first and second stanzas affirms, however, his missing image is a trope for the female counterpart who would complete him. Her absence or indifference, her failure to match feeling with his feeling, is in turn a figure for something missing in himself. It is as if for Rossetti "the mirror stage" were not the discovery of one's self (the *Ideal-Ich*) in the mirror but the discovery of a vacancy there, an empty glass.

The structure of "The Mirror" is "the same" as that in "Body's Beauty." In fact, all Rossetti's work consists of two intersubjective patterns, a desired one "which might have been, yet might not be," and its asymmetrical mirror image, which always and irrevocably exists. This double intersubjective structure is, like all such models, with difficulty distinguished, if it may be distinguished at all, from a solipsistic relation of the self to itself. The Other, however totally other, is still experienced as part of myself or as something I wish were part of myself. In "Willowwood," the four-sonnet sequence within *The House of Life*, Love grants the Narcissus-like poet the privilege of kissing his beloved's lips. These rise to meet his lips at the surface of a "wood-side well": "her own lips rising there / Bubbled with brimming kisses at my mouth" (*W*, p. 91). It is a phantom kiss, though, and of course he kisses his own imaged lips.

The desired side of this mismatched pair of patterns is expressed in "The Stream's Secret." It is a wish for future joy, the Might-still-be which stands as a future anterior for Might-have-been. This Might-still-be remains always Not-quite-yet. The mirror, which has been vacant of any images but hollow shadows of unfulfilled desire, will (or will never) become suddenly full, the reflection of a double, completed image. The lovers, in this impossible imaginary encounter, will view their joint image in the stream's mirror and then, no longer needing the mediation of any mirror, will look only in one another's eyes:

> So, in that hour of sighs
> Assuaged, shall we beside this stone

> Yield thanks for grace; while in thy mirror shown
>   The twofold image softly lies,
> Until we kiss, and each in other's eyes
>   Is imaged all alone.
>
> Still silent? Can no art
> Of Love's then move thy pity?
>   ("The Stream's Secret," *W*, p. 117)

The stream is still silent and does not tell Love's secret, since there is no secret to tell. The mirror's secret is that there is no secret. "Love's Hour," the hour when "she and I shall meet...stands...not by the door" (p. 117), however much the poet strains to believe that it does. The ultimate things unuttered are here and now, on the surface of the stream's mirror, not at the bottom of some abysmal depth. The stream will always remain vacant of any twofold image. Instead there is always, as the present without presence of crisis, the contrary image there. This image is the incongruous double of the desired one. It is the pattern, in fact, of "Willowwood," or, altered, of "Body's Beauty," or, in a different form, of "The Mirror," or, in a different form again, of "The Portrait," or, different still, of "Love's Nocturn." In this antithetical system, I look in the mirror and see not my own image but that of my female counterpart who looks not at me but at herself, subtly of herself contemplative, or, as in "The Portrait," I see her image still remaining after her death. This death is experienced, uncannily, as if my own image should remain in the mirror when I was no longer standing before it:

> This is her picture as she was:
>   It seems a thing to wonder on,
> As though mine image in the glass
>   Should tarry when myself am gone.
>   ("The Portrait," *W*, p. 169)

In "Love's Nocturn," the counterstructure takes the form of the poet's imagining that he meets his own image "face to face," as he is "groping in the windy stair" leading down to the place where all dreams are.[4] That image he would send to his lady's sleep, but he fears another image already usurps his place. His image must return then to the dream-fosse, having enjoyed one kiss not of the lady's lips but of their reflection in her mirror:

> Like a vapour wan and mute,
> Like a flame, so let it pass;

One low sigh across her lute,
  One dull breath against her glass;
  And to my sad soul, alas!
    One salute
  Cold as when Death's foot shall pass.
        ("Love's Nocturn," *W*, p. 72)

I have emphasized the differences among all these versions of the counter-pattern not only to confirm what I said earlier about the relation of incongruity between any work and the context it "mirrors," even the immediate context of other work by the same maker, but also to suggest that this counter-pattern always manifests itself differently. More precisely, each of its exemplars must be aberrant and none must be governed by an archetype. This pattern denies the existence of any archetype or model, the exact repetition of which might turn loss into completion. Ultimately, this structure may never be fixed in a definitive version, any more than Rossetti's personified beings, Love, Death, Sleep, and so on, may be systematized into a coherent counter-theology. Against this perpetually wandering structure is always set the primary structure of lover and beloved meeting face to face in a perfect match.

"Structure" here is a misleading term, not only because of its currently fashionable resonances, and not only because it does not cover all that is in question here, but because, like any possible term, it begs the questions it should keep open. It reinstates the metaphysical or "logocentric" assumptions that this "double triangle" dismantles. This "structure," "system," or "figure," this "emblem," "hieroglyph," "polygram," or "multigraph," is a complexity that cannot be unified. It remains incoherent or heterogeneous, always doubled and redoubled in repetitions that subvert rather than reinforce. Its heterogeneity lies not only in its resistance to conceptual unification or logical interpretation, but in its combining in an uneasy mélange: concept ("speculation"); figures of speech (the mirror image as image for image); figures, in the sense of persons in their relations (those reflected in the mirror); graphic or representational elements (the mirror itself, the Pre-Raphaelite woman, her landscape); and narrative material (the story of disastrous love Rossetti always tells). How can one name this except reductively, or in a figure that refigures the problem?

Perhaps Rossetti's own final figure for a sonnet, combining as it does graphic and verbal elements, might do best. Having called the sonnet a "moment's monument," carved "in ivory or in ebony," with "flowering crest impearled and orient," like some ornate coat of arms, picture and words combined, he defines the sonnet, in the sestet of his sonnet about the sonnet, as a coin. The obverse and converse of this coin combine a double, simultaneous orientation toward the experiences of the self or "soul" and toward that unnameable power, or absence of power, "Life," "Love," "Death," that governs the Soul. It is the coin itself, the double work of art – not the soul which one side of it reveals – which is, in all senses of the idiom, "due to" the Power. If the coin's face "reveals / The Soul," the "Power" is that unutterable thing of which the coin's converse is the revelation. At the same time, the converse acts as a frail screen protecting the Soul from that revelation. Or perhaps one might better say that it is the dumb sliver of metal between which keeps obverse and converse, Soul and Power, apart, both for good and for ill:

> A Sonnet is a coin: its face reveals
> 　The Soul, – its converse, to what Power 'tis due: –
> Whether for tribute to the august appeals
> 　Of Life, or dower in Love's high retinue,
> It serve; or, 'mid the dark wharf's cavernous breath,
> In Charon's palm it pay the toll to Death.
> 　　　　　　("Introductory Sonnet," *W*, p. 74)

A final, concentrated "example" of this double-faced coin is "Memorial Thresholds." This poem substitutes doorway for window or mirror and proposes two possibilities: that the threshold remain permanently vacant, or that it be filled once more, in the memorial reduplication of a déjà vu, with the form of the beloved. Here, she is imagined as having once actually stood in the same doorway somewhere, of which the new threshold is a repetition:

> City, of thine a single simple door,
> 　By some new Power reduplicate, must be
> 　Even yet my life-porch in eternity,
> Even with one presence filled, as once of yore:
> Or mocking winds whirl round a chaff-strown floor
> 　Thee and thy years and these my words and me.
> 　　　　　　("Memorial Thresholds," *W*, p. 101)

Why is it that the doorway, in Rossetti's numismatics of art, remains always empty? What is the meaning of the discovery that the mirror's secret is its vacancy? A placing of Rossetti's double-pattern of presence mirrored by absence in relation to the long tradition of such doublings may help to unriddle the secret of this secret. My discussion must be brief and incomplete because there would be no end to the labyrinthine wanderings of the critic who attempted the absurd task of a topographical mapping of all the "ways and days" intricately interwoven in this *topos* of the memorial threshold, window, or glass.

The places within this place would include: the glasses of the Apostle Paul in First and Second Corinthians, with their echo of Genesis, a passage in 1 James (l.21–25); the paradigm of the mirror in Book 10 of *The Republic* and the mirror in *The Sophist* (239d); the speech of Aristophanes in *The Symposium;* the Narcissus story in Ovid's *Metamorphoses;* the great passage on "Speculation" in the interchange between Ulysses and Achilles in Shakespeare's *Troilus and Cressida;* Eve's admiration of her own image in Book 4 of *Paradise Lost;* passages in Rossetti's more immediate predecessors, such as Shelley's " Alastor" and "Epipsychidion"; the Fuseli of so many nightmarish doors, windows, and mirrors; Tennyson's "Mariana" and "The Lady of Shalott." Finally, among Rossetti's contemporaries or successors, there would be: George Meredith, who recapitulates and reinterprets the interplay between Ovid and Milton, Narcissus and Adam, in *The Egoist;* Baudelaire's Dandy who *"doit vivre et dormir devant un miroir"*[5] Whistler's *The Little White Girl* and Swinburne's poem on this painting, "Before the Mirror"; Mallarmé's *Herodiade;* a splendid passage at the beginning of Thomas Hardy's *Far From the Madding Crowd;* Wilde's *The Picture of Dorian Gray;* Yeats's "Ribh Denounces Patrick"; all those mirrors in Picasso; the eerily uncanny moment in Freud's *"Das Unheimliche"* when he sees his own image in a mirror but does not recognize it as his own, and detests it (the reverse of the pattern in Rossetti's "The Mirror," where the image is not his own); Benjamin's essay on the photograph and the loss of aura in Baudelaire;[6] Beardsley's illustrations for Belinda's toilet in *The Rape of the Lock* ; and lastly all those paradigmatic mirrors of our own day, in Jacques Lacan's "The Mirror Stage," or in Luce Irigaray's *Speculum of the other woman*, an investigation in part of the whole tradition of the mirror-structure from Plato to Freud as it bears on the question of the male interpretation of sexual difference.[7]

This seemingly diverse and miscellaneous set of references, discontinuous points in the sky of Western culture, are in fact rigorously organized into a repeated constellation, or rather a double constellation, a Gestaltist duck-rabbit, like that big dipper which is either Charles's wain or the great bear, depending on how one looks at it. In all these texts, a complex asymmetrical structure is present in one form or another, in one degree or another of completion or explicit expression. Indeed, this structure is "fundamental" in all Western "thought" and "literature," in the sense that it both affirms and endangers any fundament or ground. The structure involves a pair which becomes potentially subverted by a triangular relation among three persons or images, though it remains precariously balanced. This stable triangle is then incongruously mirrored in another triangle which parodies it and so undermines its stability.

This complex structure is the speculative as such, the reflective or the theoretical, the positing, hypothetically, as an image, of what may be seen and known, in a movement of thinking and seeing which is also a working or making. This movement goes out from itself in order to strive to return to itself in a confirmation of itself by way of an other which is or should be the perfect image of itself, not really other than itself. Even God, it seems, cannot know himself until he has gone outside himself and so can see himself outside himself.[8] Speculation (from *speculum*, mirror), theory (*theoria*, seeing, as in "theatrical"), art or poetry (*poesis*, making), and imitation (*mimesis*, miming, as in the great mirror/doorway scene in the Marx brothers' *Duck Soup*) – all come together in the crisscross of reflections in the mirror of this double paradigm.

The pattern of completion within this paradigm is the perfect mirroring of one male figure by another, by its own image in the glass. To the speculative, the theoretical, the poetic, and the mimetic can be added the self-generating, self-sustaining, and constantly self-transcending relation of the dialectical as another name for this system of reflections. The image of the mirrored and mirroring pair, in the tradition of this motif, oscillates between being the mirroring of male by male, in perfect match, Narcissus completing his own image in the pool, and being the mirroring of male by female, in another form of perfect matching, concave matching convex, as in the androgynous couple in Aristophanes' speech in *The Symposium*.

My focus here will be on a version of this paradigm which in one way or another adds a third figure, Echo in the Narcissus story, the fascinated male watching the woman who is subtly of herself contemplative in Rossetti's poem, or, as in a novel by a male author with a female protagonist, the intimate relation of indirect discourse in which a male narrator follows the thoughts and feelings of the heroine as she thinks about herself, as in the chapter of "Clara's Meditations" in Meredith's *The Egoist*.

Such a triangle remains stable, a sure support for ontological ground, only so long as it is all male or only so long as the female is defined as the adequate "image" of the male, a case of good rather than bad mimesis. An example of the all-male triangle is the Trinity: Father, Son, and Holy Ghost; the One, his filial image, and the relation between them; or God, his perfect image, the Son, and that creation fabricated by God in the image of the Son, so that the world as a whole and every part of it separately has the countenance of God and is signed with his genuine signature. An example of the second would be the definition of Eve in *Paradise Lost* as created in the image of Adam, who is in turn created in the image of God: "He for God only. She for God in him."

The female as third, however, or, more dangerously yet, as the doubled pair watched by a male spectator, the woman as two out of three, always introduces the possibility of a mismatching, a deflection of the closed circuit of reflections. The female, according to a sexist tradition going back to Plato and Aristotle, is an imperfect male, missing one member. The female introduces the deconstructing absence, the perpetual too little or too much that makes it impossible for the balance to come right and so keeps the story going, whether it is the story of an unassuaged desire which Rossetti always tells, or whether it is the story of thought which that love story tropologically represents. Theoretically, the woman opens up the triangle beyond any hope of closing it again or of filling the gap. This gap is the echoing cavern where false images are, that place of shades and shadows, for example, in Rossetti's "Love's Nocturn" which doubles the real bodies of men, "as echoes of man's speech / Far in secret clefts are made" (*W*, p. 71).

It should be clear now, as clear as one's own face in the glass, what this double triangle of mirrored images in Rossetti "means." Or is it? The double triangle records the moment of confrontation with the loss of the *Logos* – head sense or patron of meaning, caption. Its meaning is the absence of meaning, decapitation, decollation. God in speculation looks at himself in the mirror of the world, having engendered his material counterpart, the creation, by way of his mirror image, the Son. Man, too, along with the rest of the world, is "in the image of God created," as Lilith says sardonically in Rossetti's "Eden Bower" (*W*, p. 110). Man, then, in imitation of God, as God's mimic or mime, looks in the mirror and sees a sister-image there that does not fit him. Or, in the version of this that has been my interest here, the male writer or artist takes an interest in the situation of the female who looks in the mirror and discovers her lack, the missing man, as when Tennyson's Mariana says, finally, "He will not come." This interest in what is more than or different from himself becomes, for such a male artist, fascination. It is fascination by a plus-value which in the end leads to the loss of all in spendthrift speculation.

The prolonged instant of specular fascination, drawing the male spectator into the abyss, is a version of what I call "the linguistic moment." This is the moment when signs are cut off from any extralinguistic grounding and become fascinating in themselves, in their self-sustaining and self-annihilating interplay. The momentum of this moment may make it an eternal instant. It becomes the prolonged, persisting time of poise or lack in a present which is no present. It has no presence, since it engages the signs of something missing, that is, signs as such. The sign by definition is the presence of an absence. There is nothing beyond such a moment. It cannot be gone beyond in any dialectical or speculative *Aufhebung*. It remains balanced interminably in sterile repetition, in a horrible parody of the self-engendering and self-mirroring of God.

The specular encounter, when the male looks in the mirror and does not find his image there, does not even find the answering look of his female counterpart, but sees a woman seeing herself, is the linguistic moment. In this moment occurs the dismantling of that male speculative system which ought to lead to absolute knowledge of the self by itself. Possession becomes dispossession; appropriation, expropriation. The male is entangled in the web of Lady Lilith's hair, drawn by the Siren in the tree into the Orchard Pit, put into a perpetual state of Might-have-been or Might-yet-be. What he writes or paints thereafter is constructed over the abyss of his loss, as Rossetti rescued the manuscript of *The House of Life* from his self-slain wife's coffin. He had put the manuscript just between her cheek and her hair. Such writing is without ground, like the words whirled by the mocking wind round a chaff-strewn floor in "Memorial Thresholds," in a repetition of the failure of poetic language at the end of Shelley's "Epipsychidion." As in the case of the imagined long love embrace in "The Stream's Secret," the linguistic moment suspends things over the gulf of their absence, as a matter of Might-have-been and Might-yet-be but never Is-now. The Now is an empty mirror, a stream that tells no secrets.

The speculative moment of fullness and its subversive counterpart are necessary to one another. Each implies the other and is surreptitiously present in any of its expressions. Nevertheless, they may not be combined or reconciled in any way, dialectically or otherwise. Rather, they set up in their relation an ungovernable oscillation that inhibits thought from proceeding, short-circuiting it in a feedback phenomenon. One finds oneself in a double blind-alley of thinking and feeling in which one cannot decide which corridor to take, since each corridor leads, manifestly, to a blank wall. Aesthetic art, the art of Rossetti and the Pre-Raphaelites generally, is, as Pater says, an art which satisfies that strange inversion of homesickness known to some, the desire to get as far away from home, from the "real world," as possible. Home, for Rossetti, figures death, the Orchard Pit. Therefore anyone would wish to escape from it into a world of shadows or of signs referring to prior signs, for example, into that poetry about poetry or strange second flowering after date Pater describes. The world of shadows or of signs, however, lies in the pit. Lilith and her counterparts in Rossetti's work draw men, precisely, into a realm of shadows. Either way, you have had it. The Medusa face of Rossetti's woman, since she draws her power from the annihilating energy of signs, is equally fatal in face-to-face or in mirrored encounter.

To mention Medusa is to remember Freud's "Medusa's Head" and "The Taboo of Virginity."[9] According to Freud, the male fears equally that the female will or will not possess the phallus. For Lacan, the phallus is not the penis, but what the penis stands for, the head or source of meaning, and therefore the grounding of the interplay among signs. The double horror of the phallic female makes up an essential part of the mirror structure I am discussing here. It is present, for example, in Herodias' image of herself as a reptile, in Mallarmé's poem, and in the terror that her own hair inspires in her. It is present as one moment in John Hollander's splendid version of the Lilith story in Canto 7 of *The Head of the Bed*:

> He dared not move
> Toward her one leg, toward her covered places
> Lest he be lost at once, staring at where
> Lay, bared in the hardened moonlight, a stump
> Pearly and smooth, a tuft of forest grass.[10]

The emblem of the girl with the penis is present in Rossetti, too, in the Lilith of "Eden Bower," who whispers to the snake: "To thee I come when the rest is over; / A snake was I when thou wast my lover. / I was the fairest snake in Eden" (*W*, p. 109), or in the monumental figure of *Mnemosyne*. In Rossetti's painting, the shape and position of Mnemosyne's lamp mime an erect phallus. Rossetti's caption for the painting calls attention to the winged mobility of this oddly shaped lamp: "Thou fill'st from the winged chalice of the soul / Thy lamp, O Memory, fire-winged to its goal" (*W*, p. 229). The doubleness here is the doubleness of the two-faced coin: the soul, on the one hand, and the source of energy for the activity of memory, on the other hand. The relation between soul and memory is that coming and going, toward the past, toward the future, in a perpetual interchange moving toward a "goal" it never reaches, by way of a recollection of the permanent "Might-have-been yet might not be."

In Rossetti's version of the game of "Phallus, Phallus, who's got the Phallus?," the balance among a set of alternating possibilities never comes right. There is always one too many or one too few, not enough to go around, or one left over. This always leaves an Old Maid, or a Wild Card that governs the game but remains outside it, always somewhere else, neither King nor Queen, but Jack of Displacement. If the woman does not have the phallus, there is no ground. If she has it, she must have it as phantasm, as shadow, as that which is never where it is, hence there is no ground. If she has none, then I do, or do I? If she has one, then I must, mustn't I? If she does, then I don't. She's got it. If she doesn't, then I don't, or fear I may not. Either way, I've had it, or haven't had it, in a constant oscillation of possession and dispossession which can never be stilled into a stable, motionless system.

The Medusa solidifies me, turns me to stone, and so, as Freud says, I have no loss to fear. On the other hand, as he also says, my petrifaction is my horror at my confrontation of an absence, and so I fall into the Orchard Pit. On the one hand, art may be the result of the Medusa's effect, a fixed thing in language or in graphic form of what can then safely be confronted in mirror images or in the shadows of art. This submission to the Medusa is both good and bad, both true and false art, undecidably. On the other hand, art may itself be the Medusa's head that petrifies and makes permanent the flowing and the soft, so that *Mnemosyne* stands there permanently for the beholder safely to see, as though she were reflected in a mirror. This in its turn is both good and bad, both submission to the Lilith figure and triumph over her.

The uncanniness of the double mirroring structure lies in this permanent undecidability. Does the art of poetry which presents this system induce a loss? Does it force me as spectator to submit to Lilith's snare? Or does it ward off this loss apotropaically? Does it serve as a frail screen keeping me from unutterable things? Does it save me by mirroring the Medusa or the Lilith figure, freezing her in the double mirror of an art which moves back and forth from painting to poetry in a play of reflections which does not stay still long enough to be caught? There is no way to tell. It is always both and neither. The mirror keeps its secret to the end.

Medusa, it happens, is present as such in Rossetti's work, present as a double work of art in which picture and verse give form once more to all that double system, the two-faced coin of the mirror motif in Rossetti. This double work of art expresses once more the double attitude toward that double system I have tried to catch. With the final ambiguous admonition of "Aspecta Medusa" – against seeing, against theory, and in praise of mirror images – I shall end:

> Andromeda, by Perseus saved and wed,
> Hankered each day to see the Gorgon's head:
> Till o'er a fount he held it, bade her lean,
> And mirrored in the wave was safely seen
> That death she lived by.
>   Let not thine eyes know
> Any forbidden thing itself, although
> It once should save as well as kill: but be
> Its shadow upon life enough for thee.
>
>   (*W*, p. 209)

Notes

1 Dante Gabriel Rossetti, "Body's Beauty," ll. 5–8, Sonnet 78, *The House of Life* in *Works*, ed. William M. Rossetti (London, 1911), p. 100. Further citations will be from this edition, identified as *W*, followed by the page number.

2 William Butler Yeats, "The Statues," l. 22, *Collected Poems* (London, 1950), p. 323.

3 Walter Pater, "Aesthetic Poetry," in *Walter Pater: Three Major Texts*, ed. William E. Buckler (New York, 1986), p. 520.

4 See A. Dwight Culler's excellent discussion of Rossetti's motifs of the windy and winding stair: "The Windy Stair: An Aspect of Rossetti's Poetic Symbolism, " *Ventures Magazine* 9, no. 2 (1969): 65–75.

5 Charles Baudelaire, *Oeuvres Complètes* (Paris, 1961), p. 1273.

6 Walter Benjamin, *"Über einige Motive bei Baudelaire,"* in *Illuminationem* (Frankfurt am Main, 1969), pp. 201–45; trans. Harry Zohn, "On Some Motifs in Baudelaire," in *Illuminations* (New York, 1969), pp. 155–200.

7 See Luce Irigaray, *Speculum of the other woman*, trans. Gillian C. Gill (Ithaca, 1985); and Jacques Lacan, "The mirror stage as formative of the function of the 'I,' " in *Écrits*, trans. Alan Sheridan (New York, 1977), pp. 1–7.

8 For the Hegelian recapitulation of this movement of speculation and the wordplay it involves, see Jean-Luc Nancy, *La remarque spéculative* (Paris, 1973).

9 Sigmund Freud, "Medusa's Head," trans. James Strachey, *International Journal of Psycho-Analysis* 22 (1941): 69–70; and "The Taboo of Virginity," trans. James Strachey, in *The Standard Edition of the Complete Psychological Works of Sigmund Freud* (London, 1957), 9:191–208.

10 John Hollander, *The Head of the Bed* (Boston, 1974), p. 11.

3

Browning's Anxious Gaze

Ann Wordsworth

In *On Heroes, Hero-worship and the Heroic in History*, Carlyle writes "Poetic creation – what is this too but *seeing* the thing sufficiently – the Word that will describe the thing follows of itself from such clear intense sight of the thing. The seeing eye – it is this that discloses the inner harmony of things. To the poet, as to every other, we say, first of all, *see*." Browning agrees, for he writes to Joseph Milsand about his volume *Men and Women*: "I am writing ... lyrics with more music and painting in them than before so as to get people to hear and see."

And yet, this act of seeing which Carlyle acclaimed so confidently, how uncannily it manifests itself if one rejects an idealist account of its nature in favour of a psychoanalytical one: how quickly then "the inner harmony of things" dissolves, once the matchings of a reflexive consciousness are no longer assumed. For what Carlyle's directive takes for granted are two notions which psychoanalytical theory rejects: the presence of a unified consciousness and the primacy of representation. And this in itself might make one want to reconsider the critical commonplaces that take too easily this matter of making people see.

Browning's work so hauntingly calls for a more subtle reading than falls to his lot as purveyor of experience – and yet could the dramatic monologues be discussed at all without assuming "a literature of empiricism"? Is it possible to account for their success and the pleasure

Wordsworth, Ann. 1979. "Browning's Anxious Gaze." In *Robert Browning: A Collection of Critical Essays*, edited by Harold Bloom and Adrienne Munich, pp. 28–38. Englewood Cliffs: Prentice Hall Inc. Reproduced with permission of Ann Wordsworth.

Victorian Poets: A Critical Reader, First Edition. Edited by Valentine Cunningham.
© 2014 John Wiley & Sons, Ltd. Published 2014 by John Wiley & Sons, Ltd.

they provide without the expected appeal to empathy and identification? More precisely, is it possible to draw in a psycho-aesthetics, Lacan's account of "the pacifying Apollonian effect of painting," and coordinate it with Harold Bloom's theory of poetry, the relation of influence and the revisionary processes – that is, to use two accounts of creative effects that take scant heed of the categories of perception and experience?

According to Bloom, the hardest thing in reading Browning is to distinguish the literal from the figurative and vice versa.[1] So it is obvious that this matter of getting people to see turns on more than a heightened sense of vision and a tapping of experiential wisdom. How fortunate then that one of Lacan's most interesting seminars, *Of the Gaze as Objet Petit a*,[2] should be on the scopic drive and that this should show how the gaze, the relation of desire, structures the visual field beyond the organizations of the conscious system.

It is the factitiousness of the analytic experience that Lacan's work centres on, its indifference to relations of truth and appearance. "In our relation to things, insofar as this relation is constituted by the way of vision and ordered in figures of representation, something slips, passes, is transmitted from stage to stage and is always to some degree eluded in it – that is what we call the gaze" (ibid., p. 73). This drift is not accounted for in theories of geometral vision; for they do no more than map space, and contain so little of the scopic itself that, as Diderot proves, this mapping can be reconstructed without loss for the touch of a blind man. Anamorphosis, the disarrangement of geometral space by a skewed perspective, shows more of what is missed by the reflexive consciousness; hence the power of the anamorphic object in Holbein's painting *The Ambassadors*, where the viewer is shown his own eclipse as he turns back to see the enigmatic shape as a human skull. However, it is not the presence of symbols which organizes the field of the visible, but the gaze itself, which does not only look but also *shows* – that is, forms as desire like the dream (itself a gratuitous showing), and situates the perceiver where he cannot any longer say "After all, I am the consciousness of this. …"

There is another dislocation; unconscious desire is not humanized. Lacan makes this clear when he is questioned at the end of a seminar, "When you relate psychoanalysis to Freud's desire and to the desire of the hysteric, might you not be accused of psychologism?" Lacan's answer is that there is no original subjectivity at stake: desire is an object in the unconscious functioning, and not to be confused with events and relationships in biographical life (ibid., p. 13). So it is never a matter of relating creative processes to psychobiographical details – unless perhaps to show a blurring of the process by unmanageable biographical material, as, say, in *The Professor* or *Oliver Twist*.

So, art and the spectator, art and artists, are bounded neither by the empirical relations of geometral space nor by shared subjectivities, but, according to Lacan, by the field of the scopic drive – a field orientated by the eye, whose appetite the painting feeds, and which is satisfied not by representations but by what Lacan calls the *trompe-l'oeil* and the *dompte-regard*, the lure and the taming of the gaze. The first, which in poetry might be the lure of *its* representations (in Browning, "Men and Women"), satisfies and attracts, not because of its fidelity to experience, but because through the pretence of representation we glimpse our relation to the unconscious. When Plato protests against the deception of art, his contention is not that painting gives an illusory equivalence to the object. "The painting does not compete with appearance, it competes with what Plato designates for us beyond appearance as being the Idea" (ibid., p. 112). What solicits us in painting is shown quite boldly in the pleasure given by a technical *trompe-l'oeil* – that moment of shifted focus when the illusion does not move with the eye, when it vanishes as what it feigned and emerges as something else not subject to appearance, in Lacanian terms, the "objet petit a," the unrepresentable object of desire. And this relation between *trompe-l'oeil* and *objet a* could also be the unconscious structuration beyond the slide of literal and figurative in Browning's poetry, the troping movement which Bloom shifts across the formal divisions of grammar and rhetoric into the revisionary processes, the inter-play of rhetorical, psychological and imagistic moves which constitutes poetic energy. If the lure of art, its allure, is this glimpsing, then it accompanies the intra-poetic relations that Bloom describes by the uncanny dissolution of precursor-poet into *objet a*: unconscious and formal processes merge under the auspices of a seeing eye, though not indeed as Carlyle intended.

The other move that Lacan describes, the *dompte-regard*, the taming of the gaze, is the *showing* that gratifies the appetite of the eye; yet this also has no reference to representation, for it is not an optical pleasure that is described. As it functions in relation to the unconscious, the eye is voracious, possessed by *invidia*, the envy exemplified by St. Augustine as he gazed on his brother at his mother's breast: "the envy that makes the subject pale before the image of a completeness closed upon itself, before the idea that the *petit a*, the separated *a* from which he is hanging, may be for another the possession that gives satisfaction" (ibid., p. 116). The pacifying effect of art is that it permits the laying down of this gaze by its recognition of the eye's desire. As if the painter said – how different his tone from Carlyle's – "You want to see. Well, take a look at this. …" And this effect, which Lacan calls "the taming, civilizing and fascinating power of the function of the picture," is what has never been well described before, the Freudian sublimation. Might it not be found also in the assuagement of the voracious unrest which marks creative anxiety, in the poet's power to acknowledge desire and lack in the formulations of poet-and-precursor?

There is one more move in this seminar *Of the Gaze* which can be drawn in. Critics insist on Browning's power to think himself into character and events – indeed this virtuosity is seen as his main achievement ("one's normal processes of judgment are well nigh suspended and one emerges from the experiences of the poem dazzled by the illusion of having actually penetrated an alien being and a remote period of history," as J. W. Harper puts it). To settle the question of how the subject places himself within the scopic field, Lacan uses the analogy of mimicry. This is not simply a matter of adaptation – that is, behaviour as bound up with survival means – but a series of functions manifesting themselves outside any bio-logistic explanation. Travesty, camouflage, intimidation, all have structural and psychic implications. "All reveal something in so far as it is distinct from what might be called an *itself that* is behind" (ibid., p. 99): camouflage, the production of the background; travesty, the breaking up of being between itself and its semblance; intimidation, the extension of being by overvaluation. All the moves suggest that imitation is not a faithful representation, but rather the subject's involuntary insertion within an unconscious function. The parallel between mimicry and art is taken for granted by Roger Caillois, whose work Lacan quotes; it is used with more reserve by Lacan himself. But here too there are implications for Browning criticism. If mimicry (travesty, camouflage, intimidation) were embodied in the representations of the dramatic monologues, Browning would be screened from the full play of influence anxiety while still inscribing the poet-precursor relation within the poems. Character and events would no longer be transcriptions of experience but signs of a defensive energy – a creative play that slips, passes and eludes capture altogether as representation.

The difficulty by now, of course, is obvious enough: the factitiousness of Lacanian description could hardly be further from the robust pleasures of recognition that Browning's readers expect. Instead of the assurance of a heightened vision, there is only a glimpse of processes so obscure that consciousness has no sense of them. But there are advantages in such a reading. The narrative ingenuities that are so admired soon pall and yet critics are still ready to accept tacitly Oscar Wilde's verdict: "Yes, Browning was great. And as what will he be remembered? As a poet? Ah, not as a poet. He will be remembered as a writer of fiction, as the most supreme writer of fiction, it may be, that we have ever had."[3] No matter, it seems, that Wilde's assumptions about fiction ("men and women that live") go unquestioned, and that this in its turn presupposes a neglect of Browning's early poetry and a simplistic account of his poetic development (an overall movement from the confessional Shelleyan monodramas to the achieved objectivity of the later poems after a radical break in 1842). In place of this, it is surely possible to suggest the presence of creative processes which form around the obsessive preoccupations of the belated poet and which gain power from the transindividual linking of art and unconscious functioning. And this would mean questioning idealist accounts of poetic language (its unique power to match human consciousness),[4] although substantiating its indifferent and inexhaustible energies. If the monologues are not as Wilde describes them, supreme fictions, but rather fictive substitutions, *trompe-l'oeil* displacements of creative lack and desire, then reading them would involve a slide away from representations and a recognition of a mimicry whose relation is with the envy of the scopic drive, with the *objet a* reformed as the precursor. This process centres formally in the play between literal and figurative; its material is not just the historic figure, the event but the use of these representations as displacements – richly dramatised effects behind whose *trompe l'oeil* are glimpsed the figurations of desire and lack condensed as the relation to the precursor.

How is this shown? All the monologues at first reading seem like anecdotes, held together by solid figures, animated by a plot with ironic undertones and psychological nuances. *My Last Duchess*: the subject seems so clearly and movingly apparent, disturbing only in the ambivalence the reader feels through his own admiration of the Duke's style. Surely then, it is just a matter of seeing how the dramatic irony works out, of making a choice such as is offered, say, in *The Browning Critics* – a choice between Browning's witless Duke and Browning's shrewd Duke?[5]

If one no longer centres on the referents, the characters, but tries to reconstitute the other scene, then a very different movement emerges – a beautifully complex play on the obsessive themes that haunt the creative mind, chiefly *invidia*, the fear, anger and avenges of influence anxiety. Ostensibly, the clash in the poem is between life and art – the warmth and carnal beauty of the woman and her subjection to the Duke's murderous fantasy. But behind this lies the relation of poet and precursor, doubly disguised insomuch as the precariousness of the belated poet is masked as a helpless subjection to critical misjudgements; in effect, J. S. Mill's critical misreading of *Pauline* stands in as a cover for Browning's misprision of *Alastor*. At the narrative level the poem can seize a triumph over the tyrannies that master it. The Duke intends the listening envoy to judge his last Duchess as he does, but her erotic charm escapes his description and we see her not as the mute victim of his fantasies but in her own involuntary triumph over them. Nevertheless anxiety is in the poem too. The figurations are entirely unstable and shift from level to level as literal narrative, compensatory fantasy, representations of psychic processes. Though the Duchess is obliterated, her presence hauntingly survives, figuring indifferently as poetic victory over detractors, or as precursor, negated but still active. The poem plays on the aporia between literal and figurative, in a non-relational movement whose enigmatic activity is beautifully idealised by who but Shelley in *The Defence of Poetry*:

> The mind in creation is a fading coal which some invisible influence like an inconstant wind awakens to transitory brightness; this power arises from within, like the colours of a flower which fades and changes as it is developed, and the conscious portions of our nature are unprophetic either of its approach or of its departure.

The Duke unintentionally allows a presence to revive; whereas all he meant to do was draw back a curtain, show a picture, lift a shroud. And amidst the poem Shelley's fading coal is ablaze again – indifferently, as the presence of the precursor, as the *objet a*, whatever it is that tames and allures in the pulsations of literal and figurative, that is, in poetry.

In the monodramas, direct dramatizations of creative experience, this play is not made; but it is in the two poems *Porphyria's Lover* and *Johannes Agricola in Meditation*, first printed in Fox's *Monthly Repository*, January 1836, six years before the supposed break. In *Porphyrias Lover*, the play of substitutions moves from the narrative surface of character and macabre action to another secret act of violence. By murder the lover transforms his wayward mistress into his puppet-doll – so too would the poet reduce his precursor. But barbarous action is only one part of the poem, the surface logic of a jealous panic, casting its power over the defiant resistances of sexuality and of the master poem. Under this is the mimicking – a blackly comic play of the creative mind, shuffling and redealing the cards of our mortality time, change, age, infidelity, death. When played straight, as in Rossetti's *House of Life*, "a hundred sonnets on the theme of one lover's fight against time," the mind is given its victory in visionary claims like those of Tennyson in section XCV of *In Memoriam*. Time and change are abolished; the erotic moment sustains itself against all mortal erosions, suspends laws, defies death, creates its own space and time. But in *Porphyria's Lover*, in the redealing of the substitutions, the erotic and creative triumph is got through murder not vision. Death is the trump card. Inconstancy and belatedness are overcome by dealing death to the mistress – and to the precursor – controlling them forever. Both the lover who knows time and change are destroying his erotic bliss, and the poet who knows his poems are too late, achieve their desire by an act of violence – a victory as false as it is vain. The poem turns back against vision and against all experiential wisdoms, against the acceptance of sexual loss, against the solaces of the compensatory imagination. It is derisive and uncanny and has great sustaining energy, for if the dramatic monologues are indeed fictions about influence anxiety and the struggle of the poet to gain priority, then any poem which plays and works this theme, however indirectly, wins the poet some power over his creative anxieties and readies him for his open triumph over them.

This is not the standard description of the monologues. As *Johannes Agricola* was printed as a companion poem in the 1845 volume, it might be interesting to take a more orthodox look at this second of the pair. In such terms it is a typical dramatic monologue, and so in studying it we shall be dealing with what Robert Langbaum in *The Poetry of Experience* calls "empiricism in literature." "We might even say," he writes, "that the dramatic monologue takes as its material the literary equivalent of the scientific attitude – the equivalent being, when men and women are the subject of investigation, the historicizing and psychologizing of judgment." Hence Langbaum adds Johannes Agricola to Tennyson's St Simeon Stylites as another example of "religious buccaneering," and shows that "though Browning intends us to disapprove of Johannes' Antinomianism, he complicates the issue by showing the lofty passion that can proceed from the immoral doctrine." This brings the reader to the characteristic tension between sympathy and moral judgment which draws him into the dilemma of the monologue, loosening him from his customary moral certainties and offering him the new insights of an empiricist and relativist age. Thus we learn to read from within the material itself, no longer dependent on our own external standards of judgment. It is a logical development of romantic inwardness and is uniquely achieved as an effect of the form, "that extra quantity,"

Langbaum explains, "which makes the difference in artistic discourse between content and meaning."

Clearly the orthodox reading is very different from Bloom's, for whom "every poem ... begins as an encounter *between poems*," for whom "acts, persons and places ... must themselves be treated as though they were already poems, or part of poems. Contact, in a poem, means contact with another poem, even if that poem is called a deed, person, place or thing".[6] Whether it is with the precursor, or the unconscious, or with both, this encounter engenders poetry, and to recall it restores the sense of Browning's uncanny energy, which the standard description reduces to lessons in nineteenth-century humanism.

In *Johannes Agricola* there is the same shift from literal to figurative as in *Porphyria's Lover*, and the same shuffling of effects, though this time they belong to religious and not erotic experience. Again the subject is not the imaginative triumph unmediated, but rather the triumph deliberately askewed. Johannes is God's child:

> For as I lie, smiled-on, full-fed
>   By inexhaustible power to bless,
> I gaze below on hell's fierce bed
>   And those its waves of flame oppress
>   Swarming in ghastly wretchedness:
>   Whose life on earth aspired to be
> One altar smoke, so pure – to win
>   If not love like God's love for me,
>   At least to keep his anger in.

Do we really hesitate here between sympathy and judgment? Are we not rather drawn in by the recognition of desire to watch the speaker's impermissible bliss as he lies "smiled-on, full-fed," our envy pacified by the poet's acknowledgement? And through the displacement do we not glimpse the poet's desire for such a creative gratification that no rival can threaten him?

> Priest, doctor, hermit, monk grown white
>   With prayer, the broken hearted nun,
> The martyr, the wan acolyte,
>   The incense-swinging child – undone
> Before God fashioned star or sun!

And after all, isn't the poem really a brazen mimicry of Shelley's *Ode to the West Wind?*[7]

The mysterious moment that Bloom places between 1840 and 1842 marks, not a change from solipsism to humanistic concerns, but a displacement of the dramas of creative life on to fictive substitutes. The movement is therefore not from a pastiche of Romanticism to an authentic Victorian voice, but from a poetry too dangerously open to desire and death to a deflection, screening, mimicking of the same themes – a movement towards the polymorphic, towards processes which play and replay the original themes through parallels and equivalences at a narrative level. It is not an ironisation of the early poems, a progress from delusion to insight. Sordello, like Alastor and Hyperion, dies, not as a punishment but as a gratification of desire. The pattern is a dangerously repetitious one – both a vicious circle and a dead-end – and if poetry were only the release of our primordial narcissisms, it would perhaps always involve a surreptitious privileging of beautiful and enigmatic deaths. But great poems are not just narcissistic reveries, and Bloom's theory of revisionism is a powerful attempt at defining a creative process which is as necessary and constitutive to the writing of poetry as the Freudian dream-work is to the encounter with the unconscious. Hence the triumph of *Childe Roland* over both *Sordello* and the monologues.

Sooner or later, Browning realized the creative cost of the early poems. He never devalued *Sordello* as a poem, and his fellow poets Swinburne and Rossetti read it deeply, but after it he realigned his material, displacing it onto all the substitutes, imitations, travesties of vatic intensities which flicker in and out of ordinary life – erotic and religious fantasies, deathbed reveries, self-projections, narcissisms. Browning shifts ground, not because he is too multifaceted and red-blooded to stay with Shelleyan idealism, but because poems like *Sordello* – unless achieved through the full processes of revisionism – can end only in submission to the death-wish. The shift produces a near-inexhaustible defensive play over the now latent theme, the same old one: the desire of the creative mind for priority. And if this is not Browning's greatest poetry, it is only because it is a play which brings him closer and closer to the moment in which the full revisionary process can be achieved.

Notes

1 Harold Bloom, *Poetry and Repression* (New Haven, 1976), 175.
2 Jacques Lacan, *The Four Fundamental Concepts of Psychoanalysis*, trans. Alan Sheridan (London, 1977), 67.
3 *The Artist as Critic*, ed. Richard Ellmann (New York, 1968), 345.

4 Movingly described by Geoffrey Hartman in his account of the paradox of the human imagination ("that it cannot at the same time be true to nature and true to itself"): "If poetry, then, is a way of expressing statements of identity, we may not think that the value of simile, metaphor, and poetic symbols in general stands in proportion to 'points of likeness.'... Neither effect nor value come from each relation taken separately; they both exist as a function of an immediately perceived identity, and this identity reposes upon the mind's capacity for non-relational and simultaneous apprehension" (Geoffrey Hartman, *The Unmediated Vision* [New Haven, 1954], 45).

5 *The Browning Critics*, ed. Boyd Litzinger and K. L. Knickerbocker (Lexington, Ky., 1967), 329.

6 Harold Bloom, *A Map of Misreading* (Oxford, 1975), 70.

7 In Lacanian terms, "mimicry" is not, of course, a synonym for the literary term *parody*. See above.

4

The Pragmatics of Silence, and the Figuration of the Reader in Browning's Dramatic Monologues

Jennifer A Wagner-Lawlor

Alberto Schön has observed that silence is a concept rarely personified: "There scarcely exists a silence 'made man.' In the various myths it is the divine word that prevails and if anything it is the men who observe the silence (mystic) in an attempt to approach [the] gods."[1] Silence under such circumstances indicates consensus, and indeed more than consensus – absolute faith, awe, recognition of an ineffability before which there is no need to talk. The rarity of a silence "made man" makes its appearance the more noteworthy – and in this essay I would like to explore a sighting, as it were, that has been too little discussed.

The dramatic monologue is a genre that was not invented by nineteenth-century poets, but it was certainly taken up and fully exploited for the first time by them, particularly Robert Browning. Since then, the critical spotlight has been focused primarily upon the figure of the speaker, a typically eloquent rhetorician whose admirably complex manipulations of his auditor have been the study of literary critics. Browning critics have long noted that the typical speaker of a Browning monologue is aggressive, often threatening, nearly always superior, socially and/or intellectually, to the auditor. The auditor on the other hand cannot help but hear, as it were; he is, by generic definition,

Wagner-Lawlor, Jennifer A. 1997. "The Pragmatics of Silence and the Figuration of the Reader in Browning's Dramatic Monologues." In *Victorian Poetry*, 35, iii (Fall) pp. 287–302. Reproduced with permission of Jennifer Wagner-Lawlor.

Victorian Poets: A Critical Reader, First Edition. Edited by Valentine Cunningham.
© 2014 John Wiley & Sons, Ltd. Published 2014 by John Wiley & Sons, Ltd.

absolutely silent, a passive receptor of a verbal tour de force that leaves him no opportunity for response – indeed, that often actively discourages him from doing so.

The generically mandated silence of the auditor is not, therefore – to return to Schön's observation – a mystic silence, or even the silence of a faithful Moses receiving the Word. Far from being a silence of consensus, the auditor's is often a silence of intimidation. This is surely the intent of many a Browning speaker: by silencing his auditor, the speaker accomplishes his own typically narcissistic self-delineation, puts himself in the spotlight, keeps the body of the implied listener, the "you" of the poem, not only in shadow but as shadow. Foregrounding the aggression and rhetorical power of the speaker has thus tended to allow the effacement of the second-person addressee in favor of exploring the complex brush-work in the speaker's self-portrait.

Recent linguistic theories of silence, however, make possible closer attention to the shadowy figure of the second-person addressee. Viewed in terms of communicative acts, represented or otherwise, the silent listener is absolutely crucial; the dramatic situation itself is obviously only created by the presence of the other, and he is necessary for the delineation of the speaker's self-portrait.[2] Recent work on the pragmatics of silence has outlined the many ways in which silence is clearly not mere absence of speech, but is itself heavy with communicative value; there is communication structured through silence, just as through speech.[3]

In particular, what Adam Jaworski calls the "bipolar valence of silence" provides an altogether different lens through which to view the dynamics of the dramatic monologue. Turning aside from the success with which the speaker controls his narcissistic self-delineation, this essay will explore how the pragmatic ambiguity of second-person silence in monologues highlights the tension between consensus and resistance. This tension is a central characteristic of the genre – what any dramatic monologue is "really about" – because it clarifies the genre's ultimate irony: dramatic monologue ends up spotlighting the silent auditor precisely by effacing him/her in shadow. Like a stage whisper intended for all to hear, the shadowy figure who is the auditor cannot help but be seen finally by the figure for whom that auditor is obviously a stand-in – the reader.

My argument is that dramatic monologue thus constructs the image of the audience through the very silence it enforces upon the textual auditor. The genre self-reflexively figures its own problems of interpretation, and of the freedom of the reader in the effaced, voiceless shadow of the implied listener, who emerges from obscurity as the figure of the reader. The reader too may be silent, at least at first – but as the nature of the speech act in which s/he vicariously participates becomes clearer, s/he will not likely remain so. Through the performance of interpretation, the reader distinguishes her/himself from both the speaker and the auditor; in doing so, the reader both fulfills, but also ironically undermines, the speaker's apparent tyranny over the communicative situation that makes up the discourse of the poem.

1

The landmark work on dramatic monologue appeared in 1957 from Robert Langbaum, whose book, *The Poetry of Experience*, outlines the tension in all dramatic monologues between what he called "sympathy" and "judgment." That is, the reader's own response to the speaker swings between a sympathetic identification with him, no matter how strange or disturbed that speaker may be, and a more objective, distanced judgment. Since Langbaum published his work, most criticism on dramatic monologue has concerned itself with that speaker and with his verbal self-delineation – how it is accomplished, how the textual auditor or we, the "real readers," are lured into the speaker's verbal webs, and how irony springs the verbal traps that have been set. It is the will of the speaker that dazzles and disturbs, and the last thirty years of criticism are right in following Langbaum by pronouncing that the dramatic monologue is a post-Romantic resistance to the dangers of Romantic subjectivity.[4]

The merits and impact of Langbaum's thesis have always been unquestionable; and yet in focusing upon our relation with the speaker, subsequent analyses of the form have tended to underplay the degree to which we are also sympathetic with the implied listener, who complicates the scheme that Langbaum sets forth. The body of that shadowy figure, the text's implied listener, that "you," is intentionally kept out of the spotlight by the speaker, whose sole purpose is an often narcissistic self-delineation. Two perfect examples of this are the infamous Duke of Browning's "My Last Duchess," and the charismatic title scoundrel of "Fra Lippo Lippi." But suppose one were to ask, rather than the usual "what does the speaker's rhetoric mean," a different question: "What does the auditor's silence 'mean'?"

From the perspective of linguistic pragmatics, the aggressive narcissism of the speaker, who does not let the auditor speak, sets up a violation of "access rights" to discourse. Mary Louise Pratt notes that in any such circumstance, having "agreed" to become an audience, we "at most...can indicate our displeasure by some nonverbal means, like facial expression or body posture." Indeed, we sometimes learn that despite their silence, the auditors of dramatic monologues do in fact communicate to the speaker: we occasionally discern this when the speaker – say the Duke or Lippi – corrects or modifies his remarks in evident response to some gesture or facial expression from the listener. But as Pratt goes on to point out, in such a case "audiences in this sense are indeed captive, and speakers addressing audiences are obliged to make the captivity worthwhile."[5]

In most of Browning's monologues, however, this contract of pragmatic obligation and expectation is crucially not the voluntary one that Pratt most often discusses.[6] While the reader may be said to have "chosen" to "hear" a particular dramatic monologue, the textual listener often has not. The listener in the typical Browning monologue recognizes the speaker's superior position of power; given the latter's aggressive, sometimes even menacing nature, the apparent passivity of the silent listener seems at once the more remarkable, and yet the more understandable. Again, think of Browning's Duke of Ferrara. Who would dare to question or pose an objection to the behavior he is revealing to us? The silence of the auditor, a mere envoy, is not so surprising; he is quite simply in no position to dissent.

This leads to a second point: the auditor is participating not in a voluntary or "chosen" silence but in what linguists call "imposed" silence, which Paolo Scarpi defines as occurring "when one of the two [speakers] recognises the influence or supremacy of the other. . . . *Choice* and *imposition* can express respectively assertion and recognition of leadership."[7] The imposed code of silence is grounded in fear, adds Scarpi, and while its pragmatic implication is "consensus," in actuality verbal communication has merely been "suspended" by the intimidated listener. Such an imposed silence is dangerous because, as Scarpi puts it, "it may coincide with oblivion, negation and the loss of the individual identity."[8] "Exactly so!" the narcissistic Browning speaker might agree, as he sets up, usually far from innocently, a system of imposed silence that is necessary for his own self-delineation. The listener's silence means either assent, or, at the very least, a recognition of and acquiescence in a system that places the speaker himself at the center; as Deborah Tannen points out, silence is always a "joint production" (p. 100). The silence of the addressee is a perceptibly oppressive one, particularly as by generic definition he is unable to break the situational silence, whether in agreement or disagreement, whether in comprehension or misunderstanding. And caught as we are in the same verbal web as we read, without any clearly discernible response from the textual auditor, we tend to turn always back toward the speaker, complicitous ourselves now in his self-portraiture.

The position of the addressee is therefore ambiguous, and in the silence that maintains that ambiguity, the speaker can impose what meaning he will. A remarkable acknowledgment of this ambiguity appears at the end of the strange poem "Porphyria's Lover"; having strangled his lady with a long strand of her own hair, the speaker wonders aloud that "yet God has not said a word!" It is unclear whether the lover expects to hear approval or disapproval from God. Even had God spoken, however, Porphyria's lover would most likely have heard nothing anyway, so maniacally, indeed criminally, extreme is his solipsism.

The ambiguity of the figure of the addressee is rooted in the ambiguity of silence itself – and in fact such bivalence is characteristic of the functions assigned to silence by linguists. Jaworski names at least five possible functions of silence in communication, each one bearing positive and negative values. As noted earlier, Jaworski calls this the "bipolar" nature of silence, and naturally the value can be assigned only by looking at the context of the speech act. So, for example, silence's "revelatory function" may either make something known to a person, or may hide information.

More relevant to the argument of this essay is the function Jaworski calls the judgmental: positively, silence can signal assent and favor; negatively, it signals dissent or disfavor. This function parallels Langbaum's description of the reader's relation to a monologue speaker as either "sympathetic" or "judgmental." But at the level of the poem itself, so tight is the speaker's control that it seems difficult to know which value is to be attributed to the silence of this particular communicative event. Tannen notes that "whether or not silence is uncomfortable in interaction hinges on whether or not participants feel something should be said, in which case silence is perceived as an omission" (p. 96). It is interesting to turn this remark back upon Porphyria's lover again, who clearly does see God's silence as an omission – and yet who does not recognize in his last line's repressed whisper of conscience the voice of God; the lover has effectively silenced even Him.

The same sort of ambiguity is present in "Andrea del Sarto," in which the silence of the painter's wife, Lucrezia, is motivated not by fear, as in "My Last Duchess," but by indifference. I can never imagine her listening to del Sarto's words, but rather for the whistle-signal of her "cousin" outside. Del Sarto's monologue is to some degree a delay tactic to keep her indoors with him for once. While, however, she is temporarily held captive by the painter's desire to speak – and perhaps by a momentary but shallow sense of politeness – the apparent irrelevance of his speech to her behavior or thoughts is thematized in the poem precisely as the painter's own, crushing fault. His irrelevance is in fact the gist of his self-portrait – for which he knows he will be judged as an artist, and for which he judges himself now as a man. The poem exploits the ambiguity of silence: Lucrezia at once humors and dismisses him, as he seems well aware, by sitting with him at all; he wonders, hopelessly, if her acquiescence is a mark of favor. And yet simultaneously, she rejects him by not disagreeing with his negative self-delineation. Her judgment of him, and her worst punishment as well, is implicit in her very silence.

2

While the relevance of the speaker's narrative to the auditor may be ambiguous, that ambiguity of silence in Browning's monologues is clarified when one acknowledges that what is in question here is not a "real" conversation, but a literary representation of one, or an imitation speech act. This communicative situation obviously changes everything, from the problem of relevance, to the problem of silence – and what I will be arguing in the remainder of this essay is that these two problems conflate within the figure of the reader.

While the implied auditor of the poem, the "you," remains generically imprisoned within the situational parameters defined by the speaker, and thus remains passively mute, the reader, though aligned with that auditor, is not so compelled. Jack Selzer points out that "real readers" may or may not identify with the implied reader of a text – here, the second-person addressee of a monologue – and he promotes Iser's "more flexible account" of the reading process, which "allows for an active reader who may well choose to remain quite distinct from the role suggested by the implied reader."[9] The sooner the reader, "active and yet text-based," as Selzer puts it, recalls his nonidentity with the poem's "you," the sooner the ambiguity of silence may clarify into the active silence of dissent, and the violation of H. P. Grice's maxim of relevance within the Cooperative Principle justified at the extratextual level.[10] As Pratt notes, we the actual readers assume in such circumstances that the narrative will be "relevant" and worth hearing. But within the context of the poem, even that will sometimes be unclear for the dramatic monologue's addressee. These narratives often seem directed by the speaker toward him/herself, and the dismissal of the relevance of his narrative for the auditor is matched by control of access rights to the implied "conversation."

Pratt also points out that the reader of a literary work may in theory always be "attending to at least two utterances at once – the author's display text and the fictional speaker's discourse, whatever it is." This duality "is not always exploited by the author" (p. 174) – but it is, I am arguing, essential to the very nature of the dramatic monologue. Pratt adds that all literary texts have "display-producing relevance" or "tellability," which we the audience, voluntarily reading such a text, will search for. And the distinction of the dramatic lyric is that its relevance may lie less in the particular narratives that make up the poems than in the pragmatic dynamics that these poems do – indeed must – highlight. In real speech, the auditor of a narrative will always have the opportunity to respond to the relevance of the speaker's discourse – even if not to his face. This is obviously impossible in the dramatic monologue, which begins and ends with that discourse. The monologue must assume a relation of consent, a relation of assent as generically preestablished, and it forces the auditor into a position of passive receptivity, whether voluntary or not. The relevance of the speaker's narrative to anyone but himself need not be immediately apparent, and cannot necessarily be found within the poem itself. Sometimes the speaker is, within the context of the poem, nearly speaking to himself, as in "Porphyria's Lover," or, to cite another nineteenth-century masterpiece, in D. G. Rossetti's "Jenny," in which the auditor is the sleeping prostitute. There could be no greater sign of the "irrelevance" of speech than the silence of those recipients, one dead, the other asleep.

Dramatic monologue's generic demand for silence is, as suggested above, at least a pragmatic violation – an enforced listening – and from that source springs the prevailing sense of "danger" or threat to the auditor that characterizes so many of Browning's monologue situations. From this violation too may stem the negative response of actual contemporary readers to Browning's work; some readers supposed that the speaker's characteristic pragmatic hostility toward his auditor paralleled Browning's disdain toward the reader. While not accusing him of that exactly, John Ruskin did complain to Browning of the obscurity of his work. The great critic and others, in considering that obscurity willful, also thought it to be a kind of violation of the author-reader contract: "You are worse than the worst Alpine Glacier I ever crossed," groused Ruskin, "Bright, deep enough surely, but so full of clefts that half the journey has to be done with ladder and hatchet."[11] An excerpt from Browning's famous response points out how entirely that eminent critic had simply misread his work because they had different conceptions of that contract:

> We don't read poetry the same way, by the same law; it is too clear. I cannot begin writing poetry till my imaginary reader has conceded licences to me which you demur at altogether. I *know* that I don't make out my conception by my language; all poetry being a putting the infinite within the finite. You would have me paint it all plain out, which can't be; but by various artifices I try to make shift with touches and bits of outlines which *succeed* if they bear the conception from me to you.[12]

Browning expects, in other words, more cooperation from the reader in the bringing forth of meaning than Ruskin and other contemporaries were accustomed to grant. And while Browning's speakers characteristically "flout" or "exploit" (as Grice would put it) one or more maxims pertaining to the Cooperative Principle, the reader may well be forced to supply the "logic" of a monologue's implied conversation by stepping out of the conversational context of the poem. While the silence of the auditor in the poem represents a failure of language, it is a failure any responsible literary reader, searching for meaning or "tellability" as Pratt suggests, cannot abide.

Auditor and reader must, therefore, part ways, and the issue of silence is crucial here. For the auditor, silence signals a failure of language, but silence can also, according to Tannen, offer an alternative to the reader: "Personal exploration is the existence of cognitive activity underlying silence; the failure of language refers to its social function" (p. 100). Whereas the auditor's silence may represent an involuntary consensus, the silence of the actual reader, who is forced to step out of the place of the noninterpretive auditor, may signify the opposite. This silence is the space of the open resistance of the will of the speaker by the interpretive will of the reader. In pragmatic terms, the reader (unlike, for example, either the "next duchess's" envoy or the languid Lucrezia) may become "impolite" in a manner that the textual listener, too intimidated or too acquiescent to challenge the speaker's superiority, dares not be.[13] In hermeneutical terms, the reader has become an interpreter.

An intratextual aesthetic communication between two fictional protagonists shifts into an extratextual public communication, or, I could also say, into an inter-textual public communication. These terms I borrow from Ernest W. B. Hess-Lüttich, whose article on the pragmatics of literary communication describes the kind of shift I want to mark:

> As soon as the recipient also takes over the role of an observer of the whole process, for instance as critic, linguist, or psychologist, another metacommunicative level has to be taken into account.... This second communicative relationship is by no means a mere addendum, but structurally implied within the text itself. And the role of the audience is by no means only that of passive perceivers: perception is a very active interpreting process.[14]

This is "a structural prerequisite of dramatic tension," adds Hess-Lüttich, as well as of "other classic dramatic devices," including irony (p. 237).

The aggressive monologuist would strategically discourage us from interpretation. But such aggression, while perhaps intimidating the auditor, may well provoke the reader to recall his difference from that auditor, and to disalign him- or herself from the shadowy textual stand-in.[15] In responding, in interpreting, the reader is transforming the monologue, at the metacommunicative level, into a kind of dialogue.[16] Pratt describes such a situation well:

> The fictional speaker thus produces a lack of consensus, and the author implicates that this lack of consensus is part of what he is displaying, part of what he wants us to experience, evaluate, and interpret. He may intend us to replace the speaker's version with a better one, question our own interpretive faculties, or simply delight in the imaginative exercise of calculating "what's really going on." (p. 199)[17]

Yuri Lotman concurs in this description, asserting that "between text and audience a relationship is formed which is characterized not as passive perception but rather as a dialogue. Dialogic speech is distinguished not only by the common code of two juxtaposed utterances, but also by the presence of a common memory shared by addresser and addressee" (p. 81).

If this is the case, a crucial irony emerges: by discontinuing the sympathetic identification that the reader shared with the listener, the reader does acknowledge the speaker's construction of himself through language; the self-portrait has been successfully completed. However, the textual status of the monologue ends up being crucial for the speaker – for it betrays him. The speaker, however narcissistic he may be, only exists through figuring himself in language. Only the real reader, distinct from that "you" in the poem, has the freedom, gained at the expense of the speaker himself, to realize the speaker's self-portrait fully – that is, to interpret.

There is no larger gap or indeterminacy in dramatic monologue than that passive, silent, listening figure. But his very silence is precisely what induces the reader to what Wolfgang Iser calls the "constitutive activity" that is interpretation – that is, indeed, the emergence of the aesthetic object.[18] This conforms to Robert Browning's remark concerning the role of what we would now call "the ideal reader":

> It is certain…that a work like mine depends more immediately [than acted drama] on the intelligence and sympathy of the reader for its success – indeed were my scenes stars it must be his co-operating fancy which, supplying all chasms, shall connect the scattered lights into a constellation – a Lyre or a Crown. (Woolford, p. 27)

This same passage points at the very real influence of the author as well; he, after all, is putting the stars in their places, if not lighting the space between one and another well. It seems no wonder in this light that so many of Browning's monologues are self-reflexively about art itself: the poems are pointing as precisely toward the paradigmatic structure of their own "correct" interpretation as the extraordinary passage just quoted, and Browning indicates the way toward a "process aesthetics," rather than toward the more traditional "product aesthetics."[19]

To put it another way, while the potential effect or force of a dramatic monologue remains unfulfilled with respect to the auditor, who has been effaced through his own enforced silence, that force is effected at a different level; access is gained in the relation of that utterance to the real reader. The hierarchy set up by the speaker himself is thus undermined by the poem's own status as text, without which it would be difficult in some poems to know that anything had been "communicated" to the auditor at all.[20] The speaker has therefore both gained and lost, because his demand for identity is accomplished at his own expense, simultaneously undermined by something or someone not in his control, free of the system of silence the speaker has established – the subjectivity of the real reader. Jack Selzer would call such a figure the "resisting reader" (p. 171), a term that he borrows from feminist theorists (particularly Judith Fetterley) in an effort to connect this moment of disalignment from the textual auditor, implied or not, to a more general dialogism.[21] But this resistance is obviously gained only through the textual status of the poem itself.

Lotman concludes that the "collective memory" that textuality alone makes available to the real reader shifts the orientation of the "structure of the audience" such that it "acquires a character that is different in principle" (p. 84). In the context of dramatic monologue, Lotman's description of the audience's "character" acquires a force greater even than that of the pun: it pinpoints the figuration of the audience in and through the dynamics of reading a dramatic monologue. I mean "figuration" in two senses here: the emergence of the auditor/reader as a subjective figure standing in opposition to the speaker; and, the troping of audience generally through the emergence of a "you" that is not the textual auditor, but the reader outside the text.

The discernment of the reader rather than the speaker has been an implicit subject of such poems all along – certainly it has been one focus of the "drama" of dramatic monologue. "And what easy work these novelists have of it!" wrote Browning to Elizabeth Barrett in 1845:

> A Dramatic poet has to *make* you love or admire his men and women, – they must *do* and *say* all that you are to see and hear – really do it in your face, say it in your ears, and it is wholly for *you*, in *your* power, to *name*, characterize and so praise or blame, *what* is so said and done . . <if you don't perceive of yourself,> there is no standing by, for the Author, and telling you: but with these novelists, a scrape of the pen – out blurting of a phrase, and the miracle is achieved.[22]

Note in this passage the ambiguity of the poet's admonition "if you don't perceive of yourself"; he certainly meant "by yourself" – and yet, in the context of my argument, I cannot help hearing also Browning's insistence on the reader's awareness of him/herself as a figure, both as a subjective self, and as a trope.

This figuration or troping of the reader is best illustrated by returning to the poem that has become the touchstone of so many discussions of dramatic monologue, "My Last Duchess." I have touched down on this poem throughout the essay, and would like to make the implicit reading constructed over the course of these pages more explicit henceforth. So much attention is paid the Duke and his rhetorical manipulation of the envoy that little attention is paid the third figure present, the painted figure of the Duchess herself. Her "imposed silence," to recall Scarpi's terms, does "coincide with oblivion," since she is both silent and dead. And yet, is she truly oblivious? Literally, of course, the answer is yes. Figuratively, however, reports of her death may have been exaggerated. For what is most remarkable about this figure? That she looks "as if she were alive" (l. 2), so much so that "never read / Strangers like you that pictured countenance" without "[seeming] to want to ask, if they durst, / How such a glance came there" (ll. 6–12). The picture so accurately portrays the essential generosity of spirit that brought out the "half-flush" (l. 19) that animates her face in life and death alike, that the Duke realizes he has not, in fact, escaped his irritation at and by her at all.

This painted portrait powerfully provokes the desire for dialogue about its subject, and the reason for this is not simply because the Duchess is so strikingly "there" as if alive, but also because she is so silent in her very presence. Her image alone tells a story that strangers "read," and while the Duke would control the interpretation of this visual text, he betrays a recognition that the viewer's interpretation must already have begun. A man obsessed with possession, whether of property or persons, the Duke is finally possessed himself (in the other sense) by the life-like figure, with its immortalized "glance" over which he has no more control now than he did before; the sympathetic glance that "went everywhere" (l. 24) and the blush that favored all continue to do so. The resistance to the Duke's narcissistic self-delineation, to put it another way, comes from the "liveliness" of the painting itself; the Duchess' life-in-death acts upon the Duke as a ghostly provocation, and his acknowledgment of the beauty and candor of her painted face, epitomized by the heightened color of her blushing cheek, belies his story of her supposed betrayal of the Duke himself.

The constant play of interpretation that the reader requires is made possible, in other words, by the image of the Duchess herself; the glance that sees the joy of the world, and the "spot of joy" that marks the spirit that so animated her countenance, are continuously undermining the "authoritative version" of the story that would reduce her from subject to object. I argued earlier that it is textuality that betrays the Duke; that betrayal is clearly figured here in the visual text of the portrait, the very "truthfulness" of which exposes the need for, even demands, a (re)reading of her gaze. The painting is a textual *trompe l'oeil*, the subject and object shifting back and forth like figures in a carpet; it is also a figuration of the shifting relationship of reader to text. Far from being effaced, the Duchess is time and time again brought back to life by the Duke's pathological sensitivity to an unguided, and therefore free, reading of that face.

This portrait is finally an ironical figuration of none other than the actual reader, who like the Duchess is a presence, "alive" because s/he is ultimately beyond the control of the Duke's attempted rhetorical and, therefore, hermeneutical tyranny; we, like the Duchess, are at once inside and outside the frame of the Duke's own verbal self-portrait. On the one hand, the will of the interpreting subject, provoked by the silence of the envoy and portrait alike, is constantly reanimated, as resistant to the Duke as that now monumentally indeterminate spot of joy; on the other hand, the reader, like the Duchess, keeps the Duke alive, the dynamics of reading and interpretation in play. She tropes the event of interpretation; the Duke's mistake is to assert what is clearly not true – that his painting is "merely an object." He ignores what he himself senses in his own compulsion to talk: that the significance, the meaning of the painting, is determined by interpretive operations that are simply beyond his control. Through these operations, the figures of the Duchess and of the reader alike necessarily emerge as strongly as that of the Duke himself.

Perhaps what Browning was attempting to achieve was what Patrocinio Schweikart calls the caring reader, "absorbed in the text but not effaced by it," who "gains a dual perspective through reading both the self and the text in question, and enacts a reciprocal relationship – an 'interanimation' – among author, text, and reader that is mutually respectful and liberating."[23] The ironic freedom of the Duchess' gaze, preserved forever by the portrait's evidently uncanny likeness and "liveliness," thus tropes the actual reader's freedom as interpreter – a freedom that is, to go back to Pratt, rooted in the very textuality of this interpretive event: "Given such a guarantee [that the Cooperative Principle can be restored in any work of literature by the concept of implicature], the Audience is free to confront, explore, and interpret the communicative breakdown and to enjoy the display of the forbidden" (p. 215).

Such an achievement makes sense in the context of Browning scholarship that has established both Browning's Victorian fear of the self-imprisonment of the Romantic subject, and his active resistance to tyranny of any sort, whether political or domestic.[24] This proposed freedom of the reader through the text may be analogous to arguments from recent Whitman scholars, particularly Kerry C. Larson and C. Carroll Hollis, who have outlined the way in which Whitman's poetry highlights, rather than obscures, the rhetorical or persuasive nature of literature, and foregrounds what Larson calls the "achievement of assent as an active and indeed central feature of its drama."[25] Whitman's aim, argues Larson, is to override the mediations between "I" and "you."

Browning certainly does not attempt that kind of Whitmanian conflation. The reading offered here of "My Last Duchess" may well prompt one to ask whether then the figure for the author in this text must not be the Duke. But unlike the Duke, Browning is not demanding the "rhetoric of enthrallment," as David E. Latané puts it (p. 28), that goes along with political tyranny; rather, Browning is highlighting a rhetoric not only of obscurity, but also of indeterminacy, which may perplex (hence his "aesthetics of difficulty"), but carefully does not enthrall, does not tyrannically demand identity of speaker and listener, any more than of author and reader. His monologues do reinforce a cooperative (or what Schweikart would call "interanimating") model of reading by highlighting or even thematizing the inability of the actual reader to remain wholly sympathetic to either the text's speaker or, for that matter, to the text's auditor. And this is, once again, the reader's particular freedom, that s/he can exploit and explore with a variety of interpretive approaches the significant textual silences that s/he alone can make speak.

I began this essay by quoting Alberto Schön: "There scarcely exists a silence 'made man.'" What I am suggesting is that in the Browning dramatic monologue the figure of the silent auditor does emerge, in and through the shift from the passive to the active mode of silence, within the reader. The discernment of the second-person auditor is only possible through the reader's own more distant, objective, and possibly resistant response to the speaker. With the full force of irony, the self-image that the speaker would delineate is only achieved when the reader distinguishes her/himself from the shadowy passivity of the listener's silence, and pulls away from a sympathetic association with that manipulated figure. And in turn, the reader, while performing the action of constituting the speaker, will also delineate – in her own image – the form of the silent listener. In this kind of poem, silence is "made man," created in the image of the second-person "I" that refuses to be effaced, that is, the "you," the reader.[26]

Notes

1 "Silence in the Myth: Psychoanalytic Observations," in *The Regions of Silence: Studies on the Difficulty of Communicating*, ed. Maria Grazia Ciani (Amsterdam: J. C. Gieben, 1987), p. 9.

2 Psychoanalysts have explored the parallel therapeutic situation: Lacan, for example, asks this: "Then who is this *other* to whom I am more attached than myself, since, at the heart of my assent to my own identity, it is still he who wags me?" (Quoted by Paul Kugler, *The Alchemy of Discourse: An Archetypal Approach to Language* [Lewisburg: Bucknell Univ. Press, 1982], p. 98.) On the creation of "ego" or subjectivity through language – and the notion that it is only through language that we are conscious, are "subject" at all, see: Emile Benveniste, "Subjectivity in Language," chap. 21 in *Problems in General Linguistics*, trans. Mary Elizabeth Meek (1966; Coral Gables, Florida: Univ. of Miami Press, 1971), pp. 223–30; Ann Banfield, "Where Epistemology, Style, and Grammar Meet Literary History: The Development of Represented Speech and Thought," *NLH* 9, no. 3 (Autumn 1977): 415–54. For the relation of subject-construction and dramatic monologue, see Rosemary Huisman, "Who Speaks and For Whom? The Search for Subjectivity in Browning's Poetry," *AUMLA* 71 (May 1989): 64–87; E. Warwick Slinn, *Browning and the Fictions of Identity* (Totowa: Barnes & Noble, 1982); Slinn, "Consciousness as Writing: Deconstruction and Reading Victorian Poetry," pp. 54–68 in *Critical Essays on Robert Browning*, ed. Mary Ellis Gibson (New York: G. K. Hall, 1992); Slinn, "Some Notes on Monologues as Speech Acts," *BSN* 15 (Spring 1984): 1–9; and Herbert Tucker, "Dramatic Monologue and the Overhearing of Lyric," in *Lyric Poetry: Beyond New Criticism*, ed. Chaviva Hošek and Patricia Parker (Ithaca: Cornell Univ. Press, 1985), pp. 226–43.

3 See: Adam Jaworski's *The Power of Silence: Social and Pragmatic Perspectives* (Newbury Park: SAGE Publications, 1993); Wayne C. Anderson, "The Rhetoric of Silence in the Discourse of Coleridge and Carlyle," *South Atlantic Review* 49 (January 1984): 72–90; and articles by Muriel Saville-Troike, Anne Graffan Walker, and Deborah Tannen in *Perspectives on Silence*, ed. Deborah Tannen and Muriel Saville-Troike (Norwood: Ablex Publishing Corporation, 1985).

4 See Carol Christ, "Self-Concealment and Self-Expression in Eliot's and Pound's Dramatic Monologues," *VP* 22 (1984): 217–26; Lee Erickson, *Robert Browning: His Poetry and His Audiences* (Ithaca: Cornell Univ. Press, 1984); Constance W. Hassett, *The Elusive Self in the Poetry of Robert Browning* (Athens: Univ. of Ohio Press, 1982); Robert Langbaum, *The Poetry of Experience: The Dramatic Monologue in Modern Literary Tradition* (London: Chatto & Windus, 1957; repr. Norton, 1971); Loy D. Martin, *Browning's Dramatic Monologues and the Post-Romantic Subject* (Baltimore: Johns Hopkins Univ. Press, 1985); J. Hillis Miller, *The Disappearance of God: Five*

Nineteenth-Century Writers (Cambridge: Harvard Univ. Press, 1963); E. Warwick Slinn, *Browning and the Fictions of Identity*; Herbert F. Tucker, Jr., *Browning's Beginnings: The Art of Disclosure* (Minneapolis: Univ. of Minnesota Press, 1980).

5 Mary Louise Pratt, *Toward A Speech Act Theory of Literary Discourse* (Bloomington: Indiana Univ. Press, 1977), pp. 106–7.

6 See Cynthia Goldin Bernstein, "'My Last Duchess': A Pragmatic Approach to the Dramatic Monologue," *The SECOL Review* 14 (1990): 127–42.

7 Paolo Scarpi, "The Eloquence of Silence: Aspects of a Power Without Words," in Ciani, p. 23.

8 Ciani, p. 37. See also Maeterlink, who says that passive silence is "the shadow of sleep, of death, or non-existence" (quoted by John Auchard, in *Silence in Henry James: The Heritage of Symbolism and Decadence* [University Park: Pennsylvania State Univ. Press, 1986], p. 13).

9 Jack Selzer, "More Meanings of *Audience*," from *A Rhetoric of Doing: Essays on Written Discourse in Honor of James L. Kinneavy*, ed. Stephen P Witte, Neil Nakadate, and Roger D. Cherny (Carbondale: Southern Illinois Univ. Press, 1992), pp. 166–7.

10 See H. P. Grice, *Studies in the Way of Words* (Cambridge: Harvard Univ. Press, 1989). Chap. 2, "Logic and Conversation," outlines Grice's concept of the Cooperative Principle, its several corollary maxims (such as "relevance"), and the many ways in which the "quasi-contractual basis" (p. 29) of any conversational situation may be disrupted or pushed aside.

11 December 2, 1855, published in David J. De Laura, "Ruskin and the Brownings: Twenty-five Unpublished Letters," *John Rylands Library Bulletin* 54 (1972): 326–7.

12 December 10, 1855, in W G. Collingwood, *The Life and Work of John Ruskin*, 2 vols. (London: Methuen, 1893), 1:200. David E. Latane, Jr., outlines what he calls an "aesthetics of difficulty"; he discusses the relationship of this aesthetic to audiences and, consequently, market forces, that preferred simplicity, or at least "accessibility,"in literature (see chap. 1 of *Browning's Sordello and the Aesthetics of Difficulty* [University of Victoria / English Literary Studies (No. 40 in the ELS Monograph Series, 1987)], pp. 15–39).

13 The pragmatics of politeness, and particularly of the politeness of and in literary texts, are relevant here. See Roger D. Sell's article on this in the collection of essays he edited entitled *Literary Pragmatics* (London: Routledge, 1991). Tannen also discusses "silence and negative and positive politeness" in *Perspectives on Silence*, pp. 97 ff.

14 Ernest W. B. Hess-Lüttich, "How Does the Writer of a Dramatic Text Interact With His Audience?," in Sell, pp. 235–6.

15 For a parallel view from a Browning critic, see John Maynard: "Most of these generally too open fax receivers," says Maynard, "provoke our contempt. Hearing the silence audible of the listener, we break into our own noisy response. It is almost as if Browning has found a poetic gadget

to provoke reader response" ("Reading the Reader in Robert Browning's Dramatic Monologues," *Critical Essays on Robert Browning*, ed. Mary Ellis Gibson [New York: G. K. Hall, 1992], p. 74). Maynard concludes that we should read the reader "not to define the ideal interpretive position, but to explore the range of response – experiences – the poem generates.... If we begin with the listener in the poem in order to decide where to position the cameras of our various readers, we had better be prepared for a variety of listeners as well" (p. 76). Also see Latané, who explores the dynamics of the audience "in and out" of the text; Maynard, "Browning, Donne,and the Triangulation of the Dramatic Monologue," *John Donne Journal* 4, no. 2 (1985): 253–67; and John Woolford, who is one of the few Browning critics who recognizes the significance (both in the sense of "importance" and in the sense of "signifying") of silence. He anticipates my own argument in suggesting that it is the silence of the second-person consciousness that most severely complicates Langbaum's thesis *(Browning the Revisionary* [London: Macmillan, 1988]).

16 See Rosemary Huisman's "Who Speaks and For Whom? The Search for Subjectivity in Browning's Poetry," *AUMLA* 71 (May 1989) for her conclusion that the term "dramatic monologue" is a misnomer, given the dialogic relation between speaker and reader that emerges (p. 83).

17 Yuri Lotman is not talking about dramatic monologue specifically, but about literary texts generally when he remarks that "orientation toward a certain type of collective memory, and consequently toward a structure of the audience acquires a character that is different in principle. It ceases to be automatically implied in the text and becomes a signified (i.e. free) artistic element which can enter the text as part of a game." See Yuri Lotman, "The Text and the Structure of Its Audience," *NLH* 14, no. 1 (Autumn 1982): 84.

18 My description of the pragmatics of dramatic monologue parallels the reading process as described by Iser in his "Interaction between Text and Reader," in *The Reader in the Text: Essays on Audience and Interpretation*, ed. Susan Suleiman and Inge Crosman (Princeton: Princeton Univ. Press, 1980), pp. 106–19. As Iser says, "If the blank is largely responsible for the activities described, then participation means that the reader is not simply called upon to 'internalize' the positions given in the text, but he is induced to make them act upon and so transform each other, as a result of which the aesthetic object begins to emerge. The structure of the blank organizes this participation, revealing simultaneously the intimate connection between this structure and the reading subject. This interconnection completely conforms to a remark made by Piaget: 'In a word, the subject is there and alive, because the basic quality of each structure is the structuring process itself.' The blank in the fictional text appears to be a paradigmatic structure; its function consists in initiating structured operations in the reader, the execution of which transmits the reciprocal interaction of textual positions into consciousness" (p. 119).

There is a fascinating relationship here between the problem of intersubjectivity and recent game theory, as applied to pragmatic or hermeneutic processes. I noticed while researching this paper that the trope of "game-playing" – from "boxing" to "feint" (Maynard, Sinfield) – turned up both in discussions of dramatic monologue, and in abstract accounts of the reading process. See Elizabeth W. Bruss, "The Game of Literature and Some Literary Games," *NLH* 9, no. 1 (Autumn 1977): 153–72; John Maynard; Pia Teodorescu-Brînzeu, "The Monologue as Dramatic Sign," *Poetics* 13 (1984): 136; Yuri Lotman, "The Text and the Structure of Its Audience," p. 84; Christopher Collins, "The Poetics of Play: Reopening Jakobson's 'Closing Statement,'" chap. 3 in *The Poetics of the Mind: Literature and the Psychology of Imagination* (Philadelphia: Univ. of Pennsylvania Press, 1991), pp. 47–66.

19   I borrow these terms from Nils Erik Enkvist, "On the interpretability of texts in general and of literary texts in particular," in Sell, pp. 24–5.

20   See Wolfgang Iser, *The Act of Reading: A Theory of Aesthetic Response* (Baltimore: Johns Hopkins Univ. Press, 1978): "Only when the recipient shows by his *responses* that he has correctly received the speaker's intention are the conditions fulfilled for the success of the linguistic action" (p. 57).

21   For a fuller exploration of the "dialogic element" in dramatic monologue, see Ashton Nichols, "Dialogism in the Dramatic Monologue: Suppressed Voices in Browning," *VIJ* 18 (1990): 29–51. Here of course lie the full implications of ideology's insinuations through silence, for as Scarpi notes, "Silence...becomes a necessary condition for not being excluded from the 'centre.' The myestes who takes part in the celebration of the Mysteries in silence corresponds to the citizen who obeys the 'law' (and how else but in silence?). Indeed, silence is revealed to be one of the conditions necessary to be admitted to the 'centre.'...Silence...assumes the form of an adhesion to the 'law' which the initiate carries for ever depicted on his body [in tribal initiations]" (Ciani, pp. 30–1). Silence becomes, Scarpi concludes, a "discriminating tool with regard to those who are out....It assumes the form of a type of 'discourse' of the order." In his *Marxism and Literary Criticism* (London: Basil Blackwell, 1990), Terry Eagleton also pinpoints the connection between ideology and silence: "It is in the significant *silences* of a text, in its gaps and absences, that the presence of ideology can be most positively felt. It is these silences which the critic must make 'speak.' The text is, as it were, ideologically forbidden to say certain things....Far from constituting a rounded coherent whole, it displays a conflict and contradiction of meanings; and the significance of the work lies in the difference rather than unity between these meanings" (pp. 34–5).

22   </> indicate Browning's insertion of material in his own text; August 10, 1845, in *Letters of Robert Browning and Elizabeth Barrett Browning*, ed. Elvan Kintner, 2 vols. (Cambridge: Belknap Press of Harvard Univ. Press, 1969), 1:150.

23 Quoted by Selzer, "More Meanings of *Audience*," p. 171.

24 See the early pages of Woolford's *Browning the Revisionary* on the dynamics of reading in Browning's monologues. Also interested in the reader's silence is Joseph A. Dupras; see his "'My Last Duchess': Paragon and Parergon," *PLL* 32, no. 1 (Winter 1996): 3–18.

25 Kerry C. Larson and C. Carroll Hollis, *Whitman's Drama of Consensus* (Chicago: Chicago Univ. Press, 1988), p. 6; also see C. Carroll Hollis, *Language and Style in Leaves of Grass* (Baton Rouge: Louisiana State Univ. Press, 1983). I am grateful to my colleague Paul Naylor for pointing out this connection, and also for commenting on a draft of this essay.

26 This essay is an expanded version of a paper presented at the 1993 Modern Language Association convention in Toronto. The panel, sponsored by the Linguistic Approaches to Literature division, was put together by Professor Cynthia Bernstein of Auburn, and I would like to thank her for her encouragement. I am also grateful to Professor David Herman of North Carolina State University, whose valuable and thorough comments on a draft of this essay helped direct revisions.

5

Dramatic Monologue and the Overhearing of Lyric

Herbert F Tucker

His muse made increment of anything,
   From the high lyric down to the low rational.

(Don Juan III.Ixxxv.5–6)

I would say, quoting Mill, "Oratory is heard, poetry is overheard." And
he would answer, his voice full of contempt, that there was always an
audience; and yet, in his moments of lofty speech, he himself was alone
no matter what the crowd.

(The Autobiography of William Butler Yeats)

I

"Eloquence is *heard*, poetry is *overheard*. Eloquence supposes an
audience; the peculiarity of poetry appears to us to lie in the poet's utter
unconsciousness of a listener. Poetry is feeling confessing itself to itself,
in moments of solitude." "Lyric poetry, as it was the earliest kind, is
also, if the view we are now taking of poetry be correct, more eminently
and peculiarly poetry than any other."[1] Thus wrote John Stuart Mill in
1833, with the wild surmise of a man who had lately nursed himself

Tucker, Herbert F. 1985. "Dramatic Monologue and the Overhearing of Lyric." In *Lyric
Poetry: Beyond New Criticism*, edited by Chaviva Hošek and Patricia Parker, pp. 226–43.
Ithaca: Cornell University Press. Reproduced with permission of Cornell University
Press.

Victorian Poets: A Critical Reader, First Edition. Edited by Valentine Cunningham.
© 2014 John Wiley & Sons, Ltd. Published 2014 by John Wiley & Sons, Ltd.

through a severe depression, thanks to published poetry and its capacity to excite intimate feeling in forms uncontaminated by rhetorical or dramatic posturing. One listener Mill's characteristically analytic eloquence is likely to have found at once was Robert Browning, who moved in London among liberal circles that touched Mill's and who in the same year published his first work, the problematically dramatic *Pauline: A Fragment of a Confession*, to which Mill drafted a response Browning saw in manuscript. Browning's entire career – most notably the generic innovation for which he is widely remembered today, the dramatic monologue – would affirm his resistance to the ideas about poetry contained in Mill's essays. Indeed, as early as *Pauline* Browning was confessing to the open secret of spontaneous lyricism, but in ways that disowned it. What follows is emphatically the depiction of a bygone state:

> And first I sang as I in dream have seen
> Music wait on a lyrist for some thought,
> Yet singing to herself until it came.
> (ll. 377–79)

In this complex but typical retrospect the poet of *Pauline* figures as an eavesdropper on his own Shelleyan juvenilia, themselves relics of a dream of disengaged and thoughtless youth from which the sadder but wiser poet has on balance done well to awaken. Browning's enfolding of a lyrical interval into a narrative history sets the pattern for the establishment of character throughout his subsequent work, a pattern knowingly at odds with the subjectivist convention that governed the reading of English poetry circa 1830 and to which Mill's essay gave memorable but by no means unique voice.[2]

To the most ambitious and original young poets of the day, Browning and Alfred Tennyson, the sort of lyricism Mill admired must have seemed "overheard" in a sense quite other than Mill intended: heard overmuch, overdone, and thus in need of being done over in fresh forms. Among their other generic experiments in the lyrical drama (*Paracelsus*, *Pippa Passes*), the idyll ("Dora," "Morte d'Arthur"), and the sui generis historical epic form of *Sordello*, during the 1830s Tennyson and Browning arrived independently at the first recognizably modern dramatic monologues: "St. Simeon Stylites" (1842; written in 1833) and the paired poems of 1837 that we now know as "Johannes Agricola in Meditation" and "Porphyria's Lover." These early monologues were not only highly accomplished pieces; within the lyrical climate of the day they were implicitly polemical as well. The ascetic St. Simeon atop his pillar, exposed to the merciless assault of the elements, stands for an exalted subjectivity ironically demystified by the historical contextualization that is the generic privilege of the dramatic monologue and, I shall argue, one of its indispensable props in the construction of character. Browning's imagination was less symbolically brooding than Tennyson's and more historically alert, and he launched his dramatic monologues with speakers whose insanities were perversions, but recognizably versions, of the twin wellheads of the lyrical current that had come down to the nineteenth century from the Reformation and the Renaissance. The historical figure Johannes Agricola is an antinomian Protestant lying against time as if his soul depended on it; and Porphyria's lover, though fictive, may be regarded as a gruesomely literal-minded Petrarch bent on possessing the object of his desire. Each of Browning's speakers, like St. Simeon Stylites, utters a monomaniacal manifesto that shows subjectivity up by betraying its situation in a history. The utterance of each stands revealed not as poetry, in Mill's terms, but as eloquence, a desperately concentric rhetoric whereby, to adapt Yeats's formulation from "Ego Dominus Tuus," the sentimentalist deceives himself.

What gets "overheard" in these inaugural Victorian monologues is history dramatically replayed. The charmed circle of lyric finds itself included by the kind of historical particularity that lyric genres exclude by design, and in the process readers find themselves unsettlingly historicized and contextualized as well. The extremity of each monologist's authoritative assertion awakens in us with great force the counter-authority of communal norms, through a reductio ad absurdum of the very lyric premises staked out in Mill's essays, most remarkably in a sentence that Mill deleted when republishing "What is Poetry?": "That song has always seemed to us like the lament of a prisoner in a solitary cell, ourselves listening, unseen in the next."[3] ("Ourselves"? How many of us in that next cell? Does one eavesdrop in company? Or is that not called going to the theater, and is Mill's overheard poetry not dramatic eloquence after all?) Tennyson's and Browning's first monologues imply that Mill's position was already its own absurd reduction – a reduction not just of the options for poetry but of the prerogatives of the unimprisoned self, which ideas like Mill's have been underwriting, as teachers of undergraduate poetry classes can attest, for the better part of two centuries. Tennyson and Browning wanted to safeguard the self's prerogatives, and to that extent they

shared the aims of contemporary lyrical devotees. But both poets'
earliest dramatic monologues compassed those aims through a
more subtle and eloquent design than the prevailing creed would
admit: a design that might preserve the self on the far side of, and
as a result of, a contextual dismissal of attenuated Romantic lyricism and its merely soulful claims; a design that might, as Browning
was to put it in the peroration to *The Ring and the Book* (1869),
"Suffice the eye and save the soul beside" (XII.863). St. Simeon,
Johannes, and Porphyria's lover emerge through their monologues
as characters: poorer souls than they like to fancy themselves but
selves for all that, de- and re-constructed selves strung on the tensions of their texts.

II

Both Tennyson and Browning proceeded at once to refine their generic
discoveries, though they proceeded in quite different directions.
While Tennyson kept the dramatic monologue in his repertoire, he
turned to it relatively seldom; and with such memorable ventures as
"Ulysses" and "Tithonus" he in effect relyricized the genre, running
its contextualizing devices in reverse and stripping his speakers of
personality in order to facilitate a lyric drive. Browning, on the other
hand, moved his dramatic monologues in the direction of mimetic
particularity, and the poems he went on to write continued to incorporate or "overhear" lyric in the interests of character-formation.
"Johannes Agricola" and "Porphyria's Lover" had been blockbusters,
comparatively single-minded exercises in the construction of a lurid
character through the fissuring of an apparently monolithic ego. The
gain in verisimilitude of Browning's later monologues is a function of
the nerve with which he learned to reticulate the sort of pattern these
strong but simple monologues had first knit. The degree of intricacy
varies widely, but the generic design remains the same. Character in
the Browningesque dramatic monologue emerges as an interference
effect between opposed yet mutually informative discourses: between
an historical, narrative, metonymic text and a symbolic, lyrical, metaphoric text that adjoins it and jockeys with it for authority. While each
text urges its own priority, the ensemble works according to the
paradoxical logic of the originary supplement: the alien voices of history and of feeling come to constitute and direct one another. Typically
Browning's monologists tell the story of a yearning after the condition

monomaniacal perversity with which he has put a stop to her egalitarian smiles. Each perversity so turns on the other as to knot the text up into that essential illusion we call character. Hence the Duke's characteristic inconsistency in objecting to the "officious fool" who, in breaking cherries for the Duchess, was not breaking ranks at all but merely executing his proper "office" in the Duke's hierarchical world. Hence, too, the undecidable ambiguity of "My favour at her breast": the phrase oscillates between suggestions of a caress naturally given and of an heirloom possessively bestowed, and its oscillation is what makes the star of dramatic character shine. Such a semantic forking of the ways, like the plotting of spontaneity against calculation in Fra Lippo's "*mistr...manners*" revision, blocks reference in one direction, in order to refer us to the textual production of character instead.

Because in grammatical terms it is a paratactic pocket, an insulated deviation from the syntax of narrative line, the Duke's recounting of his Duchess's easy pleasures wanders from the aims of the raconteur and foregrounds the speech impediments that make her story his monologue.[9] Moreover, the Duke's listing is also a listening, a harkening after the kind of spontaneous lyric voice that he, like the writer of dramatic monologues, comes into his own by imperfectly renouncing. Lyric, in the dramatic monologue, is what you cannot have and what you cannot forget – think of the arresting trope Browning invented for his aging poet Cleon (1855), "One lyric woman, in her crocus vest" (l. 15) – and as an organizing principle for the genre, lyric becomes present through a recurrent and partial overruling. This resisted generic nostalgia receives further figuration intertextually, in "My Last Duchess" and many another monologue, with the clustering of allusions at moments of lyric release. Here "The dropping of the daylight in the West" falls into Browning's text from major elegies, or refusals to mourn, by Milton ("Lycidas"), Wordsworth ("Tintern Abbey," "Intimations" ode), and Keats ("To Autumn"); and the Duchess on her white mule so recalls Spenser's lyrically selfless Una from the opening of *The Faerie Queene* as to cast the Duke as an archimage dubiously empowered.

Amid the Duke's eloquence the overhearing of poetry, in this literary-historical sense of allusion to prior poems, underscores the choral dissolution that lurks in lyric voice. Furthermore, it reinstates the checking of such dissolution as the mark of the individual self – of the dramatic speaker and also of the poet who, in writing him up, defines himself in opposition to lyrical orthodoxy and emerges as a distinct "I," a name to conjure with against the ominous: "This grew; I gave commands" (l. 45). Toward the end of his career, in "House" (1876) Browning would in his own voice make more explicit this engagement with the literary past and would defend literary personality, against Wordsworth on the sonnet, as just the antithesis of unmediated sincerity: " ' "With this same key / Shakespeare unlocked his heart," once more! / Did Shakespeare? If so, the less Shakespeare he!" (ll. 38–40). Poetry of the unlocked heart, far from displaying character in Browning's terms, undoes it: Browning reads his chief precursor in the English dramatic line as a type of the objective poet, the poetical character known through a career-long objection to the sealed intimacies of the poem à *clef*.

IV

In 1831 Arthur Hallam gave a promising description of the best of Tennyson's *Poems, Chiefly Lyrical* (1830) as "a graft of the lyric on the dramatic." The Victorian dramatic monologue that soon ensued from these beginnings was likewise a hybrid genre, a hardy offshoot of the earlier hybrid genre in which the first Romantics had addressed the problem of how to write the long modern poem by making modern civilization and its discontents, or longing and its impediments, into the conditions for the prolonging and further hearing of poetry: the "greater Romantic lyric." The genre M. H. Abrams thus christened some years ago has by now achieved canonical status, but a reconsideration of its given name from the standpoint of the dramatic monologue may help us save it from assimilation to orthodox lyricism by reminding us that the genre Abrams called "greater" was not more-lyrical-than-lyric but rather more-than-lyrical. Despite a still high tide of assertions to the contrary, the works of the first generations of Romantic poets were on the whole much less lyrical than otherwise.[10] Once we conceive the Romantic tradition accordingly as a perennial intermarriage, which is to say infighting, of poetic kinds, we can situate the Victorian dramatic monologue as an eminently Romantic form. In correcting the literary-historical picture we can begin, too, to see how fin-de-siècle and modernist reactions to the Browningesque monologue have conditioned the writing, reading, and teaching of poetry, literary theory, and literary history in our own time.

At the beginning of Browning's century Coleridge remarked, "A poem of any length neither can be, nor ought to be, all poetry." By the end of the century Oscar Wilde, looking askance at Browning's achievement, took up Coleridge's distinction, but with a difference: "If he can only get his music by breaking the strings of his lute, he breaks them, and they snap in discord.... Meredith is a prose Browning, and so is Browning. He used poetry as a medium for writing in prose."[11] The difference between Coleridge's and Wilde's ideas of what a poem should be is in large part a difference that the dramatic monologue had made in nineteenth-century poetry, a difference Browning inscribed into literary history by inscribing it into the characteristic ratios of his texts. Wilde and others at the threshold of modernism wanted Mill's pure lyricism but wanted it even purer. And through an irony of literary history that has had far-reaching consequences for our century, the Browningesque dramatic monologue gave them what they wanted. Symbolist and imagist writers could extract from such texts as *Pauline* and "Fra Lippo Lippi" – and also, to sketch in the fuller picture, from the Tennysonian idyll and most sophisticated Victorian novels – lyrical gems as finely cut as anything from the allegedly naive eras, Romantic or Elizabethan, upon which they bestowed such sentimental if creative regard. The hybrid dramatic monologue, as a result of its aim to make the world and subjectivity safe for each other in the interests of character, had proved a sturdy grafting stock for flowers of lyricism; and the governing pressures of the genre, just because they governed so firmly, had bred hothouse lyric varieties of unsurpassed intensity. These lyrical implants it was left to a new generation of rhymers, scholars, and anthologists to imitate, defend, and excerpt in a newly chastened lyric poetry, a severely purist poetics, and a surprisingly revisionist history of poetry.[12]

The fin-de-siècle purism of Wilde, Yeats, Arthur Symons, and others was polemically canted against the example of Browning; yet it remained curiously, even poignantly, in his debt. Consider, for example, Symons's resumption of a rhetoric very like Mill's, as he praises Verlaine in *The Symbolist Movement* (1899) for "getting back to nature itself": "From the moment when his inner life may be said to have begun, he was occupied with the task of an unceasing confession, in which one seems to overhear him talking to himself."[13] The pivotally wishful "unceasing," which distinguishes Symons's formulation from Mill's, also betrays a kind of elegiac overcompensation. Mill had dissolved audience in order to overhear poetry as if from an adjacent cell; Symons, writing at an appreciable historical remove from the achievements of Verlaine, is by contrast trapped in time. Symons's overhearing of poetry resembles less Mill's eavesdropping than the belated Browningesque audition of a poignant echo, and the symbolist movement he hopes to propel is fed by an overwhelming nostalgia that creates from its own wreck the thing it contemplates. The nostalgia for lyric that throbs through the influential versions of the poetic past Symons and his contemporaries assembled sprang from a range of cultural causes we are only beginning to understand adequately.[14] But we can observe here that the rhetorical pattern into which their lyrically normed historiography fell was precisely that of the poetic genre that had preeminently confronted lyricism with history in their century: the dramatic monologue. It is as if what Symons championed as the "revolt against exteriority, against rhetoric,"[15] having repudiated the "impure" Browning tradition in principle, was condemned to reiterate its designs in writing. The symbolist and imagist schools wanted to read in their French and English antecedents an expurgated lyric that never was on page or lip. It was, rather, a generic back-formation, a textual constituent they isolated from the dramatic monologue and related nineteenth-century forms; and the featureless poems the fin-de-siècle purists produced by factoring out the historical impurities that had ballasted these forms are now fittingly, with rare exceptions, works of little more than historical interest.

Virtually each important modernist poet in English wrote such poems for a time; each became an important poet by learning to write otherwise and to exploit the internal otherness of the dramatic monologue. When the lyrical bubble burst within its bell jar, poetry became modern once again in its return to the historically responsive and dialogical mode that Browning, Tennyson, and others had brought forward from the Romantics.[16] And upon the establishment of Yeats's mask, Pound's personae, Frost's monologues and idylls, and Eliot's impersonal poetry, it became a point of dogma among sophisticated readers that every poem dramatized a speaker who was not the poet. "Once we have dissociated the speaker of the lyric from the personality of the poet, even the tiniest lyric reveals itself as drama."[17] We recognize this declaration as dogma by the simple fact that we – at least most of us – had to learn it, and had to trade for it older presuppositions about lyric sincerity that we had picked up in corners to which New Critical light had not yet pierced. The new dogma took (and in my teaching experience it takes still) with such ease that it is worth asking why it did (and does), and whether as professors of poetry we should not have second thoughts about promulgating an approach that requires so painless an adjustment of the subjectivist norms we profess to think outmoded.

The conversion educated readers now routinely undergo from lyrical to dramatic expectations about the poems they study recapitulates the history of Anglo-American literary pedagogy during our century, the middle two decades of which witnessed a great awakening from which we in our turn are trying to awaken again. Until about 1940 teachers promoted poetry appreciation in handbooks and anthologies that exalted lyric as "the supreme expression of strong emotion...the very real but inexplicable essence of poetry," and that throned this essential emotion in the equally essential person of the poet: "Lyrical poetry arouses emotion because it expresses the author's feeling."[18] By 1960 the end of instruction had shifted from appreciating to understanding poetry, and to this end a host of experts marched readers past the author of a poem to its dramatic speaker. John Crowe Ransom's dictum that the dramatic situation is "almost the first head under which it is advisable to approach a poem for understanding" had by the 1960s advanced from advice to prescription. In Laurence Perrine's widely adopted *Sound and Sense* the first order of business is "to assume always that the speaker is someone other than the poet himself." For Robert Scholes in *Elements of Poetry* the speaker is the most elementary of assumptions: "In beginning our approach to a poem we must make some sort of tentative decision about who the speaker is, what his situation is, and whom he seems to be addressing."[19]

That such forthright declarations conceal inconsistencies appears in the instructions of Robert W. Boynton and Maynard Mack, whose *Introduction to the Poem* promotes the familiar dramatic principle but pursues its issues to the verge of a puzzling conclusion. The authors begin dogmatically enough: "When we start looking closely at the dramatic character of poetry, we find that we have to allow for a more immediate speaker than the poet himself, one whom the poet has imagined speaking the poem, as an actor speaks a part written for him by a playwright." But then Boynton and Mack, with a candor unusual in the handbook genre, proceed to a damaging concession that dissolves the insubstantial pageant of the dramatic enterprise into thin air: "In some instances this imagined speaker is in no way definite or distinctive; he is simply a voice." (When is a speaker not a speaker? When he is a "voice," nay, an Arnoldian "lyric cry.") With this last sentence Boynton and Mack offer an all but lyrical intimation of the mystification inherent in the critical fiction of the speaker and suggest its collusion with the mysteries of the subjectivist norm it was designed to supplant.[20] It may well be easier to indicate these mysteries than to solve them; what matters is that with our New Critical guides we seem to have experienced as little difficulty in negotiating the confusions entailed by the fiction of the speaker as we have experienced in converting ourselves and our students from lyrically expressive to dramatically objective norms for reading.

Why should we have made this conversion, and why do we continue to encourage it? Why should our attempts at understanding poetry through a New Criticism rely on a fiction that baffles the understanding? These are related questions, and their answers probably lie in considerations of pedagogical expediency. One such consideration must be the sheer hard work of bringing culturally stranded students into contact with the historical particularities from which a given poem arises. Life (and courses) being short, art being long, and history being longer still, the fiction of the speaker at least brackets the larger problem of context so as to define a manageable classroom task for literary studies. To such institutional considerations as these, which have been attracting needed attention of late, I would add a consideration more metaphysical in kind. The fiction of the speaker, if it removes from the study of poetry the burden, and the dignity, of establishing contact with history, puts us in compensatory contact with the myth of unconditioned subjectivity we have inherited from Mill and Symons in spite of ourselves. Through that late ceremony of critical innocence, the readerly imagination of a self, we modern readers have abolished the poet and set up the fictive speaker; and we have done so in order to boost the higher gains of an intersubjective recognition for which, in an increasingly mechanical age that can make Mill's look positively idyllic, we seem to suffer insatiable cultural thirst. The mastery of New Critical tools may offer in this light a sort of homeopathic salve, the application of a humanistic technology to technologically induced ills.

The thirst for intersubjective confirmation of the self, which has made the overhearing of a persona our principal means of understanding a poem, would I suspect be less strong if it did not involve a kind of bad faith about which Browning's Bishop Blougram (1855) had much to say: "With me, faith means perpetual unbelief / Kept quiet like the snake 'neath Michael's foot / Who stands calm just because he feels it writhe" (ll. 666–68). The New Criticism of lyric poetry introduced into literary study an anxiety of textuality that was its legacy from the Higher Criticism of scripture a century before: anxiety over the tendency of texts to come loose from their origins into an anarchy that the New Critics half acknowledged and half sought to curb under the regime of a now avowedly fictive self, from whom a language on parole from its author might nonetheless issue as speech. What is poetry? Textuality a speaker owns. The old king of self-expressive lyricism is dead: Long live the Speaker King! At a king's ransom we thus secure our reading against the subversive textuality of what we read; or as another handbook from the 1960s puts it with clarity: "So strong is the oral convention in poetry that, in the absence of contrary indications, we infer a voice and, though we know we are reading words on a page, create for and of ourselves an imaginary listener."[21] Imaginative recreation "for and of ourselves" here depends upon our suppressing the play of the signifier beneath the hand of a convention "so strong" as to decree the "contrary indications" of textuality absent most of the time.

Deconstructive theory and practice in the last decade have so directed our attention to the persistence of "contrary indications" that the doctrine espoused in my last citation no longer appears tenable. It seems incumbent upon us now to choose between intersubjective and intertextual modes of reading, between vindicating the self and saving the text. Worse, I fear, those of us who are both teachers and critics may have to make different choices according to the different positions in which we find ourselves – becoming by turns intertextual readers in the study and intersubjective readers in the classroom – in ways that not very fruitfully perpetuate a professional divide some latter-day Browning might well monologize upon. I wonder whether it must be so; and I am fortified in my doubts by the stubborn survival of the dramatic monologue, which began as a response to lyric isolationism, and which remains to mediate the rivalry between intersubjective appeal and intertextual rigor by situating the claims of each within the limiting context the other provides.

In its charactered life the dramatic monologue can help us put in their places critical reductions of opposite but complementary and perhaps even cognate kinds: on one hand, the transcendentally facesaving misprisions that poetry has received from Victorian romanticizers, Decadent purists, and New Critical impersonalists alike; on the other hand, the abysmal disfigurements of a deconstruction that would convert poetry's most beautiful illusion – the speaking presence – into a uniform textuality that is quite as "purist," in its own way, as anything the nineteenth century could imagine. An exemplary teaching genre, the dramatic monologue can teach us, among other things, that while texts do not absolutely lack speakers, they do not simply have them either; they invent them instead as they go. Texts do not come from speakers, speakers come from texts. *Persona fit non nascitur.* To assume in advance that a poetic text proceeds from a dramatically situated speaker is to risk missing the play of verbal implication whereby character is engendered in the first place through colliding modes of signification; it is to read so belatedly as to arrive only when the party is over. At the same time, however, the guest the party convenes to honor, the ghost conjured by the textual machine, remains the articulate phenomenon we call character: a literary effect we neglect at our peril. For to insist that textuality is all and that the play of the signifier usurps the recreative illusion of character is to turn back at the threshold of interpretation, stopping our ears to both lyric cries and historical imperatives, and from our studious cells overhearing nothing. Renewed stress upon textuality as the basis for the Western written character is a beginning as important to the study of poetry now as it has been for over a century to the writing of dramatic monologues and to the modern tradition they can illuminate in both backward and forward directions. But textuality is only the beginning.

Notes

1 John Stuart Mill, *Essays on Poetry*, ed. F. Parvin Sharpless (Columbia, S.C., 1976), pp. 12, 36. The quotations come from two essays of 1833, "What is Poetry?" and "The Two Kinds of Poetry."

2 Ideas like Mill's abound, for example, in Macaulay's 1825 essay "Milton," in *Critical and Historical Essays* (London, 1883): "Analysis is not the business of the poet" (p. 3); "It is the part of the lyric poet to abandon himself, without reserve, to his own emotions" (p. 6); "It is just when Milton escapes from the shackles of the dialogue, when he is discharged from the labour of uniting two incongruous styles, when he is at liberty to indulge his choral raptures without reserve, that he rises even above himself (p. 8). Comparing Mill's writings with T. S. Eliot's "The Three Voices of Poetry" (1953), Elder Olson, *American Lyric Poems* (New York, 1964), p. 2, concludes that "the study of the question has not advanced much in over a hundred years." Olson's conclusion retains its force after two decades. See Barbara Hardy, *The Advantage of Lyric* (Bloomington and London, 1977), p. 2: "Lyric poetry thrives, then, on exclusions. It is more than usually opaque because it leaves out so much of the accustomed context and consequences of feeling that it can speak in a pure, lucid, and intense voice."

3 *Essays on Poetry*, p. 14.

4 Genre theorists have often observed this distinction, though usually in honoring the exclusivity of lyric. For Babette Deutsch, *Potable Gold* (New York, 1929), p. 21, the essential distinction lies between prose and poetry: "The one resembles a man walking toward a definite goal; the other is like a man surrendering himself to contemplation, or to the experience of walking for its own sake. Prose has intention; poetry has intensity." According to Kenneth Burke, *A Grammar of Motives* (1945; Berkeley and Los Angeles,

1969), p. 475, *"The state of arrest* in which we would situate the essence of lyric is not analogous to dramatic action at all, but is the dialectical counterpart of action." Olson, "The Lyric," [*PMLA*], 1 (1969), 65, says of lyrics that "while they may contain within themselves a considerable narrative or dramatic portion, that portion is subordinate to the lyrical whole.... Once expression and address and colloquy become subservient to a further end as affecting their form as complete and whole in themselves, we have gone beyond the bounds of the lyric." For a recent view of Browning opposed to that of the present essay see David Bergman, "Browning's Monologues and the Development of the Soul," *ELH*, 47 (1980), 774: "For Browning, historicity only prettifies a work.... History, the creation of a concrete setting, has never been a major focus for Browning." I would reply that history is indeed a major focus for Browning—one of the two foci, to speak geometrically, that define his notoriously elliptical procedures.

5   *Ion* 534; Sharon Cameron, *Lyric Time* (Baltimore and London, 1979), p. 208. See also the quirky Victorian theorist E. S. Dallas, *Poetics* (London, 1852), p. 83: "The outpourings of the lyric should spring from the law of unconsciousness. Personality or selfhood triumphs in the drama; the divine and all that is not Me triumphs in the lyric."

6   Although Browning never wrote such a monologue, he glanced at its possibility in "The Englishman in Italy" (1845), with its vision of "Those isles of the siren" (l. 199) and its audition of a song "that tells us / What life is, so clear"; "The secret they sang to Ulysses / When, ages ago, / He heard and he knew this life's secret /1 hear and I know" (ll. 223 – 27). Life's secret, needless to add, goes untold in Browning's text.

7   Letter of 11 February 1845, in *Letters of Robert Browning and Elizabeth Barrett Barrett, 1845–1846*, ed. Elvan Kintner, 2 vols. (Cambridge, Mass., 1969), 1:17.

8   Jerome Christensen, "'Thoughts That Do Often Lie too Deep for Tears': Toward a Romantic Concept of Lyrical Drama," *Wordsworth Circle*, 12:1 (1981), 61. For an appropriately genealogical testimonial to the pedagogical virtues of the dramatic monologue see Ina Beth Sessions's postscript to "The Dramatic Monologue," *PMLA*, 62 (1947), 516n: "One of the most interesting comments concerning the dramatic monologue was made by Dr. J. B. Wharey of the University of Texas in a letter to the writer on January 17, 1935: 'The dramatic monologue is, I think, one of the best forms of disciplinary reading – that is, to use the words of the late Professor Genung, "reading pursued with the express purpose of feeding and stimulating inventive power."'" Among the earliest systematic students of the genre in our century were elocution teachers; their professional pedigree broadly conceived goes back at least to Quintilian, who recommended exercises in impersonation *(prosopopoeia)* as a means of imaginative discipline. See A. Dwight Culler, "Monodrama and the Dramatic Monologue," *PMLA*, 90 (1975). 368.

9   David I. Masson, "Vowel and Consonant Patterns in Poetry," in *Essays on the Language of Literature*, ed. Seymour Chatman and Samuel R. Levin (Boston, 1967), p. 3, observes that "where lyrical feeling or sensuous description occurs in European poetry, there will usually be found patterns of vowels and consonants." For more general consideration of the linguistics of lyric, see Edward Stankiewicz, "Poetic and Non-poetic Language in Their Interrelation," in *Poetics*, ed. D. Davie et al. (Gravenhage, 1961), p. 17: "Lyrical poetry presents the most interiorized form of poetic language, in which the linguistic elements are most closely related and internally motivated." Note that Stankiewicz, following the Russian Formalists, here refers not to psychological inwardness but to the nonreferential, automimetic interiority of language itself.

10 Arthur Hallam, "On Some of the Characteristics of Modern Poetry, and on the Lyrical Poems of Alfred Tennyson," in *The Writings of Arthur Hallam*, ed. T. Vail Motter (New York, 1943), p. 197; M. H. Abrams, "Structure and Style in the Greater Romantic Lyric," in *From Sensibility to Romanticism*, ed. Frederick W. Hilles and Harold Bloom (New York, 1965), pp. 527–60. On the Romantic mixture of lyric with other genres see Cameron, *Lyric Time*, p. 217; Christensen, "'Thoughts,'" pp. 60–2; Robert Langbaum, "Wordsworth's Lyrical Characterizations," *Studies in Romanticism*, 21 (1982), 319–39. Langbaum's earlier book *The Poetry of Experience* (1957; rpt. New York, 1963), which places the dramatic monologue within Romantic tradition, should be consulted, as should two responses that appeared, almost concurrently, two decades later: Culler, "Monodrama," and Ralph W. Rader, "The Dramatic Monologue and Related Lyric Forms," *Critical Inquiry*, 3 (1976), 131–51.

11 Coleridge is quoted in Frederick A. Pottle, *The Idiom of Poetry* (Ithaca, 1941), p. 82. Wilde's comments occur in "The Critic as Artist" (1890), in *Literary Criticism of Oscar Wilde*, ed. Stanley Weintraub (Lincoln, Neb., 1968), p. 202.

12 Victorian writers were divided as to the chronological priority of lyric over other genres. For Dallas, as for Mill, "Lyrics are the first-fruits of art" (p. 245), while Walter Bagehot contends that "poetry begins in Impersonality" and that lyric represents a later refinement ("Hartley Coleridge" [1852], in *Collected Works*, ed. Norman St. John-Stevas, I [Cambridge, Mass., 1965], pp. 159–60). As to the normative status of lyric, however, the later nineteenth century had little doubt. Summaries and bibliographical aids may be found in Francis B. Gummere, *The Beginnings of Poetry* (New York, 1901), p. 147; Charles Mill Gayley and Benjamin Putnam Kurtz, *Methods and Materials of Literary Criticism* (Boston, 1920), p. 122; W. K. Wimsatt, Jr., and Cleanth Brooks, *Literary Criticism: A Short History* (New York, 1966), pp. 433, 751–2. For representative belletristic histories of poetry from a nostalgic, fin-de-siècle perspective see John Addington Symonds, *Essays Speculative and Suggestive* (London, 1893), pp. 393 ff.; Edmund Gosse, "Introduction" to *Victorian Songs: Lyrics of the Affections and Nature*, ed.

E. H. Garrett (Boston, 1895); and Arthur Symons, *The Symbolist Movement in Literature* (1899; rpt. New York, 1958) and *The Romantic Movement in English Poetry* (New York, 1909). On the influence of F. T. Palgrave's *Golden Treasury* (1861; rev. 1981), an anthology that "established, retroactively and for the future, the tradition of the English lyric," see Christopher Clausen, *The Place of Poetry* (Lexington, 1981), p. 67.

13   Symons, *The Symbolist Movement*, p. 49.

14   Marxian approaches now offer the most promising and comprehensive explanations of the fortunes of lyric as a product of industrial culture, yet recently published Marxian analyses evaluate the social functions of lyric very differently. For Theodor W. Adorno, "Lyric Poetry and Society" (1957; trans. Bruce Mayo, *Telos*, 20 [Summer 1974], 56–71), "The subjective being that makes itself heard in lyric poetry is one which defines and expresses itself as something opposed to the collective and the realm of objectivity" (p. 59); in contrast, Hugh N. Grady, "Marxism and the Lyric," *Contemporary Literature*, 22 (1981), 555, argues that "the lyric has become a specialized, though not exclusive, genre of Utopian vision in the modern era."

15   Symons, *The Symbolist Movement*, p. 65.

16   Olson, "The Lyric," p. 65, in distinguishing the "verbal acts" of lyric from those of more elaborated forms, himself acts fatally on the strength of a simile: "The difference, if I may use a somewhat homely comparison, is that between a balloon inflated to its proper shape, nothing affecting it but the internal forces of the gas, and a balloon subjected to the pressure of external forces which counteract the internal." But a balloon affected only by internal forces (i.e., a balloon in a vacuum) would not inflate but explode. That the "proper shape" of a poem, as of a balloon, arises not from sheer afflatus but as a compromise between "internal" and "external" forces is precisely my point about the framing of the dramatic monologue – as it is, I think, the dramatic monologue's (deflationary) point about the lyric.

17   Wimsatt and Brooks, *Literary Criticism*, p. 675; see also Cleanth Brooks and Robert Penn Warren, *Understanding Poetry* (1938; rev. ed. New York, 1950), p. liv. Don Geiger, *The Dramatic Impulse in Modern Poetics* (Baton Rouge, 1967), pp. 85–95, provides a capable overview of the persona poetics of the New Criticism.

18   Oswald Doughty, *English Lyric in the Age of Reason* (London, 1922), p. xv; Walter Blair and W. K. Chandler, eds., *Approaches to Poetry* (New York, 1935), p. 250.

19   Ransom is quoted in William Elton, *A Glossary of the New Criticism* (Chicago, 1949), p. 38. *Sound and Sense*, 2nd ed. (New York, 1963), p. 21; *Elements of Poetry* (New York, 1969), pp. 11–12.

20   Robert W. Boynton and Maynard Mack, *Introduction to the Poem* (New York, 1965), p. 24. On p. 45, to complete the circuit, the authors equate the "voice" with "the poet." They thus return us through a backstage exit to Clement

Wood's definition of lyric in *The Craft of Poetry* (New York, 1929), p. 189, as "the form in which the poet utters his own dramatic monolog." Compare the dramatic metaphor in Benedetto Croce's 1937 *Encyclopedia Britannica* article on "Aesthetic": "The lyric...is an objectification in which the ego sees itself on the stage, narrates itself, and dramatizes itself" (quoted in Wimsatt and Brooks, *Literary Criticism*, p. 510). For Geoffrey Crump, *Speaking Poetry* (London, 1953), p. 59, the reverse seems true: "an element of the dramatic is present in all lyrical poetry, because the speaker is to some extent impersonating the poet."

21   Jerome Beaty and William H. Matchett, *Poetry: From Statement to Meaning* (New York, 1965), p. 103.

6

Matthew Arnold's Gipsies
Intertextuality and the New Historicism

Antony Harrison

In spite of his immense wisdom and his mysterious breadth, [the Gypsy] had a human weight, an earthly condition that kept him involved in the miniscule problems of daily life.
Gabriel Garcia Marquez, One Hundred Years of Solitude

Byron found our nation, after its long and victorious struggle with revolutionary France, fixed in a system of established facts and dominant ideas which revolted him. The mental bondage of the most powerful part of our nation, of its strong middle class, to a narrow and false system of this kind is what we call British Philistinism. That bondage is unbroken to this hour ....

. . . [But] as the inevitable breakup of the old order comes, as the English middle class slowly awakens from its intellectual sleep of two centuries, as our actual present world, to which this sleep has condemned us, shows itself more clearly, – our world of an aristocracy materialised and null, a middle class purblind and hideous, a lower class crude and brutal, – we shall turn our eyes again . . . upon this passionate and dauntless soldier of a forlorn hope.
Matthew Arnold, "Byron" (1881)

Harrison, Antony. 1991. "Matthew Arnold's Gipsies: Intertextuality and the New Historicism." In *Victorian Poetry*, 29, iv (Winter), pp. 365–83. Reproduced with permission of Antony Harrison.

Victorian Poets: A Critical Reader, First Edition. Edited by Valentine Cunningham.
© 2014 John Wiley & Sons, Ltd. Published 2014 by John Wiley & Sons, Ltd.

In 1881 Matthew Arnold could still identify with Byron as a poet, gipsy, an outcast wandering Europe and writing verses in futile rebellion against the values and behavior of the social class of England that had produced him. But Arnold's image is, as we all know, a sentimental idealization of the real Byron, and Arnold's implicit identification with him is equally sentimental, if not wholly disingenuous. Approaching the age of sixty, Arnold had served two five-year terms as Professor of Poetry at Oxford, was only three years away from the Chief Inspectorship of Schools, and just two from a Civil List Pension given "in public recognition of service to the poetry and literature of England." With a score of influential books behind him, Matthew Arnold had become a public institution, more of a myth than a man. Yet his identification with the position of social rebel dates from his earliest days. Park Honan describes Arnold passing his fourteenth year (the year he first read Byron) "in the grandest juvenile defiance of the fact that he was an Arnold."[1] His rebellious inclinations, notorious during his Oxford years, were never quelled but profitably channeled as he aged. By consistently challenging the dominant (materialist and spiritually barren) ideologies of his era, he gradually emerged as the preeminent intellectual authority of late Victorian England.

By this account it is perhaps unsurprising that a central, indeed mythic figure in Arnold's poetry of 1843 to 1866 is the gipsy, a cultural outsider. In "To a Gipsy Child by the Sea-Shore" (begun in 1843 or 1844), "Resignation" (begun in 1843), "The Scholar-Gipsy" (1853), and his great elegy "Thyrsis" (1866), varied but prominent images of gipsies take on totemic value. These figures have more than merely personal and temperamental significance for Arnold and his poetry. They serve him, ultimately, as crucial ideological tropes, especially insofar as they exploit conventional stereotypes of the gipsies, who were coming increasingly under public scrutiny at mid century. As is clear from the first appearance of a gipsy figure in his work, Arnold imbued these cultural outcasts with a special burden of intertextual and philosophical significance. Investigating the historical and literary contexts surrounding the production of Arnold's poems that feature images of gipsies provides a partial set of answers to the kind of question a new historicist critic might well ask but that seems not to have occurred to commentators with other theoretical orientations: "Why gipsies?"[3] Exploring the implications of those contexts using new historicist strategies (which I shall describe shortly) reveals that a gipsy trope operates throughout Arnold's cultural criticism, as well as his poetry, to position and define him as a writer whose power – like that of Byron – accrues in part from the equivocal quality of his professed estrangement from a society he, unlike Byron, desires not to escape but to transform. Arnold's poetic assaults on the false values of that society begin with a challenge to its most formidable literary titan from the 1840s, William Wordsworth, and quickly proceed to capitalize on the burgeoning popular interest in gipsies during the 1850s and 1860s.

The New Historicism

Just over two decades ago, "the structuralist controversy" unsettled the world of academic literary studies in this country. A decade later the powerful influence of what had previously been an exclusively European linguistic, philosophical, and critical renaissance was visible here as well. The "controversy" resolved itself into a growing tradition of competition among theoretical schools and of debate about the value of poststructuralist literary theory. This state of affairs was disrupted, however, by an unexpected development: early in the 1980s "the new historicism" emerged as a critical methodology. Practitioners of this revisionist form of historical literary scholarship, especially in Renaissance and Romantic studies, began formulating theoretical grounds for their work. Prominent among them were Louis Montrose, Stephen Greenblatt, and Jerome McGann, whose theoretical and practical criticism was so original and provocative that it changed fundamental ways of thinking about the social and political operations of literature. The effectiveness of their work is apparent: new historicist citicism has proliferated within the last five years in all areas of literary analysis.[4] In his 1988 *SEL* survey of the year's work in nineteenth-century literature, David Riede could thus assert the "triumph of the New Historicism," apparently without fear of contradiction.[5] As a result of this methodological "victory," however, the new historicism no longer remains a unitary theoretical phenomenon (and, in fact, it never was one). If publications are to serve as an index, a great variety of new historicisms are now being successfully practiced throughout Anglo-American critical circles.[6]

Despite such variety, it is possible to hazard a few generalizations. New historicist criticism attempts to refigure the socio-cultural field in which particular literary works were produced, resituating these works in relation not only to other texts (canonical and non-canonical) in a variety of genres, but also in relation to contemporaneous socio-political institutions and events, as well as discursive and non-discursive practices.[7]

Attention to previously ignored historical particulars surrounding the production and/or reception of a literary work can suggest the kinds of issues or questions the work appeared to respond to at the moment of its composition or publication. Such particulars might also demonstrate how the work intervened not only in ongoing disputes and struggles for dominance in the arena of literary activity, but also in the larger social, political, or cultural debates of the day.

In refiguring a particular socio-cultural field, the new historicist is not limited to analysis of literary texts, nor exclusively to a single set of procedures. He or she crosses the boundaries of disciplines because the critical inquiries of new historicism often have directly to do with theological, anthropological, political, or sociological matters. The tools of non-literary disciplines can therefore be of immense help in coming to understand the interrelations among a host of events, debates, and values at a given historical moment. Similarly, the new historicist also frequently displays the influence of procedures for textual and cultural analysis provided by other critical methodologies, such as deconstruction, psychoanalysis, or semiotics.

In this essay, for instance, I focus at first on the intertextual aspects of Arnold's earliest gipsy poems. These works should be viewed as critical responses to Wordsworth's poems (particularly the Intimations Ode and "Gipsies"), as well as to his poetic procedures and ideological inconsistencies. I then discuss an array of fictional and non-fictional texts available to Arnold that purported to report facts, but often promulgated myths, about gipsies. These circulated with unusual frequency in early- to mid-Victorian England, and they influenced Parliamentary investigations, blue-book reports, and ultimately the passage of laws directly related to gipsy life and culture. Similarly, I remark on the economic circumstances (the progress of capitalism) that helped to generate such texts and laws. Matthew Arnold's gipsy poems were produced in these literary, social, and political contexts. His central trope in four major poems is thus appropriated not only from Glanvill's *Vanity of Dogmatizing*, but also from an important controversy that attracted a great deal of public discussion during the period in which the poems were written and published (1843–66).

As these comments may suggest, a basic assumption of new historical analysis is that every expressive act is embedded in a network of material and ideological practices that are historically particular, and that all texts – literary and nonliterary alike – circulate, as it were intravenously, within the body of a culture. Consequently, no literary text is to be revered over others because it provides special access to universal (that is, non-historical) truths about human nature or experience. All texts embody definable and historically particular values and ideas. Therefore, recovering the historical contexts surrounding the production and distribution of a text is a crucial task for the new historicist critic.

If the operations of every text are ideological, manifesting struggles for dominance among systems of values and ideas at a particular historical moment, the critic is similarly trapped by his or her own historical perspectives and ideological dispositions and thus must proceed with an unusually high level of sensitivity to his or her "situatedness." Indeed, as I later argue, Arnold used the gipsy trope so centrally in his poems precisely because he understood this truth. Interested in history as the grounds of cultural exegesis, the new historicist must also be aware of the textuality of history. Not just history as a process, but documentary discussions of any particular moment of history are treated as narratives. The conclusions reached by the new historicist critic are therefore inevitably tentative and contingent upon gaps in the narrative that remain to be filled. Arnold appears also to have understood this perspective on narratives, which we now loosely term "deconstructive," and after 1852 he made use of it as a rhetorical strategy in the gipsy trope to resist ideological consistencies and commitments, and to wrest cultural power from the hands of his middle-class opposition.

Intertextual Matters

"To A Gipsy Child by the Sea-Shore" is a pessimistic, if not morose, elegy that visibly reinscribes and transvalues Wordsworth's Intimations Ode. Arnold's gipsy child, with its "gloom" and "meditative guise," is at once muse and philosophical father of the man who speaks in this poem: "With eyes which sought thine eyes thou didst converse, / And that soul-searching vision fell on me" (ll.15–16). The infant's knowledge of the world, as the speaker projects it, is complete. It has "foreknown the vanity of hope" and "Foreseen [its] harvest," yet endures with a "funereal aspect" and "the calm…of stoic souls," "drugging pain by patience" (ll. 39–40, 46, 29, 13). Unlike Wordsworth's child who trails "clouds of glory" into this world, Arnold's already possesses the sober eye of maturity, its "slight brow" surrounded by "clouds of doom" (l. 4). And even as the speaker imagines the gipsy child growing up, possibly to forget its stoical infant wisdom, he makes no mention of any precorporeal "joy," the real subject of Wordsworth's poem and object of his speaker's "obstinate questionings." In visions of the child's prospective getting and spending – Arnold's "winning" in the "thronged fields" (l. 58) of a Darwinian existence – the speaker refuses to accept the possibility that the child will ever wholly forget its present "majesty of grief" (l. 68). The most positive memory the speaker can evoke for this infant employs metaphors of the Fall:

> Not daily labour's dull, Lethaean spring,
> Oblivion in lost angels can infuse
> Of the soiled glory, and the trailing wing.
> (ll. 54–56)

Arnold's reinscription of Wordsworth appropriates his images, along with his abstract and weighty diction, only to subvert his precursor's proclaimed faith in a joy at the heart of human existence. This child's thoughts, unlike those of Wordsworth in his Ode, are not disturbed by "longings vain" or any "superfluity of joy" (ll. 9–10). The gipsy child thus becomes a cipher through whom Arnold can ventriloquize his nihilism, anticipating the critique of Wordsworth articulated in the preface to his edition of Wordsworth's poetry published thirty-four years later: "His poetry is the reality, his philosophy...is the illusion."[8] As Arnold further explains, "the 'intimations' of the famous 'Ode,' those corner-stones of the supposed philosophic system of Wordsworth, – the idea of the high instincts and affections coming out in childhood, testifying of a divine home recently left, and fading away as our life proceeds, – this idea, of undeniable beauty as a play of fancy, has itself not the character of poetic truth of the best kind; it has no real solidity" (Super, 4:49).

Arnold's intertextual assault upon Wordsworth in his gipsy poems is, however, more complex than this close reading of the language in "A Gipsy Child" alone indicates. For Wordsworth had also written about gipsies and viewed them in clear ideological terms. Arnold, who belatedly proclaimed himself a Wordsworthian, certainly knew Wordsworth's poem, "Gipsies." Its 1807 version reads in full:

> Yet are they here? – the same unbroken knot
> Of human Beings, in the self-same spot!
>   Men, Women, Children, yea the frame
>   Of the whole Spectacle the same!
> Only their fire seems bolder, yielding light:
> Now deep and red, the colouring of night;
>   That on their Gipsy-faces falls,
>   Their bed of straw and blanket-walls.

– Twelve hours, twelve bounteous hours, are gone while I
Have been a Traveller under open sky,
　　Much witnessing of change and chear,
　　Yet as I left I find them here!

The weary Sun betook himself to rest.
– Then issued Vesper from the fulgent West,
　　Outshining like a visible God
　　The glorious path in which he trod.
And now, ascending, after one dark hour,
And one night's diminution of her power,
　　Behold the mighty Moon! this way
　　She looks as if at them – but they
Regard not her: – oh better wrong and strife
Better vain deeds or evil than such life!
　　The silent Heavens have goings on;
　　The stars have tasks – but these have none.[9]

This is an extraordinary work from the pen of the professedly empathetic poet of the "primary affections of the human heart," a poem that reflects – as Arnold might well have observed – a wholly Philistine provincialism and lack of curiosity, along with a suffocating captivity to the puritan values of "Hebraism." This poem clearly betrays the liberal, humanitarian ethos that Wordsworth's 1798 poems and his famous "Preface" to the *Lyrical Ballads* define as fundamental to valuable poetry.

The speaker in "Gipsies" begins openly uncomprehending: these people, their customs and their reason for being, are wholly alien to him, as is their community, which Wordsworth describes as a mere "knot." They constitute a "Spectacle," always a disparaging term in his lexicon.[10] As a "Traveller under open sky, / Much witnessing," the speaker contrasts his own industrious activity with the gipsies' apparent immobility and passivity, his sensitivity to the natural world with their obliviousness to it: "they regard [it] not." Although an admitted outsider who has only the slightest acquaintance with the gipsy sociality, he sits in judgment upon them. The coda of this poem is stridently didactic. Wordsworth's bourgeois arrogance and insularity, qualities Arnold consistently condemns, are obvious here, and, more importantly, so is the basis of his judgment in the entirely external aspects of the gipsies' lives rather than their inward qualities as "human Beings." In this poem we find Wordsworth demonstrating none of the compassion for his fellows that elsewhere, especially in pieces from *Lyrical Ballads*, energizes his work. Indeed, the racist overtones of "Gipsies" subvert Wordsworth's early liberal and Romantic poetic ethos, which Arnold in his maturity appropriated and revised along classical lines.

The speaker's ideological stance in this lyric radically diverges from the ideal of human perfection Arnold articulates in his later essays on culture. That ideal, we recall, requires "an inward spiritual activity, having for its characters increased sweetness, increased light, increased life, increased sympathy" (Super, 5:108). Refusing any real contact with the gipsies, Wordsworth in this poem hardly embodies Arnold's premier "*social idea*": that "the men of culture are the true apostles of equality...those who have had a passion for diffusing, for making prevail, for carrying from one end of society to the other, the best knowledge, the best ideas of their time," that is, for "humanising" knowledge (Super, 5:113). It comes, then, as no surprise that, early in his essay on Wordsworth, Arnold insists that "composing moral and didactic poems...brings us but a very little way in poetry" (Super, 4:45).

Yet the impact "Gipsies" made upon Arnold is apparent from linguistic echoes of the poem and transvaluations of its critique of gipsies in "Resignation," begun in 1843 but not published until 1849. A formal and structural revision of "Tintern Abbey," this sinuous lyric finally advocates the supreme value of the poet's life, resigned in several senses: detached or withdrawn from the world; willing to accept all vicissitudes; and willing also to accept the fate of reinscription (re-signing), a fate here enacted upon Wordsworthian texts by Arnold himself. The life of the gipsies in "Resignation," is contrasted with that of the contemplative poet who attains "not [Wordsworthian] joy, but peace," a consequence of "His sad lucidity of soul" (ll. 192, 198):

> Before him he sees life unroll,
> A placid and continuous whole –
> That general life which does not cease
> Whose secret is not joy, but peace;
> That life, whose dumb wish is not missed
> If birth proceeds, if things subsist;
> The life of plants, and stones, and rain,
> The life he craves – if not in vain
> Fate gave, what chance shall not control,
> His sad lucidity of soul.
>
> (ll. 189–198)

Unlike this idealized poet, the gipsies – who, as in Wordsworth's poem, "In dark knots crouch round the wild flame" (l. 118) – appear constitutionally unable to attain tranquillity and detachment. They cannot compare past and present, nor can they "reason" about mortality ("time's busy touch") and the inevitable "decay" of their own culture, as "Crowded and keen the country grows," with "The law [growing] stronger every day" (ll.133–135). Inaccessible to the higher poetic consciousness,

> they rubbed through yesterday
> In their hereditary way,
> And they will rub through, if they can,
> To-morrow on the self-same plan,
> Till death arrive to supersede,
> For them, vicissitude and need.
> (ll. 138–143)

This, despite the fact that

> Signs are not wanting, which might raise
> The ghost in them of former days –
> Signs are not wanting, if they would;
> Suggestions to disquietude.
> (ll. 123–126)

Although this speaker claims to possess high levels of both semiotic and historical awareness ("Signs...might raise / The ghost...of former days"), and although he is not (like Wordsworth's speaker) wholly unsympathetic to the gipsies' plight, his attitude toward the gipsies remains equivocal. He generates an image of their mindless passivity and fatalism in order to aggrandize the stature of the ideal poet. In doing so, he suppresses any consciousness that their situation is socially and economically determined. As a "migratory" underclass, they lack the speaker's privileges of education, leisure, and wealth. They are in no position to make serious life choices at all. Yet Arnold's speaker is aware that their "decay" or displacement from the country-side is both a sign and product of the economic times, a result of an expansion of the Anglo-Saxon population directly tied to industrial capitalism. Unlike the speaker of Wordsworth's "Gipsies," Arnold's speaker is sensitive to social and political developments that pose a threat to traditional gipsy culture, and to the extent that they are endangered wandering outcasts, he identifies with them. Like him (and Fausta, his auditor),

> They, too, have long roamed to and fro;
> They ramble, leaving, where they pass
> Their fragments on the cumbered grass.
> And often to some kindly place
> Chance guides the migratory race,
> Where, though long wanderings intervene,
> They recognise a former scene.
> The dingy tents are pitched...
> ....
> They see their shackled beasts again
> Move, browsing, up the gray-walled lane.
>   (ll. 109–121)

The speaker in this poem exposes his limited political understanding and inadequate social vision, urging the gipsies to recover the "fragments" of their past in order to reconstitute their present and future lives as a "placid and continuous whole." This he attempts to persuade "Fausta" to do and apparently has himself done. Finally, for him as for Wordsworth, these alien people remain ciphers, despite his partial identification with and incomplete compassion for them.

Arnold's attitude toward the gipsies here, hovering somewhat obtusely between idealization and criticism, in fact replicates the extremes of contemporary response to "the gipsy problem" in England during the 1840s and 1850s. Ironically, through its critique of gipsy culture as well as through its intertextual resonances, Arnold's position calls attention to the self-righteous provincialism of Wordsworth's attack upon the gipsies some forty years earlier. But Arnold's equivocal perspective in this poem allows for important re-visions of gipsy figures (and gipsy culture) in his own poems of 1853 and 1866.

Victorian Gipsies and "The Scholar-Gipsy"

In a familiar letter to Arthur Hugh Clough written the year "Resignation" was published (on September 23), Arnold laments his sense of personal isolation, angst, distraction, and immobility. He sees himself as a representative product of a corrupt society:

These are damned times – everything is against one – the height to which knowledge is come, the spread of luxury, our physical enervation, the absence of great *natures*, the unavoidable contact with millions of small ones, newspapers, cities, light profligate friends, moral desperadoes like Carlyle, our own selves, and the sickening consciousness of our difficulties: but for God's sake let us neither be fanatics nor yet chaff blown by the wind.[11]

The substance of this critique is, of course, central to "The Scholar-Gipsy," in which Arnold laments "this strange disease of modern life," with its "sick fatigue," "its languid doubt," its manifold "disappointments," "its sick hurry, its divided aims," and "Its heads o'ertax'd." In a distinct turn from his equivocal use of the gipsy figure in "Resignation," Arnold – some seven years after the initial composition of that poem – now presents the gipsy as an ideal Other, the speaker's imaginary hero whom he warns to

> fly our paths, our feverish contact fly!
> For strong the infection of our mental strife,
>   Which, though it gives no bliss, yet spoils for rest;
> And we should win thee from thy own fair life,
>   Like us distracted, and like us unblest.
> (ll. 221–225)

By 1849 the placid and harmonious, distanced perspective on life maintained by the ideal poet of "Resignation" was beyond the grasp of Arnold, who immersed himself compulsively in the public issues of the day. The idealized scholar-gipsy is immune to such issues because he is alien to the society plagued by them. Arnold envied such immunity. In the same letter to Clough, he explains:

> When I come to town I tell you beforehand I will have a real effort at managing myself as to newspapers and the talk of the day. Why the devil do I read about Ld. Grey's sending convicts to the Cape, and excite myself thereby, when I can thereby produce no possible good. But public opinion consists in a multitude of such excitements. (*Letters to Clough*, p. 111)

Perhaps less incendiary than Lord Grey's proposal to establish a penal colony at the Cape of Good Hope, the controversy over the status and future of the gipsies in English society had constituted one such "excitement" for the British public since the early 1840s. By 1852 the directions of the public discussion, both in the periodical press and in fiction, had changed significantly.

Beginning in 1842 "the gipsy problem" was much in the news. A long controversy simmered over this "intriguing people who from time out of mind had flouted convention" (Behlmer, p. 231). As Arnold must have been aware, the gipsy presence in England "struck some reformers as an intolerable affront to the values of modern civilization," precisely those Hebraic middle-class values (industry, wealth, pragmatism, respectability) that Arnold attacks as Philistine throughout his prose works of the 1860s. Attitudes toward the mysterious gipsies generally reflect the social values and cultural dispositions of those who discuss them. During the second half of the century gipsies became the objects of both romantic idealization and "systematic harassment" in England (Behlmer, p. 232). Widely considered an "'alien' race and culture," the gipsies "existed on the fringes of society, and of the economic and political spheres, and this marginality to, or rejection of, a conventional, settled mode of life made them suspect and unwelcome." They represented a threatening cultural Other, "to be feared for the implicit threat their existence posed to a method of thinking that was increasingly to stress immobility and regularity, and to be resented for remaining apart from the pressures towards conformity, whether legal, institutional, cultural or [social]…Yet they were also envied for managing to retain some independence and individuality."[12]

In 1842 *The Times* featured a number of articles on the gipsies, reflecting the public's inconsistent attitude toward gipsy culture. On October 12 readers were reassured that "the New Forest Gypsies were an honest lot who, in return for a little straw to cushion their beds, acted as farmers' watchdogs against poachers." But a month later "the same tribe stood accused of suffocating sheep by forcing wool down their throats" (Behlmer, p. 234). That same autumn two sensational articles described the "stately funerals and shunning ceremonies in which Gypsy renegades were banished from their tribes" (Behlmer, p. 235). Even more noteworthy was the retirement in 1847 of the Reverend James Crabbe from his exotic and well-known mission at Southampton (begun in 1829), where he had attempted to care for but also convert the New Forest gipsies.

The gipsies remained in the news as much for the threat they posed to the values of the respectable middle classes (and the scenery of the English landscape) as for the mysteriousness of their customs and social organization. They were special targets of repression in 1849, when "England's new county constabularies launched a campaign against mendicancy in all its forms" and several years later when "rural police redoubled their efforts to drive all Gypsy tents off public land" (Behlmer, pp. 235–6). Gipsies were much discussed in the reports of the Select Committee on Police of 1852 and 1853. In 1856, when the County Constabulary Act was passed, "methods of surveillance, harassment and persecution became increasingly efficient, and there are many references to the constant pressures exerted by the police on the travellers, driving them from the rural roads into the towns. On occasions, camps were raided and the people persecuted simply on suspicion they might have stolen something" (Mayall, p. 155).

Books and periodical essays about the gipsies appeared regularly throughout the forties, fifties, and sixties, when Arnold was composing most of his poetry. These works exerted a strong influence on popular opinion. In 1843 Crabbe himself published *A Condensed History of the Gypsies*. In the previous year the fifth edition of Samuel Roberts's popular book, *The Gypsies; their Origins, Continuance, and Destination* (first published in 1836) had appeared, and in the following year the Reverend J. West's *A Plea for the Education of the Children of the Gypsies* came out. Also in 1844, W. Howitt's *The Rural Life of England* focused on the lifestyle and movements of English gipsy tribes. During the forties articles on gipsy life were to be found in a wide variety of magazines and institutional organs, from *Fraser's* (which often published essays by Thomas Arnold), the *New Edinburgh Review*, and *Sharpe's London Magazine* to *The Church of England Magazine*.[13]

The public interest in gipsy life and customs is most fully revealed by the success, between 1841 and 1851, of fictional and semi-fictional works by George Borrow.[14] *The Zincali; or, An Account of the Gypsies of Spain* (1841), though published by John Murray in a small edition, was hailed as the "prize book" of the season by *The Dublin University Magazine* and went through two additional printings in 1843 when Borrow's new book, *The Bible in Spain* became an enormous popular success,[15] establishing itself as "one of the great books of mid-century Britain" (Collie, p. 183) and drawing further attention to *The Zincali*. *The Bible in Spain* also raised strong expectations for Borrow's second major work about gipsies, *Lavengro*, published in 1851. Although reviews of *Lavengro* were uniformly bad, they were numerous, and, for better or worse, among Victorian readers of fiction Borrow had by mid century aroused a powerful interest in gipsy life, language, and customs.[16]

Inspired in part by Borrow's work, a number of major literary figures became fascinated with gipsies, including Carlyle, Bulwer Lytton, Swinburne, and George Eliot (who published her poem *The Spanish Gypsy* in 1868). Matthew Arnold was, it seems, even more intimately familiar with Borrow than these writers. Arnold's "The Forsaken Merman," which appeared along with "A Gipsy Child by the Sea-Shore" in his 1849 volume of poems, for example, makes use of George Borrow's version of the story from his 1825 review of J. M. Thiele's *Danske Folkesagen* (Honan, p. 89).

The Zincali appeared during Arnold's first year at Oxford, with its second and third printings coming in 1843, the year Arnold won the Newdigate prize with his poem, "Cromwell," and "settled on poetry as his *vocation*. This was his calling, his star, his reason for being. … He reconciled this [newly] serious view of himself with his idle Oxford days, and though still looking for timewasting pursuits he also wrote" and read voraciously (Honan, p. 70). In 1844 he picked up a copy of Joseph Glanvill's *The Vanity of Dogmatizing*, which discusses the Oxford "lad" Arnold memorialized as the Scholar-Gipsy. The experiences of this student, as Glanvill describes them, remarkably prefigure those George Borrow mythologized in his much discussed *Lavengro*. The publication of this book in 1851 may have prompted Arnold's work on "The Scholar-Gipsy" in 1852 or 1853. (Arnold originally titled the poem "The Wandering Mesmerist.") At the time, similarities between Borrow's descriptions of his early life with the gipsies and Glanvill's myth would have struck Arnold with uncanny force.[17] *Lavengro* replicates many passages of *The Zincali*, which begins, "I can remember no period when the mentioning of the name of Gypsy did not awaken feelings…hard to be described, but in which a strange pleasure predominated." Like Arnold's Scholar-Gipsy, Borrow felt a natural kinship with the gipsies and studied their culture extensively:

> Throughout his youth he had frequently come across and spent time with groups of gypsies.… He had consorted with them on Mousehold Heath and other such places near Norwich; had met them at horse-fairs and prizefights; had lived with them, sometimes, and been accepted by them.… In all these places, he had been accepted by the gypsies, partly because he had taken the trouble to learn their language…and partly because of a scarcely definable feeling of kinship he and many gypsies immediately felt for one another. (Collie, pp. 162–3)

As Borrow observes at the outset of *The Zincali*, "the gipsies themselves account for it on the supposition that the soul which at present animates my body, has at some former period tenanted that of one of their people."[18] Borrow claims to have been initiated into many mysteries of gipsy culture.

Glanvill's Oxford scholar also joined "a company of vagabond gipsies" and learned their secrets. Arnold redacts the story in the notes to his text:

> Among these extravagant people, by the insinuating subtilty of his carriage, he quickly got so much of their love and their esteem as that they discovered to him their mystery.… [He told his acquaintances that] they had a traditional kind of learning among them, and could do

wonders by the power of imagination, their fancy binding that of others: that [he] himself had learned much of their art, and when he had compassed the whole secret, he intended, he said, to leave their company, and give the world an account of what he had learned. (Allott, p. 357)[19]

Thus, Arnold's scholar is a particular student of "the secret [of the gipsy] art" of ruling "as they desired / The workings of men's brains" so that they "can bind them to what thoughts they will" (ll. 45–48). His *"one* aim, *one* business, *one* desire," once the long-awaited "spark from heaven" has fallen, is to impart that secret to the world (ll. 152, 120). In the meantime, this mythical figure remains elusive: in and out of the public eye and the social world, glimpsed on occasion by maidens, farmers, housewives, and possibly even by "dreaming" speaker of the poem, who ultimately admonishes the phantom Gipsy to flee all contact with those contaminated by "this strange disease of modern life" (l. 203).

If we read "The Scholar-Gipsy" in the dual contexts of Arnold's other works about gipsies and public discussions, both factual and fictional, of "the gipsy problem" in mid-Victorian England, coming to terms with this difficult poem is increasingly complicated. As David Riede has recently demonstrated, the poem is, on the one hand, so deeply resonant of various literary intertexts – including Milton, Wordsworth, and Keats – that its vision is relegated "to a literary never-never land where it can have no real contact with modern life."[20] On the other hand, as we have seen, the poem is topical. It presents a comprehensive and damning – albeit highly generalized – critique of the cultural values that dominate the historical moment of its composition. A transitional poem, "The Scholar-Gipsy" is thus overtly ideological and political. Its subject is the attainment of power in the social world, and any reader of 1853 even superficially acquainted with public issues of the day would have read "The Scholar-Gipsy" (as well as Arnold's other gipsy poems) with an awareness of the controversy over English gipsies and seen it as a peculiar extension of the romantic interest elicited by images of gipsies in recent literature, especially the work of Borrow.

The Acquisition of Cultural Power

David Riede suggests that Arnold's removal of his Scholar-Gipsy from the "gradual furnace of the world" so that he might live forever

may anticipate Arnold's later critical strategy of disinterestedness, of removing oneself from the fray to preserve a sense of the ideal, but it also anticipates the problem of that strategy – anyone so distanced from society cannot be effective or meaningful within it. By corporealizing his ideal in such a tangible form as the Gipsy, Arnold cut off the possibility of absorbing it. The Gipsy and the ideal are preserved, but only on the outskirts of society. Poetic reverie is, in a sense, banished or outlawed, or at the very least rendered irrelevant. It can have no practical influence on life. (Riede, p. 142)

But as Arnold repeatedly emphasizes (most notably in "The Function of Criticism at the Present Time"), practical influence is, from the perspective of the ideal critic – who is also a critic of the narrow but culturally hegemonic systems of value and belief we know as ideology – the least desirable kind of influence to have: "The critic must keep out of the region of immediate practice in the political, social, humanitarian sphere if he wants to make a beginning for that more free speculative treatment of things, which may perhaps one day make its benefits felt even in this sphere, but in a natural and thence irresistible manner" (Super, 3:275). Throughout his critical writings Arnold, by his example, insists precisely on the need for equivocation – a free play of ideas which disallows the taking of rigid ideological positions and allows for changes of mind and heart. Insofar as "The Scholar-Gipsy" illustrates this repudiation of narrow doctrinalism, it is a poetic manifesto that prefigures the central beliefs and procedures of his later prose criticism.

From the outset of the "Preface" to *Poems* (1853) in which "The Scholar-Gipsy" first appeared, Arnold decries "modern problems" and the consequent "doubts" and "discouragement" that afflict his contemporaries. "The confusion of the present times is great," he acknowledges (Super, 1:8), and he therefore concludes by idealizing writers like himself who, with steady and composed judgments, reject their own historical eras as "wanting in moral grandeur," ages of "spiritual discomfort." Like the speaker of "The Scholar-Gipsy," Arnold the critic laments that "it is impossible for us, under the circumstances amidst which we live, to think clearly, to feel nobly ... to delineate firmly" (Super, 1:15), and therefore to write significant poetry.

The "circumstances" Arnold cites result from industrialism, which has produced an era wholly dominated by the middle class, which Arnold always disparages in his later essays, but out of which he himself emerged. As he acknowledges in *Culture and Anarchy*, "almost all my attention has naturally been concentrated on my own class, the middle class, with which I am in closest sympathy, and which has been, besides, the great power of our day" (Super, 5:139). Beginning with his prose works of the 1850s, it is, of course, Arnold's ambition to reform and regenerate, indeed to assist in refining and "perfecting," the middle class so that its power in the world may be justified. As John Storey has observed, unlike Marx, who "attacked the middle class as representatives of an oppressive and exploitative system [,] Arnold attacked them to change them, in order to secure their future – not to close it."[21]

In *A French Eton* (1864) Arnold envisions the day when his goals will have been accomplished:

> In that great class, strong by its numbers, its energy, its industry, strong by its freedom from frivolity, not by any law of nature prone to immobility of mind...in that class, liberalised by an ampler culture, admitted to a wider sphere of thought, living by larger ideas, with its provincialism dissipated, its intolerance cured, its pettiness purged away – what a power there will be, what an element of new life for England! Then let the middle class rule, then let it affirm its own spirit, when it has thus perfected itself. (Super, 2:322)

But it is Arnold himself – a cultural outsider but a social insider – who will direct and control the process of reform. Like his mysterious Scholar-Gipsy, Arnold desires to attain a position of power over middle-class values, behavior, and tastes and "rule... / The workings of men's brains." Edward Said is exactly right in asserting that Arnold appears to have viewed society

> as a process and perhaps also an entity capable of being guided, controlled, even taken over. What Arnold always understood is that to be able to set a force or a system of ideas called "culture" over society is to have understood that the stakes played for are an identification of society with culture, and consequently the acquisition of a very formidable power.[22]

Arnold's appetite for such power becomes, to some extent, suppressed in his prose writings, but explicit in a letter to Clough in 1853, the year of the Preface, "The Scholar-Gipsy," and his altered sense of vocation: "I catch myself desiring now at times political life...and I say to myself – you do not desire these things because you are really adapted to them, and therefore the desire for them is merely contemptible" (May 1, 1853; *Letters to Clough*, p. 135). After 1853, Arnold's desire for "political" activity and influence expressed itself in an alternate and finally more secure, prestigious, and enduring line of work to which he was adapted – that of cultural sage and prophet. In that work, Arnold immediately hit upon the characteristic discursive mode and critical stance that we have already witnessed in the equivocal relationship he deliberately establishes between himself and his Philistine middle-class audience.

The gipsy, as Arnold manipulates that figure in his poems, develops as a proleptic metaphor for this relationship and for Arnold's self-positioning in his prose works of cultural criticism. The trope initially embodies Arnold's stoicism and early skepticism (in "Gipsy Child"). It then serves as a contrast to his image of the ideal poet detached from worldly activity ("Resignation"). By 1853, however, the trope projects his realization that attaining power over men's minds requires not merely poetic detachment, but an often ostensibly self-contradictory stance of simultaneous estrangement from society and involvement with it ("The Scholar-Gipsy"). Thus, the mid-century interest in gipsies and the controversy surrounding their cultural past and social future at first provided Arnold with an important and intertextually sanctioned poetic metaphor, but eventually suggested an invaluable critical identity whose essential feature was elusiveness and whose central rhetorical strategy was mystification, that is, textual mesmerism.

The value of the gipsy trope in understanding Arnold's success becomes especially clear if we recall the portions of Glanvill's text that Arnold omits in his own note to "The Scholar-Gipsy":

> In the practice of [the gipsies' *Mystery*], by the pregnancy of his wit and parts, [the Scholar] soon grew so good a proficient, as to be able to out-do his Instructors.... [Upon meeting with two former classmates, he] told them, that the people he went with were not such *Impostours* as they were taken for, but that they had a *traditional* kind of *learning* among them, and could do wonders by the power of *Imagination*, and that himself had learnt much of their Art, and improved it further then themselves could.... [Later, to explain how he knew his friends' exact words spoken in his absence, the scholar told them] that what he did was by the power of *Imagination*, his Phancy *binding* theirs; and that himself had dictated to them the discourse, they held together, while he was from them. (Tinker and Lowry, p. 206)

For Arnold the "secret" of the gipsies' "art" is inseparable from their position as cultural aliens, their peregrine lifestyle, and their uncertain origins – in short, the exotic aura surrounding them that confounds expectations of predictability in their behavior.

112

In another context, Wendell Harris has demonstrated how Arnold himself cultivates precisely such an aura in the self-representations of his prose works. By promoting singularly elusive values in these works, Arnold was able to gain unprecedented influence over the directions of Anglo-American culture in the late nineteenth and early twentieth centuries. Further, the power he acquired was in direct proportion to the gipsy-like, mesmeric qualities as well as the elusiveness of cultural doctrines whose "secret" force lay ultimately in their refusal to acknowledge ideology – that is, any single and consistent, politically implicated system of values – as power. As we shall see, Arnold's strategy for attaining a position to "perfect" the middle classes is exposed in his last major poem dominated by a gipsy trope, "Thyrsis."

In a lucid discussion of nineteenth-century and contemporary responses to Arnold's cultural criticism, Harris has analyzed the consequences of Arnold's often self-contradictory and mystifying prose: above all, it has succeeded in "binding" generations of middle-class readers and thinkers to a liberal humanist system of values. "Arnold," he acknowledges, "has offered any number of hostages to denizens of the deconstructive abyss. If we wish to demonstrate that the significant words in any discourse appeal to a hierarchy that might be reversed in another discourse, or are employed in several senses, or necessarily imply the existence of their opposites, or are indeterminate in meaning outside the context of each use, Arnold has almost done the work for us."[23] In other words, the central precepts of Arnold's critical writings are self-deconstructing, consciously deferring precise meaning to such an extent that the ideals and values he propounds in a given essay – such as "The Function of Criticism at the Present Time" – constitute a "rich range of perspectives that finally refuse to coalesce" (Harris, p. 124). Notions such as "seeing the object as in itself it really is" and measuring all ideas by "the best that has been known and thought in the world" leave themselves open to a wide variety of interpretations, subject only to Arnold's overarching emphasis on "a free play of ideas." Thus, Harris can lament that "Arnold's manifest failure to bring his major arguments into a convincing unity – not a unity to defy the deconstructionist, but simply one to satisfy our ordinary practical sense of coherence – has seemed to authorize readers to detach whatever single slogan especially appeals to them and develop it for their own purposes" (Harris, p. 125). The articulation of values and ideals in Arnold's prose after 1853 becomes a process of continual deferral, displacement, and redefinition in which (as Marjorie Levinson has argued in connection with Wordsworth's poetry) "the constitutive and deconstructive moments" are inseparable.[24]

But Arnold's elusive abstractions conform to his wholly relativistic view that social and cultural criticism of genuine value must always operate both synchronically and diachronically. He thus writes to the future as well as the present, engaged with issues of the moment but from a desired perspective of "timeless" detachment. He is aware of his captivity to "the present age," while – like Byron's heroes – defiantly resisting, indeed denying, that situatedness. As a result, his work is self-reflexive in its use of a language of historical and ideological relativism: "The Arnoldian program decrees that no one ideology, no one scheme of social reformation, can be exempt from continual comparative evaluation. Nor can any one critical evaluator – Arnold included – be presumed infallible.... Precisely because all values and beliefs are ideological, no single mode of thought can replace the free play of mind" (Harris, p. 130).

Because "the free play of mind" must, ideally, be incessant, the notion expressed in "The Scholar-Gipsy" that it might end with the appearance of a singular "light from heaven" – followed by the revelation of a "secret" to "control men's brains" and diffuse that light – is fallacious, as Arnold makes clear in "Thyrsis," where the figure of the Scholar-Gipsy reemerges. In 1853 Arnold's estranged and mysterious, eponymous hero had appeared in eternal pursuit of the ultimate ideology. Yet, thirteen years later, in "Thyrsis," Arnold revises the conceptualization of this quest in order to accommodate the gipsy stance he has adopted as a cultural critic during those years. Placing supreme value on the free play of ideas, Arnold projects a set of indeterminate and mystifying ideals that constitute an anti-ideology defined poetically as "A fugitive and gracious light... / Shy to illumine" ("Thyrsis," ll. 201–202). In confessing that "I must seek it too," Arnold insists upon the extent to which this symbol wholly eschews Philistine cultural values:

> This does not come with houses or with gold,
> With place, with honour, and a flattering crew;
> 'Tis not in the world's market bought and sold.
> (ll. 202–205)

Ultimately, Arnold's power over the future was cunningly realized outside of "the world's market," where diverse ideologies compete for dominance. Arnold's triumph resulted from an ostensible rejection of ideology as power.

Through the deployment of the discursive strategies I have described, Arnold became a "ruler" of the structure and values of

Anglo-American educational and cultural institutions, not only during his own lifetime but also with later generations. As Park Honan has observed,

> in his poetry and critical prose, Arnold introduced a new, subtle, comparative attitude to central problems in Western society and culture, and helped to form the modern consciousness. An understanding of him is really more useful to us than an understanding of any other Englishman of the last century.... He is a very great critic: *every* English and American critic of distinction since his time has felt his impact. (Honan, pp. vii–viii)

Like the original Scholar-Gipsy from Glanvill's text, Arnold was able to "dictate" the cultural "discourse" of his own and later historical eras, in part by appropriating the mysterious influence popular images of the gipsies had attained over the Victorian imagination.[25]

Notes

1 Park Honan, *Matthew Arnold: A Life* (New York, 1981), p. 26.
2 The dates of composition for the four poems by Arnold I discuss in this essay are provided in *Arnold: The Complete Poems*, ed. Miriam Allott (1979). All quoted passages from Arnold's poems will be cited parenthetically by line numbers from this edition
3 A superficial explanation of Arnold's prolonged attachment to gipsy motifs in his poetry is provided by George K. Behlmer: "precisely because the Gypsies stood apart from the mainstream of urban-industrial life, they held a special fascination for the critics of that life." "The Gypsy Problem in Victorian England," *VS* 28 (1985): 232.
4 H. Avram Veeser, ed., *The New Historicism* (New York, 1989), provides a helpful introduction to this methodology. Other important practitioners of the new historicism include Jonathan Arac, Catherine Gallagher, Marjorie Levinson, Leah Marcus, Jane Marcus, Judith Lowder Newton, and David Simpson. For discussion of the interrelations among intertextuality, ideology, and the new historicism, see my *Victorian Poets and Romantic Poems: Intertextuality and Ideology* (Charlottesville, 1990).
5 David G. Riede, "Recent Studies in the Nineteenth Century," *SEL* 28 (1988): 713.
6 Veeser's collection cited above demonstrates the diversity of new historicist criticism. as well as the array of controversial issues it raises.
7 See Louis Montrose, "Professing the Renaissance: The Poetics and Politics of Culture," in Veeser, p. 17.

8   All quotations from Arnold's prose works will be taken from *The Complete Prose Works of Matthew Arnold*, ed. R. H. Super, 11 vols. (Ann Arbor, 1960–77). Further citations to volume and page number will appear parenthetically. The present quotation is from 4:48.

9   William Wordsworth, *Poems, in Two Volumes, and Other Poems, 1800–1807*, ed. Jared Curtis (Ithaca, 1983), pp. 211–12. The most extensive discussion of Wordsworth's poem in its historical and biographical contexts appears in David Simpson's *Wordsworth's Historical Imagination: The Poetry of Displacement* (New York, 1987), pp. 22–55.

10 For example, see *The Prelude*, Book 8, ll. 676–81.

11 *The Letters of Matthew Arnold to Arthur Hugh Clough*, ed. H. F. Lowry (Oxford, 1932), p. 111.

12 David Mayall, *Gypsy-Travellers in Nineteenth-Century Society* (Cambridge, 1988), p. 92.

13 See Mayall, pp. 245–56, for a useful bibliography of nineteenth- and twentieth-century literature on the gipsies in England.

14 In 1857 Borrow published the work that made him famous for later generations, *The Romany Rye*. For a brief summary of pre-Victorian literary treatments of gipsydom, see Simpson, pp. 43–6.

15 "'This is a most remarkable book,' exclaimed *The Examiner*: 'Apart from its adventurous interest, its literary merit is extraordinary. Never was a book more legibly impressed with the unmistakable mark of genius.' The *Athenaeum*: 'There is no taking leave of a book like this.' The *Dublin University Magazine*: 'We have had nothing like these books before…The Zincali was the prize book of last season, and *The Bible in Spain* is likely to be the favourite of the present one.'" Michael Collie, *George Borrow, Eccentric* (Cambridge, 1982), p. 177.

16 As is suggested by Collie's account (p. 210) of public expectations of *Lavengro*.

17 See, for example, Collie, pp. 46ff. Dwight Culler also suggests the influence of Borrow upon Arnold, especially in "The Scholar-Gipsy." See his *Imaginative Reason: The Poetry of Matthew Arnold* (New Haven, 1966), p. 193. Allott cites "The Wandering Mesmerist" as the original title for "The Scholar-Gipsy" on Arnold's list of poems for his 1852 volume (p. 356).

18 George Borrow, *The Zincali* (London, 1841), p. 1.

19 For the full text from Glanvill, see C. B. Tinker and H. F. Lowry, *The Poetry of Matthew Arnold: A Commentary* (London, 1940), pp. 205–6.

20 David Riede, *Matthew Arnold and the Betrayal of Language* (Charlottesville, 1988), p. 142.

21 John Storey, "Matthew Arnold: The Politics of an Organic Intellectual," *Literature and History* 11 (1985): 221.

22 Edward Said, *The World, the Text, and the Critic* (Cambridge, Massachusetts, 1983), p. 10.

23 Wendell Harris, "The Continuously Creative Function of Arnoldian Criticism," *VP* 26 (1988): 122.

24 Marjorie Levinson, "Back to the Future: Wordsworth's New Historicism," *SAQ* 88 (Summer 1989): 647.

25 Despite a number of recent critics who disparage or deny Arnold's power, Jonathan Arac – like Edward Said – convincingly affirms it: "[I] emphasize not Arnold's weakness but his power, both in those prophetic moments and in the present, for I find that the debate between 'Wittgenstein' and 'Nietzsche' in current criticism is also the struggle for control over one element in the Arnoldian apparatus." Further, in his own day, Arnold, "associated...with the power of the growing educational bureaucracy, the traditional university, and the new world of publishing, ...could feel confident that culture was a power. ... It is an agency of Enlightenment, like so many of the characteristic modes of power in its time and ours, and like the panoptic eye of Bentham, its vision is productive. Culture produces both the synoptically seen 'tradition' and what Irving Babbitt called the 'all-seeing, all-hearing gentleman' who is the subject of that tradition – that is, empowered to a certain vision by means of a certain blindness" (*Critical Genealogies: Historical Situations for Postmodern Literary Studies* [New York, 1989], pp. 117, 132).

7

A New Radical Aesthetic
The Grotesque as Cultural Critique: Morris

Isobel Armstrong

William Morris's *The Defence of Guenevere and Other Poems*, a revolutionary work in Ruskin's sense and probably in ours, was published in 1858, some years after the innovative periods in the work of Arnold and Clough. Yet Morris belongs here [after a discussion of Arnold and Clough] because like them he contends with an individualist and expressive account of poetry and dissents from it. But whereas they orientate themselves through redefining a classical tradition, Morris deliberately aligned himself with what might be called a 'gothic' reading of culture. This early volume, with its debts to Froissart and Malory, is often seen as an anticipation of the 'medievalising' mode of Pre-Raphaelite poetry which came into prominence in the 1860s; or its Arthurian themes are seen to assimilate it to Tennyson's *Idylls of the King* which began to be published in 1859; or it is elided with the relaxed prolixity of Morris's own later work in *The Earthly Paradise* (1868–70). This later poem, however, is quite unlike Morris's first volume. It is a cycle of alternating classical and Teutonic legends, and advises its readers to 'Forget six counties overhung with smoke' and to retreat into the past or to an idealised past. In it Arnold's poetry of moral composure and consolation seems to have modulated into a source of therapeutic beauty to redress the damage done by work in an industrial society. But *The Defence of Guenevere* is none of these things. It has no precedent or sequel. Its boldness lies in its seizing of

Armstrong, Isobel. 1993. "A New Radical Aesthetic: The Grotesque as Cultural Critique: Morris." In *Victorian Poetry: Poetry, Poetics and Politics*, pp. 232–51. London: Routledge. Reproduced with permission of Taylor & Francis.

Victorian Poets: A Critical Reader, First Edition. Edited by Valentine Cunningham.
© 2014 John Wiley & Sons, Ltd. Published 2014 by John Wiley & Sons, Ltd.

the possibilities of myth and legend which had been theorised through the post-Coleridgean and conservative tradition and redefining them for a radical aesthetics. If Clough is the democratic poet of contemporary realism and Arnold the liberal poet of the history of objectified action, Morris takes myth, the most potent material for conservative poetics, and rethinks it for a different politics. A fresh account of work, gender, consciousness and language shapes this volume. In a deceptively simple language, without density, but with a highly energetic and laconic compactness, it is written with remarkable innovative freedom which extends to both metrical experiment and narrative condensation. Overlaying narrative with drama, with internal monologue and with lyric and ballad refrain, it makes temporality and utterance problematical and enigmatic by exploiting the multiple disjunctions between different forms. Brilliance of colour and intensity of optical detail detach the act of vision and perception from other experience, force them into hyperconscious significance, and make it necessary to consider what the nature of *seeing* is. Where Tennyson defamiliarises associative patterns, Morris dissociates vision by aberrant distortion and selection.

These procedures emerge from a dialogue with Ruskin's social and aesthetic theory and in particular with his account of the 'Grotesque' element of gothic art, in *The Stones of Venice* (1851–3). Here Ruskin elaborated an alternative to Arnoldian positions. Morris, of course, wrote under the spell of Dante Gabriel Rossetti and was closely associated with the Pre-Raphaelite group: as a comparison between Rossetti's 'The Blessed Damozel' and Morris's 'Rapunzel' suggests, there are strong affinities between them.[1] But Morris seems to have cut his way through some of the confusions of Pre-Raphaelite thought, helped by Ruskin who, before he met the group, had defended Pre-Raphaelite painting in letters to *The Times* in 1851 and 1854, and had probably managed to give there a more coherent account of Pre-Raphaelite principles than they could themselves.[2] Morris's reading of Tractarian literature, of medieval texts, of Benjamin Thorpe's *Northern Mythology*, and his passion for gothic architecture, was given a political focus by Ruskin which is not immediately apparent in Pre-Raphaelite writing in *The Germ* (later *Art and Poetry*) or in the journal which Morris himself supported, *The Oxford and Cambridge Magazine*, periodicals which had a short life and a restricted coterie readership in the early 1850s.[3] But a brief consideration of the principles of *The Germ* and its relation to Ruskin does indicate where Pre-Raphaelite thought and that of Ruskin intersect.[4]

The Germ (1850) was prefaced by W. M. Rossetti's sonnet which asserts that the cardinal principle of all artistic creation must be to ask the question, 'Is this truth?' Accordingly, the aesthetic of *The Germ* has often been seen as a call for a return to 'nature', a claim made by all new movements, and, helped by a frequently confused and contradictory exposition in the articles of *The Germ*, one which it is easy in this case to dismiss.[5] W. M. Rossetti, writing under the pseudonym John L. Tupper on 'The subject in art', in the first and third issues of January and March 1850, seems to be having it both ways: 'A writer ought to think out his subject honestly and personally, not imitatively, and ought to express it with directness and precision; if he does this we should respect his performance as truthful...individual genuineness in the thought, reproductive genuineness in the presentment'.[6] This looks like an attempt to square the expression of an inner subjectivity with accuracy of external representation, and an idealist and a mimetic theory consort uneasily. The same is true of Dante Gabriel Rossetti's prose piece, 'Hand and Soul': 'In all that thou doest work from thine own heart, simply'.[7] W. M. Rossetti's subsequent gloss, that the piece is about painting what 'your own perceptions and emotions urge you to paint', rather than didactic topics, as a way of affecting 'the mass of beholders', compounds the problem.[8] But it is a comparatively bold and innovative attempt to formulate a number of new principles: to move away from expressive theory by attempting to extend a *visual* theory to language and poetry in general, to move away from the terms in which the 'subject' in art was being discussed by assuming that, just as in painting, no object is *intrinsically* more suitable than another for depiction in the literary text, and to claim that such an art has social implications – it can reach all classes if it attends to 'the semblance of what in nature delights'.[9] This was something the Rossettis never lost sight of. W. M. Rossetti published *Democratic Sonnets* in 1907.

The word 'semblance' denotes the shift being made in Pre-Raphaelite theory: it is a rudimentary attempt to move the ground of discussion from expression to *representation*. In *Modern Painters*, the first two volumes of which had appeared in 1843 and 1846, Ruskin insisted on the fallacy of mimetic fidelity to the detail of the external world; instead the educated eye of the trained and exact vision, a democratic vision because seeing is the fundamental capacity of us all, paints the *experience* of what it sees as faithfully as possible.[10] Such an account of representation makes self and world indispensable to one another and avoids the one-sidedness which gives primacy either to the human subject or to objects. Hence the rather clumsy attempt we have seen W. M. Rossetti making to hold subject and object in equipoise. But hence also his constant emphasis on the importance of physical, sensory excitement and arousal as well as mental excitement, on response to the external rather than expression, and his belief that any representation contributes to 'the general happiness of man', 'however wild' – even hangings and executions – as long as their handling is consistent with 'rational benevolence'.[11] Hence F. G. Stephens (also known as John Seward) could argue that 'Closer communion with nature' and 'exact adherence to all her details' was liberating to the eye because all that exists in the external world is open to representation.[12] His instance is early Italian painting, but such painting is a model because of its procedures rather than being a style to copy.

The reason why *The Germ* looks eclectic, holding together a Benthamite language of 'rational benevolence', a certain aestheticism and even an element of redefined Tractarian thought, can be explained by its attempt to bring the post-Benthamite and Coleridgean traditions together on the ground of visual representation, fusing the aesthetic of the poetry of sensation with a democratic art. It is significant that W. M. Rossetti reviewed Clough's *Bothie* enthusiastically with a real understanding of its project (he thought, on the other hand, that Arnold's interest in antiquity suggested that he was 'no longer young': Arnold was not yet 30), and that Browning's *Sordello* was vigorously defended – 'Read Sordello again'.[13]

The idea of representation through the visual and, by extension, the verbal sign, is the strength of Pre-Raphaelite thought. It returns to an interest in language which was the possession of earlier decades. For despite the very considerable production of theories of poetry at this time, the framework of expressive theory to which they belonged made form and language a curiously superfluous attribute of poetry. E. S. Dallas, for instance, democratic because he believed that the poetic faculty was common to all men and because a non-didactic poet 'is no preacher of the law, he reads no riot act', was constrained in his avowedly Kantian and idealist account of representation by his understanding that the poet projected internal experience into form.[14] Feeling comes first, expression follows as a secondary manifestation of feeling. The link between the manifestation of feeling in language and primary feeling is mysterious because feeling is involuntary and unconscious and therefore unknowable, a private, psychologised Kantian noumenon behind the appearance of language. This psychological account of poetry takes different forms in the 1840s and 1850s and crosses political and religious divisons. One finds it in Keble's Oxford Lectures on Poetry, where the pressure of feeling builds up to the point of madness unless it can be displaced indirectly into symbol. Language is seen rather as a barrier to be crossed than as a representative structure. In fact, for Keble language conceals rather than represents.[15] One finds such a view being disseminated in F. W. Robertson's *Two Lectures on the Influence of Poetry on the Working Classes* (1852). Because the source of poetic feeling is unconscious and 'uncalculating', it can only be given indirect expression in external form in symbol which is mysterious and ultimately inadequate, finding 'finite words for illimitable feeling'.[16]

Ruskin sharpened Pre-Raphaelite aesthetics by developing a notion of representation as the mediation between experiencing self and the world, by formulating an account of Grotesque art in a way which enabled it to open up possibilities for a new kind of myth, and by making the form of art materially dependent on the kind of *work* undertaken in a society at any given time. Art is a form of labour and does not exist over and against work. In a modern society, he believed, it is thus available to management and organisation by the state, as is any sensible political economy.[17] His thought enabled Morris to produce a book of poems exploring the modern Grotesque (for the Grotesque is not confined to its particular historical manifestation in gothic Europe), exploring the ways in which modern poetic form and consciousness are materially shaped by the form and nature of work in nineteenth-century society. Its medieval content, ballad and folk lyric, are not a simple proxy or disguise for contemporary conditions. Nor are they even a form of analysis conducted by the latter-day reflective poet on naive material to expose the modern condition, for that would be to grant the poet a certain exemption from history even as he analyses his condition. As Walter Pater remarked much later of Morris's subsequent work, but in words more apposite to *The Defence*, this poetry uses that of a past age 'but must not be confounded with it'.[18] The poems are not concerned either directly or indirectly with work or politics. Instead they are an attempt to *be* the form in which modern consciousness shaped by work and labour sees, experiences and desires, to be what it imagines and the myths it needs to imagine with. Its assumption is that a modern consciousness needs to imagine the past in this way, not that the past will be a tool for analysis. For, as Pater saw, this 'past' is 'no actual form of life' but a sublimated form projected above but produced by the 'realities' of another historical situation, the nineteenth century.[19] It is significant that the last poem in *The Defence* is entitled 'In Prison'. These poems inhabit the enclosing perspectives of the modern consciousness which sees only 'the loophole's spark' and hears the wind beyond. Its reading of signification and the visual sign, the banners which flap 'over the stone', seen, but above and beyond the beholder, is conditioned and made problematical by the narrow loophole.[20] One of the conditions of the Grotesque, Ruskin says, is distortion, the gap between imagined possibility and realisation.[21]

A little more needs to be said about the Grotesque as cultural critique before *The Defence* can be discussed. The Grotesque is not a sign of degeneration or decadence. Indeed, it is the vital possession of a healthy culture and takes different forms in different periods. A key to the modern Grotesque is Ruskin's comment on Holman Hunt's painting, *The Awakening Conscience*. He rebuts the charge of slavish detail, saying that the Pre-Raphaelites aim to paint what is possible within the field of vision. But Hunt's picture, and the intensity and minuteness of its depiction (a girl starting up from her lover's knees as they sit before the piano), pose a problem, and Ruskin's argument is precisely that the picture problematises vision and makes it aberrant because

> Nothing is more notable than the way in which even the most trivial objects force themselves upon the attention of a mind which has been fevered by violent and distressful excitement. They thrust themselves forward with a ghastly and unendurable distinctness, as if they would compel the sufferer to count, or measure, or learn them by heart.[22]

One thinks of Galahad's vision of drops of melted snow on his steel shoes and 'bunches of small weeds' between the tiles of the floor he stares at in 'Sir Galahad, a Christmas mystery story'.[23] In 'King Arthur's Tomb', Lancelot measures the walls he rides past as a way of both remembering and of repressing memory.[24] The rider in 'The Little Tower' measures time and space by landmarks which are psychological defences but which turn into real defences when he besieges the tower, and ransacks the materials of the landscape he has passed to provide barriers and armaments.[25]

Such intensely perceived detail, however, has more behind it than the psychological justification by which we might defend, for instance, Tennyson's 'Mariana' (though it is significant that this, like 'The Lady of Shalott', was a key poem for this group).[26] In *The Stones of Venice*, in his chapter on 'The nature of gothic', Ruskin associated the Grotesque of gothic with a 'Disturbed Imagination'.[27] He thought it important enough to devote a whole chapter to it in the third book, and in his own very gothic, detailed and idiosyncratic way he makes it clear that the 'Disturbed Imagination' is one of the essentials for the possibility of a properly free, democratic art. He arrives at this paradox through an argument which is often misunderstood.

To begin with, his view of gothic is more complex than that of Pugin, who saw a movement from the pure morality of a nobly organised feudal society to religious decline reflected in cultural artefacts.[28] Likewise he differs from Carlyle; though he sees the ignoble form of the Grotesque as a sign of the decadence of Venetian religion, he does not concur with Carlyle in believing that there was ever any ideal feudal society of the past.[29] Gothic architecture occurs at a time when work and art come together, when the workman was allowed, within the constraints of the social organisation, a limited measure of freedom and spiritual autonomy. Thus the gothic may be a reflection of such freedom but it is also an art of *resistance* to bondage, of the religious principle and 'revolutionary ornament', a moment when the individual consciousness gave material form to art within a corporate social organisation and found a way of representing certain attributes of freedom.[30] Savageness, or energy, Changefulness, or a subtle and flexible refusal of the servile principles of order, Naturalism, or a celebration of fecundity, Rigidity, or an assertion of will and independence, Redundance, or a love of excess and generosity, are all possible forms in combination with the Grotesque. The gothic artist was in bondage, but could give form to this bondage in a way that the modern operative cannot in the division of labour – 'It is not, truly speaking, the labour that is divided; but the men'.[31] Then follows the frightful account of the slavery of the modern glass-bead-maker, hands trembling with a fine palsy created during the incessant action of cutting glass rods, so that work mimes and becomes a form of illness in itself.

It is the Grotesque which affords one of the few modes of self-representation for modern slavery and one of the few forms of representation in cultural production. For the Grotesque, springing from the imagination, is a form of play and the form taken by the play instinct. Because play is a reaction to work and thus a disturbance or movement of the mind it must take a fanciful or distorted form (the analogy is with the displacement of the Freudian joke). But the kind of play we can exercise *must* be conditioned by the material circumstances of our work – a typically paradoxical but logical gothic formulation which politicises play. It is *not free* play, in Schiller's sense. At this point Ruskin's divisions and subdivisions proliferate and often disguise the dialectical nature of the Grotesque and its ideological significance. The Grotesque can take a wholly ludicrous or fearful form and both forms can be culturally healthful or decadent. There are four subforms of Grotesque, which attempt to account for the organisation of work and the economic structure in different societies (free, artistocratic, post-feudal and capitalist-industrial or slave societies: though these are not exact, since Ruskin's point is that very different structures can produce equivalent forms of exploitation and that at times all four kinds of play coexist in the same society). Only two need concern us. There is the Grotesque of those forced to play, with the release of a kind of fantastic extremity in reaction to the captivity and imprisonment of labour. Such release, 'whether in polity or art', Ruskin comments, cannot be exaggerated in importance, clearly believing that this maintains the stability of the bourgeois state.[32] There is the Grotesque, always taking the form of the 'Terrible', of those who cannot play at all, either from pride in status, or from repression, or because they are 'utterly oppressed with labour' – like the glass-bead-makers.[33]

It is the last form of the Grotesque which preoccupies him, the Grotesque of those who cannot play, for this is at least a means of giving negation and oppression representation. This Grotesque is forced to experiment with the terrible in an irregular but mystified way, unable to explain it (presumably because oppressed consciousness cannot understand the conditions of oppression), and is characterised by both love and fear of God (dialectically related feelings, where lack is displaced and returns to God as fullness either of desire or dread). Extravagant and distorted excitement and intensity result from the apathy of oppression ('he is stone already') which forces itself to feel.[34] Satire and vulgar humour (the dialectical opposite of apathy) which *need* the proper aggression of indecency to represent the protest against oppression are further manifestations of the terrible Grotesque. The terrible Grotesque is the form taken by working-class protest. But in the nineteenth century, Ruskin says, it can only be represented in daily language and not in art because 'the classical and Renaissance manufactures of modern times' have 'silenced the independent language of the operative, his humour and satire'.[35] It is now only the *object* of study by middle-class authors such as Dickens. In poetry, perhaps, the work of poets such as Thomas Hood would be analogous to this middle-class research into the working class. Not a working-class poet, not quite Fox's gentlemanly looker-on either, but speaking for working-class suffering in poems like 'The Song of the Shirt' or writing popular satirical lampoons such as 'Miss Kilmansegg and Her Precious Leg' (1841–3), the story of a woman whose money takes the literal form of prosthetic aid in the shape of a solid gold leg, with which she is eventually killed by her husband, Hood is to some extent a ventriloquist for the working class.

The third and for Ruskin possibly the most important category of the enslaved Grotesque is 'diseased and ungoverned imaginativeness', and a wildness of the 'mental impressions' (one thinks here of the analysis of Hunt's picture). Disorder is the embodiment of the sense of failure and incompleteness of the 'human faculties in the endeavour to grasp the highest truths'.[36] It is the condition of the enslaved mind which longs for transcendence of the material but experiences an incomplete transcendence. Ruskin's comment that this is a distorted form of the sublime helps to gloss his discussion here. The sublime moment is an experience of annihilation in the face of overwhelming external circumstance, but is actually invested with power when consciousness comprehends annihilation as meaningful. But different historical conditions govern the sublime and the Grotesque. Logically the conditions of the enslaved consciousness call forth a desire for meaning, for a transcendent explanation of oppression, but oppression itself resists the recuperation of this condition as meaningful and thus a wayward, deviant and fantastic perception is substituted for transcendence, the more fantastic the more the enslaved consciousness strives to overcome its conditions. Indeed, the more consciousness strives to find a norm or an ideal by which the aberrance of the Grotesque can be measured, the more its correctives turn out to become distortions in themselves. The result is the broken mirror of perception, a vision 'with strange distortions and discrepancies, all the passions of the heart breathing upon it in cross ripples, till hardly a trace of it remains unbroken'.[37]

This Grotesque takes the form of the fragmentation of dreams (which are akin to madness), visions and the displacement of symbol which registers a gap between the symbolic sign and what it represents. The symbol is either iconographically narrowed and literalised (used as if it were a rebus – the example Ruskin gives is Jacob's ladder) or else the sign is estranged and representation is seen as the *veil* of meaning, a meaning we cannot reach or penetrate (we might think here of those accounts of poetry discussed above which make language the inadequate embodiment of inexpressible feeling). Above all the terrible Grotesque manifests itself in superstition and the paralysis of reason and the overexcited fancy in the face of death. For death, disturbing 'the images on the intellectual mirror', is regarded with fear and trembling, with fitful and ghastly images, by the enslaved consciousness.[38] An obsession with death is the logical outcome of the oppressed condition for which the literal annihilation of death is its counterpart, and in the face of which it has no means of transcending itself.

All these forms of the Grotesque can manifest themselves in creative or debased ways. The presence of the Grotesque in its 'full energy' is possible even in conditions of oppression and its morbid but powerful

126

energy is the mark of a particular kind of cultural power.[39] But again, Ruskin observes, workmen in present-day England are only allowed expression of the disturbed imagination in 'gesture and gibe, but are not allowed to do so where it would be most useful'.[40] That is, it is not incapacity but the social structure which oppresses working-class representation of oppression. Caricature is the vestigial form of the Grotesque generally available. But this tends not to be possible for the working class. One could instance the prevalence of parody and pastiche in nineteenth-century poetry in endorsement of Ruskin's analysis.

The importance of the theory of the Grotesque is that it is a theory of representation based on a social and not a psychological analysis, seeing psychological experience as determined by cultural conditions. In its gothic proliferation and comprehensiveness, cryptic and idiosyncratic formulations, odd categories and juxtapositions, in its need to totalise and systematise, in its moral indignation, it is easy to see it as a romanticised and anachronistic analysis of unestranged labour, as Ruskin's myth. Though elements of Ruskin's work can be interpreted in such a way, this would be a fundamental misreading. It is uncompromising in its understanding that the cultural production of a whole society and its consciousness will be formed by the nature of its dominant form of work. It does not see art in terms of progression or cultural continuity or a disinterested ethical tradition to which a way must be found of giving access for the underprivileged. It is stark here in its understanding that in nineteenth-century England the working class have been inhibited from actively evolving a form of art which belongs to them. On the other hand, it is unique in its understanding that in oppressed societies art is possible as a form of resistance and finds a cultural space for itself by making the representation of the Grotesque a form of analysis. It is alone at this time in finding an alternative to moral or psychological and individualist theory. Perhaps it owes something to Hegel's *Aesthetics*, where modern art is made structurally dependent on culture, and where the disjunction of form and idea is seen as the typical representation of modern consciousness, but the attention to labour, though Hegelian in essence, is Ruskin's original contribution.[41] *The Stones of Venice*, with the two lectures on *The Political Economy of Art* (1857), where Ruskin was concerned with the economic consequences of the integration of art into state organisation, and particularly with the possibilities of trade-union activity, form a political analysis with a coherence which was not to be seen elsewhere, even in the later prose of Morris. Bizarre, perverse at times, this is Ruskin's myth in the sense that it is an imaginative and passionate discourse.

127

In what sense is Morris's *Defence of Guenevere* in dialogue with Ruskin? In what ways might it be a manifestation of the modern gothic or Grotesque? For Ruskin helps one to understand the extraordinary nature of Morris's experiment. At the same time Morris responds to Ruskin with some important modifications of his aesthetic. The Grotesque makes for the double poem because it is the embodiment of distortion. The poem becomes intrinsically a form dislocated by the aberrant vision, which simultaneously calls forth as an absence the possibilities from which it deviates. The representations of the disempowered consciousness constitute expressions of a subjectivity. But since those representations become a form of resistance for the oppressed, resistance embodies critique, as the disempowered discourse exposes the limits of its perceptions in its struggle to find meaning, limits imposed by its form of life. Morris explores these possibilities. One would also expect to find, in an exploration of the modern Grotesque, the experiences and forms which are constitutive for the consciousness which cannot play. We would expect to see, that is, less the portrayal of the condition of oppression than its own *representations*. It is important to see that in *The Defence* Morris is not dramatising the conditions of a remote medieval society in a state of oppression but finding this notional society as the one which the disempowered modern consciousness *must* create. It is the Grotesque creation of the longings of modernity, the representations of and by the nineteenth-century subject. So *The Defence* is an intensely analytical work.

Of the three forms of the modern Grotesque posited by Ruskin – the forms of a predetermined and involuntary apathy, of mockery and of diseased and involuntary imaginativeness – one would expect to find only two in the work of a middle-class poet such as Morris. For the representations of mockery belong to the dispossessed and deprived. However, the middle-class poet does ventriloquise the forms of a notional past populace in the sparse, terse, laconic ballad quatrain and the persistent refrain which Morris handles with such virtuosity, the reconstructed language of an imagined peasant class. The operative is present by omission in this poetry through one of Morris's most startling metonymic devices. The overdetermination of the hand seen in dissociation and isolation, and with almost hallucinatory intensity as a virtually estranged object, the woman's hand in particular, is everywhere in this poetry. The blood half-transparent in the hand as it is held to the light ('The Defence of Guenevere'), the veins which 'creep' in the hand ('Praise of My Lady'), hands caressing hair, face, lips, one another, clutching, waving. The hand is invested as erotic sign and yet the hand is also the sign of instrumentality and agency as it manipulates objects, often objects of consumption, cups and clothes, holds shields or swords in disturbing disconnection from the body. The 'hand', of course, names the nineteenth-century operative on whom depends the leisure for the construction of this world of castles and towers and gardens, sinisterly emptied of the signs of servility except for the soldiers designated by their weapons as 'Spears'. The emptiness becomes so insistent that it constitutes a Grotesque technique for revealing repression. The modern Grotesque *cannot* represent the worker who cannot represent himself except by omission.

The woman's hand leads to an important modification or extension of Ruskin's gothic here. The sense of lack which returns love or fear to God is directed towards women in this volume as well as to God. In 'Sir Galahad' a compensatory vision of the divine is granted to the knight, who seems specifically excluded from the sexual love experienced by Palomydes and Lancelot. The poem can be read as the transcendence of physical love by spiritual love, as the lesser knights, who have substituted sexual love for spiritual, fail: the poem ends, 'In vain they struggle for the vision fair'.[42] Or it can be read as the disturbed and deprived imagination's *substitution* of spirituality for sexuality as the neurotic intensity of Galahad's longing is displaced into the idealism which conjures the Sangreal and its attendant and subordinated female saints. Sexual longing and desire are scarcely absent from the poems, experienced with a consuming intensity by men for women and by women for men. The void of pathological sexual longing, which empties out the consciousness and fills the self with a sense of powerlessness and loss is the organising feeling in poem after poem. These are perhaps the great poems of desire in the nineteenth century. For Ruskin desire is the central experience of the enslaved consciousness and motivates the modern Grotesque, but by defining desire in sexual terms and introducing the question of gender, Morris takes Grotesque representation into different and problematic areas.

The taboo on overt reference to sexuality is everywhere broken. A sign of this transgressive movement is the unremitting and exaggerated visual concentration on women's hair, let down and flowing, a Victorian code for released sexual feeling. The position of women in these poems is contradictory and paradoxical. They are disempowered and passive, waiting, longing and dependent on vicarious male action for representation or nullified by male rejection ('The Sailing of the Sword', 'The Blue Closet', 'The Tune of Seven Towers', 'Old Love'). On the other hand, they exert a curiously coercive power, motivating violence even when they are seen as objects of possession ('The Judgment of God', 'The Gillieflower of Gold'). They are horribly punished when they assert themselves ('Golden Wings', 'The Haystack in the Floods'), but they are involuntarily the *distorting* factors in the social structure in a way which causes profound suffering both to themselves and to men. The cathexis of frustrated passion in 'A Good Knight in Prison', which forces an almost deranged perception of colour and detail as the bee on the sunflower signifying sexuality assumes a disproportionate intensity, issues in appalling carnage when the opportunity to escape occurs. 'Spell-bound' restages repeated phases of mutual longing and separation in the present, the past, the past of that past, in hypothetical, remembered and immediately experienced narrative which insists that mutual suffering is the norm where relationships are pulled awry and deflected by a 'wizard', the superstitious figuring of distortion as magic by the Grotesque imagination which can only mystify explanation and make it fantastic.

The title poem of the volume, 'The Defence of Guenevere', both a protection or repression of her situation and a representation of her case, as the two senses of 'defence' suggest, epitomises the malfunctioning of Grotesque hermeneutics when women's sexuality is defined in terms of the deviating and distorting element. Both senses of the word 'defence' suggest displacement and this is what occurs. 'God knows I speak truth, saying that you lie': a lie is literally a distortion, and Gauwaine draws out a corresponding distortion in Guenevere.[43] She claims that Gauwaine distorts the truth by accusing her of adultery. Her love for Lancelot is a pure love and therefore not amenable to such a description; but her defence becomes progressively more deviant the more she offers a corrective to the 'lie'. She struggles with the contradiction between the intense spiritual importance attached to the liberating power of transcendent mutual passion and the equal importance attached to loyalty in wedlock. The paradox of the 'pure' woman is that the more she argues for the intensity and beauty of her experience, the more she has to repress its sexual nature and the more she argues for the purely legal status of her marriage the less she should have reason to do so if there has been no transgression of it. The more she argues that she has not transgressed the more transgressive she becomes. She is forced into dishonesty and misrepresentation because of the contradictions in which she lives. Guenevere sees her parable concerning the choice between two cloths, one red, one blue, as the representation of the complete ambiguity of choice and responsibility in a situation where the chooser is blind to the implications of her choice: but they are rather a representation of the complete contradiction between one interpretation of sexual loyalty and another. Guenevere's monologue is not in fact about an awakening conscience but about an awakening to incompletely understood contradiction, and that is why it is the title poem. For in this volume it is women who are most exposed to the contradictions of the consuming Grotesque desire for transcendence.

The numbness of being experienced by oppressed consciousness is redressed by a corresponding need for intensity in proportion to its numbness. Pater, inadvertently expressing the very desire for intensity which is the object of Morris's critical analysis, writes of the 'sharp rebound' in modern art to 'the elementary passions – anger, desire, regret, pity and fear'.[44] In Morris's volume this is not a return to simplicity but a Grotesque recourse and assent to violence. Extreme physical cruelty and torture meet Sir Peter in 'Sir Peter Harpdon's End' when he becomes victim instead of victor in an unexpected reversal. It is the counterpart of the end he had planned for his rival, as the title punningly suggests – his *aim* as well as his end or death. His aim goes awry and the peripeteia of his death becomes less a moral reversal or the occasion of pity and fear than an orgiastic exchange of violence. The recurrent violence in the book is either completely brutal – when Robert is defeated in 'The Haystack in the Floods', his enemies 'ran, some five or six, and beat/His head to pieces at their feet' – or it is romanticised, like the violent death of the dead lovers bleeding from wounds on horseback in 'Concerning Geffray Teste Noire' – or it is aestheticised in the pageantry of single combat marked by emblem and favour.[45] This is not chivalric but Grotesque combat. The fighter in 'The Judgment of God' is urged by his father to cheat by deflecting the gaze of his opponent: 'Swerve to the left'.[46] At the same time he represents single combat as a symbolic economy of simple and straightforward *exchange* between individuals, of blood for blood, right for wrong, which will terminate the endless cycle of revenge even though he knows that butchery will be the result whether he wins or loses. As if recognising the inadequacy of this analysis, his thoughts are deflected to the love of the woman he rescued from assault. Disregarding the fact that this was a communal rescue he rests his sense of truth – and identity – on the private compact between them, assuming that the public combat can be solved 'My father's crafty way'.[47] The breakdown of the ethics of single combat comes about from the separation of private from public ethics and identity: in the end the fighter's symbolic status does not synchronise with his actions. But neither can the private, compensatory lovers' compact be independent of communality or seen as a separate economy, for the lady was won in warfare, and belongs to the economy of public exchange, and, it is enigmatically hinted, belongs to the web of aggression which has issued in the duel.

Here Morris extends Ruskin's insights into the structure of oppression. The more complex the social origin and public responsibility for action becomes, the more complex questions of right and wrong, the more isolated the individual will become, interpreting all conflicts on the model of individual responsibility, assuming the paramount importance of his agency in the public sphere, which is supported by a mystified privacy. The model of single combat is not an adequate representation for the complexities of relations in social groups but it is the only one the Grotesque consciousness can arrive at. It is interesting that in the third volume of *Modern Painters* (1856) Ruskin introduced a typically indirect and two-edged commentary on the Crimean war. He acknowledged the importance of individual heroism and even appeared to glorify the crimson wave of carnage which occurred. But his main point is that such sacrifice could only be justified, not because it led to the defeat of the Tsar but to the realignment of Britain and France in the concord of civilised friendship and social bonds as their traditional enmity was abandoned.[48] The Crimean war, the first European modern war, reported and photographed and interpreted by modern media, turned out to possess a complexity far beyond the model of war as a single combat between nations, an understanding dearly bought by its carnage. This traumatic understanding is embodied in Morris's poems, as the Grotesque fascination with violence refuses to match the complexities from which it emerges. Violence is the Grotesque's oversimplification of the complexities to which the numbed consciousness cannot respond.

The longing for meaning, and the sense of the failure of perception in the oppressed state which calls forth an ever more wayward and pathological fantasy, mean that consciousness pours inventive energy into the vision and the dream, and into the symbol which either reveals too much of the literal or conceals too much of the noumenal. Representation registers a gap between sign and *meaning*. The protagonists of these poems in fact rarely dream ('Sir Galahad' and 'The Wind' are exceptions), but they are *in* the world of the dream. The terse, gnomic narrative is structured with the gaps, elisions and displacements of dream work, where objects are juxtaposed with startling vividness but without relational explanation in an unremitting and almost tiring metonymic intensity, isolated in space. Temporality contracts or expands with dream logic, a subsidiary part of the narrative suddenly assumes disproportionate importance, or it will be arranged as the interventions of multiple, fractured utterances. The poems inhabit an explanationless world, as actions, events and refrains mismatch with one another. The narrative of 'Concerning Geffray Teste Noir', for instance, deviates from what seems to be the story of an ambush into a secondary tale of the discovery of dead lovers which then assumes primary importance – what really is 'concerning' the narrator is not Teste Noir but a woman's skeleton and the power of the woman both to disrupt and to confirm masculinity. That *women* die and become deeply implicated in masculine conflict haunts and disturbs him, as if the death of the woman's body signifies a special negation and horror. He remembers his father's horrified and horrifying reaction to the discovery of women's bones in the burning church of Beauvais, 'Between a beast's howl and a *woman's* scream' (my emphasis).[49]

In 'Golden Wings' the causal relation between Jehane's departure from the castle, its destruction and her murder, is never explained. The 'slain man's stiffened feet' of the final sinister line, protruding grotesquely from the 'leaky boat', may be those of enemy or friend.[50] The violation is presented without context, like the 'green' apples (another feminine symbol) which hang against the mouldering castle wall. Even brilliant emblematic and heraldic colour, the epitome of unambiguous signification, obfuscates and confuses. The insistent refrain of 'Two red roses across the moon', incorporating emblems of love and chastity, seems to bring opposites together and to assert the permanence of the signifying colours, gold and red. The refrain punctuates the narrative of a ride to and from battle (where routine slaughter takes place) and the return of a knight to his lady when he has victoriously cut down the enemies in their scarlet and blue. All the actions of the poem occur at noon, the decisive point of division in the day. Gold dominates in the last stanza – 'there was nothing of brown', the stains of battle, the colour of mundane experience, but also the colour achieved from mixing together scarlet and blue.[51] This, of course, is exactly what the slaughter has achieved, as the differentiating marks of opposition both within the enemy side and between it and the victors have been annihilated. The totality of annihilation which the dominance of 'gold' seems to require and the necessity for the conversion into 'brown' of all that is other to gold are immediately apparent. So too is the dependence of the refinement of the golden world on brutality. But gold, too, mixed with red, the colour of both love and war by the end of the narrative, would also become brown, and the *same* colour would signify both the alliance of gold and war and gold and love in a collapse of meaning which throws customary interpretations awry. Grotesque colour here poses a riddle of meaning, and Morris's poems often acquire the arcane and incomplete nature of the riddle, embodying the baffled and fantastic hermeneutic dislocation of the Grotesque consciousness.

'Rapunzel' and 'The Wind' are poems where Morris explores the Grotesque most elaborately. 'Rapunzel' shares the figure of the lady in the tower (Tennyson's 'The Lady of Shalott' and 'Mariana', as has been suggested, motivate many Pre-Raphaelite poems, indicating the intersecting circles of conservative and post-Benthamite thinking which Mill predicted would occur) with Dante Gabriel Rossetti's 'The Blessed Damozel', which was published in the second issue of *The Germ*. It is useful to compare the two poems, since Rossetti's poem works through an immersion in the Grotesque, whereas Morris's poem explores the Grotesque as resistance and objectifies it. Rossetti's poem rests on a simple yet bold reversal. Sensuous longing and physical desire are placed in heaven, itself a physical barrier, a golden bar or rampart, a bar which the bosom of the Damozel can make warm with her flesh, as in Keats's 'The Eve of Saint Agnes' the earthly Madelaine transfers warmth to her jewels. The lover, whose words occur in parenthesis to denote his separation, defines his separation in terms of infinite distance in space and time and the loss of a sense of materiality and physical reality. Rossetti, like Clough but far removed from his empiricism, is exploring the Tractarian orthodoxy concerning symbol. Ruskin, not without reason, had detected signs of Tractarian and 'Romish' thought in the work of the Pre-Raphaelites, and though subsequently assured of the contrary (the Rossettis were Anglicans) it is the case that this poem meditates the notion of presence and the symbol which takes the transcendent mystical body to be represented by the outward sign.[52] Newman had said in *Tract 90* that the material body sets 'bounds', like the Damozel's ramparts, to spiritual presence, and makes us think in terms of degrees of nearness or farness, unlike spiritual presence, which has nothing to do with physical measurement.[53] But the Damozel, who asks for the intensity of earthly love in heaven – 'Only to live as once on earth/With love' – is presented in a deeply physical and erotic way, and certainly makes the speaker aware of degrees of farness as she becomes unobtainable and distant in heaven.

The poem is asking in what way we perceive the mystical body through the physical body and how we invest the material with significance. The Damozel is literally invested, or clothed, with symbolic garments and emblems, three lilies, seven stars, a white rose. Her robe, 'ungirt from clasp to hem' both conceals and reveals her body.[54] It is only through material signs and analogy that the speaker can grasp her language, which is like the voice of stars, the song of birds, the sound of the bell, like and not like, concealing and revealing, steps on the 'stair' which leads from earth to heaven. But if these literal signs 'bridge' the gap between earth and heaven and reach the 'Occult, withheld' experience, there is a sense in which 'likeness' as an identity of mystical and physical simply returns us repeatedly to the material. The promised new knowledge is simply a form of the old, since we can only know through the physical. Hence the acute despair of physical loss which ends the poem: 'And then she cast her arms along/The golden barriers,/ And laid her face between her hands,/And wept'.[55] Once the physical presence of love is removed there is nothing. The poem is at once a passionate account of the necessity of the incarnation of symbolic meaning, when the seen guarantees the unseen, and a sceptical discourse on the idea of the transfiguration of the erotic by the mystical: there may simply be only the manifestation of the physical or the erotic in all its fullness. The 'robe' which is the physical body conceals and reveals nothing but itself. Thus there is no stair or bridge to the unknown, and the mystical body is a case of the emperor's – or Damozel's – new clothes, as the woman's body figures nothing but itself. Perhaps that is why, despite or perhaps because of its beauty, the Damozel can remind us of one of Rossetti's 'stunners'.

The problem with the occulted nature or symbol for this poem is literally a problem of *translation*. Because there is no reversible relationship between the seen and the unseen, because we necessarily start from the seen and not the other way round we are caught in material representation. When the Damozel is 'translated' to heaven, therefore, she becomes the more intensely perceived as physical and sexual being the more ethereal she supposedly is. With her disappearance the 'clothes' of the Carlylean symbol (for this is a highly eclectic poem fusing a number of discourses of symbol just as it fuses Crashaw-like extravagance and Victorian lushness) do not become infinitely renewable as, in the last stanza, the narration moves from the visible to the merely heard '(I saw her smile.)...(I heard her tears.)'. The poem ends with a parenthesis not placed *between* two linguistic structures but followed by a void. The intensity of affective diction – 'The light thrilled towards her' – seems to be motivated by an anxiety lest language should break down altogether when the last evidence of the Damozel's presence disappears: 'She ceased'.[56]

'Rapunzel', like 'The Blessed Damozel' , takes the image of separation as its central figure, as Rapunzel's yellow hair creates a 'path' or 'stair', as the Prince and the Witch call it, between the tower where she is imprisoned by the power of the Witch and the ground below. As in Rossetti's poem, the body of a woman bears the full weight of symbolic meaning, but whereas Rossetti's poem is a discursive and reflective meditation on the symbolic conversion of the body, Morris presents Rapunzel's hair in mysterious metonymic isolation – it does not even belong to her as she is forced to let it down to the foot of the tower and turn it into a ladder at the Witch's instigation. The golden hair falls 'fathoms' below her, a word which allies with the 'waves' and 'ripples' by which it is described to suggest an amorphous substance out of her control. Like the iconography of Jacob's 'ladder' which Ruskin instances as a form of Grotesque symbol, it is seen with a narrow concentration and enigmatic intensity which literalises its function as stairway. Morris dramatises the fairy story in terse and laconic episodes and disperses the events between several consciousnesses so that no single perspective has authority. Rossetti's poem moves between two visual fields, that of the Damozel and the excluded speaker. Morris persistently triangulates relationships, seen variously from above or below by the participants – the Prince, the Witch, Rapunzel. The Witch's perspective changes constantly, magically belonging to the tower or the ground. Rapunzel invokes Mary and Saint Michael from the vestigial Christian tradition she brings to her defence: the Prince sees Rapunzel through the eyes of the court and through the song of a minstrel. The power of the gaze is not invested in a single vision but moves erratically as different perspectives intersect and diverge.

The golden hair, literally a mediating entity as demons or princes climb up or down it, becomes a symbol of mediation, but it is a fetishised symbol. The Victorian fetishising of hair as a sign of sexuality is clearly at issue here, but Ruskin had also used a related metaphor in *The Political Economy of Art* (1857) which is relevant. Speaking to a Manchester audience and using the idea of weaving as a metaphor for wealth, he talked of the 'golden net' of the world's wealth, entangling and destroying like a spider's web, or liberating when used in the social good. The price of anything never represents its value but 'the degree of desire' rich people have to possess it (in fact, he recommended coming off the gold standard for this reason).[57] Thus the net of money is a signifying system for Ruskin. The importance of the hair as fetishised symbol in the poem is not that it can be given a specific meaning but that it is implicated in desire and is substituted for different things in different ways. It is demonised as 'Devil's bats' swing on it like spiders; it is the object of struggle to the death as knights fight over emblems of it.[58] It is idealised as 'paths of stars' or a 'golden cord', or narrowly literalised so that it is used as if it *were* the object it symbolises.[59] Or it is seen, as the Prince and minstrel see it, as an obfuscating 'film' or 'veil' of gold, as Ruskin's Grotesque symbol which is experienced as veiling meaning.[60] The symbol becomes aestheticised, the opposite of literalisation, as the veil of representation takes on an independent life, creating reference out of its own distortions.

The minstrel sings of the hair as 'veil', as his refrain has it, existing "Twixt the sunlight and the shade', made by the 'rough hands' of a warrior.[61] The veil is created by the illumination and blind spots of individual vision, but the gaze also depends on the immaterial but palpable play of light and shade in the external world. The song testifies to the complexity of the gaze and the meaning of the hair. The 'veil' of symbol is always, even here, subject to the individual's 'degree of desire'. The minstrel renames Rapunzel as Guendolen, and though she is liberated into a new language, naming the hare-bells as they become more specific than the 'blue flowers' seen from the tower (a subtle way of suggesting a new perspective), her name is imposed on her as much as the name of the Witch Rapunzel, which at least signified the double identity of light and shade. In the song 'Guendolen now speaks no word', and in the life of the court she is subject to the new social taboo of marriage.[62] The marriage is a protection, a happy ending, but an equivocal one. The Witch from hell forbids men access to her golden hair.

Rapunzel/Guendolen has the vision of the oppressed consciousness which cannot play. Even her tear is absorbed by the marble parapet's 'red stains' as if to emphasise her powerlessness (unlike the Damozel of Rossetti's poem who gives warmth to her golden parapet).[63] The Prince, too, though to a lesser extent, is subject. He can only gain access to Rapunzel when he has assumed the warlike identity urged upon him by his guardians in the 'council-hall', when he works rather than dreams. His identity, and that of Rapunzel, is created for him by the Minstrel's song. Even when he sings the song to 'express' his own situation he is mediating another's representation of himself. The oppressed consciousness's fascination with death is apparent after the consummation of love when he asks 'did you ever see a death?'[64] This abruptness is typical of the non-sequiturs of the poem, a curious question to ask after a consummation. Love and death seem to come to his mind as linked extremities, terminal moments which are the counterparts of one another.

137

Death broods over *The Defence*, a never repressed nemesis. The Blake-like, gnomic refrain of 'The Wind' asks questions of the life force and energy represented by the wind. Is it sad, kind, unhappy, in its blindness as it seeks out the 'lily-seed'? Its indifferent, predatory purposiveness seems to be not the opposite but beyond or the other side of the death wish, a pleasure principle without awareness of pleasure. This collapsing of opposites occurs throughout the poem, where all experiences, however discrete, are related in contiguity rather than difference. An orange, its juice, we later learn, like blood, lies on a green chair hanging 'with a deep gash cut in the rind', and it is not immediately clear whether the orange is an actual or a represented fruit woven into the cloth, art or life, for the dragons on the cloth 'grin out in the gusts of the wind', moved by action in the external world as if they may be living.[65] Memory falls into dream, love is displaced by death, as the inexplicable fantasy of Margaret supersedes memory. Margaret, dead under a bier of life-giving spring daffodils, seems to be associated with cyclical movement of the seasons, and thus with death rather than life, for spring is inevitably superseded in time by another season. Finally, 'in march'd the ghosts of those that had gone to the war', and it is not clear whether these ghosts are part of the Margaret dream or whether they 'really' approach the speaker in a waking vision.[66] In either case the ghost is ambiguous here, for a ghost can be the return of the dead or of the living who are ghosts of their former selves. Their heraldic colours, once painted by the dreamer, but now 'faint', and thus unreadable, are the antithesis of the brilliant and hallucinatory colour of objects at the start of the poem. Nevertheless, they are complementary, for a brilliant and fantastic intensity is one of the needs of the consciousness experiencing the faded sense of lack and numbness, of the person who cannot play, the male hysteria which belongs to the heart of stone. This, above all the poems, is Morris's Crimean-war poem. The ghostly return of the ghosts is a return from the death of war to a civil *society* of death.

Ruskin always insisted that the Grotesque was not a sick or degenerate form, though it could be under certain historical conditions. It is Morris's achievement that he analyses the Grotesque through its manifestations, simultaneously inward with and external to it, actively expressing its longings and at the same time analysing the structure of its determining conditions and politics. It is this which gives these poems the energy of resistance, whether it is in the need to break through oppression and escape as Rapunzel and Jehane of

'Golden Wings' attempt to do, or in the need to experience phenomena with extraordinary hyperaesthetic intensity. For intense
feeling, grief and madness are forms of resistance rather than disease
in Morris's texts. Thus he produces a double poem which both
expresses and *reads* the Grotesque. Ruskin believed that the education of the eye was the essential democratic need, for 'the eye is a
nobler organ than the ear' and through it we obtain or put into form
'nearly all the useful information we are to have about this world'
(*The Political Economy of Art*).[67] He spoke of the distance of the verbal
and the written sign in comparison with the ocular, though he was
probably one of the first critics to think of the verbal, written and
visual sign as texts. The Pre-Raphaelites are often thought to have
brought the vividness of the pictorial into their writing, but rather
they brought the problematical gaze of the Grotesque vision. Morris's
reading of the Grotesque gaze is as much a verbal as a visual matter.
The dream syntax and articulation of Morris's Grotesque, whether at
the level of a single line or phrase or a syntagmatic sequence of narrative, require a double act of seeing and reading and are highly
organised linguistically. Its simplicity is of the utmost sophistication
because it is about misprision rather than mastery. His poems compel
the reader to go through the processes of interpreting and relating,
misprision and adjustment, actively, by refusing explanation and
context for the transgressive and disturbing material they present.
The associative process envisaged by Hallam and Tennyson commands assent and shocks by subterfuge. Morris's poems ask for dissent and shock by enabling a reader to see the distortions of Grotesque
vision even while he remains within them. Popular, immediate,
simple in form, democratically accessible, they nevertheless expose
the 'ripple', as Ruskin called it, on the mirror. In this way they aim for
the democratic self-education of the reading eye. It is interesting that
in 'The Wind' Margaret is reading a text before she is so violently
deflected by the dreamer.[68]

Notes

1   Morris shared accommodation with Rossetti at Red Lion Square from
    November 1856 until May 1859. See Philip Henderson, *William Morris. His
    Life, Work and Friends*, Harmondsworth, 1973, 56–78.
2   Letters to *The Times*, 13 May 1851, 30 May 1851, 5 May 1854, 25 May 1854.
    The Works of John Ruskin, E. T. Cook and A. Wedderburn, eds, 39 vols,
    London, 1903–12, XII, 319–35.

3 Henderson, *William Morris*, 30–1.

4 *The Germ*, January–April 1850, first two numbers January and February. Later renamed *Art and Poetry, being Thoughts towards Nature*, dated respectively March and May 1850. Folded thereafter. *The Oxford and Cambridge Magazine*, 12 monthly nos, January–December 1856.

5 W. Holman Hunt, *Pre-Raphaelitism and the Pre-Raphaelite Brotherhood*, London, 1905, 150. Consider Carol T. Christ, *The Finer Optic: The Aesthetic of Particularity in Victorian Poetry*, London, 1975, 55, as an example of an intelligent critic who attempts to unify the disparate positions of the Pre-Raphaelite Brotherhood under a discussion of detail and accuracy.

6 *The Germ*, facsimile reprint with Introduction by W. M. Rossetti, London, 1901, 16.

7 *The Germ*, 1 (January 1850), 31.

8 *The Germ*, facsimile reprint, 1901, 18.

9 *The Germ*, 1 (January 1850), 14.

10 Cook and Wedderburn, III, *Modern Painters*, 31–8, 25–32.

11 *The Germ*, 1 (January 1850), 17–18.

12 *The Germ*, 2 (February 1850), 58.

13 *Art and Poetry*, 4 (May 1850), 192.

14 E. S. Dallas, *Poetics: An Essay on Poetry*, London, 1852, reference to Kant, 157; quotation, 291.

15 See my *Victorian Poetry* (1993), Part I, pp. 71–4. See also ibid., p. 341.

16 Rev. F. W. Robertson, *Two Lectures on the Influence of Poetry on the Working Classes*, London, 1852, 11, 59.

17 See ' "A Joy for Ever"; (and its price in the market), Two lectures on the political economy of art', in Cook and Wedderburn, XVI, 5–176.

18 Walter Pater, *Westminster Review*, N.S., XXXIV (October 1868), 300.

19 Ibid., 300–1.

20 W. Morris, *The Defence of Guenevere and Other Poems* (1858), London, 1896 (1858 reprint), 247.

21 Cook and Wedderburn, XI, *The Stones of Venice*, iii, 135–95.

22 Letter to *The Times*, 25 May 1854, in Cook and Wedderburn, XII, 334.

23 *The Defence*, 46.

24 Ibid., 26.

25 Ibid., 174–7.

26 Millais based a painting on 'Mariana' in 1850. For the Pre-Raphaelite interest in Tennyson see Laura Marcus, 'Brothers in their anecdotage: Holman Hunt's *Pre-Raphaelitism and the Pre-Raphaelite Brotherhood'*, *Pre-Raphaelitism Reviewed*, Marcia Pointon, ed., Manchester, 1989, 1–21, 15.

27 Cook and Wedderburn, X, *The Stones of Venice*, ii, 184: see also XI, *The Stones of Venice*, iii, 178–80, paras. 59–60.

28 A. W. Pugin, *Contrasts, or a Parallel between the Architecture of the 15th & 19th Centuries*, London, 1836, 3: 'I will proceed, first, to shew the state of Architecture in this country immediately before the great change of

religion; secondly, the fatal effects produced by that change of Architecture; and, thirdly, the present degraded state of Architectural taste, and the utter want of those feelings which alone can restore Architecture to its ancient noble position'.

29   Cook and Wedderburn, XI, *The Stones of Venice*, iii, 134.
30   Cook and Wedderburn, X, *The Stones of Venice*, ii, 188, 196–201, paras. 9, 17–22.
31   Ibid., 196.
32   Cook and Wedderburn, XI, *Stones of Venice*, iii, 154.
33   Ibid., 155.
34   Ibid., 169.
35   Ibid., 173.
36   Ibid., 166, 178.
37   Ibid., 179.
38   Ibid., 185.
39   Ibid., 187.
40   Ibid., 191.
41   Hegel's *Aesthetics* is a text composed by his contemporary H. G. Hotho, from Hegel's notes (and students' notes) for lectures given in Berlin in the 1820s. Hotho's editions were published in 1835 and 1842. The first English translation, *The Introduction to Hegel's Philosophy of Fine Art*, trans. Bernard Bosanquet, was first published in 1886.
42   *The Defence*, 56.
43   Ibid., 4.
44   Walter Pater, *Westminster Review*, N.S., XXXIV (October 1868), 300–12: 305.
45   *The Defence*, 222.
46   Ibid., 169.
47   Ibid., 173.
48   Cook and Wedderburn, V, *Modern Painters*, iii, 410–17, paras. 33–9.
49   *The Defence*, 143.
50   Ibid., 214.
51   Ibid., 225.
52   Ibid., 121.
53   J. H. Newman, *Tract Ninety, or Remarks on Certain Passages in the Thirty-Nine Articles* (1841), A. W. Evans, ed., London, 1933, 69.
54   *The Germ*, 2 (February 1850), 80.
55   Ibid., 83.
56   Ibid.
57   Cook and Wedderburn, XVI, 'A Joy for Ever...lectures on the political economy of art', 86.
58   *The Defence*, 121.
59   Ibid., 117, 119.
60   Ibid., 121.
61   Ibid., 131.

62 Ibid.
63 Ibid., 115.
64 Ibid., 125.
65 Ibid., 188.
66 Ibid., 193.
67 'A Joy for Ever', 90–1.
68 This chapter has benefited greatly from my reading of Lindsay Smith's unpublished Ph.D. thesis on Ruskin, *The Enigma of Visibility: Theories of Visual Perception in the Work of John Ruskin, William Morris and the Pre-Raphaelites*, University of Southampton, 1989. [Published as: *Victorian Photography, Painting and Poetry: The Enigma of Visibility in Ruskin, Morris and the Pre-Raphaelites* (Cambridge: Cambridge UP, 1995).]

8

Alienated Majesty
Gerard M Hopkins

Geoffrey Hill

Among the numerous consequences of the era of so-called 'protest art' is the irrational embarrassment of the current reaction against the theme of protest, or of political writing in general. Whatever the excesses and affectations of the 1960s and '70s may have done to harm the cause of poetry, there is nonetheless a real connection between it and politics: as real now, if we could disclose its true stratum or vein, as in the Tudor court poetry of Skelton, Surrey, and Wyatt or in the political sonnets of Milton or in the relation that exists between Wordsworth's 'Preface' to *Lyrical Ballads* and his tract *On the Convention of Cintra*, or between Whitman's editorials for the *Brooklyn Daily Eagle*, and other papers, and *Leaves of Grass*. As the word 'politics' has been rendered so suspect, I have opted in these chapters on alienated majesty[1] for the term 'civil polity', gleaned from the title-page of Josiah Royce's last book, *The Hope of the Great Community*, published posthumously in 1916, where the author is referred to as 'Late Alford Professor of Natural Religion, Moral Philosophy and Civil Polity at Harvard University'.

Civil polity – let us make the claim – is poetry's natural habitat. To approach Emerson, Whitman, and Hopkins in terms of this claim is to place particular emphasis upon the nature of 'alienated majesty', Emerson's fine phrase in which he perhaps spoke more profoundly than he knew of the powerfully inhibiting element in New England society.[2] This element simultaneously restricted and enlarged powers

Hill, Geoffrey. 2008. "Alienated Majesty: Gerard M. Hopkins." In *Collected Critical Writings*, edited by Kenneth Haynes, pp. 518–31. Oxford: Oxford University Press. Reproduced with permission of Oxford University Press.

Victorian Poets: A Critical Reader, First Edition. Edited by Valentine Cunningham.
© 2014 John Wiley & Sons, Ltd. Published 2014 by John Wiley & Sons, Ltd.

of the imagination in Emerson, Whitman, and Dickinson, in Hawthorne, Thoreau, and Melville. Moreover, in all these writers I sense that the alienated majesty is the body and spirit of civil polity itself. The greatest crisis affecting civil polity during their lifetimes was obviously the [American] Civil War, though in Emerson's case the passing of the Fugitive Slave Law by the governing body of the Commonwealth of Massachusetts in 1851 took more out of him – more even than the death of his son nine years previously and certainly more than was exacted by his sidelines experience of the War itself.

If the life and work of Gerard Hopkins appear at first sight alien to the New England context, that particular frisson may not be altogether inappropriate to the argument, since aliening, alienness, even alienism – as well as self-estrangement, the reverse to the brave face of Emersonian self-reliance – are here being placed under review. Hopkins, however, remains an outsider of a more elusive kind. He comes across as being remarkably whole, even when riven by affliction and desolation; he is the same man in his late poems as he is in his sermons and retreat-notes; his introspection, which is that of the Ignatian *Spiritual Exercises*, is quite other than the introspection of Emerson, Dickinson, or Melville. His rejection of Whitman is fierce but entirely without affectation, which is more than can be said of Dickinson's.

Hopkins was acquainted with Whitman's poetry: a selection, edited by William Rossetti, had appeared in England in 1868; within three years of its appearance Whitman received greetings and praise from Swinburne and Tennyson. In 1874 George Saintsbury reviewed a new British edition of *Leaves of Grass* in the *Academy*, a review which Hopkins read. There is no way, of course, that Whitman could have known anything about Hopkins.

On the face of it, Hopkins represented everything which, in *Democratic Vistas*, Whitman urged American writers and readers to reject: Europe's 'feudal, ecclesiastical, dynastic world',[3] to the idioms of which Hopkins, on first sight, appears to cleave. As a follower of St Ignatius of Loyola and a student of the Ignatian *Spiritual Exercises* he took into his devotional life and language the terms which, in the 1530s, Ignatius, himself a member of the warrior caste, a *caballero*, had written into his book of instructions: 'if anyone would refuse the request of such a king, how he would deserve to be despised by everyone, and considered an unworthy knight' ('The Kingdom of Christ').[4]

> I caught this morning morning's minion, king-
> dom of daylight's dauphin,

and so on.[5] Moreover, within the immediate context of late-middle Victorian England, Hopkins, when he allowed his mind to attend to politics (which in fact he did fairly frequently) was, except in certain matters pertaining to Ireland, a thoroughgoing Tory Imperialist: 'I enclose a poem, the Bugler. I am half inclined to hope the Hero of it may be killed in Afghanistan', that is, killed heroically defending some vulnerable outpost of the Empire, the Raj.[6]

At the same time, Whitman recognized power when in its presence, and he could scarcely have missed its presence in Hopkins's poetry if only he had read it. A minor *leitmotiv* in these chapters on alienated majesty is Whitman's 'It is time the English-speaking peoples had some true idea about the verteber of genius, namely power'.[7] 'Verteber', a form of the word as given in Noah Webster's *American Dictionary* in 1828 and 1832, would have appealed to Hopkins, who emphasized the 'naked thew and sinew' in his observations on the admirable way in which some writers could use rhythm and syntax; Dryden, in particular, Hopkins admired for this quality, calling him 'the most masculine of our poets'.[8] Moreover, Whitman's rejection of Europe and its literature is more qualified by detail than the brief quotation from *Democratic Vistas* suggests. In a lengthy footnote within that piece, he points to works of world literature including those by Shakespeare, Cervantes, Milton, and Goethe as providing 'models, combined, adjusted to other standards than America's, but of priceless value to her and hers'.[9] Nor is *Democratic Vistas*, of 1867–70, the only place in which we find a greater degree *of finesse* in his treatment of European literature. In one of his *Brooklyn Daily Eagle* pieces ('"Home" Literature' of 11 July 1846) he condemns William Cowper for teaching 'blind loyalty to the "divine right of kings"', a crime for which he would have condemned the then two-year-old Hopkins had his seer's vision foreknown several poems and numerous letters, and he also denounces 'Walter Scott…Southey, and many others' who 'laugh to scorn the idea of republican freedom and virtue'. But when he dismisses the 'tinsel sentimentality of Bulwer', the 'inflated, unnatural, high-life-below-stairs, "historical" romances of Harrison Ainsworth',[10] not only is Whitman forthrightly, entirely, correct in his critical judgement, he is also markedly close in pitch of attention to Hopkins, another fine, albeit informal, critic of modern letters:

> If anything made me think the age Alexandrine (as they say), an age of decadence (a criticism that they sling about between the bursting Yes and blustering No, for want of more things to say…), well, it would be to see

how secondrate poetry (and what I mean is, not poetry at all) gets itself put about for great poetry.[11]

Or:

Now [Browning] has got a great deal of what came in with Kingsley and the Broad Church school, a way of talking (and making his people talk) with the air and spirit of a man bouncing up from the table with his mouth full of bread and cheese and saying that he meant to stand no blasted nonsense.[12]

Hopkins disliked what he called 'bluster', as his comic portrayal of Robert Browning's poetry and Charles Kingsley's muscular Christianity reveals; and it is likely that he would have seen Whitman as a blusterer also ('I sound my barbaric yawp over the roofs of the world');[13] unjustly because, as James Wright showed, in a beautifully appreciative essay, Whitman is one of the most delicate of poets, and with a gift of parody and self-parody to equal Hopkins's.[14] But, of course, we know why Hopkins, while admitting that he knew his own mind to be 'more like Whitman's than any other man's living', objected to his American senior. It is because Whitman was 'a very great scoundrel'; and he was a scoundrel, in Hopkins's eyes, because he claimed to be 'indifferent' to moral and doctrinal issues which Hopkins took as matters essential to salvation.[15] Whitman understood or appeared to understand sensuality as good; to Hopkins the line between sensuous and sensual was as fine-drawn as it had been for Milton, who introduced the word 'sensuous' into English.

To repeat: how Whitman would or would not have responded to the poetry of Hopkins is entirely a matter for speculation. It is conceivable that he might have been drawn, as so many readers of Hopkins have in fact been drawn, into the error of regarding him as a wild nature poet of a power to rival Keats and Shelley who unfortunately fell among Jesuits and whose gift was consequently repressed. The contrary opinion needs here to be stated, that the *Spiritual Exercises* not only saved Hopkins from repression and despair but also gave to his poetry those distinguishing features which set the seal of greatness upon it.

Hopkins had dedicated himself to poetry some considerable time before he realized that he most truly and powerfully desired to dedicate himself to the service of Christ and the salvation of his own soul. He told Dixon that he had burnt his early verse 'before I became a Jesuit and resolved to write no more, as not belonging to my profession, unless it were by the wish of my superiors'.[16] As to that section of the *Exercises* headed 'A consideration to obtain information on the matters in which a choice should be made', its particular significance for his situation may have increased rather than diminished during the twenty years in which he was a member of the Society:

> Once an immutable choice has been made there is no further choice, for it cannot be dissolved, as is true with marriage, the priesthood, etc. It should be noted only that if one has not made this choice properly, with due consideration, and without inordinate attachments, he should repent and try to lead a good life in the choice he has made. Since this choice was ill considered and improperly made, it does not seem to be a vocation from God, as many err in believing, wishing to interpret an ill-considered or bad choice as a divine call. For every divine call is always pure and clean without any admixture of flesh or other inordinate attachments.[17]

The suggestion may here be made that a poetic gift, working to the pitch evident even in Hopkins's early work, is always inordinate in its demands. There is a certain poignancy in rereading, in this light, Emerson's words from the essay 'Experience': 'if one remembers how innocently he began to be an artist, he perceives that nature joined with his enemy'.[18] At the age of fifteen Hopkins 'innocently...began to be an artist'; but poetry, such as he was to write in his later years, is not an innocent occupation, even when, as in most cases, it escapes being confronted by the demands of a vocation such as his.

Hopkins offered his great ode, 'The Wreck of the Deutschland', composed during the first half of 1876 with the permission and indeed the encouragement of his superior, to the Society, to the English Catholic Church, and to the English people; in the trust, as Norman H. MacKenzie says, that it would 'win over to the truth widening circles of Englishmen'.[19] When it failed to win over even the editor of *The Month*, Hopkins returned, so far as the Society cared or was aware, to the production of 'little presentation pieces which occasion called for'.[20] His genius, henceforth, was in hiding; though not in the half-surreptitious way which he attributes to his bird-watching 'heart' in 'The Windhover'.[21]

This crucial episode reveals, however, the strength of mind with which Hopkins lived according to the rule. He avoided two errors of romantic sentiment. First, there is no evidence that he ever sided with his genius against his vocation. He did not regret having taken vows. Secondly, he made no attempt 'to interpret an ill-considered or bad choice' – what Emerson wryly terms the innocent beginnings of the artist's life – as 'a divine call'.

Here too the line between the understanding and misunderstanding is very thin-drawn; our misunderstanding, not Hopkins's. His early sonnet 'Where art thou friend', of April 1865, has been read as 'in effect a dedication of his poetry to Christ's service'.[22] Such a sense of dedication, at that stage in his spiritual life, need not be taken as a misjudgement. If MacKenzie is right in his 'Note on Missing Poems' it was shortly thereafter, in the fall of 1865, that Hopkins began to sense that his 'deepening religious devotion was challenging his future as a secular poet'.[23] I interpret 'secular' as 'pertaining to the world of literary success or fame' rather than as 'choosing worldly themes or subjects' since Hopkins's poetry could scarcely ever have been described as 'secular' in the latter sense. The secular world in the other sense, acknowledged and then put aside, figures in the generous letter of understanding and comfort addressed to his former teacher, the Anglican Church historian and minor poet Richard Watson Dixon, in June 1878:

It is sad to think what disappointment must many times over have filled your heart for the darling children of your mind...For disappointment and humiliations embitter the heart and make an aching in the very bones. As far as I am concerned I say with conviction and put it on record again that you have great reason to thank God who has given you so astonishingly clear an inward eye to see what is in visible nature and in the heart such a deep insight into what is earnest, tender, and pathetic in human life and feeling as your poems display.[24]

Such a letter may help clarify our understanding in several ways. First, it makes evident that the mind and heart which could offer this kind of consolation in such full measure, and yet measure the rightness of each phrase, would not at this time (just less than two years after the rejection of 'The Wreck of the Deutschland') be deluded into fancying that public fame or notoriety as a poet might be construable as an alternative form of 'divine call'. Secondly, it suggests that Hopkins is able to envisage that talk of poetry could constitute, when called for (which would not be often), part of the dutiful, necessary language of charity, and that, in performing this office, he finds it appropriate to use the commonplaces of natural religion, moral philosophy, and civil polity. Such phrases as 'a deep insight into what is earnest, tender, and pathetic' are, taken by themselves, no different from Josiah Royce's 'very deep insight into the meaning of life'.[25] Here, as in a myriad other instances around us, it is context that effects the change in quality. Such language, in Royce's *William James and Other Essays*, is not the best he can do, merely the best he permitted himself to do, for a Phi Beta Kappa Oration or Commencement Address.

There are ways of offering up commonplace to the greater glory of God. Hopkins and in his way Whitman can do this; as Lincoln can. Others cannot. What Whitman offers up, in *Drum-Taps*, are phrases that represent the verbal strivings of the common soldiers of the Union army, as they endeavour to bring home the unspeakable nature of what they have been forced to endure and to witness: 'tumultuous now the contest rages',[26] 'a desperate emergency',[27] 'Faces, varieties, postures beyond description',[28] 'I see a sight beyond all the pictures and poems ever made',[29] 'O the bullet could never kill what you really are, dear friend'.[30] Very finely, these half-defeated phrases of common endurance are matched by long lines of great exactitude: 'The glisten of the little steel instruments catching the glint of the torches';[31] and both the half-articulate and the minutely articulate are imperceptibly combined into a formal generosity of cadence that does duty for them both:

> Comes before me the unknown soldier's grave, comes the inscription
>   rude in Virginia's woods,
> *Bold, cautious, true, and my loving comrade.*[32]

'Inscription rude': the rough inscription, that Whitman ensures shall be confronted by his readers although, as his endless revisions to *Leaves of Grass* make clear, he is himself anything but a rough inscriber.

'Comrade' is a key-word for Whitman: his language is comradely with half-dead phrases ('postures beyond description') as it is with the young men who uttered them and are dead. It is his equivalent of Hopkins's dutiful, necessary language of charity.

'Common', the commonness of common soldiers, their common suffering, the commonness of their slang and platitudes, is a key-term in Whitman's polemic of civil polity, in the transcendent commonness of *Democratic Vistas*:

> Grand, common stock! to me the accomplish'd and convincing growth, prophetic of the future; proof undeniable to sharpest sense, of perfect beauty, tenderness and pluck, that never feudal lord, nor Greek, nor Roman breed, yet rival'd.[33]

And this is to be distinguished sharply from what he elsewhere calls 'the mean flat average':

> To-day, in books, in the rivalry of writers, especially novelists, success, (socall'd), is for him or her who strikes the mean flat average, the sensational appetite for stimulus, incident, persiflage, &c, and depicts, to the common calibre, sensual, exterior life.[34]

It will readily be observed that between the two phrases 'grand, common stock' and 'the common calibre' – as they occur in context – there stands a *massif* of contrary implications; and yet the bulk of the divide itself is substantially built up around the word *common*. Both examples occur within some thirty pages of the same work, *Democratic Vistas*. That Whitman here perceives, more clearly than most Whitmanites of the succeeding century and a half, that a 'grand common stock' shall not find its destiny realized in the 'common calibre', the 'mean flat average', is an insight which registers itself semantically rather than discursively. It goes some way towards explaining why Whitman, like Emerson and indeed like Hopkins, invested so heavily in the idea of *genius*. 'Genius' was to them as 'intrinsic value' was to Ruskin. Together, 'genius' and 'intrinsic value' are caught, without hope of success, in the crisis of civil polity to which I have attached Emerson's phrase 'alienated majesty'. For Whitman, in the years following Lincoln's assassination and with emancipation betrayed by reconstruction, it was the mean flat average that increasingly alienated the grandeur of the common stock.

'I find within my professional experience now a good deal of matter to write on.'[35] If I did not already know whose words these are, I have no reason to suppose that I could identify the author. They are found in a letter from Hopkins to Robert Bridges (14 August 1879). To the same recipient, Hopkins writes, 'The state of the country is indeed sad, I might say it is heartbreaking, for I am a very great patriot' (16 June 1881).[36] Six months later, he writes to Dixon: 'My Liverpool and Glasgow experience laid upon my mind a conviction, a truly crushing conviction, of the misery of town life to the poor and more than to the poor, of the misery of the poor in general, of the degradation even of our race, of the hollowness of this century's civilisation' (1 December 1881).[37]

Concern for civil polity coexists with Hopkins's ever increasing devotion to the service of Christ and the salvation of his own soul. To understand the nature of this coexistence, the chapter 'Academic Theology and Hopkins's Self-Consciousness' in Walter J. Ong's *Hopkins, the Self, and God* (1986) helps us; as do Christopher Devlin's notes to his edition of *The Sermons and Devotional Writings of Gerard Manley Hopkins* (1959), in which he glosses several passages in Duns Scotus's *Scriptum Oxoniense* to indicate reasons why Hopkins should care for him so greatly. According to Scotus, 'the self-perfection to which man aspires is in the natural order' although 'the achievement of it requires supernatural aid'.[38] The idea that the kingdom of original justice was not rendered wholly inaccessible by the consequences of the Fall had a particular attractiveness for Hopkins, as did the radical suggestion, also originating with Scotus, that 'God the Son's descent into creation' was 'an act of love which would have taken place in one form or another' whether or not the Fall had taken place.[39] One can see the consequences of this Christology in the foundation and development of Hopkins's theological politics. He was a commonweal man through and through, and if 'Christ's humanity was God's first intention in creating', a far stronger light is thrown upon the idea of humanity's eternal status in the divine polity than if the Incarnation is understood wholly as an act of redemption consequent upon the Fall.[40]

'Now *what was the common weal*? what was the joint and common good of that kingdom?'[41] Hopkins's rhetorical question was raised and answered, by himself, in the presence of the Sunday evening congregation at St Francis Xavier's Church, Liverpool, 18 January 1880, in a sermon on the text 'Thy kingdom come'. Hopkins's answer to his own question was not straight out of Ignatius:

> it was that God should be glorified in man and man glorified in God. Man was created to praise, honour, and serve God, thus fulfilling God's desire in bringing him into being and by so doing to save his soul, thus fulfilling his own desire, the desire of everything that has being. He was created to give God glory and by so doing to win himself glory. This was the good that first commonwealth aimed at, this was its common weal.[42]

The foundation of this declaration is certainly that of *The Spiritual Exercises*, but the final impression and expression have been shaped by Hopkins; as he might have said himself, he has put his own stress on it. I have the feeling, when reading such a passage, that this is something from a very late response to Hobbes: a belated but powerful addition to a sequence which began in the mid-seventeenth century with Bramhall's *A Defence of True Liberty* (1655) and Clarendon's *A Brief View and Survey of the Dangers and Pernicious Errors to Church and State* (1676) and was continued in the first half of the eighteenth century by Bishop Butler's *Fifteen Sermons* of 1726. If there seems something anachronistic, even archaic, in this way of presenting these issues, it should be added that there is something anachronistic, possibly archaic, in anyone's following *The Spiritual Exercises*, set down in the early 1530s, in the midst of a progressive, increasingly secularist age; which is to say that Hopkins was thoroughly committed to his position and knew that his position committed him to appearing, to hostile Liberalism, two or three centuries behind the times.

One of the most grievous losses to modern English poetry is the 'great ode' to Edmund Campion which in September 1881 Hopkins told Bridges he had begun,[43] but which a month later he told Dixon had been 'laid aside',[44] no trace of it remains. St Edmund Campion (beatified in 1886, canonized in 1970) was one of the English Jesuit martyrs of the reign of Queen Elizabeth I, and Hopkins's ode, described by him as 'something between the *Deutschland* and [Dryden's] *Alexander's Feast*, in sprung rhythm of irregular metre',[45] had been intended as a celebration of the three hundredth anniversary of Campion's martyrdom, 1 December 1881.

The late sonnet 'Tom's Garland: Upon the Unemployed' is so unwieldy largely because Hopkins, in 1888, is attempting to compose a variant upon a mid-seventeenth century political sonnet, such as Milton, or perhaps even Hobbes, might have written. Hopkins offers what he calls a 'crib' for the poem, sent to Bridges in February 1888:

> Must I interpret it ['Tom's Garland']? It means then that, as St. Paul and Plato and Hobbes and everybody says, the commonwealth or well ordered human society is like one man; a body with many members and each its function; some higher, some lower, but all honourable, from the honour which belongs to the whole.[46]

There is little point in objecting that Hopkins has failed to take the individual stress of either St Paul or Plato or Hobbes in so lumping them together, because the added 'and everybody' clearly indicates that the sentence is intended to be read as one of good-humoured exasperation.

Even so, 'Tom's Garland' is to be judged as a passionately serious effort to match navvies' labour with imaginative toil. In terms of consequence and effect this is a far stretch from Coleridge's intention when he wrote, in *The Friend*, of requiring 'the attention of my reader to become my fellow-labourer',[47] though Hopkins's massive strenuosities in this poem may be indirectly derived from that source. We have to say that if, as Ong claims, Hopkins was 'inside his own epoch in history, at home in his own age',[48] 'Tom's Garland' is a strange way of showing this to be the case, or we must add that his at-home-ness produces some strange metaphysical children, or 'darling children of [the] mind' as he expressed it in his letter to Dixon. MacKenzie observes that the poem may have been influenced by Ford Madox Brown's sonnet 'Work' which he wrote to accompany his painting of the same title. MacKenzie adds that Brown's well-known painting 'illustrated Carlyle's teachings on the need for all men to have some work to do, whether with brawn (like the navvies shown excavating in Hampstead) or brain (like two onlookers, Carlyle and the controversial social philosopher F. D. Maurice)'.[49] The problem with the theme of 'alienation' is that, understood purely as a *topos*, it in no way prevents the philosopher who proposes it from being thoroughly at home in the world he trounces and castigates, like that couple of well-to-do loungers in Brown's painting, pleasantly observing the navvies' labour and seemingly entirely satisfied to have matters remain like that. But 'Tom's Garland' is a much stranger piece of work than Brown's painting. There is a likelihood, it has been observed, that Hopkins intended to write a burlesque element into this poem. There would be good precedent for it, in Milton's political sonnets such as 'On the New Forcers of Conscience under the Long Parliament', 'On the Detraction which followed upon my writing Certain Treatises', 'A book was writ of late called *Tetrachordon*', though it must be added that Milton's three sonnets wed terseness to the burlesque. Whereas they are terse and on target, Hopkins is not. In describing his intentions in 'Harry Ploughman', the companion piece to 'Tom's Garland', Hopkins said that he 'wanted the coda for a sonnet which is in some sort "nello stilo satirico o bernesco"', i.e. in the burlesque satirical style, after the manner of the early sixteenth century Italian poet Francesco Berni, known for his comic and satirical attacks on individuals written in the form of the caudate sonnet. Hopkins added, 'It has a kind of rollic at all events'.[50]

The noun 'rollic' appears to be derived from the verb 'to rollick', 'to frolic, sport, or romp, in a joyous, careless fashion', a dialect word, introduced into polite letters early in the nineteenth century. This verb and its noun and adjective were employed, throughout the century, by a bevy of second-order humourists, notably in the magazines, *Blackwood's Magazine, Pall Mall Gazette, Macmillan's Magazine, Fraser's Magazine, The Saturday Review*.[51] An equally significant word applied by Hopkins to 'Tom's Garland' itself as well as to 'Harry Ploughman' is 'robustious'. The *Oxford English Dictionary* states that it was in 'common use during the 17th century. In the 18th it becomes rare, and is described by Johnson (1755) as "now only used in low language, and in a sense of contempt". During the 19th it has been considerably revived, esp. by archaizing writers'.[52] Both 'rollick' and 'robustious' are more appropriate to Hopkins's own gloss on 'Tom's Garland' (provided in his letter of 10 February 1888 to Bridges) than they are to the sonnet itself, which he finally described, in the same letter, as being 'very pregnant... and in point of execution very highly wrought. Too much so, I am afraid'.[53]

In principle we ought not to object to a sonnet being simultaneously 'robustious' and 'very highly wrought'. Both terms combine well to describe the vernacular artifice of Milton's political sonnets. In principle again, such a combination could, in Hopkins's case, relate closely to one of his sharpest creative realizations: the relation of ' monumentality' to 'bidding'. 'Bidding' is Hopkins's term for 'the art or virtue of saying everything right *to* or *at* the hearer... and of discarding everything that does not bid, does not tell'. Hopkins goes on to make one of his most penetrating observations: 'It is most difficult to combine this bidding, such a fugitive thing, with a monumental style'.[54] It is the key to what is right and wrong in his own poetic method; to what is strong and weak in Keats's poems of 1819–20 ('To Autumn', the unfinished 'Hyperion'); and to what, in Wordsworth or Tennyson, strikes us as noble simplicity rather than mere verbosity or canting. It allows us to realize the very different factors which assure, on the one hand, the triumph of Whitman's 'Song of Myself' and the more limited but real success of Wilfred Owen's half-rhyme and para-rhyme in his ode 'Insensibility'. Whitman knows that if he can say the objective details 'right *to* or *at* the hearer', over a sufficiently long span, the bidding will transform itself into its own form of monumentality. Owen recognizes that he can at one and the same time annul and confirm our expectations of customary monumentality:

> But cursed are dullards whom no cannon stuns,
> That they should be as stones.[55]

And he further recognizes that half-rhyme, which sustains order and expectation while maintaining its scepticism of them, also draws bidding power into the extremities of the lines. The genius of Hopkins's own late poetry – 'That Nature is a Heraclitean Fire and of the comfort of the Resurrection', 'Thou art indeed just, Lord...' – is itself a structural compounding of bidding with monumentality: 'Mine, O thou lord of life, send my roots rain'.[56]

If civil polity is poetry's natural habitat, there are implications for such poems as 'Tom's Garland', which is markedly political and which, by the final line, has revealed itself as one of the most grotesquely unnatural of nineteenth-century poems. There is a natural explanation for this, but this in itself is part of the problem. 'Tom's Garland' is grotesque as Carlyle in 'Shooting Niagara' is grotesque or as Ruskin is in *The Storm Cloud of the Nineteenth Century.* Ong suggests that 'Hopkins, like Newman, had very little if any of the defensiveness which betrays intellectual insecurity and freezes the mind'.[57] But Hopkins is *not* like Newman, and 'Tom's Garland' is rigid with 'intellectual insecurity', or insecure intellectualism, in every line. Hopkins's own description of Scotus's disrelation to his age – 'a kind of feud arose between genius and talent',[58] the genius being Scotus, the talent that of his detractors – is more intimately and painfully true of Emerson and Carlyle. The feud between genius and talent took place within themselves, and the talent was closely attached to projections and self-projections of civic alienation. Alienation – thrown-ness – is real and deadly, but Carlyle is not thrown by any aspect of civil polity and Emerson is brutally thrown by polity perhaps only once, in the passing of the Massachusetts Fugitive Slave Law of 1851. Civil polity, in the form of Emerson's 'communities of opinion',[59] is sufficiently alienating, simply in and of itself, as Emily Dickinson clearly perceived; you do not need to adopt alienated attitudes to excite its attention. Alienated majesty signifies a reality, however, even if not an actuality. In this it resembles intrinsic value with which it has an oblique interrelationship; a direct link, even, in Emerson's essay 'Self-Reliance'. Alienated majesty is tied by a law of opposites to a variety of Emersonian positives – 'transcendent destiny', 'the integrity of your own mind', 'intrinsic right', 'the independence of solitude',[60] 'inscrutable possibilities', 'the great and crescive self, rooted in absolute nature',[61] 'the essence of genius'.[62]

It is appropriate to end with a confusion of this term 'genius', at once a word of Romantic elitism and one of the most democratic of attributes. That the word can be associated with democracy is due, in no small part, to the work of Emerson, Whitman, and Hopkins. Democratic does not mean egalitarian. In Whitman's words, 'Great genius and the people of these states must never be demeaned to romances';[63] as Emerson writes, 'Genius is power; Talent is applicability'.[64] Emerson again, 'The great genius returns to essential man.'[65] Devlin observes of Hopkins that his 'view of genius (at least of poetic genius) was that it was a seeming approach to being a whole specific nature, "so that each poet is like a species in nature and can never recur"'.[66] The issue is held in common by the three writers: it is the endeavour to conceive a uniting of individual genius to the genius of the commonwealth. In the fourth of the sermons preached by Hopkins at St Joseph's, Bedford Leigh (23 November 1879), the Christ presented to us is one who 'by acts of his own human genius' founded 'this Catholic Church…its ranks and constitution, its rites and sacraments'.[67] It will be objected that a hierarchical institution cannot be democratic, but what it cannot be, in the world's terms, is egalitarian, even though it teaches equality before God. It may be further objected that these are exactly the terms on which Hopkins must be sharply differentiated from Emerson and Whitman. The burden of these three chapters has been to find that objection unsustainable, insofar as all three writers know democracy to be alienated from its proper majesty by the egalitarian and the mean.

Hopkins writes in his journal of 1872, 'I thought how sadly beauty of inscape was unknown and buried away from simple people and yet how near at hand it was if they had eyes to see it and it could be called out everywhere again'.[68] In such a passage, he unites one of his most essential terms, 'inscape', with civil polity. He is perhaps like Wordsworth and surely like Ruskin, a Tory democrat. I do not believe, however, that he would have quarrelled with Whitman – a democrat but no Tory – when he claimed, of American poets wedded to the American nation, 'of them a bard is to be commensurate with a people'.[69]

Notes

1 'Alienated Majesty: Ralph W. Emerson' and 'Alienated Majesty: Walt Whitman', precede this chapter on Hopkins in Hill's *Collected Critical Writings*, ed. Kenneth Haynes (Oxford, Oxford University Press, 2008).

2 Ralph W. Emerson, *Essays and Lectures*, ed. Joel Porte (New York: Viking, 1983), p. 259 ('Self-Reliance'); cf. *Collected Works of Ralph Waldo Emerson*, 6 vols. to date (Cambridge, MA: Belknap Press, 1971–), vol. 2, p. 27.

3 Walt Whitman, *Complete Poetry and Collected Prose*, ed. Justin Kaplan (New York: Viking, 1982), p. 933; cf. Walt Whitman, *Prose Works (1892)*, 2 vols., ed. Floyd Stovall (New York: New York University Press, 1963–4), vol. 2, p. 366.

4 *The Spiritual Exercises of St. Ignatius*, tr. Anthony Mottola (Garden City, NJ: Image Books, 1964), p. 67.

5 Gerard M. Hopkins, 'The Windhover', ll. 1–2; cf. *The Poetical Works of Gerard Manley Hopkins*, ed. Norman H. MacKenzie (Oxford: Oxford University Press, 1990), p. 144.

6 Gerard M. Hopkins, *The Letters of Gerard Manley Hopkins to Robert Bridges*, ed. Claude Colleer Abbott, rev. impression (London: Oxford University Press, 1955), p. 92 (8 Oct. 1879).

7 Whitman, *Complete Poetry and Collected Prose*, p. 887 (*Specimen Days*); cf. Whitman, *Prose Works (1892)*, vol. 1, p. 250.

8 Hopkins, *Letters to Bridges*, pp. 267–8 (6 Nov. 1887).

9   Whitman, *Complete Poetry and Collected Prose*, p. 959; cf. Whitman, *Prose Works (1892)*, vol. 2, p. 393.

10 Walt Whitman, *The Journalism*, 2 vols., ed. Herbert Bergman et al. (New York: P. Lang, 1998–2003), vol. 1, p. 463; cf. Walt Whitman, *The Gathering of the Forces*, 2 vols., ed. Cleveland Rodgers and John Black (New York: G. P. Putnam's Sons, 1920), vol. 2, pp. 243–4.

11 Hopkins, *Letters to Bridges*, p. 275 (25 May 1888).

12 Gerard M. Hopkins, *The Correspondence of Gerard Manley Hopkins and Richard Watson Dixon*, ed. Claude Colleer Abbott (London: Oxford University Press, 1955), p. 74 (12 Oct. 1881).

13 Whitman, 'Song of Myself', l. 1333 (section 52); cf. *Complete Poetry and Collected Prose*, p. 247 and Walt Whitman, *Leaves of Grass: A Textual Variorum of the Printed Poems*, 3 vols., ed. Sculley Bradley et al. (New York: New York University Press, 1980), vol. 1, p. 82.

14 See James Wright, 'The Delicacy of Walt Whitman', *Collected Prose*, ed. Anne Wright (Ann Arbor, MI: University of Michigan Press, 1983), pp. 3–22.

15 Hopkins, *Letters to Bridges*, p. 155 (18 Oct. 1882).

16 Hopkins, *Correspondence of Hopkins and Dixon*, p. 14 (5 Oct. 1878).

17 Ignatius of Loyola, *Spiritual Exercises*, pp. 83–4.

18 Emerson, *Essays and Lectures*, p. 482; cf. *Collected Works*, vol. 3, p. 38.

19 MacKenzie in Hopkins, *Poetical Works*, p. 320.

20 Hopkins, *Correspondence of Hopkins and Dixon*, p. 14 (5 Oct. 1878).

21 Hopkins, 'The Windhover', ll. 7–8 ('My heart in hiding | Stirred for a bird'); cf. *Poetical Works*, p. 144.

22 MacKenzie in Hopkins, *Poetical Works*, p. 270.

23 MacKenzie in Hopkins, *Poetical Works*, p. 282.

24 Hopkins, *Correspondence of Hopkins and Dixon*, pp. 8–9 (13 June 1878).

25 Josiah Royce, *William James and Other Essays on the Philosophy of Life* (New York: Macmillan, 1969), p. 52 (repr. of 1911 edn.).

26 Whitman, 'The Artilleryman's Vision', l. 9; cf. *Complete Poetry and Collected Prose*, p. 450 and *Leaves of Grass*, vol. 2, p. 506.

27 Whitman, 'I Saw Old General at Bay', l. 4; cf. *Complete Poetry and Collected Prose*, p. 450 and *Leaves of Grass*, vol. 2, p. 521.

28 Whitman, 'A March in the Ranks Hard-Prest, and the Road Unknown', l. 14; cf. *Complete Poetry and Collected Prose*, p. 440 and *Leaves of Grass*, vol. 2, p. 494.

29 Whitman, 'A March in the Ranks Hard-Prest, and the Road Unknown', l. 7; cf. *Complete Poetry and Collected Prose*, p. 440 and *Leaves of Grass*, vol. 2, p. 494.

30 Whitman, 'How Solemn as One by One', l. 7; cf. *Complete Poetry and Collected Prose*, p. 454 and *Leaves of Grass*, vol. 2, p. 554.

31 Whitman, 'A March in the Ranks Hard-Prest, and the Road Unknown', l. 19; cf. *Complete Poetry and Collected Prose*, p. 440 and *Leaves of Grass*, vol. 2, p. 494.

32 Whitman, 'As Toilsome I Wander'd Virginia's Woods', ll. 11–12; cf. *Complete Poetry and Collected Prose*, p. 442 and *Leaves of Grass*, vol. 2, p. 510.

33 Whitman, *Complete Poetry and Collected Prose* 946; cf. Whitman, *Prose Works (1892)*, vol. 2, p. 379.

34 Whitman, *Complete Poetry and Collected Prose*, pp. 974–5; cf. Whitman, *Prose Works (1892)*, vol. 2, p. 408.

35 Hopkins, *Letters to Bridges*, p. 86.

36 Hopkins, *Letters to Bridges*, p. 131.

37 Hopkins, *Correspondence, of Hopkins and Dixon*, p. 97.

38 Christopher Devlin, in *The Sermons and Devotional Writings of Gerard Manley Hopkins*, ed. Christopher Devlin (London: Oxford University Press, 1959), p. 340.

39 Devlin in Hopkins, *Sermons and Devotional Writings*, p. 109.

40 Devlin in Hopkins, *Sermons and Devotional Writings*, p. 296.

41 Hopkins, *Sermons and Devotional Writings*, p. 59.

42 ibid.

43 Hopkins, *Letters to Bridges*, p. 135 (16 Sept. 1881).

44 Hopkins, *Correspondence of Hopkins and Dixon*, p. 76 (23 Oct. 1881).

45 Hopkins, *Letters to Bridges*, p. 136 (16 Sept. 1881).

46 Hopkins, *Letters to Bridges*, pp. 272–3 (10 Feb. 1888).

47 Samuel Taylor Coleridge, *Collected Works*, 16 vols. (Princeton, NJ: Princeton University Press, 1969–2002), vol. 4, part 1, p. 21 (*The Friend*, ed. Barbara E. Rooke, 2 parts).

48 Walter J. Ong, *Hopkins, the Self, and God* (Toronto: University of Toronto Press, 1986), p. 90.

49 MacKenzie in Hopkins, *Poetical Works*, p. 485.

50 Hopkins, *Letters to Bridges*, p. 266 (6 Nov. 1887).

51 s.v. 'rollick, *v.*', *OED*[2]. The citations to the magazines are found in this entry and under 'rollick, *n.*'

52 Hopkins, *Correspondence of Hopkins and Dixon*, p. 153 (2 Dec. 1887). , s.v. 'robustious', *OED*[2.]

53 Hopkins, *Letters to Bridges*, p. 274 (10 Feb. 1888).

54 Hopkins, *Letters to Bridges*, p. 160 (4 Nov. 1882).

55 Wilfred Owen, 'Insensibility', ll. 50–1; cf. *The Poems of Wilfred Owen*, ed. Jon Stallworthy (New York: Norton, 1986), p. 123.

56 Hopkins, 'Thou art indeed just, Lord…', l. 14; cf. *Poetical Works of Gerard Manley Hopkins*, p. 201.

57 Ong, *Hopkins, the Self, and Cod*, p. 92.

58 Gerard M. Hopkins, *Further Letters of Gerard Manley Hopkins*, ed. Claude Colleer Abbott, 2nd edn. (London: Oxford University Press, 1956). p. 349 (letter to Coventry Patmore, 3 Jan. 1884).

59 Emerson, *Essays and Lectures*, p. 264 ('Self-Reliance'); cf. *Collected Works*, vol. 2, p. 32.

60 Emerson, *Essays and Lectures*, p. 260, 261, 263 ('Self-Reliance'); cf. *Collected Works*, vol. 2, p. 28, 31, 230.
61 'inscrutable possibilities': Emerson, *Essays and Lectures*, p. 475, 487 ('Experience'); cf. *Collected Works*, vol. 3, p. 32, 44.
62 Emerson, *Essays and Lectures*, p. 269 ('Self-Reliance'); cf. *Collected Works*, vol. 2, p. 37.
63 Whitman, *Complete Poetry and Collected Prose*, p. 19; Whitman, *Prose Works* (1892), vol. 2, p. 451.
64 *Emerson in His Journals*, ed. Joel Porte (Cambridge, MA: Belknap, 1982), p. 304 (Mar.–Apr. 1843); cf. Ralph W. Emerson, *Journals and Miscellaneous Notebooks*, 16 vols., ed. William H. Gilman et al. (Cambridge, MA: Belknap, 1960–82), vol. 8, p. 373.
65 Emerson, *Essays and Lectures*, p. 280 ('Self-Reliance'); cf. *Collected Works*, vol. 2, p. 49.
66 Devlin in Hopkins, *Sermons and Devotional Writings*, p. 278.
67 Hopkins, *Sermons and Devotional Writings*, p. 37.
68 Gerard M. Hopkins, *The Journals and Papers of Gerard Manley Hopkins*, ed. Humphry House and Graham Storey (London: Oxford University Press, 1959), p. 221.
69 Whitman, *Complete Poetry and Collected Prose* 7 ('Preface' to *Leaves of Grass* [1855]); cf. *Prose Works (1892)*, vol. 2, p. 741.

9

Fact and Tact
Arnoldian Fact-finding and Q Tactlessness in the Reading of Gerard Hopkins

Valentine Cunningham

The great scholar-critic-editor F. W. Bateson keenly followed Mathew Arnold in linking critical judgement with valuation – distinguishing the 'best' from the rest, seeing aesthetic judgement as necessarily involving moral and social assessment, ideological and political consideration. 'Value is also fact'. Importantly, his repeated nagging at 'The Mode of Existence of a Literary Work of Art' involved asking what 'constraints' – 'conventions, traditions, and assumptions' (Bateson's global term was 'contexts') were 'imposed by the text'; and so attempting 'to put theoretical limits on interpretation'. Imposing such limits, the formidable theorist René Wellek agreed, was 'surely one of the most urgent problems of literary study today'.[1] [...]

For help in determining critical limits – and, I should say, with instructive force for all critical practitioners – Bateson kept renewing his own and his readers' acquaintance with 'that remarkable passage' at the end of Matthew Arnold's 'The Function of Criticism at the Present Time' where Arnold speaks of knowing and judging, and applying now fresh knowledge to the literary object, now invoking principles in treating it, all in the quest for truth about the scrutinised work:

> The English critic of literature…must dwell much on foreign thought, and with particular heed on any part of it, which, while significant and fruitful in itself, is for any reason specially likely to escape him. Again, judging is often spoken of as the critic's one business, and so in some

Cunningham, Valentine. 2000. "Fact and Tact: post-Arnoldian Fact-Finding and Modern Q Tactlessness in the Reading of Gerard Hopkins." In *Essays in Criticism*, 51, I (January), pp. 119–38. Reproduced with permission of Oxford University Press.

Victorian Poets: A Critical Reader, First Edition. Edited by Valentine Cunningham.
© 2014 John Wiley & Sons, Ltd. Published 2014 by John Wiley & Sons, Ltd.

sense it is; but the judgement which almost insensibly forms itself in a fair and clear mind, along with fresh knowledge, is the valuable one; and thus knowledge, and ever fresh knowledge, must be the critic's great concern for himself. And it is by communicating fresh knowledge, and letting his own judgement pass along with it – but insensibly, and in the second place, not the first, as a sort of companion and clue, not as an abstract lawgiver – that the critic will generally do most good to his readers. Sometimes, no doubt, for the sake of establishing an author's place in literature, and his relation to a central standard (and if this is not done, how are we to get at our *best in the world?*) criticism may have to deal with a subject-matter so familiar that fresh knowledge is out of the question, and then it must be all judgement: an enunciation and detailed application of principles. Here the great safeguard is never to let oneself become abstract, always to retain an intimate and lively consciousness of the truth of what one is saying, and, the moment this fails us, to be sure that something is wrong. Still, under all circumstances, this mere judgement and application of principles is, in itself, not the most satisfactory work to the critic; like mathematics, it is tautological, and cannot well give us, like fresh learning, the sense of creative activity.[2]

It's a recipe, of course, against critical parochialism, against maintaining narrow approaches to what is envisaged as expanding textual signification, in keeping with the Europeanism of much of the nineteenth century's best criticism – the Germanism of Carlyle and George Eliot, Arnold's own Francophilia. Arnold is clearly saddened when texts prove incapable of being freshened by new readings. He craves the critical creativity of constant renovation. This creative reading is highly moral. The critic and the criticism are to be fairminded. The critic is to speak the truth. The critic is a person with principles: principles in the fullest sense, it would appear, moral ones intussuscepted by aesthetic ones, in a radical convergence of the moral and aesthetic impossible to unpick, where *fairness* (as here) and *sincerity* (a few lines later in the essay) – key components one would guess in the famous *disinterestedness* which is repeatedly invoked in the essay – denote a moralised critical disposition (the critic's person) and a moralised critical practice (the critic's readings). It's a headily enticing mix, cognate with Arnold's notion of literature's intrinsic goodness and the goodness it does readers and cultures: at their best these goods are all at once both aesthetic and moral. And the critic's goal is to 'do most good to his readers', which means 'he' comes armed with principles, rather than with theories. The critic is no abstract lawgiver. 'The great safeguard is never to let oneself become abstract.' So this is a set of theoretical statements giving critical preeminence to things not theoretical; it's a programme for an eminently practical criticism, for an empirical moral-aesthetic work to be performed on knowable textual items – Arnold's famous seeing 'the object as in itself it really is'. It's a work of judging; of weighing moral-social-aesthetic merit; of striving 'to get at our *best in the world*' ('I am bound', he says a little later, 'by my own definition of criticism: *a disinterested endeavour to learn and propagate the best that is known and thought in the world*'); and so, in the end, a canon-forming work ('establishing an author's place in literature'). But coming to a 'valuable' judgement is dependent upon knowledge. Valuable judgements will arise as an 'almost insensible' consequence of applying 'fresh knowledge': 'knowledge, and ever fresh knowledge, must be the critic's great concern for himself. Criticism, Arnold summarises in his essay's penultimate paragraph, 'must be sincere, simple, flexible, ardent, ever widening its knowledge'. The world is big, phenomena are plentiful, the present is 'copious and complex', a 'vast multitude of facts awaiting and inviting...comprehension' (as he put it in 'On the Modern Element in Literature'); critics can never know enough; and texts are knowable objects participating in this great copiousness. So the knowing of literary objects not only allows for the bringing up of new knowledge; it relies on it.

What Arnold holds out is an exhilarating, if rather daunting, intersubjective (to use a favourite Bateson word) contract between reader and text. It's a vision of 'The Function of Criticism at the Present Time' drawn animatedly into Bateson's own early announcement of 'The Function of Criticism'. It would be central to the practices of the Arnoldianly titled Bateson journal *Essays in Criticism*, which contained that manifesto in 1953. It's a vision Bateson found endorsed in T. S. Eliot's own Arnold-tribute essay also entitled 'The Function of Criticism', and which Bateson is in turn endorsing, and endorsing not least Eliot's very Arnoldian declaration that the 'most important qualification' for critical work 'is that a critic must have a very highly developed sense of fact'.[3] Bateson's title for the lead-chapter of his book *The Scholar-Critic* was 'The Sense of Fact'. The run, the line, of inheritance and tradition was being made clear. And it's furthered by one of Bateson's starriest Oxford disciples, Christopher Ricks, also an editor of *Essays in Criticism*, in his explicit advocacy in his essay 'Literature and the Matter of Fact' of criticism as an Arnold-Eliot-Batesonian matter of principled empiricism engaging with factuality and factual truth-telling and factual truth-seeking on the part of both texts and readers.[4]

[...]

Of course the nature of Arnold's literary 'object' and the 'knowledge' we're to bring to it – what Eliot and Bateson and Ricks call 'fact' – needed some close specifying. And they got it. Bateson, the textual critic, the editor and general editor of texts, well knew the flexible force of the textual crux and the critical ponderability of the necessary emendation. [...] But such an empirical and principled recognition of potentials for textual differences and variances scarcely sustains a theory of textual imponderability. The huge range of variant readings in the textual object known as *Hamlet* does not make it less present as an object for reading, but rather makes it more present, gives the more substance for the critical dredger to get its teeth into. And textual variants come high up Bateson's list of Arnoldian facts. He talked of 'the honourable department of external evidence known as textual criticism'. This was in a large consideration of Arnoldian and Eliotic fact, the article entitled 'Shakespeare's Laundry Bills: The Rationale of External Evidence' (what value Shakespeare's laundry bills might have was, of course, first raised in Eliot's 'The Function of Criticism').[5] External evidence and critically applicable 'fact' comprised for Bateson a very wide field. It embraced all the contextual materials which were and are the concerns of traditional literary scholarship – historical, social, biographical evidence, data from all the various modalities of the modes of production of the literary work, all 'the ancillary disciplines provided by scholarship'. As Wellek had nervously noted, even value was for Bateson 'fact'.

And facts were needed precisely as controls. They would work as a preventive to 'neurotic critical fantasy', as the grounds of objectivity in the intersubjective relation between reader and text, a prophylactic against any wilfully free play with signifiers.[6] But there was an obvious rub in the Arnold-Eliot enthusiasm for fact and more fact: how to judge, to value, the facts the critic wished to adduce, how to tell a good fact from a bad, how in fact to test relevance (Eliot's 'fact' needed, Bateson said, restatement as *'relevant fact'*[7]). How to stop a boundlessness of factuality which might in practice turn out to be not distinguishable enough from a dubious postmodern vision of utter textual boundlessness.

Arnold seems to assume that the classically trained gentleman reader will simply know about which bits of 'fresh knowledge' will be truly refreshing: he'll have the right touchstones, the appropriate touch for what's relevant, by dint of being born into the right cultural group and being exposed to the right kind of Oxonian training. T. S. Eliot is vague, too, though you can tell his critical wind is blowing from more or less the same quarter as Arnold's. A 'highly developed sense of fact' is, he says, 'by no means a trifling or frequent gift. And it is not one which easily wins popular commendations. The sense of fact is something very slow to develop, and its complete development means perhaps the very pinnacle of civilisation. For there are so many spheres of fact to be mastered, and our outermost sphere of fact, of knowledge, of control, will be ringed with narcotic fancies in the sphere beyond'.[8] Bateson rejected Eliot's 'unsavoury class consciousness' and 'sheer snobbery',[9] and was certainly not one for approving the Winchester–Oxford version of the best pathways in education as they are plainly set out in Eliot's *Notes Towards the Definition of Culture* (1948). But still he can only invoke 'the more responsible approach of the sensitive adult' – as opposed to 'adolescent literary enthusiasm'.

The responsibility and sensitivity of the mature reader. Responsible and sensitive, or as Christopher Ricks's reformulation of this cautionary principle restates it: principled and tactful. 'My enterprise', says Ricks – the one of respecting 'The Matter of Fact' – 'is partly an argument, partly a plea. I need to add that I don't consider this matter, in my handling of it, to be one of theory but rather of principle and tact'. They mean well, these guiding terms; and one can see clearly enough their point as guides to good practice; but they aren't terribly hard-edged. You can see them letting in more scope for readings and excuses for readings than their proponents would always like. They're all terms with a certain unbuttoning subjectivity about them. Indeed Ricks goes on to say that 'I should myself be grateful for a disinterested theoretical – better still philosophical – exploration of the whole business'.[10] But as this group of critical guidelines stands – knowledge/ fact brought to bear on textual objects, tested for relevance on the basis of responsibility and sensitivity or principledness and tact – they certainly have their distinct uses in helping chart and steer criticism through the murky waters of reading, in practice, as well as in theory.

Take the fate of Gerard Manley Hopkins's poem 'Felix Randal'. It's an example which springs instantly to mind when there's any suggestion of how 'fresh knowledge' can change (and change at a stroke) the meaning and the reception – the intersubjective existence, as Bateson would put it – of a literary text. It's an example, too, which, because of its now central place in Queer Studies, that busy branch of 'theoretical' enterprise, not only takes us right up to the place where distinctions between critical theory and principle cry out to be made (an opposition more or less explicit in the Arnold passage, and one made very explicit in Ricks's engagement with the matter of factuality'[11]), but which also raises most prominently – as the many highly ideological post-Foucauldian reading practices which involve political 'outing' of various sorts tend to – issues very much of relevance, responsibility, sensitivity and tact.

Thinking about possibilities and limits for critical practice in relation to 'Felix Randal' is not least attractive because a reading of it once appeared, and in the way of many a confident, and would-be finalising, reading from the mid twentieth century, under the heading 'The Meaning of a Poem'. This claim on *the* meaning came from Bateson's distinguished literary contemporary George Orwell. [...] 'The Meaning of a Poem' was a talk produced in the India Section of the BBC in which William Empson also worked, beamed to India on 14 May 1941, and printed in *The Listener*, 12 June 1941.[12] It's not at all bad, for its time, which is to say given the state of knowledge in 1941 about Hopkins and his poem and the audience to which it was originally broadcast.

As every commentator has been, Orwell is specially drawn to the word for the horseshoe the dead farrier Felix Randal once 'fettled' – 'Didst fettle for that great grey drayhorse his bright and battering sandal'. *Sandal* is heralded as a very happy accident of rhyming, *Randal* leading to *sandal*. (It never occurs to Orwell, nor indeed to anyone else, that the verbal progression might have been the other way around and that Hopkins could have chosen the name Randal because he wanted to get the metaphoric sandal in.) Very nicely, Orwell points out that sandals mean differently in India than in Britain: 'I ought to perhaps add that the word "sandal" is more impressive to an English reader than it would be to an oriental, who sees sandals every day and perhaps wears them himself. To us a sandal is an exotic thing, chiefly associated with the ancient Greeks and Romans. When Hopkins describes the cart-horse's shoe as a sandal, he suddenly converts the cart-horse into a magnificent mythical beast, something like a heraldic animal.' This is well said, and a fine recognition of readerly context, a most tactful approach by the Englishman with Burmese experience to differences of knowledge among different implicit readers. It is not the last word on contexts for sandals, however. The atheist Orwell is immune to many of the poem's Christian contexts (not all, but many), and so has not thought of the sandals worn by religious in the Catholic tradition, nor of Jesus's sandals, whose latchet John the Baptist felt unworthy to unloose – knowledge about sandals which a Christian reader might have thought of in the very first place, and which later readers would vigorously invoke, before thinking of eastern sandals (middle-eastern, so to say, before eastern). But Orwell's adduced acquaintance with Burmese and Indian sandals and sandalwearers does add to everyone's knowledge, as well as clearing things up specifically for Indians. And Orwell is not bad either on other bits of verbal knowledge. He's looked up the priestly narrator's words *fettle* and *road* ('Ah well, God rest him all road ever he offended') and found they're old (Saxon, pre-Chaucerian) and dialectal. Orwell knows Hopkins made 'technical studies' of 'the old Saxon poets', and here are results from that interest. Applied to Randal's case they suggest old, pastoral, rural activity. It's a view Orwell applies with vigour. The smith becomes a rural black-smith; encountering *farrier* and *forge* as well as *fettle* has evidently brought old poetic associations with village smithies under spreading chestnut trees springing to mind. And the knowledge brings other contextualities crowding in. Felix Randal becomes 'a man living at a particular moment of time, the latter part of the nineteenth century, when the old English agricultural way of life – the old Saxon village community – was finally passing away'. 'The special power' Hopkins 'has of re-creating the atmosphere of an English village would not belong to him if it were not for the purely technical studies he had made made, earlier in his life, of the old Saxon poets.' Orwell's accumulating critical wisdoms, built on the Arnoldian accrual of knowledge, on a great respect for the Eliotic sense of fact, remained, more or less, the story of Felix Randal for some years afterwards. Orwell did not get on to *random* (*random grim forge*) as a technical or trade term meaning built of rough and irregular stones – that would have to wait until W. H. Gardner's curiosity about an adjective which looks regular enough took him to the dictionary where the regular usage suddenly looked most irregular. This piece of knowledge, a fact, which Gardner's third edition of Bridges's collection of Hopkins's poems (1948) made public, straightaway transformed the sense of Felix Randal's character greatly, if not utterly: most readings since 1948 have wanted to keep the regular sense of random alongside the irregular one, to invoke ambivalence, and so to go on talking about Randal's insouciance, his randomness of spirit ('wild and random hardiness': Paul L. Mariani; 'noisy and almost wild enjoyment of life...part of the whole scene – the forge built of random or rough stone': J. R. Watson[13]). And so perhaps they should.

But if post-Orwellian readers pondered the difference Gardner's dis-covery about *random* made, it would only be to afforce Orwell's sense of an old-fashioned tradesman, and not unsettle the rural scenario he'd built. At least, there was still no suggestion that the poem, which was well enough known to have been written in Liverpool during Hopkins's vexed period at St Francis Xavier's, Salisbury Street, in one of industrial England's greatest cities, actually featured a hero from the big city. In 1959 Christopher Devlin boldly declared that Hopkins 'experienced *Felix Randal*' at Bedford Leigh, the small Lancashire manufacturing town with that odd Victorian blend of mill and mine and adjacent fields, where he worked before going on to Liverpool. 'The poem was written in Apr. 1880; but the events described seem to have taken place' some months earlier, when Hopkins was at Bedford Leigh.[14] Paul Mariani, a mighty man for dictionary facts (*randal*, he found out, is an Anglo-Saxon word meaning shield and so reaches out to the sacramental protection the priest in the poem offers his parishioner; *rand* is a strip of leather used in the making of shoes; *randall* is an obsolete variant on *random* meaning a gallop or a disorderly life; so 'Felix's boisterous, random life is given direction by the viaticum, metamorphosing randal to "bright and battering sandal"', which makes one wonder about sensitivity and tact in the applying of 'fact') – Mariani worries over the Bedford Leigh assumption about a poem patently written in Liverpool. The facts of dating and place of composition bother him enough to make him argue the point: 'The tone of the first line of the poem strongly suggests that Hopkins had learned the news of the blacksmith's death at second hand, as if he had ministered to him for a while, then had not heard from or of him, and only afterwards heard of his death. This suggests that the blacksmith was not from Liverpool, where Hopkins had been stationed for less than four months when the poem was written, but was rather from Bedford Leigh'.[15]

But all this, all based upon resorts to facts, or to such facts as existed at the time, simply fell into irrelevance when in 1973 in the *TLS* Alfred Thomas reported the existence, and the death on 21 April 1880, seven days before Hopkins wrote his poem, of the Liverpool farrier Felix Spence, aged 31, a parishioner of Hopkins who lived at 17 Birchfield Street, was ministered to by Hopkins in his illness, whose death was entered in the St Francis Xavier parish register by Hopkins, and whose name was read out in the church on Sunday 25 April among those who had recently deceased. The *TLS* piece reproduces a copy of the death certificate from the General Register Office at Somerset House in London, and one of the parish register for 25 April, the Fourth Sunday after Easter, in Hopkins's hand.[16] There's no doubt that Felix Spence is Hopkins's Felix Randal. Here, emphatically is knowledge, fresh knowledge, matter of fact, and critically relevant fact, all of it instantly changing our sense of the poem, clearing away Orwell's carefully constructed house of rural cards and the Bedford Leigh school. So much for the temerity of claiming 'The Meaning' of this poem as if for evermore.

Alfred Thomas, the factual bit now firmly between his teeth, had much more of would-be factual interest to offer. The name Randal, he suggests in the same *TLS* article, was probably suggested to Hopkins by two Roman Catholics he knew of, the renowned English Jesuit Randal Lythgoe, and the 'genial' local Lancastrian Randal Lightbound. Mariani had already hit on Randal Lightbound (he's mentioned in Hopkins's correspondence);[17] Father Lythgoe was all Alfred Thomas's own work. Facts, again, and by no means irrelevant offerings, but not possessing the utterly refreshing impact of the unearthing of Felix Spence. Less valuable facts, Arnold might say.

But just to endorse Arnold's expectation that fresh knowledge would succeed fresh knowledge, it has to be observed that this wonderful Felix Spence *trouvaille* would not be the last word on the poem. Indeed this discovery of a real proletarian male model for the poem's subject can be seen as actually helping criticism keep on going in its ever renewing expectations. Here, for instance, was a new light, or sidelight, on Hopkins's well recognised use of colloquialisms in 'Felix Randal' and more generally in his poetry. This poem's resort to non-educated turns of speech could now be read as implying a lot more than before about the sort of real contacts – male, proley, desired, feared – behind Hopkins's use of such ordinary speech registers. Eric Griffiths's fine sense of how Hopkins used the 'colloquially familiar' in his poems, 'the grind of colloquial against religious idiom', acquires a quiet but distinctly real, as opposed to a merely invented or fantasy, frame with the arrival of Felix Spence on the scene.[18] And so does the great interest Queer theorists have taken in Hopkins's dealings with male subjects.

What's especially of interest here is how so much of what is offered as 'theoretical' or theorised reading – neo-historicism, post-colonialism, feminism, Q Studies, *et si qua alia* – owes far more to the sense of fact than any instigation from what can be really labelled as theory. Queer Studies, and Colonialism, and Feminism involve, of course, like Bateson's Value, fact. Which is ironic enough, given the historical tendency of literary 'theorists' to despise mere facts, and deplore the Arnoldianism they signify, as belonging to a mere and too humble-minded empiricism. But unsurprisingly, what's greatly apparent from inspections of readings coming under such headings is how greatly they stand in need of the principled checks of sensitivity and tact – the proper checks of openly factual critical business. If the Felix Spence story is a parable of how fresh knowledge makes all the difference in reading a text, the Queer readings of 'Felix Randal' amount to a parable or allegory of just how necessary is tact – sensitivity of critical touch – in handling the facts and the fresh political perspectives on those facts which the new Foucauldianised criticalisms are anxious to trade in. And this latter is a most piquant parable, too, because 'Felix Randal' is so much about tactility.

Joseph Bristow is rather expert, in his influential article of 1992 on 'Hopkins and the Working-Class Male Body',[19] at digging out fresh knowledge, but he's less good at making it relevant. With an eye on the bright and battering sandal, he begins with Hopkins's January 1888 'Retreat Notes' about John the Baptist feeling unworthy to undo Jesus's 'shoe latchet' – a meditation on John as expert in middle-eastern sandals ('I know the difference between a light sandal and the soldier's heavy *caliga*'), on Jesus as being 'as well-shod as a traveller, soldier on the march, or farm-labourer in the forest', and on Christ in his big footwear (a man sporting, by implication, the imperial soldierly military *caliga*, no lame wearer of a *caligula*, or little boot, he), his heavy tread able to 'grind hearts to powder'. This parallel passage from the notebooks is illuminating fresh knowledge (I haven't found anyone else using it). But it's not made really relevant, as it might be, to 'Felix Randal', being left hanging in the air of a general inspection of weedy Hopkins's liking for huge proletarian males and of a 'masculine poetics' in which various 'stresses' converge: aesthetic (poems made up of stresses), religious (God the Jesuit's trampling master), and homosexual (Hopkins's masterful-submissive relations with big parishioners and men off the street). There's much apparent truth in this general account of Hopkins's work and imagination, but it entails some weird mistakings and strange constructions in reading 'Felix Randal'. This labourer, we're told, 'could be seen "battering" out horseshoes'; but he couldn't: the battering is done by the great horse's horseshoes, not by their farrier. And fettling is a matter of smaller blows. 'Even though on the brink of death, the farrier, not the priest, stands out here as an emblem of power'. But, actually, it's the horse, as much as if not more so than the farrier, who is the powerful one ('great gray...battering'); the horse drives on out of the poem, leaving the dead smith behind; and the priest comes nowhere in the big body contest. In other words, the critic is failing to perceive the link it looked as if he would make, and which his noticing of the big footwear in Hopkins's meditation on the baptised Jesus points so brightly towards – namely an association in the poem between the lordly dray-horse and the Jesuit's mighty Christ of the Gospel's footwear encounter. Hopkins evidently turns in his poem from disturbing recollections of the attractively bodied farrier to a more morally acceptable and sublimating vision of the horse's bodily might – a focus all the more acceptable as an alternative to the smith's somatic attractions because its battering, mastering power can remind Hopkins of Christ, the plough-pulling 'stallion stalwart' hurling aside earthly hearts under his great trampling feet in the poem 'Hurrahing in

Harvest'. Alerted by his own footwear delvings Bristow might have remembered that by now well known strange letter of Hopkins, about the May Day horse parade in Liverpool just after Felix Spence's death, in which the handsome horses are admired at the expense of the 'base and bespotted figures and features of the Liverpool crowd', men not at all like the fine and manly Norwegians hanging about the Liverpool streets waiting to take passage to America.[20] In Liverpool it was safe for a priest to admire big horses, when he might rather have wished to spend more time with manly Norwegians – but Bristow eschewed availing himself of that fact too.

These failures with fact are clear failures of tact. The critic tramples all over the poem. 'Only when the priest has mastered Felix Randal's body can he remain with [that means, I think, *can he recall*] the physical power of one who formerly shod "the great grey drayhorse".' But there is no mastering of parishioner by priest in the poem at all – rather there's a most delicate play of tender touchings given, and tender touchings resisted, in a most tactfully presented sequence of worried contacts and might-be touchings between the male priest and poet and his male parishioner and poetic subject. The priest anoints the sick man, in a sacramental touch. He offers him the sacramental bread or wafer, the sweet food of the eucharist, a tender tendering from hand to mouth ('since I had our sweet reprieve and ransom / tendered to him'). It's a relationship of mutual endearing ('This seeing the sick endears them to us, us too it endears'), rooted in bodily exchanges – the priest's comforting words (which come from his tongue: 'My tongue had taught thee comfort'), the priest's tear-drying touch ('My . . . touch had quenched thy tears'), the returned touch of the tears on the priest's heart ('Thy tears that touched my heart'). The mirrored repetitions and reciprocations of words enact these interactions of the two male bodies: 'endears . . . to us, us too . . . endears'; 'My tongue . . . thy tears, Thy tears . . . my heart'; 'My . . . touch . . . quenched thy tears, Thy tears . . . touched my heart'; 'touch . . . touched'. One verbal juxtaposition and exchange, which is manifestly felt to be pressing in all the time on the encounter, never, however, occurs: *my touch, thy touch*. And, in fact, there is a quenching, a refusal, of touch going on within the acknowledging and the granting of touching. The touch of the priest which quenched Randal's tears was a putting to an end of the very means of the smith's touching the priest in his heart. Within this moving interchange, the touching of the priest by the man, a perfectly acceptable sacerdotal emotionality one would guess, there is emergent a merely human emotionality the priest recognises and everywhere in the poems fears. That's why the priest has to step back, repress himself, resume his role as a 'eunuch for the kingdom of heaven's sake' (the vocation the 'terrible sonnet' 'Thou art indeed just, Lord' chides God about), put an end to his being touched by those tears. Hence, perhaps, those coolnesses which have worried most readers since commentary on this poem began – the 'O is he dead then', and 'Ah well, God rest him', and the too distancing egotism of 'This seeing the sick endears them to us, us too it endears'. In the context of feared contactings, these sound like a careful denying of aroused interest akin to the self-cautionings of 'The Bugler's First Communion', where the priestly narrator allows himself the luxury of imagining a lovely tactility greater than his religion will condone (the lovely youth 'Yields tender as pushed peach' to the priest's teaching), but then quickly warns himself off ('Let me though see no more of him'). The priest must be for other bodily contacts than these, for prayerful kissings, divinely directed erotic encounters, a tongue-work with God in prayer, no doubt for victory over such earthly temptations ('I have put my lips on pleas/Would brandle [shake] adamantine heaven with ride and jar, did/Prayer go unregarded'). The poet-priest must make tactful withdrawals; is compelled to go very tactfully around the attractions of bodily tactility; is most anxious to remain virginally intact for God.

This is a far cry from the Q theorists' rather blunt touchings upon Hopkins's sensitivities about these touching matters: the simple, one-way touchings and endearings of Bristow's paraphrasings; the downright 'perversity' of Hopkins's 'unconscious thought' about Christ's body in Gregory Woods's thorough-going follow-ups on Bristow in his *History of Gay Literature*, with its too knowing talk of the 'exuberant orality' of Hopkins's poems (where knowingness is a poor substitute for knowledge), and its curious dwelling on the disturbingly attractive 'sweat' of Felix Randal, a part, it's alleged, of Hopkins's sexual excitements over smelly labourers.[21]

There is no mention at all of sweat in 'Felix Randal'. Woods has imported this proletarian smelliness from other Hopkins poems. The only possible olfactory word in this poem is *sweet*. But communion wafers don't smell. That sweetness is rather a matter of taste. Surely the critic has not misread 'our sweet reprieve' as 'our sweat reprieve'? Perish the thought. But the battering brusqueness of the analysis hereabouts does make a crude mistaking seem more than a little possible. Certainly the traditional critical hesitations abundant in pre-Queer Studies days seem more sensitive to the poem's flustered encounters

('Young and naked innocence existing dangerously poised among surrounding dangers': Charles Williams – a Christian who knew a thing or
two about sexual temptation; 'most complex states of intense feeling':
Humphry House – who lost his faith and so might be thought to know
about complex currents of feeling).[22] Our undismayed current access to
the facts about Hopkins's fraught sexuality, our open eyes to what the
letters and journals and sermons as well as the poems seem to be touching on sexually speaking, our licence to raise freely questions which
were once thought fit only for critical undertones, indeed the large present 'theoretical' imperative to confront in writings once repressed items
of whatever description, are none of them excuse for abandoning critical tact in all its forms. It's not the least of the important instructions
arising from this whole post-Arnoldian disposition of critical thought,
this Batesonized corner of distinguished critical theorising, that our
inevitably widening knowledge about how texts work and what they
do makes critical sensitivity, the principledness of tactful handling of
texts, all the more necessary than ever.

Notes

1 René Wellek, 'The Literary Theories of F. W. Bateson', *E in C*, XXIX,
   ii, 112–3.
   [...]
2 Matthew Arnold, 'The Function of Criticism at the Present Time' (= 'The
   Functions of Criticism...' in *The National Review*, ns I (November 1864)),
   Essays in Criticism (1865); *Lectures and Essays in Criticism*, The Complete
   Works of Matthew Arnold, ed. R. H. Super, vol. iii (Ann Arbor, 1962),
   pp. 282–3, as quoted in F. W. Bateson, 'The Sense of Fact', in *The Scholar-
   Critic: An Introduction to Literary Research* (1872), pp. 5–6. 'That remarkable
   passage', in F. W. B., 'The Function of Criticism', *E in C*, III, i, 3.
3 T. S. Eliot, *Selected Essays* (1932; 3rd enlarged edn., 1951, 1969 repr.), p. 31.
4 Christopher Ricks, *Essays in Appreciation* (Oxford, 1996), pp. 280–310.
   [...]
5 F. W. B., *Shakespeare Jahrbuch* 98 (1962), pp. 51–63; reprinted in F. W. B., *Essays
   in Critical Dissent* (1972), pp. 37–48.
6 'The Sense of Fact', in *The Scholar-Critic*, p. 25.
7 'Shakespeare's Laundry Bills', in *Essays in Critical Dissent*, p. 39.
8 *Selected Essays*, p. 31.
9 F. W. B., 'Criticism's Lost Leader', in *The Literary Criticism of T. S. Eliot*, ed. D.
   Newton-de Molina (1977), quoted in Wellek, 'The Literary Theories of F. W.
   Bateson', p. 113.

10 'Literature and the Matter of Fact', p. 283.

11 See Ricks's 1985 essay 'Literary Principles as against Theory' – a not entirely formed piece, I think, but still a forceful one, which preceded the 1990 lecture on 'The Matter of Fact', but succeeds it in *Essays in Appreciation (1996)*, pp. 31–2.

[...]

12 'The Meaning of a Poem', in *The Collected Essays, Journalism and Letters of George Orwell*, vol. ii, *My Country Right or Left, 1940–1943*, ed. Sonia Orwell and Ian Angus (1968; Harmondsworth, 1970), pp. 157–61.

13 Paul L. Mariani, *A Commentary on the Complete Poems of Gerard Manley Hopkins* (Ithaca and London, 1970), p. 166; J. R. Watson, *The Poetry of Gerard Manley Hopkins* (Harmondsworth, 1987), p. 106.

14 In *The Sermons and Devotional Writings of Gerard Manley Hopkins*, ed. Christopher Devlin (1959), pp. 5, 279.

15 Mariani, *Commentary*, p. 170, and nn. 7 and 8.

16 Alfred Thomas, 'Hopkins's "Felix Randal": The Man and the Poem', *TLS* , March 1971, pp. 331–2.

17 Mariani, *Commentary*, p. 170 n. 7.

18 See Eric Griffiths, *The Printed Voice of Victorian Poetry* (Oxford, 1989), pp. 276, 336.

19 Joseph Bristow, '"Churlsgrace": Gerard Manley Hopkins and the Working-Class Male Body', *JELH*, 59/3 *(1992)* 694–711.

20 Quoted by e.g. Norman White, *Hopkins: A Literary Biography* (Oxford, 1992), p. 325.

21 Gregory Woods, *A History of Gay Literature: The Male Tradition* (New Haven and London, 1998), pp. 171–3.

22 Charles Williams, in his introduction to *Poems of Hopkins* (1930); Humphry House, in his review of Elsie Phare, *The Poetry of Hopkins* (1933), *TLS*, 25 January 1934, p. 59; both in *Gerard Manley Hopkins: The Critical Heritage*, ed. Gerald Roberts (London and New York, 1987), pp. 175, 265.

10

'A Thousand Times I'd be a Factory Girl'
Dialect, Domesticity, and Working-Class Women's Poetry in Victorian Britain

Susan Zlotnick

> I would not leave thee, dear beloved place,
> A crown, a sceptre, or a throne to grace,
> To be a queen – the nation's flag unfurl –
> A thousand times I'd be a Factory Girl!
>
> Ellen Johnston, "Address to Napiers' Dockyard,
> Langefield, Anderston"

In 1857, Edwin Waugh penned the most famous dialect poem of the century, "Come Whoam to thi Childer an' Me," an unqualified celebration of the simple domestic joys available to the working man around his own hearth. But it is Waugh's "Down Again!" – a humorous account of childbirth in a working-class family – that best encapsulates the dialect tradition's problematic relationship with the women it enshrined:

> "What's o' thi hurry, Jem?" said he,
> As I went runnin' by:
> "I cannot stop to talk to thee;
> We'n someb'dy ill," said I.
> "Who is it this time?" cried owd Clem;
> "Is it Nan, or litle Ben?"

Zlotnick, Susan. 1991. "'A Thousand Times I'd be a Factory Girl': Dialect, Domesticity, and Working-Class Women's Poetry in Victorian Britain." In *Victorian Studies*, 35, i (Autumn), pp. 7–27. Reproduced with permission of Indiana University Press.

Victorian Poets: A Critical Reader, First Edition. Edited by Valentine Cunningham.
© 2014 John Wiley & Sons, Ltd. Published 2014 by John Wiley & Sons, Ltd.

> "Nawe, nawe," said I, "it's noan o' them;
> *Our Betty's down again!"*
>
> (ll. 41–48)

"Down Again!" presents childbirth from the husband's vantage point and thus ignores the most important actor as well as the true laborer – the pregnant wife – in order to focus on the husband's activities during delivery:

> I never closed my e'en that neet,
> Till after break o' day;
> For they keep me runnin' o' my feet,
> Wi' gruel, an' wi' tay:
> Like a scopperil° up an' down i' th' hole,   *spinning-top*
> I're busy at th' owd job
> Warmin' flannels, an' mendin' th' fires
> An' tentin'° stuff o' th' hob.   *looking after*
>
> It wur getten six or theerabout;
> I're thrang° wi' th' gruel-pon;   *busy*
> When I dropt mi spoon, an' shouted out,
> "How are yo gettin' on?"
> "We're doin weel," th' owd woman said;
> "Thou'd better come an' see;
> There's a fine young chap lies here i' bed;
> An' he wants to look at thee!"
>
> I ran up i' my stockin'-feet;
> An' theer they lay! By th' mon;
> I thought i' my heart a prattier seet
> I ne'er clapt e'en upon!
> I kissed our Betty; an' I said, –
> Wi' th' wayter i' my e'en, –
> "God bless yo both, my bonny lass,
> For evermoore, Amen!
>
> "But do tak care; if aught went wrang
> I think my heart would break;
> An' if there's aught i' th' world thou'd like
> Thou's nought to do but speak:
> But, oh, my lass, don't lie too long;
> I'm lonesome by mysel';
> I'm no use without thee, thou knows;
> Be sharp, an' do get weel!"
>
> (ll. 65–96)

The poem never exploits the irony whereby the husband complains of the burdensome toil of fetching doctors and making tea – "I never closed my e'en that neet, / Till after break o' day"– while his unseen and unheard wife labors in childbirth. Instead, it concludes with a sudden turn toward the sentimental, the father's welcome to his new-born son, and thus reaffirms the strong ties of love and affection that bind the working-class family together. With its unwillingness to make visible the invisible laboring wife, "Down Again!" embodies the controlling irony of the dialect tradition: it is a class-based literature that consistently denies working women their class identity by refusing to recognize them as laborers.

Written by and for the urban working classes of northern Britain, dialect literature reigned as the dominant, even hegemonic, form of working-class expression in the quiescent decades after the mid-century demise of Chartism and before the late-Victorian resurgence of trade union agitation. As Martha Vicinus notes in *The Industrial Muse*, her pioneering study of working-class literature, it was one of the more successful attempts by the Victorian proletariat to "create and sustain a distinctive literature in the face of bourgeois economic and cultural control" (2). Yet, if we understand dialect literature to be a distinct working-class voice, we must at the same time acknowledge it to be a distinctly male one. Like the literary tradition of which it forms a part, dialect writing is an almost exclusively male province: Vicinus could locate "only some half-dozen volumes" written by working-class women in the entire nineteenth century (5).

To explain the disparity between the stacks full of poetry and prose published by working-class men in the nineteenth century and the piti-fully few volumes produced by working women – which if ranged together would scarcely fill up a single shelf – one has to consider more than just the conditions under which most Victorian working-class women lived. Underfed, undereducated and overworked, the Victorian working-class woman did not have the requisite room of her own, nor the time and energy to pursue what must have seemed like the lei-surely self-indulgence of literary creation. But then, neither did the working-class male, who was marginally better fed and educated than his female counterpart, yet suffered from a material condition of life that seems on the face of it just as hostile to the production of literature. If nineteenth-century working-class men and women shared, both met-aphorically and literally, the same room, we must look beyond material explanations for the disparity that exists, and this search will lead us back to dialect literature. For one factor, usually ignored, that may have contributed to the silence of Victorian working-class women is the prevailing intellectual and literary conditions among the working classes themselves.[1] By examining the poetry of Edwin Waugh, one of the most popular of the dialect poets, and two female worker/poets active in the 1860s and 1870s, Fanny Forrester and Ellen Johnston, this essay aims to show how the dialect discourse was itself inimical to female self-expression. Like the laboring wife in Waugh's "Down Again!" working-class women were silenced by the dialect tradition, which, in its adherence to the ideology of domesticity, made it difficult for working women to write of their own experiences as women who worked.

I

Contemporary critics agree that dialect was a profoundly conservative literary movement.[2] By offering up either nostalgic portraits of the pre-industrial worker or sentimentalized sketches of the contemporary working class home, dialect literature fashioned a potent image of the working class as generally immune to the incursions of industrialism, a fact which has led Brian Maidment to conclude that "the inspiration of the industrial muse was a complex one, as so little of the [dialect] verse was directly about industrial culture" ("Prose" 31). After the failure of Chartism, the working class and its writers turned inward by turning indoors, embracing the ideology of domesticity, and participating in an apotheosis of the home and family similar to that of the Victorian middle classes. Although domesticity evolved out of the Evangelical movement in the early 1830s, it quickly spread to the larger middle-class world, where it became the dominant – if frequently contested – ideology.[3] By the 1850s, it began to extend its reach to working-class circles and there remained for the rest of the century, a largely unattainable but nevertheless potent ideal.

Importantly, historians no longer agree that an ascendant bourgeoisie forced the working class to accept the ideological hegemony of domesticity. Taking exception with this interpretation, feminist historians contend that working-class men freely embraced the domestic ideology and adopted a representation of waged work that excluded women in order to restrain female competition in the workplace and hence secure their own imperiled patriarchal interests, challenged by the rise of the self-possessed, wage-earning factory woman. As Barbara Taylor observes in her study of socialism and Victorian feminism, *Eve and the New Jerusalem*, "the wage-earning wife, once seen as the norm in every working-class household," became in the middle decades of the nineteenth century "a symptom and symbol of masculine degradation" (111). Of course, the reinscription of working-class women as, ironically, women who do not work departs radically from laboring-class traditions, in which wives and husbands were considered joint partners in the domestic venture. The invention of the non-working working-class wife did not so much restore the old order of things as engender a new one to fit the new conditions of the nineteenth century. But it quickly, even if incorrectly, became associated with the better times before the coming of the factories. By appropriating the domestic discourse, the dialect poets wedded themselves to a backward-glancing ideology, one that envisioned domesticity as a return to a status quo, the natural order of things believed to have existed before the disruptive birth of the factory system.[4]

Thus, in the process of being imaginatively transformed into a paradise for husbands, the working-class home became a place unaltered by and secure from the unaccountable changes occurring in the outside world. For example, when the wife in Edwin Waugh's "Come Whoam to thi Childer an' Me" pleads with her husband to return home, she tempts him with some homespun pleasures:

> Aw've just mended th' fire wi' a cob°; *lump of coal*
> Owd Swaddle has brought thi new shoon°; *shoes*
> There's some nice bacon-collops o' th' hob,
> An' a quart o' ale-posset i' th' oon°. *oven*
> (ll.1–4)

The key to the attraction lies not only in the promise of domestic comfort, but in the mythic quality of the moment, its historical indeterminateness: Waugh could be sketching a hearthside scene of fourteenth-century life, since nowhere does the poem acknowledge the existence of an urban, industrial milieu. In the closed world of dialect domesticity, the home became not only an antidote to modernity but the repository of working-class traditions, as if the lost village community, abandoned in the nascent moments of industrialization, had been resurrected inside the worker's cottage.

Given the alienating conditions of industrial England, it is not surprising that working men would wish to seek refuge from the workaday world of the factories, even if that refuge took the form of poetic fantasies. Nevertheless, despite its considerable surface charm, "Come Whoam" implicitly acknowledges the tensions inherent in the domestic ideal, even while it affirms working-class domesticity. Presenting two irreconcilable points of view, the poem takes the form of a dialogue between a homebound wife and an errant husband. Lonely, fretful, and left at home to tend children and darn socks, the wife laments her absent husband:

> When aw put little Sally to bed,
> Hoo° cried, 'cose her feyther weren't theer,   *she*
> So aw kiss'd th' little thing, an' aw said
> Thae'd bring her a ribbin fro' th' fair;
> An' aw gav' her her doll, an' some rags,
> An' a nice little white cotton-bo' °;   *bow*
> An' aw kiss'd her again; but hoo said
> 'At hoo wanted to kiss thee an' o.
>
> An' Dick, too, aw'd sich wark wi' him,
> Afore aw could get him upstairs;
> Thae towd him thae'd bring him a drum,
> He said, when he're sayin' his prayers;
> Then he looked i' my face, an' he said,
> "Has th' boggarts° taen houd o' my dad?"   *bogeymen*
> An' he cried whol his e'en were quite red: –
> He likes thee some weel, does yon lad!
> (ll. 9–24)

When her wandering mate finally returns from pursuing his own pleasures, he problematically proclaims both his right to a "bit of a spree" and his enduring affection for home:

> "God bless tho' my lass; aw'll go whoam
> An' aw'll kiss thee an' th' childer o' round;
> Thae knows that wheerever aw roam,
> Aw'm fain to get back to th' owd ground;
> Aw can do wi' a crack o'er a glass;
> Aw can do wi' a bit of a spree;
> But aw've no gradely° comfort, my lass,   *proper*
> Except wi' yon childer an' thee."
> (ll. 41–48)

With unabashed sentimentalism, the poem embraces a domesticity that it cannot quite endorse: the husband's wanderlust testifies to the limitations of the domestic ideal. The simple comforts offered in the opening stanza fail to satisfy the husband, and even though he insists there's no place like home, he also hints that it's no place he particularly wants to be, thus leaving his wife with the sad futurity of many more such silent, solitary evenings. However, by letting the husband have the last word, Waugh effectively irons over the tensions his poem raises, and "Come Whoam" concludes on a note of domestic concord. In the end, the poem contains the contradictions embodied in the domestic ideal, and thus it contributes to the mythologizing impetus of dialect poetry by actively translating the working man's cottage into the husband's castle.

II

But however understandable this translation may be, like much dialect poetry "Come Whoam to thi Childer an' Me" depends upon the effacement of women's waged labor. While the domestic ideal envisaged every working-class wife supported by her husband, the reality usually fell far short of this goal because, quite simply, only the most prosperous and skilled workers could afford to keep an unemployed wife at home in any degree of comfort, and a large percentage of working-class women continued to add to their families' incomes after marriage. A glance at the few published autobiographies of Victorian and Edwardian working-class women reveals that these individuals did not expect their wage-earning days to end with their marriage vows.

Certainly Lucy Luck, whose autobiography is reprinted in John Burnett's *Useful Toil*, held no such illusions about married life. Born in 1848 and brought up in a workhouse, Luck eventually marries, bears seven children and never stops adding to the family income. A straw-plaiter by trade, she confesses at the end of her life that "I always liked my work very much and although I had trouble with it when I first learnt, it has been a little fortune to me. I have been at work for forty-seven years, and have never missed one season, although I have a large family" (77). While justly proud of her achievements, Luck has no sense that working for five decades and raising a large family is an extraordinary accomplishment. But then, given what we know of the lives of Victorian working-class women, it most likely was not. Contrary to popular belief, women did not stop working when they got married; in fact, they frequently had to stay in the labor market to supplement the family's income until their children were old enough to earn for themselves.

Yet domesticity so dominated working-class culture that the domestic ideal was for years accepted as fact by historians, and only recently has scholarship begun to insist on the regularity with which working-class wives continued to earn money after marriage. Of course, women's working patterns varied according to the specifics of regional economies, but in the cotton districts of Lancashire, the center of dialect activity, a long tradition of married women's work existed. But this is a truth one would never grasp from reading dialect poetry.[5]

Moreover, and perhaps even more problematically, dialect domesticity denied women credit for the unwaged as well as the waged work they performed. Whether earning a wage or not, most working-class women had the primary responsibility of housekeeping, frequently a daunting task in urban settings where, as Robert Roberts recalls in *The Classic Slum*, a first-hand account of life in turn-of-the-century Salford, housewives fought a constant battle with "ever-invading dirt" and "wore their lives away washing clothes in heavy, iron-hooped tubs, scrubbing wood and stone, polishing furniture and fire-irons" (37). Yet dialect domesticity consistently refused to elevate housework to the status of work, noble and ennobling human labor that required skill, organization and intelligence. Rather, in its need to set off the domestic realm (the site of natural relationships between men and women, parents and children) from the industrial realm (the site of unnatural, alienated relationships between men and masters, workers and machines), dialect literature reconceived housework not only as "not work," but as one of woman's duties, or, more precisely, one of her natural functions, like breathing and childbearing.

This conception of domestic work is certainly the unstated assumption in Edwin Waugh's "Dinner Time," a poem about failed domesticity. When the husband returns home for his mid-day meal only to discover the house in a state of disarray, he complains bitterly to his wife:

> "Thou's nought to do, fro' morn to neet,
> But keep things clean an' straight,
> An' see that th' bits o' cloas° are reet°,   *clothes/right*
> An' cook one's bit o' meight;
> But thou's never done it yet, owd lass:
> How is it? Conto tell?"
>
> (ll. 41–46)

181

The husband first belittles the wife's labor, and then he devalues it completely; apparently, as the husband subsequently insists, only sheer laziness and a weakness for gossip keep her from it. Although the poem opens with the wife's frantic attempts to put supper on the table, it closes with the husband's threat to leave the home and dissolve the family.

> "No wonder that hard-wortchin' folk
> Should feel inclined to roam
> For comfort to an alehouse nook,
> When they han noan at whoam.
>
> I'm fast: 1 don't know what to say;
> An' I don't know what to do;
> An' when I'm tired, at th' end o' th' day,
> I don't know where to goo.
> It makes me weary o' my life
> To live i' sich a den:
> Here, gi's a bit o' cheese an' loaf,
> An' I'll be off again!"
>
> (ll. 53–64)

Nowhere in the poem does Waugh undermine the husband's point of view, so that "Dinner Time" obscures the adversities of housekeeping in a working-class home lacking all modern amenities and ignores the talent required to feed, clothe and care for a family. Lady Florence Bell contends in *At the Works* (1907), an account of late-nineteenth-century life in a Yorkshire iron town, that it was frequently a woman's managerial abilities (rather than her husband's industrial capabilities) that determined the economic well-being of the family:

> the key to the condition of the workman and his family, the clue, the reason for the possibilities and impossibilities of his existence, is the capacity, the temperament, and, above all, the health of the woman who manages his house; into her hands, sometimes strong and capable, often weak and uncertain, the future of her husband is committed, the burden of the family life is thrust. (171)

Unlike Lady Bell, Waugh cannot acknowledge the wife's unpaid domestic duties as valuable, difficult labor because to do so would undermine the home as the antithesis of the factory, the opposition upon which domesticity depended.

Ultimately, dialect poetry not only devalued women's contributions to the domestic economy, but it strove to deny their efforts completely by encouraging working-class women to engage in acts of self-effacement and to erase – as much as possible – all traces of their domestic labor. Dialect poets usually made this suggestion in the form of the advice poem, a subgenre of dialect poetry in which, frequently, an old man or woman offers household hints to the newly married. Almost invariably, the dispenser of wisdom informs a young bride that although the secret to a happy marriage lies in the spotless purity and perfect orderliness of her domestic arrangements, a well-run home also renders invisible the labor involved in its upkeep. Somewhat ironically, these working-class poets seem to be advocating a fetishized domestic space where only the "commodity" (the cooked food, the clean house), and not the labor required to produce it, would be disclosed to the homeward-bound worker.

Clearly it is this lesson in concealment that the superannuated uncle in Samuel Laycock's "Uncle Dick's Advoice to Wed Women" tries to impart to his newlywed niece when he informs her that:

> When it's weshin' day, get done as soon as yo' con;
> Awill assure yo' it's very unpleasant for John
> To come into th' heawse ov a nooin' or neet
> An' foind th' dirty clooas spread abeawt his feet....
>
> Oh! It's grand when one enters th' inside o' the'r cot,
> An' fonds 'at th' woife's made it a heaven ov a spot;
> An' her stondin' theer, bless her, to welcome yo' in,
> Wi' o 'at's abeawt her as clean as a pin!...
>
> Let 'em feel – when the'r wark's done – 'at th' loveliest spot'
> At the'r is under heaven, is th'r own humble cot,
> Ah' ther's lots o' poor fellows aw've known i' mi loife,
>
> At's bin driven fro' whoam bi a slovenly woife:
> When they'n come in at neet, weaned eawt wi' th'er toil,
> I'th stead o' being' met wi' a sweet, lovin' smoile,
> Ther's nothing but black-lookin' holes meet the'r ccn,
> An' a woife an' some childer, a shaum to be seen.
>
> (ll. 13–56)

As Laycock's last stanza reveals, it is from the body of the housewife that the effects of domestic labor must primarily be erased.

In this regard, Uncle Dick's friendly advice does not differ from the "toothsome advice" a young married woman receives in Edwin Waugh's poem of the same name. "Toothsome Advice" echoes "Uncle

Dick's Advoice to Wed Women" in its insistence that the ornamental appearance of the wife will attract – like a sexual magnet:

"Thou mun keep his whoam pleasant an' sweet;
An' everything fit to be seen;
Thou mun keep thi hearth cheerful an' breet;
Thou mun keep thisel' tidy an' clean
A good-temper't wife will entice
To a fireside that's cosy an' trim;
Men liken to see their wives nice;
An' I'm sure that's so wi' your Jem."

(ll. 25–32)

By asserting the desirability of the working-class wife only when she conceals the marks of her class identity (the dirt, the fatigue), Waugh reverses the middle-class fascination with the sexuality of the working-class woman. Moreover, while neither Waugh nor Laycock would demand that the working man, exhausted from his labors, arrive home cheerful and tidy, both expect the working wife to transform herself at the end of each day into a decorative object more befitting a bourgeois matron with a staff of servants than the poor drudge that she frequently was. Evolving as it did out of the peculiar conditions of middle-class life, the domestic ideal never fit the economic realities of the working class, and the only way the dialect poets could make it fit was, oddly enough, by eroding the class differences between middle- and working-class women. The practical and pernicious effect of this erosion was that dialect literature, which claimed a certain authenticity as the voice of the industrial working class, came to define the working-class woman in terms that ignored her class conditions.

A yawning and unbridgeable gap existed between the domestic ideal – which overlooked women's waged work and devalued their unwaged work – and the necessities of survival for working-class families in Victorian Britain. The ideal demanded that working-class women reproduce, albeit in a less opulent form, the bourgeois world inside the worker's cottage, a demand that the working-class wife could rarely achieve, and then only through small acts of daily heroism. Drearier than the rosy pictures sketched by the dialect poets, working women's lives were filled with long days of overexertion, as Roberts observes:

realists among the old working class today remember, and with sadness, not King Edward's "lovely ladies" and tea on the lawn at Hurlingham, but the many women broken and aged with childbearing well before their own youth was done. They remember the spoiled complexions, the mouths full of rotten teeth, the varicose veins, the ignorance of simple hygiene, the intelligence stifled and the endless battle merely to keep clean. Unlike many in the middle and upper classes, fondly looking back, they see no "glory gleaming." They weep no tears for the past. (41)

Dialect writers, however, were not realists; they were idealists, if somewhat pragmatic ones. Tied to the working-class communities they spoke to and for, they fully understood that every working-class home did not meet the impossible standards of the domestic ideal. Certainly Edwin Waugh, who abandoned his own wife and children to the workhouse and took up with a wealthy Irish widow before penning his famous poem (Vicinus, *Ambiguities*), comprehended something of the ideal's tentative nature. Still, the ideal seems to have held emotional and imaginative sway over the British working classes. "Home, however poor, was the focus of all…love and interests," Roberts recalls. "Songs about its beauties were ever on people's lips. 'Home sweet home,' first heard in the 1870s, had become 'almost a second national anthem' " (53). But whether it was honored more in the breach or in the observance, by focusing almost exclusively on women's role in the home the ideology of domesticity neglected the diversity of working-class women's experience in nineteenth-century Britain, where there were few occupations – from coalmining to fishing – in which women did not actively engage. Ultimately, in their single-minded devotion to the domestic ideal, dialect poets robbed working-class women of the realities of their lives as workers.

III

Although the domestic ideal gained currency among the working classes around 1850, its complete ascendancy was neither immediate nor complete, especially among working women. Admittedly, many women saw in the ideal some possible relief from the twin burden of waged work and housework they carried. But not all embraced it, and those who did dispute its imposition lacked a language to articulate their discontents. As historian Barbara Taylor has shown in her investigations of the women who wrote letters to the "Woman's Page" of the *Pioneer*, a popular Owenite trades union journal of the 1830s, working-class women in the early part of the nineteenth century could evoke the traditional language of radicalism – of the rights of man and woman – to fight their battles. They could, and frequently did, argue against all "artificial aristocracies" *(Pioneer* 273), whether of class or of gender. But Chartism, the next great wave of working-class radicalism after Owenism, eventually repudiated the revolutionary feminism of its predecessor by heralding the domestic ideal and the ideology of domesticity left working-class women without a solid foundation on which to base a critique of their unequal position in Victorian society at the same historical moment when gender inequities were being reasserted and reinscribed into a system of separate spheres. This situation, which divested women of an oppositional discourse when they stood in the greatest need of it, created myriad difficulties for working-class women writers like Fanny Forrester and Ellen Johnston, two worker-poets whose experiences fell outside the narrow confines of Victorian domesticity.

Granted, neither Fanny Forrester nor Ellen Johnston is usually located within the dialect camp, and thus comparing them to a dialect poet like Edwin Waugh may seem arbitrary at best, misleading at worst. However, I would counter, both women were active during the height of dialect poetry's popularity, and they emerged from the same social and geographical milieu that spawned the major dialect figures. Moreover, the Scottish-born Johnston, heir to the tradition of Robert Burns, occasionally used the Scots dialect; and even though Forrester wrote exclusively in standard English, she published the majority of her poems in *Ben Brierley's Journal*, a magazine edited by one of the masters of dialect prose, Ben Brierley. Most important of all, the two women confronted the domestic ideal in their work, and their writings record that confrontation. It is through Forrester's and Johnston's texts that we can begin to gauge the formative (and deforming) pressures the discourse of domesticity exerted on working-class women's writings.

To frame Forrester's and Johnston's later collisions with domesticity, it might be useful to consider first the poetry of a woman who did not write from within or against domesticity. Active at mid-century and publishing in *The People's Journal*, a magazine run by the reform-minded, middle-class Howitts and dedicated to finding a wider reading audience for working-class poets, a Chorley factory worker who signed herself "Marie" was not enmeshed in the Victorian cult of domesticity. Consequently, she could freely configure herself as a worker and a woman without lapsing into contradiction. For example, the subject matter of Marie's "Labour," a Carlylean paean to the creative powers of work, would not alone make it a remarkable poem; however, what distinguishes it from working-class poetry written later in the century is the imagery Marie deploys to realize her vision of the better world that can be created through dint of hard work. Unlike Edwin Waugh, who in "Down Again!" effaces the labor of women's childbirth, Marie turns to childbirth as a metaphor for all human labor:

> When great nature, in sore travail,
> Bringeth forth her child –
> Some old nation in convulsion,
> With new freedom wild! –
> Some long-borne and huge injustice
> That in dumbness stood,
> Pouring out its new-born utt'rance
> In a jargon flood!
> 'Tls but nature's heart
> Beating in her children's bosom,
> Bidding wrong depart.
> Ages are her fleeting moment, –
> World-times are her years –
> In immensity she singeth
> 'Mid the shining spheres.
>
> "Hark, hark, to God's heart beating;
> Time is on the wing,
> Labour is the only worship
> Any soul can bring!"
> (ll. 61–79)

Syntactical irregularities aside, by heralding labor's infinite capacity to form worlds anew the poem celebrates creativity as procreativity: work is both natural and "naturally" feminine. Instead of envisioning women's work as a perversion of the natural order, Marie can represent woman as a natural worker because women and work were not divorced in her mind.

Marie embraces the larger political struggles of her fellow workers and produces poems full of class-conscious rhetoric, bearing such outsized heroic titles as "Idealise the Real and Realise the Ideal," "Fellow Workers," "The Indomitable Will," and "Encouragement." Like some latter-day figure of Liberty leading the people, Marie writes to advance the cause of the working classes:

> Though ignored our lowly lot,
> Scornful glances harm us not;
> We accept our homely fate;

And a beauteous life create; –
From earth's bosom, brown and bare,
Flowerets draw their colours rare;
And though we are seeming stinted
All our days are rainbow-tinted
By our noble will!

Come there failure or success,
We march on in earnestness;
Nought can come amiss or wrong,
If the soul be true and strong,
On, and up, courageously!
And our banner's motto be
"Hope and work, with heart and hand –
Naught can finally withstand
Those of earnest will!"
("The Indomitable Will," ll. 37–54)

Significantly, Marie represents the class struggle from the position of the first person plural and includes herself in the empowering "we" of class solidarity. By identifying herself as a worker without needing the qualifying adjectives of gender, Marie reveals an understanding of the word "worker" that encompasses both men and women.

In the two decades dividing Marie from Fanny Forrester, we can place the triumph of the domestic ideal. By the mid-1870s, the confluence of woman and worker called up contradictory and self-defeating images in the poetry of Fanny Forrester, the pseudonym of a young female operative from Manchester who entered a dye-works at the age of twelve and was publishing regularly in *Ben Brierley's Journal* by the time she reached twenty. Her poetry ranges from somewhat lugubrious narratives of urban living to vaguely Romantic invocations of the pre-industrial past. However, when focused on Manchester life, her poetry reveals the impediments a working-class woman faced when attempting to write about factory girls in the golden age of domesticity.

To some degree, Forrester was aware of her dilemma. In "The Lowly Bard," published in 1873, Forrester's humble male poet "mourns the incompleteness of his lyre" (8), a dissatisfaction justified by his inability to find an appropriate poetic voice for the subject of the poem, working-class women in the industrial city. Although Forrester wishes to make heroines out of mill hands, she knows that they are not conventionally heroic, and the tension between the poetic language of Victorian femininity and the prosaic reality of her female operatives threatens the poem's intelligibility:

> O'er great looms slight figures lowly stoop
> And weary shadows cross their girlish faces
> That like frail flowers o'er stagnant waters droop....
> Toil, toil to-day, and toil again tomorrow:
> Some weave their warp to reach a pauper grave!
> Naught of romance doth gild their common sorrow;
> Yet ne'er were heroines more strong – more brave.
>
> (ll. 22–28)

Forrester uses the clichéd comparison of drooping flowers and mill girls even though she understands the inadequacy of romantic language to capture and record the lives of her weavers. Despite the willowy weakness and fey feminine charm Forrester attributes to her workers, in the end she destabilizes her own characterization of them by acknowledging their strength and bravery. Enmeshed in a representational system that could only see factory women as victims (frail flowers needing the shelter of the domestic nook), Forrester cannot articulate coherently the lives of mill hands like herself, and if she stumbles into contradictions, it is because a working woman in the 1870s was a contradiction, at least ideologically.

Unable to translate her own experiences of survival and success into poetic forms, Forrester invariably depicted the industrial milieu as anathema to female life: her inaugural piece in *Ben Brierley's Journal*, the three-part "Strangers in the City," which appeared in the spring of 1870, recounts the woeful tale of a young Irish woman who migrates to the city and dies shortly thereafter, worn out by her daily contact with the mill. But this tragic emplotment runs counter to what we know of the outlines of Forrester's life. For in spite of her own early hardships, Forrester eventually became a popular contributor to *Ben Brierley's Journal*, arousing so much reader interest that in 1878 the magazine took the unusual step of printing a biographical notice, in which, interestingly enough, Brierley acknowledges how extraordinarily disconnected the poetry is from the poet's life:

> she writes of fields and flowers as of things with which her earlier years were unacquainted, as treasures only reflected in books, or dreamt of in her dreams, and with which her soul yearns for companionship. We are assured that beyond the range of Peel Park [in Manchester], outward nature has hitherto been a sealed book to her. (37)

Brierley alludes to the fact that poems with urban settings like "The Lowly Bard" and "Strangers in the City" stand out as exceptions because most of Forrester's poetry recalls, in a plangent and irreconcilable voice, a sanitized, picturesque world "where the little brooks are singing through the valleys all the day" (l. 2) that the poet could never possibly have known ("Homeless in the City" 42). He surmises, no doubt correctly, that her inspiration comes from books – most likely from volumes full of Romantic nature poetry and dialect literature, neither genre providing her with a language for representing the lives of modern mill women with anything other than self-pity or evasion: nature poetry offered a condemnation of the urban milieu while dialect domesticity tendered a similar critique of wage-earning women. Forrester ends up achieving an easy pathos in her poetry but nothing like lyrical truth, and even the pathetic effect she produces is undermined by the contradictions that inevitably emerge between the domestic ideology and certain realities that Forrester cannot completely suppress.

IV

It is against the backdrop of domesticity – which presented working-class women with the problem of representing themselves in a representational system that effectively denied their existence as workers – that we must set the achievement of Ellen Johnston, a Scottish mill hand born in the mid-1830s. Johnston, who labelled herself "the Factory Girl," is one of the few working-class women to publish a volume of poetry in the mid-1800s and, as far as I have been able to ascertain, the only one who made life in the mills the chief subject of her writing. A self-professed "self-taught scholar" (7), Johnston tries to resolve the dilemma facing working-class women writers like Forrester by turning to the Romantic tradition of rebellion, a literary model that encourages the oppositional, confrontational stance Johnston adopts in her 1867 *Autobiography, Poems and Songs.*[6] Casting herself as Romantic rebel, Johnston engages in Miltonic inversions, transforming the heaven of working-class domesticity into a hell and, in turn, Blake's "dark, Satanic mills" into a personal paradise. As a result, she breaches the walls of the working-class home and lets some light shine into the unexposed and unexplored corners of the domestic ideal.

In the autobiographical preface to her poems, Ellen Johnston flatly rejects domesticity and reinvents herself as a Romantic heroine.

She proudly boasts that "mine were not the common trials of every day life, but like those strange romantic ordeals attributed to the imaginary heroines of 'Inglewood Forest' " (5); and, in fact, the story of her life does resemble something out of Byron's poetry or an over-plotted Victorian romance. When her father decides to emigrate to America, her mother refuses to go and, shortly after hearing false reports of her husband's death, she remarries, only to die from the shock when he unexpectedly returns years later. Meanwhile, left fatherless in Scotland, Johnston undergoes the first of her uncommon trials, one she alludes to as "the mystery of my life" (9), and while she remains highly circumspect throughout, she manages to convey the fact that as a child she suffered at the hands of her abusive (and perhaps sexually abusive) stepfather, whose attentions forced her as a young girl to run away from her mother's house "for safety and protection" (9).

Given her early history, it is scarcely surprising that Johnston never sentimentalizes the domestic sphere. Indeed, when the home appears at all in her poetry, it does so as a den of terror, as in "The Drunkard's Wife," a harrowing account of her aunt's unhappy marriage to an alcoholic. Ellen Johnston could have scripted her life as a domestic tragedy – as a cautionary tale about failed domesticity – but since she sees herself not as a victim but as a bohemian free-spirit, she chooses rather to celebrate herself and her life with Whitmanesque energy, exalting her homelessness and embracing the open road as a symbol of her liberation. She compares herself to a wandering Jew and proudly recalls her life's travelogue: "I have mingled with the gay on the shores of France – I have feasted in the merry halls of England – I have danced on the shamrock soil of Erin's green isle" (6). Even more daringly, she openly proclaims her moral wanderings and then, true to form, refuses to repent the birth of an illegitimate daughter:

> I did not ... feel inclined to die when I could no longer conceal what the world falsely calls a woman's shame. No, on the other hand, I never loved life more dearly and longed for the hour when I would have something to love me – and my wish was realized by becoming the mother of a lovely daughter on the 14th of Sept, 1852. (11)

Having read an abundance of nineteenth-century fiction, Johnston knows that a proper Victorian lady, on becoming a single mother, should engage in some self-destructive display, but she gamely declines to play the role of the shame-ridden woman. Glorifying her outcast state, Johnston rejoices in the motherhood that brands her a fallen woman.

Of course, as a woman who worked in a factory and wrote poetry, Johnston was already outside the categories of conventional representation, at least in the eyes of her upper-class readers, for whom the autobiographical preface was written. "Self-taught writers were regarded as much as social phenomena as writers of serious poetry" (85), Maidment reminds us in "Essayists and Artizans." Wealthy Victorians were as interested in the lives of working-class poets as they were in the poetry itself, and Johnston's awareness of the fact that part of her celebrity – at least among her "betters" – derived from her class status rather than her poetic skills prompted her to write "An Address to Nature on its Cruelty":

> Learned critics who have seen them [her verses]
> Say origin dwells within them;
> But when myself perchance they see,
> They laugh and say, "O is it she?
> Well, I think the little boaster
> Is nothing but a fair imposter;
> She looks so poor-like and so small,
> She's next unto a nought-at-all;
> Such wit and words quite out-furl
> The learning of 'A Factory Girl.' "
>
> (ll. 11–20)

Surely for the aristocratic readers of her autobiography, like the Duke of Buccleuch and the Earl of Enniskillen, both of whom appear on the subscriber list, "the factory girl" would have been beyond the pale of respectable representation, which situated the pure woman in the domestic space. Perhaps trumpeting herself as a (sexually) fallen women in the autobiography allowed her to be comfortable with what she ideologically already was: a woman who had fallen out of her proper sphere. In fact, one senses that, at least imaginatively, Johnston relishes her status as a fallen woman, finding power and a transformational energy in her emancipation from the constraints of Victorian womanhood.

By reversing the social and moral hierarchy of working-class domesticity, Johnston's factory poems sustain the rebellious posture that she assumes in the autobiographical preface. "Kennedy's Dear Mill," which

Johnston probably wrote as an occasional piece to commemorate a company function, upends the tropes of dialect poetry:

> And freedom's glorious shrine
> Is center'd in thy walls;
> No tyrant knave to bind,
> No slavish chain enthrals.
> The workers are as free
> As the sunshine on the hill;
> Thy breath is liberty
> Oh! Kennedy's dear mill.
>
> (ll. 40–48)

While the dialect poets usually figure the working-class home as an escape from the regimentation and regulations of factory life, in "Kennedy's Dear Mill" Johnston locates her freedom in a weaving shed, and then, to complete her break with the domestic discourse, she claims to find a home in Kennedy's mill and a family among her fellow mill workers. In Johnston's poetry, the mill rather than the home emerges as the emotional center of her life, so that all the affection and familial loyalty (and even the air of sanctification) that the dialect poets ascribe to the domestic sphere, she transfers to the factory:

> Thou hast a secret spell
> For all as well as me;
> Each girl loves thee well
> That ever wrought in thee.
> They may leave thy blessed toil;
> But, find work they will,
> They return back in a while
> To Kennedy's dear mill.
>
> (ll. 17–24)

In fact, to be out of work for Johnston is to be removed from her spiritual home and to become an expatriate from paradise, a "factory exile" who writes love poems full of passionate longing for the mill she left behind: "Thou lovely verdant Factory! What binds my heart to thee? / Why art thou centered in my soul, twined round my memory?" ("The Factory Exile," ll. 1–2).

One could explain Johnston's factory effusions as a subtle parody of the dialect tradition's over-sentimentalization of the home, but her attachment to the factories seems sincere, grounded both in the treasured freedom she associates with mill life and in the sense of self-worth, perhaps not otherwise available to an unwed mother in Victorian Scotland, it affords her. If one considers the generally low status of the Victorian working-class woman, and the even lower status of domestic labor, factory work provided Johnston with one of the few areas in which she could achieve a certain standing and dignity. Frequently boasting of her prowess at the loom and relating all the praises her various employers have heaped upon her, Johnston seems to be as proud of her weaving skills as she is of her poetic ones; her self-confidence is bolstered by the knowledge that she is a sound craftsman, a skilled worker with words and with wool.

Nevertheless, while Johnston may have found in the radical strain of Romantic thought a paradigm that allowed her to validate her identity as a factory girl, she is also liberated by having no specific models from "high" art on which to pattern her industrial verses. Although Johnston borrowed the revolutionary posture of the Romantics, the Romantic poets left behind no body of factory poetry with which Johnston needed to contend. But when Johnston takes her subject matter as well as her revolutionary stance from the Romantic tradition, the pressures exerted by male literary models and the ideology of femininity enclosed within them transform her sexual politics. In fact, it is at these moments that Johnston and Forrester most closely resemble one another. Johnston's few non-industrial poems, mixed cocktails of Scott and early Wordsworth, reaffirm certain conservative notions of femininity that her autobiographical material repudiates. In one particularly Wordsworthian effort, the heroine of an ersatz lyrical ballad entitled "The Maniac in the Greenwood" is rejected by her lover and confirms her maidenly modesty and innate femininity by going mad. However, at the same time and in the same volume, Johnston's autobiography recounts a life that contains considerably more trying events than an unhappy love affair. Johnston survives incidents of child abuse, periods of unemployment, a bout of illness, and the experience of single parenthood, and through it all she retains a remarkable degree of optimism and emerges from the text as a resilient individual, the spiritual kin of the stalwart Lucy Luck. Like Fanny Forrester's poetry, Ellen Johnston's, when it follows male literary models that embody conventional Victorian notions of femininity, cannot approximate the truth of a working woman's life. Johnston's text, which juxtaposes autobiography and a scattering of poems straining to emulate canonical forms, opens up and lays bare the gap between male literary traditions and the working-class woman's realities.[7]

Perhaps the lesson to be learned from Johnston's *Autobiography, Poems and Songs* is that the most revealing source of information we have on working-class women's lives remains the autobiography. Of course, that statement does not intend to deny the obvious fact that an autobiography is a fictional ordering of personal recollections, but it is a fiction that gives us access to the way an individual wishes the world to see him or her. As Susan Stanford Freidman argues, women's autobiographies often reveal a self at odds with dominant cultural representations:

> A white man has the luxury of forgetting his skin color and sex. He can think of himself as an "individual." Women and minorities, reminded at every turn in the great cultural hall of mirrors of their sex or color, have no such luxury.... Alienation is not the result of creating a self in language, as it is for the Lacanian and Barthesian critics of autobiography. Instead, alienation from the historically imposed image of the self is what motivates the writing, the creation of an alternate self in the autobiographical act. Writing the self shatters the cultural hall of mirrors and breaks the silence imposed by male speech. (39–41)

Johnston's autobiography and autobiographical factory poems may be the closest we can come to sharing the private vision of one Victorian woman directly involved in industrial labor in the decades after mid-century.

However, in spite of her ample achievements, Johnston may have shattered one hall of mirrors only to have moved to another room in the patriarchal fun house. For while Johnston can exuberantly proclaim that "A thousand times I'd be a Factory Girl," the epic celebration of herself throughout the *Autobiography, Poems and Songs* comes at a price: she may find a liberating voice in the rhetoric of Romantic rebellion, but that voice traps her into reinforcing the governing cultural assumptions about the immorality of "working girls." Johnston can only present herself to the reader as a fallen woman, and in spite of her avowed enthusiasm for mill life, Johnston nonetheless acknowledges that to be a female factory worker is to have fallen out of one's proper sphere: she upends the domestic ideal only to reaffirm its hegemony in working-class culture. But even if, in the final analysis, she fails to escape the dominance of the domestic ideal, Johnston succeeds in articulating experiences that could not be reconciled with the dictates of domesticity. But who knows how many women, lacking Johnston's daring, confrontational zeal, were dissuaded from writing about their own lives as women and workers? While the discourse of domesticity cannot alone account for the silence of working-class women in the Victorian period, clearly dialect literature, that pure distillation of working-class domesticity, reinforced it. Dialect may have embodied some of the dreams and desires of the Victorian working man, but by refusing to grant the working-class woman her class status, it muted her voice.

Notes

1 David Vincent first broke with purely materialist explanations to account for the scarcity of working-class women's writings when, in *Bread, Knowledge and Freedom*, he considered the emotional and intellectual conditions of the working class and argued that their low self-esteem and the lack of "the self-confidence required to undertake the unusual act of writing an autobiography" accounted for the absence of working women's autobiographies (8–9).

2 In *The Poorhouse Fugitives*, Brian Maidment contends that dialect poetry "is largely a search for a lost 'history' of ordinary people, most usually associated in their world with a rural/industrial village life which just pre-dates urbanization and the factory system" (231). Vicinus points out that the choice of the dialect itself was an attempt to forge a connection with the past: "the spoken dialect belonged to the past and to the country in the minds of many city dwellers" (*Industrial* 190). And in the preface to his anthology of dialect verse, *Songs of the People*, Brian Hollingworth observes that after its golden age in the 1850s and 1860s, dialect poetry quickly degenerated into an antiquarian and rather nostalgic attempt to conserve a dying culture and language" (5).

3 One need look no further than Florence Nightingale's *Cassandra* for an excoriating contemporary critique of domesticity. Many middle-class women, however, found a way to challenge the domestic ideal from inside through its ideological concomitant – female influence. For example, domestic ideologues, like Anna Jameson, employed the idea of a woman's moral influence to transcend the domestic sphere and annul the public/private divorce; in her widely-circulated social treatise of 1856, *The Communion of Labour*, Jameson asks her readers if they wish to deny women "the power to carry into a wider sphere the duties of home – the wifely, motherly, sisterly instincts, which bind them to the other half of the human race" (119). This broad interpretation of domestic ideology gave middle-class women some access to the public sphere, through the limited means of female philanthropic endeavors. Clearly though, the notion of female influence and philanthropy would have been useless in a working-class context.

4 For the fullest analyses of the implications of the working-class adoption of domesticity, see Taylor's chapter on "Sex and Class in the Post-Owenite Era," and Lown.

5 Moira Machonachie quotes the following figures for female employment, taken from the 1851 census: out of a population of 7,043,701 adult women, 2,846,097 were in paid employ and 500,000 worked in family businesses. The prevalence of working wives in Victorian Britain – and the grave economic consequences for women resulting from the adoption of the domestic ideal – is discussed by Rose; Lown; Alexander; and Osterund.

6 Julia Swindells fleshes out the literary influences of Johnston's autobiography, particularly her indebtedness to such Romantic figures as Sir Walter Scott.

7 Johnston's celebrations of factory life owe an unacknowledged debt to the "low" tradition of the broadside, which as Vicinus notes, often praised the "liveliness and vitality of factory towns" (*Industrial* 53). But by explicitly aligning herself with Byron, Scott and Wordsworth, Johnston attempts to locate herself within the canonical tradition of English literature, and in this sense, she shares much in common with the working-class writers whom Vicinus identifies as seeing literature as their vocation. I think Forrester's poetry also reveals a desire on the part of the author to "participate in English literary culture" (140).

Works Cited

Alexander, Sally. "Women's Work in Nineteenth-Century London: A Study of the Years 1820–1850." *The Rights and Wrongs of Women*. Ed. Juliet Mitchell and Ann Oakley. Harmondsworth: Penguin, 1976. 59–111.

Bell, Florence. *At the Works*. 1907. London: Virago, 1985.

Brierley, Ben. "Fanny Forrester." *Ben Brierley's Journal* 23 Jan. 1875: 37.

Burnett, John, ed. *Useful Toil: Autobiographies of Working People from the 1820s to the 1920s*. Harmondsworth: Penguin, 1984.

Forrester, Fanny. "Homeless in the City." *Ben Brierley's Journal* Mar. 1870: 42.

—— "The Lowly Bard." *Ben Brierley's Journal* Nov. 1873: 265.

Freidman, Susan Stanford. "Women's Autobiographical Selves." *The Private Self: Theory and Practice of Women's Autobiographical Writings*. Ed. Shari Benstock. London: Routledge, 1988. 34–62.

Hollingworth, Brian, ed. *Songs of the People*. Manchester: Manchester UP, 1977.

Jameson, Anna. *The Communion of Labour*. London, 1856.

Johnston, Ellen. *Autobiography, Poems and Songs of Ellen Johnston, the Factory Girl*. Glasgow, 1867.

Laycock, Samuel. "Uncle Dick's Advoice to Wed Women." *The Collected Writings of Samuel Laycock*. Ed. George Milner. Manchester, 1908. 98–9.

Lown, Judy. "Not So Much a Factory, More a Form of Patriarchy: Gender and Class During Industrialisation." *Gender, Class and Work*. Ed. Eva Gamarnikow et al. London: Heinemann, 1983. 28–45.

Machonachie, Moira. "Women's Work and Domesticity in the *English Women's Journal*." *Studies in the History of Feminism*. Ed. Sally Alexander. London: U of London Dept. of Extra-mural Studies, 1984.

Maidment, Brian. "Essayists and Artizans – The Making of Nineteenth-Century Self-Taught Poets." *Literature and History* 9 (1983): 74–91.

—— *The Poorhouse Fugitives: Self-Taught Poets and Poetry in Victorian Britain.* Manchester: Carcanet, 1987.

—— "Prose and Artisan Discourse in Early Victorian Britain." *Prose Studies* 10 (1987): 30–41.

Marie. "Idealise the Real and Realise the Ideal." *The People's Journal* 4 (1851): 175.

—— "The Indomitable Will." *The People's Journal* 4 (1851): 63.

—— "Labour." 1850. Maidment, *Poorhouse.*

Osterund Nancy Grey. "Gender Divisions and the Organization of Work in the Leicester Hosiery Industry." *Unequal Opportunities: Women's Employment in England, 1800–1918.* Ed. Angela John. Oxford: Blackwell, 1986. 45–68.

The Pioneer, or Grand National Consolidated Trades' Union Magazine. 1833–34. New York: Greenwood Reprint Co., 1968.

Roberts, Robert. *The Classic Slum: Salford Life in the First Quarter of the Century.* 1971. Harmondsworth: Penguin, 1988.

Rose, Sonya O. "'Gender At Work': Sex, Class and Industrial Capitalism." *History Workshop Journal* 21 (1986): 113–31.

Swindells, Julia. *Victorian Writing and Working Women.* Minneapolis: U of Minnesota P, 1985.

Taylor, Barbara. *Eve and the New Jerusalem: Socialism and Feminism in the Nineteenth Century.* London: Virago, 1983.

Vicinus, Martha. *The Ambiguities of Self-Help.* Littleborough, Lancashire: George Kelsall, 1984.

—— *The Industrial Muse: A Study of Nineteenth-Century British Working-Class Literature.* New York: Barnes, 1974.

Vincent, David. *Bread, Knowledge and Freedom: A Study of Nineteenth-Century Working Class Autobiography.* London: Methuen, 1981.

Waugh, Edwin. "Come Whoam to thi Childer an' Me." *Poems and Lancashire Songs.* Manchester, 1859. 64–5.

—— "Dinner Time." Hollingworth 68–9.

—— "Down Again!" Hollingworth 70–1.

—— "Toothsome Advice." *Poems and Songs.* Ed. George Milner. Manchester, 1893. 136–7.

11

'The fruitful feud of hers and his'
Sameness, Difference, and Gender in Victorian Poetry

Dorothy Mermin

When women poets began in the Victorian period to win real acceptance in the ranks of high culture, the problems particular to women writing poetry were to a significant extent those of men as well. Men too, in an age of religious uncertainty and drastic social change, felt excluded from the bardic, prophetic confidence of the past and from their Romantic predecessors' intimate sense of a poetry-sustaining life in nature. As lines of gender demarcation became exceptionally rigid, the gendered division between private and public spheres marked poetry itself – and especially lyric – as feminine and private even though publication belonged to the masculine sphere. While most women writers suffered galling constraints on their freedom to move beyond domestic seclusion, many male writers found the public world of bourgeois masculinity alien and disagreeable. On a formal level, the conventional gendering of the speaking subject as male and the object as female, with the wide-ranging polarization it imposed, was problematic for both men and women. But outside conventional gender structures – assuming one could escape them – lurked the threat of undifferentiated sameness, with the double danger of sexual transgression (more evident for men than for women, and becoming increasingly clear as the

Mermin, Dorothy. 1995. "'The fruitful feud of hers and his': Sameness, Difference, and Gender in Victorian Poetry." In *Victorian Poetry*, 33, I (Spring), pp. 149–68. Reproduced with permission of Dorothy Mermin.

Victorian Poets: A Critical Reader, First Edition. Edited by Valentine Cunningham.
© 2014 John Wiley & Sons, Ltd. Published 2014 by John Wiley & Sons, Ltd.

century progressed) and the loss of the essential structures that defined both poetry and the self.[1]

In interlocking elegiac verses on her female predecessors, "Felicia Hemans: To L.E.L., Referring to Her Monody on the Poetess," and "L.E.L.'s Last Question," Barrett Browning places herself in a poetic tradition in which women write to one another instead of being written about by men: a world without gender difference, in which identities keep threatening to merge. Both poems describe Landon as projecting or seeking her own image everywhere. "Felicia Hemans" begins:

> Thou bay-crowned living One that o'er the bay-crowned Dead art bowing,
> And o'er the shadeless moveless brow the vital shadow throwing,
> And o'er the sighless songless lips the wail and music wedding,
> And dropping o'er the tranquil eyes the tears not of their shedding! –
>
> (ll. 1–4)[2]

Hemans' tearful example creates Landon's tears, which drop into Hemans' eyes so that they seem to be shedding those tears together. Landon's "Stanzas" in fact echo Hemans' "Bring Flowers": "Bring flowers! thus said the lovely song; / And shall they not be brought / To her?"[3] – turning the poem's author into the object of its exhortation. But Barrett Browning wants to break the chain, even as she joins it: "No flowers for her! no need of flowers, albeit 'bring flowers!' thou saidest" (l. 8). "Nor mourn, O living One, because her part in life was mourning" (l. 17).

But the first alternative the poem offers is another form of mirroring:

> Lay only dust's stern verity upon the dust undreaming:
> And while the calm perpetual stars shall look upon it
> solely,
> Her sphered soul shall look on *them* with eyes more
> bright and holy.
>
> (ll. 14–16)

The real alternative is Jesus, who projects his qualities onto the dead poet without reflecting hers: "The whiteness of His innocence o'er all her garments, flowing" (l. 27). Landon's "Stanzas" leave Hemans "laid" in the "breast" of "quiet mother-earth" (ll. 105–107); Barrett Browning substitutes contiguity with a male divinity for absorption into female nature, leaving Hemans "on" the "bosom" (l. 26) of Jesus.

If Landon rejoices like Hemans in Jesus, she can hope for the same happy end: "as thy dust decayeth / May thine own England say for thee, what now for Her it sayeth" (ll. 29–30). She will become in her turn object rather than subject; and what England will say is that her death is quieter and therefore better than her poetry:

> "Albeit softly in our ears her silver song was ringing,
> The foot-fall of her parting soul is softer than her.
>   singing!"
>
> (ll. 31–32)

Landon can only replicate her predecessor after all; and the best replication is silence.

In "L.E.L.'s Last Question," similarly, the poet is chided for seeking a mirror of herself. The "last question" is: "'Do you think of me as I think of you?'" Barrett Browning dislikes what she sees as the monotonous emotionality of Hemans' and Landon's poetry, trapped in conventionally feminine themes and tones:

> And little in the world the Loving do
> But sit (among the rocks!) and listen for
> The echo of their own love evermore –
> "Do you think of me as I think of you?"
>
> (ll. 11–14)

But her own poem remains trapped in the same theme, if not quite the same tone, echoing Landon's question seven times in nine stanzas, until in the final stanza the poet hears Jesus addressing the question to herself. As in "Felicia Hemans," the poem breaks out of the hall of mirrors only by having God assert his primacy as subject, returning the woman poet once again to the position of silence.

These poems describe a female poetic tradition that eludes a system of differences geared to the male subject, only to find itself trapped in a world of undifferentiated sorrow and forced to seek a new principle of difference in religion – Christ's divinity, not his gender – that also requires their silence. Male poets, too, struggled against the traditionally gendered system of poetic difference and confronted the difficulties and impasses that the struggle entailed. In this essay I shall try to suggest some of the ways in which these issues, which are central to Victorian women's poetry, are played out in the work of their male contemporaries.

Dorothy Mermin

1 Questioning the Subject: Dramatic Monologue

The distinctively Victorian form, the dramatic monologue, calls attention to and problematizes the status of the speaking subject. For women poets this is the overriding, inescapable question; and men too formulate it surprisingly often in terms of gender. According to Isobel Armstrong, nineteenth-century women poets (Hemans, Landon) "'invented'" the dramatic monologue as a way to counter and control the poetic objectification of woman.[4] Women poets most often use dramatic monologues to allow female speakers to express passion, rage, and rebellion against social constraints (e.g., Barrett Browning's "Bianca among the Nightingales" and "Mother and Poet," Rossetti's "Cousin Kate" and "'The Iniquity of the Fathers upon the Children,'" Webster's "A Castaway"), and female speakers in such poems as Browning's "James Lee's Wife," Tennyson's "Rizpah," and Arnold's "A Modern Sappho" (the strongest expression of erotic desire in all of Arnold's work) are similar voices of the unimpeded subjectivity that dramatized female speakers, but not female poets in anything that might be mistaken for their own voices, were conventionally allowed.[5] In contrast and complement to such affirmations of the female speaking subject who exists only as a fictional construct, Tennyson and Browning in their most famous early dramatic monologues explore the stresses and pathologies of the subject-object relations that actually obtained in poetry.

In "Ulysses" and "Tithonus" the integrity of the self turns out to depend on the structures of difference created by gender. Ulysses renounces the roles of husband, father, and ruler for a comradeship that amounts almost to identity ("My mariners, / Souls that have toiled, and wrought, and thought with me" [ll. 45–46]); he is nostalgic for the days when he "drank delight of battle with his peers"; he leaves the "aged wife" with whom he is mis-"matched" (l. 3) to seek "the great Achilles, whom we knew" (l. 64); and he loses the selfhood that depends on difference. "I am become a name" (l. 11), "I am a part of all that I have met" (l. 18), he says as he prepares to sail off into an ever-receding emptiness.[6] Tithonus, similarly, is "A white-haired shadow roaming like a dream" (l. 8), "all I was, in ashes" (l. 23), and like Ulysses he wants to leave a woman from whom he feels an absolute alienation ("how can my nature longer mix with thine?" [l. 65]) to return to an undifferentiated sameness: "I earth in earth forget these empty courts, / And thee returning on thy silver wheels" (ll. 75–76). Insofar as "Tithonus" is an allegory of art and the artist, it suggests the hopelessly alien, shimmeringly redundant femininity (woman, goddess, natural

202

phenomenon) of the poetic object. The two poems together represent the desire to escape the dependence of the male poetic subject on the female object, and also the dissolution of self that escape would entail.

Browning's monologues obsessively explore both the moral corruptness of that dependence and the impossibility of getting away from it. "My Last Duchess," which is generally taken as the prototypical dramatic monologue, is also the prototypical study of the objectification of woman in art; and it shows how speaker, poet, and reader all inevitably participate in the objectifying act. The Duchess embodies the feminine virtues of naturalness, spontaneity, and non-judgmental sympathy, virtues impossible to either the author or the reader of an ironic poem like this one. A male painter turns the Duchess into a work of art; the Duke – the only person in the poem with the power of speech – controls the painting both physically and through his explication of it; and the poet himself, with the reader's complicity, controls and explicates the Duke. Anyone who has heard students discuss "My Last Duchess" will recall the relish with which they diagnose the Duke's immorality, pounce on his self-betrayals, draw the curtain on the discussion with the self-satisfaction of superiority and control, and perhaps even experience aesthetic pleasure as they do so – mimicking in every aspect, that is, the Duke himself. Poems like "Porphyria's Lover," "Andrea del Sarto," and "Cleon" have similar themes and similar effects in the classroom, while critics and teachers have unselfconsciously indulged in the pleasure of detecting the moral failings of almost every dramatic monologuist in the Victorian canon – over-exercising the moral "judgment" that Robert Langbaum taught us was definitive of the form while forgetting the sympathy he equally enjoined.[7] In terms of gender politics, the achievement of "My Last Duchess" is to make the male speaking subject the object of scrutiny and control and by doing so to demonstrate the inevitable complicity of poet, reader, critic, and critic of critics (as in this account) in his objectifying act.

"The Bishop Orders His Tomb" presents a man who tries to become what women poets felt they had to be: both subject and object of art. Imagining that his existence will be fixed, as women's so often were, in an artistic representation commemorating his death, he endeavors simultaneously to create and to become that work of art:

> I fold my arms as if they clasped a crook,
> And stretch my feet forth straight as stone can point,
> And let the bedclothes, for a mortcloth, drop
> Into great laps and folds of sculptor's-work.
>
> (ll. 87–90)[8]

203

Having blurred the boundary between subject and object, his wandering thoughts confound distinctions between life and death (he expects his sculpted self to hear and see and feel), spirit and matter, religion and aesthetics, Christianity and paganism, and male and female: "Saint Praxed at his sermon on the mount" (l. 95). The poem's heavy-handed insistence on his manifold moral failings reminds us of the almost universal nineteenth-century condemnation of self-consciousness and self-display, particularly in regard to women, and its inhibiting effect on women poets. And as the bishop transforms himself into an object to be looked at, his remembered mistress undergoes the opposite transformation. He recalls her first as the object of his rival's envy, "so fair she was" (l. 5), then as his sons' "tall pale mother with her talking eyes" (l. 96), and finally as merged with the sons' predatory gaze: "Ever your [the sons'] eyes were as a lizard's quick, / They glitter like your mother's for my soul" (ll. 104–105). But in the last line of the poem he reverts to his original pleasure in her beauty as a cause of envy, "so fair she was" (l. 125). For his unresponsive sons are leaving, his orders will not be carried out, and he could not in any case turn himself into a stone carving. So conventional gender roles are restored. Throughout Browning's career, the destructiveness of male subjectivity and the impossibility of escaping it prove as unresolvable – and as poetically enriching – a subject for Browning as the struggle to become subject rather than object of poetry does for women.[9]

2 Androgyny

Attempts to revise conventional gender roles appear most obviously in poems that work towards an androgynous ideal, which generally turns out to mean appropriating almost all desirable qualities and powers to one's own gender, leaving very little for the other. The woman of the future evoked at the end of *The Princess*, while growing "like in difference" (vii.262), will retain "the childlike in the larger mind" (vii.268) and "set herself to man / Like perfect music unto noble words" (vii.269–270), while the man will add "sweetness" and "moral height" to his "wrestling thews that throw the world" (vii.265–266). Arthur Hallam in *In Memoriam* harmonizes oppositions in an ideal unity: public-private, doubt-faith, reason-emotion, body-spirit, God-nature, human-divine, and underlying them all and reflected in almost all of them, male-female. Formally, too, gendered opposites merge, as in *The Princess* with its admixture of lyric to narrative: elegy was a masculine form and religious doubt a theme reserved for men, but the poem presents itself as a kind of diary: fragmentary, spontaneous, unpremeditated, and as such feminine. But it takes shape around an interlocking series of binary oppositions that are inherently hierarchical: "O loved the most, when most I feel / There is a lower and a higher" (cxxix.3–4). Ideally, they merge, like "Sweet Hesper-Phosphor, double name / For what is one, the first, the last" (cxxi.17–18). Hallam is "Known and unknown, human, divine" (cxxix.5); "mixed with God and Nature" (cxxx.11); "manhood fused with female grace" (cix.17). But the fusion is radically unequal: the unknown soars above the little that can be known, the divine incorporates and surpasses the human, Nature fades into an almost transparent veil for God, and manhood fuses not with womanhood but with a single feminine quality, the "grace" that perfects the man. The simple "Sweet-hearted" woman who thinks that "doubt is Devil-born" is juxtaposed to Hallam's complexity: "Perplext in faith, but pure in deeds" (xcvi.2, 4, 9). Women appear in the poem as figures for Tennyson's relationship to Hallam, or, in the case of his sisters Emily and Cecilia (whose marriage to another of Tennyson's friends provides the occasion for the epilogue), as links between men: Tennyson's fantasy of Hallam living to marry Emily concludes with Tennyson and Hallam dying at the same time and taken by Christ "as a single soul" (lxxxiv.44) – having apparently forgotten about Emily.

Barrett Browning's and Christina Rossetti's images of androgyny show a complementary exclusiveness. Aurora Leigh's professional accomplishment and personal autonomy are crowned by love and marriage, while Romney loses his eyesight, his ancestral house, his work, and his philosophy. He is allowed to marry and adore, like a woman, but forbidden both man's work and woman's, perhaps because he has tried to combine the two in an androgyny of his own: the philanthropy for which he is so harshly punished encompassed political activity and social theory (defined in the poem as male) as well as visiting sickbeds, feeding and making a home for the poor, and other forms of feminine nurturing. Similarly, the sisters in Rossetti's *Goblin Market* achieve both heroic action and maternal and sororal fulfillment although – or rather, because – the only men in the poem are little goblins who disappear when the sisters have stolen their power. In each case the androgynized version of the author's own gender expands to fill the intellectual, moral, and social space available.

With more explicit visions of androgyny, however, come a shudder and recoil. In a draft for *The Princess*, Tennyson wrote:

> And if aught be comprising in itself
> The man, the woman, let it sit [apart]
> Godlike, alone, or only rapt on heaven—
> What need for such to wed? or if there be
> Men-women, let them wed with women-men
> And make a proper marriage.
>
> (Poems, 2:290n)

Barrett Browning's two sonnets to George Sand (written before *Aurora Leigh)* take for granted as Tennyson does that female intellect and genius violate the lines of gender – Sand is a paradoxically "large-brained woman and large-hearted man" ("A Desire," l. 1), "True genius, but true woman" ("A Recognition," l. 1) – and associate androgyny with sexual transgression. Sand is urged to transcend sensuality, first for an angelic purity that would culminate in quasi–maternal same-sex embraces – "child and maiden pressed [i.e. would press] to thine embrace / To kiss upon thy lips a stainless fame" ("A Desire," ll. 13–14) – and then for "unsex[ed]," "unincarnate" life in heaven ("A Recognition," ll. 13–14). The first sonnet foreshadows Aurora's relationship with Marian Erle and her child, in which Aurora plays out the possibilities of taking a male role in the courtship and marriage plots, and the second shows the fears Barrett Browning had to overcome before she could conceive Aurora's triumphant combination of career and marriage. In these sonnets androgyny is allowable only without sex.

In his four-sonnet sequence "Hermaphroditus," addressed to the statue in the Louvre, Swinburne presents the idea of androgyny literally, sensuously lingering precisely where other poets shied away. As Ovid tells the story, the youth Hermaphroditus refused the love of the nymph Salmacis, but when he dove into her pool she pressed against him until they merged in one body. Fleeing the feminine, he becomes it. Swinburne, like Ovid, takes a male point of view: his androgyne is a feminized man, just as Barrett Browning's Sand is a masculinized woman, and a conventional gender hierarchy is implicit in the poem. The nymph is more a natural object than a woman, and the melting of Hermaphroditus' manhood is presented as effete and shocking. But while for Ovid it is a tale of horror, for Swinburne it is one of delectable sadness:

> I saw in what swift wise
> Beneath the woman's and the water's kiss

> Thy moist limbs melted into Salmacis,
> And the large light turned tender in thine eyes,
> And all thy boy's breath softened into sighs.
>
> (IV)[10]

The infusion of female grace that Tennyson admired in Hallam is here
literal and complete:

> Sex to sweet sex with lips and limbs is wed,
> Turning the fruitful feud of hers and his
> To the waste wedlock of a sterile kiss.
>
> (II)

Swinburne in his customary fashion carries a theme other poets
approach with trepidation and indirection into full explicitness, and
makes it clear why others did not. The androgyne has become almost
without disguise the object of the poet's homoerotic desire.[11] And while
the gendered poetic conventions of difference (the "fruitful feud of his
and hers") often inhibited fructification for women poets, they had
given men endless possibilities for readjustment, renegotiation, and
exploration, with an edge of transgressive danger – possibilities that
"Hermaphroditus" fulfills and, by doing so, forecloses.

3 The Disappearance of the Object

The basic gender distinction of poetic convention – male speaker, female
object – troubled women's entrance into poetry. If they are the speakers,
who are the objects? They examine this problem in variants of quest
romance and the story of Sleeping Beauty. In Rossetti's "The Dead City"
and Barrett Browning's "The Lost Bower" and "The Deserted Garden"
questers arrive at the magical place but find no object there; Rossetti's
speaker leaves, acknowledging failure, and Barrett Browning's bower
and garden can be found only by a child, not by a woman.[12] Browning's
"'Childe Roland to the Dark Tower Came'" and Swinburne's "A
Forsaken Garden" also describe quests that find no gendered object, but
these poems are hymns of triumph over old conventions rather than,
like Barrett Browning's and Rossetti's, records of defeat.

In "'Childe Roland'" not only has gender vanished; the whole oppositional structure of experience and values has collapsed. Roland
confounds the distinction between truth and lies, glorious past and

inglorious present, success and failure, innocence and guilt, self and nature, presence and absence, and subject and object. The poem itself seems to confound sense and nonsense – an appearance Browning encouraged. The poem came on him "as a kind of dream," he said; "I did not know then what I meant…, and I'm sure I don't know now."[13] It was written in the shadow of the acknowledged or suspected moral collapse of the two most important male authority figures in Browning's life: his recently widowed father was publicly revealed to have written foolish love letters to a woman who sued him for breach of promise, and the essay he had just written on Shelley was haunted by rumors of Shelley's cruel abandonment of his first wife. These offenses threatened the moral foundations of masculine identity as established in relationships with women. In "'Childe Roland'" there are no such relationships: there is only Roland's acceptance of identity in failure with his fellow-questers. He himself (women being absent) is both subject and object of the quest. His arrival at the tower – or rather, in an allegory of self-recognition, his realization that he is already there – is also a self-presentation to his "peers." He "discovers" himself in the double sense of finding and revealing:

> There they stood, ranged along the hill-sides, met
> To view the last of me, a living frame
> For one more picture!

Presenting himself to their gaze, however, he also looks at them:

> in a sheet of flame
> I saw them and I knew them all.

And he asserts his own subjectivity:

> And yet
> Dauntless the slug-horn to my lips I set,
> And blew. *'Childe Roland to the Dark Tower came.'*
> (ll. 199–204)

Browning created what seemed an impossibility to Barrett Browning and Rossetti in their early quest-poems, a speaker who is both subject and object – and he does so by erasing all forms of difference, starting with gender.[14] The mystification surrounding the poem, however, suggests the difficulty of doing so.

In "A Forsaken Garden," the gendered object, the desiring, questing subject, and the quest itself have all disappeared together. "Through branches and briars if a man make way" (l. 14) to this version of Sleeping Beauty's palace or the garden of love, he will find nothing but wind. "All are at one now, roses and lovers" (l. 57). Without oppositional relationships, there is no life:

> Not a flower to be pressed of the foot that falls not;
>   As the heart of a dead man the seed-plots are dry;
> From the thicket of thorns whence the nightingale calls not,
>   Could she call, there were never a rose to reply.
>
>   (ll. 25–28)

The earth will shrink and crumble until absence conjures up a single presence that like the garden itself is also an absence, both subject and object: death. "As a god self-slain on his own strange altar," the poem concludes, "Death lies dead" (ll. 79–80).[15]

"Hermaphroditus" and "A Forsaken Garden" present as theme the blurring of boundaries, the melting of one thing into another, that Swinburne's poetry typically enacts as style. As John Rosenberg says, Swinburne "is obsessed by the moment when one thing shades off into its opposite, or when contraries fuse."[16] Good and evil, love and hate, presence and absence, pleasure and pain, male and female, but also sound and sense, sense and nonsense, seriousness and self-parody typically flow into each other. For instance:

> Or they loved their life through, and then went whither?
>   And were one to the end – but what end who knows?
> Love deep as the sea as a rose must wither,
>   As the rose-red seaweed that mocks the rose.
> Shall the dead take thought for the dead to love them?
>   What love was ever as deep as a grave?
> They are loveless now as the grass above them
>   Or the wave.
>
>   (ll. 49–56)

In this intricate dance elements blur and fuse: homonyms ("whither," "wither") rhyme and merge in significant relationship; the rose and the sea join in seaweed that looks like a rose; the short final phrase, which seems to float as a syntactically vague afterthought, suggests that the lovers are under both sea and earth; and the word "love" pervades the stanza even as love itself is declared to be absent. The foregrounding of sound, the bewildering repetitions, and the speed with which the verses hurry us onward enhance the dislocating effect of such locutions. T. S. Eliot complained that in the lines "Time with a gift of tears; / Grief with a glass that ran" (from *Atalanta in Calydon*) Time and Grief have exchanged allegorical properties, and that Swinburne's poems often offer only "the hallucination of meaning." But that, of course, is the point, as Rosenberg points out;[17] Swinburne's unexpected images conjure up images of time's hourglass and grief's tears, and what passes before our eyes is a blur of superimposed objects.

According to Robert Buchanan in his notorious attack on "the fleshly school of poetry" (in which Swinburne is a prominent member),

> the fleshly gentlemen...aver that poetic expression is greater than poetic thought, and by inference that the body is greater than the soul, and sound superior to sense; and that the poet...must be an intellectual hermaphrodite, to whom the very facts of day and night are lost in a whirl of aesthetic terminology.[18]

Buchanan notes the influence of *Sonnets from the Portuguese* behind Dante Rossetti's fleshly sonnets; and critics complained that Barrett Browning's poems, too (especially her early long works, *The Seraphim* and *A Drama of Exile*), were misty, opaque, obscure, foregrounding language rather than objects or ideas.[19] The first stanza of "Felicia Hemans," with its long lines, swinging music, suspended syntax, structures of opposition that blur into sameness, and interweaving repetitions of words and sounds, works much as Swinburne's verses do. It simultaneously affirms and denies: "less" is affixed four times to Swinburnean monosyllables and negations are immediately negated:

> And o'er the shadeless moveless brow the vital shadow
> > throwing,
> And o'er the sighless songless lips the wail and music
> > wedding.
>
> > > (ll. 2–3)

The poem both enacts and renounces the very idea of "wedding." Don't give life to the dead (ll. 1–4); don't bring her flowers (ll. 7–8), since flowers belong to different kinds of stories (ll. 9–12), but only dust for dust (l. 14) – but the poem weds itself to its predecessors' music, and it is full of flowers (the word appears six times). Women's poetry, like Swinburne's Time and Grief, superimposes new stories on old ones, as in their variants of quest romance, or in love poems where the half-remembered voices of male lovers haunt our readings and confuse our response, or in the complex argument about women's poetry that underlies the Christian consolation of "Felicia Hemans" and "L.E.L.'s 'Last Question.'" Such superimpositions recreate an old story only to show how women's versions have to be different; and as with Swinburne unless we see that the mismatch between the new poem and the old ones we sense behind it is precisely the point, the poems will seem thin and shallow, with only the hallucination of meaning.

The foregrounding of verbal complexity in conjunction with an apparent confounding of systems of difference, in defiance of conventional gender values and to the apparent detriment of discursive meaning, is used by other Victorian poets too, even when gender distinctions superficially remain intact. In Morris' "The Defence of Guenevere," written in the intricately woven form of terza rima, the self-protective strategy of Guenevere's speech is to display herself as an erotic object in order to disguise the fact of her sexual transgression and confound the distinction between truth and lies:

> say no rash word
> Against me, being so beautiful; my eyes,
> Wept all away to grey, may bring some sword
>
> To drown you in your blood; see my breast rise,
> Like waves of purple sea, as here I stand;
> And how my arms are moved in wonderful wise,
>
> Yea also at my full heart's strong command,
> See through my long throat how the words go up
> In ripples to my mouth.
>
> (ll. 223–231)[20]

The content of speech dissolves into its physical embodiment, while the speaker invites her audience to admire the parts of her body (her eyes, her throat) with which she looks and speaks, and which she cannot herself see. And in Christina Rossetti's "Sleeping at Last," with its wonderfully interweaving repetitions, the dead woman has ceased to be either subject (no more "pangs" and "fears" [l. 6]) or object ("out of sight of friend & of lover" [l. 3]):[21]

> Fast asleep. Singing birds in their leafy cover
> Cannot wake her, nor shake her the gusty blast.

> Under the purple thyme & the purple clover
> Sleeping at last.
>
> (ll. 8–11)

Angela Leighton remarks that "certain images, of laughter, music, entombment, heartlessness and whiteness, figure, in the work of many [Victorian women] poets, as signs of a condition of suspended reference, of playful nonsense, achieved against the moral cost of what it means to be a woman."[22] Browning, Swinburne, and Morris achieve a similar kind of nonsense against the moral cost of being a man.

In Swinburne, says Eliot, "the meaning and the sound are one thing," which for Eliot is almost – but not quite – as it should be: for while "language in a healthy state presents the object, is so close to the object that the two are identified," Swinburne goes too far: "They are identified in the verse of Swinburne solely because the object has ceased to exist."[23] Swinburne is the extreme case of what appalls Eliot in Victorian poetry. Approached from the perspective of women's poetry, the loss of the "object," which for Eliot means the fall into vague subjectivity or mere Tennysonian music that defined Victorian poetry for modernist critics, carries with it the breakdown of the oppositional structure that required and affirmed the masculinity of the poetic subject. It marks the feminization of Victorian poetry.

4 Matthew Arnold

Eliot's insistence on "the object" echoes Arnold's critical efforts to construct an escape from the impasses of subjectivity. The Greek poets, Arnold says, did not engage in modern poetry's "dialogue of the mind with itself" – a phrase that could define the self-mirroring art for which Barrett Browning admonishes Landon, as well as "'Childe Roland'"; instead, they knew how to find "a sufficiently grand, detached, and self-subsistent object for a tragic poem."[24] Arnold as critic, like Eliot, wants to assert the independent existence of "the object" and to disengage it from feeling and from language; the task of modern criticism is "'to see the object as in itself it really is.'"[25] In Arnold's poetry, however, the feminine object is often elusive or absent, and the masculine subject is correspondingly problematic.

One of Arnold's most persistent themes (in "Mycerinus," "The Scholar-Gipsy," *Sohrab and Rustum,* and many other poems) is the disinclination to grow up into a hard, unpoetical adult masculinity. His juvenilia, like Barrett Browning's, show a marked distaste for the role assigned him by the conventions of gender in both poetry and life. Like Barrett Browning, he seems as a child to have conceived of poetry in large part as a question of travel. Barrett Browning, whose brother went away to school and would be allowed (she wrongly supposed) freedom to range the world, daydreamed of dressing as a boy so that she could be Byron's page, or lead an army against the Turks to liberate Greece and teach their classical language to Greek islanders;[26] she saw travel and poetry as male prerogatives. Arnold, who was sent unhappily away to school and knew all too well that men were expected to lead armies and defend and teach classical culture, seems to have daydreamed about staying home. Some poems written when he was thirteen play out this theme. His earliest surviving verses, "Mary Queen of Scots on her departure from France," represents Mary's lament at leaving the "Land of my earlier, happier days" (l. 9); she is on a boat heading for Scotland, where she will find (the reader knows) disasters and death.[27] "The First Sight of Italy" urges an undefined addressee alternately to travel and to stop, and (in the last three of ten stanzas) to come home. And in "Lines written on first leaving home for a Public School" the unhappy speaker tries to reassure himself that the thought of home will cheer him along the "dreary path" (l. 10) through "the maze of life" (l. 22), which he imagines in terms of metaphorical battle (l. 9) and unmitigated gloom. But to travel is also, as for the young Elizabeth Barrett, to be a Byronic poet: the Italy of "The First Sight" is "the Poets' ceaseless story" (l. 35), and Arnold's early poems show the powerful influence of Childe Harold's pilgrimage through Italy.

In poems in which travel is structured as a quest, correspondingly, the disturbance of gender roles means that, as in Barrett Browning's "The Lost Bower" and "The Deserted Garden" and Rossetti's "The Dead City," the speaker arrives at what should be a place of erotic and imaginative fulfillment but finds no "other" there. Instead, he finds a mirror in which he sees himself. "Stanzas from the Grande Chartreuse" begins with a quest-like approach to an enclosed, secluded, magical place, in which the speaker eventually recognizes his likeness to the monks who receive him. He dissociates himself from aggressively masculine "Sons of the world" (l. 161) with their "exulting thunder" (l. 164), "pride of life," and "tireless powers" (l. 167), and ranks himself with the monastic "children reared in shade" (l. 169) who cannot leave their secluded childhood home to join the armies, hunters, and "Gay dames"

(l. 185) of grown-up life. (The fact that the night Arnold spent at the Grande Chartreuse was part of his honeymoon, and that his wife was not allowed to come in with him, reinforces the association of the monastery and the loss of gender opposition.) For a woman, the absence of an object other than the self at the end of the quest exemplifies the exclusion of women from poetry; the speakers leave and cannot return. But for Arnold in the same situation the Grande Chartreuse is a trap, like Childe Roland's tower. "Fenced early in this cloistral round" (l. 205), he and the monks cannot leave their "desert" (l. 210). Whereas women feel excluded from poetry, Arnold's speaker feels excluded from life.

The absence of gender opposition can also doom the quest of an Arnoldian lover who yearns for what "The River" describes in Platonic terms as the "twin soul which halves [his] own" ("Too Late," l. 4). The speaker in *Switzerland* "dream[s]" that "two human hearts might blend/In one" ("Isolation. To Marguerite," ll. 38–39), and laments that would-be lovers who were once "Parts of a single continent" ("To Marguerite – Continued," l. 16) have broken apart into separate islands. "A Farewell" begins at the end of a lover's moonlight journey on horseback across a bridge and up a "steep street" (l. 7), "Led by [Marguerite's] taper's starlike beam" (l. 8). Marguerite is there, thoroughly feminine, and expecting a thoroughly masculine man:

> women – things that live and move
> Mined by the fever of the soul –
> They seek to find in those they love
> Stern strength, and promise of control.
>
> (ll. 21–24)

But he is her counterpart, not her opposite: "the bent of both our hearts/ Was to be gentle, tranquil, true" (ll. 47–48). They both have androgynous yearnings:

> I too have felt the load I bore
> In a too strong emotion's sway;
> I too have wished, no woman more,
> This starting, feverish heart away.
> I too have longed for trenchant force,
> And will like a dividing spear;
> Have praised the keen, unscrupulous course,
> Which knows no doubt, which feels no fear.
>
> (ll. 29–36)

But the aggressively phallic masculinity he claims to have desired is depicted not only as morally negative but also as antithetical to the qualities of feeling and sympathy that in Arnold's view characterize true poetry; and in fact the lack of masculine firmness – the strong emotions, the "feverish heart" – that disqualifies him for being loved also implicitly characterizes him as a Byronic poet:

> this heart, I know,
> To be long loved was never framed;
> For something in its depths doth glow
> Too strange, too restless, too untamed.
> (ll. 17–20)

Like Barrett Browning's sonnets to George Sand, "A Farewell" suggests that androgyny is tolerable only in a desexualized life beyond this world. The speaker sometimes attributes the failure of their love to Marguerite's sexuality: in "Parting" he is driven from her by the thought that she has kissed and embraced other men (ll. 65–70), and many years later in "The Terrace at Berne" he imagines her having returned to France (home of sexual license) and taken up "riotous laughter," rouge, and lace (ll. 21–24). In the afterlife they will be innocent children basking "in the eternal Father's smile" ("A Farewell," l. 61), not lovers but brother and sister (l. 78). But meanwhile their love is thwarted by her sexuality and desire for difference and by the unmasculine qualities that make him a poet.

Arnold's poetry, like Swinburne's, often haunts the boundary between sea and land where symbolic opposites meet and mingle. This boundary-blurring structure is basic to his poetic imagination, as it is to Swinburne's, although whereas Swinburne glories in confusion, Arnold generally, as in *Switzerland*, includes an edge of resistance or at least of regret. Two of the poems written when he was thirteen show that this structure was ingrained in his imagination, and that like young women poets when they approached adolescence he had trouble adapting to the gender role thrust upon him by literary and social convention. "Reply to a declaration that he would not live by the Sea, made in verse by H. H." asserts the poet's love for hills and fields and his even greater love for the ocean as a source of poetic scenes and stories, and sets up a series of oppositions:

> To you be the pleasures of soft green fields,
> And tales round the fireside,

215

> But to me be the murmur of ocean's wild wave
> And the ebb and the flow of his tide.
>
> May you wake from your sleep at the nightingale's voice
> And I at the sea fowl's cry.
>
> (ll. 45–50)

But he is not really choosing the excitement of the sea rather than the pleasures of domesticity; he means to live at the seashore and look at the life he desires – as women in Victorian literature so often do – from a window: "May you look from your window on Nature's green garb, / And I on the wave dashing high" (ll. 51–52).

"Lines written on the Seashore at Eaglehurst," written at about the same time, imagines naiads moving from undersea halls of coral and glens on the "wooded shore" (l. 9), and then pictures the "barrier firm and stiff" (l. 29) of the castle-crowned cliff that opposes the waves' attempt to "lave" (l. 27) its foot. The ocean (which is male) seems to stand in for the poet: it is driven by imaginative longings for lovely "scenes" (l. 36) which make it emulate the boundary-crossing behavior of the female naiads who in generally artistic fashion revel and sing and decorate things with flowers; but "while his fancy takes its fill / His waves must roll below" (ll. 39–40). Phallic power defends the boundary against the incursions of imagination.

"The Forsaken Merman" elaborates this early poem into a story which structures gender and imagination in the same terms. The merman haunts the shoreline like the ocean that "Still restlessly…struggles on / O'er seaweed fair, o'er shell and stone" ("Lines," ll. 31–32), and is repulsed by the town and church as the ocean at Eaglehurst is by the cliff and the castle, whereas Margaret, like the naiads, has moved back and forth. "The Forsaken Merman" sets up and then complicates a set of superimposed oppositions between male and female, natural and human, family and society, human and divine. The location of happiness and virtue shifts back and forth between the chambers of the sea and the white-walled town. Margaret leaves her family to answer the call of religion, thereby becoming "faithless" (l. 121) to another set of values; although her Christian faith is a feminine virtue, it leaves her husband to take care of the children; and the merman keeps slipping out of his own point of view to see things from hers, even as she (he imagines) slips from her joy in the town to yearnings for the sea-children whom she at the same time imagines as irrevocably alien: "the cold strange eyes of a little Mermaiden / And the gleam of her golden hair" (ll. 106–107). Nothing is stable except sorrow, loss, and the merman's returns to the shoreline across which his imagination endlessly moves like the ocean's "fancy" at Eaglehurst. In "The Forsaken Merman" the border of sea and land also marks the separation of men and women, but it is a boundary across which conventional gender differences disappear; and the loss of those differences, as in "A Farewell," makes love impossible even as it creates a poem.

Arnold's poetry, like that of his major female and male contemporaries, explores the disparity between the gender conventions that structured English poetry and the complexities of gender relations as they were experienced and perceived by Victorian poets. Like Barrett Browning's, the records of his early ventures into poetry show his discomfort with the gender role assigned him by society and poetry alike. Like both Elizabeth Barrett and Robert Browning, he finds the conventional subject-object relations of poetry psychologically difficult or morally offensive. And as for many of his contemporaries, the struggle against them informs much of his poetry even when he finds those relations inescapable, or to be escaped only at great moral cost. More perhaps than any of his male contemporaries, he struggled against the difficulty of a situation in which poetic structures were still framed for male subjects but poetry's qualities were those associated with women.

Many years ago I chose to write my doctoral dissertation on Matthew Arnold, half-consciously inspired by the feeling that his predicament in some ways prefigured my own alienation, as a woman, from the cultural tradition presented and represented to me by the, Harvard English Department. I now think that in some important sense all the Victorian poets, male and female, can be read as women.

Notes

1 Herbert Sussman remarks that "much of the best recent work on Victorian masculinities has been produced by feminist critics who have turned their methods to the study of men's art and men's psyches" ("The Study of Victorian Masculinities," *Victorian Literature and Culture* 20 [1992]: 366–77). Particularly useful studies of male responses to the gender issues of Victorian poetry include Barbara Charlesworth Gelpi, "The Feminization of D. G. Rossetti," in *The Victorian Experience: The Poets*, ed. Richard A. Levine (Columbus: Ohio Univ. Press, 1982), pp. 94–112; U. C. Knoepflmacher, "Projection and the Female Other: Romanticism, Browning, and the Victorian Dramatic Monologue," VP 22 (1984): 139–59; Herbert Sussman, "Robert Browning's 'Fra Lippo Lippi' and the Problematic of a Male Poetic," VS 35 (1992): 185–200; and Alan Sinfield, *Alfred Tennyson* (Oxford: Blackwell, 1986). Sussman defines the problem as the "disjunction between entrepreneurial

Dorothy Mermin

manhood and the romantic ideal of the poet" ("Robert Browning," p. 186). In *Be a Man! Males in Modern Society* (New York: Holmes &. Meier, 1990), Peter N. Stearns describes the ideals of manhood moving in the first two-thirds of the nineteenth century away from androgyny, as gender was "being called upon to take on new symbolic importance" (p. 110).

2 *The Complete Works of Elizabeth Barrett Browning*, ed. Charlotte Porter and Helen A. Clarke, 6 vols. (New York: Thomas Y. Crowell, 1900), 2:81.

3 *Life and Literary Remains of L.E.L.*, ed. Laman Blanchard, 2 vols. (Philadelphia, 1841), 1:5–7.

4 Isobel Armstrong, *Victorian Poetry: Poetry, Poetics and Politics* (London: Routledge, 1993), p. 326.

5 According to Lawrence Lipking, "Prior to the rise of the novel [the poetry of abandoned women] seems the *only* sort of literature that attracted male and female authors equally" (*Abandoned Women and Poetic Tradition* [Chicago: Univ. of Chicago Press, 1988], p. xxiii). Men poets used the female voice in such poems, Lipking says, not as the other but to express feelings they couldn't express in the male voice (p. xx).

6 *The Poems of Tennyson*, ed. Christopher Ricks, 3 vols. (Berkeley: Univ. of California Press, 1987). Alan Sinfield reads "I am a part of all that I have met" in political terms as "the imperialism of the imagination": "Ulysses *is* the hegemonic: he is the colonizer who requires ever more remote margins to sustain his enterprise" (*Alfred Tennyson*, p. 53). Barrett Browning, in contrast, shuddered in revulsion from the Jamaican slave-plantations from which her family had drawn its fortune, although, as with the poetry of her female predecessors, she recognized her own involvement in what she sought to renounce.

7 Robert Langbaum, *The Poetry of Experience: The Dramatic Monologue in Modern Literary Tradition* (1957; New York: W. W. Norton, 1963).

8 Robert *Browning: The Poems*, ed. John Pettigrew and Thomas J. Collins, 2 vols. (New Haven: Yale Univ. Press, 1981).

9 On Browning's attempts to examine or escape the position of the male poetic subject who dominates the female object see Knoepflmacher, "Projection and the Female Other," and Adrienne Auslander Munich, *Andromeda's Chains: Gender and Interpretation in Victorian Literature and Art* (New York: Columbia Univ. Press, 1989).

10 *The Complete Works of Algernon Charles Swinburne*, ed. Sir Edmund Gosse and Thomas James Wise, 20 vols. (London: William Heinemann, 1925). Identity and difference are central themes in *Atalanta in Calydon*. "I am fire, and burn myself" (l. 1805), says the murderous mother, Althea: "I feed and fill my body...even with flesh / Made of my body. Lo, the fire I lit / I burn with fire to quench it" (ll. 1870–2). Identity is destruction, while "division" (a recurrent word in the poem) can be bad, as in "the dividing of friend against friend" (l. 839), but is also the foundation of language: "Sweet articulate words / Sweetly divided apart" (ll. 751–2). And yet, "words divide and rend; / But silence is most noble till the end" (ll. 1204–5).

218

11 Richard Dellamora says that "Hermaphroditus," "remarkable for its approach to the experience of the receiver in anal intercourse, is marked with the language of moral anxiety and disapproval" (*Masculine Desire: The Sexual Politics of Victorian Aestheticism* [Chapel Hill: Univ. of North Carolina Press, 1990], p. 83).

12 See Dorothy Mermin, "The Damsel, the Knight, and the Victorian Woman Poet," *CritI* 13 (1986): 64–80.

13 William Clyde DeVane, *A Browning Handbook* (New York: F. S. Crofts, 1935), p. 204.

14 The other two poems that Browning wrote on the first three days of 1852, "Women and Roses" and "Love among the Ruins," deal with the failure and the success, respectively, of the male pursuit of beloved women. In "Love among the Ruins," the happy pastoral version of "'Childe Roland,'" distinctions collapse in a positive way until at last the happy lovers will "extinguish sight and speech / Each on each" (ll. 71–72) and conclude that "love is best" (l. 84). The Essay describes Shelley as the ideal type of the subjective poet, whose poetry shows not the external world, but himself. Harold Bloom brilliantly explicates "'Childe Roland'" in "Browning's *Childe Roland*: All Things Deformed and Broken," *The Ringers in the Tower: Studies in Romantic Tradition* (Chicago: Univ. of Chicago Press, 1971). Knoepflmacher points out that "it is significant that there should be no females in that poem of pure projection" (p. 147).

15 Insofar as this is a Christian allusion (like Donne's "Death, thou shalt die"), Swinburne's chain of identities, like Barrett Browning's, needs religion to bring it to an end; but this end is not a reassertion of difference.

16 John D. Rosenberg, "Swinburne," *VS* 11 (1967): 149. On the relation between Swinburne's style and issues of gender, as perceived by Victorian critics, see Thai's E. Morgan, "Mixed Metaphor, Mixed Genre: Swinburne and the Victorian Critic," *VN* 73 (1988): 16–19. Morgan notes that the "exclusion of anything that appears feminine or effeminate from the canons of good style entails the exclusion of women from the position of speaker or writer, and hence their exclusion from the political power than may be gained through rhetoric" (p. 18).

17 T. S. Eliot, "Swinburne as Poet," *Selected Essays* (New York: Harcourt Brace, 1950), pp. 284, 285. Rosenberg, p. 133.

18 "The Fleshly School of Poetry: Mr. D. G. Rossetti," *Contemporary Review* 18 (October 1871): 335.

19 Buchanan, p. 342. Reviewing Poems (1844), *John Bull* saw "a mere conglomeration of glittering verbiage," and *The Spectator* found "affecta- tion, and a diffusive verboseness," complaining that "sometimes the style, sometimes the metre, sometimes the images, are so quaint and pecu- liar that the attention is fixed upon mere secondary objects" (*The Brownings' Correspondence*, ed. Philip Kelley and Ronald Hudson, 11 vols. to date [Winfield, Kansas: Wedgestone Press, 1984–], 9: 331, 325).

20 William Morris, *The Defence of Guenevere, and Other Poems*, ed. Margaret A. Lourie (New York: Garland, 1981).

21 *The Complete Poems of Christina Rossetti: A Variorum Edition*, ed. R. W. Crump, 3 vols. (Baton Rouge: Louisiana State Univ. Press, 1979–1990).

22 Angela Leighton, *Victorian Women Poets: Writing Against the Heart* (New York: Harvester Wheatsheaf, 1992), p. 7.

23 T. S. Eliot, *Selected Essays*, pp. 283, 285.

24 Preface to First Edition of Poems (1853), *The Complete Prose Works of Matthew Arnold*, ed. R. H. Super, 11 vols. (Ann Arbor: The Univ. of Michigan Press, 1960–77), 1:1, 7. "Object" as Arnold uses it is a slippery term; the "eternal objects of poetry," he says here, are "human actions" (p. 3), but elsewhere it has very different meanings.

25 *On Translating Homer, Complete Prose Works*, 1:140; "The Function of Criticism at the Present Time," *Complete Prose Works*, 3:258.

26 *The Brownings' Correspondence*, 1:361.

27 *The Poems of Matthew Arnold*, ed. Miriam Allott (London: Longman, 1979). The topic was probably not of his own choosing, since one of his siblings seems to have written a similar poem at the same time (*Poems*, pp. 711–13), but it is significant that a female speaker is used to express an unambiguously unmanly reluctance to leave home.

12

'Eat me, drink me, love me'
The Consumable Female Body in Christina Rossetti's Goblin Market

Mary Wilson Carpenter

When Alice falls down the rabbit-hole she behaves, as Nancy Armstrong has pointed out, like a typical shopper – picking out and then putting back a jar of orange marmalade from the shelves of the rabbit-hole.[1] Later, she discovers that objects in Wonderland tend to come inscribed with such unsubtle advertising ploys as "eat me" or "drink me." Noting that all Alice's troubles seem to "begin and end with her mouth," Armstrong relates Alice's dilemma to "a new moment in the history of desire," a moment when the burgeoning "consumer culture" based on British imperialism changed the nature of middle-class English femininity (p. 17). *Alice in Wonderland* (1865) demonstrates the logic that links the colonial venture to the appetite of a little girl through the image of a "double-bodied woman" – a conflation of non-European women with European prostitutes and madwomen, all three of which were thought to exhibit the same features of face and genitals and, more crucially, to display the disfiguring results of unrestrained "appetite."[2] Victorian consumer culture both produced objects of desire and dictated that little Alices must learn to control their desires, in imagined contrast to women of the "dark continents" and prostitutes on the dark streets of their own cities.

So runs Armstrong's persuasive reading of a Victorian "children's" classic known to as many adults as children. Christina Rossetti's poem,

Carpenter, Mary Wilson. 1991. "'Eat me, drink me, love me': The Consumable Female Body in Christina Rossetti's *Goblin Market*." In *Victorian Poetry*, 29, iv (Winter), pp. 415–34. Reproduced with permission of Mary Wilson Carpenter.

Goblin Market, first published in 1862, suggests its location in the same intersection of imperialist culture and consumer capitalism that Armstrong elucidates *for Alice in Wonderland*.[3] Opening with the sensuous advertisement of exotic fruits hawked by goblin men to innocent young women, Rossetti's poem presents an explicitly articulated image of a marketplace in which female "appetite" is at stake. But whereas in Carroll's narrative, according to Armstrong's reading of it, "*all possibility for pleasure splits off from appetite and attaches itself to self-control*," in Rossetti's poem female appetite is simply re-directed toward another female figure, where it is provoked, encouraged, and satiated in the undeniably homoerotic text of the poem (p. 20; Armstrong's emphasis). Lizzie urges Laura to "Hug me, kiss me, suck my juices" as well as to "Eat me, drink me, love me" (ll. 468, 471). While Laura is said to loathe this "feast" proffered on her sister's body, it makes her leap and sing "like a caged thing freed" (l. 505). The result of Laura's totally unrestrained, orgiastic consumption of the "juices" on her sister's body is her restoration to life and health and, I will argue, to desire. The female body in the poem is subject to "consumption" as a commodity – as Laura's near-fatal experience demonstrates – but it is also "consumable" as a regenerative and self-propagating "fruit," as Lizzie's example shows us.

If *Alice in Wonderland* is structured on the "problem" of female desire in the imperialist marketplace, then Christina Rossetti's *Goblin Market* presents a startlingly different assessment of female sexual appetite. Yet the drive to evoke and regulate female appetite is not unique to the Rev. Charles Dodgson's children's story or even to children's literature conceived by Victorian clergymen. Charles Bernheimer argues that for nineteenth-century French male artists and novelists, the image of the prostitute stimulated representational strategies to control and dispel the fantasmatic threat of female "sexual ferment."[4] These artists associated the female body with "animality, disease, castration, excrement, and decay" (p. 2). Bernheimer acknowledges that in writing his book he "had to confront powerful expressions of disgust for female sexuality" (p. 4). As the nineteenth century progressed, the fear of "contamination" by the prostitute's unrestricted sexuality was given medical justification in France by "theories of degenerate heredity and syphilitic infection" (p. 2). Similarly, as Judith R. Walkowitz shows, the passage of the Contagious Diseases Acts in England in the 1860s suggests that prostitution was increasingly perceived there also as a dangerously contaminating form of sexual activity, one "whose boundaries had to be controlled and defined by the state."[5]

Even closer to Christina Rossetti's artistic context was her brother Dante Gabriel Rossetti's poem about a prostitute, "Jenny," which articulates a typical construction of female sexuality as diseased and contagious appetite:

> For is there hue or shape defin'd
> In Jenny's desecrated mind,
> Where all contagious currents meet,
> A Lethe of the middle street?[6]

If, as Armstrong argues, the 1860s represent a new moment in the history of desire in which consumer culture changed the nature of middle-class English femininity, both producing the desire for objects and structuring femininity in relation to that desire, then what accounts for the radically different representation of female appetite in *Goblin Market*? How was it possible for Christina Rossetti, devout Victorian practitioner of what Jerome McGann has called a "severe Christianity," to produce a poem in which fear of the contagion of the female body is radically disavowed?[7] And is it nonetheless possible to locate a "deviant counterpart" – the "double-bodied" figure of the prostitute-cum-African or -Asian woman – as a structuring figure repressed from *Goblin Market*?

D.M.R. Bentley has recently speculated that Christina Rossetti may have written *Goblin Market* with the intention of reading it not to children but to the inmates – "fallen women" or prostitutes – of the St. Mary Magdalene Home, Highgate, where she is known to have volunteered during the 1860s.[8] However much this possibility may alter our perception of the poem, Rossetti's intentions are not my concern here. Rather, I would propose that the foundation of Anglican Sisterhoods associated directly with the two churches which Rossetti is known to have attended, and the work of those Sisterhoods with homeless, destitute, and fallen women, gave the poet access to a uniquely feminocentric view of women's sexuality and simultaneously opened her eyes to its problematic position in Victorian culture. In particular, her immediate experience with the interaction between prostitutes and women's religious communities may have constructed Rossetti's representation of a "marketplace" in which "appetite" puts a woman at risk, but where her salvation is to be found not in controlling her appetite but in turning to another woman.

Like the other "fruits of empire," women's bodies were vended in the streets surrounding the churches, and zealous churchwomen like

Christina Rossetti went out to "buy" them back. But these shoppers were themselves commodified by the market in which they bargained, their own bodies and appetites implicated in the exploitative sexual economy they sought to resist and evade. In this scene of "compulsory heterosexuality," *Goblin Market* suggests that female erotic pleasure cannot be imagined without pain, yet the poem not only affirms the female body and its appetites but constructs "sisterhood" as a saving female homoerotic bond.[9]

While *Goblin Market* pushes the normative realm of heterosexual marriage to the margins of its narrative – invoking husbands only by implication in the final lines of the poem – that normative realm with its inscription of gender, class, and racial hierarchies is nevertheless exhibited in the poem which followed *Goblin Market* in its 1862 edition (Crump, I, p. 26).[10] In that little-discussed poem, "In the Round Tower at Jhansi," I find a final comment on what *Goblin Market* is, and is not, about.

Sisterhoods and the Female Gaze

The extraordinary homoerotic energies of *Goblin Market* seem particularly unaccountable in relation to the familiar assessment of Christina Rossetti as a devout Anglo-Catholic spinster who lived out her entire life with her mother, sister, and elderly aunts. William Rossetti described her as a "devotee," instancing her "perpetual church-going and communions, her prayers and fasts, her submission to clerical direction, her oblations, her practice of confession" – a catalog that suggests a religious practice stripped of much social interaction and certainly of all pleasure.[11] Yet the histories of Christ Church, Albany Street, and All Saints' Margaret Street, and of the Sisterhoods founded at these two churches produce a very different reading of the Oxford Movement that constructed both Rossetti's religious practice and her poetic texts. Far from McGann's conception of a "severe Christianity," the "Church" as represented in these histories appears to have been a hotbed of social reforms and sexual tensions generated by those reforms. The work of the newly formed Anglican Sisterhoods proved to be inseparable from the "work" of "fallen women," producing an unprecedented mingling of "pure" and "tainted" women. Moreover, as Martha Vicinus has noted, the Anglican Sisterhoods empowered women, validating their work and values.[12] The feminism and intense homoeroticism of *Goblin Market* are fully accountable when read intertextually with this unconventional "social text" of the Victorian Anglican church.

In speaking of the homoeroticism of the poem as "accountable," I am assuming, as Mary Poovey states, that "the representation of biological sexuality, the definition of sexual difference, and the social organization of sexual relations are social, not natural, phenomena."[13] Rather than reading *Goblin Market* as "expressing" by virtue of the poet's creative genius an "inner" and unaccountable desire – a reading which might be called a humanist Freudian interpretation – I look for the "origins" of Rossetti's representation of female sexual desire in the complex interactions between the social institutions and texts of her culture. Thus, I will argue that the characteristics of the historical institution of "sisterhood" unique to Christina Rossetti's churches constituted a social and discursive matrix which enabled the production of a radical subjectivity in *Goblin Market*: that is, a female speaker or subject of discourse which does not take up the conventional phallocentric position, in which the female body is the object of a male gaze.[14] In a text exemplary of the Oxford Movement's "women's mission to women," as I will show, the female body is represented as the object of a female gaze, and in *Goblin Market* we find a similarly radical female subjectivity.

What I will be arguing here is that the writer, though determined by the ideological structuring of her society, may also be emancipated in some degree by exposure to unconventional or disruptive ideological discourses. Such "uneven developments," as Poovey says, result from the different positioning of individuals within the social formation, and from the different articulation of the ideological formulation by different institutions, discourses, and practices (p. 3). While Marxist or materialist readings may position the writer as the "simple" subject of the dominant ideology, subjectivities are constituted at the intersection of multiple and competing discourses.[15] This multiplicity accounts for such "uneven developments" as a powerfully feminist and homoerotic text written by a devout Victorian lady poet.

Previous attempts to link *Goblin Market* with Rossetti's associations with "sisters" and "fallen women" have focused on her involvement with the institution at Highgate, despite William Rossetti's recollection that this work did not begin until 1860, while the manuscript of *Goblin Market* is dated April 27, 1859. So little is known about the 1850s in Christina Rossetti's life that they have been described as the "grey years."[16] Scholars have relied largely on William's reminiscences, but these are often vague and spotty and may also be inaccurate, as demonstrated in his comments to Mackenzie Bell about Christina's church-related work:

> She was (I rather think) an outer Sister – but in no sort of way professed – of the Convent which Maria afterwards joined – Also at one time (1860–'70) she used pretty often to go to an Institution at Highgate for redeeming 'Fallen Women' – It seems to me that at one time they wanted to make her a sort of superintendent there, but she declined – In her own neighbourhood, Albany Street, she did a deal of district visiting and the like.[17]

William's use of the term "Convent," which suggests an enclosed community of women, to refer to the All Saints' Sisterhood which Maria joined in 1873 shows how unacquainted he must have been with the Sisterhood and its activities, for it was primarily a nursing order which occupied an ever increasing number of buildings adjacent to All Saints' Church and administered various institutions both in London and outside it. The headnote, "House of Charity, " which Christina penciled in on her poem, "From Sunset to Star Rise," and which William thought referred to the Highgate institution, may have referred to the All Saints' Home run by these Sisters, since the Rev. W. Upton Richards described it as an institution entirely dependent on voluntary gifts and commended to the "Christian charity of all."[18]

William's statement that Christina did district visiting in "her own neighbourhood, Albany Street" may also be misleading, as this implies that she did this kind of work only after March, 1854, when the Rossetti family moved to 45 Upper Albany Street. Since the Rossetti women began attending Christ Church in 1843, it seems probable that Christina participated in its social work and reform efforts well before 1854 (Battiscombe, p. 30). Built in 1837 at the instigation of William Dodsworth, a fiery young preacher who was then the incumbent at the Margaret Street Chapel (whose remaining parishioners went on to build All Saints' Church), Christ Church was characterized by "zeal" for social reform from its beginnings.[19] According to Canon Burrows, who became the incumbent in 1851, Christ Church became "the leading church in the [Oxford] movement," and the scene of sermons by such well-known preachers as Archdeacon Manning, Dr. Pusey, and Dr. Hook (Burrows, p. 14). Doubtless much more important to Christina Rossetti and her sister Maria was the fact that the first Anglican Sisterhood since the Reformation was founded there.

Pusey seems to have been the guiding force for the formation of this Sisterhood, which some thought might "save" certain Anglican members from converting to Roman Catholicism while others despaired that it would only further encourage such "Romanising."[20] Pusey's desires for the Sisterhood, however, appear to have been intimately linked with his grief for his own daughter, who died tragically on the very day of the meeting which decided to establish such a community (Cameron, p. 31). Pusey thought that for a Bishop to have anything to do with the Sisterhood, which should consist simply of a few young women living together, would be to violate "the sacredness of domestic charity and devotion" (Cameron, p. 32). His close and even tender relationship with the Sisters began on March 26, 1845, when the first two aspirants arrived. As Pusey later wrote to Keble, "We (i.e. Dodsworth and myself) had a little service with them on Wednesday; they were in floods of tears, but in joy" (Cameron, p. 33).

If Pusey imagined a sanctified domestic enclave of perpetual daughters, others – particularly the women who either entered or founded such Sisterhoods – seem to have had quite a different vision. Far from seeking out an ecclesiastical version of the patriarchal families most of them were leaving, they saw themselves as embarking on a new and independent existence in which they would undertake useful, important work. The Park Village Sisters are reported to have immediately begun to visit the "low Irish people" and the brothels in their district (Williams and Campbell, p. 23).[21] Before founding the All Saints' Sisterhood, Harriet Brownlow Byron took a nursing course.[22] She then began the work of this Sisterhood by taking homeless women and orphan girls right into the house where the Sisters lived, the All Saints' Home. By 1862 this "Home" occupied four buildings on Margaret Street, and the Sisters' various enterprises eventually occupied every building on Margaret Street as far as Great Titchfield Street. By 1866 they were conducting an asylum for aged women, an industrial school for girls, an orphanage, a home for incurables, two convalescent homes, and the nursing service for the entire University College Hospital, in addition to teaching in the district nightschool and nursing the sick poor in their own homes.[23]

Unlike the more successful All Saints' Sisterhood, the Park Village Sisterhood encountered many difficulties, finding itself at the center of fierce religious controversy in Christ Church.[24] Throughout the years of 1849 and 1850 Dodsworth – increasingly convinced that he should convert to Catholicism – was preaching sermons at Christ Church of such a nature that Pusey said "he wished he could induce the sisters to read their Bibles during his sermons or shut their ears."[25] One of the Sisters was actually kidnapped by a "Miss White" and taken to a Roman

Catholic convent. She was eventually released, only to be assailed and accused of "apostasy" the following Sunday as she tried to enter the door of Christ Church (Williams and Campbell, pp. 81–2). Christina Rossetti could hardly have escaped involvement in the parish turmoil. She was at this time engaged to James Collinson, who had converted from the Roman Catholic to the Anglican Church to further his court-ship of Christina. During the early months of 1850, Collinson decided that he must rejoin the Catholic Church, and upon hearing this, Christina decided to end their engagement. The Rev. Mr. Dodsworth "romanized" on the last day of 1850.[26]

Despite such disruptions, both Christ Church and the Sisterhood moved ahead vigorously with new plans for ministering to the poor. A second church was to be built at the south end of the parish near "the notoriously evil York Square," where brothels flourished because of the nearby Cumberland Barracks (Coombs, pp. 9–12). On July 15, 1849, the laying of the foundation stone for "St. Mary Magdalene" was planned, with the congregation to make a procession from Christ Church to the site.[27] John Keble, who preached the sermon, hinted that troublemakers might be encountered and begged the congregation to "go reverently…as we pass through the streets of Babylon." The "long tramping procession" accordingly wound its way silently through the "sordid district" (Coombs, p. 13). A little over a year later, in September, 1850, Pusey laid the foundation stone for the "House of Religion," which was to be occupied by the Sisters of Park Village but was also intended to accommodate fourteen homeless women, forty orphan girls, and fourteen "ladies" (Coombs, p. 15). This building was very near the site for the new St. Mary Magdalene Church (and therefore near the brothels). On All Saints' Day (November 1) in 1850, Pusey also laid the foundation stone for what would become the extravagantly beautiful All Saints' Church, built on the site of the old Margaret Street Chapel.

Christina Rossetti, her sister Maria, her mother Frances, and her aunts could all have been a part of that unprecedented outdoor proces-sion through the neighboring "red light" district to the site chosen for the new church.[28] That Christina and one of her aunts were very much caught up in the new fervor for women's work with the needy is known from the fact that they were among some "ladies of the [Christ Church] congregation" who joined the Park Village Sisters and others in volun-teering to go with Florence Nightingale to the Crimea in December, 1854.[29] Nightingale rejected Christina on the grounds that she was too young, but her aunt was accepted.

Neither the Park Village nor the All Saints' Sisters had a mandate for working with "fallen women," but their work with "homeless women" and "orphan girls" would in fact have been inseparable from work with "fallen women."[30] Other Anglican Sisterhoods which were newly forming at this time, however, displayed a predominant interest in work with prostitutes. The first Sister at St. Mary's, Wantage, felt called to penitentiary work and founded a penitentiary there in 1850, despite the distress of the Vicar, who had wanted this Sisterhood to be dedicated to educational work. The Clewer Sisterhood was formed because three women moved into a "House of Mercy" in 1851, simultaneously undertaking the religious life and the work of the "penitentiary."[31] This "House of Mercy" had been founded two years earlier by a Mrs. Tennant, a laywoman living in the village of Clewer who offered to take the "abandoned women" of the parish into her own home. She was said to have an unparalleled ability to control the "most undisciplined and impassioned natures" of these women and to attach them to herself "in a marvellous manner" (Cameron, pp. 58–9).

Such enthusiasm for work with prostitutes and willingness to share living-quarters with them was not confined to religious sisterhoods. Josephine Butler, who led the Ladies' National Association in its campaign against the Contagious Diseases Acts, began her career by taking women from the workhouses, jails, and streets of Liverpool into her own home, where she devotedly nursed them herself. Walkowitz reports that by 1878 the LNA leadership had actually grown wary of the "rescue impulse," recognizing by then that there were "a 'hundred women' who would engage in rescue work for the 'one' who would bravely enter the political arena to combat the acts" (Walkowitz, p. 133).

The St. Mary Magdalene Home at which Christina Rossetti worked in the 1860s may have been staffed by lay "sisters" who committed themselves to the work but took no permanent religious vows. According to its Annual Reports, St. Mary's "sisters" were to be divided into two groups, "approved sisters" and "sisters under probation," either of whom were to be free to resign at any time.[32] Christina Rossetti's work at St. Mary's in the 1860s appears to have been only a continuation of her involvement with the "rescue work" which had appealed to the desires of British women in general, and Anglican Sisterhoods in particular, including the two Sisterhoods associated with the churches attended by the Rossetti women. *Goblin Market*, written sometime during the late 1850s, is inscribed by the turbulent history of "women's mission to women" in the Oxford

Movement during this period. In this ecclesiastical "female world of love and ritual," how was the female body and its "appetite" represented?[33]

I would like to begin by noting that ecclesiastical discourse constituted saving "sisters" and "fallen women" together, as if part of a unitary entity. In a preface to two sermons on penitentiary work, W. J. Butler, Vicar of Wantage, wrote that, "so soon as the evil [prostitution] was fairly faced…nothing could quell it so much as purity and tender love, that these would foster habits of prayer and industry and faith in virtue and goodness,…the lack of which had occasioned so fearful a moral wreck."[34] The Sisters' "purity and tender love" are defined by the "moral wreck" so in need of them.

Like the discourses of nineteenth-century male artists, the discourses of the Oxford Movement also reveal a fear of "contamination." But while the male artists' imagery suggests a fear of physical and moral pollution from the prostitute's body, male clerics appear to have feared that the sisters would be contaminated by the attractions of the "fallen women" and their way of life. In a sermon preached at St. Mary's Home, Wantage, in 1861, Samuel Wilberforce, the Bishop of Oxford, displays this anxiety by taking as his opening subject the prevailing notion that those who work to reform the corrupted are themselves liable to be corrupted. He also labors to disprove the idea that institutions such as St. Mary's tended to "discredit homely virtue and to throw a gloss over vice" (*On Penitentiary Work*, p. 5). In a second sermon preached on the same occasion, Henry Parry Liddon indicates that the "decay" of prostitution begins with a woman's "act of rebellion," and that this first act of rebellion is generally followed by a second and a third, such that "you find yourself in the presence of a new and formidable force – the force of habit" (p. 19). This habit of rebellion, he suggests, must be met by "a counter-habit of purity" (p. 20).

These sermons thus articulate a fear that, far from experiencing "disgust for female sexuality" or "sexual repulsion," the sisters who worked with fallen women might themselves be "corrupted" by these living examples of active female sexuality and "rebellion." In an 1867 sermon to the Parochial Mission-Women Association, Canon Burrows' text fairly resonates with the fear that rescue work might encourage the development of an unwomanly sense of authority, and that after going into the streets, mission women might not return exactly as they had been before. Noting uneasily at the outset that he was not often called upon to "address a body so largely composed of women" and that there were many "Managers and Superintendents here today," he takes as his theme the imperative of maintaining a proper sense of humility amidst the heady excitement of this mission work:

> "Many of you, Mission Women, must be tempted to think…when you find yourselves associated with rank and talent, the clergy co-operating, congregations applauding, and all men speaking well of you, that surely success is certain; but you come together to-day to the House of God, to humble yourselves."[35]

Commenting that "yours is woman's work, and a true woman's best work is modest, retiring, humble, self-sacrificing," Burrows reminds his feminine audience of "the special deference to authority" involved in their "constitution" and urges his hearers to be always willing to "take the lowest place" and to be "persistent" in humility (pp 7, 9, 11). He mentions that these mission women not only have no house or institution, no official dress, but that they almost always work singly. They go out on the streets and bring women in to the Mission room, the School, the Church. They must never forget, he concludes, that they should be "the servant of all" (p. 11).

Although always organized hierarchically and on the assumption that class differences were part of God's plan and not to be interfered with, the Oxford Movement actually fostered associations between middle-class church women and working-class women on the belief that the former could help prevent the latter from "falling." In 1856 Upton Richards founded an organization called the All Saints Confraternity for Girls and Young Women.[36] According to the 1866 Manual, the association was intended for the "mutual help and encouragement of Girls and Young Women wishing to lead a Christian life amidst the difficulties and temptations of the world." The Objects of the Confraternity further specified that the organization was to help "carefully brought up" and pious girls retain their beliefs and good behavior after they were sent out into the world to earn a living.[37]

These objectives obviously suggest another possibility for an intended audience for *Goblin Market*, which certainly can be read as a cautionary tale for girls and young women wishing to lead a Christian life amidst the temptations of the "world," for which read the streets of London. Again, however, my interest is not to speculate on an "intended" audience but rather to examine certain texts produced by or for the Confraternity which I believe are paradigmatic of female relations in the Oxford Movement, and to read in them a construction of the female gaze that I think is highly pertinent to the reading of *Goblin Market*. In this construction of the female gaze we may find a "look" exchanged between women that constitutes an unorthodox (feminine) subjectivity.

Class difference and hierarchy clearly structured the Confraternity, like all of the Sisterhood enterprises. In 1866 its membership consisted of sixty "members" and twenty "Lady-Associates," headed by a "Superior-General" or the Rev. Upton Richards, and a "Sister-Superior," who was one of the All Saints Sisters.[38] But these rigid demarcations of class and authority do not appear in the Confraternity hymns to the Virgin Mother, or to the Virgin's mother, St. Anne. In a hymn to St. Anne I find a particularly significant revision of Jacques Lacan's construction of the "mirror stage" as the moment when the infant first perceives itself as a coherent image. In Lacan's theorization of this moment, the infant is constituted by its perception of this mirrored image, an image which the mother who holds the infant only "guarantees." In short, the infant, not the mother, is the subject here.[39]

If we take the Confraternity hymn to St. Anne as textual exemplar, we read in it instead an egalitarian exchange of gazes between the Virgin's mother and the future Virgin Mother:

> Blest among women shall thy daughter be!
>   Yes, highly favoured above every other;
> The little one reposing on thy knee,
>   (Believe, and fear not) shall be GOD'S own Mother.
>
> The clear, grave eyes that now look up to thine,
>   In the calm faith that sheds its radiance o'er her,
> Thus shall they gaze upon the form divine
>   Of God's bright Angel, as he stands before her.
>   (*Manual*, pp. 65–6)

There are several important points here. For one, it is the gaze of the infant daughter which is represented as guaranteeing the mother's subjectivity. The Virgin's mother looks down on the "little one reposing" on her knee, and in the infant's mirroring gaze sees the promise of a future divine motherhood. Rather than beginning (and ending) with the infant and ignoring the mother as anything but "guarantee," it starts (though it does not end) with the mother.

Another interesting difference is the hymn's explicit construction of the gaze between two feminine subjects. The hymn virtually excludes males from this female exchange, and what is male appears only as prophetic image that grants permission to the mother's gaze: the female child can be taken as "object" because she is validated by the divine form of the angel who will announce that she is a virgin mother. The hymn thus authorizes the female gaze to take a feminine object as its focus.

The infant daughter here, however, obviously functions as subject herself: her look "up" to the mother's look is already a gaze upon a future "form divine" that is in turn a guarantee of her subjectivity. As such, I think the exchange can be said to undo the hierarchy of mother and daughter as it does of infant and "mirror." How shall we describe the relationship constructed by such an exchange of looks between female subjects? As "sisterhood" – a "sisterhood" which represses hierarchical differences and permits the female gaze to feast on the female form.

Goblin Market and Feminine Guessiness

Criticism of *Goblin Market* can be divided into two camps in the reading of Lizzie and Laura: one camp assumes that Laura represents the "fallen woman" and Lizzie the "pure woman," or that Laura is a type of Eve and Lizzie a type of Mary; the other camp asserts that the poem does not construct either sister as morally superior and that Lizzie is as much "redeemed" by her confrontation with the goblins as Laura is by ingesting Lizzie's "antidote."[40]

I take my stance very much in this second camp, for it seems to me the poem quite deliberately denies any suggestion of categorical differences between the two women. That is, the text excludes any suggestion of sexual, racial, class, or any other kind of hierarchical difference between the two women – or girls, since the difference between sexual maturity and childish innocence also seems to be blurred. We cannot find in the text of this poem or in the illustration Dante Gabriel designed for it of the two "golden heads" any suggestion of Armstrong's "double-bodied woman." On the contrary, even after Laura has eaten of the goblin fruits – an act many readers regard as synonymous with a "fall" – the poem constructs them in what Jerome McGann appropriately calls "unspeakably beautiful litanies" of identical innocence (p. 253):

> Like two blossoms on one stem,
> Like two flakes of new-fall'n snow,
> Like two wands of ivory.
> (ll. 188–198)

I would like to suggest that the poem excludes difference between the two girls or women in order to focus on women's common plight as

233

commodities in the linked capitalist and sexual economies. By erasing categorical differences between Laura and Lizzie, the poem can construct those various characterological differences among women which make them vulnerable to the market, on the one hand, but which the poem, on the other hand, argues "sisters" can also capitalize upon in order to rescue each other from exploitation.

Christina Rossetti's own reflective interpretation of Eve and her "fall" in an 1882 work of biblical commentary, *Letter and Spirit*, is relevant here:

> It is in no degree at variance with the Sacred Record to picture to ourselves Eve, that first and typical woman, as indulging quite innocently sundry refined tastes and aspirations, a castle building spirit (if so it may be called), a feminine boldness and directness of aim combined with a no less feminine guessiness as to means. Her very virtues may have opened the door to temptation.[41]

So it appears with Laura in *Goblin Market* – her very virtues open the door to temptation. She combines a "feminine boldness and directness of aim" with "sundry refined tastes and aspirations." She exhibits a "castle-building spirit," if so we may read the heroic similes which describe her as stretching her "gleaming neck" and being like a "moonlit poplar branch," or a "vessel at the launch / When its last restraint is gone" (ll. 81–86).

But she also exhibits a "feminine guessiness as to means." Untutored in the deceptive strategies employed in the goblin market, she gets herself in for more than she bargained for. Although her desire to indulge "refined tastes" for the exotic and delicious fruits hawked by the goblin men is nowhere condemned in the poem, Laura finds that in consuming those fruits a part of herself has also been "consumed." What has been stolen from her in this shady transaction is her "desire" itself, a desire which far exceeds that for real fruits, however exotic.

Yet we should not fail to notice how infinitely more potent as locus of desire these "fruits" are than that pathetically domesticated jar of marmalade that is supposed to tempt Alice. The very words for these fruits are quite literally mouth-filling and sensuously delectable, but they are also packed with metaphorical and associational meanings. Both a woman and the product of her womb may be called a "fruit," but with what different valences! And "fruits" can refer to the profits of any kind of enterprise – economic, spiritual, or sexual.

The poem, moreover, specifically links the fruits to "the fruits of empire": these are not just common, home-grown English apples and cherries, but also a rich variety of gourmet fruits imported from foreign climes – pomegranates, dates, figs, lemons and oranges, "citrons from the South." These are luxury fruits that appeal to "sundry refined tastes" such as have been cultivated by Britain's colonial empire. That Rossetti associated the availability of such luxuries with the capitalistic exploitation of the poor is clearly indicated in her 1892 commentary on the Book of Revelation, *The Face of the Deep*, where she identifies her country with the apocalyptic Babylon and assails it with prophetic wrath: "'Alas England full of luxuries and thronged by stinted poor, whose merchants are princes and whose dealings crooked, whose packed storehouses stand amid bare homes, whose gorgeous array has rags for neighbours!' "[42]

Amidst this market with its packed storehouses and gorgeous array, Laura, who has not a single "copper" in her purse, is taken in by the crooked dealings of the goblin men. When they tell her she does not need any money because they will be happy with a "'golden curl," she hands over this emblem of her virginity with only a single tear. Her "feminine guessiness as to means" – her naiveté about the marketplace – has condemned her to a loss far greater than she knows.

So far it would almost be permissible to read the poem as a sort of feminist guide to shopping: watch out for those so-called bargains, sister, especially the ones offered by the funny little men – you'll be taken for a lot more than you know. But to read it as such a sororal cautionary tale is to neglect what the poem has to say about the importance of looking. While one can get into trouble by satisfying the desire to look and listen, the trouble is precisely the loss of that desire. Christina Rossetti herself wanted to name the poem, "A Peep at the Goblins," but when her brother Dante Gabriel suggested *Goblin Market*, Christina accepted this as a "greatly improved title."[43] Yet while the poem is certainly about the "traffic in women," it also seems to be about the desire to "peep." Even more interestingly, the poem does not appear to condemn this voyeuristic desire in itself but rather to represent its risks in the goblin market.

Thus, Laura at first warns Lizzie, "We must not look at goblin men," as well as "We must not buy their fruits." But apparently sensing her sister's weakening control, Lizzie responds, "Laura, Laura, / You should not peep at goblin men" (ll. 42, 43, 48, 49). Lizzie sticks her fingers in her ears and shuts her eyes, but Laura lingers and looks, "Wondering at each merchant man."[44]

When she returns after having made her unwittingly disastrous bargain, and "sucked and sucked and sucked" the goblin fruit until her lips were sore, Lizzie meets her "at the gate / Full of wise upbraidings" (ll.141–142)." 'Dear, you should not stay so late, / Twilight is not good for maidens," she reminds her sister primly, and now already too late tells her the sad tale of Jeanie who "lies low" because she loitered so (ll. 143–163). But when Laura first suffers agonies because of the frustration of her "baulked desire," and then, like her "kernel-stone," begins to dry up, dwindle, and face the prospect of a "sandful" sterility (how painful that "sandful" is!), Lizzie is jarred out of her maidenly correctness by her sister's "cankerous care." After taking the prudent precaution of supplying herself with a silver penny, Lizzie ventures out, "And for the first time in her life / Began to listen and look" (ll. 327–328).

The narrative thus clearly affirms woman's listening and looking – Lizzie needs to listen and look, the line suggests, or she will remain merely a happy little bird in her closed domestic cage. The decision to confront the goblins of the twilight, to open her eyes and unstop her ears, is as crucial to Lizzie as the recovery of desire will be to Laura. So long as Lizzie remains safely behind her garden gate, she will never know desire or taste its fulfillment and she will be no better off – though her case will be different – than her sister, whose desire has been stolen from her. The sisters represent women's double plight in the Victorian sexual economy: either risk becoming a commodity yourself, or risk never tasting desire, never letting yourself "peep."

The poem demonstrates for us how listening may be as seductive as looking: the goblins laugh when they spy Lizzie "peeping," and they slither towards her in a fascinating cacophony of sounds that fills the ear just as the earlier listing of fruits fills the mouth. These sounds are full of sinister, sexual, spell-binding implications – snake-like, we might say.

But looking and listening are not enough to accomplish the poem's desire for Lizzie here. She must also suffer, putting up at first with name-calling, then with what we would call sexual harassment and physical abuse. The goblins push her and jostle her, rip her dress, tear out her hair, and step on her feet. Finally, they try to force their "fruits" into her mouth. Under this treatment, Lizzie is transformed into a heroic and unviolated figure. The list of similes here interestingly refers both to colonial and sexual economies: she's like a "fruit-crowned orange tree" beset by wasps and bees, or like "a royal virgin town" beleaguered by a fleet "Mad to tug her standard down." Laughing in her heart, Lizzie gleefully lets the goblins "syrup" her face with their juices, but she keeps her mouth shut. The goblins are unable to penetrate her. When she leaves the glen, the penny jingling in her purse is testimony that she got what she wanted for a smaller price than she thought she might have to pay. The price was only "a smart, ache, tingle" – not so bad, under the circumstances.

Ecstatically, she offers Laura the "juices" of her sexual knowledge, spread over the surface of her bruised body:

> She cried "Laura," up the garden,
> "Did you miss me?
> Come and kiss me.
> Never mind my bruises,
> Hug me, kiss me, suck my juices
> Squeezed from goblin fruits for you,
> Goblin pulp and goblin dew.
> Eat me, drink me, love me;
> Laura, make much of me:
> For your sake I have braved the glen
> And had to do with goblin merchant men."
> (ll. 464–474)

Laura clings about her sister, "kissed and kissed and kissed her," and is transformed in her turn. Though the juice is "wormwood" to her tongue, and she "loathes" the feast, she appears to experience a masochistic orgy – writhing like one possessed, leaping and singing, and beating her breast. In simile, she streams upward like an eagle toward the sun, like a caged thing freed, like a flying flag when armies run. And then she falls – falls like a mast struck by lightning, like a tree uprooted by the wind, like a waterspout that falls into the sea. She falls, "pleasure past and anguish past," into a deep sleep, from which she awakens as innocent as ever, and quite healthy.

Lizzie appears to have restored her sister by recirculating the erotic energies first set into motion by the goblin market. Inviting her sister to feast on her instead of on the goblin fruits produces a saving satisfaction. But all such exchanges involve the paying of some price, and here the price is pain – a pain which seems always to originate from the "goblin merchantmen." However, the pain does not seem to be part of a sadistic-masochistic pairing. Rather, the pain which accompanies the women's erotic pleasure appears to be the inevitable effect of that dimly glimpsed other world that frames and constructs the sisters' relationship to each other. Nevertheless, within their own sphere, sisters can do a lot for each other. Or, as Laura teaches the little ones to sing, "there is no friend like a sister."

In the end, however, we must acknowledge that the poem accomplishes this transformative sisterhood by pushing the heterosexual world to its margins – husbands are not completely excluded, they are implied in the last paragraph – and by wiping out all reference to class or racial differences as if they did not exist. That they did exist, and that they determine the vision in *Goblin Market* of non-hierarchical sisterhood, is demonstrated by the poem which has been placed immediately after *Goblin Market* in the 1862 volume. This poem, "In the Round Tower at Jhansi, June 8, 1857," carries in its title the specific reference to time and place, and to empire and colony, that has been excluded from *Goblin Market*.

The title of the poem refers to an incident in what was called the "Indian Mutiny" but was actually part of the Indian rebellion against the British Empire, an incident in which a young white officer reportedly shot first his wife and then himself in order to protect her from the threat of rape by "The swarming howling wretches below." These "wretches below" are, presumably, the Indian troops. In this poem, then, we find the traces of the imperialist discourse missing from the preceding poem: the purity of the (English) female body here is constituted by its absolute difference from "The swarming howling wretches below." Lizzie's consumable body is, after all, offered to an equally blond sister – those "wretches below" on the London streets have not been invited to the saving feast.

I have suggested that *Goblin Market* constructs a radically different view of the female body and its appetites, and that the poet's access to the social and discursive matrix of the Oxford Movement's "women's mission to women" accounts for this radical discourse. Read in this context, the poem articulates women's common vulnerability to sexual and economic exploitation while affirming the bodies and appetites that are implicated in that exploitation. But "In the Round Tower at Jhansi" demonstrates that *Goblin Market* achieves this seemingly radical vision of women's bodies through its deliberate exclusion of racial and class differences. Like that first and typical woman, Christina Rossetti's work is still limited by a "feminine guessiness as to means."

Notes

1 Nancy Armstrong, "The Occidental Alice,"*Differences* 2 (Summer 1990): 3–40.

2 Armstrong, p. 9. On the "double-bodied image," see also Sander Gilman, "Black Bodies, White Bodies: Toward an Iconography of Female Sexuality in Late Nineteenth-Century Art, Medicine, and Literature," in Henry Louis Gates, Jr., ed. *"Race," Writing, and Difference* (Chicago, 1985), pp. 223–61.

3 All references to *Goblin Market* are to *The Complete Poems of Christina Rossetti*, ed. R. W. Crump (Baton Rouge, 1979), vol. 1, pp. 11–26. Perhaps the "eat me" and "drink me" labels in *Wonderland* are already a more restrained

and heterosexually-oriented version of Lizzie's "eat me, drink me, love me," for "Lewis Carroll" (Rev. Charles Dodgson) not only knew Rossetti well but was extremely enamored of little girls and very likely to have been intrigued by *Goblin Market*. See *The Annotated Alice*, ed. Martin Gardner (Harmondsworth, England, 1960), pp. 11–13, and U. C. Knoepflmacher's "Avenging Alice: Christina Rossetti and Lewis Carroll," *NCL* 41 (1986): 302, 311.

4 Charles Bernheimer, *Figures of Ill Repute: Representing Prostitution in Nineteenth-Century France* (Cambridge, Massachusetts, 1989), p. 2.

5 Judith R. Walkowitz, *Prostitution and Victorian Society: Women, Class and the State* (Cambridge, 1980), p. 3.

6 *The Poetical Works of Dante Gabriel Rossetti*, ed. William M. Rossetti (London, 1911), p. 39. D.M.R. Bentley points out that Dante Gabriel turned "intensively to the fallen-woman theme between 1853 and 1858," and that William Rossetti stated that "Jenny" was finished toward 1858, though revised in 1869 ("The Meretricious and the Meritorious in *Goblin Market*: A Conjecture and an Analysis," in David A. Kent, ed., *The Achievement of Christina Rossetti* [Ithaca, 1987], p. 60). *Goblin Market*, dated April 27, 1859, would appear to have been written in roughly the same period as "Jenny."

7 Jerome J. McGann, "Christina Rossetti's Poems: A New Edition and a Revaluation," *VS* 23 (1980): 254.

8 "The Meretricious and the Meritorious in *Goblin Market*," p. 58.

9 See Adrienne Rich's foundational analysis of the strategies universally employed by cultures to make heterosexuality compulsory by discouraging and even punishing homosexuality, thus coercing women into "choosing" heterosexuality. Rich theorizes that all women remain more attached to their mothers than men do, and that all women are therefore part of a "lesbian continuum." See "Compulsory Heterosexuality and Lesbian Existence" in Ann Snitow, Christine Stansell, and Sharon Thompson, eds., *Powers of Desire: The Politics of Sexuality* (New York, 1983), pp. 177–205.

10 As Dorothy Mermin comments, "This is a world in which men serve only the purpose of impregnation" ("Heroic Sisterhood in *Goblin Market*," *VP* 21 [1983]): 114.

11 *The Poetical Works of Christina Georgina Rossetti*, with memoir and notes by William Michael Rossetti (London, 1924), p. lv.

12 Martha Vicinus, *Independent Women: Work and Community for Single Women, 1850–1920* (Chicago, 1985), p. 83.

13 Mary Poovey, *Uneven Developments: The Ideological Work of Gender in Mid Victorian England* (Chicago, 1988), p. 2.

14 Laura Mulvey, referring to Jacque Lacan's theory, explains how "the unconscious of patriarchal society" structures Western narrative so that woman is the object of the male gaze ("Visual Pleasure and Narrative Cinema," reprinted in Constance Penley, *Feminism and Film Theory* [New York, 1988], pp. 57–68).

15 Terrence Holt's otherwise insightful reading of sexual and economic exchange in *Goblin Market*, for example, is limited by its reading of the language of the poem exclusively in relation to a dominant phallocentrism. Not surprisingly, Holt ignores the female homoeroticism of the poem. See " 'Men sell not such in any town': Exchange in *Goblin Market*," *VP* 28 (1990): 51–67.

16 Georgina Battiscombe, *Christina Rossetti: A Divided Life* (New York, 1981), p. 76.

17 Mackenzie Bell, *Christina Rossetti: A Biographical and Critical Study* (Boston, 1898), p. 60. Interestingly, William's letter goes on to document the interaction between Christina's church-related social work and the consumer culture of her day. One thing which occupied Christina "to an extent one would hardly credit," William writes, "was the making-up of scrapbooks for Hospital patients or children – This may possibly have begun before she removed to Torrington Sq[uare]: was certainly in very active exercise for several years ensuing – say up to 1885. When I called to see her and my mother it was 9 chances out of 10 that I found her thus occupied – I daresay she may have made up at least 50 biggish scrapbooks of this kind – taking some pains in adapting borderings to the pages etc. etc." These scrapbooks, no longer extant but presumably compiled from popular magazines and newspapers, suggest the poet's interest in popular culture.

18 *Poetical Works*, p. 485. Diane D'Amico, in "Christina Rossetti's 'From Sunset to Star Rise': A New Reading," (*VP* 27 [1989]: 95–100) has also pointed out that William was probably mistaken in this surmise, not only because "House of Charity" is never used in the records for this institution, but because an Anglican institution for the "fallen" was much more usually referred to as a "House of Mercy." Concluding that Christina's note, "House of Charity," probably refers to some other institution – perhaps the House of Charity in Soho – D'Amico suggests that the poet probably worked in more than one charitable institution.

19 Canon Burrows described its foundation as "a time of fervour and revival of church principles." By January, 1839, only a year and a half after its founding, for example, the congregation had set up schools in which no fewer than 871 district children were enrolled. See Henry W. Burrows, *The Half-Century of Christ Church, Albany Street, St. Pancras* (London, 1887), pp. 12–14.

20 Allan T. Cameron, *The Religious Communities of the Church of England* (London, 1918), pp. 28–34.

21 Thomas Jay Williams and Allan Walter Campbell, *The Park Village Sisterhood* (London, 1965), p. 23.

22 Pitkin Guide, *All Saints Margaret Street* (London, 1990), p. 18.

23 *All Saints' Church, Margaret Street*. Reprinted from *The Orchestra* (London, [1866]).

24 The Park Village Sisterhood merged with the Devonport Sisterhood in 1856. See Chapter 12 in Williams and Campbell, *The Park Village Sisterhood*, pp. 112–17.

25 Joyce Coombs, *One Aim: Edward Stuart*, 1820–1877 (London, 1975), p. 11.

26 Battiscombe, pp. 55–7. Burrows, p. 22.

27 So far as I have been able to determine, there was no connection between this church and the St. Mary Magdalene institution at Highgate.

28 Christina visited Collinson's family (James Collinson himself was not there) at Pleasley Hill during August 1849, but there is no evidence that she was not in London during July 1849. See *The Family – Letters of Christina Georgina Rossetti*, ed. William Michael Rossetti (London, 1908), pp. 5–8; also Lona Mosk Packer, *Christina Rossetti* (Berkeley, 1963), p. 35.

29 Janet Galligani Casey, in "The Potential of Sisterhood: Christina Rossetti's *Goblin Market*," *VP* 29 (1991): 63–78, also gives an account of Rossetti's interest in Nightingale and the "sisterhood movement," but argues that "sisterhood" in the poem "potentially includes the experience of both sexes" (p. 63).

30 Walkowitz notes that women who moved into prostitution were most often girls in their late teens, living outside the family, in fact often half or full orphan, and frequently having previously been casual maids of all work. See *Prostitution and Victorian Society*, p. 19.

31 Cameron, pp. 43, 59. Interestingly, these two Sisterhoods which took work with prostitutes as their primary focus grew to be two of the largest Anglican communities (Vicinus, *Independent Women*, p. 72).

32 First organized under a council formed by the Bishop of London in 1854, this "penitentiary" at Highgate was known originally as "Park House" but called "St. Mary Magdalene's" in order to give it a "distinctive name." See Deed to the London Diocesan Penitentiary, St. Mary Magdalene, London Guildhall Library, MS. 18532 and the Annual Reports of the London Diocesan Penitentiary, St. Mary Magdalene's, London Guildhall Library, MS. 18535. The institution is not listed among those institutions supervised by the All Saints' Sisterhood, nor is it mentioned in accounts of the Park Village Sisters. Cameron notes that "The House of Mercy," North Hill, Highgate, was taken over by the Clewer Sisters in 1901 (p. 65).

33 Carroll Smith-Rosenberg, "The Female World of Love and Ritual" in *Disorderly Conduct: Visions of Gender in Victorian America* (New York, 1985), pp. 53–76.

34 *On Penitentiary Work. . . . Two Sermons Preached At the Opening of the Chapel of St. Mary's Home, Wantage, July 30, 1861, by Samuel [Wilberforce], Lord Bishop of Oxford, and Henry Parry Liddon, MA, with a Short Preface on Sisterhoods, by W.J. Butler, MA, Vicar of Wantage* (Oxford and London, 1861), pp. iv–v.

35 *Parochial Mission-Women Association. A Sermon Preached at St. James's, Westminster, on June 20th, 1867, by the Rev. H. W. Burrows, B., Perpetual Curate of Christ Church, St. Pancras* (Oxford and London, 1867), pp. 4–5.

36 Although there is no evidence that Christina Rossetti was a member of this particular organization, a Young Women's Friendly Society was organized

at Christ Church for the benefit of servant girls. Tea, Bible lessons, and other "religious recreations" were offered on Sunday afternoons (*Half-Century of Christ Church*, p. 34). Maria Rossetti not only worked with this society but wrote a series of letters (dated 1860–1) to the young women in it, published *as Letters to My Bible Class on Thirty-Nine Sundays* (London, n.d. [1872]).

37 *The Manual of the Confraternity of All Saints, for Girls and Young Women, in connection with the All Saints' Home, 82, Margaret Street, Cavendish Square,* 2nd ed. (London, 1866), p. 1.

38 In a notice to the public, the Superior of the All Saints' Home stated that "women of a superior class are received to be trained for Nursing the Sick Poor in Hospitals; and for Private Nursing in the Families of the rich" ("Nurses for the Sick, in Private Families," All Saints' Home, 82, Margaret Street, Cavendish Square [1862]). Vicinus comments on the "upper-class character" of the All Saints' and Clewer Sisterhoods and notes that both were known as "fashionable" (*Independent Women*, pp. 55–6).

39 Jacques Lacan, "The mirror stage as formative of the function of the I as revealed in psychoanalytic experience," in *Écrits: A Selection*, trans. Alan Sheridan (New York, 1977), pp. 1–7. As Jane Gallop notes, "In Lacanian models she [the mother] is the prohibited object of desire; in object-relations she is the mirror where the infant can find his or her subjectivity. In either case her only role is to complement the infant's subjectivity; in neither story is she ever a subject" ("Reading the Mother Tongue: Psychoanalytic Feminist Criticism," *CritI* 13 [1987]: p. 324).

40 Helena Michie, for example, speaks of Laura and Lizzie as representing aculturally constructed difference between sisters, in which one sister is the "fallen" and the other the "unfallen," one the "sexual" and the other the "pure woman," in "'There is No Friend Like a Sister': Sisterhood as Sexual Difference," *ELH* 56 (1989): p. 404. Jerome McGann typifies the other reading which argues that without Laura's "precipitous act the women would have remained forever in a condition of childlike innocence" and that "Lizzie's timidity is by no means condemned, but its limitations are very clear," in "Christina Rossetti's Poems," p. 250).

41 Christina Rossetti, *Letter and Spirit* (London, [1882]), p. 17.

42 *The Face of the Deep: A Devotional Commentary* (London, 1892), p. 422.

43 *Poetical Works*, p. 459; Crump, 1:234.

44 We should not overlook the fact that "merchant man" also refers to a cargo-carrying ship.

13

Browning's Corpses

Carol T Christ

In 1801, Pierre Giraud, a prominent French architect and a figure in the Revolution, published a book, *Les Tombeaux, ou essai sur les sépultures*, in which he describes a procedure for dissolving the human body in order to convert it into an indestructible substance with which to make portrait medallions, quite literally, of the dead. The technique was not new; a seventeenth-century German inventor had discovered that the soil produced by the decomposition of human bodies could be used to produce a very fine glass; Giraud proposes substituting industry for nature. He envisions a cemetery, in the middle of which is a crematory oven that converts human corpses to a vitrifiable material. From the glass thus obtained can be made a new form of the human body, incorruptible and imperishable. Giraud writes:

> One need only have a heart to understand how consoling it would be to a sensitive soul to possess a bust of a pleasing material that would have the inestimable advantage of being both the portrait and the actual substance of a father, mother, wife, child, friend, or any other individual who was dear to us.[1]

Unfortunately, the glass is not sufficiently fluid to make a bust, so Giraud settles upon a medallion. There would be enough glass, Giraud speculates, for two medallions, one which the family could take with them when they traveled, the other to be displayed in the cemetery,

Christ, Carol T. 1995. "Browning's Corpses." In *Victorian Poetry*, 33, iii–iv (Autumn–Winter), pp. 391–401. Reproduced with permission of Carol T Christ.

Victorian Poets: A Critical Reader, First Edition. Edited by Valentine Cunningham.
© 2014 John Wiley & Sons, Ltd. Published 2014 by John Wiley & Sons, Ltd.

where it would have an edifying effect upon visitors: "How many children would spontaneously, from their earliest youth, be turned away from the path of crime and dissipation at the mere sight of the portraits of their virtuous ancestors" (p. 514).

The story of Giraud's medallions bears an interesting similarity to Jeremy Bentham's instructions about his dead body. Bentham left orders that his body be dissected after his death so that mankind might reap some benefit from his disease. He saw his act as an example of the utility principal, one that offered itself in opposition to the contemporary horror of medical dissection. After his body was dissected, however, Bentham, like Giraud, provided for a certain reversal of the dismembering he had authorized. He instructed that his skeleton be reassembled, complete with his mummified head, dressed in his own clothes, and set up for people to view. This effigy he called the auto-icon, a representation, like Giraud's medallions, constituted of the thing itself. It was, to Bentham, a further example of the principle of utility, of the uses of the dead to the living. Obviously, Bentham felt, people after his death would want a representation of him. What better representation than one constituted from his body itself?

These two anecdotes point to a set of preoccupations characteristic of nineteenth-century attitudes toward death. There was, on the one hand, an intense anxiety and concern about bodily dissolution, reflected in public debates about the proper disposal of corpses and the healthful location of cemeteries, in the widespread fear of dissection, which was seen as a mutilation appropriate only to murderers, in an equivalent repugnance toward cremation, and in an interest in new methods of embalming that would preserve the body intact for as long as possible after death. There was, on the other hand, a taste for elaborate funerary monument seen not only in the newly designed cemeteries of the age but in those mourning objects, intended for the home, so characteristic of the Victorian sensibility – chimney piece-ornaments, firescreens, funeral teapots, and the like. The two preoccupations are of course related; funerary monument – a kind of mourning work – undoes the bodily dissolution that is the work of death. As we can see in Bentham's and Giraud's plans for the disposition of corpses, or, more modestly, the common practice of making mourning jewelry from the hair of the dead, the ideal funerary monument is the body itself, perfectly disposed for the resurrectionary trumpet.

The value that Victorian culture placed upon the representation of the dead carried important implications for literary representation.

Literature, particularly poetry, was often used to perform a kind of mourning work. Much as the Victorians created material objects that were effigies for the dead, Victorian writers often sought to substitute the literary work for the dead body. A reversal of divine incarnation, the flesh becomes word, and the art object presents itself as the auto-icon. One can think of numerous examples – Tennyson's attempt in *In Memoriam* to connect body to text in a way that restores Hallam's presence, his identification in "The Lady of Shalott" of the Lady's dead body with self-definition as an aesthetic icon, Hopkins' project in "The Wreck of the Deutschland" to transform the dead body of the tall nun to the Word of God, or any number of paintings and poems by the Pre-Raphaelites, which present a dead woman's body as the ultimate aesthetic image.[2] This focus upon the dead body's construction as image does not occur only in poems of memorialization but in other poems as well, frequently those about poetry. Furthermore, poets do not always maintain the ideal construction of such activity one sees in *In Memoriam* but reflect upon it critically and ironically. Browning is a case in point. He frequently stages poems in the presence of a corpse. These poems, I will argue, reflect importantly upon his understanding of writing poetry. Like Bentham, he sees the dead body as the object that can constitute its own representation. However, he portrays this attempt as a macabre project on the part of the living to use corpses to support their own fictional construction of reality.

In his famous comment about "The Bishop Orders His Tomb at Saint Praxed's Church," Ruskin said that he knew of no other piece of modern English, in prose or poetry, in which there is so much told of the Renaissance spirit. Various models for the Bishop's tomb have been suggested, despite the fact that it seems unlikely the Bishop's "nephews" will follow his orders, and we all no doubt have in mind an image of a Renaissance tomb, with its recumbent figure on the top, which fits the Bishop's description. Yet the Bishop's imagination of his transformation to his own funerary monument is distinctly Victorian. The moments of fear – almost panic – in the poem when the Bishop feels he has lost the assent of his nephews to his plan are marked by a terror of bodily dissolution:

> What do they whisper thee,
> Child of my bowels, Anselm? Ah, ye hope
> To revel down my villas while I gasp
> Bricked o'er with beggar's mouldy travertine.[3]

Or, toward the end of the poem:

> There, leave me, there!
> For ye have stabbed me with ingratitude
> To death – ye wish it – God, ye wish it! Stone –
> Gritstone, a-crumble! Clammy squares which sweat
> As if the corpse they keep were oozing through.
>
> (ll. 113–117)

Through the design of his tomb, the Bishop preserves his body intact. He imagines it, like Giraud's medallions, as both image and substance, an auto-icon, which, like that of Jeremy Bentham, will remain in the world he inhabited. The poem treats the Bishop's design with deep irony, understanding his attempt to become his own funerary monument as his last futile grasp at power.

"The Bishop Orders His Tomb" is in some ways unique among Browning's poems that concern themselves with the dead body, for the Bishop is contemplating his own death rather than the death of another. Far more frequent in Browning's poetry is the situation in which he positions the speaker in the presence of a corpse – "Porphyria's Lover," "Evelyn Hope," "A Grammarian's Funeral," "Gold Hair: A Story of Pornic," "Apparent Failure." Browning is typical of writers of the period in this regard; it is characteristic of Victorian literature not only to stage deathbed scenes,[4] but to stage scenes in the presence of a corpse – Victor Frankenstein's galvanization of his creature, Heathcliff's exhumation of Catherine, Dr. Woodcourt's examination of Nemo's body. These moments – in which a character confronts a corpse – are often importantly implicated in the writer's understanding of what literature does. In Browning's poetry in particular, the animation of corpses is closely connected to his conception of the dramatic impulse and to the form of the dramatic monologue.

In his monumental work, *The Hour of Our Death*, Philippe Aries argues that the nineteenth century was characterized by a fundamental change in social attitudes toward death, a change from a concern with one's own death to a concern with the death of the other, whose loss and memory inspired a new cult of tombs and cemeteries, which, in the most ideal descriptions of their function, became the source of familial and civic virtue (Aries, pp. 409–558). As the examples of Giraud and Bentham demonstrate, this memorialization involves a complex exchange. The living preserve the memory, even the substance of the dead in acts of memorial that are often conceptualized in terms of industrial or social productivity. The dead become thus available for a kind of appropriation through which they inform the identity of the living. This process sometimes involves a deliberate fetishism, one explicitly recommended by several of Comte's disciples in their writings on the cemetery. Pierre Lafitte writes, "The material object is for us, and for the whole human species, both the symbol and the substance of the deceased" (Aries, p. 542). Positivism should embrace this spontaneous fetishism, incorporate it into the tomb and the cemetery, and thus give it a public character, in order to develop the sense of continuity in the family, the city, and the race.

In a poem like Tennyson's *In Memoriam*, one can see an ideal version of the cult of the dead that I have been describing, and one can see as well the way in which literature in its capacity to re-present the dead can be essentially connected to such memorialization. But there are less ideal ways of construing the relationship of the artist to the corpse, ways with which Browning showed an uneasy fascination.

In the first book of *The Ring and the Book*, Browning presents an image of the poet's art as resuscitation. Carefully distinguishing man from God, who alone has the power to create original life, he asserts that man, repeating God's process in "due degree,"

> May so project his surplusage of soul
> In search of body, so add self to self
> By owning what lay ownerless before, –
> So find, so fill full, so appropriate forms –
> That although nothing which had never life
> Shall get life from him, be, not having been;
> Yet, something dead may get to live again.[5]

He names Elisha as his ideal antecedent, who, coming into a house where there is a corpse,

> lay upon the corpse, dead on the couch,
> And put his mouth upon its mouth, his eyes
> Upon its eyes, his hands upon its hands,
> And stretched him on the flesh; the flesh waxed warm.
> (I.765–768)

The story suggests that Browning's ideal image of the poet is the resurrectionist, who, like the physician that Karshish hears of from Lazarus, brings the dead back to life. However, "resurrecting" was a specialized profession in the nineteenth century, the stealing of bodies from graves in order to sell them to doctors and medical students for dissection.[6]

The passage from *The Ring and the Book* contains besides Elisha another image of the poet, a magician who chances upon some "Rag of flesh, scrap of bone, in dim disuse" (1.753) which he animates and then leads forth "By a moonrise through a ruin of a crypt" (1.757). Thus, existing together with the ideal sense of the poet as one who, Christ-like, resuscitates the dead, is one who, more like Frankenstein, collects pieces of bodies and galvanizes them into life. Even in Browning's ideal sense, the poet must "add self to self" (1.724), own "what lay ownerless before" (1.725); the question for Browning is whether such animation of bodies is bringing the dead back to life or robbing graves to create phantoms.

In the beginning of the Pope's monologue, Browning returns to the image of the corpse in an episode that seems strangely disproportionate to the argumentative burden that it carries. Facing the burden of his decision about the murder of Pompilia, the Pope is reflecting upon the fallibility or infallibility of the judgment of popes. Reading a history of the popes of Rome in anticipation of the day when the next page "shall be stretched smooth o'er my own funeral cyst" (10.23), the Pope relates the story of a "ghastly trial" (10.29), in which one of his predecessors, Stephen, disinters his rival for the see, places him upon Peter's chair, and appointing a Deacon to be "advocate and mouthpiece of the corpse" (10.52), tries the corpse to determine, "Hath he intruded or do I pretend" (10.65).

The grotesqueness of the episode makes it jump out of its context to reflect more generally upon the poem itself. The grisly trial that the Pope relates bears an uneasy relationship to the poetic act in which Browning himself is engaged. Like Stephen, Browning has taken a dead pope from the grave and provided an advocate and mouthpiece of the corpse. Like Stephen, he requests a judgment – hath he intruded or do I pretend? In one sense, the question raises the issue of historical authenticity that Browning had pondered in the first book – is this the thing itself, the real Pope resuscitated through the poet's creative powers, the real "he" intruding, or is it mere pretense? But what makes the moment in the Pope's monologue such an eerie one is the negativity of the two terms, intrude and pretend, a negativity that makes the Pope and the corpse rivals for a single legitimate power. Thus, if we judge the dead the genuine article, we make the resurrectionist a fraud, but if we judge the corpse a fraud, we give its resurrectionist legitimacy. Unlike the way in which Browning had constructed the poet's authority in Book I as depending on genuine resuscitation, the incident here implies that the dead threatens the legitimacy of the one who disinters him, that only by exposing the pretense, the artifact, the fiction of the corpse, can he secure his own authority. The need to enact this ghastly ritual suggests how fragile this authority is. In order to sustain it, the poet must continually restage such encounters with a corpse, in which his mouthpiece can own what he fears the corpse may possess.

"Porphyria's Lover" is a case in point. Many readers have noticed the way in which the speaker, before the murder, attributes all action to Porphyria and presents himself as eerily passive. When Porphyria enters the room:

> straight
> She shut the cold out and the storm,
> And kneeled and made the cheerless grate
> Blaze up, and all the cottage warm;
> Which done, she rose, and from her form
> Withdrew the dripping coat and shawl,
> And laid her soiled gloves by, untied
> Her hat and let the damp hair fall,
> And, last, she sat down by my side
> And called me. When no voice replied,
> She put my arm about her waist,
> And made her smooth white shoulder bare,
> And all her yellow hair displaced,
> And, stooping, made my cheek lie there,
> And spread, all o'er, her yellow hair,
> Murmuring how she loved me.
> (ll. 6–21)

In these lines, the speaker not only presents himself as the passive object of Porphyria's attentions, almost as if he were a small child, but attributes all action and passion that seems his own to her. When he kills her, he reverses the situation; she becomes the passive object of his affection. Yet the way in which his actions mirror those that he had previously projected as hers suggests that the speaker finds in the murder a way to share a single life between the two of them:

> her cheek once more
> Blushed bright beneath my burning kiss:
> I propped her head up as before,
> Only, this time, my shoulder bore
> Her head, which droops upon it still.
> (ll. 47–51)

The psychoanalytic work that has been done with necrophilia argues that its root is a fantasy of emptying the mother of all life until she becomes a corpse, which the necrophiliac then introjects and identifies with himself.[7] Fundamental, then, to necrophilia is the drive toward female identification, based upon the fantasy that the mother is in sole possession of authentic life. "Porphyria's Lover" in many ways conforms to this description, for the speaker derives all definition from Porphyria in the beginning of the poem, a definition he appropriates in its second half, with even a suggestion of female impersonation: "my shoulder bore her head."

The necrophilia of "Porphyria's Lover" is grotesque, but the poem depends upon such grisly pretense, creating its odd and uneasy humor through the kinship of the lover's animation of Porphyria and Browning's animation of him. Like the trial of Formosus, the poem suggests that the poet secures his own office through grotesque fictionalization of the dead through which he distorts and appropriates its face. "Evelyn Hope" provides another example. The poem begins as a conventional lament for the unlived life of a girl dying young. In the first stanza, the speaker seeks to depict her bedroom without change and yet realizes that he cannot do so; the second stanza for the most part dwells upon the life that has been cut off. The third stanza, however, contains a startling shift – from the unlived life of Evelyn Hope to the unlived life of the aging speaker; her death is a denial of his possibility. The speaker then proceeds to undo his loss – a loss of something he has never had – by making a move characteristic of Browning; he appropriates what he presents as an authoritative vision of the future – "No, indeed! for God above / Is great to grant as mighty to make" (ll. 25–26). He then uses that vision to project a plot past an event which had seemed to establish final closure. One of the problems of plotting that most engages Browning, as it does a number of his contemporaries, is the projection of narrative beyond death. He does this in a number of ways – in his representation of mediumship, in his creation of deathbed scenes which establish either a different structure of time or different mode of existence for the speaker, or in his use of resurrection as endpoint or subject of poems. In part, of course, this projection of narrative after death is related to the kind of deferral of closure in Browning's poetry that Herbert Tucker has demonstrated so brilliantly.[8] The animation of corpses, however, not only defers closure but reverses it, converting a death narrative to a life narrative, to reconstitute the body, as Giraud and Bentham do, in art. This reconstitution has less to do in Browning's poetry with grief for the death of the other than concern for the self. By animating the dead, Browning's speakers seek to secure their own trajectory. In "Evelyn Hope," the speaker asserts his claims not only to her but to much experience beyond the present moment – of men, ages, climes. His imagination of their future meeting, moreover, involves his memory of her youth and beauty, now dependent on his recall:

> But the time will come, – at last it will,
>   When, Evelyn Hope, what meant (I shall say)
> In the lower earth, in the years long still,
>   That body and soul so pure and gay?
> Why your hair was amber, I shall divine,
>   And your mouth of your own geranium's red.
>   (ll. 33–38)

He transforms her loss to his gain.

Yet there is clearly an irony in "Evelyn Hope" as there is in all of Browning's poems in which the speaker makes so fictional a projection about the dead body. The poems on the one hand enact a fantasy about life's confirmation while they expose its hollowness, a kind of enthroning of corpses that mirrors the death of the self that erects them. The rather grotesque poem, "Gold Hair: A Story of Pornic," presents this irony directly in the story it tells. The poem relates the anecdote of a beautiful girl, who, dying young, begs to be buried with her gold hair untouched. Hair seems to be the feature of the dead body that the Victorians most frequently used as a synecdoche for the intact corpse; indeed, as such, it often functions as a screen for the decaying body. Recall, for example, Lizzie Siddal's hair, which allegedly continued to grow after death; the role that hair plays in "Porphyria's Lover"; or even the practice of making mourning jewelry from the hair of the deceased. In "Gold Hair," it first seems as if the girl's hair will function in this way as the enduring token of her beauty, but the priest of the church in which she is buried decides to disinter the corpse when some boys find a gold piece in the vicinity of the coffin. When the diggers lift the rotten planks of the coffin lid, they discover, wedged amid the girl's skull, a mint of money, which she had apparently hidden in her hair. The poem takes a vindictive and gleeful pleasure in exposing the greed of the girl who had seemed "too white," "an angel before the time" (ll.I, 67), and the church too gets considerable profit from the demystification; the gold enables it to build a new altar. In "The Bioeconomics of *Our Mutual Friend*," Catherine Gallagher argues that the economy of the novel requires the body's deanimation as a condition of valuable life; it transforms corpses to wealth, a process suggested in the utility Bentham finds in dissection or Giraud in cremation.[9] Browning's poem, too, accomplishes such a transformation, even in its sardonic rendering of the beautiful corpse, that suggests the need to appropriate the dead body to the use of the living.

Usually, however, the exchanges that Browning portrays are less material, as in the poem "Apparent Failure," in which he portrays his visit to the Paris morgue. Like Dickens, who also made literary capital out of his trips to the Paris morgue, Browning invests and exercises his literary identity in his visit. He begins the poem in response to the epigraph he takes from a Paris newspaper, "We shall soon lose a celebrated building," with the words, "No, for I'll save it," and when he comments that Petrarch's Vaucluse makes proud the Sorgue, the next line, by parallel logic, calls for a writer whose literary habitation of the Paris morgue will ensure its renown. When Browning views the drowned bodies in the morgue, he imagines their slabs as thrones and makes up stories about them. They are, he asserts, suicides, whose investment in political ambition, revolutionary politics, and gambling yielded a poor return. These melodramatic plots, Browning's domestication of the scene in imagining the slabs as beds over which their tenants hang their hats and coats, and the pious resurrectionary sentiment with which he ends the poem are all attempts to make the face of death more comfortable. Browning thus "owns," to use his word, these ownerless corpses, rationalizes their disturbing aspect. But the odd, grotesquely jocular way he addresses them – "How did it happen, my poor boy? / You wanted to be Buonaparte / And have the Tuileries for toy" (ll. 37–39) – signals his discomfort in the face of "this," as he says in Stanza 6, "poor fellow that is blue" (ll. 46–47). The awkward jauntiness of tone that Browning tries to maintain makes this poem not a very successful one, but it nonetheless reveals the problem that the corpse typically presents in Browning. The corpse seems to require a fictional animation that secures the identity of the observer, as if he must transform the potentiality of his own death through artifact. Yet the clarity of the pretense involved, and the grotesqueness and the exaggeration of the fictions, reveal more pointedly the corpse within.

In one of the early *Cantos*, Pound tells the story of one Pedro, who disinters his murdered queen, sets her corpse upon the throne, and compels the very courtiers who had murdered her to do her homage. The story bears an uncanny similarity to that of Formosus and suggests similar anxieties – that the poet may set up corpses upon thrones to secure his own pretense. Browning's poetry in this, as in much else, provides a parodic reflection of the social transformations of his culture. I wrote at the beginning about the way in which funerary monument undoes the bodily dissolution that is the work of death. Tennyson's and Arnold's elegiac poetry demonstrates the ways in which literature itself was involved in the cult of funerary remembrance so central to the culture. Browning's corpses imply a less ideal construction of the dead body, a fetishism not the source of civic virtue, but of the self's pretense in the face of death. Such pretense paradoxically depends upon the death it seems to wish to efface, a compulsive reencounter with the sight it transforms. The grotesque pretense in which Browning involves his characters as well as the extravagant make-believe of the poetry itself suggests an understanding of art as just such extravagant pretense, exercised to secure the authority it reveals as hollow.

When one looks at the history of the dramatic monologue subsequent to Browning, it is striking how often it involves a thematics of the dead. In *The Spoon River Anthology* and in any number of poems by Hardy, Jarrell, Frank Bidart, the poet makes the dead speak. These poems suggest that not merely Browning's personal psychology or even the social history of the period but an impulse of the form itself is involved with the habitation of corpses. It do the dead in different voices, one might say of the dramatic monologue, to provide an advocate and mouthpiece of the corpse.

Notes

1 Quoted in Philippe Aries, *The Hour of Our Death* (New York: Vintage Books, 1982), p. 514.
2 For an analysis of the relation between portraiture and the dead body, see my essay, "Painting the Dead: Portraiture and Necrophilia in Victorian Art and Poetry" in *Death and Representation*, ed. Sarah Webster Goodwin and Elisabeth Bronfen (Baltimore: Johns Hopkins Univ. Press, 1993), pp. 133–51).
3 Robert Browning, *The Poems*, ed. John Pettigrew and Thomas J. Collins. 2 vols. (Yale Univ. Press, 1981), 1:414, ll. 63–6. All further quotations from Browning's poems are taken from this edition
4 See Garrett Stewart, *Death Sentences: Styles of Dying in British Fiction* (Cambridge: Harvard Univ. Press, 1984), for an analysis of death scenes in Victorian fiction.
5 *The Ring and the Book*, ed. Richard D. Altick (New Haven: Yale Univ. Press, 1971), Book 1, ll. 723–8. All further quotations from *The Ring and The Book* are taken from this edition.
6 See Albert Hutter's essay, "The Novelist as Resurrectionist: Dickens and the Dilemma of Death," DSA 12 (1983): 1–39.

7   See, for example, H. Segal, "A Necrophiliac Phantasy," *Institute Journal of Psychoanalysis* 34 (1953): 98–101, and Sidney Tarachow, "Judas, the Beloved Executioner," *Psychoanalytic Quarterly* 29 (1960): 538–9.
8   Herbert F. Tucker, *Browning's Beginnings: The Art of Disclosure* (Minneapolis: Univ. of Minnesota Press, 1980).
9   Catherine Gallagher, "The Bioeconomics of *Our Mutual Friend,*" *Zone* #5 (1989): 345–65

14

A E Housman and 'the colour of his hair'

Christopher Ricks

'Oh who is that young sinner with the handcuffs on his wrists?' In 1895, A. E. Housman dealt swingeingly with the imprisonment of Oscar Wilde, whose first trial had been in April and who was sent to Reading Gaol in November. His crime: the giving of homosexual offence. The world's judgment (Housman's poem fiercely urged) is as unjust as taking a man 'to prison for the colour of his hair'.

Why, of all capricious gravamina, did Housman seize upon this? Because, while flamboyantly arbitrary, the colour of one's hair had come to represent just such a cruel perversion of injustice. Arbitrary though punishment for the colour of one's hair is, there was nothing arbitrary about Housman's choosing it as his indictment. For it had become a type of the arbitrarily unjust, and so – itself by way of being a tradition – it was the more sharply fitted to the case, a case where there converged with it another good old English tradition, the punitive repudiation that is now dubbed homophobia.

To bring into play, footnotable play, the precedents *in re* the colour of one's hair, is not only to see Housman's instance of preposterous crime as at once impertinent and pertinent, but to take the measure of the poem's *saeva indignatio*.

Laurence Housman, who in 1937 (a year after his brother's death) respectfully chose to publish this unreleased poem,[1] was right to see it as a poem of protest against society's laws, but he was limited in seeing the poem as that only. The poem's protest, as often in Housman, is

Ricks, Christopher. 1997. "A E Housman and 'the colour of his hair.'" In *Essays in Criticism*, 47, iii (July), pp. 240–55. Reproduced with permission of Oxford University Press.

Victorian Poets: A Critical Reader, First Edition. Edited by Valentine Cunningham.
© 2014 John Wiley & Sons, Ltd. Published 2014 by John Wiley & Sons, Ltd.

partly against that part of life which is society's doing and wrongdoing, but is more largely against all else. Society's laws, yes, but nature's too, and, above all, the laws of 'Whatever brute and blackguard made the world'. This, even a chorus of priests might have to acknowledge:

> Oh wearisome condition of humanity!
> Born under one law, to another bound:
> Vainly begot, and yet forbidden vanity,
> Created sick, commanded to be sound:
> What meaneth Nature by these diverse laws?
> (Fulke Greville, Chorus Sacerdotum,
> from *Mustapha)*

What meaneth Society by these perverse laws? 'The laws of God, the laws of man' (*Last Poems* XII): there the sway and the swaying constitute the even-handed scales of Housman's handy-dandy.

> Oh who is that young sinner with the handcuffs on his wrists?
> And what has he been after that they groan and shake their fists?
> And wherefore is he wearing such a conscience-stricken air?
> Oh they're taking him to prison for the colour of his hair.
>
> 'Tis a shame to human nature, such a head of hair as his;
> In the good old time 'twas hanging for the colour that it is;
> Though hanging isn't bad enough and flaying would be fair
> For the nameless and abominable colour of his hair.
>
> Oh a deal of pains he's taken and a pretty price he's paid
> To hide his poll or dye it of a mentionable shade;
> But they've pulled the beggar's hat off for the world to see and stare,
> And they're haling him to justice for the colour of his hair.
>
> Now 'tis oakum for his fingers and the treadmill for his feet
> And the quarry-gang on Portland in the cold and in the heat,
> And between his spells of labour in the time he has to spare
> He can curse the God that made him for the colour of his hair.

It was not until thirty years after Laurence Housman published the poem that there appeared – likewise after its author's death – his essay on his brother's love and friendship, 'A. E. Housman's "De Amicitia"'.[2] (The Latin has all the decent lack of obscurity of a learned language.) Laurence Housman's words, which manifest a tender probity, are well-known but they remain unexhausted:

> I do not pretend to know how far my brother continued to accept throughout life, in all circumstances, the denial of what was natural to

him, but I do know that he considered the inhibition imposed by society on his fellow-victims both cruel and unjust. That fact is made abundantly plain in the poem which, after considerable hesitation, I decided to publish, even though its literary merit was not high – the one beginning

'Oh who is that young sinner with the handcuffs on his wrists?'

It refers quite evidently to those who inescapably, through no fault of their own, are homosexual – having no more power of choice in the matter than a man has about the colour of his hair, which, as the poem says, he may hide out of sight, or dye to a 'more mentionable shade,' but cannot get away from.

Here, then, was a poem expressing contemptuous anger against society's treatment of these unhappy victims of fate, and a sympathy which went so far as to imply no blame. That poem he had left me at liberty to publish: had he objected to publication he would either have so marked it – as he did one or two others for literary reasons – or would have destroyed it. My only reason for hesitation was that its meaning was so obvious, that intelligent readers would be unlikely to refrain (nor did they) from making the true deduction; and my brother had relatives still living to whom this might give pain. I felt nevertheless, that the risk must be taken; it was something of a public duty that I should make known so strong an expression of feeling against social injustice [...][3]

This is admirably executed, down to the duly dry touch – what with prison and infringements of liberty – of 'That poem he had left me at liberty to publish...' The brotherly paragraphs are truthful, and yet they are not the whole truth. For Laurence Housman's exclusive emphasis, tripled, upon society ('imposed by society', 'society's treatment of these unhappy victims of fate', 'social injustice'), has the effect of narrowing the poem's perturbation, as though – were society to be so good as to abolish its prohibitive laws – all would be well. Not so.

> How small, of all that human hearts endure,
> That part which laws or kings can cause or cure.[4]

Samuel Johnson, like A. E. Housman, was a radical conservative, and Johnson's great apophthegm, aware of society's injustices, is aware too of life's condition.

For one reason why 'Oh who is that young sinner...' should not be seen only as social protest is its famously being a sombre pendant to two poems which Housman did publish, next year (1896), consecutively too: *A Shropshire Lad* XLIV, 'Shot? so quick, so clean an ending?', and XLV, 'If it chance your eye offend you'. Laurence Housman found in his brother's copy of *A Shropshire Lad*, alongside XLIV, the newspaper cutting which has since become famous. Dated August 1895, it quotes a letter by a young Woolwich cadet who had committed suicide, racked by cowardice and despair at his sexual nature while spurred to self-slaughter by 'as yet': 'I thank God that as yet, so far as I know, I have not morally injured, or "offended," as it is called in the Bible, anyone else'. When Housman congratulates this dead young man, it is with no sense, no implication, that the man had been wrong to feel shame at his sexual self.

> Shot? so quick, so clean an ending?
> Oh that was right, lad, that was brave:
> Yours was not an ill for mending,
> 'Twas best to take it to the grave.

Housman these days is liable to find himself harshly judged by the new censoriousness that has replaced the old much worse one; his shade may be told that he was a household traitor to his sexual nature (and others') by lacking pride in being 'gay'. Out, out. But Housman wrote what he meant; the poem praises the young man for doing something not only 'brave' but 'right'; and when it goes on immediately 'Yours was not an ill for mending', there is no reason to suppose that for the poet, in this poem or elsewhere, the ill *was* an ill for mending, being after all not truly an ill at all but only deemed so by a social injustice that the mending of man's laws would rectify. It is not social condemnation only that gives such balanced obduracy to Housman's line 'Souls undone, undoing others', or to the stanza that had set the soul before us:

> Oh soon, and better so than later
> After long disgrace and scorn,
> You shot dead the household traitor,
> The soul that should not have been born.

There are the clean lines of admiration:

> Undishonoured, clear of danger,
> Clean of guilt, pass hence and home.

But the admiration is along lines which invoke honour (a magnificently positive double negative, 'Undishonoured'), an invocation that resists any emancipated or enlightened insistence that there is in homosexuality no dishonour or guilt of which one should yearn to be 'clean'. So too,

Housman's ensuing poem, *A Shropshire Lad* XLV, comes to an end in praise of the healthy courage that had brought itself to put an end, not to something which was not really sick at all (merely deemed so, socially, wrongly), but to soul-sickness:

> And if your hand or foot offend you,
>   Cut it off, lad, and be whole;
> But play the man, stand up and end you,
>   When your sickness is your soul.

The Biblical injunction to be willing to inflict upon oneself the cutting-off of hand or foot is inestimably more grave than to cut one's hair or 'dye it of a mentionable shade'. But 'the colour of his hair' constitutes a tradition, secular and Biblical, that is germane to the conviction that Housman's poem, tragically, should not be restricted to social protest.

It had been, earlier in the nineteenth century, Macaulay who had given new life to an old association of injustice with the capricious indictment of the colour of one's hair.[5] He launched a flight of ferociously precise fancy in his essay on 'Civil Disabilities of the Jews' (*Edinburgh Review*, 1831).

> The English Jews are, as far as we can see, precisely what our government has made them. They are precisely what any sect, what any class of men, treated as they have been treated, would have been. If all the red-haired people in Europe had, during centuries, been outraged and oppressed, banished from this place, imprisoned in that, deprived of their money, deprived of their teeth, convicted of the most improbable crimes on the feeblest evidence, dragged at horses' tails, hanged, tortured, burned alive, if, when manners became milder, they had still been subject to debasing restrictions and exposed to vulgar insults, locked up in particular streets in some countries, pelted and ducked by the rabble in others, excluded every where from magistracies and honours, what would be the patriotism of gentlemen with red hair? And if, under such circumstances, a proposition were made for admitting red-haired men to office, how striking a speech might an eloquent admirer of our old institutions deliver against so revolutionary a measure! 'These men,' he might say, 'scarcely consider themselves as Englishmen. They think a red-haired Frenchman or a red-haired German more closely connected with them than a man with brown hair born in their own parish. If a foreign sovereign patronises red hair, they love him better than their own native king...'

And so inexorably on, in Macaulay's Swiftian fantasy exposing cruel realities. The Civil Disabilities of the Jews have constituted an incitement to criminal dealings and to the law's injustices. To this intersection (alive in Housman's poem) of hair-colour and the law's injustices, and to an implication of Macaulay's seizing *red* hair, I shall return.

In John Locke's earlier supposition in 1689 – more calm, more level, and no less telling – it had been black hair that was postulated, this in relation to religious toleration:

> Suppose this business of religion were let alone, and that there were some other distinction made between men and men, upon account of their different complexions, shapes and features, so that those who have black hair, for example, or grey eyes, should not enjoy the same privileges as other citizens; that they should not be permitted either to buy or sell, or live by their callings; that parents should not have the government and education of their own children; that they should either be excluded from the benefit of the laws, or meet with partial judges: can it be doubted but these persons, thus distinguished from others by the colour of their hair and eyes, and united together by one common persecution, would be as dangerous to the magistrate, as any others that had associated themselves merely upon the account of religion?[6]

Here too 'the laws' are crucial; here too there is the yoking, once again scornful, of 'the colour of their hair' with religion, an association which is, I suggest, to be glimpsed in Housman's poem.

But it is the greatest legal historian, and legal thinker, of Victorian England, Sir James Fitzjames Stephen, who furnished the crucial stage by which this yoking of crime and the colour of one's hair, previously pressed into service by Locke and Macaulay, may arrive at Housman and sexual opprobrium. Stephen had written on Macaulay, mentioning the argument that 'Jews ought to be allowed to sit in Parliament', in the *Saturday Review* (18 August 1866). He had written expansively there (9 March 1867) on Locke's letters on toleration, and he further referred to these in the preface to the second edition of his *Liberty, Equality, Fraternity* (1874).

Two arguments in Stephen's *Liberty, Equality, Fraternity* converge.

Pondering the age-old intricacy of the relations between morality and the law, Stephen deplored not only Mill's liberalism but his laxity. For Mill, turning a blind eye towards an inconvenient inconsistency, had seen nothing wrong in continuing to find publicly criminal such conduct as should, by Mill's own arguments, have been a matter for private life only. On the general proposition, Stephen is insistent:

> Other illustrations of the fact that English criminal law does recognize morality are to be found in the fact that a considerable number of acts

which need not be specified are treated as crimes merely because they are
regarded as grossly immoral.

'Which need not be specified': Stephen's reticence is not a matter of
laying his finger against the side of his nose or upon his lips. His
modern editor specifies. 'Stephen here refers to what the Victorians
generally called "unnatural vice". Sodomy was a capital crime until
1861' (R. J. White).[7]

Stephen proceeded at once to indict Mill for paltering.

I have already shown in what manner Mr Mill deals with these topics. It
is, I venture to think, utterly unsatisfactory. The impression it makes
upon me is that he feels that such acts ought to be punished, and that he
is able to reconcile this with his fundamental principles only by subtleties
quite unworthy of him. Admit the relation for which I am contending
between law and morals, and all becomes perfectly clear. All the acts
referred to are unquestionably wicked. Those who do them are ashamed
of them. They are all capable of being clearly defined and specifically
proved or disproved, and there can be no question at all that legal punishment reduces them to small dimensions, and forces the criminals to
carry on their practices with secrecy and precaution. In other words, the
object of their suppression is good, and the means adequate.

Yet it is characteristic of Stephen that at this point he should turn away
from too eager a prosecution, with a breadth of mind and a genuineness of concession seldom found in a conservative thinker – and far too
seldom acknowledged by liberals to be even possible to a conservative
thinker:

In practice this is subject to highly important qualifications, of which I
will only say here that those who have due regard to the incurable weak-
nesses of human nature will be very careful how they inflict penalties
upon mere vice, or even upon those who make a trade of promoting it,
unless special circumstances call for their infliction.

This caveat, which is quite other than a rhetorical move, is a form of
'however' – one that is duly followed by a further 'however', turning
the argument back to Stephen's axis of conviction:

It is one thing however to tolerate vice so long as it is inoffensive, and
quite another to give it a legal right not only to exist, but to assert itself in
the face of the world as an 'experiment in living' as good as another, and
entitled to the same protection from law.[8]

Such is Stephen's judicious position on 'grossly immoral' acts and their criminality. It is in the next chapter of *Liberty, Equality, Fraternity* that the colour of one's hair enjoys its day in court:

> The rule, 'All thieves shall be imprisoned,' is not observed if A, being a thief, is not imprisoned. In other words, it is not observed if it is not applied equally to every person who falls within the definition of a thief, whatever else he may be. If the rule were, 'All thieves except those who have red hair shall be imprisoned, and they shall not,' the rule would be violated if a red-haired thief were imprisoned as much as if a black-haired thief were not imprisoned. The imprisonment of the red-haired thief would be an inequality in the application of the rule; for the equality consists not in the equal treatment of the persons who are the subjects of law, but in the equivalency between the general terms of the law and the description of the particular cases to which it is applied. 'All thieves not being red-haired shall be imprisoned' is equivalent to 'A being a thief with brown hair, B being a thief with black hair, C being a thief with white hair, &c., shall be imprisoned, and Z being a thief with red hair shall not be imprisoned.'

Given the prejudice against red hair, it is good of Stephen to invert his instance so that, for once, red hair would be favoured. What is striking, though, and is the sort of thing that might strike such a fancy as Housman's, is that Stephen moves immediately to a relating of red hair to an imaginable psychopathology:

> In this sense equality is no doubt of the very essence of justice, but the question whether the colour of a man's hair shall or shall not affect the punishment of his crimes depends on a different set of considerations. It is imaginable that the colour of the hair might be an unfailing mark of peculiarity of disposition which might require peculiar treatment. Experience alone can inform us whether this is so or not.[9]

There is a more than a hint of the sexually aberrant in this odd coupling, with 'the colour of the hair' as possibly 'an unfailing mark of peculiarity of disposition which might require peculiar treatment'. More than a century after Stephen, it has not been many years since the alternative to being taken to prison for this colour of one's hair was the meting out of peculiar treatment to rectify peculiarity of disposition. Aversion therapy against perversion. Oh who is that young patient with the limpness of the wrists?

'For the colour of his hair': what do most readers see? We see red. And this not only because of Macaulay, for Macaulay in his turn had been availing himself, so as to hold anti-Semitism up to ridicule, of the age-old prejudice against red hair. The *OED* cites, under 'red-haired', George Chapman, *Bussy D'Ambois* III i (1607), 'Worse than the poison of a red-hair'd man'. Swift needed the commonplace opprobium, in *Gulliver's Travels* IV: 'It is observed, that the Red-haired of both Sexes are more libidinous and mischievous than the rest'. Even Stevie Smith has a poem 'From the Italian: *An old superstition*':

> A woolly dog,
> A red-haired man,
> Better dead
> Than to have met 'em.

Though the colour of the hair is in Housman's poem left unspecified (grossly immoral 'acts which need not be specified'), the reiterated line is calculated to call up an ancient prejudice, prejudice being in any such case the nub.

Take, for instance, the word 'poll': 'To hide his poll or dye it of a mentionable shade'. A poll of hair may be any colour, but is likely to conjure up red, for not only is 'redpoll' many a species of bird, but there had been Peter Pindar in 1787 ('Large red-poll'd, blowzy, hard, two-handed jades'), and there was – by a coincidence, in 1895, the very year of Housman's poem and Wilde's trial – 'The celebrated...herd of Red-Polled cattle': 'The Duke of York is getting together a large and choice herd of Red-Polls' (*Westminster Gazette*, 29 March 1895).[10] There is an onomastic felicity in its having been, exactly a century later, in 1995, a scholar of the name of Whitehead whose book noted the echo of the phrase 'such a head of hair as yours' from Arthur Conan Doyle's Sherlock Holmes story 'The Red-Headed League' (1891), a story where the person with red hair is indeed innocent of crime.[11]

But if red hair were darkly called up by Housman, there might come with it a further darkness. There is, so far as I know, only one person whose name identifies a colour, and this the colour of hair, and the colour red. (Rufus *means* red, and so is another story.) *OED*:

> *Judas-coloured* (of the hair or beard) red (from the mediaeval belief that Judas Iscariot had red hair and beard):
> c.1594 Kyd: And let their beards be of Judas his own colour.
> 1695 Motteux: Observations on the Judas-colour of his Beard and hair.
> 1673 Dryden: There's treachery in that Judas-coloured beard.
> 1879 Dowden: An ugly specimen of the streaked-carroty or Judas-coloured kind.

Dryden spat this more than once.

> [Now the Assembly to adjourn prepar'd,
> When *Bibliopolo* from behind appear'd,
> As well describ'd by th' old Satyrick Bard:]
> With leering Looks, Bullfac'd, and Freckled fair,
> With two left Legs, and Judas-colour'd Hair,
> With Frowzy Pores, that taint the ambient Air.
>
>   ('Lines on Tonson')

But is Judas to be glimpsed in Housman's poem? To the colour of the hair there might be added hanging: 'In the good old time 'twas hanging for the colour that it is'. Yes, 'sodomy was a capital crime until 1861', but there might be Judas's self-infliction too. For to the compound *Judas-coloured* there may be added the compound *Judas-tree*: 'From a popular notion that Judas hanged himself on a tree of this kind' (*OED*).

The Gospel according to Saint Matthew reports that Judas 'repented himself', 'saying, I have sinned' (Housman: 'sinner', 'conscience-stricken air'); Judas 'went and hanged himself' (Housman: 'hanging'); for Judas, there was 'the price of blood', 'the price of him that was valued' (Housman: 'and a pretty price he's paid').

For there is the further compound, *Judas-kiss*. The Gospel according to Saint Matthew: 'Now he that betrayed him gave them a sign, saying, Whomsoever I shall kiss, that same is he: hold him fast. And forthwith he came to Jesus, and said, Hail master; and kissed him'. The Gospel according to Saint Luke: 'But Jesus said unto him, Judas, betrayest thou the Son of man with a kiss?' Moreover, the Judas-kiss lent itself to homosexual solicitation; Wilde was to take up the suggestion of it from within *The Ballad of Reading Gaol*, to furnish the concluding antithesis of the poem:

> And all men kill the thing they love,
>   By all let this be heard,
> Some do it with a bitter look,
>   Some with a flattering word,
> The coward does it with a kiss,
>   The brave man with a sword!

Housman, praising the cadet who had bitten a bullet, contemplated unflinchingly the thought of 'The soul that should not have been born'. Those words probably came to him from Saint Matthew:

> but woe unto that man by whom the Son of man is betrayed! it had been good for that man if he had not been born. Then Judas, which betrayed him, answered and said, Master, Is it I? He said unto him, Thou hast said.

Macaulay had needed the same verse:

> The same reasoning which is now employed to vindicate the disabilities imposed on our Hebrew countrymen will equally vindicate the kiss of Judas and the judgment of Pilate. 'The Son of man goeth, as it is written of him; but woe to that man by whom the Son of man is betrayed.'

In conclusion something must be said of why it matters whether Judas is to be glimpsed in 'Oh who is that young sinner...' One answer is that Judas widens the focus of the poem's burning glass, not away from the laws of man but beyond them to take in too the laws of God. For Judas has always provoked a great unease about divine justice. Did not God's providence, and Christ's mission, need Judas, and is not some gratitude due to him for being, at the very least, of such service? Bob Dylan and Jorge Luis Borges have this much in common, that both have pondered whether Judas Iscariot had God on his side. Here is the thinking of Nils Runeberg, Borges' Nils Runeberg:

> Skilfully, he begins by pointing out how superfluous was the act of Judas. He observes (as did Robertson) that in order to identify a master who daily preached in the synagogue and who performed miracles before gatherings of thousands, the treachery of an apostle is not necessary. This, nevertheless, occurred. To suppose an error in Scripture is intolerable; no less intolerable is it to admit that there was a single haphazard act in the most precious drama in the history of the world. *Ergo*, the treachery of Judas was not accidental; it was a predestined deed which has its mysterious place in the economy of the Redemption.
>
> Judas, alone among the apostles, intuited the secret divinity and the terrible purpose of Jesus. The Word had lowered Himself to be mortal; Judas, the disciple of the Word, could lower himself to the role of informer (the worst transgression dishonour abides), and welcome the fire which can not be extinguished. ('Three Versions of Judas')[12]

For Judas, 'dishonour abides', unlike for the cadet whom Housman had celebrated as 'Undishonoured'. It is not only society whose injustices cry out. For Housman the great blasphemer, the injustice visited upon a man damned to prison for the colour of his hair might cry out to the fellow-suffering visited upon a man damned for playing his indispensable part in the economy of the Redemption.

To this cosmic injustice there is no end in sight. Even as I write, the current issue of the *London Review of Books* (20 February 1997) contains

265

a reply by William Klassen to Frank Kermode's review of *Judas: Betrayer or Friend of Jesus.*

> Despite Professor Kermode's suggestion to the contrary, I approached my mandate to write a life of Judas with the firm conviction that Judas was a traitor and that all the Gospels were unanimous in portraying him as such. In time that conviction had to yield to the evidence.

Judas the traitor (Housman and 'the household traitor'). Of Judas it is written: 'It had been good for that man, if he had not been born'. Housman: 'The soul that should not have been born'. But would Jesus's *raison d'être* have lived had Judas not been born? What does God's plan owe to Judas's felicitous culpability?

'He can curse the God that made him for the colour of his hair'. 'My suggestion', Klassen wrote, 'that Judas was acting as a faithful Jew, carrying out not only God's will as understood by Jesus but also the will of Jesus himself, at least deserves some consideration'. As does the thought that 'Oh who is that young sinner...' is not only a Locke-located, a Macaulay-maculate, and a Stephen-steeped poem, but a Judas-coloured one.

Notes

1 *A.E.H.* (1937), p. 226: Additional Poems XVIII.
2 Annotated by John Carter, *Encounter*, vol. xxix no. 4, October 1967. Laurence Housman had died in 1959.
3 *Encounter*, pp. 36–7.
4 Among the lines supplied by Johnson for Goldsmith's *The Traveller*.
5 Here and elsewhere I am grateful to John Gross.
6 *Epistola de Tolerantia*, (1689); *Letters concerning Toleration* I; *Locke and Liberty*, ed. Massimo Salvadori, (1960), pp. 138–9.
7 Archie Burnett, whose forthcoming Clarendon Press edition of Housman's poems will be of the greatest interest and value, annotates *abominable* in 'the nameless and abominable colour of his hair' [Clarendon, Oxford, 1997]:

> *OED*'s earliest example (1366) refers to 'The abhomynable Synne of Sodomye', and the earliest example of 'abomination' 1. (1395) refers to 'abhominacioun of bodili sodomie'. Also Lev. 18:22: 'Thou shalt not lie with mankind, as with womankind: it is abomination'.

John Sparrow in a letter to the *New Stateman*, (1942, xxiii 226) related 'nameless' and 'abominable' to legal statutes against sodomy, and added: 'Another echo of this phraseology (and one with which Housman was himself doubtless familiar) occurs in Chapter XLIV of Book IV of Gibbon's

Decline and Fall of the Roman Empire: "I touch with reluctance, and dispatch with impatience, a more odious vice, of which modesty *rejects the name*, and nature *abominates* the idea."' (Archie Burnett notes that Housman in the preface to his edition of Lucan, alluded to this phrasing from Gibbon.) To these dark glosses there might be added the false etymology which long held sway. Under 'abominable', of which the true etymology is the Latin *ab* and *omen*, *OED* has:

> In med. L. and OFr., and in Eng. from Wyclif to 17th c, regularly spelt *abhominable*, and explained as *ab homine*, quasi 'away from man, inhuman, beastly', a derivation which influenced the use and has permanently affected the meaning of the word. No other spelling occurs in the first folio of Shaks., which has the word 18 times; and in *L.L.L.*, V. i. 27, Holopherness abhors 'the rackers of ortagriphie', who were beginning to write *abominable* for the time-honoured *abhominable*.

(There is a grim irony in 'time-honoured'.) *OED* has a further entry under the false spelling:

> *abhominable, abhomination*, etc., the regular spelling of ABOMINABLE, ABOMINATION, etc., in OFr., and in Eng. from their first use to 17th c, due to an assumed derivation from *ab homine*, 'away from man, inhuman, beastly', which influenced their early use, and has coloured the whole meaning of the words to the present day.

'The present day': this first fascicle of the *OED* was published in 1884. The word 'coloured' catches something for my argument.

8   *Liberty, Equality, Fraternity*, (1873, 2nd edn 1874); ed. R. J. White, (1967), p. 154.
9   *Liberty, Equality, Fraternity*, p. 186.
10   Notable in the Nineties; the first entry in the *OED* is 1891: 'The Norfolk and Suffolk Red Polled breed stands highest for dairying purposes. The Red Polls are handsome symmetrical animals of medium size'. Further *OED* citations for the breed are from 1895, 1896 and 1898.
11   John Whitehead, *Hardy to Larkin: Seven English Poets*, (1995), p. 60.
12   1944. *Fictions*, translated by Anthony Kerrigan, (1962).

15

Tennyson's 'Little *Hamlet*'

David G Riede

Tennyson's two great poems of mourning and melancholia, *In Memoriam* and *Maud*, can to some extent be seen as distinguishing between "'normal' mourning" that eventually finds hard-earned resolution in *In Memoriam* and the "'pathological' mourning" *of Maud* that is clearly a form of madness (Armstrong, *Victorian Poetry*, 255). To be sure, the mourning of *In Memoriam* is so extended and its resolution so dubious that its differentiation from melancholia is not entirely convincing, but the imposed resolution certainly makes it a more "hopeful" poem than *Maud*, which seems to have been written as a sequel to return Tennyson to his accustomed melancholy: "It's too hopeful [*In Memoriam*], more than I am myself. I think of adding another to it … showing that all the arguments are about as good on one side as the other, and thus throw men back more on the primitive impulses and feelings" (*Poems*, ed. Ricks, 1: 8). However sad and perplexed it may be, *In Memoriam* eventually disciplines the "primitive impulses and feelings" with the Christian ideology of the age, exalting "character" above the "abysmal deeps of personality." *Maud*, on the other hand, was a generic experiment designed to represent a pathological condition, evidently melancholia: "The whole was intended to be a new form of dramatic composition. I took a man constitutionally diseased and dipt him into the circumstances of the time and took him out on fire" (*Letters*, 2: 138). As critics have recognized, Tennyson's "new form" was recognizably akin to the spasmodic poems

Riede, David G. 2005. "Tennyson's 'Little *Hamlet*.'" In *Allegories of One's Own Mind: Melancholy in Victorian Poetry*, pp. 75–90. Columbus: Ohio State University Press. Reproduced with permission of Ohio State University Press.

Victorian Poets: A Critical Reader, First Edition. Edited by Valentine Cunningham.
© 2014 John Wiley & Sons, Ltd. Published 2014 by John Wiley & Sons, Ltd.

that Ludlow and Arnold characterized as allegories of the poet's own mind, though the word "dramatic" evidently distinguishes the diseased mind from the "poet's own." The autobiographical resonances of *Maud*, however, have long been recognized, and even though the speaker cannot be simply equated with Tennyson or the eponymous heroine with Rosa Baring, the poem is evidently a symbolic representation of the poet's own emotional experience, an allegory of his own mind.

Rather than being the representation of a specific woman known to Tennyson, Maud is a complex allegorical signifier of the Romantic beloved. Like the Poet's vision in "Alastor," she is the spectral figuration of the speaker's ego-ideal or "epipsyche," and the speaker's desire for her is allegorized within the courtly tradition as a quest for a queen of Romance ("Rose of the rosebud garden of girls" [i. 902]) and for the perfect beauty that is also death ("Dead perfection" [i. 83]). Like all allegorical emblems, according to Walter Benjamin, Maud is a multivalent signifier, an emblem of beauty, of death, of "Honour that cannot die" (i. 177), of Englishness ("Bright English lily" [i. 738]), of wealth and class status and even, "Cleopatra-like" (i. 216), of the Oriental erotic temptation explored in many of Tennyson's earlier poems. *Maud* is, in short, a melancholy allegory very much in the tradition of *Alastor* and *Endymion*, and as the erotic pursuit of an insistently Orientalized sexual other, it reiterates Tennyson's fusion of the imperial Romantic imagination with the imperial spirit of the age. *Maud* is especially important because it is an allegory of both the poet's own mind and Victorian pathology generally. The "constitutionally diseased" speaker is explicitly enflamed by the "circumstances of the time" and particularly the economic condition of the age, as the poem represents the "history of a morbid poetic soul, under the blighting influence of a recklessly speculative age" (Hallam Tennyson, *Memoir*, 1: 96).

The allegorical character of *Maud* is, moreover, strikingly illustrative of Benjamin's thesis that melancholy is generative of allegory: the speaker "brood[s]/On a horror of shatter'd limbs" (i. 55–56), on a "corpse in the pit" (ii. 326), and generally on graves, corpses, and death throughout, beginning with the opening account of the "Mangled and flatten'd and crushed" corpse of his father in the "dreadful hollow," pausing also on Maud's mother "mute in her grave as the image in marble above" (i. 159), an anonymous funeral urn (i. 303), the "blacker pit" of yet another grave (i. 335), and culminating in a grim hallucination of his own buried life in a "shallow grave" (ii. 244). The poem is, in effect, the allegory of a consciousness diseased by its own failure to "bury [it]self in [it]self" (i. 75) deeply enough and particularly to "bury/ All this dead body of hate" (i. 779–80).

The resultant allegory replays in sharper focus the process I have traced in the earlier poems. The multiplicity of meaning associated with Maud and the protagonist's quest imbricates the love story with social issues from the outset. Expressing his disgust with the sordid commodity culture of the age, the speaker's initial desire is not for a woman but for a national cause to heal and unify the diseased spirit of the age, specifically a chivalric, martial spirit to end the economic civil war of each against all:[1]

> When a Mammonite mother kills her babe for a burial fee,
> And Timour Mammon grins on a pile of children's bones,
> Is it peace or war? Better, war! loud war by land and by sea,
> War with a thousand battles, and shaking a hundred thrones!
> (i. 45–48)

When Maud attracts the speaker's attention away from brooding on shattered limbs, it is as a "chivalrous battle-song" (i. 383), a bugle call to action:

> She is singing a song that is known to me,
> A passionate ballad gallant and gay,
> A martial song like a trumpet's call!
> ....
> Singing of men that in battle array,
> Ready in heart and ready in hand,
> March with banner and bugle and fife
> To the death for their native land.
> (i. 164–66, 169–72)

The cure for the speaker's "diseased condition" is to replace the diseased condition of culture with a return to the chivalric spirit of the feudal past, specifically to replace "a time so sordid and mean" (i. 178) with a pursuit "of Death and of Honour that cannot die" (i. 177). The call is eventually realized not as an achieved erotic union with Maud but as a call to an Eastern war in the Crimean, and, as in "Locksley Hall" and other earlier poems, the melancholic anomie of the hero is subordinated to the demands of a militant ideology. As if recapitulating Tennyson's earlier career, *Maud* originates in a seemingly contentless melancholia and proceeds through the speaker's literal recollection of the Arabian Nights to a love synonymous with imperial appropriation of an Orientalized other and finally to outright imperial aggression as the hero enlists to fight in an Eastern war.

The "germ" of *Maud*, as Tennyson said, was the lyric "O that 'twere possible" (ii. 141–238), a poem written in 1833–4 during his early grieving for Hallam. But despite its emotional origins in Tennyson's mourning, the poem does not move toward a resolution of grief but rather displaces sadness to a mysterious, undeveloped heterosexual yearning that can have no resolution. As a result, it is not so much a poem of grief as a poem of such purely Tennysonian melancholy that Swinburne called it "the poem of deepest charm and fullest delight of pathos and melody ever written, even by Mr. Tennyson" (*Letters*, 3: 125). Harvie Ferguson has pointed out that in modern thought "melancholy has no substance of its own, that it is 'only' the sombre mirror in which being reflects itself" (xvi), and Tennyson's lyric, describing a subject haunted by a vaguely perceived phantom, seems to epitomize a vision of melancholia as the representation of a "deathlike type of pain" that is explicitly a reflection of the subject: "'Tis the blot upon the brain/ That *will show* itself without" (ii. 200–201). Quite possibly the reference to the brain rather than the mind indicates that Tennyson saw the hero's disease in terms of the age's "medical materialism," but the disease manifests itself in and as diseased signs of the times. As in Carlyle's account of the signs of the times, the deeper meaning is allegorically readable in the signs of the surface, where the infinite bodies forth the finite, and so shows itself without. The speaker can assert his own anguish, but the source of that anguish, its content, remains shadowy and undefined:

> Through the hubbub of the market
> I steal, a wasted frame,
> It crosses here, it crosses there,
> Through all that crowd confused and loud,
> The shadow still the same;
> And on my heavy eyelids
> My anguish hangs like shame.
>
> (ii. 208–14)

Maud was written, apparently, to provide a context that would make this lyric "intelligible," in effect to provide a referent, a substance for this nebulous "it," in response to "a suggestion made by Sir John Simeon, that, to render the poem fully intelligible, a preceding one was necessary. He wrote it; the second poem too required a predecessor, and thus the whole poem was written, as it were, *backwards*" (Hallam Tennyson, *Memoir*, 1: 379).

Tennyson's development of a love plot to represent the hopelessness of melancholy yearning is of a piece with the pattern traced in the early lyrics, and with the Romantic love represented by the "Alastor" poet's yearning for his insubstantial ideal likeness, with Endymion's longing for Cynthia, and with the "Kubla Khan" poet's longing for the Abyssinian maid. More specifically, however, it all but explicitly recalls the emotional entrapment of "Mariana":

> For am I not, am I not, here alone…
> Living alone in an empty house,
> Here half-hid in the gleaming wood,
> Where I hear the dead at midday moan,
> And the shrieking rush of the wainscot mouse,
> And my own sad name in corners cried,
> When the shiver of dancing leaves is thrown
> About its echoing chambers wide,
> Till a morbid hate and horror have grown
> Of a world in which I have hardly mixt,
> And a morbid eating lichen fixt
> On a heart half-turned to stone.
>
> (i. 254–67)

As in "Locksley Hall," the appropriate response would apparently be to turn from "feminine" "perversity" to mix with the world ("I myself must mix with action, lest I wither by despair" ["Locksley Hall,"l.98]).

In this case, the speaker does not explicitly embrace the imperialist fantasy of finding some dusky woman to rear his savage race, but he does envision a romance with Maud in strikingly imperialist terms. His fantasy of wedded bliss with Maud is grounded in an actual recollection of the Arabian Nights:

> i
>
> Did I hear it in a doze
>   Long since, I know not where?
> Did I dream it an hour ago,
>   When asleep in this arm-chair?
>
> ii
>
> Men were drinking together,
>   Drinking and talking of me;
> "Well, if it prove a girl, the boy
>   Will have plenty: so let it be."

iii

Is it an echo of something
Read with a boy's delight,
Viziers nodding together
In some Arabian night?
(i. 285–96)

As Ricks points out, it *is* an echo of some Arabian night, specifically *The Story of Nourredin Ali and Bedreddin Hassan (Poems,* 2: 537n). In addition, Maud is imagined as an Oriental seductress:

What if with her sunny hair
And smile as sunny as cold,
She meant to weave me a snare
Of some coquettish deceit,
Cleopatra-like as of old
To entangle me when we met,
To have her lion roll in a silken net
And fawn at a victor's feet.
(i. 212–19)

Further, Maud herself is represented in terms of wealth that resembles the bejeweled version of Oriental splendor set forth in "Recollections of the Arabian Nights": she is imagined both as the phantom of "O that 'twere possible" and as a gem: "Luminous, gemlike, ghostlike, death-like" (i. 95). She is a "pearl," a jewel (i. 352), a "precious stone" (i. 498) with a "sweet purse-mouth" (i. 71). Further, as Herbert Tucker observes, the "exotic images the hero imports for Maud's beauty (the 'Arab arch,' the curiously male peacock's crest) suggest that his fantasies of erotic dominion are imperial fantasies as well" (*Tennyson,* 419). As in the earlier poems, however, the dreams of erotic or imperial conquest are dashed. In fact, Maud's interfering brother, referred to throughout as the Sultan, interrupts the fantasy exactly as the good Haroun Alraschid did in "Recollections of the Arabian Nights." When the Sultan claims possession of his own, he makes inevitable the climactic and disastrous duel that kills the brother and dooms the speaker's love. It is at precisely this defeat of the dream that the "ghastly Wraith" (ii. 32) appears to provide the antecedent for the shadowy "it" of "O that 'twere possible." Yet this antecedent hardly gives substance to the melancholy shadowed forth as "it" – the problem is not simply that it is not substance but spirit, but that it apparently negates the most likely reading of "it" as

Maud's ghost, since Maud is still alive when it appears. The mystery only deepens around the meaning of the externalization of the "blot upon the brain."

Finally, as in the earlier poems, the seductive, unmanning imperial fantasy provides, perhaps, languorous reverie:

> There is none like her, none.
> Nor will be when our summers have deceased.
> O, art thou sighing for Lebanon
> In the long breeze that streams to thy delicious East,
> Sighing for Lebanon,
> Dark Cedar, though thy limbs have here increased,
> Upon a pastoral slope as fair,
> And looking to the South, and fed
> With honeyed rain and delicate air,
> And haunted by the starry head
> Of her whose gentle will has changed my fate,
> And made my life a perfumed altar-flame.
>
> (i. 611–22)

But this feminized, perfumed reverie must eventually give way to the masculine actualities of empire. In the case of *Maud*, masculine activity is vigorous indeed: the speaker not only kills the Sultan but joins his nation's imperial cause to fight against Eastern iniquities, to fight for the good, "to embrace the purpose of God and the doom assigned." Whether the dreadful warmongering at the end of *Maud* is attributed to Tennyson or to his speaker, it is certainly consistent with both Tennyson's earlier tendencies and with the psychological movement of *Maud* from reverie, through erotic and imperial fantasy, to actual imperial warfare and a reassuring solidarity with Englishness: "I have felt with my native land, I am one with my kind" (iii. 58).

The longing for a revival of chivalric honor in *Maud* is consistent with Tennyson's medievalism elsewhere and suggests that his "poems made on…chivalric bones" (Barrett Browning, *Aurora Leigh*, v. 198), like Morris's "Concerning Geffray Teste-Noire," are a product of melancholy brooding on the loss of a social ideal in the strife of modern commodity culture. John Lucas has persuasively argued that Tennyson as laureate had no problem as a spokesman for the chivalry idealized in the medieval rhetoric that depicted Victoria as Gloriana and Albert, in Tennyson's words, as "Scarce other than my king's ideal knight" (Dedication to *Idylls of the King*, 1.6), but in the 1850s, at the time of Maud, Englishness was clearly aligned with the commercial, commodity culture celebrated at the First Great Exhibition of 1851, but excoriated in *Maud* as a particularly vile form of civil war (i. 21–52). The deepest source of melancholia in *Maud* is the speaker's inability to align himself with the commercial spirit that he associates with a "lust of gold" that is "Horrible, hateful, monstrous, not to be told" (iii. 39–41), akin to the degrading sexual lust described by Shakespeare as "Savage, extreme, rude, cruel, not to trust" (Sonnet 129, 1.4). From this perspective, the courtly love tradition evoked by representing *Maud* as "Queen Rose of the rosebud garden of girls" (i. 902) is actively antithetical to the conditions of English culture.

A fuller account of the relation of melancholia in *Maud* to the spirit of the age is, perhaps, best achieved by considering Tennyson's reference to the work as a "little *Hamlet*" (Hallam Tennyson, *Memoir*, 1: 296). Like Hamlet, the speaker of *Maud* is melancholy because the time is out of joint, or at least because he is alienated from it. As I have discussed,[2] the Victorian age was particularly attuned to Hamlet's melancholia as "at once the sense of the soul's infinity, and the sense of the doom which not only circumscribes that infinity but appears to be its offspring" (Bradley, 108), and a similar comment by Coleridge provides a useful suggestion regarding how Tennyson's "little *Hamlet*" might be read as an experiment in genre; speaking of Hamlet's "morbid excess" of meditation on his own mind, Coleridge remarks that

> The effect of this overbalance of the imaginative power is beautifully illustrated in the everlasting broodings and superfluous activities of Hamlet's mind, which, unseated from its healthy relation, is constantly occupied with the world within and abstracted from the world without, – giving substance to shadows and throwing a mist over all common-place activities. It is the nature of thought to be indefinite; – definition belongs to external imagery alone. Here it is that the sense of sublimity arises, not from the sight of an outward object, but from the beholder's reflection upon it; – not from the sensuous impression, but from the imaginative reflex.... Hamlet feels this; his senses are in a state of trance, and he looks upon external things as hieroglyphics. (*Lectures*, 344–45)

In terms of genre, *Hamlet* seems to have served both Romantic and Victorian poets as a model of what Coleridge represents as the melancholy sublime. Writing of a time when verse drama was effectively defunct, Romantic and Victorian poets characteristically chose closet drama or even, to use the term Tennyson chose for *Maud*, monodrama, to represent a melancholic monomania akin to Hamlet's. The most obvious English example is Byron's *Manfred* with its many echoes of

Hamlet, but as Bradley and Arnold recognized, Goethe's *Faust* is an even more significant modern version of the melancholy sublime. The conspicuous Victorian examples are *Maud* itself and Arnold's *Empedocles on Etna*, so it is particularly appropriate that Arnold suppressed the Hamlet-like broodings, the melancholy of the modern world, in a phrase that applies equally well to all works that rely on hieroglyphics to shadow forth the "infinite within," to the Romantic and Victorian works I have mentioned, and to the poetic aspirations of the nineteenth century generally:

> [T]he modern critic not only permits a false practice; he absolutely pre-scribes false aims. – "A true allegory of the state of one's own mind in a representative history," the Poet is told, "is perhaps the highest thing that one can attempt in the way of poetry." – And accordingly he attempts it. An allegory of the state of one's own mind, the highest problem of an art which imitates actions! No assuredly, it is not, it never can be so; no great poetical work has ever been produced with such an aim.... Faust, itself, judged as a whole, and judged strictly as a poetical work, is defective. (*Prose Works*, 1: 8)

Coleridge's reference to "hieroglyphics" and Arnold's to "allegory" suggest a generic inheritance from *Hamlet* of greater significance than the use of dramatic form to depict melancholia. The most significant generic feature in all of these works is allegory or, more specifically, the melancholy allegory described by Benjamin.

Benjamin's discussion of allegory is all the more obviously pertinent to Tennyson's "little *Hamlet*" because it was developed to explain the seventeenth-century German tragic drama that ostentatiously used the same allegorical principles that *Hamlet* used far more indirectly (*Origin*, 191). Benjamin comments that "for *Hamlet*, as indeed for all Shakespearian 'tragedies,' the theory of the *Trauerspiel* is predestined to contain the prolegomena of interpretation" (228). *Hamlet*, like *Maud*, can be seen as a complex meditation and allegorical contextualization to cope with the figure of a ghost, and both revolve around the central character's contemplation of death and burial. "In the *Trauerspiel* of the seventeenth century," says Benjamin, "the corpse becomes quite simply the pre-eminent emblematic property" (218), as in *Hamlet* the pre-eminent emblematic properties are the dead king, the skull of Yorick, and the open grave of Ophelia, and as in *Maud* they are the corpses in the "dreadful hollow" and, eventually, the speaker's own corpse as he hallucinates his burial.

Perhaps the best way to describe allegory in this sense is to return once again to Coleridge's "Kubla Khan." In Coleridge's headnote the vision of his reverie is described as already formulated in language: "all the images rose up…as things, with a parallel production of the correspondent expression, without any sensation or consciousness of effort" (*Works*, 102). This is exactly what Benjamin describes as the spurious claim of the Romantic symbol, "which miraculously unites the beauty of form with the highest fullness of being" (164), but as Coleridge's work suggests, it is possible only in an opium-induced reverie. It is a pipe dream, and the only way to fix it in language in the waking world is by an allegory that "immerses itself into the depths which separate visual being from meaning" (165). Unlike the symbol, which is momentary and, in Blake's terms, finds "eternity in a moment," allegory is a sequential, temporal progression of signs that seek recovery, or "redemption" of the lost fullness of being, so the actual poem of "Kubla Khan" does not record the vision but only the allegory of love and the desire for recovery: "Could I revive within me/Her symphony and song" (ll.42–43). Recording loss, and separation of the sign from being, allegory is necessarily melancholy.

As we have seen,[3] Paul de Man defines post-Romantic allegory, following Benjamin, as the sequential presentation of signs that always point to anterior signs, so that the essence of the allegorical sign is "pure anteriority," and this rather strikingly calls to mind Tennyson's composition of *Maud* "as it were, *backwards*." As Tucker describes it, *Maud* "situates its hero reactively, his phase of passion having been prompted by some action anterior to the text" (*Tennyson*, 413). The poem seems almost uncannily to mesh with Benjamin's account of "the heart of the allegorical way of seeing, of the baroque, secular explanation of history as the Passion of the world; its importance resides solely in the stations of its decline" (*Origin*, 166).

As allegory, *Maud* fits neatly into the series of late Romantic poems of melancholy quest discussed earlier. Like "Kubla Khan," *Alastor*, and *Endymion, Maud* is the account of a man seeking a projection of his own ego-ideal (the "blot" upon his brain, projected without), a woman who has never really existed. Ricks has described the poem in exactly these terms, noting that Maud appears "ghostlike, deathlike, half the night long / Growing and feeding and growing" in the speaker's dreams: "[T]his unsubstantiality… is the poem's peculiar regret. It is a poem about losing someone whom you have never really had. She is at first beautiful, but as a gem, as an epitome of womankind, as a phantasmal pulse, a dreamlike vision" (Ricks, 52 [252]). Similarly, as Culler notes,

Tennyson pointed out that the "memory [presumably of the hero's betrothed in part i, section vii] is a phantasmal one which he cannot trace to its origin" (201).

Perhaps it should not be surprising that Tennyson's work resembles that of the baroque German dramatists, since his work was recognized as baroque in his own time. Walter Bagehot famously labeled Tennyson the foremost exemplar of the "ornate" poet. His interest in depicting madness, moreover, was bound to involve a representation that ostentatiously separated the language of poetry from "fullness of being," that abandoned the Romantic symbol for an allegorized mode that underscores the alienation of the speaker's mind from actuality. As has always been noted, *Maud* abounds with what Ruskin called the "pathetic fallacy," figurative language resulting from "violent feelings" that "produce in us a falseness in all our impressions of external things" (Works, 5: 205). For Ruskin such imagery is the product of a "morbid," deranged subjectivity, as it seems the natural language of madness. The sequence of pathetic fallacy in *Maud*, the sequence of morbid signs, produces a kind of morbid allegory, the perfect representation, perhaps, of melancholia.

The most obvious and most often noted pathetic fallacy in *Maud* occurs at the very outset, in the speaker's personification, or genitalization, of the blood-red lips of the "dreadful hollow" (i. 2). The allegorical significations in *Maud* may be read in a variety of ways, including, of course, as a sublimation of grief in the imperial work of the nation and as a working through in Freudian or Lacanian terms of the loss of the father emblematized by the hollow. The hollow is, of course, the "ghastly pit" (i. 5) in which the father's body was found, and its "blood-red" ledges suggest the female genitals as symbolic of death and burial in mother earth, as burial within the self, of birth and the loss of unity with the mother, and of the castrating wound that represents loss of the father and loss of the phallus as ego-ideal. The hollow is, in short, an explicit and overdetermined sign of absence and loss at the origin of the speaker's emotional life, of his desire, and of his quest. As everyone recognizes, however, the imposition of the speaker's consciousness on nature, the rampant excess of figurative meaning in the pathetic fallacy, is above all symptomatic of the speaker's morbid subjectivity, the kind of solipsistic alienation that afflicted the entrapped Mariana, the Lady of Shalott, the soul in "The Palace of Art," and, of course, the buried self hallucinated later in *Maud*, so the hollow must also be seen as an emblem of morbid solipsism itself, an emblem of melancholy.

The multivalent significance of this image and others makes it impossible or hopelessly reductive to read a single coherent allegorical plot in

Maud. Like Hamlet, the speaker thinks "too curiously," but his mad excess of meaning is itself the point. As Benjamin argues, "Overnaming [is] the linguistic being of melancholy" ("On Language," 122), and it is also the allegorical poetry of the melancholy sublime: "With every idea the moment of expression coincides with a veritable eruption of images, which gives rise to a chaotic mass of metaphors. This is how the sublime is presented in this style" (*Origin,* 173). For this reason, "the basic characteristic of allegory … is ambiguity, multiplicity of meaning" (*Origin,* 177). Still, something specific can be extracted from this sublime: clearly the "dreadful hollow," whatever else it may signify, is an allegorical emblem of death, and, coming at the very beginning of the poem, it positions all of the speaker's subsequent comments, like Hamlet's, as a gloomy contemplation of death. Further, the opening lines indicate that in the solipsistic brooding of the speaker, everything becomes an emblem of death: "And Echo, there, whatever is asked her, answers 'Death.'" As a further subtle implication that the answer "Death" is ventriloquized by the speaker, Echo answers "Death" conspicuously where the verse needs to echo, or rhyme with, "heath": the off-rhyme indicates the speaker's tendency to hear or understand nature in terms of his own imposition of allegorical meaning, just as when he variously hears the cawing of ravens once as "Keep watch and ward, keep watch and ward" (i. 247) and later as "Maud, Maud, Maud, Maud" (i. 414). As an emblem both of death and of the speaker's morbidly deranged perception and tendency to allegorize, the "dreadful hollow" is an overdetermined emblem of melancholy itself. In addition, if Walt Whitman's ear is to be trusted, the word "hollow" especially sounds Tennyson's depths: "Tennyson shows, more than any poet I know…how much there is in finest verbalism. There is a latent charm in mere words, and in the voice ringing them, which he has caught and brought out, beyond all others – as in the line, 'And hollow, hollow, hollow, all delight'" (quoted in Culler, 4–5).

The whole of *Maud,* in its incoherence, seems almost a parody of conventional allegory. Examples of morbid, deranged allegorization, ubiquitous in the poem, include the speaker's moralizing upon the "lovely shell" (ii. 49) found on the Breton coast as an ambiguous figure of either the speaker's passive fragility or his "force to withstand" (ii. 72). Another example is the whole of the famous lyric "Come into the garden, Maud" (i. xxii), with its seeming parody of courtly love allegory as the roses and lilies discourse beneath the "planet of Love" (i. 857). The effect of such imagery is to represent the pathological, hysterical structures of the speaker's emotions (Carol Christ, 26–7). They represent an allegory of the speaker's own mind, as Tennyson more or less described *Maud*: "You must remember always, in reading it, what it is meant to be – a drama in lyrics. It shows the unfolding of a lonely, morbid soul, touched with inherited madness ... The things which seem like faults belong not so much to the poem as to the character of the hero" (*Poems* 2: 517). Quite deliberately experimenting with genre, Tennyson produced an "allegory of his own mind," exactly the kind of unpoetic "multitudinousness" that Arnold deplored.

The distinctly modern Victorian quality of *Maud* is its description of the horrors of commodity culture as an especially vile form of civil war. The attack on commodity culture is overt and obvious, fore-grounded at both the beginning and end of the poem with allusions to the contemporary scandals of infanticides for insurance fraud, "When a Mammonite mother kills her babe for a burial fee" (i. 45), and of food adulteration, "And chalk and alum and plaster are sold to the poor for bread,/And the spirit of murder works in the very means of life" (i. 39–40). The counterfeit representation of bread by "chalk and alum and plaster" in itself suggests a kind of anarchic materialized allegory displacing the semiotic system of material culture. The "won-drous Mother-age" and its spirit of progress had been a source of hope in "Locksley Hall," but in *Maud* it is just the reverse:

But these are the days of advance, the works of the men of mind,
When who but a fool would have faith in a tradesman's ware or his word?
Is it peace or war? Civil war, as I think, and that of a kind
The viler, as underhand, not openly bearing the sword.
Sooner or later I too may passively take the print
Of the golden age – why not? I have neither hope nor trust;
May make my heart as a millstone, set my face as a flint,
Cheat and be cheated, and die: who knows? we are ashes and dust.

(i. 25–32)

It is because he *does* "passively take the print" of the age that *Maud* reg-isters the pathology of the age in the melancholic psyche of the individual. The point is obvious, and universally accepted among Tennyson's readers, that *Maud* represents not only an individual person "but a condition – the condition of England" (Culler, 207): "The poem makes the laureate's principal contribution to the Condition of England question, by representing that condition and the condition of its deranged hero as utterly congruent and as reciprocally determined" (Tucker, *Tennyson*, 407).

The work's most profound contribution to the "Condition of England" question takes place not at the overt thematic level but in the ideologically inflected form. To a considerable extent the ideological content is imperialist and Orientalist, and perhaps, if we take an off-hand comment of Culler's seriously, this is true at the level of form as well, since Culler describes the poem's incoherence, its leaps "from subject to subject and mood to mood" as a "wild Oriental manner" (196). The incoherence is better seen, however, as a consequence of a general loss of faith, hope, and trust in modern capitalist society. In a world emptied of the presence of God or any transcendental signific-ance, faith is reduced to a foolish "faith in a tradesman's ware or his word," and the individual can have "neither hope nor trust." As Marx's analysis of the commodity powerfully demonstrates, the system of commodity exchange and money is, like all semiotic systems, like lan-guage itself, based on an unanchored system of exchange. The thematic references to capitalist economy point to a general loss of faith, hope, and the charity that would mitigate or eliminate the civil war of economic struggle. Loss of faith in the symbolic system of commodity culture, moreover, implies a similar loss of faith in the symbolic exchange of language, and the result is a breakdown of the connections between words and things, and between words and ideas, that decon-structs language to produce the pathetic fallacies of melancholy allegory.

Maud thus enacts, at the level of form, the close connections of mel-ancholy with the systemic problems of a free market economy: "Such economies alienate workers from their products, efface for consumers the origin of their fetishized purchases, convert desire itself into an exchangeable commodity, and estrange human intelligence from a 'Nature' that at the close of the eighteenth century receded even as the mind mastered so many of its mysteries" (Guinn Batten, 1). It is perhaps an insight along these lines that leads Tennyson's speaker to idealize the suppression of desire, even if in a strongly Orientalist manner: "For not to desire or admire, if a man could learn it, were more/Than to walk all day like the sultan of old in a garden of spice" (i. 142–43). More important to Tennyson than the specific economic scandals he drew from Carlyle was Carlyle's proto-Marxist analysis of the dehumanizing cash nexus that takes the place of a stabilizing vision of truth in capitalism. Consequently, it is not surprising that, even without the help of Marx, Tennyson was able to see the end result of economic civil war as the reification of human life, with individuals reduced to wooden automatons moved only by Adam Smith's "invisible hand."

Tennyson consequently anticipates both Robert Browning and Edward Fitzgerald in characterizing the modern alienated subject as a puppet: "We are puppets. Man in his pride, and Beauty fair in her flower;/Do we move ourselves, or are moved by an unseen hand at a game/That pushes us off from the board, and others ever succeed?" (i. 126–28). *Maud* is the greatest and fullest expression of Victorian melancholy both because it thematizes the sources of melancholy in Victorian culture and, even more, because it reveals the content of Victorian ideology in its allegorical form.

Tennyson's poetry overtly illustrates both Victorian melancholy and its sublimation in imperial conquest, but it also illustrates the sublimation of melancholy in aesthetic form by demonstrating the manic pleasures of allegory. Because allegory enables the melancholic simultaneously to fill the hollow of loss with figuration and to expose the truth of history in his own terms, says Benjamin, "the only pleasure the melancholic permits himself, and it is a powerful one, is allegory" (*Origin*, 185). Strangely, Benjamin describes the pleasures of sublimation in allegory in terms particularly appropriate to my argument about Tennyson's Orientalism: "The wealth of ciphers which the allegorist discovered... may not accord with the authority of nature; but the voluptuousness with which significance rules, like a stern sultan in the harem of objects, is without equal in giving expression to nature" (184). It is, perhaps, only by chance that Benjamin's simile so propitiously fits my argument, but his general point about the pleasure of allegorization points to a fundamental connection between melancholy and aestheticism that characterizes Tennyson's poems from "Mariana" through *Maud* and that further illuminates the close connection in the later nineteenth century between melancholy and aestheticism.

Although the poetry of sensation led others into aestheticism, however, Tennyson was appalled when "he was attacked with the cry of 'Art for Art's sake'" and composed an epigram referring to the movement as "truest Lord of Hell!" (Hallam Tennyson, *Memoir*, 2: 91–2). At the same time that Tennyson was working on *Idylls of the King*, Walter Pater, Swinburne, Morris, and D. G. Rossetti were using medieval themes and sources to explore the meeting of the pagan world with Christianity, making what Pater called a "deliberate choice between Christ and a rival lover" (191), in which the poets of the "aesthetic school" all sided with the rival lover, with pagan sensuality, in order to write an uninhibited poetry of sensation. Tennyson, also using medieval material for the *Idylls*, pointedly separated himself from "Art with poisonous honey stolen from France" ("To the Queen,"l.56). Far from abandoning the theme and mode of melancholy, however, Tennyson wrote the *Idylls* as an allegory of melancholy, a tale "shadowing Sense at war with Soul" ("To the Queen," l.37). Though he did not like to be pinned down by too dogmatic allegorical readings, or, as he put it, "tied down to say '*This* means *that*'" he acknowledged that "there is an allegorical or perhaps rather a parabolic drift in the poem" (Hallam Tennyson, *Memoir*, 2: 127). In fact, Tennyson evidently conceived of the *Idylls* as early as 1833 as an allegory in which Arthur would symbolize "Religious Faith," Merlin would symbolize "Science," Mordred would be "the skeptical understanding," and so on. The poem underwent many changes over the decades of its composition, and symbolic meanings tended to shift, but in the finished *Idylls*, "Sense at war with Soul" plainly meant the sensuality of the flesh (Guinevere, Ettarre, Vivien) at war with conscience (Arthur).[4] The dialectic of personal desire at war with conscience, of course, constitutes melancholy itself, and the whole of the *Idylls* quite evidently allegorizes that dialectic. Ultimately, in this allegory, sensation triumphs and sins of the flesh unseat the conscience so that man rolls back into the beast. Still, Tennyson leaves no doubt that failure to obey the dictates of conscience is destructive at both the personal and social level. Gladstone was undoubtedly correct in saying that "Wherever [Arthur] appears, it is as the great pillar of the moral order" (quoted in Hallam Tennyson, *Memoir*, 130). As Gladstone's comment indicates, the conscience in this allegory is very obviously the internalized moral order of the age, and most obviously it rages against the perceived moral decay of the time. Unfortunately, the great pillar of the moral order inevitably sounds priggish to an almost inhuman extent, but the very severity of Arthur's repudiation of Guinevere may be regarded as the rage of the superego against the ego – the maiming rage that Freud would find to be the necessary but painful condition of civilization. Such a reading of the *Idylls* undoubtedly states the case too baldly: Tennyson himself allegorized his allegory in an attempt to ward off such readings: "Poetry is like shotsilk with many glancing colours. Every reader must find his own interpretation" (Hallam Tennyson, *Memoir*, 2: 127). For my purposes, however, it is not necessary to examine the subtleties of Tennyson's painted veil but simply to note that the *Idylls* presents both of the "two Tennysons," the spokesman of Victorian values and the poet of sensation, and that this dialogue of the mind with itself dramatizes the disastrous results when the conscience loses control but, as poetry, also illustrates the disastrous results if the conscience triumphs too fully: in Arthur's extraordinary rebuke to the groveling Guinevere, Tennyson's poetry is reduced to a smug moral superiority – the voice of a pillar, not a poet. As I will argue in the next chapter,[5] the triumph of conscience, or superego, is damaging to the poetry of melancholy because it short-circuits dialectic and leaves the poet little more than a spokesperson for official culture.

Notes

1 Tennyson's focus on commodity culture is also representative of nineteenth-century allegory as Benjamin understood it. Benjamin's emphasis on allegory as a record of ruin and decay is even intensified in his shift from German baroque drama to the modern world. As Kelley puts it [Theresa Kelley, *Reinventing Allegory* (Cambridge: Cambridge UP, 1997), 253] "whereas decay was [in German baroque culture] a melancholy, plodding affair in [the 'commodified' world] it is very nearly instantaneous and, as such, a shocking sign that decay and ruin, not continuity, make history".

2 In the book from which this chapter is taken, David G Riede, *Allegories of One's Own Mind*, 15–16.

3 Ibid., 27 ff.

4 For a discussion of Arthur as conscience see Matthew Reynolds, *The Realms of Gold, 1830–1870; English Poetry in a Time of Nation Building* (Oxford: Oxford UP, 2001), 246–7.

5 "Elizabeth Barratt and the Emotion of the Trapped", David G. Riede, op.cit., 91–133.

Works Cited

Arnold, Matthew. *Complete Prose Works*, ed R H Super, 11 Vols. (Ann Arbor: U of Michigan P, 1960–1977).

Armstrong, Isobel. *Victorian Poetry, Poetics and Politics* (London/NY: Routledge, 1993).

Batten, Guinn. *The Orphaned Imagination: Melancholy and Commodity Culture in English Romanticism* (Durham NC: Duke UP, 1998).

Benjamin, Walter. *The Origins of the German Tragic Drama*, trans John Osborne (London: NLB, 1977).

——. 'On Language as Such, and on the Language of Man', *One Way Street and Other Writings*, trans Edmund Jephcott & Kingsley Shorter (London: Verso, 1985).

Bradley, A C. *Shakespearian Tragedy* (1904), repr (Cleveland: Meridian Books, 1962).

Christ, Carol. *The Finer Optic: The Aesthetic of Particularity in Victorian Poetry* (New Haven: Yale UP, 1975).

Coleridge, Samuel Taylor. *Lectures and Notes on Shakespeare and Other English Poets* (London: G Bell & Sons, 1814).

Culler, A Dwight. *The Poetry of Tennyson* (New Haven: Yale UP, 1977).

De Man, Paul. *Allegories of Reading: Figural Language in Rousseau, Nietzsche, Rilke and Proust* (New Haven: Yale UP, 1979).

Ferguson, Harvie. *Melancholy and the Critique of Modernism: Søren Kierkegaard's Religious Philosophy* (London: Routledge, 1995).

Pater, Walter. *Selected Writings*, ed Harold Bloom (NY: Signet, 1974).

Ricks, Christopher. *Tennyson* (London & Basingstoke: Macmillan, 1972).

Ruskin, John. *Works*, ed ET Cook & Alexander Wedderburn, 39 vols (London: George Allen, 1904).

Swinburne, Algernon. *Letters*, ed Cecil Y Lang, 6 vols (New Haven: Yale UP, 1959–62).

Tennyson, Alfred Lord. *Poems*, ed Christopher Ricks, 3 vols (Harlow: Longman & Berkeley: U of Calif P, 1987).

——. *Letters*, ed Cecil Y Lang & Edgar Shannon Jr, 3 vols (Oxford: Clarendon P, & Cambridge MA: Harvard UP, 1981–90).

Tennyson, Hallam. *Alfred Lord Tennyson, A Memoir by His Son*, 2 vols (1897), repr (NY: Greenwood Press,).

Tucker, Herbert. *Tennyson and the Doom of Romanticism* (Cambridge MA: Harvard UP, 1988).

16

The Disappointment
of Christina G Rossetti

Eric Griffiths

Christina G. Rossetti sometimes disappoints a reader. The opening line of 'Golden Glories' is extreme, and characteristic: 'The buttercup is like a golden cup'.[1] Of course it is, otherwise the flower would be called something else – 'butterelectricshaver' or 'butterfrisbee'. The inane chime brings on a let-down, as when you walk upstairs and overcalculate the number of steps by one; muscular intent comes to nothing, and the foot goes through air. These let-downs are frequent in her writing, in prose as well as verse. A tale for children delights to find a mole has 'handy little hands'; her calendar of devout thoughts for adults, *Time Flies*, remarks of Saint Philip and Saint James the Less (known as such to distinguish him from Saint James the Great): 'The Gospel tells us little specially of St. Philip, and even less of St. James (the Less)'.[2] The earlier work offers 'Athirst with thirst'; 'the dreadful dread'; 'last words, and last, last words'; 'the past past'. She is still at it in her late poems from 'Time lengthening, in the lengthening seemeth long' until 'Eternity to be and be and be'.[3]

Listening in to verbal repetition throughout this poet's work, taking account of how many times she had recourse to phrases like 'day by day', 'point to point', 'star with star', 'fire from fire', the perpetual variations on sameness in her writing, you recognise that, though the buttercup which is like a cup may be a mere slip of her lip or pen, something more than clumsiness speaks through the stumbles. These verbal stubbornnesses hang on in her voice, a characteristic 'accent', as Proust

Griffiths, Eric. 1997. "The Disappointment of Christina G Rossetti." In *Essays in Criticism*, 47, ii (April). pp. 107–42. Reproduced with permission of Oxford University Press.

Victorian Poets: A Critical Reader, First Edition. Edited by Valentine Cunningham.
© 2014 John Wiley & Sons, Ltd. Published 2014 by John Wiley & Sons, Ltd.

understood that word, a feature of style, which may or may not be deliberated but which is integral to the work and to the person we find there.[4] Moments when her verbal needle seems stuck in a groove are rarely sheer collapses but rather the sound of her distinct achievement, her life-work of 'observation, ingenuity, and perseverance'.[5] Making such let-downs eloquent is her major subject as a poet. She is not only at times a disappointing poet but also, more thoroughly, a poet of disappointment, as she wrote of herself in 1888:

> I am that contented 'droner' who accounts her assigned groove the best.... I am bound to avow that even my (small) limited amount of self-knowledge certifies me that some of my actual trials are exquisitely adapted to my weak points. Do you know I suspect I find a grinding groove less galling than you do. I feel at home among anxieties and depression...[6]

Take the groove worn by repetitions in her best-known lines:

> In the bleak mid-winter
>   Frosty wind made moan,
> Earth stood hard as iron,
>   Water like a stone;
> Snow had fallen, snow on snow,
>   Snow on snow,
> In the bleak mid-winter
>   Long ago.[7]

The fivefold 'snow' is especially marked because it repeats the stanza's structural rhyme, giving the second quatrain six recurrences of the long 'o' rather than the two which the scheme requires (the vowel has already arrived in the 'moan' / 'stone' of the first quatrain). The lines stay with us partly because of this unrelenting pressure on the word 'snow', a cumulation which shows how blandly snow builds on itself, each flake so little individually and yet when joined to more of the same becoming a power able to transform the look of things. Snow is, then, like the first Christmas, barely heeded as it starts but in the end important throughout the world, over the world, when the world at last reluctantly takes its drift.[8] Some of the imaginative reach of this stanza comes from its not mentioning the birth of Christ; had only these lines survived without a title, we could not have known they concerned the Nativity. Hence the surprise when she opens the second verse with the words 'Our God', the concept of the divine appearing in her poem as suddenly as the Christ-child Himself appeared in fact.

So universal a feature of poetry as repetition – of phoneme, rhythm, word, phrase, cadence, stanza-shape – couldn't by itself help us pick out the accent of Christina G. Rossetti. From the point of view of a poet and theorist like Valéry, sensuous, linguistic persistence sheerly defines poetic language as contrasted with language which takes on practical tasks or the toils of abstract thought; poetry begins when 'the sound, I might even say the physique, of [a] little phrase returns inside me, repeats itself inside me...I enjoy hearing my lips form it again and again'.[9] Not only poets and their readers have the experience of being inhabited by some words, having them shadow or preoccupy your thought, nor is the experience always a serene, aesthetic revel. Wordsworth, in his 'Note' to 'The Thorn', takes a broad view of verbal repetition:

> ...every man must know that an attempt is rarely made to communicate impassioned feelings without something of an accompanying conscious-ness of the inadequateness of our own powers, or the deficiencies of lan-guage. During such efforts there will be a craving in the mind, and as long as it is unsatisfied the Speaker will cling to the same words, or words of the same character. There are also various other reasons why repetition and apparent tautology are frequent beauties of the highest kind. Among the chief of these reasons is the interest which the mind attaches to words, not only as symbols of the passion, but as *things*, active and efficient, which are of themselves part of the passion. And further, from a spirit of fondness, exultation, and gratitude, the mind luxuriates in the repetition of words which appear successfully to communicate its feelings. The truth of these remarks might be shown by innumerable passages from the Bible and from the impassioned poetry of every nation.[10]

There is a magnificent amplitude in his remarks, a sweep which ranges from the splutters of a person struggling in the lime of words (craving and clinging at once – 'fucking mother-fucking fucker' and the like) to inspired utterance, 'the Bible and...the impassioned poetry of every nation'. These extremes can meet, as for example in the Book of Job. Wordsworth passes from the kind of repetition which evinces a sense of lack in language to replete, luxuriating repetition with an unruffled 'There are also various other reasons why repetition and apparent tautology are frequent beauties...', as if he were merely enumerating more instances of the same phenomenon. Across this anodyne 'various other reasons' he moves between two conceptions of language, conceptions which, were we to treat them as elements of a unified theory, would be not only diverse but contradictory. At first, he speaks as if states of consciousness and their linguistic expression were identifiable apart from each other, so that a speaker might spot a mismatch between them, but in repetition of his second type words are 'not only...symbols of the passion, but... *things*, active and efficient, which are of themselves part of the passion'. In these terms, the feeling of 'mismatch' or let-down is harder to explain; there is nowhere between thought and language where we can stand and observe them failing, like two strips of patterned wallpaper, to line up exactly with each other.

Rossetti has nothing as sublime as Job, though her lyrics are comparably genuine as they bring together in utterance a 'consciousness of... inadequateness' and a grateful iteration which finds its own words somehow successful, felicitous even. A speaker can really feel both these ways and at the same time about words, troublous though this is for a theory of language to describe. As in her poem, 'Ripetizione' ['Repetition']:

> Credea di riverderti e ancor ti aspetto;
>   Di giorno in giorno ognor ti vo bramando:
> Quando ti rivedrò, cor mio diletto,
>   Quando ma quando?
>
> Dissi e ridissi con perenne sete,
>   E lo ridico e vo'ridirlo ancora,
> Qual usignol che canta e si ripete
>   Fino all'aurora.

[I thought I would see you again and I'm still waiting for you; / From day to day and always I go about craving you: / When will I see you again, sweet heart of mine, / When oh when?

I said 'when?' and I said it again with a perpetual thirst, / And I say it again and want to go on saying it, / Like the nightingale who sings, repeating itself / Right through till dawn.][11]

Italian is inherently thick with rhyme, but Rossetti laces her verse with a surplus of chiming, a surplus which both enriches its formality, stresses how rule-governed it is, and at the same time releases through the rules the inflection of a quirky, self-determining voice, a voice dutiful to excess and so not only dutiful.[12] Thus, the first three lines are threaded with internal rhymes on 'ancor', 'ognor', 'cor' ('still', 'always', 'heart'), and as these rhymes fall stably just after the middle of the line, they have the effect of confirming the patternedness of her words; they

289

are plushy, quilted even. The sudden intrusion of an extra rhyme in lines 2–3 – 'bramando / Quando' (which might louchely be rendered 'for you I have a constant yen / When') – snags the verse, though it too comes as a surplus, because it is the structural '– ando' which recurs, recurs twelve syllables before it is due at the end of the stanza. The sound comes too soon, as if in a fit of impatience, an impatience apt to the psychological burden of the poem but skewed across the broader outline of its form. In the first case of internal rhyme, the voice might be said to luxuriate over its prowess within the verse; in the second, it rather seems to kick against its own traces, cramped inside the shape it is making for itself. What is true in this detail remains true of the piece as a whole. When the poet says she has many times said 'when?' and 'vo'ridirlo ancora' ('I want to go on saying it'), what is the nature of her longing to repeat herself? She would have to stop were the beloved to turn up, so perhaps she is too happy in her unhappiness to desire the satisfaction of her desire. Or she could be a Nietzschean, remorselessly willing the eternal recurrence of any and every moment of her life. Had Freud treated her, he might have diagnosed from the phrase an obsessional neurosis, the insistence of a compulsion to repeat whose very nature demonstrates not affirmation but abeyance of an individual will. Then again, any or all of these scriptings for the poem would be rejected by someone who maintained that the 'I' here is a purely 'lyric I' whom it would be a category-mistake to confuse with the historical person who used to sign herself 'Christina G. Rossetti'. The desire to 'go on saying' of a 'lyric I' is not to be understood psychologically but rather as part of the grammar of lyric poetry itself, a form of utterance which inherently strives for self-perpetuation and which gives us not snapshots of a particular person's emotional state at any one time but a permanent algebra of human moods.[13]

To reflect on repetition in a poem such as Rossetti's 'Ripetizione', we need the concepts of an empirical and of a 'lyric' self, distinct but related, as we also need to acknowledge the existence of both Wordsworthian kinds of repetition, the clinging lack and the exultant fullness. The poem lends itself to an impassioned voicing; it can speak the demand of a person in real distress, a person who wants an answer from another. Hearing that tune in it, we may be alerted to biographical facts about Christina G. Rossetti; we respond to that aspect of the work which makes it specifically *her* poem. Equally though, the poem is dextrously composed in the traditional hendecasyllabics of Italian verse with various other marks of self-conscious literariness; there is no linguistic feature of the text which indicates the gender of speaker or beloved, and the enfolding mellifluousness, as it were the contentment of the words one with another, could suggest to us a more equable voicing, one in which the poem answers to itself and entertains with some placidity a future in which there is no satisfaction to come other than the confidence that desire will not fade away into mutism. We should not choose between these versions, for it is through their confluence that the poem has been made. In 'Ripetizione', a composed and a suffering voice are poignantly in each other's earshot; such a doubled consciousness can actually occur to any of us, and does so on those occasions when we hear ourselves thumping a favourite tub, telling a joke we have told before, playing again our tune. It is just that Rossetti has given this doubled consciousness a pleasurably definite shape, as we mostly cannot manage to do.

Schopenhauer raises these details of literary practice to grand heights when he defines the 'nature of the lyric proper':

> It is the subject of the will, in other words, the singer's own willing, that fills his consciousness, often as a released and satisfied willing (joy), but even more often as an impeded willing (sorrow), always as emotion, passion, an agitated state of mind. Besides this, however, and simultaneously with it, the singer...becomes conscious of himself as the subject of pure, will-less knowing, whose unshakable, blissful peace now appears in contrast to the stress of willing that is always restricted and needy. The feeling of this contrast, this alternate play, is really what is expressed in the whole of the song, and what in general constitutes the lyrical state. In this state pure knowing comes to us, so to speak, in order to deliver us from willing and stress. We follow, yet only for a few moments; willing, desire, the recollection of our own personal aims, always tears us anew from peaceful contemplation...Therefore in the song and in the lyrical mood, willing (the personal interest of the aims) and pure perception of the environment that presents itself are wonderfully blended with each other.... The genuine song is the expression or copy of the whole of this mingled and divided state of mind.[14]

I set aside the many metaphysical commitments Schopenhauer makes in this sharp and lofty passage (the special sense that 'will' has for him, his belief that 'pure, will-less knowing' is possible, and so on). I take the passage simply as a contribution to understanding the grammar of many lyrics. A state of arrested and contemplated 'personal aims' often occurs explicitly in the story of a lyric, as when Keats praises and laments the position of the 'Bold lover' on the Grecian urn: 'never, never canst thou kiss, / Though winning near the goal'.[15] The depth of

Schopenhauer's suggestion lies in his discerning such a state within composer, protagonist and reader of a lyric. Keats not only envisaged the permanence for the lover of a 'so near and yet so far', he delineated it by curving his words around the line-end – 'kiss, / Though' – thus dramatising the metrical pause as an instant of ever-verging; nor did he only delineate it, he took pleasure in the interstice and offered it for our responsive pleasure, so that he and we too may analogously experience through language the lover's erotic outreach and its intrinsic curb. Whether or not the lyric has a story which pivots on such a Keatsian stillness, Schopenhauer claims that there is an inherent dynamism in the lyrical state. His account attributes this dynamism to our being in search of a satisfaction beyond the present and simultaneously aware of our own longing as if it were a natural phenomenon whose beauty we observe and wish to preserve (imagine you are hungry and manage to regard your hunger not in relation to your own desires but as something with a place in the world, an endangered species which you wish to maintain in being).

Schopenhauer's formulation would be improved by recasting it into a less psychological vocabulary, for his words could mislead some into believing that he offers a 'reader-response' account of lyricism. The necessary modifications are made by splicing the philosopher's terms with those Wordsworth chooses for his comments on repetition in the 'Note' to 'The Thorn'. The lyric's 'stress of willing' then appears in that repetition which is unsatisfied and craving, a repetition through which language and consciousness present themselves as letting each other down, ill-assorted, unhappily married; the lyric's 'blissful peace' and 'pure perception of the environment' transpire in that other kind of repetition which is fond and grateful, and for which language and consciousness are not extrinsic one to the other but coupled as 'active and efficient' parts of each other. This splicing is justifiable because the demanding, willing consciousness treats language and the natural world alike merely as potential suppliers of something the consciousness lacks; similarly both Schopenhauerian 'knowing' and Wordsworthian gratitude discover themselves *in* the natural world and language, which they may regard desirously but which they can also leave be. Thus interpreted, the dynamism of lyric appears wholly in the aspect-shifts of verbal design, in the possibility, for example, of voicing 'Ripetizione' now this way and now that, and entails no speculation about the psychology of the writer's empirical self, whether or not, say, she was agitated by love at some time and later placated by a nightingale.

292

Angela Leighton contrasts Rossetti's work with that of one of her predecessors, L.E.L.: 'She has taken [the] well-worn woman's pose 'to heart', but somehow emptied it of all the cloying appeal of the earlier poet's verse, retaining only the shell – the exquisite, formal shell of rhyme and metre – which holds almost no emotional purpose or petition in it at all.... Rossetti's most explicitly heart-broken verses verge on being...insouciant jests'.[16] There is a truth in this, though not put right. Poems do not have insides and outsides; to talk as if they did usually leads to valuing the supposed emotional content (which amounts to no more than paraphrasable sentiment) over the intent processes of composition. Such delusive terms arise from misinterpretation of the aspect-shift inherent to expressively shaped language, by which the utterance may appear demanding or self-replete, afflicted or achieved, and should be understood as both. Nor does the phrase 'insouciant jests' capture that 'artlessness of expression – a quality in which the poetess was by no means deficient',[17] as William Rossetti demurely says, for the lithe, self-conscious hollowness which Leighton has noticed in the poems is thoroughly souciant, though what it most cares about does not always correspond to a present-day sense of priorities. Angela Leighton's book is on *Victorian Women Poets*; naturally then, she compares Rossetti principally with other women. This concentration sometimes has the unfortunate effect, as in other studies of female writers, of attributing a gender-specificity to features of writing which have in fact no such quality. As here, where Leighton implies that to be a 'creature of doubleness',[18] is particularly the fate of women who write, whereas this is normal also for male writers, Byron for example. Indeed, it is a speciality in the tradition of masculine self-pity.

Consider a 'Song' Rossetti wrote when she was eighteen:

> She sat and sang alway
>   By the green margin of a stream,
> Watching the fishes leap and play
>   Beneath the glad sunbeam.
>
> I sat and wept alway
>   Beneath the moon's most shadowy beam,
> Watching the blossoms of the May
>   Weep leaves into the stream.
>
> I wept for memory;
>   She sang for hope that is so fair:
> My tears were swallowed by the sea;
>   Her songs died on the air.[19]

Why 'alway' rather than 'always'? The *OED* notes that 'alway' was first confused with and then superseded by 'always', at least 'in prose, *alway* surviving only in poetry or as an archaism'. The dictionary's last illustrations of the form in prose come from the King James Bible, which is probably where Rossetti found the word in sayings such as 'I am with you alway, even unto the end of the world' (Matthew 28.20). 'In poetry or as an archaism': there's a mine in that 'or'. Perhaps the lexicographer who wrote the note thought of poetry and archaism as options within the same range of thing (as when we offer 'tea or coffee'). That, anyway, is the point of the word in these lines – poetry survives in this poem *as* an archaism. 'Song' is an intricate time-loop: two stanzas tell us that something happened unchangingly; it was ever thus, she sang and I wept, but the final lines reveal that this is now a past perpetuity, for both songs and tears are gone. She underlines the 'then' / 'now' contrast by giving the first two stanzas the same rhyme-words, changing to a new set in the last quatrain. Yet the poem which declares the passing of songs is still called 'Song', and is a song, of sorts; it falls into a twisted ballad-stanza, not the 8686 of common measure but recognisably akin to that in its 6886, preserving as it does the abab rhyme-scheme of much folk-poetry. Her voice in the poem reminisces about poetic shapes that have gone before, like someone trying to hum a melody she can't quite get back.

This is why the 'for' in 'I wept for memory' has such depth of ambiguity: it may be that she wept because she had memories, whether happy or sad, or that she wept because she had once had memories but has now lost even them. Similarly, she 'sang for hope' may mean that she sang because she had hope, or she may have sung for it as people are sometimes required to sing for their suppers. Salt tears return at the close to their natural home, the sea, and songs evaporate into air, into thin air. But then an 'air' in English is another word for a song, which is what the poem's title promised; the piece is back where it started, has eventually itself become a thing of the past, though the past is now its element. Emily Dickinson wrote to Mrs Holland: 'Dear Sister. The Things that never can come back, are several – Childhood – some forms of Hope – the Dead –'.[20] The remark is eminently Dickinsonian; it states with electric sternness a series of half-truths. After all, our language speaks not without reason of 'second childhood', and she may have spoken too soon when she denied the resurrection of the dead. Her piercing phrase, 'some forms of Hope', though, goes to a heart of Rossetti's lyricism.

The customary forms of a poetic tradition, such as the ballad-stanza which she pleats and turns in 'Song', spring eternal in any breast sufficiently familiarised with them, and are 'forms of Hope' just by being

designs in time and making it seem, while they last, that time is suscep-
tible of design and not intrinsically waste. Which is not to say that
Christina G. Rossetti had what might be called a 'positive outlook'.
Heaven forbid. She knew that hope may be a vampire which is not
easily laid to rest, and found this side of her writing both wretched and
funny, as she wrote to her brother, Dante Gabriel: 'If only my figure
would shrink somewhat! For a fat poetess is incongruous especially
when seated by the grave of buried hope'.[21]

Those were different times; they even used the word 'poetess'. Along
with its sense of rhythm, it is the past's sense of humour which is hardest to recall. The two senses have close relations with each other, as the
importance of 'timing' to both shows. When Rossetti makes her arch
joke about the incongruity of being fat and yet known to the public for a
fascinating melancholy, she both fills and parodies a rôle; similar effects
occur constantly in her poems. As in 'Maiden-Song', another work
which sets poeticality in a persistent but irretrievable past – 'Long ago
and long ago, / And long ago', it begins, adding to complete the line,
'still'. 'And long ago still', one of three 'merry maidens' sang out; she

> Trilled her song and swelled her song
> With maiden coy caprice
> In a labyrinth of throbs,
> Pauses, cadences...[22]

The manuscript shows that she had trouble, as well she might have
done, with the word 'cadences'; her editor gives in the textual notes
on the last line I quote: 'Pauses, [illegible erasure] <cadences>'. The
first two lines here have a familiar swing to them which goes awry in
the third and fourth lines, awry to the extent of failing to rhyme at a
point where the other stanzas rhyme, coming out with only the assonance of 'caprice' / 'cadences'. The mismatch of these two words is a
bold stroke not a blunder, for it enables her to reveal 'cadences' as a
portmanteau-word formed from 'maiden ' and 'caprice'. This is
thought-provoking: within the framing pastiche-ballad which begins
and ends 'long ago', we are to hear a 'labyrinth of throbs, / Pauses,
cadences', a complex interiority. There is a temptation to regard this
interiority as what is most authentically Rossetti's about the poem.
Yet the distinctive swerve on 'cadences' can be heard only through
the less wayward rhythms which surround it; if these lines are
somehow more 'personal', this personality exists in relation to the
rest of the poem not as an item to its container but as a voice singing

in an acoustic which has a liveliness of its own, inseparably one with the sound the voice makes within it.

The lilt in Rossetti's work, which often derives from ballad, folk-song, or nursery rhyme, has been taken by some of her recent critics as representing a conformed world, regular, regulated even. There co-exist (this story goes) with that world and its style of utterance, other, more volatile inflections, a speech which is improperly her own. Critics line up idiomatic speech-rhythms as tokens of the individual and composed verserhythms as marks of socialisation, and come to hear her poems as arenas for a combat between self and society; they incline to say that, at least in her rhythmic imagination, she subverts, undermines, interrogates the order of her society. The next steps are easily taken. Her society was patriarchally ordered; literary conventions may be identified with social conventions which they replicate; thus, her voice's off-beats and asymmetries sound the true note of her being-a-woman. There is an appeal to this way of thinking; simplifications have their charm. Yet the implicit notion of how an individual's voice makes itself heard in a language which does not belong exclusively to that individual is incoherent, as if individuality showed itself only in deviation from a norm; the belief that there is something especially female about idiolectal features is groundless; the relation presumed between literary and social conventions does not exist, and, even if it did, it would not follow that a literary variation from the conventional entails a critique of the convention – artists vary on the past of their arts for many reasons, including a desire to refresh the conventional and keep it alive. What is traditional in Rossetti's poetry is quite as much hers, and hers as a woman, as is her re-inflecting of the tradition.

It is not agreeable to name individuals guilty of such *bêtises*, which are anyway endemic in literary criticism at present, but it would be more invidious not to do so. Consider then Isobel Armstrong writing about the idiomatic qualities of Elizabeth Barrett Browning's *Sonnets from the Portuguese*:

> The aim of 'Sonnets' is to redefine 'the whole/Of life in a new rhythm', as Elizabeth Barrett Browning puts it in Sonnet VII, and the sliding cadences, the deliberate elisions and metrical freedoms which break away from the established regularities of the sonnet form are clearly intentional. The late caesuras and enjambement declare an attempt to dissolve the customary forms and restrictions.[23]

'Freedoms' stand in antithesis to 'established regularities', 'customary forms' are synonymous with 'restrictions' and need to be 'dissolved'. As Professor Armstrong's chapter is about 'women's poetry', it is not mentioned that all the prosodic features identified may be found in sonnets by Barrett Browning's male predecessors, found so often as to be countable among the 'established regularities of the sonnet form'. Angela Leighton is still more explicit: 'The idea that metrical correctness is equivalent to moral propriety continued into the nineteenth century, at least as far as women's poetry was concerned. Anna Barbauld had laid down the rules, in the previous century, in "On a Lady's Writing": "Her even lines her steady temper show, / Neat as her dress, and polished as her brow."'[24] Mrs Barbauld was much respected, perhaps especially by men, but her word was not law, nor do her words as quoted here say that 'metrical correctness is equivalent to moral propriety'. Is there reason to believe that this equivalence was thought to apply particularly to women's poetry? In 1861, Ruskin wrote Dante Gabriel Rossetti a sour letter about his sister's poems: 'I sate up till late last night reading poems. They are full of beauty and power. But no publisher... would take them, so full are they of quaintnesses and offences. Irregular measure (introduced to my great regret, in its chief wilfulness, by Coleridge) is the calamity of modern poetry.... your sister should exercise herself in the severest commonplace of metre until she can write as the public like'.[25] Coleridge lived an irregular life, though Ruskin does not equate this with his irregular metres. As it happens, thirty years earlier Coleridge had himself blamed the young Tennyson in similar terms: 'The mischief is that he has begun to write verses without understanding what Metre is.... Tennyson's verses are neither fish nor flesh in respect of construction. I can't scan them'; he prescribed for Tennyson, as Ruskin did for Christina G. Rossetti, a régime of exercise in 'well known and strictly defined metres'.[26] English writers have failed to hear each others' verse as verse at least since Jonson opined that Donne for not keeping of accent deserved hanging.[27] To be misheard is not exclusively a woman's privilege.

These critics have heard aspects of Rossetti's verse but are led astray by theoretical conceptions and political preconceptions when they try to describe those aspects. She can indeed make poetical graces bitter in the mouth, as when she turns her characteristic, syncopating internal rhymes to acrid effect:

> If I might see another Spring –
> Oh stinging comment on my past
> That all my past results in 'if' –...[28]

where the self-interrupting syntax is capped by the premature chime of 'Spring' with 'stinging'. Or again, in her fierce rendering of Psalm

137, notable for the vehement iterations she adds to her original. Where the King James reads 'Happy shall he be, that taketh and dasheth thy little ones against the stones', she writes:

> By the waters of Babylon
>   Tho' the wicked grind the just,
> Our seed shall yet strike root
>   And shall shoot up from the dust…[29]

which genteelly veils the infanticidal gloating of the psalm while at the same time spinning from its words a web of violent implication: the 'seed' of God's covenant with Abraham is made vegetable, strikes rather than takes root, as if its very germination willed injury, 'root' accelerates into 'shoot', a precocious burgeoning into vengeance. 'Spring' / 'stinging', 'root' / 'shoot': she speaks of her own woes and those of ancient Israelites with the same impetuosity of internal rhyme. But 'impetuosity' is not the right word, for these anticipative rhymes are timed by a trained ear. The rhythmic catch in her voice is instinct with the experience of time, particularly with the experience of waiting, during which time most makes itself felt. Stanzaic shapes are models of timed experience, periodicities, so premature rhymes, if heard as 'bending the rules', get ahead of themselves, while they also, if heard as extravagantly obedient to the requirements of pattern, school us to patience.

Such rhymes in her work are instances of lyric's double-aspect, its stilled longing; they show one way she learned to live with unsatisfied desire. As her desire was so religiously set, so informed with readings of the Bible, that for her 'to live' and 'to wait' approach synonymy, her voice naturally takes the same contours whether her subject is the thought of another spring or remembering Jerusalem. Scripture resounds in 'Twice', her most acutely disappointed poem:

> I took my heart in my hand
>   (O my love, O my love),
> I said: Let me fall or stand,
>   Let me live or die,
> But this once hear me speak –
>   (O my love, O my love) –
> Yet a woman's words are weak;
>   You should speak, not I.
>
> You took my heart in your hand
>   With a friendly smile,

With a critical eye you scanned,
   Then set it down,
And said: It is still unripe,
   Better wait awhile;
Wait while the skylarks pipe,
   Till the corn grows brown.

As you set it down it broke –
   Broke, but I did not wince;
I smiled at the speech you spoke,
   At your judgment that I heard:
But I have not often smiled
   Since then, nor questioned since,
Nor cared for corn-flowers wild,
   Nor sung with the singing bird.

I take my heart in my hand,
   O my God, O my God,
My broken heart in my hand:
   Thou hast seen, judge Thou.
My hope was written on sand,
   O my God, O my God;
Now let Thy judgment stand –
   Yea, judge me now.

This contemned of a man,
   This marred one heedless day,
This heart take Thou to scan
   Both within and without:
Refine with fire its gold,
   Purge Thou its dross away –
Yea hold it in Thy hold,
   Whence none can pluck it out.

I take my heart in my hand –
   I shall not die, but live –
Before Thy face I stand;
   I, for Thou callest such:
All that I have I bring,
   All that I am I give,
Smile Thou and I shall sing,
   But shall not question much.[30]

Why is the poem called 'Twice'? Perhaps the title glances at the pro-
verbial 'once bitten, twice shy', meaning: once I offered my heart to
someone, but never again. This burned child does not fear the fire,

though; she makes a second offering of her heart, this time to God. The poem does not tell us how to understand the relation, if there is one (or more than one), between the human beloved and the divine. Little happens in the story, or rather, what happens is a momentous let-down, an erotic bathos: the man says 'thanks but no thanks'. The story ends before we know how God responds to the second offer (in this, it is life-like). 'Twice' inhabits what Hopkins, in devout parody of the liturgical 'world without end', termed a 'world without event'.[31] In this vacated world, words occur redoubledly; *they* are what happens twice (at least). Clasped about each other, at once spasmic and psalmodic, her words come back on her : 'I took', 'you took', 'take Thou'; 'Let me fall or stand', 'let Thy judgment stand', 'Before Thy face I stand'; 'you scanned', 'take Thou to scan'; and so on. Such intense recapitulation suggests that the title may have the further sense of a musical instruction to repeat a piece, so that 'Twice' obeys what Beckett called 'the beautiful convention of the "da capo"'.[32] As in Hebrew lyric, verbal doublings and parallel-isms both vent a self-assertive human will and also create with that will's vehemences a shape in which it prepares to conform itself to God's will, so that what she said of Psalm 102 is true of her 'Twice', 'this woeful complaint is still a song: even while he lies under the Divine indignation and wrath the penitent sings and makes melody in his heart to the Lord'.[33]

Her finest stroke comes when she anticipates the rhyme to come on 'wince' in the third stanza: 'But I have not often smiled / Since then, nor questioned since' – the understatement of 'not often', the run-on past 'smiled' which insists we don't dwell on the word and so per-haps implies the smile itself was faint, the fall of the voice onto 'since', arriving too soon at the beginning of the line but then re-arriving in its formal place as the terminal rhyme. That repeated 'since' tells how drastic the rejection was: everything since then is merely more 'since'-ness, a long anniversary of what did not come right. The voice turns sharply onto 'since' but with what curve of larynx it is impossible to say: we may hear her as self-pitying, indignant, derisive, numb. The word stands at an ethical junction from which it is possible to move in the direction of many attitudes. Anthony Harrison is sure which route she took: '"Twice" operates at a level of cultural criticism dif-ferent from that of "Light Love" and "An Apple-Gathering". The attack implicit in its four [sic] brief stanzas is upon the powerlessness of women in a rigid patriarchal society'.[34] The one reproachful word the poem utters is 'heedless' which does not add up to much of an 'attack'; Rossetti nowhere specifies the social context of the encounter, probably because she rightly thought such disappointments happen in all societies, nor does she regret her 'powerlessness' because power would have been no help to her (does Professor Harrison suppose she might have *compelled* the response she desired had she but had a gat to hand?). She does not embark on 'cultural criticism' but submits herself to divine judgment. Readers nowadays may be disappointed by her lack of socio-political pugnacity but these regrets do not excuse misprision of her work. Particularly not when, as with this poem, the work is brave and individually achieved while the pretence that she was engaged in feminist critique just recycles a slack and canting sentimentalism, a refusal to face, or even countenance, the disappointment that waits for all of us, male, female, or excluded middle.

Why does God appear in stanza four of 'Twice' (as with His arrival in the second verse of 'A Christmas Carol', there has been no sign of Him before)? Today's wisdom is prompt to explain; Rossetti must be sublimating. Adrienne Rich could have fingered her as one who 'like Simone Weil, like St. Teresa, like Heloise, . . . substitutes a masculine God for the love of earthly men (or women) – a pattern followed by certain gifted imaginative women in the Christian era'.[35] In a sense, this is true, as it is equally true that Adrienne Rich substitutes the love of earthly women (or men) for God – a pattern followed by certain gifted imaginative women in what is called the post-Christian era. Freud's hypotheses about the origins of religious belief have for many become articles of faith, but if we preserve a scepticism even about Freud, we may find more to say about God in 'Twice'. He crosses her mind, I think, because of all human experiences the one which gives you the most piercing sense of what divine judgement might be like is an erotic venture of your self such as she makes in the poem. All of you at such a time is at issue. An extreme of dread, then, is that on the Last Day God might decline to take me back to His place. This is why Rossetti often alludes in this poem to Scriptures about death and judgment.[36] Her eschatological shadowings and the specific instance of erotic disappointment figure and measure each other. There was an end of sorts to her world when she was turned down, and the breakage of her hopes can be understood as emblematic of how all human designs are frail; conversely, that fragility is a universal human condition, that the world will end and all suffer some cut-off of what they have known and desired, reminds her she is not the only being on the face of the earth deserving of pity. Nor does the poem quite end with its own concluding words, for a last sense of 'Twice' is an ethical version of the musical *da capo*: what calm the poem achieves about its own pain is not something possessed once and for all, but will have to be worked towards again, patience being an incessant rehearsal of itself.

William Rossetti remarked of his youngest sister 'She was replete with the spirit of self-postponement, which passed into self-sacrifice whenever that quality was in demand'.[37] Self-postponement' is a good word for what shows of her in her writing; formally and substantively, hers is an art of longings delayed but not abandoned. Her renunciations were temporary; she spared herself and others the fanatic altruism of the young George Eliot with her view that 'All self-sacrifice is good'.[38] Her foregoings, though, went too far for some later tastes. Virginia Woolf knew what Rossetti lacked: 'she starved herself of love, which meant also life'.[39] What this coarse remark means is that Rossetti had, so far as we know, not much of a sex-life which, according to Virginia Woolf, for a woman means not much of a life full stop. Rossetti lived all but her last eight years with her mother, whom she loved passionately, but Woolf doesn't count this, or any of the poet's other intimate and devoted relations, as 'love'; it was beyond Woolf to conceive that a love of God might be love too.

Rossetti's prose yields many compounds made with 'self-': 'self-oblation', 'self-mistrustful', 'self-restriction', 'self-sifting'.[40] Her values are not comforted or comforting, but they can be respected. When, for example, she writes

> And as the poor never cease out of the land and are in various degrees standing representatives of famine, this self-stinting seems...to be the rule and standard of right living; not a desperate exceptional resource, but a regular, continual, plain duty.[41]

her words continue to make a sane and decent admonition. It is not necessary to be a Christian to recognise the eloquence, the ardour of the following passage in which she tries to bring out the power of redemption as it re-orients our being in the created world and that world's bearing on us:

> Not merely all the inhabitants thereof, but the earth itself is dissolved; and Christ alone bears up the pillars of it...In judgment upon man, or in sympathy with him, all is disjointed, unstrung, enfeebled; all faints, fails, groans, travails in pain together...
> And Christ, on Whose sinless head our sins were made to converge, willed also that on Himself should centre the short-coming, failure, disappointment, which balk us at every turn.[42]

She sounds for a moment like Hopkins, especially in her turning-inside-out of the word 'self-centred' so that it expresses Christ's will 'that on Himself should centre' all the abeyances and thwartings which cross the path of human selves. It is, though, necessary for the appreciation of so great a passage to try to open yourself imaginatively to forms of life and belief which may be very different from your own; this, unfortunately, is something many writers about literature are currently not prepared to do.[43]

F. D. Maurice was alert and sober about the complexities at issue hereabouts:

> To enter into the meaning of self-sacrifice – to sympathise with any one who aims at it – not to be misled by counterfeits of it – not to be unjust to the truth which may be mixed with those counterfeits – is a difficult task...[44]

He was introducing Charles Kingsley's *The Saint's Tragedy*, a polemical drama about the life of St. Elizabeth of Hungary, who gave up for the religious life her immense earthly wealth and her attachment to husband and children. Charlotte Brontë had a fair sense of the play's merits and failings: 'Faulty it may be, crude and unequal, yet there are portions where some of the deep chords of human nature are swept with a hand which is strong even while it falters. We see throughout (I *think*) that Elizabeth has not, and never had a mind perfectly sane'.[45] St Elizabeth of Hungary's story became a centre of considerable interest after Kingsley's play (1848), particularly to Rossetti because her one-time fiancé, James Collinson, decided to produce a large, historical painting on the subject. The life of this medieval saint focussed a more general concern in the late eighteen-forties, a concern that can be put in a word: nuns.

At the Reformation, religious orders for men and women were dissolved, and for centuries thereafter forbidden in this kingdom. From about twenty years before Kingsley's play, there had been a growing movement to revive these orders. Southey in 1829 lamented that England had no Sisters of Charity such as the Béguines; small groups of Roman Catholic nuns began to work in England again in the late eighteen-thirties. Marian Rebecca Hughes became in 1841 the first Anglican woman since the Reformation to take religious vows, secretly in the church of St Mary the Virgin at Oxford. The first sisterhood took up residence at 17, Park Village West in Easter Week, 1845; from opposite directions, the nuns and the female Rossettis converged for divine service on Christ Church, Albany Street. By the time Maria Francesca

Rossetti entered the novitiate at the All Saints' Sisters of the Poor in 1873, some forty Anglican sisterhoods had been established; they had been mocked in *Punch* and aroused sufficient concern to require a report from a Select Committee of Parliament on conventual and monastic institutions (1870).[46]

There were several kinds of worry about the sisterhoods. Walter Walsh considered them 'not only Popish, but also Pagan in [their] origin', comparable to 'priestesses of Freya'; he hinted that some of them died in suspicious circumstances: 'Nuns are buried within those [convent] walls, though whether their deaths were properly registered or not is more than I can say'.[47] Walsh was an ecclesiastical guttersnipe, but many of his concerns were shared by more respectable observers. In *Sisterhoods in the Church of England*, a Miss Goodman claimed that the religious vow of obedience produced 'spiritual despotism and terrorism' in the communities.[48] There was great resistance to all religious vows from many bishops, though, as is the custom of the Anglican hierarchy, their views were inconsistently expressed and went largely ignored by those they most affected. There was, in fact, no solid ecclesial or theological argument against religious orders for women; the suspicion and resentment directed at the sisterhoods expressed rather a foggy, socio-sexual ethos. Bishop Tait opined in 1865: 'I believe no blessing will ever come on work, however self-denying, which is undertaken to the neglect of those higher duties which belong to home life, and which are imposed directly by God Himself'. G. H. Lewes shared the bishop's domestic Erastianism: 'The grand function of woman, it must always be recollected, is, and ever must be, *Maternity*: and this we regard not only as her distinctive characteristic, and most endearing charm, but as a high and holy office'.[49] The unctuous blather about 'higher duties' and 'high and holy office' shows its true nature in Lewes's brutal 'function'. Supporters of the sisterhoods were among the few at that time to credit women with a choice of life not determined by their rôle in reproducing the species. Thus, J. M. Neale was unusual in saying that virginity '*is* a higher and holier state' than marriage and maternity, as Pusey was unusual in defending sisterhoods from the control of the male clergy: 'I think it is a wrong ambition of men to wish to have the direction of the work of women. I should fear that it would be for the injury of both. Women ought to understand their own work, the education and care of young women; or they would not be fit for it at all'.[50]

Victorian nervousness about groups of women detached from their families and under rules of their own devising was exacerbated by sexual tremors. The period was not one of pre-Freudian 'innocence' about the entanglement of erotic and religious desires; its difference from the twentieth century lies rather in the fact that no single theory of that entanglement had established so powerful a monopoly of explanation as has Freud's in our time. Kingsley speaks out through his mouthpiece, Walter, berating medieval Puseyites: 'I have watched you and your crew, how you preach up selfish ambition for divine charity and call prurient longings celestial love, while you blaspheme that very marriage from whose mysteries you borrow all your cant'. He turns to sub-Shakespearean metaphors of sexual queasiness in characterising the pious aspirations of young women as 'pert fancies; / This fog-bred mushroom-spawn of brain-sick wits', and arranges that Elizabeth's dying words should hint that her heart is set towards reunion with her dead husband, much though the priest, Conrad, tries to stage manage her as an ascetic saint:

ELIZ[ABETH],	Now I must sleep for ere the sun shall rise,
	I must be gone upon a long, long journey
	To him I love.
CON[RAD].	She means her heavenly Bridegroom –
	The Spouse of souls.
ELIZ.	I said, to him I love.[51]

The phrase 'the spouse of souls' marks Conrad as thoroughly un-English; no decent Protestant would use such a risqué term. The Bishop of London, for example, had objected to the description in their Rule of the Park Village sisters as 'spouses of our Lord'.[52] Something other and more than prudery operates here, though prudery was also at work, nor do we face only apprehensiveness about a volatile mix of female desire and Catholic mysticism. A more general question arises, one which Rossetti touched on when pondering the verse 'God is Love' (I John 4.16): 'Beyond a doubt "God is Love": it is my own conception of love which may not in truth be love'.[53] Theologians may expand this thought to the vast issue of whether terms understood in and through human experience (such as 'love') can be applied in any intelligibly analogous sense to a God who transcends human experience, but they can hardly make the thought deeper than it is in Rossetti's plain words. The confluence of erotic and religious vocabularies in Rossetti's work, as in many liturgical contexts or in the carping about sisterhoods, puts this question repeatedly and from many angles; that she had no answer to the question does not prove she was unaware of it. Indeed, this might rather show how well she understood it.

The third of Rossetti's 'Three Nuns' describes a woman's entry into the religious life:

> My heart trembled when first I took
>   The vows which must be kept;
> At first it was a weariness
>   To watch when once I slept.
> The path was rough and sharp with thorns;
>   My feet bled as I stepped;
> The Cross was heavy and I wept.
>
> While still the names rang in mine ears
>   Of daughter, sister, wife;
> The outside world still looked so fair
>   To my weak eyes, and rife
> With beauty; my heart almost failed;
>   Then in the desperate strife
> I prayed, as one who prays for life,
>
> Until I grew to love what once
>   Had been so burdensome.
> So now when I am faint, because
>   Hope deferred seems to numb
> My heart, I yet can plead; and say
>   Although my lips are dumb:
> 'The Spirit and the Bride say, Come.'[54]

She wrote this section in 1850, and never published it, for reasons which may have included its nearness to the bone of her relation to Collinson but also probably involved its nearness to the knuckle of ecclesiastical controversy about sisterhoods (the poem's 'vigils', 'fasts' and 'vows which must be kept' are all notably Romanizing). Consider the line 'I prayed, as one who prays for life'. She may pray 'for life' in the sense of wishing again for her life before she entered the convent, harking back along some of her rhymes to a world 'rife / With beauty' in which she might have been called 'wife'; she may pray for her life because the struggle with those old desires is so desperate she fears she will die; she may pray for a true life of devotion which she has not yet attained, a life of devotion which she hopes will yield the life eternal. She has at any rate taken a perpetual vow of lifelong prayer. The passage dramatically suggests a complex state of the soul, and yet is aptly quiet in its drama, as in the so hushed intimation of the change that comes over the nun, an intimation carried by Rossetti's extra internal rhyming of 'still', 'still' in the penultimate stanza with the eventual 'Until' at the beginning of the last verse. Henry James took a *novella* to arrive at a similar, inquiring poise over the many aspects of a woman's disappointment, renunciation and ability to make a new life – the last sentence of *Washington Square*: 'Catherine, meanwhile, in the parlour, picking up her morsel of fancy-work, had seated herself with it again – for life, as it were'.[55]

The rhyme-sound which completes the last stanza of 'Three Nuns' ('numb' / 'dumb' / 'Come') is the same sound which completed the opening stanza of the first monologue in the set (she rhymes on it nowhere else in the poems):

> Shadow, shadow on the wall
> Spread thy shelter over me;
> Wrap me with a heavy pall,
> With the dark that none may see.
> Fold thyself around me; come:
> Shut out all the troublesome
> Noise of life; I would be dumb.[56]

We hear, arching over the whole sequence, how these distinct women have become sisters to each other through a shared life. They remain individuals, though, because Rossetti varies the seven-line stanza they have in common, giving them different rhyme-schemes and syllabic distributions. We also gauge through the recurrence of rhyme how long these women wait in their night-watches, for Rossetti has made 'Three Nuns' not only a sequence but also a cycle. She wrote that 'human life is in two sections, life terminable and life interminable',[57] and this sounds gloomier than perhaps she intended, for 'interminable', though meant to mean 'everlasting', somehow doesn't have the same ring.

The last line of 'Three Nuns' quotes almost the last words of the Bible, Revelation 22.17: 'And the Spirit and the bride say, Come'. The sacred text ends with confidence that Christ will come quickly, as it had begun by prophesying 'things which must shortly come to pass' (Revelation 1.1). Rossetti opens her commentary on this book : 'At the end of 1800 years we are still repeating this "shortly"'; she discovers in this still repeating a 'fellowship of patience' with Saint John.[58] The nun finds it difficult to say the words which say what she longs for; she says them with dumb lips, and perhaps she only quotes them – they are placed within inverted commas. This is not surprising because the words entail an apocalyptic resignation of the self and its whole world;

the most world-weary might find them hard to utter. The words are there, though, in the silence of the page, on her heart's lips, evermore about to be said. This liminal aspect to the utterance is the verge of lyric, for, as Schopenhauer does not make clear in his argument, if it is possible to desire an end to the self and its willing (as it is), that desire will itself by the inherent dynamism of lyric be stilled, known, perpetuated through blissful acquiescence in its own unsatisfaction, its disappointment. For the lyric poem the world ends only in the line next after last.

Dora Greenwell remarked: 'A Christian is too deeply pledged to a foregone conclusion to be bold and fearless in tracking out ultimate truth'.[59] There are more ways of foregoing a conclusion than Dora Greenwell imagined. Orthodox Christians cannot be pledged to a foregone conclusion because theirs is an eschatological faith, and the Last Things are yet to be. Rossetti had an orthodox Christian temperament, whatever her doctrinal allegiances, which is to say that she spent a deal of her time waiting for the end. Her faith resolves itself not into the atemporal conclusions of a philosophical system but into handling time, both as she went about her daily life and through the composed timing of her poems, such timings as, for example, the suspension across a stanza-break at 'I prayed, as one who prays for life, // Until I grew to love what once / Had been so burdensome' – how long was the time before 'Until'? Evidently, the break can't be long sustained when reading the poem aloud but the dip or loft of the voice a reader must make to indicate the stretch of sense over the formal break stands for what may have been years passed in attendance.

'How long?' is a question her poems often ask, implicitly or explicitly:

> Heaven is not far, tho' far the sky
>   Overarching earth and main.
> It takes not long to live and die,
>   Die, revive, and rise again.
> Not long: how long? Oh, long re-echoing song!
> O Lord, how long?[60]

Once again, anticipative rhyme ('long' / 'song') strains at the leash and accents the verse with her own inflection, individuates not only the verse but also the question 'how long?', a question fundamental to Judaeo-Christian scripture – Cruden's *Concordance* lists more than fifty occurrences. Rossetti speaks here as her self and as all believers in the divine promise. If asked 'how long is Rossetti's "Yet a little while"?', we ought to answer 'six lines' or 'about twenty seconds' and also 'several thousand years, and still not finished'.

Rossetti might not have appreciated, but, having in the relevant sense no 'foregone conclusion', she would have understood one great joke in *Endgame*:

CLOV: Do you believe in the life to come?
HAMM: Mine was always that.[61]

One of her favourite Biblical quotations was Proverbs 13.12. 'Hope deferred maketh the heart sick'; she rarely mentions the second half of the saying, 'but when the desire cometh, it is a tree of life'.[62] The phrase comes in poems which speak out of her actual woes:

> I looked for that which is not, nor can be,
>   And hope deferred made my heart sick in truth:
> But years must pass before a hope of youth
>   Is resigned utterly.[63]

She was eighteen when she wrote this, and may be thought of as looking forward to giving up her 'hope of youth' (the poem ends by reverting to, not resigning, hope). The lyric self is also very old, and the poem can read as if she were freed from hope's exactions. That doubleness of aspect can be heard in the ambiguity of cadence at the end of this stanza, where the voice may collapse on the dactyl of 'utterly', as if despondently, or sustain the word so the rhyme with 'nor can be' is heard and thus not quite 'let go' the word or hope. She also regards her state of deferred hope as the lot of any Christian, so that she adopts the same phrase to stress the patience with which Saint John waited for the second coming, describing his as 'a life...of great austerity and mortification; a life surely of hope deferred and desire waited for, and eyes that failed for looking upward'.[64] Sometimes her balance of personal and liturgical senses for 'hope deferred' is less than poised. In 'Ye Have Forgotten the Exhortation' an angel tries to comfort a bereaved soul with thoughts of the final perfection of the world; the title is from Hebrews 12.5 which speaks of how God chastens those He loves. The soul is unconsoled by this thought:

ANGEL: Bury the dead heart-deep;
           Take patience till the sun be set;
           There are no tears for him to weep,
           No doubts to haunt him yet:
           Take comfort, he will not forget: –

> SOUL: Then I will watch beside his sleep;
> Will watch alone,
> And make my moan
> Because the harvest is so long to reap.
> ANGEL: The fields are white to harvest, look and see,
> Are white abundantly.
> The harvest moon shines full and clear,
> The harvest time is near,
> Be of good cheer: –
> SOUL: Ah, woe is me;
> I have no heart for harvest time,
> Grown sick with hope deferred from chime to chime....
> O Lord, my heart is broken for my sin:
> Yet hasten Thine Own day
> And come away.
> Is not time full? Oh put the sickle in,
> O Lord, begin.[65]

At 'The fields are white to harvest', the Angel alludes to Christ's words about the imminence of the world's end (John 4.35); Rossetti clips and twists the word 'har(ves)t' to thoughts of her 'heart'. To have 'no heart for harvest time' means both that the soul feels her heart is unworthy to be harvested but also, more drastically, that she is no longer in the mood for the second coming; she has waited ages and can't be bothered any more. As Rossetti wrote, 'It is possible to be so disheartened by earth as to be deadened towards heaven'.[66] She has 'grown' like a crop, but the crop is worthless, for what she has 'grown' is 'sick'. The 'chime to chime' along which hope has been deferred may be the regular chimes of bells which summon to religious observance; the chimes are also those of verse itself, its vain completenesses, patternings which offer the satisfaction only of themselves, promises, promises. When she asks the Lord to 'come away', we can hardly tell Him apart from death – 'Come away, come away death', as the Clown sings in *Twelfth Night*. Which is only right for He is her death; she will die in Him, of that at least she thinks she can be sure.

Impatience would be a natural response to this writing of hers with its 'tedious indomitable grace'[67] of patience. Some readers, the cheerier, the empowering sort, incline to wish she'd give herself a shaking, realise there are plenty more good fish in the sea, and that one should never say die. These are the people whom Florence Nightingale considered noxious in the sick-room, with their 'shower-bath of silly hopes and encouragements':

'I really believe there is scarcely a greater worry which invalids have to endure than the incurable hopes of their friends'.[68] The same is true of the sick at heart and their encouragers, for, as Nightingale's shrewd phrase 'the incurable hopes of their friends' suggests, it is hope not hopelessness the heart-sick suffer from. Rossetti volunteered for work with Nightingale in the Crimea but was turned down; her nursing was done only at home, except in that for a poet of her quality, with her cast of attention, the whole earth is her hospital and time itself the patient over whom she keeps her vigil. Writing verse is actually more like nursing than current taste in poetry or poets often care to recognise, like nursing in its detailed, rhythmic solicitudes, its close acquaintance with fevers, and its slowly-learned but steady power to live with the hard truth that sometimes you can do more for others, by way of pleasant distraction or of good advice, than you can for yourself. Poets, like nurses, should not raise expectations. The reason why this is so was well stated long ago by William Empson:

> it is only in degree that any improvement of society could prevent wast-age of human powers; the waste even in a fortunate life, the isolation even of a life rich in intimacy, cannot but be felt deeply, and is the central feeling of tragedy. And anything of value must accept this because it must not prostitute itself; its strength is to be prepared to waste itself, if it does not get its opportunity.[69]

It was Rossetti's strength as a poet to find tunes for waste and isolation, for the sense of missed opportunities, the drag of waiting, the yearning for a cure, while giving these abysmal states enough shape to make us able to sustain them, even, oddly, enjoy seeing how we look in them. As, for instance, in her poem on 'Ascension Day', which characteristically does not follow the upward trajectory of the ascending Christ but hangs back with the apostles who were left behind, persistent and bereft:

> For as a cloud received Him from their sight,
>   So with a cloud will He return ere long:
> Therefore they stand on guard by day, by night,
>   Strenuous and strong.
>
> They do, they dare, they beyond seven times seven
>   Forgive, they cry God's mighty word aloud:
> Yet sometimes haply lift tired eyes to Heaven –
>   'Is that His cloud?'[70]

These apostles are living in Victorian England. They stand as if at a great railway-terminus, scanning the crowds, the clouds, which throng before them, waiting for an announcement, wondering if He will be on time, if His train is even now drawing in: '"Is that His cloud?"' – no, that's the sleeper service. There is something absurd about people's behaviour when they are waiting, the ways they try to mask their dependence on something beyond their control, their pronounced unconcern ('It really doesn't bother me if he *never* comes'), their whis-tlings, pretended absorption in a time-table, and restlessness. From which it does not follow that the beliefs which keep them waiting are absurd.

Notes

1 Quotations from Rossetti's poems are from *The Complete Poems of Christina Rossetti*, ed. R. W. Crump, (Baton Rouge, 3 vols., 1979–90), and give volume, page and line numbers; thus for this instance, II, 95,l. 1.

2 *Speaking Likenesses*, (1874), repr., Jan Marsh (ed.), *Christina Rossetti: Poems and Prose* (1994), 343; *Time Flies, A Reading Diary* (*1885*, repr., 1897), 83.

3 Respectively, 'The Convent Threshold', I, 64,l. 99; 'A Bird's-Eye View', I, 135, l. 59; 'The Prince's Progress', I, 105, l. 374; "The Iniquity of the Fathers Upon the Children", I l. 177, l. 500; 'Time lengthening...', III, 275,l. 1 and l. 7.

4 Proust discusses 'accent' often in *A la recherche....*; see, for example, in the edition of Jean-Yves Tadié et al., (Paris, 1987, 4 vols.), I, 42; I, 543; III, 759–61.

5 These are the qualities Florence Nightingale singled out as constituting a good nurse. See her *Notes on Nursing: What It Is, and What It Is Not*, (1860, repr., New York, 1946), 65.

6 Letter to Caroline Gemmer, 3 January 1888, quoted in Antony H. Harrison, *Christina Rossetti in Context*, (Brighton, 1988), 82.

7 'A Christmas Carol', I, 216–217,ll. 1–8.

8 Two of her comments on snow in *Seek and Find: A Double Series of Short Studies of the 'Benedicite'*, (1879), provide apt glosses: 'The beauty of snow needs no proof. Perfect in whiteness, feathery in lightness, it often floats down without hesitation as if it belonged to air rather than to earth: yet once resting on that ground it seemed loath to touch, it silently and surely accom-plishes its allotted task; it fills up chasms, levels inequalities, cloaks imper-fections...', *65*; 'If aught which endures or which is eternal be likened to snow, it is on occasion of its brief revelation to mortal eyes...', 222.

9 I translate from 'Poésie et pensée abstraite', (Oxford, 1939), repr. in *Oeuvres*, ed. Jean Hytier, (Paris, 1957, 2 vols.), I, 1325. All subsequent translations are mine, except where otherwise noted.

10 'Note' to 'The Thorn', in *Lyrical Ballads*, (1800), eds. R. L. Brett and A. R. Jones, (1963, rev. ed., 1965), 289.

11 III, 311, ll.1–8.

12 Isobel Armstrong treats Rossetti's repetitions subtly in her *Victorian Poetry: Poetry, Poetics and Politics*, (1993), 352.

13 The early Nietzsche presents an emphatic version of lyricism along these lines; see *Die Geburt der Tragödie aus dem Geiste der Musik*, (Leipzig, 1872), section 5: 'Only this lyrical I is not identical with that of the waking, empirical person, but with that I which alone has true being, the eternal I which rests at the very basis of things', trans, from *Friedrich Nietzsche: Werke*, ed. Karl Schlechta, (Munich, 1966, 3 vols.), I, 38.

14 *Die Welt as Wille und Vorstellung*, (1819), trans, by E. F. J. Payne as *The World as Will and Representation*, (Indian Hills, 1958; repr. New York, 1969, 2 vols.), I, 249–50.

15 'Ode on a Grecian Urn', ll. 17–18, from the edition of Miriam Allott, (1970, corrected ed., 1975), 535.

16 Angela Leighton, *Victorian Women Poets: Writing Against the Heart*, (Brighton, 1992), 76.

17 W. M. Rossetti, 'Memoir', in *The Poetical Works of Christina Georgina Rossetti*, (1904), lxi.

18 Leighton, op. cit., 76.

19 'Song', I, 58, ll. 1–12.

20 Letter of late 1881, in T. H. Johnson (ed.), *The Letters of Emily Dickinson*, (Cambridge, Mass., 1958; 3 vols.), III, 714.

21 Letter of 4 August 1881, in W. M. Rossetti (ed.), *The Family Letters of Christina Rossetti*, (1908), 95. The dead Christ is, evidently, her prime 'buried hope'; compare Hegel's astonishing sentence in his account of some unhappinesses of the Christian self: 'Therefore it is only the *grave* of that in which it lives that can become a presence to this consciousness', trans. from *Phänomenologie des Geistes*, (1807), ed. Gerhard Göhler, (Frankfurt a.M., 1970), 131.

22 I,113, ll. 118–21.

23 Armstrong, op. cit., 356.

24 Leighton, op. cit., 38.

25 Letter of c. 20 January, 1861, in W. M. Rossetti (ed.), *Ruskin: Rossetti: Preraphaelitism: Papers 1854 to 1862*, (1899), 258–9.

26 *Table Talk*, ed. Carl Woodring, (Princeton, 1990, 2 vols.), I, 367–8.

27 In conversation with William Drummond of Hawthornden, 1618–19, repr. in *Ben Jonson*, ed. Ian Donaldson, (Oxford, 1985), 596.

28 'Another Spring', I, 48, ll. 17–19.

29 'By the waters of Babylon', III, 282, ll. 25–2836.

30 I, 124–6, ll. 1–4837.

31 'In honour of St. Alphonsus Rodriguez', in Norman H. Mackenzie (ed.), *The Poetical Works of Gerard Manley Hopkins*, (Oxford, 1990), 200.

32 Beckett, *Proust*, (1931), repr. in *Proust and Three Dialogues with Georges Duthuit*, (1965), 92.

33 *The Face of the Deep*, 90. Compare her comment on one of her favourite Biblical tags: '"Vanity of vanities", as "Solomon in all his glory"…states and restates it, amounts to so exquisite a dirge over dead hope and paralysed effort that we are almost ready to fall in love with our own desolation…', *Seek and Find*, 272.

34 Harrison, op. cit., 124.

35 Adrienne Rich, *On Lies, Secrets, and Silence: Selected Prose 1966–1978*, (New York, 1979), 95.

36 For example: Isaiah 38. 1–3; Malachi 3.2; Matthew 5. 29 and 7. 26–27.

37 'Memoir', loc. cit., lxvii.

38 George Eliot, *The George Eliot Letters*, ed. G. S. Haight, (New Haven and London, 1954–178, 8 vols.), I, 268.

39 Diary entry for 4 August 1918, in Anne Olivier Bell, (ed.), *The Diary of Virginia Woolf* (1977–184, 5 vols.), I, 178.

40 Respectively, *The Face of the Deep*, 16, 61; *Seek and Find*, 293; *Time Flies*, 2.

41 *The Face of the Deep*, 202.

42 *Seek and Find*, 169–70.

43 For instance, Elaine Showalter observes 'The feminine novelists did share the cultural values of Victorian middle-class women, and they clung to the traditional notion of femininity', *A Literature of Their Own: British Women Novelists from Brontë to Lessing*, (Princeton, 1977), 97. She does not attempt to justify 'clung to', it being clear to her that rational beings could have no other relation to a 'traditional notion'. Isobel Armstrong praises some of Adelaide Anne Procter's poems because 'Neither "A Parting" nor "A Woman's Answer" retreats to celibacy or virginity as an alternative to marriage', (Armstrong, op. cit., 337), where 'retreats' assumes a view of marriage as the properly 'advanced' state, at least for women. Spinsters, it seems, are backward, except when truly avant-garde practitioners of extra-marital sex.

44 'Preface' to Charles Kingsley's *The Saint's Tragedy*, (1848), in Kingsley, *Poems*, (1871, repr. 1889), xix.

45 E. C. Gaskell, *The Life of Charlotte Brontë*, (1857, 3rd ed., 1857), quoted from the edition of Alan Shelston, (1975, repr. 1985), 456–7.

46 This sketch is indebted to: P. F. Anson, *The Call of the Cloister: Religious Communities and Kindred Bodies in the Anglican Communion*, (1955; 2nd ed., rev. and ed. by A. W. Campbell, 1964); T. J. Williams and A. W Campbell, *The Park Village Sisterhood*, (1965); Michael Hill, *The Religious Order: A study of virtuoso religion and its legitimation in the nineteenth-century Church of England*, (1973); Geoffrey Rowell, *The Vision Glorious: Themes and Personalities of the Catholic Revival in Anglicanism*, (Oxford, 1983).

47 *The Secret History of the Oxford Movement*, (1897, third ed., 1898), 165 and 192.

48 Margaret Goodman, *Sisterhoods in the Church of England: With Notices of Some Charitable Sisterhoods in the Romish Church*, (1863, 3rd ed., 1864), 110.

49 Bishop Tait, quoted in Anson, op. cit., 303; G. H. Lewes, quoted in Showalter, op. cit., 68.

50 J. M. Neale, *Annals of the Virgin Saints*, (1846), xxvi; Pusey, letter of 14 January 1856, quoted in Hill, *The Religious Order*, 232.

51 Kingsley, *The Saint's Tragedy*, loc. cit., respectively, 121, 31, 138.

52 Anson, op. cit., 230.

53 *The Face of the Deep*, 476.

54 'Three Nuns', III, 192–3, ll. 187–207.

55 *Washington Square*, (1880, repr. Harmondsworth, 1971), 174.

56 Three Nuns', III, 187, ll. 1–7.

57 *The Face of the Deep*, 99.

58 *The Face of the Deep*, 9.

59 Quoted in Leighton, op. cit., 124.

60 II, 266, ll. 1–6. This poem was given the title 'Yet a little while' when it appeared in *Verses*, (1893); it was untitled on first publication in *The Face of the Deep*, where it forms part of her commentary on the 'shortly' of Revelation l.1.

61 Samuel Beckett, *Fin de partie*, (1957), translated by the author as *Endgame*, (1958), in *The Complete Dramatic Works*, (1986), 116.

62 In *Time Flies*, 80–1, where the second half is for once mentioned, it is glossed as referring to 'the Cross of Christ Crucified'.

63 I, 51, ll. 1–4.

64 *Called To Be Saints: The Minor Festivals Devotionally Studied*, (1881, repr. 1906), 72.

65 III, 229–30, ll. 18–34, 46–53.

66 *The Face of the Deep*, 527.

67 *The Face of the Deep*, 68.

68 Nightingale, op. cit., 98, 96.

69 *Some Versions of Pastoral*, (1935, repr. 1968), 5.

70 II, 232–3, ll. 21–28.

17

Stirring 'a Dust of Figures'
Elizabeth Barrett Browning and Love

Angela Leighton

This word is not enough but it will have to do.
(Margaret Atwood, "Variations on
the Word *Love*," 83)

Not only is the word "love" not enough; it is also too much. Its meaning is prolific. Love serves, as Atwood specifies, for the lacy, heart-shaped card, the expensive body lotion, the patriotic war song; even, perhaps, for the cool copulation of slugs. "Then," she adds, "there's the two / of us" (83).

Variations on the word "love" range from a creed to a cliché, a psychosis to a social contract, a pious mysticism to a crude commercialism. Personal or political, holy or obscene, literal or metaphorical, to talk about love as opposed, for instance, to sex, marriage or desire, is to have a constant problem of reference. It would be easier not to talk about it at all. Yet this problem of reference is part of the point. Love, in a way, includes sex, marriage and desire, but it also suggests something more: a residue – sentimental and nostalgic, maybe – of all the quantifiable terms of our social and sexual politics. Love is something left over: – just a superfluous word, perhaps.

The twentieth century's reaction against the Victorians, as well as its obsession with them, tends to focus on the problem of love. The

Leighton, Angela. 1999. "Stirring 'a Dust of Figures': Elizabeth Barrett Browning and Love." In *Critical Essays on Elizabeth Barrett Browning*, edited by Sandra Donaldson, pp. 218–32. New York: G K Hall and Co. Reproduced with permission of Angela Leighton and the Browning Society.

Victorian Poets: A Critical Reader, First Edition. Edited by Valentine Cunningham.
© 2014 John Wiley & Sons, Ltd. Published 2014 by John Wiley & Sons, Ltd.

continuing popularity of works such as *The Barretts of Wimpole Street*, for instance, bears witness to our own fascination with hypocrisy and repression. We flatter ourselves at the spectacle of the Victorians' sexual mystifications. We *enjoy* the "repressive hypothesis" (Michel Foucault, 10) which seems to confirm our superior sexual enlightenment. Yet, it may be, that far from being the detectives of the Victorians' hidden *crimes passionnels*, we are, ourselves, the criminals; ourselves, the "Victorians." The theory of repression is one which depends on reducing the open possibilities of love to the closed meaning of sex.

Meanwhile, however, our own repression goes unnoticed. Having made no secret of sex, we have, perhaps, to invoke Foucault again (35), made a verbose and degraded secret of love. Sentimentalised, commercialised or simply ridiculed, love is, it may be, our own peculiarly obsessive taboo. We speak of it scornfully, guiltily or coyly. Yet, somehow, we do go on speaking about it. In all its debased and specific variations, love offers us still a possibility of meaning – a precarious idealism. It is, as Atwood concludes:

> a finger-
> grip on a cliffside. You can
> hold on or let go.
> (83)

Psychoanalytical and feminist discussions of love, while assimilating it into the Oedipal drama, on the one hand, or into the discourse of sexual politics, on the other, have also, often, felt something unaccounted for. Freud has influentially linked love with narcissism, but both Lacan and Kristeva have since wanted to loosen that connection. "The lover is a narcissist with an *object*" (250), Kristeva declares. Feminist critics, particularly in the early seventies, have been emphatic in denouncing the oppressive ideology of romantic love. Shulamith Firestone, for instance, asserts that "love, perhaps, even more than childbearing, is the pivot of women's oppression today" (142), and Kate Millett, similarly, dismisses love as no more than a pious Victorian excuse for "sexual activity" (37), particularly the sexual activity of women. Other feminist critics, however, have sought to distinguish love from the social and psychological inequalities which vitiate it. Love, for de Beauvoir, when "founded on the mutual recognition of two liberties" (677), might still be an ideal for the future. Thus, however much decried or explained, love continues to suggest something over and above the calculable power-structures of society or of the mind – something, perhaps, to be desired.

It is this superfluity of meaning which Roland Barthes celebrates in *A Lover's Discourse*. Rejecting the antagonistic or reductive descriptions of love in Christian, psychoanalytical and Marxist discourse (211), he turns, in his linguistic bereavement, to the language of imaginative literature. In particular, he turns to the wordy, profligate, posturing conventions of the literature of Sensibility. It is Goethe's *Werther* which, above all, offers innumerable examples of the discourse of love. Such a discourse, which indulgently "puts the sentimental in place of the sexual" (178) is, in fact, Barthes claims, the scandalous subject of today.

This reversal of priorities reiterates the principles of a long tradition. As Denis de Rougemont argues in *Love in the Western World*, romantic love, which is rooted in the courtly literature of the twelfth and thirteenth centuries, constantly resists its material expenditure in either sexual satisfaction or social final gratification. In that postponement, the lover finds time to speak. "Passion and expression are not really separable" (173), de Rougemont claims. Rather, it is a passion *for* expression which characterises romantic love. In this tradition, "the sentimental" does not aim to become "the sexual," but rather to postpone it.

Juliet Mitchell, in an essay on "Romantic Love," complains that de Rougemont generalises entirely from the experience of the male. The love of women is different, she claims. For, while man's love is "the poetic utterance of a free, aspiring subject," woman's love remains the "opiate of a trapped sexual object" (108). The trouble with this distinction, however, is that it confirms as an absolute the very difference it would condemn. Mitchell's assertion that the "romantic love of women looks forward, forward to marriage" (114) is one which seems to assign to women only the bourgeois domestication of love, and denies them its rebellious, imaginative energies. The evidence of women's literature, from the letters of Heloise to the poems of Adrienne Rich, tells a different story.

"Marriage in the abstract," Elizabeth Barrett Browning wrote to Miss Mitford in February 1846, at a time when her thoughts might well have been running on marriage, "has always seemed to me the most profoundly indecent of all ideas...." She adds: "I have always been called romantic for this way of seeing" (III, 160). It is one of the sad ironies of EBB's reputation as a poet that later generations have called her "romantic" for quite different reasons. She has gone down in literary history as the invalid poetess, who was swept off her couch, and rescued from a tyrannical father, by a charming poet with whom she eloped to Italy. As testimony to this eminently satisfying romance, she wrote, everyone knows, *one* poem: "How do I love thee? Let me count

the ways" (Sonnet XLIII). Many of EBB's most appreciative critics have found the *Sonnets from the Portuguese* something of a stumbling block. For instance, Alethea Hayter complains of having a "Peeping Tom sensation" (105) when reading the Sonnets, though, surprisingly, she never feels it when reading the "love letters" (106). Recent feminist critics, such as Gilbert and Gubar and Cora Kaplan, tend to pass over these ideologically unfashionable poems. Somehow, their subject and their inspiration, which lack the larger sexual politics *of Aurora Leigh*, strike contemporary critics as naked and naive. They are, it is said with wearying regularity, simply too "sincere."[1]

However, it may be that sincerity is an inhibition of our own expectations, rather than a fault of the poems. The story of the popular romance continues to overshadow our reading. But the emotional drama of the Sonnets has, in fact, little to do with a despotic father, an invalid daughter and a miraculous elopement. Instead, that drama is to be found in the close and self-conscious connection with the love letters – themselves a highly *written* text. It is as a literary performance, rather than an autobiographical statement, that I want to look again at the writing of these poems.

To read the Sonnets afresh, in conjunction with the letters, is to become aware of an intricately answering and over-wrought writing of love. In both poems and letters, sincerity of feeling is not so much the motivation as the point in question. The correspondence, which has been hailed as one of the great documents of romantic love, is in fact as prolix and literary as any other substitution of "the sentimental" for "the sexual." The passion of these letters is a passion of too many words, at odds with life and the heart's true feelings. For all their intimate wrangling, the general effect of the letters is of a highly constructed and self-referential piece of collaborative writing.

It is true that Robert's are the more contorted, defensive and equivocal letters. But the idea that Elizabeth was the inspirationally simpler and sincerer poet of the two reflects, as Daniel Karlin (52) points out, much more on Robert's need to idealise her than on any quality of her verse. She no more "communicates with godlike directness" (205) than he does. The *Sonnets from the Portuguese*, in particular, elaborate many of the anxieties of the letters about the possibility of communicating the heart's true feelings. The theatrical landscapes and stylised imagery of these poems distances them, strangely, from the real scene of love. Furthermore, there is a certain, quietly playful instability of reference in the Sonnets, which gives them an air of being very often only half serious.

> BELOVED, thou hast brought me many flowers
> Plucked in the garden, all the summer through
> And winter, and it seemed as if they grew
> In this close room, nor missed the sun and showers.
> So, in the like name of that love of ours,
> Take back these thoughts which here unfolded too,
> And which on warm and cold days I withdrew
> From my heart's ground. Indeed, those beds and bowers
> Be overgrown with bitter weeds and rue,
> And wait thy weeding; yet here's eglantine,
> Here's ivy! – take them, as I used to do
> Thy flowers, and keep them where they shall not pine.
> Instruct thine eyes to keep their colours true,
> And tell thy soul their roots are left in mine.
>
> (Sonnet XLIV)

As Elizabeth waited during those many months of courtship for Robert to visit her, or for his letters to arrive, she wrote the poems which she offered in return for all his flowers, but which she did not show him until three years after their marriage. However, it is not only his actual gifts of flowers which she remembers and requites in this last of her Sonnets, but also the many shared double meanings of flowers throughout the correspondence. Flowers are the connecting image of love and poetry, of passion and expression. The first gift was Robert's, in that opening letter with its extraordinarily direct declaration of literary esteem: "so into me has it gone, and part of me has it become, this great living poetry of yours, not a flower of which but took root and grew – oh how different that is from lying to be dried and pressed flat, and prized highly and put in a book…" (I, 3). Yet, of course, the having been "put in a book" is precisely the original tenor of these flowers, just as it will be their last in EBB's sonnet. Flowers begin as poems, "pressed flat and put in a book," and only later spring roots in the heart.

This opening gambit supplies both correspondents with a wealth of playful variations on the theme of flowers. In them, the usual priorities of what is lived and what is written are upset. Poetry, Elizabeth declares, "is the flower of me." She adds that "the rest of me is nothing but a root, fit for the ground and the dark" (I, 65). Between the flower and the root, between poems and life's "ground," there is a discrepancy; just as later, in the sonnet, there is a break between the flower's expression and the "heart's ground" from which it comes. These flowers, though once grounded, have been plucked. Obedient to her imagery, Robert repeats the idea: "this is all the flower of my life which you call forth and which lies at your feet" (I, 352). But the flower which is uprooted is not really life's; it is poetry's and love's. Robert tells her: "this is my first song, my true song – this love I bear you" (I, 352). Love is already the song, and the flower is already what it might become: a poem. For Elizabeth it did; and, as if in proof of what flowers might be, she returned, so many years later, her own small "anthology" of poems, which she had not yet dared "put in a book."

The play on flowers throughout the courtship offers a continual, delightful, metaphorical substitution of one thing for another: poems, flowers, life, love, memories, flowers and poems, again. The "ground" of these figurative transformations ought to be the heart, but it is just as often already a book of poems. Heart and book are subtly inter-changeable, as if in quiet acknowledgement of the fact that they were interchangeable at the start: "I love your verses with all my heart, dear Miss Barrett" (I, 3). This witty and self-conscious play on flowers, however, throws into dark relief that comment of Robert's, when he remembered how a "strange, heavy crown, that wreath of Sonnets (was) put on me one morning unawares" (*Robert Browning and Julia Wedgwood*, 114). Whether the "wreath" was one of laurels for her, or of death to himself, remains to be guessed.

The *Sonnets from the Portuguese* were published in 1850 and, as William Going has noted, they resuscitated an outworn genre (19). The amatory sonnet sequence, before the Victorian flowering of the form, was largely confined to the sixteenth century. It is, therefore, as Cynthia Grant Tucker points out, a "literary mode" clearly associated with "a bygone age," and riddled with "old generic postures and conventions" (353). One of these "generic postures" which the Victorians revived, for reasons that may have been socially contemporary as well as imagina-tively nostalgic, was that of the woman who waits. One particular poem, which stands at the threshold of the age, seems to have been profoundly influential in the recovery of this pose:

> All day within the dreamy house,
> The doors upon their hinges creak'd
> The blue fly sung in the pane; the mouse
> Behind the mouldering wainscot shriek'd,
> Or from the crevice peer'd about.
> Old faces glimmer'd thro' the doors,
> Old footsteps trod the upper floors,
> Old voices called her from without.
> She only said, "My life is dreary,

> He cometh not," she said;
> She said, "I am aweary, aweary,
> I would that I were dead!"
> (Tennyson, "Mariana," 90)

Tennyson's "Mariana" captures, not only the ennui of the woman's waiting, but also the pressure of a literary tradition behind that waiting. Only a woman could be so trapped in hopelessness. But at the same time, Mariana's is no more than an old literary pose – a waiting, in the courtly tradition, which is almost for its own sake. Tennyson's poem is ghostly with literariness. Not only is it a text, written on the inspiration of another text; but it also seems to want to go back in time to its literary original. The house suffers from the dilapidation of ages, and the past haunts its precincts in those "Old faces," "Old footsteps," "Old voices." The "dreamy house" is actually a house *of* dreams: from the antique. Although the atmosphere of courtly love is curiously decadent for the Victorian poet, and the passion of expectation somehow stale, the "old generic postures and conventions" are the same: Mariana waits.

Dorothy Mermin writes that a "woman poet who identified herself with such a stock figure of intense and isolated art would hardly be able to write at all" (68).[2] But this is not quite true. "I am like Mariana in the moated grange and sit listening too often to the mouse in the wainscot" (I, 87), Elizabeth informs Robert. The figure of Mariana offers her both a literally apt, and a subtly desirable, description of herself. "For have I not felt twenty times the desolate advantage of being insulated here and of not minding anybody when I made my poems?...and caring less for supposititious criticism than for the black fly buzzing in the pane?" (I, 263), she asks. Tennyson's imagery of fixation and distraction offers EBB, as it will Christina Rossetti, an eerily appropriate picture of herself. To be the maiden in the tower, the woman at the window, the dreamer in the prison, is to inhabit a literary tableau which is very close to the facts of life. Certainly, Elizabeth waited, and kept Robert waiting. Christina Rossetti made a life's work of waiting – and turned away any lovers who did come. Her poem "Day-Dreams" is "Mariana" from another, equally disconcerting, angle:

> Cold she sits through all my kindling,
> Deaf to all I pray:
> I have wasted might and wisdom,
> Wasted night and day:
> Deaf she dreams to all I say.
> ("Day-Dreams," 333)

It is as if these women poets sometimes choose to inhabit the "dreamy house" of Mariana, but with attention turned inwards to its poetic possibilities: to the "Old voices" which still echo in the ruined house of love. The "lover's discourse," Barthes claims, "is no more than a dust of figures stirring according to the unpredictable order, like a fly buzzing in a room" (197).

If the love poetry of the Victorians very often stirs "a dust of figures" from the antique, EBB's *Sonnets from the Portuguese*, which have by turns delighted or embarrassed readers for their sincerity, are certainly no exception.

> THOU hast thy calling to some palace-floor,
> Most gracious singer of high poems! where
> The dancers will break footing, from the care
> Of watching up thy pregnant lips for more.
> And dost thou lift this house's latch too poor
> For hand of thine? and canst thou think and bear
> To let thy music drop here unaware
> In folds of golden fulness at my door?
> Look up and see the casement broken in,
> The bats and owlets builders in the roof!
> My cricket chirps against thy mandolin.
> Hush, call no echo up in further proof
> Of desolation! there's a voice within
> That weeps...as thou must sing...alone, aloof.
>
> (Sonnet IV)

This is much more Mariana in the moated grange than it is EBB in Wimpole Street. The imagery of courtly luxury and mouldering decay belongs to a long tradition of romantic love, which the poet inhabits like the ruined house itself. She sits, picturesquely, amid a scene of desolation, listening, like her prototype Mariana, for the "lifted latch," and aware of too many echoes. The whole poem is a stage-setting of love in some "far countree" of the imagination. Singing, playing, dancing, weeping, are all decorous items of a drama self-distanced in time and feeling. It is this tapestried effect of the language which gives to the *Sonnets from the Portuguese* their atmosphere of a "bygone" passion. This is not a spontaneous, but a remembered and remote poetry of love, haunted by figures stirring from another time, another literature: "bats and owlets builders in the roof!"

However, at their best, these Sonnets also have a quietly discordant sense of humour. They are not just period pieces. "My cricket chirps against thy mandolin" is a welcome interruption of that too consistently "golden" music, attributed to Robert, the serenader. Thus the courtly or mythological imagery is frequently subjected to small witticisms and pranks of action. The moments when the instrument proves out of tune, angels collide, a god turns out to be a porpoise, the poet's hair is liable to catch fire, or a mystic shape draws the speaker familiarly "by the hair" – these are moments when the static iconography of courtly love is playfully disrupted, and the once immovable lady is caught up in a quite lively drama. It remains, however, a bookish drama, dependent on the written tangles of the letters, much more than on the actual events in Wimpole Street. The minstrels, princes, angels, palm trees and porpoises of these Sonnets belong to that rarefied, but fertile, drama of the correspondence, where the two poets find occasion to be both in love, and also practising for poems.

To fix the *Sonnets from the Portuguese* as an autobiographical record of a true romance is to miss their literary playfulness, their in-jokes, even, at times, their competitive ingenuity. But above all, it is to miss their sense of the other, remote, difficult language of love, which is inherited from a long-ago of literature, and which threatens to substitute its "Old voices" for the new; its flowers of poetry for real flowers. This is the danger, but also the "desolate advantage," of writing about love. Through the gruellingly *written* story of the letters and the Sonnets there is felt, in counterpoint to love's earnest, love's other language, which is separate, strange and insincere.

"As for me," Elizabeth writes at one point, "I have done most of my talking by post of late years – as people shut up in dungeons, take up with scrawling mottos on the walls" (I, 13). The scene of writing, for this woman poet, is the prison; so that, she suggests, all her letters will have the desperate and dissociated quality of a writing on the wall. This, already at the beginning, rejects Robert's idealisation of her as the poet of unmediated expression. Her woman's confinement means that all her writing will seem like vivid, but hardly decipherable, "mottos." Certainly, the experience of reading Elizabeth's letters must soon have disabused Robert of his idealising simplification. As he admits, he was frequently bewildered by her twists of logic. Often, she puts him "'in a maze'" (I, 474); he is jealous of her "infinite adroitness" (I, 533); he is beaten by her seeming to turn his "illustrations into obscurations" (I, 558); till, at one point, he turns on her almost violently, with the declaration: "Sometimes I have a disposition to dispute with dearest Ba, to wrench her simile-weapons out of the dexterous hand...and have the truth of things my way and its own way, not hers" (I, 562). This peevish insistence on the truth being his own betrays the extent to which Robert felt threatened by Elizabeth's own rhetoric. The "truth of things" is at risk in the very similes she wields so dexterously and combatively.

The quarrels of these lovers are not so much quarrels of feeling, as of etymologies and meanings. They censor each other's scripts, and cavil at each other's turns of phrase. They both, also, contend passionately to have the last word. "I *must* have last word," Robert insists, "as all people in the wrong desire to have – and then, no more of the subject" (I, 80). But immediately, Elizabeth makes her own claim to be last: "but suffer me to say as one other last word, (and *quite, quite the last this time!*)…" (I, 82). As each new dispute develops between them, the imposition of a last word continues to be laid down. "Therefore we must leave this subject – and I must trust you to leave it without one word more." She adds, with pointed vagueness, "too many have been said already" (I, 179). Too many words is the danger and the temptation of romantic love. Towards the end of the correspondence, Robert admits how often his letters have "run in the vile fashion of a disputatious 'last word', 'one word yet'" (II, 1058). Yet, the continuing drama of the last word was to prove a fecund source of poetry to him. The poem he wrote, years later, to thank Elizabeth for her Sonnets, affectionately recalls the contentious wordiness of the letters: it is "One Word More."

The literature of romantic love is always, in a sense, a word too many. Self-expression becomes its own goal. As de Rougemont puts it, romantic love "tends to self-description, either in order to justify or intensify its being, or else simply in order to keep *going*" (173). One word more is one more poem. Yet, this very creative resourcefulness of words risks being at odds with a sense of the truth. It is perhaps to Elizabeth that Robert ascribes the weary plea of that other poem of a last word, which recalls the furious verbalising of the letters. The speaker of "A Woman's Last Word" begs:

> Let's contend no more, Love,
> Strive nor weep:
> All be as before, love,
> – Only sleep!
>> ("A Woman's
>> Last Word", I, 539)

Love may be, on the one hand, a rhetoric of too many words, but, on the other hand, love also seeks to put an end to words altogether. "I love you because I *love* you" (I, 245), Robert insists, offering the redundancy of the logic as an emotional security. But such security is achieved at the cost of words. As Barthes puts it, "I love you because I love you" is a line that marks "the end of language, where it can merely repeat *its last word* like a scratched record" (21). Yet, a poem must be more than "a scratched record." There are times when Robert sounds trapped between the minimalist statement of love, which Elizabeth demands of him, and the one word more that must be written, if poems are to continue. "I turn from what is in my mind," he declares, "and determine to write about anybody's book to avoid writing that I love and love and love again my own, dearest love – because of the cuckoo-song of it" (I, 329).

When EBB attempts to write the "cuckoo-song," the reductive obviousness of it risks spoiling the poem:

> SAY over again, and yet once over again,
> That thou dost love me. Though the word repeated
> Should seem "a cuckoo-song," as thou dost treat it,
> Remember, never to the hill or plain,
> Valley and wood, without her cuckoo-strain
> Comes the fresh Spring in all her green completed.
> Belovèd, I, amid the darkness greeted
> By a doubtful spirit-voice, in that doubt's pain
> Cry, "Speak once more – thou lovest!" Who can fear
> Too many stars, though each in heaven shall roll,
> Too many flowers, though each shall crown the year?
> Say thou dost love me, love me, love me – toll
> The silver iterance! only minding, Dear,
> To love me also in silence with thy soul.
>
> (Sonnet XXI)

Between the silence of the soul and the poem's proliferating figures – between words which are not enough and those which are too much – the poet lover must negotiate a kind of truth. In this sonnet EBB fails to find it, perhaps for insisting too much on the "cuckoo-song" at the expense of a more playful rhetoric.

There is one delightful passage in a letter of Elizabeth's where she directly confronts the problem of living and loving so much in words. She is correcting Robert's "The Book of the Duchess" and is puzzled at having seemed to have lost a "bad line" which she cannot locate in the poem. She realises, with undisguised pleasure, that she must have written the line herself. "And so it became a proved thing to me," she relates, "that I had been enacting, in a mystery, both poet and critic together – and one so neutralizing the other, that I took all that pains you remark upon to cross myself out in my double capacity...and am now telling the story of it notwithstanding. And there's an obvious moral to the myth, isn't there? for critics who bark the loudest, commonly bark at their own shadow in the glass, as my Flush used to do long and loud...and as I did, under the erasure." She continues, irresistibly: "And another moral springs up of itself in this productive ground; for, you see...quand je m'efface il n'y a pas grand mal' " (I, 145).

In this fine piece of structuralism before its time, the "productive ground" of meaning is the act of writing itself. From that "productive ground" many flowers may grow, and many kinds of morals may spring. It is indeed a fertile origin. Thus, as Elizabeth cancels her own line, she also cancels herself, her face in the mirror, her role as critic and her role as bad poet. But, in the end, as she gaily tells, someone is left over from all the cancellations, to tell "the story of it notwithstanding." Out of a "bad line" she spins a good tale, and out of her self-effacement she irresistibly pursues the proliferating figures of a game of words. In any case, one might ask, what was she doing *writing* in Robert's poem?

"'Quand je m'efface il n'y a pas grand mal.'" The lover's discourse, according to Barthes, "proceeds from others, from the language, from books." He concludes, "no love is original" (136). The "dreamy house" is haunted by other voices. The text of feeling has been written already. This *déjà vu*, or rather, *déjà écrit*, inevitably turns the lover's passion into a pose; the lover's poem into another, older one. Feeling suffers the anxiety of having been preempted by literature.

The innumerable references to other texts in the letters, as well as the innumerable self-references to the act of writing, bear witness to this pressure. For instance, it is not only Tennyson's "Mariana" which supplies a figure of love, but also EBB's own poem "Catarina to Camoens." Catarina was the courtly lady loved by the poet Camoens, but she died while waiting for him to return from his long travels. The poem is the last and only word of one who experienced love so entirely in the "sentimental" that all she experienced was a set of lovely phrases. As she repeats the line from one of Camoens' own songs: "'Sweetest eyes were ever seen!'" (3, 124), she wonders what use to her either the sweetness of her eyes, or the sweetness of his poem, will be, once she is dead.

Sonnets from the Portuguese, as is well known, is the title that was suggested by Robert, as a disguise. It hints at a translation – specifically, it hints at Camoens, some of whose works had been translated by Felicia Hemans, and who was well known to the Victorian public in

Strangford's translation as well. The title thus serves as a distraction from the autobiographical origins of the Sonnets. But the title hints at Camoens by way of EBB's own, very popular, "Catarina to Camoens." In a sense, therefore, "from the Portuguese" means, not only from Camoens, but also from Catarina – the woman who waited, to no avail. Like Christina Rossetti, in her *Monna Innominata* sonnets, EBB seems to speak from the generic pose of the unknown lady of the courtly tradition – anonymous and foreign – whose indefinitely postponed love becomes the occasion for poems instead. The title thus stresses the effect of distance, in time and place, which the language of the poems themselves underlines.

That the *Sonnets from the Portuguese* take their place in a long, self-conscious tradition of literary writing about love is also suggested by one other possible connotation of the title. In 1678, there appeared in English translation a series of five letters, written allegedly by a Portuguese nun to her unfaithful lover. The *Portuguese Letters*,[3] as they were known, started a vogue for writing "à la portuguaise," – in a style of declamatory despair which later became the stock-in-trade of the literature of Sensibility. Through the posturing rhetoric of the nun's grief there runs a vein of almost self-satisfied achievement. "And it is not your Person neither that is so dear to me," she asserts, "but the Dignity of my unalterable Affection" (17). It is in the cause of love alone, that she is driven to tell "at every turn how my Pulse beats" (21). That the Portuguese Letters were probably fictitious, and not written by a nun at all, only makes them the more characteristic of a literature in which feeling is a matter of fine words, and truth a matter of convention. The very name of the nun is resonantly premonitory of that most stereotypical name in the literature of Sensibility: "Ah wretched *Mariane!*" (5) she exclaims.

Thus the title, *Sonnets from the Portuguese*, is one that teases with a wealth of literary connotations. It proposes a translation; it remembers another poem; it echoes, perhaps, the highly literary disposition of the Portuguese nun herself. However, the sense of derivativeness – the sense of a text remembering some other original – is a connotation which finds support, not only in these specific references, but also in a recurring anxiety about the language of feeling, expressed in the letters of both poets. The "dust of figures stirring" in the title of *Sonnets from the Portuguese* is not just a dust flung in the eyes of "Peeping Tom" readers. It is not just a decoy. It is also a quiet revelation. The idea of translation – of mediating what is remote and foreign – of writing at a distance from the original – is an idea that finds considerable support in certain preoccupations of both Robert's and Elizabeth's letters.

Elizabeth's early descriptions of herself as a prisoner "scrawling mottos, on the walls," with its admission of a displaced intensity and of an alienated sensibility, is one which then gathers a cluster of related images in the course of the correspondence. Taking her cue, at first, from Robert's unnerving declarations of having a double nature, Elizabeth gradually recognises the same doubleness in herself. Far from being the prototype of the inspirationally direct poet, she too knew the discrepant passage from consciousness to writing, from love to love poetry. That Robert also eventually recognised this equivalent obliquity in *her* work is perhaps revealed by one of those characteristically answering images between the letters and the poems. Near the start of the correspondence, Elizabeth acknowledges that all Robert's verse is a dramatic displacement of himself: "your rays fall obliquely rather than directly straight," she admits, and adds, humbly, "I see you only in your moon" (I, 22). This sense of the moon, as the indirect reflector of light, is remembered, and returned, perhaps, in that resonant line from "One Word More," where Robert calls Elizabeth: "my moon of poets!" (I, 742). She too, he seems to admit, has her unknown, dark side, and her own mediations of the light.

The idea that feeling is often refracted, and expression mediated, is one which finds a recurring description in the letters. After Elizabeth returned that first, over-enthusiastic letter of Robert's, in which, it seems, he declared his feelings for her too impetuously or fulsomely, he retaliated by assuring her, in his reply, that she had mistaken both him and his intentions. Cruelly driving the message home, he stressed that there were "huge layers of ice and pits of black cold water" in his character, and that those were his "true part" (I, 74). Elizabeth was haunted by the implications of this simile for years. At the time, however, she answered with unaggrieved dignity: "Well – if I do not know you, I shall learn, I suppose, in time. I am ready to try humbly to learn – and I may perhaps – if you are not done in Sanscrit, which is too hard for me" (I, 79). A little later, in her frustration at being idealised out of her own true nature, she retorted with a similar image, and begged Robert to "determine to read me no more backwards with your Hebrew, putting in your own vowel points without my leave" (I, 87). He, in his turn, jumped at the opportunity offered by her mis-reading and mis-correcting one of his poems: "So you can decypher my *utterest* hieroglyphic?" (I, 153) he mocked, hinting again that the language of his true self might be indecipherable.

The idea of the illegible script, the strange text, the foreign language, frequently has a double reference, to the heart and to the book, to the

329

self and the poem. Reading and writing thus become the primary gestures of love's drama, subject to all the tricky and deceptive calligraphies of the heart. The difficulty of knowing the true from the false, the sincere from the convention, the familiar from the foreign, is a dilemma exacerbated by the very verbal nature of romantic love. The more the difference is insisted on, the more elusive does it become. Thus, even as Robert expresses his ambition to write the perfectly self-expressive, unmediated text – "'R.B. a poem'" (I, 17) – he is frustrated by the difference between the two. The self does not translate easily into poetry. For when he reads "the language" of himself to himself, he reads a "spiritual Attic" (I, 38), communicable to none.

But it is not only Robert who defensively distances himself in doubleness and foreignness. The same split is felt by Elizabeth. When, towards the end of *Aurora Leigh*, Romney enthusiastically claims to have understood her at last, after reading her poems, Aurora answers curtly:

> You have read
> My book, but not my heart; for recollect,
> 'Tis writ in Sanscrit, which you bungle at.
> (*Aurora Leigh*, VIII, 475–7)

That "recollect" goes all the way back to the letters, and is Elizabeth's pointed response to the fear that Robert himself was "done in Sanscrit."

Thus, the idea that the language of the heart is hard to learn, easily misunderstood, dauntingly foreign, is one that runs through the letters. Such a language is likely to be archaic and difficult – perhaps permanently beyond reach. Elizabeth might assure Robert that "you could turn over every page of my heart like the pages of a book" (I, 274–5), but she cannot promise that the language in which the book is written will be understood. The evidence of many of the letters is that it will not. For if "writ in Sanscrit," it is "too hard." It will remain untranslatable.

The language of romantic love, even when written in the heart, is a language likely to be foreign, strange, dead. It is written already, out of old codes, old conventions, old poems, perhaps. The difficulty of making it legible again is the constant anxiety of the lover poet. To write about love, originally and uniquely, might be, in fact, to engage in an act of translation. "I have done some work," Elizabeth responds evasively, "only it is nothing worth speaking of…lyrics for the most part, which lie written illegibly in pure AEgyptian" (I, 145). Her own suggested title for the Sonnets is only another obstructively remote and puzzling derivation to add to all these others: "from the Bosnian" she proposed.

This, then, is the troubling legacy of romantic love. It is the legacy, not of an original passion, but of an old language; not of a sincere feeling, but of a poem. The literature of romantic love, even as it seeks to be the heart's expression, is likely to be something else: mottos, hieroglyphs, Sanscrit, Hebrew, Attic, AEgyptian, Bosnian: – a "dust of figures." To these one must add the distant, literary, untranslated derivation of EBB's own love Sonnets: "from the Portuguese."

Notes

1 For two exceptions, see Dorothy Mermin, "The Female Poet and the Embarrassed Reader: Elizabeth Barrett Browning's *Sounds from the Portuguese*," *English Literary History*, 48 (1981), 351–67, and Angela Leighton, *Elizabeth Barrett Browning* (Brighton, Harvester, 1986), chapter five.
2 Dorothy Mermin, "The Damsel, the Knight, and the Victorian Woman Poet," *Critical Inquiry*, 13 (1986), 64–80.
3 I am grateful to a member of the audience at the "Victorians and Love" conference, April 1987, for directing me towards these.

Bibliography

Atwood, Margaret, *True Stories* (London, Jonathan Cape, 1982).
Barrett Browning, Elizabeth, *Aurora Leigh*, intro. Cora Kaplan (London, The Women's Press, 1983).
—— *The Complete Works of Elizabeth Barrett Browning*, 6 vols., ed. Charlotte Porter and Helen A. Clarke (New York, Thomas Y. Crowell, 1900).
—— *The Letters of Elizabeth Barrett Browning to Mary Russell Mitford: 1836–1854*, 3 vols, ed. Meredith B. Raymond and Mary Rose Sullivan (New York, The Browning Institute and Wellesley College, 1983).
—— *The Letters of Robert Browning and Elizabeth Barrett Barrett: 1845–1846*, 2 vols., ed. Elvan Kintner (Cambridge, Mass., Harvard University Press, 1969).
Barthes, Roland, *A Lover's Discourse: Fragments*, trans. Richard Howard (New York, Hill and Wang, 1978).
Browning, Robert, *The Poems*, 2 vols., ed. John Pettigrew, supplemented and completed by Thomas J. Collins (Harmondsworth, Penguin, 1981).
—— *Robert Browning and Julia Wedgwood*, ed. R. Curle (London, John Murray, 1937).
de Beauvoir, Simone, *The Second Sex*, trans. H.M. Parshley (Harmondsworth, Penguin, 1972).

de Rougemont, Denis, *Love in the Western World*, trans. Montgomery Belgion, revised and augmented edition (Princeton, N.J., Princeton University Press, 1983).

Firestone, Shulamith, *The Dialectic of Sex: The Case for Feminist Revolution* (1970; revised edition New York, Bantam, 1972).

Foucault, Michel, *The History of Sexuality*, vol. I, trans. Robert Hurley (Harmondsworth, Penguin, 1981).

Gilbert, Sandra M. and Gubar, Susan, *The Madwoman in the Attic: The Woman Writer and the Nineteenth-Century Literary Imagination* (New Haven and London, Yale University Press, 1979).

Going, William, *Scanty Plot of Ground: Studies in the Victorian Sonnet* (The Hague, Mouton, 1976).

Hayter, Alethea, *Mrs Browning: A Poet's Work and its Setting* (London, Faber, 1962).

Karlin, Daniel, *The Courtship of Robert Browning and Elizabeth Barrett* (Oxford, Oxford University Press, 1987).

Kristeva, Julia, "Freud and Love: Treatment and Its Discontents," in *The Kristeva Reader*, ed. Toril Moi (Oxford, Blackwell, 1986).

Leighton, Angela, *Elizabeth Barrett Browning* (Brighton, Harvester Press, 1986).

Mermin, Dorothy, "The Damsel, the Knight, and the Victorian Woman Poet," *Critical Inquiry*, 13 (1986), 64–80.

—— "The Female Poet and the Embarrassed Reader: Elizabeth Barrett Browning's *Sonnets from the Portuguese*," *English Literary History*, 48 (1981), 351–67.

Millett, Kate, *Sexual Politics* (London, Virago, 1977).

Mitchell, Juliet, "Romantic Love," in *Women: The Longest Revolution* (London, Virago, 1984).

The Portuguese Letters, in *The Novel in Letters: Epistolary Fiction in the Early English Novel 1678–1740*, ed. Natascha Wurzbach (London, Routledge & Kegan Paul, 1969), 3–21.

Rossetti, Christina, *The Poetical Works of Christina Georgina Rossetti*, ed. William Michael Rossetti (London, Macmillan, 1928).

Tennyson, Alfred, *The Poems of Tennyson*, ed. Christopher Ricks (London, Longmans, 1969).

Tucker, Cynthia Grant, "Meredith's Broken Laurel: *Modern Love* and the Renaissance Sonnet Tradition," *Victorian Poetry*, 10 (1972), 351–65.

18

'Love, let us be true to one another'
Matthew Arnold, Arthur Hugh Clough, and 'our Aqueous Ages'

Joseph Bristow

I

Few would argue with the claim that Matthew Arnold's 'Dover Beach' stands as the paradigmatic Victorian poem where the burden of the literary past weighs heavily on each and every anxious line. Caught in the 'Wordsworthian matrix' analyzed by U. C. Knoepflmacher,[1] this elegaic lyric revises its chief precursor to such a strenuous degree that it provides an ideal example for a canonical criticism interested in the waning of vatic authority during the mid-nineteenth century. Invoking not only Wordsworth's poems about the feared invasion of Napoleon at Dover in 1803, but also concentrating its attention on Sophoclean tragedy, Arnold's speaker finds himself engulfed by 'the turbid ebb and flow/Of human misery' (16–17).[2] The poem moves between celebrating a universal model of human tragedy and engaging with a particular understanding of several of the most urgent social and political upheavals of the late 1840s. In one respect, this restless tidal movement enacts a recursive pattern of disaster where the military ambitions of Louis Napoleon III, in reviving those of his uncle, extend both the Oedipal tragedies of Sophocles and the benighted Battle of Epipolae

Bristow, Joseph. 1995. "'Love, let us be true to one another': Matthew Arnold, Arthur Hugh Clough and 'our Aqueous Ages.'" In *Literature and History*, series 3, 4, I (Spring), pp. 27–49. Reproduced with permission of Manchester University Press.

Victorian Poets: A Critical Reader, First Edition. Edited by Valentine Cunningham.
© 2014 John Wiley & Sons, Ltd. Published 2014 by John Wiley & Sons, Ltd.

recorded in Thucydides' *History of the Peloponnesian War*. But, in another sense, the speaker's anguish derives from his acknowledgement of an immediate crisis in the Christian world. His eagerness to join with the ranks of Sophocles and Wordsworth – exemplary figures from the ancient and modern periods respectively – emerges from the loss of religious faith in Victorian Britain. Horace Mann's 'Report on the Religious Census' (1851) counts among the best-known works from this period that expressed alarm at the millions of working-class non-attendants at church services. So in Arnold's poem we discover what E. D. H. Johnson influentially calls the 'alien vision of Victorian poetry',[3] and it is fair to say that 'Dover Beach' condenses a typically mid-nineteenth century set of fears that may be quickly identified in many poems by his contemporaries. Generally regarded, then, as a pre-eminent representative for his age, Arnold's saddened speaker discloses that his nostalgic longing for contact with the glories of the past is built upon his perception of spiritual abandonment in the present.

It is fair to say that this account of 'Dover Beach' sums up the traditional view of the central place and high status enjoyed by this poem within English literary history. Yet the immense amount of critical attention bestowed upon this famous work has turned it into a monument that represents the most pressing intellectual issues, not just of the mid-Victorian period, but also those of modern liberal humanists who identify in this poem a voice that speaks to a form of universal experience where love promises to mend the ruptures of historical change. Small wonder, then, that 'Dover Beach' serves as Gerald Graff's main example for staging his debate about the transformed climate which subverted many of the longstanding orthodoxies of English studies in the 1980s. Explicating the recent conflicts between traditional and oppositional approaches to the Western tradition, Graff plays off the remonstrations of an Older Male Professor (who claims that 'Dover Beach' concerns 'universal human experience') against those of the Young Feminist Professor (who complains of Arnold's 'phallocentric discourse').[4] My concern here, however, is not to allot the poem to either of the camps that Graff schematically opposes against one another. Although my interest lies instead in the sexual ebbs and flows of this and several other poems both by Arnold and by his close friend, Arthur Hugh Clough, the evidence supplied by the works of both poets suggests that masculine desire at this time is neither masquerading as universal nor presenting itself as solely or assuredly phallic. In their writing, masculinity is in an intensely conflicted state. If one question vexes their poetry more than anything else, it is that same-sex comradeship and sexual love for women have rival claims on the affections of their male protagonists. Numerous passages from some of Arnold's and Clough's best-known lyrics and narrative poems disclose that the transition from the fraternal support offered by their public-school (Rugby) and then Oxonian (Balliol) undergraduate community to taking the hand of a woman in marriage was fraught with anxiety, not least because the anticipated pattern of their lives was at this time being disrupted by very rapid alterations in the class structure.

Like many young Victorian men who found themselves at a loss when coming to terms with main upheavals of the 1840s – the pan-European revolutions, the religious agnosticism pervading British culture, and the potential turmoil promised by Chartism – Arnold and Clough developed their intellectual life in an atmosphere of disappointment and uncertainty. As Arnold informed his mother, after attending a Chartist rally at Kennington Green, he 'should be sorry to live under their government'.[5] In this respect, since his speaker feels overtaken by the pace of history, Arnold makes in 'Dover Beach' a characteristic move to resist its onward march towards democracy. Gazing towards the retreating 'Sea of Faith' (21), his speaker finally appeals to the redemptive spirit of love. What has been until line 28 a solitary voice gains in rhetorical confidence when it locates another presence directly in its midst: 'Ah, love', he declares, 'let us be true/ To one another' (29–30). Like Wordsworth, notably in 'Tintern Abbey' – a poem that provides the template for several of Arnold's lyrics – this persona shifts his attention away from universal musings to the implied auditor of his noble thoughts. She is the woman – like Wordsworth's unnamed but implied sister, Dorothy – with whom he wishes to share 'the world, which seems/ To lie before us like a land of dreams' (30–31). Moral resolution and poetic closure are only possible when the silent woman's assumed reciprocity to his desires has been addressed. These culminative sections amount, according to Park Honan, to 'the most deeply felt seventeen lines ever written by a modern poet'.[6] But, more specifically, they also express – as a number of lines warily disclose – thwarted sexual desires. His meditation upon Sophocles and Wordsworth may be read as the confused outpourings of an intellectual who is not at all well-practised in the art of seduction, and whose discomfort with women is more than a little evident.

One later poet, together with several commentators on the poem, makes exactly this point. 'Dover Beach' proved memorable enough in 1960 for Anthony Hecht to write a swingeing parody of Arnold's high seriousness. Hecht's unamusing title, 'The Dover Bitch: a Criticism of

Life', lays bare the sexual subtext to be discerned in Arnold's revealing metaphors for religious belief. In 'Dover Beach', the 'Sea of Faith/… once… /Lay like the folds of a bright girdle furled' around the earth (21–23). The 'shingles', too, are conspicuously 'naked' (28). There is, in the light of these displaced sexual interests, something coyly Victorian about the repressiveness of this brief poem whose plaintive tones may be thought to linger on a sense of post-coital triste (notably, the 'melancholy, long, withdrawing roar' [25]). 'Dover Beach', therefore, may be viewed as a failed prelude in courtship, since the elegaic tone hints at an unconsummated relationship for where the speaker's displays of erudition would appear to be compensating for his sexual inadequacy. With this point in mind, Lionel Trilling and Harold Bloom assert that Arnold 'is too ready to ascribe his own failure of nerve, erotically speaking, to a larger crisis in the history of culture'.[7] Compounding various kinds of failure, then, 'Dover Beach' has a distinguished place in the cultural consciousness – for its post-Romantic sense of belatedness, for the manner in which it bears witness to a fading Christianity, and for its inhibited sexual energies. Yet the 'love' named in the penultimate section of Arnold's poem is not necessarily the 'bitch' of Hecht's invention who 'had read/ Sophocles in a fairly good translation'.[8] I want to argue that it could also be the kind of man who was versed in the ancient Greek of the original. And, furthermore, I wish to show how this poem is one among several by Arnold and by Clough that points to some of the most problematic tensions within the ascendant ideology of 'separate spheres' for men and women.

For 'separate spheres' was from the outset a doctrine that contained the seeds of its own subversion. Although proponents of this system of moral conduct, which came into its own in the late 1830s, insisted that 'woman's mission' was to be subordinate to men, they none the less laid a significant emphasis on woman's superior position, since it was she who was protected from a transforming industrial world where corruption was perceptibly rife. In domestic seclusion, so this argument went, women were unsullied by the everyday hardships of the public realm. It comes as no surprise that writers such as Sarah Lewis and Sarah Stickney Ellis would champion the capacity of women to maintain stability in the home, seeing women's role as a morally regenerative one. In his review of Ellis's influential manual on women's duty, A. W. Kinglake observed that he could not help but 'look at works written by women upon the science of domestic government with a kind of good-humored suspicion… by saying that they make us remember that treatise on horsemanship which the tailor detected as having decidedly come from the pen of the chestnut mare.' It is, above all, Ellis's claim that 'England, as a nation, has little to boast of beyond her intellectual and her moral power' to which Kinglake most forcefully objects. For such an assertion, he claims, fails to observe that 'England...is illustrious by force of her arms.'[9] Kinglake is, in other words, implying that Ellis's patriotic zeal elevates the feminine moral and regenerative principle at the expense of ignoring the masculine one enshrined in the nation's military prowess. In this respect, 'woman's mission' could appear to be staked on very false claims indeed. Commenting on the supreme moral authority ascribed to women by Ellis and Lewis, Judith Newton observes that such writers 'in their tendency to place men at the bottom of industrial capitalist and domestic ills and in their tendency to isolate women like themselves as social heroes, challenged the power relations of their world and in the process entertained a view of mid-nineteenth-century society which middle-class men, by and large, did not share'. But, as Newton's passing comments on Arnold's 'The Buried Life' demonstrate, the female presence that haunts the closing lines of that poem signals that he was only too aware of the increased moral influence exerted by middle-class women at this time. She notes that this alteration in gender relations occurred at a time when 'Classical liberal and middle-class ideology were undergoing a shift.' It was, she argues, a period in which a 'series of booms and depressions sharpened the edge of class conflict'.[10] Scholarly young men, to say the least, were feeling more and more embattled, and their sense of dispossession frequently sounds throughout the poetry of this time. In the strained friendship between Arnold and Clough, we can see for sure how the university-educated poet was torn between his Oxonian loyalties and his desire for a consoling form of femininity. The main trouble for these men was that middle-class women increasingly appeared to have greater moral influence than the post-Romantic poet could readily assert for himself.

The purpose of this essay, therefore, is to consider how poems such as 'Dover Beach' demonstrate why the need for a scholarly community (enshrined in Sophocles, Wordsworth, and Thucidydes) is wholly incommensurate with another 'love' that could – I will argue – be either male or female. Although numerous studies suggest that 'Dover Beach' was written as a tribute to Arnold's wife, Frances Lucy Wightman, during their deferred honeymoon in 1851, there was another 'love' whose presence haunts, if not the 'naked shingles', then the 'Sea of Faith' itself. The 'love' invited to 'Come to the window' (6) and 'Listen' to the 'grating roar/ Of pebbles' could not so implausibly be Clough.

For Clough notoriously declined to subscribe to the Thirty-Nine Articles, and so resigned his fellowship at Oriel College, Oxford. In making this suggestion, I am not trying to concoct a previously unknown homoeroticism between Arnold and Clough – although there was, without doubt, an intense intimacy between them. Instead, my discussion focuses on the pronounced antagonism between same-sex affections and other-sex desires historically situated in what one of Clough's protagonists calls 'our Aqueous Ages'.[11] This is, metaphorically, a time of fluidity that alludes to two closely related things. The 'Aqueous Ages' signal change from enjoying the independent life of a bachelor to becoming a respectable married man. They also point to that wider sphere of social and political changes anatomized in each succeeding clause of 'Dover Beach'.

It is hard not to notice how water saturates the poetry of both Arnold and Clough, either centrally or on its receding margins. Attending to the predominant metaphors of Arnold's lyrics, William A. Madden asserts that this writer may be described temperamentally as a 'poet of water'.[12] From 'The Forsaken Merman' to the six short poems comprising the 'Marguerite' sequence, the all-encompassing tide figures as a realm of inestimable loss. On a similar note, Robindra Kumar Biswas celebrates the 'great sea' as 'that subtle and profound symbol of bewilderment, indeterminacy, flux, and chance which dominates' Clough's work.[13] This snared metaphorical resource, however, is frequently associated with the threatening – if not alienating – presence of women. Yet rarely have critics explored the complexity of the sexual meanings that are carried on the cross-currents of the tides, streams, and rivers that ebb, flow, and course through these poets' works. Only in Tony Pinkney's study of Arnold's Northern seas is there a critical account of the gendered troubles figured by the tidal movements of these writings.[14] Pinkney's project is to demonstrate that this sea is the medium incorporating – or, better, sublimating – the repressed 'other' of Arnold's paranoid classicism. He is, in other words, saying that the sea – so frequently associated with the Goths' violent sacking of Rome – connotes a degrading and anarchic physicality against which Arnold would later pitch his belief in culture. This subversive Gothic element, argues Pinkney, frequently unleashes its repressions, and the thickening medium it condenses takes the form of a fearful and unapproachable femininity. What Pinkney calls the 'oceanic', however, is not solely Arnold's problem. The poetry of both Arnold and Clough discloses acute conflicts within male homosocial desire whenever they draw on these highly manipulable oceanic images.

But Arnold's and Clough's shared concern with their 'Aqueous Ages' should not obscure the fact that they were writing almost entirely opposed kinds of poetry. The differences of style, technique, and philosophical outlook that lie between them point to one of the major divisions in middle-class poetic practice in the late 1840s and 1850s. Their 'love' was unquestionably structured around a passionate disagreement about the role and function of poetry. In this respect, Arnold's correspondence to Clough, and Clough's 1853 review of Arnold's *Poems* count among the most significant documents for comprehending a more widespread crisis in mid-Victorian poetry. The strongly felt lack of consensus about what a poem should be led to forms of experimentation that gave rise to such new phenomena as the 'persona' – the antecedent of the modernist 'mask'. Such transformations in the genre also meant that critical debates about poetry became intensely politicized. For Arnold and Clough, the antithetical nature of their respective poetic practices was so great that it became a decisive factor in the eventual collapse of their friendship. But, as their writings reveal, there was another reason why they had to forgo their love for one another. For in poetry they found a kind of fluidity that they often figured in feminine – or, more precisely, feminized – terms. They plunged the depths of a potentially volatile medium where objects of desire and poetic ideals repeatedly failed to coalesce. The genre in which they worked was, in a sense, militating against their gender.

II

So, first of all, it is useful to examine the basis of these poets' Oxonian 'love' for one another. In the years immediately following their graduation, Arnold's impassioned attachment to Clough could not have been more effusive. 'Dover Beach' echoes the intimate salutations of Arnold's warmest letters to the friend to whom he had 'clung...more in spirit than to any other man'.[15] In 1848, when Clough was in Liverpool composing *The Bothie of Toper-Na-Fuosich* – to give it its first and, as it turned out, sexually embarrassing title[16] – Arnold concluded one letter with sentences to which 'Dover Beach', according to Isobel Armstrong, bears more than a passing resemblance:[17]

> Farewell, my love, to meet I hope at Oxford: not alas in heaven: tho' thus much I cannot but think: that our spirits retain their conquests: that from the height they succeed in raising themselves to, they can never fall. Tho: this uti

possetedes principle may be compatible with entire loss of individuality and of the power to recognize one another. Therefore, my well-known love, accept my heartiest greeting and farewell.[18]

The whole letter is full of amatory declarations of this kind: 'my duck...my love...my well-known love'. Yet if the spirited intimacy of this extract is clear, the selfsame closeness of this friendship consigns some of Arnold's references to secrecy. In part, the compressed grammar is to blame for these obscurities. Although the gist of this passage is that he hopes that their friendship will last forever, the allusion to the 'uti possetedes principle' makes for some confusion. In Arnold's subjunctive declension, it translates as an esoteric 'as if you were to possess principle'; more conventionally, as 'uti possitedes', it refers to an 'as you possess principle'. Either way, the probable object of this principle of possession is Clough, and in the broader context of the letter the desire to lose individuality and recognize another person – here, presumably, his friend – is lodged against a wholehearted disappointment in women.

For these remarks come immediately after ten lines of mock-heroic verse invented by Arnold himself that disparage the female sex. 'Say this of her', Arnold writes in a commanding tone, 'The day was, thou wert not: the day will be, / Thou wilt be most unlovely'. These misogynistic remarks append an earlier comment where he declares on his tiredness with reading in French the 'fade' – that is, tasteless or insipid – Béranger, and that his exhaustion with this writer compares with a 'feeling with regard to (I hate the word) women'. As he states in the poem he has just penned, Béranger's Epicureanism and femininity shall suffer exactly the same kind of 'abhorred decay'. So, taken together, the reference to Oxford, the sexual hostility of his mock-heroic verse, and his desire to be 'in Heaven' with his friend demonstrate only too clearly how their 'love' for each other rests on a bed of disapproval towards women: such beings are too predictable by far, and so prove tiresome. It is altogether preferable to indulge in latinized banter with another university-educated man. One of Arnold's better-known comments strengthens this point. The promixity of these sexually volatile declarations to Arnold's later invective against Charlotte Brontë's *Villette* (1853) is hardly accidental. He found this novel, which stakes an urgent claim on woman's professional autonomy, to be 'one of the most utterly disagreeable books I ever read – and having seen her makes me more so'.[19] (Brontë, it is worth noting, thought Arnold insincere in his charm.)[20]

Arnold's letters to Clough are not usually cited for their same-sex interests. They are instead deployed to uphold two different axioms about his own and Clough's work. The first is to show how his unceasing revulsion with his age, in which he diagnosed a stifling *'congestion of the brain'*[21], extends his far-reaching dissatisfaction with the culture of mid-century which he bemoans at length in the Preface to his 1853 volume of *Poems*. (There Arnold famously writes: 'The confusion of the present times is great, the multitude of voices counselling different things bewildering', and so on.)[22] Second, these letters are often taken as evidence of how Clough's career was marked by failure and inconsistency. 'You ask me', writes Arnold 'in what I think or have thought you going wrong', and then elaborates this view: 'you…could never finally, as it seemed – "resolve to be thyself" – but were looking for this and that experience, and doubting whether you ought not to adopt this or that mode of being persons qui ne vous valaient pas [whom you do not value] because it might possibly be nearer the truth than your own'. This assessment of Clough's unfulfilled vocation – which Arnold concludes with a self-aggrandizing reference to his own poem, 'Self-Dependence' – concludes with this crushing judgement: 'You have I am convinced lost infinite time in this way'. Such reproving statements must without doubt have contributed to the impairment of their 'love'.

Clough's career after Rugby would indeed appear not to have realized its promise. He failed to excel in his degree and then, several years later, resigned his Oxford fellowship. The life he spent in successive posts – as head of University Hall, London; as tutor in Cambridge, Massachusetts; and, finally, as Education Officer in London – may have diminished what brief amounts of time he devoted during his vacations to writing poetry. Yet Arnold found little to praise in the substantial canon of work that Clough produced on his holidays. Arnold declared that Clough's second volume, *Ambarvalia*, was 'not *natural'*.[23] These sentiments may look odd when Arnold's intense 'love' is taken into consideration. Yet the more one examines Arnold's letters the more it seems that his investment in this friendship was driven by energies that Clough could not return in kind: *'pray* remember', he charges his friend, 'that I am and always shall be, whatever I do or say, powerfully attracted towards you…I am linked for ever with you by intellectual bonds – the strongest of all: more than you are with me'.[24] Arnold's fierce admiration for Clough is constantly matched by his blighted hopes in this idol of his Oxford days. 'I do not think', he writes in 1853, 'that we did each other harm at Oxford. I look back to that time with pleasure'.[25]

Although Clough's replies to Arnold are not extant, the significance of this friendship to him emerges in a letter to Tom Arnold, dated May 1851. There Clough states that he 'consider[s] Miss Wightman a sort of natural enemy'. 'How can it be otherwise?' he asks, 'shall I any longer breakfast with Matt twice a week?'[26] By comparison, in his own correspondence with his fiancée, Blanche Smith, Clough's trepidation in making the transition from being a bachelor to a married man comes to the fore. More than anything else, he implores her not to expect a marriage modelled on the commonplace maxims of 'separate spheres' for men and women:

> I ask no girl to be my friend that we may be a fond foolish couple together all in all to each other. If one that has dreamt of such unreality will open her eyes and look about her and consent to be what alone in plain fact she can be, a help-mate – that is a different thing…We are companions – fellow labourers – to the end of our journey here.[27]

Marriage, he implies, should enshrine the fellowship that he and Arnold enjoyed in former times. Yet, as his later letters to Blanche Smith indicate, he would eventually capitulate to the orthodoxies of the day. For there she figures as his helpless little girl whom he continues to infantilize. The point is that in the late 1840s Clough was trying to create a vision of an alternative femininity, and the sentiments he expresses here connect directly with the scheme of social and sexual relations laid out in the *Bothie*. In this poem, the arch-radical Philip Hewson marries a Highland lassie, Elspie Mackaye. She embodies qualities that several readers thought made her a most inappropriate partner for a young Oxford graduate like Hewson.[28] Their liaison not surprisingly gave offence to some reviewers of a poem that possessed a brazenly arresting mixture of student jargon and experimental hexameters. Elspie is the kind of labouring woman who, 'uprooting potatoes' (II. 5), fires Hewson's imagination, and their future exists in New Zealand where 'hath he farmstead and land, and fields of corn and flax fields' (IX. 200). There they promise to live out a life where Elspie is the newly-born Eve – the 'sole helpmate meet to be with' Adam in Eden (II. 87). Tom Paulin recognizes that she represents that 'ideal northern maiden' who is 'the British equivalent of an *aisling*, the visionary embodiment of national freedom in Irish Gaelic poetry'. So Hewson's investment in this foreign femininity, Paulin argues, is a symptom of Clough's 'desire to find a primal purity outside the social structure of 1840s Britain, though it can also be viewed as a form of sexual tourism'.[29] The liberating exuberance of the poem, then, deserts the postlapsarian condition of England for

the farthest reaches of the globe. And it does so in a prosody that deliberately affronts poetic tradition. Its form could not be more distant from
the 'over-educated weakness of purpose' that Clough found in Arnold's
Poems.[30] Clough did not live to see 'Dover Beach' in print – he died in
1861, the poem appeared in 1867 – but its tenor is similar to those earlier
poems by Arnold that displeased him. He was dismayed at how
Arnold's lyrics and poetic narratives advanced 'lessons of reflective-
ness' and 'maxims of caution', rather than the 'calls to action' that he
felt were needed by an age in transition.

Clough's poetry often makes a founding principle of these 'calls to
action' – so much so that the very word 'action' becomes a personification of sorts. The *Bothie* is an uproariously energetic poem, notably
where Elspie expresses her longings for Hewson who, for her, tellingly
figures as the sea: 'the sea there,/ Which *will* come, through the straits
and all between the mountains,/ Forcing its great strong tide into every
nook and inlet' (VII. 120–22). The hydraulic force of this sexually
charged 'tyrannous brine' (VII. 130) has overwhelmed Elspie in a recent
dream. She recalls how these surging waters tried to 'mix-in' (VII. 132)
with her, threatening to change the course of her life. The contrast with
Arnold's poetry could not be more stark. In 'Marguerite – Continued',
for example, Arnold's waves once more obstruct consummation.
Comparing each individual to an 'enisled' continent (1), the 'water
plain' (17) pushes the speaker and Marguerite further and further apart.
Although the whole poem resembles 'Dover Beach' in expressing its
'longing like despair' (12), the restless movement of the sea points to a
rather different conception of history. The seas that divide continents
here are those discussed by Charles Lyell in his controversial *Elements
of Geology* (1838), which explains how land was created when molten
lava first collided with water. Lyell's account went far to challenge biblical computations of historical time. In Arnold's poem, the painful
'severance' (22) of each island from an original land mass takes on an
aspect of humanity's original fall from grace. 'Who ordered', asks the
speaker, 'that their longing's fire/ Should be, as soon as kindled,
cooled?' (19–20). Controlled by a higher power, the sea exerts three
memorable qualities: it is 'unplumbed', 'salt', and 'estranging' (24). No
action can, in Arnold's despairing grammar, be taken against it. The
poem is, then, a prime example of the 'Stoic-Epicurean' stance that
Arnold often adopts to maintain a philosophical aloofness from the
ravages of history, and which Clough would not hesitate to mock.

In its use of a geological conception of historical time, 'Marguerite –
Continued' marks a complicated but revealing intersection with the

343

'Aqueous Ages' that preoccupy much of Clough's epistolary sequence, *Amours de Voyage*. But this is not the only historical mode that concerns Clough's poem. Mazzini's Italian revolution of 1849 is its immediate point of reference, and it is both to and from this site of struggle that the poem embarks on its intricate amatory, political, and intellectual voyage. Both 'Marguerite – Continued' and the *Amours* were composed at roughly the same time, and at least one commentator has suggested that Clough's main protagonist, Claude is an impersonation of Arnold.[31] Evidence exists to support this view. The rather haughty Claude propounds a distinctly Arnoldian 'Stoic-Epicurean acceptance' (I. 76). But altogether more intriguing is the view that Arnold's Marguerite poems chart his failed love affair with Mary Claude during his stay in Switzerland in 1847. The name Claude would, then, appear to bring Clough's interest in his friend's amours into focus. Yet the claims made upon the scant information that exists on this matter have created dissension among scholars.[32] The name of Mary Claude was doubtless known to Arnold's closest friend, and the *Amours* may be read as a rather chiding satire on Arnold's stand-offishness towards women. Claude, after all, fails to win his lady, and many of his letters to his friend, Eustace, voice opinions that compare with those oceanic and distinctly sexual disturbances that pulsate throughout Arnold's shorter poems.

Clough's satire frequently derives from Claude's scholarly high-mindedness in the face of the revolution led by Mazzini. At one point caught up in bouts of rioting, Claude informs his friend that he has been pondering Nature: the higher power that looks down on such petty disturbances with contempt. The tumult of 1849 concentrates Claude's mind on what J. C. Shairp thought to be the 'blank dejection' evident in Arnold's poetry.[33] Claude takes the kind of intellectual position that Clough would later refer to as the 'rehabilitated Hindu-Greek theosophy' that made much of Arnold's poetry so 'dismal'.[34] (Arnold told Clough that he had been reading the *Bbagavad-Gita*.[35]) But even when sending up such philosophizing, Clough's poetry refuses to succumb to the resigned tempo of Arnold's lyrics. Bouncing hexameters ceaselessly mock Claude's despondency:

'This is Nature', I said: 'we are born as it were from her waters,
Over the billows that buffet and beat us, her offspring uncared-for,
Casting one single regard of a painful victorious knowledge,
Into her billows that buffet and beat us we sink and are swallowed'.

(III. 51–54)

In this reverie, Mother Nature figures as the sea. But it is significant that, in the next few lines, she adopts a more identifiably female form. Swayed by the motion of the steamer from Marseilles to Civita Vecchia, Claude drowsily recalls the famed statue of the 'Sleeping Ariadne' in Rome. Yet, instead of retaining her repose, she begins to stare at him 'from the face of a Triton in marble' (III. 57). She is one of a great many well-known figures from classical myth that serve to indicate how his visual perception of the world is mediated through a repertoire of erudite allusions, ones elevating his intellect at the expense of immediate feeling. As this episode demonstrates, however, his learned imaginings contract the very distance that he seeks to impose on his travels in Italy, particularly where his condescending attitude towards his socially inferior fellow tourists is concerned. (Claude finds himself in the company of not so well-educated Cornish tradespeople.)

Outstaring Claude, this image of Ariadne represents a disapproving femininity – one which, like Mother Nature, threatens to chasten him. It is her reproachful countenance that leads him to reject thoughts of 'growth' – like the 'grain' that, as he puts it earlier, enjoyed 'force to develop and open its young cotyledons' (III. 40–43). Instead, he declares that 'we are still in our Aqueous Ages' (III. 59). By this phrase – which echoes Lyell's introductory discussion of aqueous rocks – he means that humanity has not progressed as far as it might have thought, since it remains unable to 'compare, and reflect, and examine one thing with another' (III. 44). These sentiments once again suggest the Arnoldian incapacity to act upon the world. Yet the specific representation of femininity in these lines provides an additional gloss on the shape and direction of Arnold's 'Marguerite' poems. Engulfed in Nature's 'waters', human life is trapped within her womb. All that Claude can do is sink back into it. In this respect, the *Amours* hint at the fear of amniotic flooding in those bitterly mediative poems that Arnold penned to his beloved in Switzerland, the woman who might have been Mary Claude.

III

But to see the *Amours* solely as a punishing satire on Arnold's worst traits while disclosing the conflicted nature of their friendship, may obscure the more general crisis in social and sexual relations that preoccupies nearly every section of this poem. From the outset, Claude's marked apprehensiveness about marriage comes right to the fore! Although he argues that the promise of fathering children – 'those/ Pure and delicate

345

forms' (I. 175–76) – has its attractions, this alone will not compensate entirely for the tiresome company of the 'feminine presence' (I. 169). Searching for an escape-route to a secure, loving, and dignified alternative to marriage, he deplores the constraining possessiveness of the nuclear family. Proposing that he might pursue a 'peaceful avuncular function' (I. 179), enjoying his future nephews and nieces, he decries how 'No proper provision is made for that most patriotic,/ Most meritorious subject, the childless and bachelor uncle' (I. 184–85). Eve Kosofsky Sedgwick observes that 'in the increasingly stressed nineteenth-century bourgeois dichotomy between domestic female space and extrafamilial, political and economic male space, the bachelor is at least partly feminized by his attention to and interest in domestic concerns'. He is a liminal figure whose position within society is potentially quite disruptive. 'At the same time', adds Sedgwick, 'his intimacy with clubland and bohemia gave him a special passport to the world of men.'[36] This is the dual masculine identity that Clough explores in the *Amours*, and he elaborates his thoughts on the bachelor's 'extrafamilial' status in a way that points to considerable fears about unregulated sexual behaviour. That society regards bachelorhood as unconventional surprises Claude in the light of what he calls 'Malthusian doctrine' (I. 183). Malthus was certainly on Clough's mind in 1848, shortly before he started work on this poem. A letter to the poet's sister, Anne, indicates how he saw sexual pleasure as the one thing that could transcend the all too evident poverty affecting the Hungry Forties. Adhering to the view that 'the more wretched a population becomes, the more rapidly it should increase', he observes that to 'live together as man and wife is sometimes the only enjoyment that people can get without immediate ready money payment or certainty of getting into debt for it'.[37] But this is not to say that sex adequately compensates for economic deprivation. It belongs, in fact, to the same cycle. For Clough believes that if the material conditions of the working classes are improved, then they will 'find the inclination to refrain' from sexual intercourse. Both the *Amours* and this letter, therefore, suggest that marriage, sex, and reproduction follow in an unwelcome pattern where physical and material needs are forever sundered. If a man is middle-class and married, he is bound to a woman in whom one has – as Claude says later – only 'an *ad-interim* solace and pleasure' (III. 143). By comparison, if a man is working-class and lacks material resources, he indulges in sex and is consequently saddled with the burden of a large family.

Yet it is not only the prospect of marriage that unsettles Claude. His future choice of profession remains equally precarious and unsure. For he, much to his frustration, does not have an inheritance to rely on. In a long section deleted from canto 1, he ponders how his own life might in such politically difficult times turn out to be socially useful: 'What can a poor devil do who would honestly earn him his victuals?' (624: 9). Entertaining all the various options – such as joining the armed forces, entering the Church, or emigrating to the colonies – he is appalled by the consequences of each. The army and navy seem redundant, since this is 'an industrial age...with "PEACE" on the calico banner' (624: 12–14). The Church, particularly in its High Anglican forms, strikes him as a 'Vast Eleusianian system of lady-and-gentleman doctrine' propounded by 'Perverts' (624: 45–46) – namely, converts to Rome. And, lastly, the pioneer has to put up with 'occasional Caffres,/ Snowy Canadian woods, penitential Australian acres,/ And the Phlegraean fields, far famed, of the Cannibal islands' (625: 61–63). Such thoughts would, within a matter of years, take shape in Clough's own mind as he sought a profession that yielded sufficient income so that the father of Blanche Smith would give his consent to her marriage to an itinerant academic. Arnold, likewise, took a post as an Inspector of Schools so that Mr Justice Wightman would allow his daughter to take the hand of a former Oxford scholar. No matter how satirically he is treated, Claude is surely addressing an issue that had equal urgency for Clough.

So, in enumerating these divergent professional paths, Claude is expressing the indignation of those young men who have no private income. They find themselves looking in vain for a suitable position after graduating from Oxford. All they can do, it seems, is compete with those who 'make their money from commerce' (624: 3), and who successfully petition for those *laissez-faire* policies that belittle the prowess of the military in protecting the nation. (It is precisely this issue that vexes the excitable hero of Alfred Tennyson's *Maud*.[38]) They see the Church increasingly taken over by 'ladylike priests and deacons' (624: 26), contaminated by Tractarian doctrine. And, as a last alternative, these highly educated men recognize that emigration means not only mixing with the natives, but being brought down to their brutish level. This unbending amalgam of class, sexual, and racial prejudices points directly at one thing: an overwhelming feeling of emasculation. Little wonder that Claude remonstrates that 'Starving meanwhile is a quiet and most inexpensive process', one that he 'can but decline to prefer' above all other things (624: 70–71).

A short and incomplete poem by Clough sharpens this strained sense of emasculation in the face of the growing power of the masses, not to say the changing structure of class relations in general. It is also here

Joseph Bristow

that Clough resorts, like Claude and Arnold, to the sea. Clough's editors provide no date of composition for the unpublished and untitled poem beginning 'The contradictions of the expanding soul', and the extant text is a copy in a fair hand by Blanche Smith. Yet, even if its status within Clough's canon is unclear, the sentiments located in these lines are plain enough. A distressed man discovers himself adrift, like a log, where 'opposing tides' (3) of thought beat and buffet him from every side. He would much prefer to be like a 'strong ship... /Well steered' (5–6). Tossed upon the tide, he is anxious for the 'manhood of our race' (2). In this respect, he appears much like Claude, except here the poem adopts a sombre – one might say Arnoldian – tone. At the mercy of the waves, his mind turns to different types of men. The first are the 'lordly scions of nobility' (15) who partly win his admiration since they are 'Manly almost to the inhuman' (20). Yet he is outraged at the 'Impudence' (17) of those laws that grant rights of inheritance to such men 'at the font' (18). The muscular strength of these nobles, which exerts itself most forcefully in the army, shows no fear, only an inexorable will to succeed. Although the speaker in many ways regrets the triumphal status of aristocratic fighters within society, he concedes that 'Earth cannot spare them yet' (27), and so resigns himself to the fact that their might shall retain its authority for many years to come.

IV

Arnold was similarly troubled by the values of brute strength attached to the noble warrior, and he too would find ways of reconciling himself to it. Here it is worth turning to the famous incident in 'Sohrab and Rustum' where the great man of war confronts his equally powerful illegitimate son. When these leaders of opposing armies clash, they are wholly unaware of their filial relation. Having fallen down and then recovered his sword, the elderly Rustum taunts his enemy: 'Girl! nimble with thy feet, not thy hands!/ Curled minion, dancer, coiner of sweet words' (457–58). And within a matter of lines he repeats this effeminizing insult (469). This adaptation of an episode recorded in John Malcolm's *History of Persia* finally leads to a celebration of soldierly honour. For Rustum, who eventually discovers that he has slain his son, declares his tragic loss. The poem closes with an elegaic description of the sun setting above the 'Chorasmian waste' (878) where the Oxus makes its ways down from the Pamirs to the Aral Sea: 'by the river marge .../... Rustum and his son were left alone' (873–74). Resting

348

together, the two warriors form a natural part of this landscape, and like the river that flows beside them they blend with elemental – if not sexual – forces that rush forth towards the 'longed-for dash of waves' (889). Echoing Achilles' lament for Patroclus in Homer's *Iliad*, Rustum's final speech to his dying son amounts to one of the most affirmative moments of close physical affection to be found anywhere in Arnold's poetry. Not surprisingly, this poem found favour with Charles Kingsley who applauded 'Sohrab and Rustum' as 'poetry written by brave men and read by brave men'. Such writing exhibited those qualities of robust manliness championed by Kingsley's pugilistic Christian Socialism. Such was Arnold's gift for adapting a historical story of tragic heroism that Kingsley implores Arnold to 'employ his great powers in giving us [a] translation of Homer'.[39]

But when the scene shifts to contemporary Victorian Britain, Arnold's personae find themselves on altogether less firm ground. 'Resignation – To Fausta' – a poem that Clough wittily satirized – reveals that the manly ideal was remote from the demands and desires of those Oxonian men who were searching for an alternative masculinity that would prove as powerful as the military strength embodied in the nobles commanding the armed forces, on the one hand, and as influential as the work undertaken by the captains of industry, on the other. The speaker of 'Resignation – To Fausta' upholds the belief that all things in nature 'bear rather than rejoice' (270). Here, once again, is the 'Stoic-Epicurean' posture where the poet 'Bears to admire uncravingly' (161) the world that lies before him. From the start, he recoils from those who are 'too imperious' (37) in their desire for power, conquest, and change. Exemplars of such rude force include pilgrims bound for Mecca, the Crusaders, the Goth, and the Hun – all of whom, he claims, live by the principle of do or die. Each group, he declares, is 'enthrall[ed]' by its 'self-ordained...labours' (14).

Not only does the resigned speaker distance himself from these uncivilized victors. His abhorrence of such 'imperious' types is also compounded by a wholesale rejection of Romantic authority. The romantic poet who despicably *'flees the common life of men'* (212) – a man who, in other words, stands above the 'general life, which does not cease,/ Whose secret is not joy, but peace' (191–92) – has no place within this scheme of things. In making these claims, the poem adopts a structure of address similar to that of 'Dover Beach'. And, once again, the same poetic precursor is there. 'Resignation – To Fausta' models its landscape on Wordsworth's 'Tintern Abbey'. In reworking this chief antecedent, Arnold's poem indicates that the Romantic ideal which seeks, in Wordsworth's phrase, to 'see into the life of things' is no longer valid.[40] Putting words into Fausta's mouth, the speaker claims how wrong she is to believe that the poet *'Breathes...immortal air'* (146–47). Instead, it is the duty of the poet to 'scan/ Not his own course, but that of man' (146–47). Should he do otherwise, he would implicitly rank among the likes of the Muslim pilgrim, the Crusader, the Goth, and the Hun, all of whom seek either triumph or self-destruction, rather than peaceful and civilized resignation. Arnold's poet attempts to steer a course between Romantic idealism and Gothic violence by declaring how he 'Surveys each happy group which fleets,/ Toil ended, through the shining streets' (166–67). Thus he can conclude he is emphatically not *'alone'* (169). One can, to be sure, detect in this ending the conflicted desire to be both integrated within *and* remain aloof from a class-divided society that characterizes Clough's anxious intellectual who is threatened by aggressive and highly physical men. To be resigned, in other words, is to be somewhere in between, on the one hand, 'each happy group' returning from their labours and, on the other, those 'imperious' brutes who survive through tyranny.

But, hereafter, Arnold's resigned speaker finds it hard to ensure that his ideal poet is placed both individually above and socially within the ordinary confines of the 'general life'. If confident in his desire to 'bear rather than rejoice', he is ultimately uncertain about what he calls 'action's dizzying eddy whirled' (227). By this he means the fundamental energy embodied in those waters that rush unimpeded through so many of his poems, notably 'The Buried Life', and which has already figured in the 'wide-glimmering sea' (85) in which he and Fausta have bathed their hands 'with speechless glee' (84). Water undoubtedly signals sexual pleasure. But the speaker does his utmost to resist its turbulent force. Here the closing lines compile a sequence of loosely connected clauses that mystify the status of this 'dizzying eddy' by designating it as an unnamed 'something that infects the world' (278). This obscure energy would seem to be just as unstoppably driven as the 'imperious' dynamism embodied in those heartless brutes who in former eras laid siege on centres of civilization. Since it is by nature nebulous, this 'something' has prompted divergent interpretations. (G. Robert Stange, for example, believes that it refers to evil, and thus departs from Arnold's Stoicism.[41]) The broken grammar of these lines suggests that the speaker is claiming that our resigned lives are not necessarily 'milder' (275) because we have forgotten this agitating and impulsive force. There again, it is possible to see how the 'something that infects the world' can never be forgotten, since it exerts an ongoing transitive power. For it continues to infect. No one can escape it. And the fact that this infection gains such prominence in the closing lines of the poem indicates that its power is altogether greater than the resigned stance which he earlier propounds. It proves, in the end, hard to accept that this persona's passive capacity to 'bear' enjoys moral superiority over the 'dizzying eddy' that invokes 'action'. He is surely as much at a loss as Clough's speaker who, while contemplating the 'contradictions of the expanding soul', bemoans his feminized position within the culture.

Clough, however, devised a distinctive style of writing that could go some way towards restoring his strength as both a poet and an intellectual who felt caught between the social authority invested in the trading classes and the enduring magnanimity of the aristocracy. For Clough's greatest resource is his vein of satiric wit that found a suitable target in the man who made him into both an idol and an emblem of failure. Clough's cynical 'Resignation – To Faustus' makes merciless fun of Arnold's poem. But this satire need not simply be seen as an irreverent answer to Arnold's agonized claims about the poet who wishes to stand implausibly both above and among the populace. Instead, Clough's satire defends another equally déclassé intellectual from confronting – as Arnold does – the loss of Romantic authority, and the forms of masculine power invested in that vatic role. Shifting the interests of Arnold's subtitle from the amatory rhetoric of Goethe's *Wilhelm Meister* to the Mephistopholean concerns of *Faust*, Clough's persona addresses an imaginary 'land of Empire' (1), a classical city that has been overrun by Goths. This world is riven between the muses and the masses – 'A sky for Gods to tread above,/ A soil for pigs below me!' (3–4) – and the gulf between them is embodied in two startling images. To begin with, there is the priest who thinks it 'fit to stop and spit/ Beside the altar solemn' (31–32). But surely worse is the working man who heedlessly urinates on any 'Corinthian column' (34) that takes his fancy. Such sights, however, do not make a cynic of the speaker. They are simply viewed as the everyday goings-on from which Nature positively derives its 'emanative power' by imbibing 'mixtures fetid foul and sour' (48–49). A 'classic land', he states, is built upon 'dirt' (42). So rather than avert his gaze from the mire, he celebrates it. In other words, he finds that he must with 'resignation fair and meet' (84) learn to 'greet… / The dirt and refuse of the street' (85–86). Once he can accomplish this, he believes, then the 'columns set against the sky' (85) – no matter how much urine is sprayed upon them – will remain 'perfect' (87). All of which points to the fact that the cloudy triumphs of a civilization subsist on the degraded soil of this society. Clough, therefore, is laying bare the repulsive mud and grime that repressively seep from the edges of Arnold's high-minded 'Stoic-Epicurean' stance.

The only working-class figures who feature among the dignified concerns of Arnold's 'Resignation – To Fausta' are a band of gypsies: a vagrant and self-contained society that enshrines ideal values exemplifying how one should 'bear rather than rejoice'. In turning to these outcasts, the poem is once again invoking Wordsworth's poetry – namely, 'Gipsies', dating from 1807. This marginal group represents a life of continuity. They follow the 'self-same plan' (141) in their 'hereditary way' (139). Theirs is an unspoiled world of resignation. But elsewhere in Arnold's work the gypsy returns in a rather different guise, and on both occasions he embodies aspects of Clough. The gypsy provides one aspect of a different kind of manhood desired by both Arnold and Clough that could create bonds within the social fabric that they felt the class divisions of mid-Victorian Britain had riven apart.

V

'The Scholar-Gypsy', which probably dates from 1853, tells a tale of two hundred years ago when an 'Oxford scholar poor,/ Of pregnant parts of quick inventive brain,' grew 'tired of knocking at preferment's door' (35), and so decided to join the company of travellers. In one sense, this 'scholar-gypsy' is a version of the Arnoldian poet who wishes to be a part of society and yet wants to survey its scene from a cautious distance. But here one can glimpse the image of the midcentury Oxonian who, like Arnold and Clough, looked to a future career in the Church, the army, or in commerce with not a little trepidation. The scholar-gypsy, unlike his fellow graduates, retains his autonomy within the 'wild brotherhood' (38) who live according to their own laws. The scholar-gypsy's resolve –since he possessed '*one* aim, *one* business, *one* desire' (152) – contrasts with those Victorian men who 'fluctuate idly without term or scope' (167). It was this verb that Arnold underlined when writing to Clough about both this poem and 'Sohrab and Rustum': 'You are too content to *fluctuate* – to be ever learning, never coming to the knowledge of truth. That is why, with you, I feel it necessary to stiffen myself – and hold fast my rudder'.[42] Pinkney points out that here Arnold is holding fast to his rudder because he fears running aground on the viscous mud that figures social and sexual instability. In accusing Clough of being a man who is 'content to *fluctuate*', Arnold is feminizing his friend as a Siren, while he remains like 'Ulysses binding himself to the mast'.[43]

But if Arnold's friend was thought lacking the 'term or scope' that characterized the mid-Victorian male intellectual, then it is significant that he canonized him in 'Thyrsis' as one who once belonged to a social set that in the past had counted the 'Gipsy-Scholar' (29) among their company. 'Thyrsis' returns Clough to an idyllic Virgilian moment, enshrining him in a tradition of pastoral elegy that is hardly apposite for a writer whose chief precursors were eighteenth-century satirists such as Alexander Pope and Jonathan Swift. This use of pastoral elegy to praise Clough would seem to be very much an act of Arnoldian appropriation, where Thyrsis became a figure that idealizes Arnold's and not his friend's poetic and political interests. It is surely significant that, although Arnold was prepared to write a stylized elegy of this kind, he refused to furnish a prefatory memoir to the posthumous edition of Clough's works.[44] Following John Milton's 'Lycidas', 'Thyrsis' duly makes it heroic gestures before the elegist discovers that he must finally turn away from the golden age and meet the demands of the present moment. Once the death of this pastoral idol has been recognized as wholly irretrievable, then the darkness of night falls like a shroud over his corpse. Yet, importantly, at this instant the night figures as a woman who – like one of the Fates – in 'ever-nearing circles weaves her shade' (132). Her 'slowly chilling breath invade[s]/ The cheek grown thin' (134–35). Although this feminized personification may appear to be following the conventions of pastoral elegy, these lines take such pains to underline the power of this deathly femininity that it is fair to claim that 'Thyrsis' discloses how the glories of his blissful undergraduate days have been destroyed by the invasive presence of women. This eerie image may well indicate longstanding fears that marriage would bring about a kind of death.

Marriage certainly terminated the 'love' that Arnold and Clough enjoyed in the countryside surrounding Oxford where the ghostly scholar-gypsy freely roved, retaining that idealized hybrid identity as both a university man and a common fellow. But this drastic change in these poets' lives stood as a figure for other transformations that called their poetic vocation into question. By examining the chief intersections between their poems, we can surely see how the intellectual rewards of an Oxford life were diminished in the face of a society that put less and less faith in the scholar, as the military pre-eminence of the landed lords, the industrial success of commercial entrepreneurs, and the growing Malthusian mass of the working classes affronted him on all sides. Relishing true intimacy only with others of his kind, this type of man was not just fearful of women, he became conscious of his own feminization. This is certainly the case for both poets, even if the sexual adventurousness of Clough's works – all the way from the early lyrics to the incomplete Chaucerian sequence entitled *Mari Magno* – seem remote from the 'long withdrawing roar' that saps the sexual energy of Arnold's speaker in 'Dover Beach'. In his prizewinning poem written at Rugby, 'The Close of the Eighteenth Century', which charts the political ructions of the modern age from the outbreak of the French Revolution, Clough would presciently exclaim: 'Lord, we are wandering on an unknown sea' (174). The 'Aqueous Ages' of the following decades would confirm Clough's need to counter the 'caterwaulings of the effeminate heart', as the eponymous hero of *Dipsychus* declares (IX. 154). But it would leave Arnold in a state of perpetual regret. 'Love, let us be true To one another': these words are assuredly tinged with nostalgia for the Oxonian companionship that his poetry had increasingly repelled. The more the distance opened between Arnold and his oceanic unconscious, the more vigorous Clough grew in his satirical treatment of that repression. But there is enough evidence to show that Clough's satire emerged from an impulse similar to that which was repeatedly expressed by the man who was the butt of his biting wit. In so doing, Clough was trying to defend himself from the troubling thought that the scholarly bachelor no longer had a privileged place within the social structure. Oxonian men of his and Arnold's generation were left instead with suggestive metaphors of fluidity: the medium in which their sense of displaced authority impossibly tried to take shape.

Notes

1   U. C. Knoeplfmacher, 'Dover Revisited: The Wordsworthian Matrix in the Poetry of Matthew Arnold', *Victorian Poetry* 1 (1963), 17–26. Equally informative on Arnold's Wordsworthian heritage is David Trotter, 'Hidden Ground within: Matthew Arnold's Lyric and Elegaic Poetry', *ELH* 44 (1977), 526–55. Algernon Charles Swinburne was among the first to remark that 'The good and evil influence of that great poet, perverse theorist, and incomplete man [namely, Wordsworth], upon Mr Arnold's work is so palpable and so strong as to be almost obtrusive in its effects': 'Mr Arnold's New Poems', *Fortnightly Review* NS 2 (1867), 414.
2   Quotations from Arnold's poetry are taken from *The Poems of Matthew Arnold*, eds. Kenneth Allott and Miriam Allott, second edition (London, 1979). Line references appear in parentheses.

3   E. D. H. Johnson, *The Alien Vision of Victorian Poetry: Sources of Poetic Imagination in Tennyson, Browning, and Arnold* (Princeton, NJ, 1952).

4   Gerald Graff, *Beyond the Culture Wars: How the Teaching Conflicts Can Revitalize American Education* (New York, 1992), 38.

5   Arnold, 'To His Mother', April 1848, *Letters of Matthew Arnold*, ed., George W. E. Russell, 2 vols. (London, 1895), I, 7.

6   Park Honan, *Matthew Arnold: A Life* (London, 1981), 235.

7   Lionel Trilling and Harold Bloom, eds., *Victorian Prose and Poetry* (New York, 1973), 593.

8   Anthony Hecht, 'The Dover Bitch: A Criticism of Life', in David J. DeLaura ed., *Matthew Arnold: A Collection of Critical Essays* (Englewood Cliffs, NJ, 1973), 54.

9   [A. W. Kinglake,] 'The Rights of Women', *Quarterly Review*, 75 (1845), 112, 115.

10   Judith Newton, 'Making – and Remaking – History: Another Look at "Patriarchy"', *Tulsa Studies in Women's Literature* 3:1–2 (1984), 131, 129. Leonore Davidoff and Catherine Hall remark that a 'tension between the notion of women as "relative creatures" and a celebratory view of their potential power lies at the heart of Mrs Ellis's writing and helps to explain her popularity': *Family Fortunes: Men and Women of the English Middle Class 1780–1850* (London, 1987), 183.

11   Arthur Hugh Clough, *Amours de Voyage*, III, 359. Quotations from Clough's poetry are taken from *The Poems of Arthur Hugh Clough*, second edition, ed. F. L. Mulhauser (Oxford, 1974). Line references appear in parentheses. Where quotations are taken from the drafts reprinted in the appendices to this edition, relevant page numbers precede line references.

12   William A. Madden, 'Arnold the Poet: (i) Lyric and Elegaic Poems', in Kenneth Allott, ed., *Writers and Their Work: Matthew Arnold* (London, 1975), 57.

13   Robindra Kumar Biswas, *Arthur Hugh Clough: Towards a Reconsideration* (Oxford, 1972), 469. It is worth comparing E. Warwick Slinn's analysis of the oceanic images that prevail in *Amours de Voyage*; Slinn's concern is with the ways in which the persona's subjective identity 'floats helplessly upon the element that allows it differentiation'. Slinn sees in the poem passages where Claude's subjectivity is both passive and active: *The Discourse of the Self in Victorian Poetry* (Basingstoke, 1991), 104.

14   Tony Pinkney 'Matthew Arnold and the Northern Sea: Goths and Gender in the Poetry', *News from Nowhere* 5 (1988), 11–27.

15   Arnold, 'To Arthur Hugh Clough', 12 February 1853, *The Letters of Matthew Arnold to Arthur Hugh Clough*, ed., Howard Foster Lowry (London, 1932), 129.

16   The *Literary Gazette* pointed out that Clough had made a blunder in his choice of title; 'fuosich' in Scottish Gaelic meant 'bearded well', and thus stood as a metaphor for the vagina. The title of the poem was adjusted to *The Bothie of Tober-Na-Vuolich* when reprinted posthumously: see Biswas, *Arthur Hugh Clough*, 264.

17 Isobel Armstrong, *Victorian Poetry: Poetry, Poetics, and Politics* (London, 1993), 209. Armstrong's respective chapters on Clough and Arnold lay particular emphasis on the tensions deriving from these poets' divergent political interests, rather than the problems of homosocial desire that inform their antithetical attitudes on radical and liberal positions.

18 Arnold, 'To Arthur Hugh Clough', 29 September 1848, *Letters to Arthur Hugh Clough*, 93. My thanks to Christina Britzolakis for advising me on Arnold's Latin.

19 Arnold, 'To Arthur Hugh Clough', 21 March 1853, *Letters to Arthur Hugh Clough*, 132.

20 Kathleen Tillotson, '"Haworth Churchyard": The Making of Arnold's Elegy', *Brontë Society Transactions* 15 (1967), 112, cited in Honan, *Matthew Arnold*, 219.

21 Arnold, 'To Arthur Hugh Clough', 12 February 1853, *Letters to Arthur Hugh Clough*, 130. Further quotations from this letter are taken from this page.

22 Arnold, 'Preface' to *Poems* (1853), 'Appendix A', in *The Complete Poems*, ed. Allott and Allott, second edition, 669.

23 Arnold, 'To Arthur Hugh Clough' [early part of February 1849], *Letters to Arthur Hugh Clough*, 98.

24 Arnold, 'To Arthur Hugh Clough', 12 February 1853, *Letters to Arthur Hugh Clough*, 130.

25 Arnold, 'To Arthur Hugh Clough', 1 May 1853, *Letters to Arthur Hugh Clough*, 135.

26 Clough, 'To T. Arnold', 16 May 1851, *The Correspondence of Arthur Hugh Clough*, ed. Frederick L. Mulhauser, 2 vols. (Oxford, 1957), I, 290.

27 Clough, 'To Miss Smith', [27 January 1852,] *Correspondence*, 301.

28 J. A. Froude informed Clough: 'I don't believe in your Elspie. If any girl in her position was ever so highly cultivated, she is an exception, and so the moral would be false': 'To Arthur Hugh Clough', 21 January 1849, in Michael Thorpe, ed., *Clough: The Critical Heritage* (London, 1972), 35.

29 Tom Paulin, *Minotaur: Poetry and the Nation State* (London: Faber and Faber, 1992), 66.

30 Clough, 'Recent English Poetry', *North American Review* 77 (1853), 12–24, reprinted in Isobel Armstrong, ed., *Victorian Scrutinies: Reviews of Poetry 1830–1870* (London, 1972), 167. Further quotations are taken from this page.

31 See Eugene R. August, '*Amours de Voyage* and Matthew Arnold in Love: An Inquiry', *Victorian Newsletter* 60 (1981), 15–20.

32 On the controversial identification of Mary Claude, see Honan, *Matthew Arnold*, 144–67; and Miriam Allott, 'Arnold and "Marguerite – Continued"', *Victorian Poetry* 23 (1985), 125–43.

33 J. C. Shairp, 'To Arthur Hugh Clough', 14 April 1853, *Correspondence*, II, 401. Shairp was similarly dissatisfied with Clough's contributions to the collection published jointly with Thomas Burbidge, *Ambarvalia*, together with the earliest draft of the *Amours*: see *Correspondence*, I, 275.

34 Clough, 'Recent English Poetry', in Armstrong, ed., *Victorian Scrutinies*, 168.

35 Arnold, 'To Arthur Hugh Clough', 4 March 1848, *Letters to Arthur Hugh Clough*, 71.

36 Eve Kosofsky Sedgwick, 'The Beast in the Closet: James and the Writing of Homosexual Panic', in Elaine Showalter, ed., *Speaking of Gender* (New York, 1989), 248.

37 Clough, 'To Anne Clough', 22 May 1848, *Correspondence*, I, 209.

38 On the debate about rival forms of aristocratic and bourgeois manhood in Tennyson's *Maud*, see Joseph Bristow, 'Nation, Class, and Gender: Tennyson's *Maud* and War', *Genders* 9 (1990), 93–111.

39 [Charles Kingsley,] Review of Matthew Arnold, *Poems, Fraser's Magazine* 49 (1854), 140–9, reprinted in Armstrong, ed., *Victorian Scrutinies*, 180, 183.

40 William Wordsworth, *Poetical Works*, eds., Thomas Hutchinson and Ernest de Selincourt (Oxford University Press, 1969), 165.

41 G. Robert Stange, *Matthew Arnold: The Poet as Humanist* (Princeton, NJ, 1967), 67.

42 Arnold, 'To Arthur Hugh Clough', 30 November 1853, *Letters to Arthur Hugh Clough*, 146.

43 Pinkney, 'Matthew Arnold and the Northern Sea', 15.

44 In 1868, Arnold informed Blanche Clough (*née* Smith) that he was 'quite sure' that he 'should neither satisfy you nor myself if [he] tried to throw into form for publication [his] recollections of [her late] husband'. In addition, Arnold remarks on the 'special point' she mentions: namely, Clough's 'resignation of his fellowship'; about this delicate matter, Arnold declares that he feels he 'could say nothing': 14 October 1868, *Letters to Arthur Hugh Clough*, 161.

19

'Poets and lovers evermore'
The Poetry and Journals of Michael Field

Chris White

What's in a Name?

Katherine Bradley and Edith Cooper were poets and lovers from 1870 to 1913. They lived together, converted to Catholicism together, and together developed the joint poetic persona of Michael Field. As aunt and niece their love was socially structured and sanctioned. As Catholics and classicists they developed a language of love between women. As Michael and Henry their life together is recorded in the surviving man-uscript journals. And as Michael Field they presented themselves to the world as Poets. (The capitalization, and the sense of the importance of this activity, is theirs.) But were they lesbians in any recognizable sense? This question relates to a developing orthodoxy of lesbian history and politics, in particular the influential thesis of Lillian Faderman in *Surpassing the Love of Men* where she discusses Michael Field, an anal-ysis which I will attempt to interrogate in this chapter.[1] I want to make an intervention in the interpretative practice employed by Faderman, whereby all loving relationships between women before the 1920s are viewed as romantic friendships, and not as sexualized or erotic. Through connecting questions of homosexual history, politics, and desire, this chapter will offer readings of poems and journal entries that build up a picture of a specific instance of homosexual history.

White, Chris. 1992. "'Poets and lovers evermore': the poetry and journals of Michael Field." In *Sexual Sameness: Textual Differences in Gay and Lesbian Writing*, edited by Joseph Bristow, pp. 26–43. London: Routledge. Reproduced with permission of Taylor & Francis.

Victorian Poets: A Critical Reader, First Edition. Edited by Valentine Cunningham.
© 2014 John Wiley & Sons, Ltd. Published 2014 by John Wiley & Sons, Ltd.

In their relationship and their work, Katherine and Edith typify many of the difficulties in deciphering the meaning and nature of love between women. Faderman's comments are based only on published extracts (a slender volume concerned primarily with their lives as Catholics) from their extensive journals covering the years 1869–1914. The scale of this material is enormous: thirty-six foolscap volumes, with several others consisting of correspondence and notes.[2] It is a remarkable resource, but it is neither assimilable to a linear narrative nor capable of being easily represented here. (There is also the problem that some words and phrases are indecipherable.) It would be a mistake, however, to assume that these journals offer anything like a straightforward access to the 'truth' about the relationship or Katherine and Edith's understanding of it, even given all the usual reservations about the mediated status of autobiography.[3] The journals were left with instructions that they might be opened at the end of 1929, and that the editors, T. and D.C. Sturge Moore, should publish from them as they saw fit. It hardly needs pointing out that at some point the journals became directed towards publication. When that was, or to whom the journals are addressed, is never clear. There is, I must assume, no truly 'private' record.

In the journals and the poetry there are copious references that may be read as lesbian. These texts are dotted with the words 'Sapphic', 'Beloved', 'Lover' and 'Lesbian'.[4] Yet it is not possible to infer that such terms indicate a same-sex sexual relationship, while Faderman argues that they are not at all sexual. I intend to demonstrate that these references are not simply definable as 'sexual' or 'non-sexual', but have their origins in more diverse sources. Any such analysis must be hedged around by considering the historically specific treatment of the Sapphic and the Lesbian.

Classical Greek literature and culture provided one way for nineteenth-century homosexual writers to talk about homosexuality as a positive social and emotional relationship. These authors appropriated the works of Plato and the myths of male love and comradeship to argue for social tolerance of same-sex love. For homosexual writers, a culture that was in the nineteenth century regarded as one of the highest points of civilization provided a precedent that was both respectable and sexual. This deployment of a Greek cultural precedent appears in Katherine and Edith's volume *Bellerophôn*, published under the pseudonyms Arran and Isla Leigh, in the poem 'Apollo's Written Grief', on the subject of Apollo and Hyacinth. This poem may be understood as a homo-political appeal for tolerance and an expression of the search for the right way of conducting a homosexual relationship:

> Men dream that thou wert smitten by the glow
> Of my too perilous love, not by the blow
> Of him who rivalled me.[5]

Apollo's love for his 'bright-eyed Ganymede' (p. 160) is presented as the best option for the boy, since he would otherwise have been consumed by Zephyrus or Zeus 'in greed' (p. 160). Apollo's love would not have proved dangerous to Hyacinth who, in 'panting for the light' (p. 159) of the sun-god, 'sufferedest the divine/Daring the dread delight' (p. 159). This poem, therefore, employs the already existing construction and terminology for homosexual love and desire. These myths remained available to readings as homoerotic archetypes or ideals.[6] This poem is not explicitly, or even obviously, a lesbian text. All of its characters are male. All the relationships are masculine relationships; between father and son, god and cup-bearer. The absence of women indicates an exclusively masculine world, where women are simply not relevant. One might imagine that alongside this world there exists another where women live together. But some of the language in which the poem speaks of homosexuality has metaphorical relationships to desire between women. The reference to 'the glow/Of my too perilous love' (III, 1, 2–3) is not like the more frequent, although usually embedded, phallic references. Where a whole canon of male – male bondings and loves exists, women had only one classical equivalent to draw upon for expressions and strategies of female – female love – the poetry of Sappho. Katherine and Edith as Michael Field, in using one of the male precedents, are taking up an available model in which to talk about same-sex desire. In order for them to use the lesbian precedent of Sappho, that classical antecedent must be recuperated from male appropriations, salaciousness or prurience.

Katherine and Edith wrote at a time when treatments of Sappho's verse were numerous and diverse. There are instances of deliberate suppression of the female pronouns, as in T.W. Higginson's translation published in 1871. In the novels of Alphonse Daudet, Théophile Gautier and Algernon Charles Swinburne, Sappho and Sapphic women were constructed as sadistic, predatory corruptors of innocent women. This emerged from male fantasies about masculine women with phallic sexualities, women who behaved like men with 'innocent' women, which does not threaten the proper balance of power between the sexes, but transplants it. It also participates in a fantasy about unnatural women who are brutalizing and corrupting of true, feminine women, thus marking off men as living in a proper relationship to femininity. And, predictably, there is the erotic value for the man in having two women on display. A standard work on Greek culture describes Sappho as 'a woman of generous disposition, affectionate heart, and independent spirit...[with] her own particular refinement of taste, exclusive of every approach to low excess or profligacy'.[7] Alternatively, another academic author declared that there was 'no good early evidence to show that the Lesbian standard was low'[8] (that is, sexual). In other versions, Sappho was portrayed as a woman falling in love with the fisherman Phaon, committing suicide when that love was unreciprocated.[9] The plurality of depictions and appropriations of Sappho indicates the extent to which she and her work became a cultural battleground, much more so than any male homosexual equivalent. Where some writers attempt to recuperate at all costs the great poet from accusations of lewdness, and others concede the love between women, but deny it as being passion of a base nature, Michael Field holds her up as a paragon among women, and puts the passion back into the poet's community of women. Michael Field's 1889 volume *Long Ago*, a series of poems based on and completing Sappho's fragments, explores the heterosexual version of Sappho, alongside poems on passion between women. They explained, in a letter of 11 June 1889, the thinking behind *Long Ago*.

> I feel I have hope that you will understand the spirit of my lyrics you who have sympathy with attempts to reconcile the old and the new, to live as in continuation the beautiful life of Greece.... What I have aspired to do from Sappho's fragments may therefore somewhat appeal to your sense of survival in human things – to your interest in the shoots and offspring of older literature.[10]

The reconciliation of the old and the new – of classical Greek culture and literature and nineteenth-century remakings of those forms and ideas – forms an important part of the conceptualization of homosexual desire, and more significantly, of the place of homosexuals in a dominantly heterosexual society. In this letter, Michael Field appeals to Pater's own analyses and interpretations in his essays and lectures on Greek studies, art, and literature.[11] Greek culture is not perceived as being mere history, a dead past of interest only to scholars and classicists. It is, rather, a potent and valid model for nineteenth-century

British culture, which, for many critics and poets, ought to be reflected in the organization and standards of their own society. In addition to the political and cultural virtues of the Greek precedent, many writers, Michael Field among them, found images, texts, and authors that provided a positive framework in which to speak about desire between two men or two women, and this framework did not require the writers to begin from a point of self-justification or to address the dominant cultural ideas about sin and unnatural sexual practices. Greek culture was perceived as a young culture, and the associated discourses that connected youth with purity and innocence preserved Greek culture from accusations of adult vice and knowledge.[12]

Long Ago contains no references to sin or corruption. Relations between women are taken as a given. The forms of those relationships are complex and in a state of negotiation. There are fickle lovers, women who would rather marry men, quarrels between lovers, reconciliations and erotic interludes among the poems about the public making of poetry:

> Come, Gorgo, put the rug in place,
> And passionate recline;
> I love to see thee in thy grace,
> Dark, virulent, divine....
>
> Those fairest hands – dost thou forget
> Their power to thrill and cling?[13]

This is no sexless romance between friends, but an exotic eroticism. The loved/desired woman in the act of lying down is passionate and divine. There is the reference to the pleasure that can be given with hands between women.

If this is one version of Sappho, there are at least two other Sapphos in *Long Ago*. One is a woman at the centre of a loving community of women, a community which she must keep safe from the intrusions of men. In poem LIV, 'Adown the Lesbian Vales', Sappho is in possession of a 'passionate unsated sense' which her maids seek to satisfy. The relationship between Sappho and her maids is premised upon a need to keep the women away from marriage: 'No girls let fall/Their maiden zone/At Hymen's call' (p. 96). The third Sappho is the heterosexual lover of Phaon:

> If I could win him from the sea,
> Then subtly I would draw him down
> 'Mid the bright vetches; in a crown

> My art should teach him to entwine
> Their thievish rings and keep him mine.[14]

This seems to be a possessive heterosexual desire, springing from a manipulative battle to win him in a destructive competition with the fisherman's work at sea. But the imagery is also quite sexy. The drawing down echoes the 'passionate recline' of the previous extract. Yet, where the focus in the latter is on Gorgo, here the focus is as much on the vetches as on the fisherman. The supposed erotic object does not stand centre stage. Instead it is the 'I' of Sappho who dominates, shaping the desire, which means annihilating the loved object. Even the seemingly heterosexual Sappho is not, in Michael Field's poetry, shown to be a truly feminine figure existing in a proper relationship to what ought instead to serve as the focus of all their desires, the masculine.

Masculinity in itself is not valued. In poem LXVI. Sappho prays to Apollo about Phaon:

> Apollo, thou alone cans't bring
> To Phaon's feeble breast
> The fire unquenchable, the sting,
> Love's agony, Love's zest.
> Thou needs't not curse him, nor transform;
> Give him the poet's heart of storm
> To suffer as I suffer, thus
> Abandoned, vengeful, covetous.[15]

I think this is a very funny poem. OK, Apollo, you don't need to turn him into something or someone else, and maybe you shouldn't curse him, although you could, and I did consider it for a while; just make Phaon like me. As he is, he's feeble and emotionally a bit inadequate, and if you make him like me, a poet, with a poet's emotional turbulence, he'd be much improved. And then I'll probably abandon him, and leave him to stew. Love with a man untransformed by a god just isn't worth the hassle.

The second and third versions of Sappho come into conflict over the issue of virginity and poetry. The love of Phaon and the inviolate women of the Lesbian community are combined in Poem XVII: 'The moon rose full, the women stood'. Sappho calls to her virginity, her 'only good', to come back, having been lost to Phaon. The inviolate state is 'that most blessed, secret state / That makes the tenderest maiden great', not the possession of a male's sexual attention. Sappho's loss of virginity effectively puts an end to her poetic gift:

> And when
> By maiden-arms to be enwound
> Ashore the fisher flings,
> Oh, then my heart turns cold, and then
> I drop my wings.

The connection between poetry and virginity is broached in *The New Minnesinger and Other Poems*, published by Katherine under the pseudonym Arran Leigh. The title poem discusses the craft of the woman-poet, 'she whose life doth lie/In virgin haunts of poesie.'[16] The virgin woman-poet, by virtue of her freedom from men, possesses the potentiality to be 'lifted to a free/and fellow-life with man' (p. 12). There appears to be a contradiction between 'free' and 'fellow-life'. With the stress placed on the 'free', there is a reverbation of the usage of 'enwound' in Poem XX. Heterosexuality as the form of the relationship between men and women is a form of bondage. If this is replaced by the 'fellow-life' of equal comradeship, an idea much employed in this period and derived from Walt Whitman,[17] then the bondage, even in relationships between men and women is at an end. But whatever 'realm' a woman endeavours to enclose, she must 'ever keep/All things subservient to the good/Of pure free-growing womanhood' (p. 13). Virginity is not sterile in this formulation: it is simultaneously pure and productive. This version of femininity offers an ambiguous challenge to the terms of patriarchal culture. It exists apart from patriarchal dictates, but includes fellowship and equality with men. It embraces the productiveness of womanhood and an all-women community, and speaks of an equality of potency between men and women. It is the 'fellow-life' that is desired, and not men or heterosexuality. Poem LII goes so far as to produce life as a woman as superior to life as a man, through the figure of Tiresias. He is "doomed" to "forego"

> His manhood, and as woman, know
> The unfamiliar, sovereign guise
> Of passion he had dared despise...
> He trembled at the quickening change,
> He trembled at his vision's range,
> His finer sense for bliss and dole,
> His receptivity of soul;

> But when love came, and, loving back,
> He learnt the pleasure men must lack,
> It seemed that he has broken free
> Almost from his mortality.[18]

Tiresias, in his youth, is said to have found two serpents, and when he struck them with a stick to separate them, he is said to have suddenly changed into a woman. Seven years later he was restored to manhood by a repeat of the incident with the snakes. When he was a woman, Jupiter and Juno consulted him on a dispute about which of the sexes received greater pleasure from marriage. Tiresias decided in Jupiter's favour that women derived greater pleasure – and Juno punished Tiresias for this slight by blinding him. Michael Field turn this myth, that is more than a little disparaging about men's enthusiasm for marriage, into a positive valuing of women. Women are not only more sensitive, more feeling, the usual attributes of femininity, they are also more capable than men of experiencing pleasure. That pleasure is not to do with the greater size of women's psyches or souls. Love equals pleasure, and women feel more pleasure. If this is read in the light of the Gorgo poem, above, then that pleasure comes to take on distinctly physical aspects. The other interesting aspect of the Tiresias poem is that it holds both genders together at the same time. At the moment of transition from female to male, Tiresias has a masculine consciousness and a feminine memory, and is an emotional hermaphrodite. While the feminine is better, the moment of transition is one of fullness, with both genders working together. Tiresias is a representation of the absence of any clear split between male and female in Michael Field's Utopian vision.

The construction of femininity in these poems is more complex than an unequivocal embrace of a non-sexual friendship. Michael Field represent Sappho as a wise, old(er) woman who remembers the rejections of youth and deplores the fickleness of younger women and their susceptibility to men. Her constancy to women, 'Maids, not to you my mind doth change' (*Long Ago*: XXXIII, p. 52), is contrasted with her reaction to the men whom she will 'defy, allure, estrange,/Prostrate, made bond or free'. To her maids she is a maternal or passionate lover, and to men she is manipulative and fickle. (The attitude to men is complicated by virtue of the poems being authored under the name of a man. The 'male' poet relates sexually to both men and women.) The volume concludes with the poem, 'O free me, for I take the leap', where Sappho flings herself from a cliff with a prayer to Apollo for a 'breast love-free'.

Michael Field's Sappho, therefore, is not the denizen of a lesbian or Lesbian idyll. Rather, she is the subject of a contradiction which emerges from those versions described above. On the one hand, Sappho the poet must be defended from accusations of immorality, while, on the other, Sappho the Lesbian must be salvaged from the Phaon myth. The Lesbian community of women is more than a society of friendship, but is also a site of poetic production and, moreover, the production of the Poet identity. Both are threatened by men and heterosexuality. The 'production' of poetry both images and guarantees the 'free' bonds of the women makers. It is a lesbian writing which, familiarly, needs to think itself as free from men, for the conditions of its own practice. It defines itself as productive, rather than anti- or non-productive, not simply to give itself the dignity that men's poetry has within the canon and practice of poetry, but also to give voice to, and thus 'have', the lesbian desires that are constructed by and construct the poetic product. This is clearly not only an account of Sappho and Lesbos, but a grappling with the nature and practice of the composite poet, Michael Field. The poetry is the result of the joint productiveness of two women.

Sexuality is not, therefore, the only interpretative category in play in *Long Ago*. The practice of Poetry is equally important, and it interweaves with sexuality. In the preface to *Long Ago* there is an ambiguous appeal to 'the one woman'. The volume is jointly authored, yet the voice of the preface is in the first-person singular. This prefatorial voice advocates worship of, and the apprehension of, an ideal of the Poet and the lover in the poetry and person of Sappho. A direct connection is made between Sappho's prayer and the prayer of this first-person voice:

> Devoutly as the fiery-bosomed Greek turned in her anguish to Aphrodite, praying her to accomplish her heart's desires, I have turned to the one woman who has dared to speak unfalteringly of the fearful mastery of love, and again and again the dumb prayer has risen from my heart –
>
> σὺ δαυτα
συμμαχος εσσο[19]

Here, the Greek is translated as 'you will be my ally'. The 'one woman' is either Sappho, a lover, or a writing partner. This ambiguity of identity is central to this volume of poetry. In *Long Ago* Michael Field are writing with Sappho the Poet, and working with Sappho, Aphrodite, and the partner in an imaginary alliance. The preface does not specify who that mastery of love is directed to. But perhaps that is the point.

In order to speak 'unfalteringly' of woman's love for woman, it is necessary for Michael Field to work in alliance with other women and other women's formulations of such love. The construction in the preface is both strategic and passionate, not a privatized emotion which continues detached from historical and social concerns. It is political, creating changes in the presentation of love between women on the basis of the available cultural models. Michael Field's appeal to 'the one woman' does not rest upon a static image of monogamous romance, which while apparently neutral and ahistorical is intimately connected with bourgeois values and patriarchal family structures, and which lesbianism has the potential to sidestep or remake.

This passage begs a series of questions about desire and speech. The dumb prayer rising, an as yet unaccomplished desire, a person who could dare to speak are all potent, and about-to-be, differentiated from the existing 'mastery'. This yearns for something that is both Utopian and physical, and the process of making one necessarily involves making the other. The metaphors of the invocation are all physical. Aphrodite's passion is not abstract, but fiery and residing in her breast. One lover turns to the other, the emotional and physical senses both contained in that reference to that action.

'The Fearful Mastery of Love'

If, in the late twentieth century, contemporary lesbians are determined to write our own dictionary of lesbian love and desire, there appears to be no such imperative behind the writings of Michael Field. Michael Field, rather than inventing a vocabulary with an unmistakable precision of meaning, deployed the language of classical scholarship, the language of love belonging to heterosexuality, the language of friendship (but never noticeably the language of blood relatives), and later the language of Catholicism. These differing languages represent a series of modulations both chronologically within their *oeuvre* and in the different forms of writing they practised. There is no single language which they employ to talk about each other and their relationship. Consequently, there is enough imprecision or ambiguity in the slippage around their words of love and desire for Faderman, misleadingly, to find sufficient material in their writings to call them romantic friends, when the terms 'romantic' and 'friend' are both so sloppy. It is, of course, equally misleading to call them lesbians. Although the term 'lesbian' is historically available, it is not a word they ever used of themselves to indicate a sexual relationship. They did, however, have other terms and metaphors.

In comparing themselves to Elizabeth Barrett Browning and Robert Browning, Michael Field asserts *'we are closer married'*.[20] Marriage was an available metaphor or conceptualization for both women to apply to their relationship. Following Edith's death, Katherine invoked the words of the marriage service when making an approach to the literary periodical the *Athenæum* to 'write a brief appreciation of my dead Fellow-Poet, not separating what God had joined, yet dwelling for her friends' delight on her peculiar & most rare gifts'.[21] In the preface to *Works and Days* God is said to have joined Michael Field both as the Poet and as 'Poets and lovers evermore' (*Works and Days* p. xix). And, as a last example, to Havelock Ellis, on the subject of his attempts to discover who wrote which piece, they asserted 'As to our work, let no man think he can put asunder what God had joined.'[22] Faderman denies that there is any sexual meaning in these statements, insisting that since they were generally so completely without self-consciousness in their public declarations of mutual love',[23] the relationship must have been 'innocent'. It is difficult to understand how someone can make a declaration of any kind without being conscious of what they are doing. In addition to this, Faderman makes the error of deciding that their love for one another *'caused* them to convert to Catholicism' (p. 211; my emphasis), since this conversion was a way to guarantee being together eternally. Faderman's specious theory appears to be based wholly upon one paragraph in the published journals, written by Edith: 'It is Paradise between us. When we're together eternally, our spirits will be interpenetrated with our loves and our art under the benison of the Vision of God' (p. 324). Faderman derives the whole of their Catholic experience from this brief extract, which was written when Edith was dying. Moreover, Faderman ignores the evidence of the rest of the journals, which reveal their faith as being a good deal more than a mere instrumentalist insurance policy, and the history and pattern of Catholic conversion at that time, with many literary figures joining the Church and some, notably John Gray and Frederick Rolfe, becoming or attempting to become priests.

Michael Field's God is not a cosy, tea-table God, nor an Old Testament God of vengeance for the wicked and just deserts for the righteous. It is a construction of God as an authority that resists what men do – which is, dividing women in the name of femininity and the family. God provides a ground for Utopian female artistic production. The language of the passage from the published journals raises both their love and their art, equally significant, to the knowledge and approval of God. The act of interpenetration is produced as the highest point of achievement for poet and lover. This is not a safe, lesbian-feminist, metaphor. The act of inter-penetration unites the two women not as Romantic Friends, but interprets the relationship as something that values it as an entering into the other's work and identity. Not surprisingly, Faderman does not comment upon it. It does not fit with the diffuse sensuality she ascribes to Romantic Friends.

Faderman bases the Romantic Friendship hypothesis on a specific construction of femininity. She presents it as the sole form of the relationship between loving women before the development of a female homosexual identity and pathology through political and scientific discourses, such as the work of the sexologists and the gay rights movements in Germany and France. Consequently, Faderman applies a modern version of relations between women to the late nineteenth century which precludes any consciousness of sexual interest. In doing so, she constructs all female friendships along the lines of the dominant culture. Faderman argues that, since sexual relationships between women were unacceptable to the dominant, and since women were constructed as the passionless gender and ignorant of sex, they could not possibly have had the knowledge, language, or experience of lesbian *desire*. Any Victorian woman, she maintains, would have been profoundly shocked by such an interpretation of their feelings, and therefore every woman's expression of love or passion must of necessity have been free from the taint of homosexual desire. Faderman does not even entertain the possibility that these women, knowing that the dominant culture condemned such feelings and relationships, could have developed their own strategies for talking about and explaining such expressions of sexuality. Instead she presumes that innocence is a superior form of loving compared to sexual experiences between women. She practises the condescension of history, and in doing so attempts to dodge the revelation of her own political agenda. Of course, Katherine and Edith did not have available to them the language, politics, and structures of contemporary lesbianism and feminism. But Faderman's insistence that they were too stupid to know any better rests upon a belief in linear progress from one age to the next. Contemporary lesbians, so the argument goes, are much wiser than their nineteenth-century sisters because they of course can see through the mechanisms used to oppress and limit women. By practising this evolutionary politics, Faderman manages to read over the top of all the strategies and devices that Michael Field, among many others, did

Chris White

deploy in order to create a cultural space for themselves. That these strategies did exist is beyond question, and they were various, from the appropriations of Greek culture to Carpenter's assertion that 'homogenic love', encompassing both male and female homosexuality, was a potentially superior social force to heterosexuality.[24]

Before going further, I want to make it clear that I am disquieted by the project of going into print criticizing another lesbian. This is an unsisterly thing to do, particularly given the open nature of this forum. Such debates ought not to be conducted in public and in a manner belonging to the practices of non-feminist, gentlemen's club scholarship. *Surpassing the Love of Men* is an invaluable catalogue of the works of hundreds of lesbians which have been suppressed or ignored. But opposition to the political agenda of the book's thesis and the new orthodoxy, which is finding such currency amongst lesbians, academic and non-academic, is in my view of paramount importance. This version of lesbianism appropriates to itself lesbian history and makes of it a reactionary sexual politics. In the introduction to *Surpassing the Love of Men* Faderman makes this claim:

> In lesbian-feminism I have found an analog to romantic friendship...I venture to guess that had the romantic friends of other eras lived today, many of them would have been lesbian-feminists. (p. 20)

My guess is that in 'Romantic Friendship' she found an analogue to radical lesbian-feminism. She displays yet another methodological error in her making of history into analogues, since this works to deny the material specificity of the past as well as the present. Both Romantic Friendship and lesbian-feminism are positions distinguished by the desexualized nature of relations between women. This denial of lesbian sexual practice is spelt out by Elizabeth Mavor in *The Ladies of Llangollen: A Study in Romantic Friendship*, a work which I believe owes a great deal to Faderman's study: 'Much that we would now associate solely with a sexual attachment was contained in romantic friendship: tenderness, loyalty, sensibility, shared beds, shared tastes, coquetry, even passion.'[25]

This reading of love declarations between women and accounts of women living together as wholly non-sexual is explained by Faderman as follows:

> Women in centuries other than ours often internalised the view of females as having little sexual passion...If they were sexually aroused, bearing no burden of proof as men do, they might deny it even to themselves if they wished. (p. 16)

370

Undoubtedly, women internalized the prescriptions of dominant ideology, but the leap from saying they took on board these prescriptions to the assumption that this internalization defined and limited all they believed and practised is quite breathtaking. In particular, it seems hardly credible that simply because women did not have penile erections they would not have recognized how sexual arousal felt and what it meant. Yet this is the outcome of the position adopted by Faderman and Mavor, which argues for a female nature utterly distinct from all things male and masculine. Both writers construct a time that is both more innocent and more separatist than our own. Lesbian separatists construct lesbianism and lesbians as superior, more creative, more sensitive, and more human. Romantic Friendship is an expression of lesbian separatism which takes the form of a relationship that is, in Mavor's words, 'more liberal and inclusive and better suited to the more diffuse feminine nature' (p. xvii) – not concentrated in an erect penis – and which, according to Faderman, 'had little connection with men who were so alienatingly and totally different' (p. 20). The prescriptions of lesbian-feminism extend even into what happens sexually between women. Two women together escape the oppression of phallic heterosexuality, but to arrive in a Utopian region of non-sexual romance and intimacy they must never behave in a manner which in any way reflects that in which men behave towards women.

Paradoxically, the Romantic Friendship hypothesis is a celebration of many of the conventional attributes of femininity as it has been constructed by patriarchy, such as passivity, gentleness, domesticity, creativity, and supportiveness, and which condemns as irretrievably phallic other characteristics generally labelled masculine, including strength, capability, activity, success, independence, and lust. In claiming women-loving women as romantic friends, the hypothesis annihilates from history all those lesbians/lovers who gave histories to (or recognized themselves in the works of) sexologists such as Havelock Ellis,[26] or who, alternatively, formed part of lesbian subcultures based on sexual preference and emotional commitment.[27] Faderman's model consigns lesbian sexual activity to a male fantasy that routinely appears in pornographic writing. She opposes the pornographic image of women's sexuality to the 'true', non-sexual history of women's relationships which, it is claimed, appears in their diaries and writings. Having lighted upon male pornographic images of lesbian sex, Faderman concludes that if men talk about women having sex through a particular discourse, then since that discourse does not appear in women's writings, women did not have sex together or relate sexually to each other.

I am not arguing that every close relationship between women was a sexual one. The point is that the evidence should be looked at without the limitations of lesbian-feminist presuppositions. The political imperative behind my argument is to avoid having lesbian and gay histories misappropriated yet again, and this time from within the ranks of gay writers. Faderman's work is a revisionist project whose critique is focused on 'non-routine acts of love rather than routine acts of oppression, exploitation or violence'.[28] On the basis that these women lovers did not behave like or pretend to be men, this position concludes that they are 'nice girls', not lesbians. As an alternative to this revisionism, I want to try to begin an account of Michael Field's work and relationship that gives them credit for awareness and strategic practice, and which has the potentiality to include within its frame of reference class, race, and power. This will reject the lesbian-feminist invention of a realm and an age of harmonious femininity where all women are equal, provided they do not indulge in politically-right-off sexual activity.

Fleshly Love and 'A Curve That Is Drawn So Fine'

In order to develop a framework in which to understand and talk about love between women in Michael Field's work, I will now go on to look at the references to desire between women, and examine the plurality of ways in which they talked about their understanding of sexual and emotional love between women.

Two instances of desire between women that are constructed as negative and unnatural appear in the journals. Travelling through Europe, Edith falls ill in Dresden, and writes: 'My experiences with Nurse are painful – she is under the possession of terrible fleshly love [which] she does not conceive as such, and as such I will not receive it.'[29] The nurse is presented as not recognizing her experience. Edith, however, does conceive of this love as fleshly. It is certainly within Edith's conceptual framework to apprehend one woman's feelings of physical desire for another woman. This instance of fleshly sin does not belong to the imagination of a pornographer. In this extract, the use of the words 'possession' and 'terrible' cannot be simply read as condemnatory, since any unwelcome sexual attentions may appear to be a terrible possession of the harasser. It is not clear, though, whether Edith would not accept fleshly love in any context, or whether it is this particular instance that is unwelcome.

The second example concerning fleshly love appears in the manuscript journal for 1908, referring to a painting they saw.

A man named Legrand – a monstrous charlatan – who can by a clever trick give the infamies of the worldly Frenchwoman – especially in unconscious self-conscious exposure to her own sex…[as manuscript] female friends together. What is to be expressed is of Satan – and the means as ugly as the matter. The people round me say 'He must be a Genius' – I answer to myself A Demon-Spawned Charlatan.[30]

I have yet to trace this painting, but it obviously enraged Edith. She can read this picture as false and disgusting. The exposure is apparently to the female gaze, but actually for the male gaze. The prurience of that gaze is expressed through that 'unconscious self-consciousness', a wink at the audience, inviting the viewer in to enjoy the scene. This 'clever trick' is that of the pornographer. Two women apparently exist for their own pleasure, but they are actually on offer as double pleasure for the male viewer.[31] The unreality of the scene is evident to Edith. Her racism is evident in her ascribing of infamies to Frenchwomen (and German women too, as evidenced by her comments on the nurse). The point is, she recognizes Legrand's painting is a false image of how women behave to one another as 'female friends'. Edith repudiates the way in which patriarchal values frame and perceive relations between women. Legrand is a charlatan; his representation bears no relation to the truth. Yet this rejection is not the same thing as denying the existence of desire between women. However, what that truth is cannot easily be deduced from the writings.

Outside of the treatment of Sappho, which is a minefield of interpretative complexity, there is very little explicit analysis of the relationship between Katherine and Edith. Their primary concern is always with Michael Field the Poet, and it is the name itself I want to focus on now because it reveals to a large extent how they conceived of their practice as poets. That male-authored publications are usually better received and taken more seriously than female-authored works is a truism. Before the adoption of the joint persona they used the pseudonyms Arran and Isla Leigh, which brought them more favourable reviews than they ever had as Michael Field, and also the assumption that they were either a married couple or a brother and sister. Perhaps this misinterpretation is what led them to adopt the single pen-name. Although Katherine and Edith used metaphors of marriage to describe their love, it would be surprising if they had wanted to be publicly portrayed as a heterosexual couple. However, 'Michael Field' cannot be regarded as a true pseudonym, since it was widely known in a literary circle that included John Gray, George Meredith, and Oscar Wilde, as well as their friends Charles Ricketts and Charles Shannon, that they were two women. Much of their correspondence is addressed to them both under the heading of Michael Field and they often signed themselves with the joint name. The name contains a compelling contradiction: they both deploy the authority of male authorship and yet react against such camouflage. Michael Field is not a disguise. Nor is it a pretence at being a man.

None the less, they were appalled when they became known to their Catholic congregation as the women behind Michael Field. Edith confronted her confessor, Goscommon:

> I say I regret it is known; but that in the same way, I am glad he, as my Confessor, knows, for it will help him to understand some things I feel he has somewhat misunderstood, & also it is for a poet with his freedom of impulse to submit to the control & discipline of the Church.[32]

This anxiety for concealment is in marked contradiction to their previous willingness to be known. Wayne Koestenbaum offers the explanation that 'their aliases gave them a seclusion in which they could freely unfold their "natures set a little way apart"'.[33] Yet that desired seclusion became impossible when they submitted to the authority of the Church. Even though their attempts to develop a framework in which to talk about their love and desires in part depended upon a screen from the world, this effort did not rest wholly upon the use of a male pen-name. Rather, the development of the poetic persona Michael Field gave them another role in which to play out their understandings of their relationship. The persona is distinct from Katherine and Edith, and separate from their pet names Michael and Henry, which were in common currency among friends. Michael Field the Poet is always presented as the highest point of their work.

Complicated shifts took place when they converted to Catholicism. Entering the Roman Catholic Church evokes from Edith the two explicit references to sexuality I have found. In the 1907 volume of the journals she wrote, 'Since I have entered the Holy Catholic Church, I have never fallen into fleshly sin',[34] which presupposes that before she joined she had succumbed to such fleshly temptation. Here fleshly sin may be a reference to masturbation, but I am doubtful, given the second reference in 1908: 'When I came into this Church a year ago [I gave] a gift that was a vow of chastity.'[35] Not practising masturbation may constitute abstinence from fleshly sin, but chastity in this context seems to involve another person. This may be an indication that before conversion, there had been a sexual or erotic relationship between Katherine and Edith.

The physicality of the relationship is not so much implicit as embedded, especially in the late poems. An unpublished poem from the manuscript journals, 'My Love is like a lovely Shepherdess', is appended with a note from the writer of the poem, Katherine.

> Edith's peach & green embroidered gown came home this evening; – after seeing her in it I brake into the 1st part of the 1st verse of this song – then came down &, at my desk, in the evening light, wrote the rest of the verses. Friday July 19th.

The first part of the first verse reads

> My Love is like a lovely Shepherdess;
> She has a dress
> Of peach & green
> the prettiest was ever seen.[36]

After this, the poem goes into a pastoral idyll, where the poet adores the shepherdess through metaphors of spring, morning, and music. But the starting point for the pastoral is the appearance of the beloved. She is 'pretty' (6), 'virgin white' (15), with a 'tender face' (10). The specificity of the poem derives from an identifiable moment in their daily life, which is valued as the proper subject of poetry, although not for publication.

From *The Wattlefold*, a volume of previously unpublished poetry which was eventually published after their deaths in 1930, comes Katherine's poem 'Caput Tuum ut Carmelus'. It opens with these lines:

> I watch the arch of her head
> As she turns away from me.

And continues in the third stanza:

> Oh, what can Death have to do
> With a curve that is drawn so fine,
> With a curve that is drawn as true
> As the mountain's crescent line?[37]

This dwelling on the physical detail of the loved/desired object makes the physical presence the representation of the identity of that object. That fine curve stands in for both the fineness of the inner self and also for how the lover conceptualizes the relationship with the loved.

That curve is a combination of art – it is drawn – and of nature – like a mountain, and this is indicative of one way in which the identity of the loved object as loved object is delineated through the poetry. While there are no explicit declarations of lesbian desire, there are these embedded constructions of identity expressed through relationship.

Edith, in one of her last entries before her death, wrote: 'We have had the bond of race, with the delicious adventure of the stranger nature, introduced by the beloved father.'[38] Since the word father is not capitalized, I hazard to guess that this is a reference to John Gray, a poet, a convert, a priest, Katherine's one-time confessor, and spiritual adviser to them both. He was also the long-time lover of the poet Marc-André Raffalovich.[39] The word 'race' here is intriguing, but again there is the notion of natures that are different. Although they had been in correspondence with Havelock Ellis,[40] there is no evidence in their work of any belief or interest in sexology, inversion, and the 'third sex'. That said, these remarks do seem to resonate with the notion of belonging to a 'breed apart'.

Their strategies for making sense of their love do not take the shape of pretending to be or believing themselves to be men, nor of understanding themselves to be romantic friends. In their treatment of their role as Michael Field and of their love for each other, Katherine and Edith construct a position of opposition against the misapprehensions and prejudices of the world. That opposition relies upon their alliance with one another, and with specific cultural formations that they recognize as expressive or reflective of that alliance. This is the impulse behind their declaration of 1893:

> My Love and I took hands and swore
> Against the world, to be
> Poets and lovers evermore....
> Of judgement never to take heed,
> But to those fast-locked souls to speed,
> Who never from Apollo fled....
> Continually
> With them to dwell,
> Indifferent to heaven and hell.[41]

The reference to Apollo marks the homoerotic nature of the relationship, and the indifference to heaven and hell seems to suggest they were refusing some large-scale social rules and norms. The roles of poet and lover are both integral to one another and essential to their rejection of the judgement of 'the world'. This is an implicitly political understanding of women as lovers, rather than a private and personal retreat from the world into Romantic Friendship.

There is no one strategy or organizing principle that they use to define themselves, a point which is demonstrated in the difference between the poem from 1893 and the prefatory poem from the 1875 volume *The New Minnesinger* by Arran Leigh (alias Katherine Bradley). 'To E.C'. refers to the 'mast'ring power' of the other woman's love, and the writer's need of that love which is 'forever voiceless' (p. vii). The 'lighter passions' will find a way 'into rhythm', and the voiceless need is premised upon the assertion that 'Thou hast fore-fashioned all I do and think' (p. vii). This difference marks the shift from a virtual silence about the love to the opening up of a framework in which to talk about that love.

Edith and Katherine's methods of explaining their love and desire are difficult to decipher because they are so unlike our own modes of explanation. But the fact that we have that trouble does not mean that they encountered the same problem. It is necessary to beware failing or refusing to recognize the complexity of the negotiations these women-loving women made. If we do, as Faderman has done, then all those negotiations made within a hostile dominant culture would lead to a particularly restricted view – a homogeneous and desexualized version. What I have attempted to do here is to begin the process of mapping out the complicated processes whereby the discourses of lesbianism might have been inscribed in the nineteenth century, and not to fall into a simplistic one-theory-fits-all position.

Notes

1 Lillian Faderman, *Surpassing the Love of Men: Romantic Friendship and Love between Women from the Renaissance to the Present* (1981; London: The Women's Press, 1985). Page references are included in the text.

2 These journals are held in British Library under the title 'Works and Days' from 1870 on. All British Library manuscript reference numbers and folio numbers indicate these texts. The published journals appeared as *Works and Days*, ed. T. and D.C. Sturge Moore (London: John Murray, 1933) hereafter referred to as *Works and Days*.

3 See Donna C. Stanton and Jeanine F. Plottel (eds.), *The Female Autograph: Theory and Practice from the Middle Ages to the Present* (Chicago: University of Chicago Press, 1987); Liz Stanley and Sue Scott (eds.), *Writing Feminist Biography* (Manchester: Manchester University Press, 1986).

4   'Lesbian' is here and elsewhere used to refer to people and things pertaining to Lesbos; 'lesbian' is used throughout to refer to sexual or emotional relationships between women.

5   Arran and Isla Leigh, *Bellerophôn* (London: Kegan Paul, 1881), p. 159.

6   Examples of homosexual treatments of Greek literature and culture from the nineteenth century include William Cory, 'Heraclitus' from *Ionica* (London: Smith, Elder, 1858); Charles Kains-Jackson, 'Antinous' from *The Artist and Journal of Home Culture*, 12 (October 1891); Walter Pater, *Greek Studies: A Series of Lectures* (1894); John Addington Symonds, *A Problem in Greek Ethics* (1883).

7   William Mure, *Critical History of the Language and Literature of Ancient Greece* (1850–7), cited in Richard Jenkyns, *Three Classical Poets: Sappho, Catullus, Juvenal* (London: Duckworth, 1982), p. 2.

8   Gilbert Murray, *Ancient Greek Literature* (1897), cited in Jenkyns, op. cit., p. 2.

9   The version of Sappho as heterosexual lover appeared in ironized form as early as 1848 in Christina Rossetti's suppressed poem 'What Sappho would have said had her leap cured instead of killing her'.

10 Michael Field to Walter Pater, 11 June 1889, in Laurence Evans (ed.), *The Letters of Walter Pater* (Oxford: Clarendon Press, 1970), p. 96.

11 See Walter Pater, *Greek Studies: A Series of Lectures* (New York: Chelsea House, 1983).

12 See John Addington Symonds, *A Problem in Greek Ethics*, the full edition (1901), and *A Problem in Modern Ethics* (1896).

13 Michael Field, *Long Ago*, Poem XXXV (London: Bell, 1889), p. 56.

14 ibid., Poem V, 'Where with their boats the fishers land', p. 8.

15 ibid., Poem LXVI, 'We sat and chatted at our ease', p. 123.

16 Arran Leigh, *The New Minnesinger and Other Poems* (1875), p. 2.

17 For nineteenth-century British homosexual usages of Walt Whitman, see, for example, Edward Dowden, *Studies in Literature 1789–1877* (1878), John Addington Symonds, *Walt Whitman: A Study* (London: Routledge, Kegan Paul, 1893), and John Addington Symonds, 'Democratic Art with Special Reference to Walt Whitman', in *Essays Speculative and Suggestive* (1893).

18 *Long Ago*, Poem LII, 'Climbing the hill a coil of snakes', p. 89.

19 Preface to *Long Ago*, p. iii; translation from Poem 78 in Josephine Balmer, *Sappho: Poem and Fragments* (unpaginated edition), [p. 58].

20 Mary Sturgeon, *Michael Field* (London: Harrap, 1922), p. 47.

21 British Library, Add. MS 46803, fo. 100ᵛ.

22 Sturgeon, op. cit., p. 47.

23 Faderman, op. cit., p. 210.

24 Edward Carpenter, *Homogenic Love, and Its Place in a Free Society* (Manchester: Manchester Labour Society, 1894).

25 Elizabeth Mavor, *The Ladies of Llangollen: A Study in Romantic Friendship* (1971; London: Penguin Books, 1973), p. xvii.

26   Case histories of female sexual inverts contained in H. Havelock Ellis, *Studies in the Psychology of Sex*, vol. 1, *Sexual Inversion* (1897) included Edith Ellis and Renée Vivien.

27   Sonja Ruehl, 'Sexual Theory and Practice: Another Double Standard', in Sue Cartledge and Joanna Ryan (eds), *Sex and Love: New Thoughts on Old Contradictions* (London: The Women's Press, 1983), p. 219.

28   Gayle Rubin, 'Thinking Sex: Notes for a Radical Theory of the Politics of Sexuality', in Carole S. Vance (ed.), *Pleasure and Danger: Exploring Female Sexuality* (London: Routledge & Kegan Paul, 1984), p. 301.

29   *Works and Days*, p. 63.

30   British Library MS, 46798 fo. 25ᵛ.

31   See E. Ann Kaplan, 'Is the Gaze Male?', in Ann Snitow *et al.* (eds), *Desire: The Politics of Sexuality* (London: Virago, 1984), pp. 321–38.

32   British Library MS, 46798, fo. 20ᵛ.

33   Wayne Koestenbaum, *Double Talk: The Erotics of Male Literary Collaboration* (London: Routledge, 1989), p. 173: he is citing Sturgeon, op. cit., p. 23.

34   British Library MS, 46797, fo. 52ᵛ.

35   ibid., fo. 77.

36   British Library MS, 46777, fo. 87.

37   Michael Field, *The Wattlefold: Unpublished Poems by Michael Field*, collected by Emily C. Fortey (Oxford: Blackwell, 1930), p. 191.

38   *Works and Days*, p. 326.

39   See, with reservation and suspicion, since he suppresses or refutes any suggestions of homosexuality, Brocard Sewell, *Footnote to the Nineties: A Memoir of John Gray and André Raffalovich* (London: C. & A. Woolf, 1968) and Brocard Sewell, *In the Dorian Mode: A Life of John Gray 1866–1934* (Padstow: Tabb House, 1983).

40   Sturgeon, op. cit., p. 47.

41   *Works and Days*, p. xix.

20

Swinburne at Work
The First Page of 'Anactoria'

Timothy A J Burnett

'He is a reed through which all things blow into music': Tennyson's two-edged compliment (*Swinburne: The Critical* Heritage, ed. Clyde K. Hyder [1970], 113), with its imputation of a fatal facility, has dogged Swinburne's reputation. Browning went even further. 'As to Swinburne's verses…they are "florid impotence", to my taste, the *minimum* of thought and idea in the *maximum* of words and phraseology. Nothing said and nothing done with, left to stand alone and trust for its effect in its own worth' (*Hyder* 115). Swinburne has been regarded as a poet whose work lacked what Dante Gabriel Rossetti called 'fundamental brainwork' (*Letters*, ed. Cecil Y. Lang [1959–62], 1.xix). Examination in some detail of part of one of Swinburne's poetical manuscripts, the only records that we have of his compositional brainwork, may throw some light on whether or not this reputation is justified. The poem chosen is 'Anactoria' which was, of course, not only one of the texts which caused the outcry at the publication of *Poems and Ballads* (1866), but also contains one of Swinburne's most famous phrases: 'the mystery of the cruelty of things'. It is also, conveniently, possessed of a particularly complicated draft.

In *Notes on Poems and Reviews* (1866) Swinburne claimed that in 'Anactoria' he had tried to reproduce the spirit of Sappho's Ode 'To a Beloved Woman', a poem which he would have known since his time at Eton. Swinburne was one among the many who have considered

Burnett, Timothy A J. 1993. "Swinburne at Work: the first page of 'Anactoria.'" In *The Whole Music of Passion: New Essays on Swinburne*, edited by Rikky Rooksby and Nicholas Shrimpton, pp. 148–58. Aldershot: Scolar Press. Reproduced with permission of Timothy A J Burnett, with thanks to Rikky Rooksby and Nick Shrimpton.

Sappho to be the greatest lyric poet of all time. She was also, for him, a symbol of the high calling and immortality of the poet. Her verse, written in the 7th century BC, has survived only in fragmentary form in the quotations of later classical writers and commentators, and in equally fragmentary papyri. It chiefly treats of affection between women, a theme which has caused the modern world to give the name of Sappho's native island to a practice which there is no evidence that she herself pursued. Although Sappho's ode is graphically descriptive of her jealousy at seeing a woman she loved seated beside a man, and although in fragment 28 she calls love the 'giver of pain',[1] and although Swinburne incorporated several lines translated from Sappho's poems in *his* poem, it is not the spirit of Sappho that is expressed in 'Anactoria' so much as that of the Marquis de Sade whose *Justine, ou les malheurs de la vertu* Swinburne had read in 1862.[2] This is true not only of the overtly sadistic passages (lines 23–36 and 103–144), but also of the philosophical (lines 148–188), where God is portrayed as the supreme sadist, the cause and essence of 'the mystery of the cruelty of things'.

In the case of the philosophical passages, study of Swinburne's draft reveals that lines 145–154 were added later, while 155–188 are not found in the manuscript at all. These are the lines closest in spirit to the philosophy of the choruses in *Atalanta in Calydon*, and their appearance out of sequence, as it were, would already have suggested that composition of the two poems proceeded coevally, even if we were not aware that a draft of lines 155–188 is to be found on folio 6b of the Fitzwilliam Museum, Cambridge, manuscript of *Atalanta*.

To quote W. R. Rutland, 'No poet ever wrote more supple rhyming couplets in iambic fives...The variety of caesura, the variations of enjambement and endstopping, and the skill with which the rhymes carry the sense instead of chopping it up, simply takes one's breath away'.[3] Swinburne himself, in a letter to Dante Gabriel Rossetti dated 22 December 1869 referred to '...my own scheme of movement and modulation in Anactoria, which I consider original in structure and combination' (*Letters*, 2:74). Perhaps by examining Swinburne's manuscript in detail we may be able to discern, however dimly, something of how this was achieved.

There are three manuscripts of 'Anactoria' known to me: the first, a draft, preserved at the Harry Ransom Humanities Research Center, at the University of Texas at Austin, is written on both sides of two folio leaves of blue wove paper (folios 1 and 2), on both sides of two folio leaves of blue laid paper (folios 4 and 5), and on one side only of two folio leaves of blue laid paper (folios 3 and 6). Folios 4 and 6 are watermarked

'Sawston/1858' and 'J & SH/ 1863' respectively. The leaves have been bound in the wrong order, and should be as follows: 1, 2, 4, 5, 3, 6. The second manuscript is the draft of lines 155–188 at the Fitzwilliam Museum mentioned above, and the third is a fair copy in the Bibliotheca Bodmeriana at Geneva. In this last manuscript the poem was originally entitled 'Philocris'.

The system of transcription employed in order to reproduce the first page of the draft may be simply explained by means of examples. Comparing line 1 of the facsimile[4] and of the transcription, it will be seen that Swinburne first wrote *lips* and then substituted *life* by writing it over *lips;* at the same time he changed *are* to *is.* When he made these changes he had got at least as far as *bitter,* so the words substituted, *life* and *is,* are italicised to show that they are substitutions within an already existing string of words. Swinburne could, theoretically at least, have come back hours or days after completing the line, and made the changes. Further along the line, however, he has written a little over half of what is probably *my,* abandoned it, and *currente calamo* substituted *thy.* In that case *thy* is not italicised. Where, as in line 4, Swinburne has deleted the first substitution and substituted a third version, as in *falters, quickens, strengthens,* the first substitution is in italics, and the second is in bold face. If there were a third, it would be in bold face italics. A fourth substitution has, happily, yet to occur.

Let us now look at the draft: Lines 1–10 may possibly have background inspiration from Sappho fragment 27 '…You burn me,…'. In Line 1 we see a change from *lips* being *bitter* (Swinburne considers *burnt*) with *my* love to the less concrete *life* being *bitter* with *thy* love. On the other hand in line 3 we see a change from the neutral *their* to the more specific, and alliterative and sibilant *soft,* and in fact Swinburne builds up a remarkable accumulation of 's's in the first five lines. In line 4 there is a change from the concept of *sight* failing to *blood* faltering – an avoidance of yet more smooth sibilant alliteration, and the substitution of a more staccato, vivid image – followed by a change of tack from *falters* through *quickens* to *strengthens* (*strengthens,* although it contains two 's's, is a harsher word than *quickens*). We also see a move from the abstract *life* to the concrete *veins.* In line 6 we see a change from the legato *that life is death* to staccato *it is not death.* In line 7 Swinburne started *I would we twain were.* He then presumably conceived an ending in two iambic feet, and therefore substituted for *were* the filler O, *thou;* he then reverted to the first version; abandoned that tack and put the agents of annihilation (the *sea* and the *fire*) in the active role, and Sappho and her beloved in the passive; after which, apart from two hesitations (*sea were* [something along the lines of *over us*] for *sea had hidden*, and juggling with *fire pyre fire* – finally preferring the smoother fricative to the more jerky plosive) the line was in its final form. Lines 8 and 9 gave Swinburne considerably more trouble. The basic concept was that fire should cleanse, purge, destroy Sappho, her beloved, and Sappho's passion together. At the same time he had to find a rhyme word for *fire*. He started with the idea of fire severing life from the lovers, abandoned that (but stored it in his memory), tried *Purged life from lips*, deleted *life from lips* (Swinburne seems to have been tempted by the image of lips while composing this section, but to have decided against it; three times he deleted *lips* or *lip*), substituted *us*, then abandoned the personal approach and substituted the general, holocaustic, concept *Consumed the earth*. It is just possible that there was an intermediate stage *Purged us, the earth* [and something else besides to be supplied], but I think not. Swinburne then dropped the general concept and returned to the personal with *Laid hold upon us like a new desire*. At that point he had a line that made sense, that rhymed and that led on to lines 9 and 10 *Severed...leaves*. Nevertheless, the poet with the fatal facility was not satisfied. Out went *like a new desire* and in came *as with hands*. Presumably the hands were to be 'of fire', and it was possibly at that juncture that *pyre* was substituted for *fire* in the preceding line. *As with hands* was then deleted, and a new concept introduced: *with the lip that cleaves* – the fire's lip, that is. The idea of fire suggested *ash*, but in the meantime there was a problem to be solved. Swinburne was pleased with the word *cleaves*, with its ambiguous, twin meanings of clinging on the one hand and separation on the other, but by using it he had lost his rhyme-word with *fire*. After some hesitation over how to begin it, he inserted the otherwise perhaps somewhat redundant line *Wilt thou fear that and fear not my desire?* Interestingly enough, the final word *desire* is immediately adjacent to deleted *desire* from the earlier attempt. There then follows the line that employs the rhyme-word *cleaves* (again, it is adjacent to its earlier, deleted, appearance) – a line full of paradox. It is *fire* that severs the bones, yet by a jump in time the bones are not blackened, but bleached. *Severed*, too, is an odd word to use of bones parted from flesh by fire, yet that was the concept intended, since Swinburne also tried the word *divided*. *Severed* had been lurking in his mind, and on the page, since there it is at the beginning of the aborted version of line 8. Yet *flesh that cleaves* implies a jump in time in the opposite direction, since flesh cleaves to the bones only before the fire has taken hold. *Bleach* and *cleaves* are linked by assonance, but express contrary ideas. It is a complicated line, and it cost Swinburne some pains to wrestle it out. There follows a fairly neutral line, line 10, and then two lines, 11 and 12, where the expression of pain rises to a higher pitch, but it remains a mutual pain. In line 12 the too monotonous *vein aches on vein* is changed to the more biting *and vein stings vein*.

At this point the order of composition becomes somewhat hard to follow, but appears to have gone thus: line 1–10, 67 and 68, 11–14, 64, 69–71 as far as *kisses*, 23–34 omitting 29–32, then 29–32, the second half of 71, 72, and finally 63–66. The exact order in which the lines were set down upon the page may be impossible to determine, but it is clear that 67 and 68 were written down, as a couplet, early on, if not first of all, since so many of the other lines curl around them, or are fitted in next to them. Moreover, they appear to be written with a different pen, and in a bolder hand. They relate to a passage of Sappho's own poetry, the 'Ode to Aphrodite', line 1, where the goddess is described as "poikilothron" – richly enthroned.

There are therefore at this point two opposed, but balanced, concepts in Swinburne's mind at the same time: Aphrodite on her throne offering comfort to Sappho; and the torments that Sappho wishes upon the faithless object of her desire. The latter concept leads on from, and was possibly inspired by, the sentiments found in lines 11 and 12, just as lines 23–24 lead on from lines 11 and 12 physically upon the page. The desire for *mutual* destruction found in lines 7–14, however, transmutes itself into a *sadistic* desire for the lingering and painful death of the beloved. It seems clear that Swinburne was not easy about these notorious lines, and was undecided whether to include them or not, if he did include them, where. In the poem as printed line 14 is separated from line 23 by the passage beginning 'Why wilt thou follow lesser loves?', a passage possibly inspired by Sappho fragment 22. '…Out of all mankind, whom do you love better than you love me?…', but which really contributes very little to the poem, unless it be to provide a brief lull of pleading, a change of tone, between the two violent passages. In the draft it is found on folio 2, following a different sadistic passage, lines 103–112. In the fair copy lines 23–34 were originally omitted altogether, and were added later in the right hand margin of folio 1. They represent the first appearance of sadism in the poem (albeit quite an early appearance) and Swinburne seems unsure how to handle it. Whatever his difficulty in placing these lines, however, he seems not, on the whole, to have had the same difficulty in composing them. Lines 23 and 24 came easily enough. Swinburne's first attempt at lines 25 and 26 reads: *Thou art over fair; I would the grave might eat / Thy body as fruit*…He then abandoned the envious sentiment at the beginning of line 25, but retained the idea of the beloved's body being consumed like fruit by the earth, reinforcing it with the image of her body being eaten by some loathsome reptile. He began: *And save the worm's no mouth could find thee sweet*, but no doubt found that trite and banal. He then strengthened it to: *And no mouth but the grave-worm's* (with its echo of ballad vocabulary) *found thee sweet*, but still unsatisfied searched for a yet more 'laidly worm', trying first *viper's*, and then at last, possibly prompted by the genitive 's', arriving at the splendidly sinister and onomatopoeic *And no mouth but some serpent's found thee sweet*.

The next line, 27, which begins a new passage, and signals a raising of the emotional pitch, came easily enough, as did 28, once Swinburne had made an 180 degree turn from *Subtle* to *Intense*, and from *soft* to *superflux*. He next wrote the first version of what was eventually to be line 34, *By soft red ways*, and probably *and shuddering*, before deleting *By soft red ways* and substituting *Veiled notes and shuddering semitones of death*. At this point it must have occurred to him that *Veiled notes* etc. would make the perfect end to the whole passage. He accordingly tried to fit in a line which would rhyme with *death* before the line which he had just finished. He first wrote *Strain out with music*, then substituted *pangs like music* for *music*, followed by *all thy breath*. To strain out with music all the beloved's breath must have seemed too far fetched, or at least ambiguous, but the idea of death accompanied by music, of the beloved's screams and dying sobs being music to Sappho's ears, an idea which seems to have been introduced when *Veiled notes* were substituted for *soft red ways*, is one which Swinburne decided to retain for the end of the passage, but which, after one further attempt *With pangs like music*, he set aside for the time being. The concept that now came into his mind, perhaps suggested by another meaning of 'strain', was that of treading life out as must is trodden out of grapes. He starts with a line-ending *and tread*, followed by *Thy life out softly till the dregs were shed*. Not happy with that, he tried two line-endings both of which, unfortunately, contain words which are, for myself at least, illegible. The first reads *and [ ] it out like [ ]*, and the second *and hurt thee sore being [ ]*. Swinburne then turned to a new variation on his theme of prolonged and painful death: *Vex thee with amorous agonies, let slip / And rein thy soul up at the* – but there he could go no further. Possibly he was thinking of reining the soul up at the something's lip, for his next attempt, adhering to the equestrian metaphor, was *And curb thy soul's half-lacerated lip*. This, however, would clearly not do, since it meant abandoning the image of holding the beloved in agony on the brink of death, whilst sadistically not allowing her to die. At last everything came right, and lines 29–32 were written out with but one hesitation,

385

the incredible line 32 – *Intolerable interludes, and infinite ill* – causing the poet, as far as can be judged from the draft, no trouble at all. After that, it only remained to balance the assonance of line 32 with the alliteration of line 33, and to substitute *Dumb tunes* for *Veiled notes*, and the passage was complete.

Surprising as it may seem after the epicene emotions and perverse passions of lines 23–34, Swinburne now returned to Aphrodite, whom he had left imperishable upon her storied seat. It is, however, clear from the draft that lines 64–66, and the second half of line 71 with line 72, were written after lines 23–34. Inspired, perhaps, by Sappho fragment 123, 'I dreamt that you and I had words, Cyprus-born', Swinburne wrote first *For sleeping*, but was then struck by another concept, that of contrasting Sappho's genius with the beloved's beauty, in the deleted line *For me she loves for my song's sake, but thee.* Abandoning that, he returned to Sappho's dream. The four lines introducing the vision of Aphrodite gave him little trouble, he incorporated the two lines (67 and 68) which he had had set down for so long, and the two and a half lines which he had added earlier, completed line 71, added line 72, and was ready to continue the dream conversation between Aphrodite and Sappho on the verso of the first leaf, incorporating the idea in the abandoned *For me she loves...* into what was to become line 74: *but thou art sweeter, sweet, than song.*

What conclusions can be drawn after studying one of Swinburne's manuscripts in this kind of detail? For one thing, and contrary to Browning's assertion quoted at the beginning of this article, it can be seen that Swinburne's text is remarkably stable. Once he has fought his way through a draft he is faithful to the result, and with very minor adjustments the final text found in the draft is the same as the text as printed. In this he may be contrasted with Dante Gabriel Rossetti, haunted, continually seeking an ideal, whose text is very unstable, and who even uses the same poem in different contexts. Beside Rossetti, Swinburne exhibits a sublime self-confidence, and seems to declare 'Quod scripsi, scripsi'.

It can be observed that Swinburne, contrary perhaps to what is generally believed of him, does proceed from the sense to the sound. He establishes the sense first, then seeks the proper sound, as in the revisions *their* to *soft* (line 3), *quickens* to *strengthens* (line 4), or *the graveworm's* to *some viper's* to *some serpent's* (line 26).

Two different moods and two different concepts can often be seen going forward at the same time and on the same page; on the one hand intense sadistic feelings towards the beloved, and on the other the vision of Aphrodite comforting Sappho. In the printed text these two passages are quite widely separated, and there is nothing to reveal how closely intertwined they were in the poet's mind. It is also possible to see the influence of one passage upon another, separated in the printed version, but clearly written under one impulse, as in the case of the two sadistic passages, lines 7–14 and 23–34. The fact that Swinburne had difficulty in deciding where to place the latter passage, conscious as he was of the effect that it would have upon his audience, can only be discovered by study of the manuscripts.

In his choice of vocabulary, Swinburne can move either from the precise to the vague, or from the general to the specific. He is not, as is sometimes supposed, for ever paring away at precision in order to achieve a vague and dreamy music. We are also reminded that poets do not compose logically, starting at line 1, and continuing through to the end. One idea sparks off another, inspiration for a line or lines strikes in the midst of the composition of an unconnected passage. Lines sometimes come into the brain and go down on the page pell-mell, and sometimes in an ordered, logical and apparently serene progression.

Finally it reminds us that we cannot lay hold of the nature of creative genius. We can trace influences, we can follow the course of ideas being worked out, but we cannot account for the sudden appearance, perfectly formed, with no struggle, of 'Intolerable interludes, and infinite ill'.

Anactoria

Folio 1

1   My <*lips*> *life* <are> *is* bitter <*burnt [ ]*> with <m[ ]> thy love; thine eyes
2   Sting me, thy tresses burn me, thy sharp sighs
3   Divide my flesh and spirit with <*their*> *soft* sound,
4   And my <sight> blood <falters> <*quickens*> **strengthens**, and my <life> veins abound.
5   I pray thee sigh not, speak not, draw not breath;
6   Let life burn down, and dream <that life> it is not death.
7   I would <we twain <were> <, **O thou**> were> the sea <were> had hidden us, the <fire> <*pyre*> **fire**
                  <(> <What> <Why fear it> (<Who> <Shalt thou>

8 Wilt thou fear that and *fear* not my desire?)
      <Severed> <Purged <*life from lips,*> us, <<Consumed the
        earth,> <Laid hold upon us <Like a new desire> <, *as with
        hands[ ]*> with the lip that cleaves>
      <Let fall <*the* white> the ash>

9 <Severed the> <Divided> *Severed the* bones that bleach, the flesh
                                        that cleaves

10 And let our sifted ashes drop like leaves.

13 Let fruit be crushed on fruit let flower on flower

11   I feel thy blood
                            against my blood; <thy
                            veins> <*my pain*> **my**
                            pain

14 Breast kindle breast <[ ]> and either burn one hour.

64 <For in my> <Saw> in her *high* place in Paphos
                        <Fill my> <Filling> <Pains thee,>
                        <Pains thee *all through*, and

12   vein throbs hard on vein.>
                        Pains thee, <and mouth> and
                        lip hurts lip, <and> *and*
                        vein <aches on> *stings* vein.

67 Saw Love, a burning flame from crown to feet

68 Imperishable, upon her <carven> *storied* seat.

69 Clear eyelids lifted toward the north and south

70 A mind of many colours and a mouth

71 Of many tunes and kisses: *and she bowed*

72 <Through> *With* all her subtle face laughing aloud,

23   I would <[ ]> my love could slay
                            thee; I am satiated

24   With seeing thee live and fain
                            would have thee dead.

25   <Thou art over fair;> I would
                            <the grave might) *earth had
                            thy body as fruit to* eat

26   <Thy body as fruit,>
                        And <save the worm's> no
                        mouth <could> but <*the
                        grave-worm's*> some <viper's>
                        serpent's <find> *found* thee
                        sweet

27   I would find grievous ways to
                            have thee slain,

28   <Subtle> Intense device, and
                        <soft> superflux of pain:

<and tread>
<Thy life out softly <till the dregs were shed> and <[ ] *it out
like*> **hurt thee sore being** [ ]>

29 Vex thee with amorous agonies <, <let slip> *sharp*>
<And <rein> *curb* thy soul's <up at the> *half lacerated lip.*>
and shake

30 Life at thy lips, <with> and hold it there to ache;
<With pangs like music> Strain
out with <music> pangs like
music all thy breath>

31 Strain out thy soul with pangs too soft to kill,

32 Intolerable interludes, and infinite ill;

2

< *By soft red ways* > <*Veiled
notes* > < *With* > **Dumb tunes**, and
shuddering semitones of death.

34

1

Relapse and reluctation of the
breath,

<For sleeping> <For me she loves for my song's sake, but thee>

63 For I beheld in sleep <her> the light that is

158 The whole music of passion

64 In her high place in Paphos, heard the kiss

65 Of body and soul that mix with <laught> eager tears

66 And laughter <through> stinging through the eyes and ears

Notes

1 All citations of Sappho are from the translation by D. A. Campbell in his *Greek Lyric, 1, Sappho, Alcaeus*, The Loeb Classical Library, Cambridge, Massachusetts and London, 1982.

2 In a letter to Richard Monckton Milnes, 18 August 1862, Swinburne wrote, 'I have just read "Justine ou les Malheurs de la Vertu"' (*Letters*, 1.53). In his notes to this letter Lang points out that Swinburne actually read *La Nouvelle Justine*, the revised version of 1797.

3 W. R. Rutland, *Swinburne: A Nineteenth Century Hellene*, 1931, 289–90.

4 The first page of the manuscript is reproduced by kind permission of the Harry Ransom Humanities Research Center, The University of Texas at Austin.

21

Naming and Not Naming
Tennyson and Mallarmé

Mary Ann Caws and Gerhard Joseph

As the author of "in the name of the author" puts it in the final commentary on a recent group of articles on anonymity, "The question *what matters who's speaking?* cannot of course be answered by the author himself (as Barthes reminds us), nor by the writer's own contemporaries (as Foucault reminds us), nor by literary theory (as we ought to remind ourselves). Questions of meaning and value can be answered only provisionally, each time a text is read by close readers like you and me." "Still," he maintains, "when we read a text that really matters, it will matter who's speaking."[1]

We think so too. In our case, who is speaking an English poem and the name behind it and who is translating them into another language, French. "Lord[s] of the senses five" ("The Palace of Art," l. 180), but especially the sense of sound, Alfred Tennyson early in life pondered the mystery of his name's sound, and Stéphane Mallarmé, the elliptical suggestor, found the epitome of the admired English poet's meaning in the reverberation of that sound through posterity. We thus explore, at the center of Symbolist links between the two major poets, the problem of what and who is named, what and who is not, and what is actually suppressed: sonorous naming, then, and refusing to name, in the name of poetry itself.

Caws, Mary Ann and Gerhard Joseph. 2005. "Naming and Not Naming: Tennyson and Mallarmé." In *Victorian Poetry*, 43, i (Spring), pp. 1–18. Reproduced with permission of Mary Ann Caws and Gerhard Joseph.

Victorian Poets: A Critical Reader, First Edition. Edited by Valentine Cunningham.
© 2014 John Wiley & Sons, Ltd. Published 2014 by John Wiley & Sons, Ltd.

I. Becoming A Name

Since the first half of our collaboration will eventually be about autho-
rial achievement of impersonality, about the "disappearance of the
speaker" within the poet's name,[2] let us open, by contrast, with the res-
onance of a personal anecdote. Many years ago one of us (Joseph) in a
graduate seminar on Victorian poetry heard its teacher, G. Robert
Stange, make the offhanded judgment that an Edinburgh newspaper
article by Mallarmé some two weeks after Tennyson's death in 1892,
"Tennyson, vu d'ici," (that is, Tennyson, seen from France), was the
most astute contemporary estimate of the English poet's qualities. Since
that time, aside from a brief summary in Marjorie Bowden's study of
Tennyson's French reputation and influence,[3] we have never run across
any critical allusion to, much less an evidentiary consideration of, that
article's putative importance. If such neglect within Anglo-American
criticism be indeed the case,[4] perhaps one reason for the silence is the
absence until recently of an English version of the article. Originally
published in French in the *National Observer of Edinburgh* on October 29,
1892,[5] reprinted in the *Revue Blanche* of December 1892, and collected in
Mallarmé's *Divagations* of 1897 and thereafter in his *Oeuvres complètes*
(pp. 527–531; notes 1590),[6] the essay was not translated into English, as
"Tennyson, Seen from Here," until 2001 by the other collaborator in this
essay (Caws), in *Mallarmé in Prose*.[7]

Since "Tennyson, vu d'ici" is now readily available in English for the
first time, perhaps this might be the moment to look at it in detail, but
to do so within the larger context of Tennyson's impact upon Mallarmé
and upon the nineteenth-century French poetic tradition more
generally.

The fact that Tennyson's early work contributed to the evolution of a
Symbolist aesthetic has been something of a critical truism for some time
now, at least since H. M. McLuhan's "Tennyson and Picturesque Poetry."
Spelling out that connection, McLuhan's essay was given a wide circulation
in John Killham's groundbreaking collection of essays in 1960, *Critical Essays
on the Poetry of Tennyson*,[8] that was instrumental to Tennyson's modern critical recuperation. What drew Mallarmé, as well as Baudelaire, Verlaine, and
other Symbolists to Tennyson, was a melopoetic tendency he attributed
specifically to the English tongue, a *musicalité intérieure*, in Mallarmé's
phrase, that they prized in Anglo-American lyricism, preeminently in the
linked poetry of Edgar Allan Poe and Tennyson. For, following what
Baudelaire read as a "quasi-fraternal [mutual] admiration" of the two
poets,[9] the French themselves persistently connected Tennyson with his

391

sound-intoxicated American equivalent and devotee. Poe, for whom its melody was poetry's essence, thus served as an intermediary between a Tennyson who claimed to know the sound values of every English vowel except those in the word "scissors"[10] and the French Symbolists, who strove for a deconceptualized perception, for a sensate "purity that knows nothing of the calculations of language."[11] Whenever Poe himself alludes to Tennyson, it is with a panegyrical verve that knows few bounds: for Poe, Tennyson is the most "pure" of the poets; he is *"the greatest* [poet] that ever lived"; the critical neglect in America of Tennyson's "magnificent genius" is "one of the worst sins for which the country has to answer."[12] And so on, with scarcely interrupted proselytizing until the very end of Poe's life in 1849.

As a conceptual extension of sheer musicality, the quality that appealed to Poe in such early poems as "Mariana," "The Lady of Shalott," and "Oenone" was what he once called their "etherisity," "a suggestive indefiniteness of meaning, with a view of bringing about a definiteness of vague and therefore of spiritual *effect*."[13] (It is this "suggestiveness" of the image, an amorphousness arising out of the contemplation of a repeated detail that attracted Mallarmé [see note 38 below]). We can thus understand how in striving for a *poésie pure* he drew upon both the music of words and their vague associations in Tennyson as well as Poe. For Tennyson is surely, as Angela Leighton has recently said, one of the century's "most memorable, sensuous, aestheticist voices. It is he who pushes language almost as far as it will go into music, whose rhymes and echoes ring on the other side of sense, who uses refrains and returns like audible embodiments of the tautology of art for art's sake."[14] And perhaps no early poem of Tennyson's illustrates such linguistic echo effects as well as "Mariana," which Mallarmé first translated into French in 1874 in the midst of his translations of Poe, and then re-translated in 1890 (versions which we examine in Part II). As McLuhan said, so representative a work of Tennyson's lyricism "is there to prove that the most sophisticated symbolist poetry could be written fifty years before the Symbolists" (p. 70).

"Mariana" is one of the two Tennyson works (the other being an 1884 translation of "Godiva," published posthumously) that Mallarmé, who spent some wretched time as a teacher of English, actually did translate into a prose poem (quoted in full in note 38). It can thus provide us with a perfect distillation of what the Symbolists took from Tennyson: an inclination from univocal verbal meaning toward the suggestive reverberation of sound. Most striking in both the English and French versions of "Mariana" is the way in which the elaboration of a concrete, particularized image within the individual verse stanza (or, in Mallarmé's case, the prose-poem paragraph) leads inexorably to the climactic contemplation, through repetition in verse after verse, of a single epiphanic phrase, "I am aweary, aweary" in Tennyson's English, "je suis lasse, lasse" in Mallarmé's French, so that the meaning of the word itself, its "matter-moulded" form (*In Memoriam* XCV 46),[15] approaches the condition of ineffability. If one thinks of other early Tennyson lyrics, one can see that the "Shalott"/"Camelot" repetitions of "The Lady of Shalott" or the "hearken ere I die" ones of "Oenone" achieve a comparable tendency – as does the "dying, dying, dying" in the bugle song of *The Princess* or the moment in *The Princess* when the wind rises and whispers to the Prince, "Follow, follow, and win." As A. Dwight Culler says about such echoing sounds of which Tennyson's beloved mantra, "far, far away," is perhaps the most deliquescent instance, "Every lyric is…in some sense an act of transcendental meditation, operating upon a particular word or phrase and inducing in the reader who can savor its shape or sound a state of transcendent wonder."[16] Whether or not such an addiction to the way musical echo effects can make "dying words live," as the poem "Far-Far-Away" would have it, is the essential Tennysonian impulse, that possibility may at any rate be read as an interpretive backformation of a Symbolist emphasis upon the force of sonal repetition. As verbal meaning yearns for the purity of elemental sound, such a gravitation in both Tennyson and Mallarmé moves from an aesthetic of particularity towards an aesthetic of sonal and visual suggestiveness; it generates a tension between the originating image and the general impression, from what is materially present (as in *Coup de dés*, etc.) to the Idea or Ideal, capturing for Mallarmé "the moment when a bird, just some bird, suddenly flies off from some branch, revealing in this moment its quality of being-an-origin, and its power of finding a meaning," as Yves Bonnefoy would have it.[17]

But such a convergence grows, for the most part, out of a French reading of the early Tennyson, the Tennyson of "Mariana" and other early lyrics. When Mallarmé comes to write "Tennyson, vu d'ici" in 1892, it is in assessment of the entire career – and in response to a newspaper's call for a French elegiac comment upon the English laureate's death. What strikes us as original in Mallarmé's assessment is its recapitulation, if in a veiled form, of a Symbolist aesthetic that moves from a tangle of particularities to the mystery of pure sound – and specifically the reverberating sound, through his audience, of Tennyson's name.

Let us summarize Mallarmé's argument as it moves toward that name: after describing the incompetence of the French daily press in trying to find the appropriate name of a French equivalent for the celebrated English laureate, Mallarmé ventures his own approximations. Knowing how "falsifying every comparison is, already by definition; and how impossible it becomes as soon as you try to associate two beings, so that the most dissimilar traits shine out, and even the most evident likeness escapes or fades into thin air," he nevertheless makes his stab at nominal precision: "when it is a matter of Tennyson, the names of Leconte de Lisle, tempered by an Alfred de Vigny and in some way or other, Coppée" come to mind. But how fleeting and mistaken, he realizes, even such nominal comparisons as his own are.

Next he tries out the misguided preferences of French popular taste with respect to the poems themselves, a faultiness usually based upon an ignorance of their actual content: there are the well-known allusions in Taine's *History of English Literature* to the mature Tennyson that do not necessitate a reading public's going back to a particular source, not to mention a close reading of that source; or the *Enoch Arden* that was drummed into the French student's head, along with grammatical foot-notes. Or, in the 1860s' and 70s' version of today's coffee-table book, the contemporary fashion of Gustave Doré meant that there was to be found on every salon table the luxurious folio binding of one of the many versions of the *Idylls of the King*. That is, in France as in England, Tennyson was the foremost of the newly commodified poets in the late nineteenth century.[18]

So much for the response of the middle-class reading public: what Pater called aesthetic criticism, or more specifically the informed commentary of a Mallarmé, can presumably do better, can render a more precise justice against the popular taste. For the poet lives, as Mallarmé said on another occasion "outside of and unbeknownst to advertisement, to the counter groaning under copies, or exasperated salesmen" (*Prose*, p. 30). In a salvage operation from popular reductiveness that foreshadows Harold Nicolson's "two Tennysons," Mallarmé prefers *Maud*, "The Lotos-Eaters," and "Oenone"; above all, the many leaves of Tennyson's poetry "are like so many tombs, the same everywhere, in which *In Memoriam* is a cemetery for a single dead man." As Mallarmé singles out now this Tennysonian gem and now that one, the particularity is quickly subsumed under a more general, a more blurred affect of sublimity because of the passage of time: "what we remember of a great poet is the so-called impression of sublimity he has left, by and through his work, rather than the work itself, and this impression, veiled in human language, pierces through in even the most common translations" (*Prose*, p. 72).

This movement from sharp particularity to blurred impression quickly fades for Mallarmé into an even more generalized condensation beyond the book, from the detailed characterization of a specific poem to the sublimity of a totalized oeuvre caught in the poet's name: thus, "The name of the poet reconstitutes itself with the entire text which, from the union of words among themselves, ends up forming just one significant text, a résumé of the whole soul, communicating itself to the passerby. It surges forth from the wide-open pages of the book which is from then on vain: for, finally genius has to take place in spite of everything, and has to be recognized despite all the obstacles and sometimes even without a reading." Thus it is through the very name, the musical and "chaste arrangements of syllables," repeated slowly again and again, "*Tennyson*, now said solemnly like this: *Lord Tennyson*" on the occasion of the poet's passing, that "the whole soul" is called forth. Tennyson's lyric wing is enshrouded within a mysterious reverberation of impersonal sound, within a plangent mantra whereby his very name, transcending his work, becomes what the Symbolists would call a "pure poèm" – just as the sheer accumulation of outward circumstance, the clutter of ominous detail upon detail opens upon the melancholic tonal purity of "je suis lasse, lasse" at the conclusion of each stanza of Mallarmé's translation of "Mariana."

In short, as Tennyson had his Ulysses affirm of himself, both for the common reader who does not read Tennyson and the poet/critic who, having internalized him, no longer needs to, Tennyson is "become a name" ("Ulysses," l. 11). In the former case, it is the brand name of commodity culture, while in the latter it is the sublime name of High Art's aesthetic introjection.[19] "Becoming a name," that is, can be an evocation of either absence or presence: when Ulysses asserts that for the citizens of Ithaca who "know not me" he is become a name, he means that, whatever his past reputation, he is now become merely a name, a signifier without a referent, a simulacrum empty of being, so why remain in Ithaca?[20] By contrast Mallarmé's own sense of the name as the consolidation of the known text is celebratory, an assertion of immediate presence: for the aesthetic critic "becoming a name" is not a Ulyssean emptying out but rather an act of symbolization (in Coleridge's, not Paul de Man's sense), an evocation of "le mystère d'un nom" as Mallarmé would put it in the passage from his "Ballets" with which we close whereby the name encapsulates the essential present thing, the "whole soul" of the poet. (In comparable fashion, the Duke of Wellington's "name" is both underscored at various points in Tennyson's "Ode on the Death of Wellington" and finally dissolved by the plethora of recurrences and rhymes that the "people's voice" [l. 146], ventriloquized by the poet, finds for the hero's "name.") Thus, what is most interesting about the Mallarmé essay is the way in which it enacts the perspectivist counter-movement in the nineties of 1) an emptying out of the poet's name for middle-class culture and 2) an idealizing, "fulfilling" of that name for avant-garde literary culture, of whom in his alienating "difficulty"[21] we can think of no better a representative than Mallarmé.

Furthermore, Mallarmé's foreign meditation upon the mystery of an English laureate's repeated name at the conclusion of his career cannot but remind us of Tennyson's own meditation on the same phenomenon at the very beginning of his life. In a conversation with John Tyndall in 1858, Tennyson famously described a state of consciousness into which he could, as a boy, throw himself by the incantation of his name, a state in which he felt a transcendence of the spirit beyond the body. As he put the matter to his son:

> A kind of waking trance I frequently had, quite up from boyhood, when I have been sitting alone. It has generally come upon me thro' repeating my own name two or three times to myself, till all at once, as it were out of the intensity of the consciousness of individuality, the individuality itself seemed to dissolve and fade away into boundless being, and this not a confused state but the clearest of the clearest, the surest of the surest, the weirdest of the weirdest, utterly beyond words, where death was an almost impossibility [sic], the loss of personality being no extinction but the only true life. (Hallam Tennyson, 2:29)[22]

It's an odd collocation that comes to mind, this mantra-like repetition of the name at the end of Tennyson's life from the perspective of Mallarmé, a poet/critic who underlines his foreignness ("vu d'ici"), and Tennyson's own internalized repetitions at the beginning of his life. On the one hand, it reminds us of Lacan's notion that our proper name, the aural equivalent of the earlier visual "mirror" as we enter the Symbolic register of language, the Law of the Father's "nom"/ "non" (hence, at some stage in Tennyson's mantra, "Tenny-*son*"?), is the source of our life-long *méconnaissance*, our self-misrecognition, our sense of strangeness and impersonality in the world, since that name is imposed upon us from the outside[23] – or even Derrida's insistence upon the "originary violence of language" implicit in any naming.[24] On the other, both Mallarmé and Tennyson are saying that the matter-moulded name, in its very movement beyond the texts of this life, leads us beyond personality and in such epiphanic force is liberating, "is no extinction but the only true life." What at any rate the defamiliarization of their naming impulses have in common, we would suggest, is part of an idealizing aesthetic mode that unites Tennyson and the Symbolists, a progress from particularity to deliquescent vagueness, from individuation to amorphous collectivity, from personality to impersonality – the self-annihilating dispersion of meaning, in the "pure work," that both deverbalizes perception and deperceptualizes words. As Mallarmé says in language that might well apply to Tennyson (and that as a matter of fact suggests that both poets prefigure T. S. Eliot's insistence upon the impersonality of poetry):

> The pure work implies the disappearance of the poet as speaker, yielding his initiative to words, which are mobilized by the shock of their difference; they light up with reciprocal reflections like a virtual stream of fireworks over jewels, restoring perceptible breath to the former lyric impulse, or the enthusiastic personal directing of the sentence.[25]

II. Not Naming, But Suggesting

In the October 1874 issue of Mallarmé's *La Dernière Mode* (*The Latest Fashion*),[26] that two-year run of a journal entirely written by the Master himself, under many disguises – running the scale from "Madame de Ponty," "Mademoiselle Satin," and "Olympia la négresse," to "IX," and "le chef de chez Brabant," et al., and a cast of invented readers, eager to know what to wear and prepare and see, and how best to travel-there appeared his translation of "Mariana" of 1830. Only the last stanza had appeared previously, in *La Revue Indépendante*, in February of that year. Mallarmé had just finished translating several Poe poems, and the editors of this first Pléiade edition of Mallarmé's works comment that Mallarmé reveals himself as a rather indifferent and weak translator – "un traducteur assez incertain" (*Oeuvres*, p. 1622). They continue their speculation by supposing that he had to fill a space in this number of *La Dernière Mode* hastily, so he just grabbed his translation of this Tennyson poem and thrust it in, wherever it would fit. It is unlikely, to be sure, that the readers, real or invented, would have known what to make of this very un-French text.

Now Mallarmé, maker of many pleats, folded much into himself, being a great gatherer, a pleater together or multi-plier.[27] Mallarmé was a famous gatherer of friends, that is, of his circle, on his celebrated

"Mardis" or Tuesday evenings, when he would lean on the mantel and hold forth – but also a gatherer of names. As Jeffrey Mehlman points out in his "Mallarmé and 'Seduction Theory,'"[28] Mallarmé had already, if awkwardly, telescoped the names of Salomé and Hérodiade in his *Noces d'Hérodiade*, of which only one scene was published in his lifetime. This was, he thought, to have been his masterpiece, which he requested his wife and daughter to destroy upon his death ("Believe me," he said with his last breath, "it would have been very beautiful"). Mehlman maintains that this Salomé/Hérodiade, a repressive (if dance-prone) heroine has a twin sister in Lady Godiva, celebrated in another of Tennyson's poems, also translated by Mallarmé, not once but twice.

That story goes like this: Georges Rochegrosse, who was perhaps planning to do a portrait of the Lady of Chester, asked Mallarmé, who had made a spontaneous oral translation of Tennyson's "Godiva," to write it out for him, which Mallarmé did, sending it almost by return,[29] proving that he knew his Tennyson. In response to Mallarmé's "Godiva," Philoxène Boyer, a friend of the painter Rochegrosse, exclaimed, "That is Tennyson himself in his thought and his very essence" ("dans sa pensée et dans sa moelle"). Mallarmé was scarcely "un traducteur incertain" to all eyes. The reader may well recognize in the Tennyson poem just those accents which would most likely have appealed to Mallarmé, such as the following:

> The deep air listened round her as she rode,
> And all the low wind hardly breathed for fear.
> (ll. 54–55)

Of course, Mallarmé recognized in this sonorous language what he was longing for in his own tongue – these were indeed those tones that the English had forgotten to recognize, as they were always innate to it: "To have given to the human voice such intonations as had never before been heard (without Tennyson, a certain music befitting to the English nation would be lacking, as I see it, and to have made the national instrument yield such new harmonies, instantly recognized as innate to it, constitutes the poet by his task and prestige" (*Prose*, p. 73).

Mehlman's interest here is in the contrast between the "massive return of the repressed" in Salomé/Hérodiade as opposed to the "progressive and activist ego [of] Godiva" (p. 108), and in their double reflection on death. The interwoven deaths of Mallarmé's mother and sister Maria give rise to a long meditation on the interrelation of the heroines and on the relation of death to seduction.

But our own reflection upon Godiva leads us in a less dark direction. The first thing we see in anyone's speaking of Godiva is this capillary curtain, her loosened locks, as she showers down her "rippled ringlets to her knee," so as to be clothed in her curls and her chastity. Mallarmé's fascination with tresses is well documented (see his poem on "La Chevelure," beginning "La Chevelure vol d'une flamme a l'extrême / Occident de désirs pour la tout déployer"; *Oeuvres*, p. 53) ("Hair in flame of flight at the extreme / West of desires to unfurl it") – with its own titular recall of Baudelaire's two poems, in prose and verse, on "La Chevelure" ("the mane of hair") and its sideways suggestion, at least for us, of this sunset at the day's "extreme," with the theme of the day's waning in "Mariana." Mallarmé, fascinated by the notion of and the sight of hair in general and in particular, remains terrified of Hérodiade's Medusa-like "massive" head of hair, just as he is of the forest. Everything enters into this madness of the mane, from Baudelaire's elucubrations on Jeanne Duval's abundant hair, curly as that of sheep ("O toison, moutonnant" in the verse version of "La Chevelure"[30]) and prose ("Un Hémisphère dans une chevelure" "A Hemisphere in a mane of hair" [1:300–301]), through Mallarmé's own untitled sonnet beginning with an evocation of an ancient East,[31] and his "Plainte d'automne" ("Autumn Lament"), where he dreams of his dead Maria, reads Latin poems, and thrusts his hand deep into the fur of his cat, that "pure animal" ("[je] plongeais une main dans la fourrure du pur animal" [*Oeuvres*, p. 270]), and suggests for the Baby Jesus in sugar or wax atop the Christmas tree for a supposed Alsatian reader of *La Dernière Mode* some curly ringlets (*Prose*, p. 94).[32]

All this sends us back to Lefébure's famous letter to Mallarmé in 1862, ironically signaling the difference between his addressee's poetry and poetic outlook and those of the English Laureate, as well as the difference in their coiffure, Tennyson's locks being curlier than Mallarmé's (*Oeuvres*, p. 1622; see note 2). One photograph of Mallarmé in 1863 (Steinmetz, pp. 176–7) shows how straight his hair could appear: his ringlets are saved for writing. That letter inaugurates explicitly what was an implicit relation of Mallarmé to Tennyson, whom he admired: an admiration which stretched over thirty years. A recent commentator about this stretch has marveled about Lefébure's ironic statement concerning the two poets, their writing, and their hair: "It is hard to imagine that Mallarmé and Tennyson spent fifty years (1842–92) on the same planet." But, he continues, no matter how trivial Mallarmé's subject matter (face cream, biking costumes, the top hat), "it's not difficult to remember why deeply unfrivolous poets such as Valéry and Celan saw Mallarmé as a master, if not the master."[33]

Clearly, biking attire and horse riding attire may differ. On Lady Godiva's unforgettable ride, the loosened locks she has wrapped about her to cover her nudity form a curtain, which the human eye penetrates at its peril. Just so the peeping Tom finds his eyes shriveled. Mallarmé's meditation on vision, in the poet Yves Bonnefoy's words, allies itself with his affection for the night and disaffection for the day,[34] even as daytime vision is associated with the despoiling of the essential mystery of poetic obscurity, at its worst a "viol oculaire" (ocular rape), as Mallarmé said to Robert de Montesquiou about the "secret" of his "Hérodiade" – "the future violation of the mystery of her being by John's look."[35] Mallarmé writes to Francois Coppée (April 20, 1868), "As for me, it's been two years now since I committed the sin of seeing the Dream in its ideal nakedness, whereas I should have been amassing between it and me a mystery of music and oblivion."[36] There is spying and there is seeing, and poetic seeing through: the music and its mystery form a protective curtain against unworthy – read unpoetic – invasion.

Bonnefoy has meditated at length on what photography does to painting, to poetry, and to us all, by the undoing of mysteriousness and the invasion of someone else. Since it reveals in such detail, it manifests its own distance, as if we were invaded by "an *other*...a no-one-knows-what other, on whom nothing you try to say takes any hold.... Non-meaning has penetrated human meaning.... someone in us wonders...who?"[37]

So Godiva enters into Mallarmé's poetic scheme of thought. But then why Mariana? First of all, given Mallarmé's fascination with groupings of all sorts, we cannot fail to appreciate such an extraordinary concatenation of names: his dead sister Marie, his wife Maria, his mistress Méry Laurent (whose name was mispronounced "Mary" by her protector, the American dentist, Dr. Evans [Steinmetz, p. 181]), Marianne of the French republic, rendering the figure of Mariana and the Latest *Fashion*, in which she so figures, an even tighter fit. The golden-haired Méry was of bounteous proportions, a good thing, since, as Mallarmé pointed out in a letter to Eugène Lefébure, he only liked "one sort of fat woman; certain blond courtesans, in sunlight, especially wearing a black dress – women who seem to shine with all the life they have taken from men" (*Selected Letters*, p. 80; see the photograph of Méry Laurent [Steinmetz, facing p. 177]). Around the name of Mariana were thus gathered a bevy of other women close to the Master, whose roles he could assume one after the other, while retaining his masterly mystery. That was precisely what he was doing in his *Dernière Mode*.

Understandably, Tennyson's "Mariana" appealed to Mallarmé's poetic temperament. The mysteriousness permeating symbolism profited from this romantic inheritance, lending it nuance and suggestion as opposed to statement. With its lengthy suspense, leading to the heroine's exhaustion at the day's end and her own expressed wish to die out, it had a natural, if not fatal, attraction for the poet so entranced with even the vocabulary of the ephemeral; "I've loved everything that has been gathered up in this word: fall" ("J'ai aimé tout ce qui se résumait dans ce mot: chute" ["Plainte d'automne, *Oeuvres*, p. 270]). It is once again the noun or name of the notion that is most suggestive.

Mallarmé's initial rendering in poetic prose of Tennyson's "Mariana" was printed in October 1874's *La Dernière Mode* as "Figure d'album no. 1" – but there was to be no "Figure d'album no. 2." Mallarmé had said that verse was for summer, and prose for the fall and its splendors: "Avec l'éclat automnal cesse le vers"; "With the splendor of autumn, verse ceases" ("Mimique," *Oeuvres*, p. 340). Mariana was translated in the autumn of 1874. Thus, this translation and indeed this "figure" were clearly a one-time venture, although the translation was retouched and recast by Mallarmé in 1890 for *Le Mercure de France* (June, 1890). It is the latter version which is reprinted in the Mondor and Aubry edition (*Oeuvres*, p. 703), with the comment by Remy de Gourmont that Mallarmé had touched it up for the new edition: "Le maître, en nous la laissant reproduire, a voulu, toujours si soigneux artiste, revoir et retoucher son travail d'alors" ("The master, in permitting us to reproduce it, wanted, the always careful artist that he was, to review it and touch up his former work") (*Oeuvres*, p. 1622). It bears within itself several of the same organizing features as Tennyson's famous poem, while having to find, like all prose poems, its cohering principle from within to compensate for its lack of verse, rhyme, and visual shape.[38]

What seems most striking in both versions of the English translation, as in the French original from the beginning to the end, is the stress on the natural waning of the day – a crucial lean toward death. The initial reference to a tomb (as the French verb "tomber") is instantly obvious: "The rusted nails fell" translated as: "Les clous rouillés tombaient." This overdetermination is carried throughout the poem: "Ses larmes tombèrent...ses larmes tombaient...L'ombre tomba" "le rayon...gisait..." "le jour pencha" rendering the English "Her tears fell...the shadow...fell..." "sunbeam lay athwart..." "day was sloping." One of the more remarkable changes occurs in a recasting of the fifth stanza of the first version to emphasize the tomb, as clearly as does the omission/suppression of the daylight in the stanza left out. In the re-translation appears an exclamation point added by Mallarmé, absent in both his initial translation and in Tennyson's poem, and which names the dark drama of the situation quite explicitly: " Et toujours, quand baissa la lune et que les vents aigus se levèrent, haut et loin, dans le rideau blanc, elle vit d'ici à là l'ombre secouée se balancer. Mais quand la lune fut très bas et les sauvages vents, liés dans leur prison, l'ombre du peuplier tomba sur le lit, par-dessus son front!" There could scarcely be a clearer reference to the tombal nature of the poem itself than the repeated accent on lowering ("baissa," "très bas") and the echo of "ombre…tomb" and the final exclamation.

Back to the usual question about Mallarmé's translation of Tennyson: why that poem? Unlike Mallarmé's first editors, who suggested that Mallarmé had thrust in his Tennyson translation as filler material for the October 1874 issue of *La Dernière Mode*, we think that Mariana finds her appropriate place in this ladies' magazine, much of which is about costume and feminine finery: she fits the pattern perfectly. She is clothed, as Godiva is not, but they both have a mane of hair curlier than that of Mallarmé, as curly as Tennyson's own, the poet in drag.

There is, to say the least, a significant gap between the first and second translations, in the latter of which Mallarmé simply brings about the blatant and unapologetic omission of the third of Tennyson's stanzas, the only one invoking the presence of daylight. In Tennyson's third stanza, beginning "Upon the middle of the night," Mariana says, for the only time, "The day is weary…" to announce the refrain: "He cometh not…I would that I were dead." What might Mallarmé's omission point to? What might he be wanting not to name here?

Tennyson's third stanza, the one Mallarmé cuts out in his retranslation, is significantly the only one in which "the day" figures in the original, where the refrain reads from "my life" in the first stanza to "myself" ("I am") in the last, and from night to day: "My life….The night….The day….My life….The night….My life….I am." Mallarmé cared immensely about the sound of language: the harmony of being depended on the unity and unison that poetry could bring about. Concerned so about words, he was crucially bothered when they were inappropriate in their sounding – the major example being his concern with how "le jour" projects a sonority longer, richer, and rounder than that of the night, "la nuit," in all its brightness of the "i" vowel: "à côté d'*ombre*, opaque, *ténèbres* se fonce peu: quelle déception devant la perversité conférant à *jour* comme à nuit, contradictoirement, des timbres obscur ici, là clair." ("Beside darkness, opaque, *shadows* is not very deep; what a disappointment we feel, confronted with the perversity that results in the paradox of the dark-sounding *jour* meaning day and the bright-sounding *nuit* meaning night" ["Crise de vers," *Oeuvres*,

p. 364].) Or as Bonnefoy phrases it, "For, united with others like it...the sound *nuit* will allow many notions to light up each other with reflections come from some other...this coming together brought about under the clear sign...in the lucidity of pure sound."[39] Far from disturbing, this continuing night harmonizes sound and sense in the refrain of Mallarmé's "Mariana": "Ma vie ....La nuit ....Ma vie ....La nuit ....Ma vie .... Je suis."

The words all rhyme, as does Tennyson's "my life is dreary...I am aweary, aweary," and indeed the poem in Mallarmé works wonderfully, with the same progression from "he isn't coming" (which Mallarmé, however, varies from Tennyson's invariable "he cometh not" to "il ne vient point," "il ne vient jamais," "il ne vient pas," to "he will not come" ("il ne viendra pas"). Perhaps the most noticeable difference between the two poems is the ellipsis of death in the last stanza: "oh! Dieu!" ends Mariana's exclamation. The death wish is totally absorbed and has no need to be reiterated after its preceding strikes and the total obliteration of the so-hated day, as Mallarmé's re-vision simply suppresses the third stanza. When it is allowed to enter the poem, it is judiciously, if not faithfully placed. First, it is innocuous and clichéd in its initial position in his fifth stanza, the "pénultième" (to use one of Mallarmé's favorite expressions): "all day"/ "tout le jour." This is no real daylight, this is just part of a temporal sequence. Then comes the whammy: for in the last stanza, in that loathed hour when the sun breaks in, like a spying eye, that hour is already seen, by Mallarmé, as dying, before the day slopes or leans to the west. For Tennyson, the sunbeam just "lay" – was simply lying there, with no indication of slope until afterwards:

> but most she loathed the hour
> When the thick-moted sunbeam lay
> Athwart the chambers, and the day
> Was sloping toward his western bower.
> (ll. 77–81)

It is clear how masculine is the day, unlike the somewhat mysterious Mariana. Now in his version of his "Mariana," Mallarmé uses a peculiar verb, applying it to the male sunbeam ("le rayon de soleil"), one which in French has a deadly note to it, for it can only mean to lie down dying or dead: "le rayon de soleil *gisait* au travers des chambres, quand le jour pencha vers le bosquet occidental." So death has entered, quite naturally ("Nature exists, and cannot be added to"; *Prose*, p. 37) right next to the

403

day, leaning to the west in its Mariana-like weariness. It thus needs no repetition in the person of Mariana, who weeps her fatigue, exclaims "oh! Dieu" and there ends the translation – this self-translation, as Mehlman would have it (p. 103). The defective (but highly effective) verb *"gisait"* here stands out as a pointer to the death of day and hope. It is the very entrance of the sunbeam that spells death to the dream. No need to spell it out again at the end, where the drama has its own power, cutting short the verbal expression, as the day is first cut out, and then cut short, made into a prose statue, a *gisant: ci-gît*: here lies …. Here in the Mallarmé rendering lies the day, felled … after a long waiting. No, he didn't come. It is a fitting tomb. We know that the prose poem often emphasizes the edges: beginnings and ends, in order to set itself off as a separate unit: so, in Mallarmé's translation, the extremity of death and the exclamation work to round off the poem, as in the Tennyson original, but with still more drastic atmosphere.

Yet we could make a case for there being, in the concision of Mallarmé's re-translation, with its deliberate literary crime against Tennyson's original, *"A salvation, precisely on both sides" (Prose*, p. 46). For Mallarmé's elegy to Tennyson, a prose equivalent to his celebrated verse *Tombeaux* for Poe, Baudelaire, and Verlaine, concludes with a double homage to the two Anglophone poets he revered: Poe and Tennyson. Referring to a "column of the temple called Poetry," he writes of Tennyson: "Let his shade be received there in the very terms of affectionate hyperbole that in his youth, illustrious but still future, Poe addressed him: 'the most noble poetic soul who ever existed'" ("l'âme poétique la plus noble, qui jamais vécut") *(Prose*, p. 73).

In her "Mallarmé and the Bounds of Translation," Rosemary Lloyd points out the difference between the literal "prosaic and lowly function of spelling out the name" described in Mallarmé's "Ballets," in that the name is "stated and not evoked," and the mystery of every naming evocation that remains crucial to the act of poetry.[40] It remains an act never to be taken lightly, so invoking the British poet's name, Mallarmé enunciates it slowly, solemnly: *"Lord Tennyson."* And then in his homage to the poet Théophile Gautier, Mallarmé salutes the "final tremor" in that poet's voice, as it awakens "for the Rose and the Lily the mystery of a name" ("éveille / Pour la Rose et le Lys le mystère d'un nom"; *Oeuvres*, p. 55).[41] That the "name" and the "noun" share in the meaning of the French "nom" doubles the significance of this mysterious quality of non-literality, of creation as appellation.

A strange and very early poem of Mallarmé, aptly titled "Sa fosse est fermée" ("Her grave is closed") and cited by Jacques Derrida in his classic article about the symbolist poet, "La double séance" ("The double session"), invokes the power of the name as noun:

> De tout que reste-t-il? Que nous peut-on montrer?
> Un nom!
>
> (From all this, what remains? What can be shown?
> A name!)
>
> (*Oeuvres*, p. 8)[42]

Mallarmé's view of poetry, prose and painting was the very opposite of spying. It was and remains a vision sufficiently powerful to share, sufficiently discreet to reveal both poet and poem without piercing the curtain of mystery – whether created by curls, ringlets, or straight lines – as all the noble stuff of poetry itself envelops every picture of a genuinely poetic rider.[43]

Notes

1   Donald W. Foster, "Commentary: In the Name of the Author," *NLH* 33 (2002): 395.

2   Stéphane Mallarmé, "Crisis in Poetry," (1886) trans. Mary Ann Caws, in *Stéphane Mallarmé: Selected Poetry and Prose*, ed. and co-trans. Mary Ann Caws (New York: New Directions, 1982), p. 75.

3   Marjorie Bowden, *Tennyson in France* (Manchester: Manchester Univ. Press, 1930).

4   Michael Temple in *The Name of the Poet: Onomastics and Anonymity in the Works of Stéphane Mallarmé* (Exeter: Univ. of Exeter Press, 1995) does consider the essay in a way relevant to our concern, pointing out that Mallarmé espoused a theory of onomastics in "Tennyson, vu d'ici" that he had initially developed in a commemorative talk on the occasion of the death of Villiers de L'Isle-Adam (pp. 9–11).

5   It was most likely Whistler who suggested to William Ernest Henley, the editor of the *National Observer*, that Mallarmé be invited to write a piece on Tennyson's death in 1892. That was the year that Whistler left London to live at 110 rue du Bac in Paris, a dwelling Mallarmé found for him.

6   Stéphane Mallarmé, *Oeuvres Complètes*, ed. Henri Mondor and G. Jean-Aubry (Paris: Gallimard, 1965). Hereafter cited as *Oeuvres* in text.

7   *Mallarmé in Prose*, ed. and co-trans. Mary Ann Caws (New York: New Directions, 2001), pp. 70–3. Hereafter cited as *Prose*. All citations of "Tennyson, Seen from Here" are from this text, which has also been reproduced in *TRB* 7 (2001): 255–8.

8   H. M. McLuhan, "Tennyson and Picturesque Poetry," in *Critical Essays on the Poetry of Tennyson*, ed. John Killham (New York: Barnes and Noble, 1960), pp. 67–85.

9   Charles Baudelaire, *Oeuvres Complètes* (Paris: Lévy, 1870), 6:22, as quoted in Bowden, p. 101. But see also the 1862 letter of his friend Eugène Lefébure suggesting to Mallarmé, in a comic vein, the "slight opposition" in the work, as well as in the curliness of the hair, between the two poets : "J'ai remarqué une ressemblance curieuse entre votre portrait et celui de Tennyson, le doux Tennyson, dont la poésie, je crois, est un peu le contraire de la vôtre. Seulement il est beaucoup plus frisé que vous" (*Oeuvres*, p. 1622).

10 Hallam Tennyson, *Alfred Lord Tennyson: A Memoir* (1897; New York: Greenwood Press, 1969), 2:231.

11 Yves Bonnefoy, "Igitur and the Photographer," trans. Mary Ann Caws, *PMLA* 114 (1999): 335.

12 Edgar Allan Poe, *The Complete Works of Edgar Allan Poe*, ed. James A. Harrison, 17 vols. (1902; repr. New York: AMS Press, 1965), 14:289; "the greatest," from an unsigned review in the *Broadway Journal* 2 (November 29, 1845), confidently attributed by Poe's biographers to him as "the sole editor and proprietor" of the *Journal*; *Complete Works*, 12:180.

13 *Complete Works*, 16:28. See Gerhard Joseph, "Dream Houses of 'Etherisity': Poe and Tennyson," in *Tennyson and the Text: The Weaver's Shuttle* (Cambridge: Cambridge Univ. Press, 1992), pp. 26–46.

14 Angela Leighton, "Touching Forms: Tennyson and Aestheticism," *TRB* 7 (2001): 230.

15 All citations of Tennyson's poetry are from *The Poems of Tennyson*, ed. Christopher Ricks, 3 vols. (Berkeley: Univ. of California Press, 1987).

16 A. Dwight Culler, *The Poetry of Tennyson* (New Haven: Yale Univ. Press, 1977), p. 5.

17 Yves Bonnefoy, "La Poetique de Mallarmé," introduction to Stéphane Mallarmé, *Igitur, Divigations, Un coup de dès* (Paris: Gallimard, 1976), p. 40. The English translation is by Mary Ann Caws.

18 In "Commodifying Tennyson: The Historical Transformation of 'Brand Loyalty,'" *The New Economic Criticism: Studies at the Intersection of Literature and Economics*, ed. Martha Woodmansee and Mark Osteen (New York: Routledge, 1999), Gerhard Joseph juxtaposes Tennyson's medievalizing use of "brand" (for "sword") in the *Idylls of the King* and the fact that an edition of his works was one of the first books (and the only work of poetry) that Frederick Macmillan brought out in 1890 to institute the publishing firm's "net book" policy. Through that policy Macmillan would provide certain books to booksellers and lending libraries on trade terms only if they would agree to sell them at a fixed net price rather than at a highly variable discount, as had hitherto been trade practice. In the assertion of such control, Joseph argues, Macmillan indulged in an early instance of what economic

historians have described as the "branding" of a commodity, in this case the branding of an author.

19 From a Marxist perspective, of course, Mallarmé's aestheticized idealism will seem a mystification, an expression of a superstructural "ideology of the aesthetic" that occluded the material base in which the market rules all. For the relevant argument that a turn from production to consumption models of human behavior in the 1870's accounts for comparable late nineteenth-century transformations in economic theory and, consequently, aesthetic taste, see Regenia Gagnier, *The Insatiability of Human Wants: Economics and Aesthetics in Market Society* (Chicago: Univ. of Chicago Press, 2000), pp. 1–18 – and, as exemplification, Joseph's argument described in n. 18.

20 Within the context of the entire poem, Erik Gray, in "Tennyson and Ulysses Becoming a Name," *TRB* 7(2000): 165–173, gives line 11 a more complex meaning. Ulysses, he argues, claims to have so completely earned the heroic epithets that constituted his name, to have so embodied those "names," that he has become them, whatever the blunted imagination of Ithaca's inhabitants. The rest of the poem thus becomes his reassertion of those epithets, those names he has earned at Troy and thereafter, so that by the end he can affirm the confidently tautological "that which we are we are" (l. 67), with no distinction between name and being.

For a reading that interprets "becoming a name" in light of Althusserian interpellation and Marxist "ideology" more generally, see Matthew Rowlinson, "The Ideological Moment of Tennyson's 'Ulysses'," *VP* 30 (1992): 273. The coherence and recognizability of Tennyson's Ulysses depends upon his interpellation, his "hailing" by name, in the various discourses of present and past that always already constitute him – including, for our purposes, the French one of this essay.

21 See Malcolm Bowie, *Mallarmé and the Art of Being Difficult* (Cambridge: Cambridge Univ. Press, 1978); and George Steiner, "On Difficulty," in *On Difficulty and Other Essays* (Oxford: Oxford Univ. Press, 1972), on the four kinds of verbal "difficulty." Mallarmé, Hölderlin, and Heidegger, Steiner says, are the best examples of the fourth kind, the ontological, that confronts us with "blank questions about the nature of human speech." "In ontological difficulty, the poetics of Mallarmé and of Heidegger...express their sense of the inauthentic situation of man in an environment of eroded speech" (p. 44).

22 Hallam Tennyson, *Materials for a Life of A. T. Collected for My Children*, 2 vols, (n.p., n.d.), 2:29. We follow A. Dwight Culler in assuming that the name Tennyson threw into the wind would have been "Tennyson" – it could, after all, have been "Alfred" (the position of Harold Nicolson, *Tennyson, Aspects of his Life, Character and Poetry* [Boston: Houghton Mifflin, 1923], p. 46), or even "Alfred Tennyson"? In *The Poetry of Tennyson* Culler entitles his chapter on the matter "Tennyson, Tennyson, Tennyson."

23 "Thus, the subject, too, if he can appear to be the slave of language is all the more so of a discourse in the universal movement in which his place is already inscribed at birth, if only by virtue of his proper name" (Jacques Lacan, "The Agency of the Letter in the Unconscious or Reason since Freud," in *Écrits: A Selection* [New York: Norton, 1977], p. 148). J. Hillis Miller makes a comparable point in his introduction to Dickens' *Bleak House* (Harmondsworth: Penguin Books, 1979): "To name someone is to alienate him from himself by making him part of a family," p. 22.

24 "There was in fact a first violence to be named. To name, to give names that it will on occasion be forbidden to pronounce, such is the originary violence of language which consists in inscribing within a difference, in classifying, in suspending the vocative absolute. To think the unique *within* the system, to inscribe it there, such is the gesture of the arche-writing: arche-violence, loss of the proper, of absolute proximity, of self-presence, in truth the loss of what has never taken place, of a self-presence which has never been given but only dreamed of and always already split, repeated, incapable of appearing to itself except in its own disappearance." ("Violence of the Letter," in *Of Grammatology* [Baltimore: Johns Hopkins Univ. Press, 1974], p. 112). Such a "disappearance" of the "proper" provides our own most relevant context for Tennyson's mystification of "Tennyson."

25 "Crisis in Poetry," in *Stéphane Mallarmé: Selected Poetry and Prose*, trans. Mary Ann Caws, p. 75.

26 Extracted in Caws, *Mallarmé in Prose*, pp. 79–94.

27 Pierre Boulez knew this, and played on the word in his superb *Pli selon pli*. Gilles Deleuze's brilliant study, *Le Pli: Leibniz et le baroque* (Paris: Editions de Minuit, 1988), centers on the word's meaning as both fold and pleat. Thus the famous "explication" or unfolding of a text, the pleats in a skirting of the issue, the gathers in a fabric or a text, and so on, make their own play on the pleat, otherwise seen) as *The Fold* (see Tom Conley's translation, *The Fold* [Minneapolis: Univ. of Minnesota Press, 1993], of Deleuze's *Le Pli)*.

28 Jeffrey Mehlman, "Mallarmé and Seduction Theory," *Paragraph* 14 (1991): 95–109,

29 Jean-Luc Steinmetz, *Stéphane Mallarmé: L'Absolu au jour le jour* (Paris: Fayard, 1998), p. 356.

30 Charles Baudelaire, *Oeuvres complètes*, ed. Claude Pichois (Paris: Pléiade, 1975), pp. 26–27.

31 Stéphane Mallarmé, *Oeuvres complètes* , ed. Carl Paul Barbier and Charles Gordon Millan (Paris: Flammarion, 1983), p. 224.

32 As for Tennyson's concern with hair beyond the covering ringlets of "Godiva," see Elizabeth G. Gitter, "The Power of Women's Hair in the Victorian Imagination," *PMLA* 99 (1984): 936–54. Gitter treats the serpentine hair of the seductress Vivien in "Merlin and Vivien" and the bartered golden ringlets of the woman in "The Ringlet" (where they are "bought

and sold, sold, sold") as part of a pervasive hair fetishism and taboo within the male Victorian imaginary. As further Tennysonian examples, see the "streaming curls of deepest brown" that the (serendipitously, for our own purposes of national comparison) French Mariana draws apart to expose her "melancholy eyes divine" in "Mariana in the South," ll. 16–19; Aphrodite's "deep hair / Ambrosial, golden round her lucid throat / And shoulder" that tempts Paris in "Oenone," ll. 173–5; and Tennyson's complaint that Holman Hunt's illustration of "The Lady of Shalott" for the illustrated Moxon edition of the poems in 1857 took licence with the control of her hair: "My dear Hunt …. I never said that the young woman's hair was flying all over the shop." "No," replied Hunt, "but you never said it wasn't." Quoted in Jennifer Gribble, *The Lady of Shalott in the Victorian Novel* (London-. Macmillan, 1983), p. 2, from G. S. Layard, *Tennyson and his Pre-Raphaelite Illustrators* (London, 1894), p. 41.

33 Chase Madar, Review of *Mallarmé in Prose*, ed. Mary Ann Caws, *TLS* (December 7, 2001): 24.

34 Yves Bonnefoy, "La Poétique de Mallarmé," p. 15.

35 Mehlman, p. 111; see also Sylviane Huot, Le *'mythe d'Hérodiade' chez Mallarmé: Genèse et évolution* (Paris: Nizet, 1977), p. 5.

36 *Selected Letters of Stéphane Mallarmé*, ed. Rosemary Lloyd (Chicago: Univ. of Chicago Press, 1988), p. 84. Hereafter cited as *Selected Letters*.

37 Yves Bonnefoy, "Igitur and the Photographer," trans. Mary Ann Caws, *A Painter's Poet: Stéphane Mallarmé and the Impressionist Circle*, ed. Jane Roos (New York: Hunter College Art Gallery, 1999), p. 21.

38 On the prose poem, see Michael Riffaterre, "On the Prose Poem's Formal Features," pp 117–33; and Mary Ann Caws, "The Self-Defining Poem: On its Edge," pp. 180–97, in Mary Ann Caws and Hermine Riffaterre, *The Prose Poem in France: Theory and Practice* (New York: Columbia Univ. Press, 1983). Mallarmé's translation of Tennyson's "Mariana," as published in *La Dernière Mode* of October 18, 1874 reads as follows:

> Les endroits à fleurs avaient une croûte épaisse de mousse très-noire, tous de même. Les clous rouillés tombaient des attaches qui tinrent la pêche aux murs du jardin. Les appentis brisés, étranges et tristes; le bruyant loquet était sans se lever: sarclée .et usée, l'ancienne paille sur la grange solitaire du fossé. Elle dit uniquement: "Ma vie est morne, il ne vient point," dit-elle; elle dit: "Je suis lasse, lasse, je voudrais êtremorte!"
>
> Ses larmes tombèrent avec la rosée du soir: ses larmes tombaient avant que les rosées n'eussent séché: elle ne pouvait point regarder le ciel suave, au matin ni le moment du soir. Après le volètement des chauves-souris, quand l'ombre la plus épaisse causa une somme dans le ciel, elle tira le rideau de sa croisée et regarda à travers les obscurités plates. Elle dit uniquement: "La nuit est morne, il ne vient pas," dit elle; elle dit: "Je suis lasse, lasse, je voudrais être morte!"
>
> A un jet de pierre environ du mur dormait une vanne à eau noircie; et au-dessus, nombreuses, rondes et petites, rampaient les mousses des marais

par grappes. Un peuplier, fort près, remuait toujours, tout vert argenté à noueuse écorce. A des lieues, nul autre arbre ne marquait 1'espace nivelé, les environs gris. Elle dit uniquement: "Ma vie est morne, il ne vient jamais," dit-elle; elle dit: "Je suis lasse, lasse, je voudrais être morte!"

Et toujours, quand baissa la lune et que les vents aigus se levèrent, haut et loin, dans le rideau blanc, elle vit d'ici à là l'ombre secouée se balancer. Mais quand la lune fut très bas et les sauvages vents, liés dans leur prison, l'ombre du peuplier tomba sur le lit, par-dessus son front! Elle dit uniquement: "La nuit est morne, Il ne vient pas," dit-elle; elle dit: "Je suis lasse, lasse, je voudrais être morte!"

Tout le jour dans la maison de rêve, les portes claquèrent sur leurs gonds; la mouche bleu chanta sur la vitre: la souris, derrière la boiserie allant en poussière, criait ou, de la crevasse regardait. De vielles faces luisaient par les portes, de vieux pas foulaient les étages supérieurs: de vielles voix l'appelaient, elle, de dehors. Elle dit uniquement: "Ma vie est morne, il ne vient pas," dit-elle; elle dit: "Je suis lasse, lasse, je voudrais être morte!"

Le moineau pépiait sur le toit, le lent tic-tac de l'horloge et le bruit qu'au vent faisait le peuplier confondaient tous ses sens; mais, le plus! elle maudit l'heure où le rayon de soleil gisait au travers des chambres, quand le jour pencha vers le bosquet occidental. Alors elle dit: "Je suis très morne, il ne viendra pas," dit-elle; elle pleura: "Je suis lasse, lasse, oh! Dieu!"

39 Yves Bonnefoy, "La Poétique de Mallarmé," p. 15.
40 Rosemary Lloyd, "Mallarmé and the Bounds of Translation," *Nottingham French Studies* 40 (2001): 23.
41 And, in his response to Jules Huret's "Inquiry about Literary Evolution," Mallarmé stresses how – unlike the Parnassians, who by showing the object entirely, "lack mystery" and deprive the reader of the joy of figuring out the relation between things, his essential requirement for poetry – the poet should proceed: "*Nommer* un objet, c'est supprimer les trois quarts de la jouissance du poème qui est faite de deviner peu à peu: le *suggérer*, voilà le rêve." ("To name an object is to suppress three-fourths of the pleasure of the poem, which is made up of guessing little by little: to suggest it, that's the ideal"; *Oeuvres*, p. 869). This clarifies the more than famous passage in "Crise de vers": "I say: a flower! And, beyond the forgetting to which my voice relegates no shape, insofar as something other than the known calyxes, there rises musically, the idea itself and subtle, absent from every bouquet." ("Je dis: une fleur! Et hors de l'oubli où ma voix relègue aucun contour, en tant que quelque chose d'autre que les calices sus, musicalement se lève, idée même et suave, l'absente de tous bouquets"; *Oeuvres*, p. 368).
42 Jacques Derrida, *Dissemination*, trans. Barbara Johnson (Chicago: Univ. of Chicago Press, 1981), p. 276; after "La double séance," in *La Dissémination* (Paris: Editions du Seuil, 1972), pp. 199–317.
43 We would like to thank Herbert Tucker, a reader for *Victorian Poetry*, for valuable suggestions we followed in both the Tennyson and Mallarmé parts of this essay.

Index

Abrams, M. H. 84
abysmality 5, 6, 35, 89, 268, 311
    see also mise en abîme
Adorno, Theodor W. 93n14
Aesthetics (Hegel) 127
Alice in Wonderland (Carroll) 221, 222
alienated majesty (Emerson) 143–4,
    150, 155
alienation 153, 155, 282
All Saints Confraternity 231–2
All Saints' Home 227, 242n38
All Saints' Sisterhood 227–8, 229
allegory
    Benjamin on 269, 276–7, 279, 282,
        284n1
    Coleridge 277
    Tennyson 269–70, 277–80, 283
Allott, Miriam 109
Ambarvalia (Clough) 341
Ambiguities (Vicinus) 185
Amours de Voyage (Clough) 341, 344,
    345–6
'Anactoria' (Swinburne)
    drafts 381, 382–6
    Sade influences 14, 381
    sense to sound 386–7
    transcription 382–4

androgyny 10–11, 204–7, 214–15,
    218n1
Anglican Sisterhoods 223, 224–5,
    226–7, 228, 303–5
antinomianism 52, 77
anti-semitism 12, 263
aporia 5, 51
appetite 221–2, 223, 230
Aqueous Age 13, 338–9, 344, 345, 354
Aries, Philippe 246–7
Aristophanes 38, 39
Aristotle 5, 23, 40
Armstrong, Isobel 8–9, 12, 202,
    296–7, 314n43, 339–40, 356n17
Armstrong, Nancy 221, 222, 223
Arnold, Matthew 1, 4, 10, 96, 111
    androgyny 214–15
    Aqueous Age 13, 338–9
    boundary-blurring 215–16
    and Clough 13, 105, 339–41
    cultural power 96–7, 109–15
    echo 23
    funerary remembrance 253
    gipsies 8, 98–9, 103–4, 112, 352
    ideology 96, 98–9, 100–2, 109, 110,
        113–14, 160
    mirroring 23

Victorian Poets: A Critical Reader, First Edition. Edited by Valentine Cunningham.
© 2014 John Wiley & Sons, Ltd. Published 2014 by John Wiley & Sons, Ltd.

Index

Index

Index